The Nonsense Factory

ALSO BY BRUCE CANNON GIBNEY

A Generation of Sociopaths

The Nonsense Factory

THE MAKING AND BREAKING
OF THE AMERICAN LEGAL SYSTEM

Bruce Cannon Gibney

hachette
BOOKS

New York   Boston

Copyright © 2019 by Do Not Bend, LLC.

Jacket design by Milan Bozic and Amanda Kain
Jacket illustration by Steve Noble
Jacket copyright © 2019 by Hachette Book Group, Inc.

Hachette Books
Hachette Book Group
1290 Avenue of the Americas
New York, NY 10104
hachettebooks.com
twitter.com/hachettebooks

First Edition: May 2019

Hachette Books is a division of Hachette Book Group, Inc.
The Hachette Books name and logo are trademarks of Hachette Book Group, Inc.

The publisher is not responsible for websites (or their content) that are not owned by the publisher.

Library of Congress Control Number: 2018959937

ISBNs: 978-0-316-47526-6 (hardcover); 978-0-316-47525-9 (ebook)

Printed in the United States of America

LSC-C

10 9 8 7 6 5 4 3 2 1

To my grandmother,

沈文玉

CONTENTS

CONTENTS

The practice of law was vulgar, but the study of it was sublime.

Oscar Wilde (attrib)/John Irving

You can't keep doing shitty things, and then feel bad about yourself like that makes it okay! You need to be better!

Todd Chavez (*BoJack Horseman*)

AUTHOR'S NOTE

This book describes law in its essentials. Law is riddled with quibbles and caveats, but in the interests of clarity, I have forgone the customary qualifiers of "generally," "for the most part," "subject to," "absent other factors," etc., save where it was important to emphasize exceptions/generality or when a concept was introduced for the first time. I have also focused on federal law, which applies nationwide.

This book presents law as it stood in 2018, though law's tremendous inertia should keep matters current for some time. The most likely and consequential shifts over the next few years will involve federal agencies and executive power (Chapters 5 and 13, especially).

The standard inflation-adjustment is CPI-U (Consumer Price Index for All Urban Consumers). Anachronistic spellings and capitalizations have been updated where sensible.

Britain plays an outsize role in American law. Because English practices dominated British and early American legal thinking, I have conflated Britain and England where doing so is reasonable.

I have omitted the last three days of a Congressional term in references to years (e.g., the 115th Congress ran from January 3, 2017 to January 3, 2019, but for simplicity, its work is denoted as for 2017 to 2018). Citations within citations are also omitted without comment by default, and I have not conformed the endnotes to the nitpicker's bible/legal citation manual, *The Bluebook*. There should only be four basic rules for citation: (1) accuracy; (2) reasonable consistency; (3) sufficient detail to give readers an impression of a source's credibility and aptness; (4) enough information that one cut, one paste, and two clicks can retrieve the source.

The Nonsense Factory

THE EXCEPTION *IS* THE RULE

The young man knows the rules, but the old man knows the exceptions.

Oliver Wendell Holmes, Sr.[1]

This book is about the increasingly serious failings of the American legal system. In the common view, law is a system of intelligible rules, made sensibly and applied evenly. That's a reasonable definition of what law should be, but not an accurate description of what law has become. Over the past century, whole fields of law have grown so bloated and confused that not even a subset of their rules can be administered consistently. To cope, law modifies or ignores its own rules on the fly, and the entire legal system is backsliding toward a regime in which the arbitrary supplants the absolute. Eventually, what calls itself law will cease to deserve the name.

There's no denying that law is bedeviled from within and without. The Trump Administration vividly reduced entire provinces of law to failed states, but that is not the only reason why the legal system needs a critique, nor is it what compelled me to write this book. Trump's actions add an undeniable relevance, but only in the same way that discovering a gas leak adds urgency to the calamity of a house already on fire. Law's crises preceded, and will outlast, Trump.

A major theme of this book is that as law becomes less lawlike, the essential goods we expect from the legal system—order, justice, legitimacy—will be in ever shorter supply. A minority of Americans already suffer these legal deficits, severely. But general legal decay consigns all of us to injustices large and small. Whether our antagonists are police, building inspectors, litigious opportunists, or Social Security benefits administrators, our legal difficulties are real, and they will get worse. These are the inevitable consequences of a system of rules self-liquidating into a chaos of exceptions.

Consider the right to trial by jury, provided by the Constitution, and American law's crown jewel. It is *The Rule.* Yet American trial courts conduct very few trials—a withering that became quite pronounced in the 1980s.[2] In criminal matters, virtually all charges are now resolved by plea bargains, each fashioned according to the unaccountable whims of a prosecutor selecting from a vast menu of crimes. These bargains are the exceptions, made ad hoc, and they leach the jury trial rule of its value. Nevertheless, the Supreme Court condones plea bargains as useful expediencies, explaining that the rules of criminal procedure have made trials dauntingly intricate and expensive. Notice that the Court does not make a *Constitutional* argument; it offers a bullet point on the management consultant's slide deck, sandwiched between "outsourcing" and "downsizing." The Court works a betrayal, and claims that it's for our own good.

Trials have also disappeared in civil proceedings, such as disputes over broken contracts, employment discrimination, cell phone overbilling, and medical malpractice. We are all potential parties to these sorts of civil disputes, and we have a right to trial by jury. Again, the Court says modern litigation is too cumbersome to fully honor Constitutional promises. The Court therefore sanctions arbitrations, privatized justice whereby stronger parties can divert troublesome litigation into fora of their own design, using whatever procedures and "judges" they deem most useful to themselves. The Court proclaims its satisfaction with these arrangements, and why not? Justice seems to be just another chore to life-hack.

How did law become so lawless? In large part, because the rot is spreading from the top: the institutions that make the rules cannot be bothered to abide by them. Congress can't even follow its own rules for making rules: to pass legislation of any importance, Congress resorts to emergency procedures that sidestep committees, open debate, and normal voting. Yet, for all the compromise and strain, Congress voids itself of surprisingly little substance. The real work of legislating is offloaded to bureaucracies, which take their own shortcuts to hustle product out the door. The net effect is that rules can be created in enormous volume, but not always well, nor in compliance with the authorizing law or the Constitution, America's ur-rule. To apply the sprawling rule book in the real world, the system's enforcers must cut corners of their own, engendering litigation that the Court must resolve. Naturally, the Court issues its own rules, barely workable in theory and mostly unusable in practice, which must be ignored in turn, and the cycle of expedience becomes fully self-perpetuating.

Notwithstanding these dysfunctions, a generally dismal reputation, and specific and well-publicized disasters, law has escaped a comprehensive critique. This is not the public's fault, but the legal community's. Scholars jealously guard their status as the definitive arbiters of legal discourse. For the most part, their work lacks scope and interconnection commensurate with claims of monopoly. Legal scholarship is overwhelmingly specialized, inward-focused, and prone to viewing grave catastrophes as mere byproducts of theoretical kinks. Law's provincial pathologists spend endless hours counting angels impaled on different pinheads, which fosters the false impression that law's problems are compartmentalized or abstract, amenable to being ignored or tweaked. In fact, most of law's problems are systemic, deriving from the same few sources—the swirl of rules and exceptions being a chief example. The whole of law is poisoned, with tangible and serious consequences, and requires a comprehensive overhaul.

To chance an extended metaphor, law is a giant factory. In a perfect world, the factory would be run according to a sensible plan, rigorously monitored, with customer satisfaction carefully scrutinized. In reality, the factory is bedlam. Every division receives instructions that are too complicated to follow and quotas that are impossible to meet. Each division tries to make its numbers by taking shortcuts, hoping that someone else will pick up the slack. Because the divisions don't communicate and quality control has taken an extended holiday, few workers realize how awful the product is. A normal factory so poorly run would be overhauled or shuttered. But law is not a normal factory: it can force people to buy whatever it produces.

Naturally, customers are not satisfied, but until they understand that the *entire* legal enterprise is at risk and demand corresponding reform, we are all victims-in-waiting. Though our tragedies will differ in kind and degree, none of us can escape the decay of a system that controls every aspect of our lives. What law needs is a wide-angle critique, and that demands a generalist, which is where I hope to be useful. Rather unusually, my legal career broadened as it progressed. I began as a securities lawyer and, had I proceeded on the normal course, I would have ended as one. I would have burrowed into my specialty for forty years, and retired believing that I had the odd luck to toil in an unusually messy corner of the law, one whose disorganization was merely a function of being too vulgar to attract the attention lavished on glitzier subjects like Constitutional law (which surely worked better). However, I quickly left law firm practice to become a general counsel, and then a private client, working with more than a dozen law firms over the years. As I spent time with legal specialists in different areas—finance, employment, health care, construction, intellectual property, and tax—I noticed important commonalities. Everyone seemed to believe *their* specialty area was a mess, yet few attorneys asked if the rest of the system was similarly afflicted. They simply assumed that the legal system *as a whole* was reasonably healthy, overseen by a Constitutional Higher Power according to some sensible plan. They didn't check if that was true. In fairness, that wasn't their job. Their job was to answer technical questions and get me off the phone before any metaphysical (and potentially unbillable) questions issued. My job here is to provide a more panoptic view.

If the panoptic view requires a generalist, the realist critique demands an expatriate.[3] Residents, especially those at law's higher ranks, have difficulty separating themselves from the very worldview that requires examination. Moreover, for all its other problems, law has, by definition, served its elites well, making it harder for them to see (or care) whether law is working for everyone else. Indeed, some traditions hold that the efficacy and morality of laws are not proper subjects for legal study—though the public surely cares about those matters, and the public is the nominal source, and intended beneficiary, of law. (Why else would it tolerate lawyers?) Furthermore, many eminent legal commentators, whatever their doctrinal perspectives, must maintain polite relationships with the legal system. One would no more expect an august professor or judge to write a broad and searing account of the legal system's failings in the *Harvard Law Review* than imagine Jeff Bezos exposing the failures of techno-capitalism in the *Wall Street Journal*. Having extracted myself from the vocation of law, I'm largely immune to these considerations. While I stand behind the text alone, to the extent my arguments have credibility beyond these pages, it's because I'm appropriately free of conflicting interests—as all lawyers, and all critics, should be.

Although I have no great responsibilities to law, I do have responsibilities to you, and they're straightforward: to inform and to entertain. I'll be glad if your reading provides some useful knowledge, such as your ability to nullify an unjust law if serving on a jury, notwithstanding the misleading instructions that judges often deliver. And I hope what follows is interesting. The law is fascinating, as the evergreen popularity of legal dramas makes plain. But the genuine article is so much more compelling and colorful than cinematic derivatives. Screenwriters might pause at having a character's liberty depend on whether a fish is a "record, document, or tangible object." But in real life, that issue went all the way to the Supreme Court, and it was a 5–4 nail-biter.[3] (The result: a fish is not a "tangible object," at least when it comes to the Sarbanes-Oxley Act. Actually, the case should have been decided

9–0, because why was government using an Enron-inspired law to hassle fishermen?)

Along the way, I hope to discredit law's central claim, which is that the legal system works as a coherent whole to produce outcomes that citizens recognize as just. Opinion polls suggest that most Americans already disdain law, but whenever we vote, call 911, sign a contract, hire a lawyer, pray that the courts provide us deliverance, or do any of the million other things in which law plays a role, we reveal our residual faith in the system. Regrettably, that faith is increasingly misplaced if this book's second theme is correct: that the law *can't* fulfill its promises—not reliably, not in its present state.

Before we proceed, let me provide one more illustration of how the chaotic, unfeeling operations of the legal factory produce perfect, and perfectly legal, absurdity. Recall that the Court (and Congress and other members of the legal firmament) have allowed corporations to force consumers—you, me, everyone—into "gotcha" arbitrations. The mere act of testing a product can be enough to shunt consumers into this world of rigged non-trials. Well, as it happens, this book is a product, and by reading any further, those legal luminaries—but emphatically *not* other readers—hereby consent to binding arbitration, per the Appendix. What the Appendix requires is that arbitrations occur at the time and place of my choosing (Antarctica is charming, I hear), with my mother as sole arbitrator. To which some of the professors, judges, and Congressmen pilloried herein might respond: that's nonsense.

Well, it might be nonsense, but it's also the law.[4]

INTRODUCTION

> Through over two hundred years of committed effort,
> our federal court system has become a model for justice
> throughout the world....Foreign jurists—especially
> those from emerging democracies who best under-
> stand the debilitating effects of injustice—uniformly
> admire...United States courts. They want to know the
> secret of our success.
>
> Chief Justice John Roberts (2013)[1]

It's not only possible, but likely, that all three branches of government are controlled by criminals. At a minimum, it cannot be proved otherwise, for the simple reason that no one truly knows what the criminal laws of the United States contain. The U.S. Department of Justice, charged with enforcing federal criminal law, can't even *count* the number of criminal provisions. The DOJ attempted a census in 1982, but after two years of intensive research, it could only say that "approximately 3,000 federal crimes" existed.[2] The difficulty was that America lacked (and lacks) a unified federal criminal code; Congress blithely sprinkles criminal provisions across the vast plain of law, a practice so unhelpful that DOJ's counting project was undertaken "for the express purpose of exposing [its] idiocy."[3] What DOJ did not appreciate is that idiots are immune to charges of idiocy, and Congress continues to play Johnny Appleseed, sowing crimes in unknowable quantity, in unknowable locations. Of course, laws that cannot be counted or found also cannot be understood or obeyed. The legal system declares that our problem—which it surely is, though it shouldn't be.

Today, the number of federal statutory crimes has grown from 3,000 to something well over 4,400, though the exact total is uncertain.[4] What can be stated confidently is that there are far more than 4,400 ways to incur criminal sanction. By 2013, federal bureaucracies had emplaced some 300,000 provisions with criminal implications.[5] To those unsettling and formidable totals must be added the various criminal laws and regulations of the fifty states and their bureaucracies, and the ordinances of the nation's 19,508 "incorporated places."[6] Of these millions of prohibitions and demands, many are trivial (Massachusetts can fine you $100 for starting the national anthem, but failing to sing it to conclusion), others verge on nonsense (Alaska's prohibition on being drunk in a bar, which police actually enforce), and some openly conflict (federal prohibitions on marijuana against state legalizations of the drug).[7] But rules are rules, no matter how inane or contradictory, no matter how fragmented or incontinently produced. What exists, we must obey; ignorance of the law is rarely an excuse. Because obedience is impossible, we all become criminals. Surely there is something deeply repellent about a legal system that condemns *everyone*, even if only technically, and even without consequences.

Voluminous as the criminal laws are, they constitute only a subset of the much larger corpus of law, though how *much* larger a corpus is destined to remain mysterious. In 2013, after endless inquiries by citizens, an exasperated researcher at the Library of Congress declared that counting the number of federal laws in force was "nearly impossible," and declined to go further.[8] (The research division's motto is *in custodia legis*, so these self-styled "legal custodians" seem to have lost track of their foster children—which seems illegal, but how are they to know?) One could plausibly argue that the unknowable superfluity of laws violates Constitutional guarantees of due process. That argument would be laughed out of court and most scholars would view it as embarrassingly unsophisticated, which speaks less about the merits of the due process argument than the mentalities prevailing in law's higher ranks, whose members accept lunacy as the cost of doing business. Law's elite (a word I use with no pejorative connotations) will happily critique any one error produced by the system, but rarely the system itself.

Yet, the system deserves a critique, because the stakes are so high. Law holds our lives and fortunes hostage. It reserves to itself the right to kill, draft, imprison, and tax us; affirm or void our marriages; regulate what we eat and drink; control how we work; and limit what we can say. Through "civil forfeiture," law can seize our property without charging us with a crime first (or, indeed, ever), a procedure law enforcement has used to line its own pockets and by which government relieved Americans of more property in 2014 than burglars did.[9] Against these powers and their abuse, citizens have limited recourse. The law grants its servants wide immunity from victims' suits to recover compensation. A cop can shoot you without financial liability, even if you've committed no crime and pose no danger, and even if the cop's conduct was otherwise unlawful, so long as it wasn't *so* grossly unlawful that no "reasonable" officer would have sanctioned it. (Law's definition of a "reasonable" officer is wildly *un*reasonable, but that's for later.) Thus, we the people, the notional source of legal power, are in practice the subjects of a discretionary and overbearing monarch named Law.

Like all monarchs, law employs swarms of courtiers to assure us of our master's benevolence. John Roberts declares American courts to be models of justice; police departments promise us their courtesy, professionalism, and respect; the Pledge of Allegiance speaks of the liberty and justice guaranteed to us by our republic of laws. When confronted with evidence that these ideals have been violated, law's PR team processes through the spin cycle: first, deny the wrong ("an unfortunate accident"), then blame the victim (a "bad hombre"), and finally, and only in the most extraordinary cases, concede the wrong while denying its importance ("one bad cop"). The formula can be applied as necessary to the corrupt Congressman, hapless bureaucrat, or abusive warden. Even Roberts's model federal judiciary now finds itself with explaining to do; in 2017, media reported that Alex Kozinski, one of the nation's most esteemed federal judges, was a serial sexual harasser. (No great surprise, given that he was investigated in 2008 for hosting an open pornography server, a matter promptly whitewashed and filed away.) So Kozinski, the erstwhile upholder of laws, seems to have broken quite a few himself, though he still found the time to mentor our newest Justice, Brett Kavanaugh. Kozinski is hardly alone. Just as local litigators knew that a sleazeball stalked the Ninth Circuit long before the media identified him, so, too, insiders know that abusers, tyrants, and crooks inhabit their own provinces of the legal system. Insiders just don't know if their experiences hold universally.

Nevertheless, if there really aren't *too* many bad apples, and most of those are promptly fished out of the barrel, then perhaps the legal system deserves our patience as it self-corrects. Brutal cops will be disciplined, corrupt Congressmen will be shamed into resignation or voted out of office, erring judges will be unseated, presidents will face legal sanction, and so forth. These comeuppances happen all the time, and are touted as proof that the system works, but that can only be true up to a point. If Volkswagen discovers a defect and issues a prompt and voluntary recall, it's fair to infer that VW has a stern commitment to quality. If VW issues dozens of recalls and only after media exposés (which is essentially what happened with VW's emissions scandals), the more plausible interpretation is that there's something rotten in Wolfsburg. Every complex system makes mistakes, but only gravely flawed systems make mistakes in volume—and law *does* make mistakes in volume.

In earlier pages, I contended that an important reason for the frequency and seriousness of legal failures is that law's constituent parts do not understand each other very well. (Nor, as we'll see, do they understand the public they serve.) I do not argue that all parts of the legal system need to *agree;* indeed, the Constitutional system of checks and balances presupposes that they often will not and should not. Rather, my argument is that when various parts of the legal system interact, they need to *comprehend* the workings of their partners. That comprehension often goes missing. For example, when Congress passes ambiguous or otherwise defective laws, judges must be able to decipher the purpose of those laws to apply them properly. To perform their interpretive feats, judges use a set of elaborate canons that they believe allow them to inhabit the minds of Congressional drafters. But empirical research shows that many legislative drafters are unaware of judicial canons, and those drafters who do know about the canons either disregard them or reject many of them outright. Accordingly, judges sometimes reach erroneous results because they have used the wrong tools. The law is filled with these sorts of misunderstandings, and as legal product passes from one department to another, defects compound.

To assess the scope of law's dysfunctions, this book takes a general tour of the American legal system (which I'll sometimes call "law," as context allows). To keep things to a single volume, this book breaks with several traditions. In legal academia, it's customary to survey all the monuments of existing scholarship, no matter how ancient or boring. That's about as gratifying as visiting the Met and allotting equal time to van Gogh's paintings and a tray of Dutch doorknobs. Close detail will be provided when it matters, but I'll leave the microscope on the shelf whenever possible, and this is for the best. (I once wrote an academic article parsing the word "scienter," which roughly means "wrongful intent." That took forty pages; holding to those standards, a book analyzing the Constitution would consume at least 300,000 pages, while a treatment of the Affordable Care Act's regulations would demand several hundred million.) Rather than going through the tiresome motions required of Respectable Contributions to Legal Discourse, this book reviews the general dynamics of the American legal system and its most consequential successes and failures.

I hope that the evidence adduced persuades you of my thesis which, to recapitulate, is that the various cogs in the legal machinery often do not mesh, leading to miscarriages of justice. For non-lawyers, this may not seem terribly ambitious. Yet, it points a gun directly at the heart of law. Law claims—indeed, *must* claim—that its parts work in harmonious comprehension. If judges don't understand how Congress works, they will misinterpret legislation. If Congress, which has delegated enormous power to executive branch bureaucracies, doesn't understand how those bureaucracies work or how much power has been given away, legislators may find their intentions disregarded, or even thwarted. And, of course, for legal actors to understand each other, they must possess a degree of self-awareness. But like the mad, forlorn Lear, they have but slenderly known themselves. Congress, for example, rarely reads or understands the legislation it passes, which is how the Senate managed to accidentally and dramatically *raise* some corporate taxes in its version of the Tax Cuts and Jobs Act of 2017.[10] The goal is to simply produce rules quickly and in volume, taming any monsters by means of exception. Worse still, law's departments, each overwhelmed by managing its own Island of Dr. Moreau, hardly realize that their beasts have escaped to breed with other creatures in a larger archipelago of deformity.

The chapters that follow examine the different parties that make, interpret, and enforce law. However, description is not enough—law doesn't simply exist; it should be effective and legitimate. Accordingly, the first chapters address what laws can do, how they can be made well, and where their limits lie. These matters are not properly addressed in American law schools, an omission that reverberates throughout the legal system for the obvious reason that law school graduates fill many critical positions in the system. Lacking a firm notion of the sane and the good, lawyers can only make undereducated guesses, using hunches informed by legal customs. These customs are more habits than heuristics, but to the extent law thinks, these are its default modes of cogitation.

Customs of the Natives

Four mental tics dominate legal thinking: slavish deference to authority, a belief in the normalcy of American law, an obsession with the past, and an unshakable belief in the power of rules. These beliefs are often deeply unhelpful and can defeat law's social purposes, but they do allow us to reliably *predict* how law will confront many problems.

Servility. Law inverts normal business mores: the customer (you) might be wrong, but the boss (officialdom) is always right. Given law's famously quarrelsome nature, servility may seem an unlikely attribute, but once a higher power clicks its heels together, lesser legal beings rapidly fall into line—assuming they understand their orders. Servility is the helpmeet of hierarchy and authoritarianism, traits that suffuse law, which is problem enough. But servility is also anti-thought, and radically constrains legal discussion: this is how ancient injustices pervade the law without provoking many systemic critiques.

To illustrate by extremes, all lawyers are trained from professional birth to view the Supreme Court with awe. The Court has accomplished some amazing things and has included some jurists of real genius. However, in the past century alone, the Court has let stand laws and orders requiring segregation, ethnic internment camps, the execution of minors (until *2005*), the suppression of free speech (about the Constitution, incredibly), the involuntary sterilization of "imbeciles," the immunization of police brutality, and the diversion of public lawsuits into private fora.[11] The last three are still on the books, supplemented by blemishes including the Court's summary resolution of the 2000 presidential election on intellectually flimsy and nakedly partisan grounds.[12] This would seem to counsel some skepticism about the Court. Yet, while lawyers vehemently debate the merits of today's decisions, they mostly avoid questioning the Court *as an institution.*

Let me provide an example by making an observation I haven't seen get much play elsewhere. The Court is supposed to provide a bulwark against executive tyranny. But a majority of the present Court helped create an over-powerful executive by articulating doctrines of presidential maximalism before they became Justices—and indeed, we can speculate that those accommodations were *why* Justices Alito, Gorsuch, Kagan, Kavanaugh, and Roberts landed on presidential short lists. If this matter is raised, it's always presented in personal terms—Nominee A being too cozy with White House

B—rather than as the institutional issue it is. When the straightest path to a Court nomination is to undermine the judiciary's role as a check or balance, the Court has a structural problem. And what holds for the Court holds for most of law. Following orders is almost always safe; questioning orders (however much questioning is deserved), is dangerous. Law expects the same when interacting with the public: we are to do as we're told, full stop.

(Ab)normalcy. The second cultural tic is American law's belief in its own normalcy, which is so deeply held as to be invisible. But American law is *not normal.* For one, it's unusually expensive, and not unrelatedly, it facilitates much weirder lawsuits (only in America would an administrative law *judge* sue a local dry cleaner, claiming damages of $67 million for a lost pair of pants).[13] American law also stands out because it employs the common law, a system used only by Britain and its imperial stepchildren.[14] Most of the world draws upon the civil law tradition, in which American standards such as judge-made law, precedent, and adversarial trial play limited roles, or none at all.[15] American law is unimaginable without the judge-precedent-trial trinity, and while that trinity makes a certain amount of internal sense, that doesn't mean the system of which it is a part is normal or necessarily good. Even John Roberts, a sophisticated jurist, fell into the normalcy trap. When John Roberts said that federal courts were "uniformly" a "model…throughout the world," he made a statement that wobbled between the merely poetic and empirically untrue. (It was also false on its face.*) America's common-law courts can't be a model to civil-law courts, any more than pilots can learn to fly by watching cowboys ride horses.

The assumption of normalcy makes it difficult to raise basic questions about American law, or to see problems that are readily visible to outsiders. For example, precedent is an established feature of American law, and most lawyers accept its value without demurral (even if they often try to evade its

---

* Roberts said that foreign judges "uniformly" admire American courts, "especially [those] from emerging democracies." But the "especially" establishes an exception, and "uniformly" doesn't admit exceptions. Roberts provides another illustration of the legal habit of setting down a universal rule, only to immediately create exceptions.

consequences, which speaks volumes). After one judge jumps off a bridge, precedent requires that every future judge take a leap, all else being equal. Other nations believe precedent helps perpetuate old mistakes, especially when, as in American law, the operating assumption is that the more ancient the precedent, the better. Even the proper name for following precedent, *stare decisis*, betrays this principle of helpless antiquarianism. Aside from being unintelligible to the public, it's also wildly perverse to render a *common*-law principle in Latin, the language of Rome, birthplace of the *civil* law system. Such is the price of historical fetishism.

Historical obsessions. On the subject of history, law is trapped in a passionate, unhealthy relationship with it. Constantly looking to a past that's remote, and whose details law occasionally and catastrophically mangles, consigns us to unhealthy regress. To interpret laws written yesterday, judges look back to the Constitution. When that document is unclear, many judges (especially "originalist" jurists) examine the practices of the Framers, which were themselves informed by legal doctrines in eighteenth-century England, which in turn derived from historical clutter accumulating since the thirteenth century. Certainly, history can provide apt lessons. When we face the same problems as the Framers, James Madison can be illuminating about the Constitution he (co-)wrote. In 1791, America had a Congress and priests, and Madison's thoughts about mixing the two remain relevant. (As it happens, Madison believed that having chaplains in Congress was an unconstitutional blending.[16]) By contrast, in 1791, America had a Second Amendment, but not gangland Glocks, so the Framers' adamancy about the right to bear arms is less revealing (if that adamancy existed, which it arguably did not). But law is a grave-robber with eclectic tastes: it plucked one trinket from the corpse while ignoring the other.

The greatest temple to erratic historiography is the Supreme Court building located at the deeply unsubtle address of 1 First Street, Washington, D.C., center of the legal universe. Leaving aside the potent symbolism of John Roberts sealing the Court's front door in 2010, which requires no decoding, what are we to make of the Court's interior? The main chamber is adorned with a bizarre sculptural history of law that would stump Lara Croft, Indiana Jones, and Robert Langdon (he of *The Da Vinci Code*).[17] Almost none of the figures depicted are relevant to, or express values even vaguely consonant with, American law: the pharaoh Menes (irrelevant, obviously), Draco (so harsh that his name lives on in "draconian"), Augustus (swept away republican government), Justinian (laid foundations for modern *civil* law), Mohammed (elaborated *sharia*, which incidentally forbids his depiction), King John (had the Pope nullify Magna Carta), and Napoleon (abolished common law as a ludicrous anachronism). Sure, it's just decoration, but it's decoration of the *family home*. Why is it there? More pertinently, what does it *mean*? The answer to the second question is simple: law should use the past seriously or not at all, and any judicial opinion drawing on history should be treated with (as judges would say) "heightened scrutiny." Thus, our narrative will delve into the historical details to present counter-narratives when appropriate.

Blind faith in rules. For law, there is no problem that cannot be solved by a rule—preferably, many rules. Unfortunately, it's very difficult to craft even *one* clear, self-contained rule. Consider the old legal chestnut, the municipal sign reading "no vehicles allowed in park." Does that apply to bicycles, motorized wheelchairs, and ambulances, or only to private cars? Or does it allow a private car in the public green, so long as the gearshift isn't in "park"? It's difficult to say on semantic grounds. Yet, parks are not overrun by wayward vehicles, because common sense and basic decency give the rule life; we understand what the municipal prohibition means to convey and even if we don't, we err on the side of caution. What makes rules work, in other words, are norms—standards of community behavior. Modern law needs both rules and norms, but if given the choice, law prefers rules (making them, that is; not necessarily following them).

Norms, however, cannot be ignored. When rules and norms conflict, citizens can become disgruntled to the point where they ignore the law or deem it illegitimate. Arguably, the entirety of modern law violates two norms central to our conceptions of justice: the norms of fair warning and even application. Many areas of law are so unknowably large that fair warning doesn't exist—even as a concept. And by granting its own officials special dispensation to ignore rules deemed too complex to follow, law also violates the norm of even application. In the end, the vast system of loopholes must reform itself into legitimacy or face an abrupt and extra-legal revolution, a process that's called (in no slight coincidence) a "state of exception."

By Way of Preview

To provide a preliminary sense for how law functions end to end, it's useful to observe one set of laws moving through the assembly line, a process that roughly tracks the order of the succeeding chapters. As we started with criminal law, we may as well continue the theme. The general purpose of criminal law is to impose order by issuing clear rules within Constitutional boundaries, with suspects apprehended fairly, charges supported by credible evidence, and cases tested in open court by equal adversaries before a jury. If there's a conviction, the sentence should be determined by a judge who fits punishment to crime, with convicts contained and rehabilitated until they can be safely discharged. This is how it works on TV and in textbooks, and for once, they have it right: this is how criminal law is supposed to work in real life. Sadly, it doesn't.

In the 1980s, Congress responded to widespread fears about rising crime with a wave of legislation. The project began in 1984, the same year that the DOJ threw up its hands at the already exasperating profusion of criminal law. Rather than study the social factors responsible for rising crime, or ponder why existing laws had failed to stem misbehavior, Congress decided to slap criminal sanctions on anything that caused opinion polls to twitch. The first product was the Comprehensive Crime Control Act of 1984 (CCCA), which debuted stringent new provisions for drug crimes, so that any user not immediately shamed into sobriety by Nancy Reagan's Just Say No campaign would be treated to a cleansing stint in the federal clink. For maximum effect, the CCCA opened the door to civil forfeitures, by which the illicit gains of the drug trade could be seized. Forfeiture arguably violated existing rules and had obvious potential to be abused, though perhaps Congress was beguiled by images of Detectives Crockett and Tubbs breaking the spine of South Floridian criminality by snapping up coke-funded Ferraris in *Miami Vice* (which premiered shortly before the CCCA passed).

Congress then passed the Anti-Drug Abuse Act of 1986. That act was cobbled together in the month following the furor over basketball star Len Bias's death by overdose of crack cocaine, whose distribution or use would now be punished much more severely than cocaine in powder form. The bill had many problems, including a real whopper: Len Bias actually died of a *powder* cocaine overdose, as was becoming clear before the Act was finalized. Congress had missed its target before it even pulled the trigger. But Congress wanted to take a dramatic stand all the same. So, in addition to harsh penalties for crack, Congress expanded the range of crimes subject to mandatory minimum sentences, a profound rebalancing of a criminal justice system about which Congress knew little and declined to know more. As one of the legislative aides involved later reflected: "We had no hearings. We did not consult with the Bureau of Prisons, or with the federal judiciary, or with DEA, or with the Justice Department."[18] The Act passed anyway, and the states pursued similar experiments.

In the 1980s, Congress also chartered the U.S. Sentencing Commission, a new bureaucracy charged with writing up the Sentencing Guidelines, in its current form a rigid and barely intelligible monster that collapses into a numbing matrix of forty-three criminal offense levels, six tiers of criminal history "points," and four sentencing "zones" by which prison terms are calculated.[19] The Guidelines reflected law's faith in rules (628 pages of them, in the latest version), but worked about as well as boarding planes by five-zone group numbers. Worse, the combination of the Guidelines, mandatory minimums, and the functional abolition of parole vaporized the existing sentencing regime almost overnight, without fully considering the ramifications.

The bureaucratization of criminal sentencing was inevitable. In important ways, bureaucracies *are* the government. Your medical and retirement benefits are formally established by Congressional acts, but in practice, what you receive and whether you receive it are decided by bureaus. Bureaucracies provide the rules, the enforcers, and in many cases, the courts—fora in which bureaucracies can sue you, using their own judges, interpreting their own rules. Bureaucracies operate beyond public control, which partially explains why they are despised. But most bureaucracies also lie beyond *Congressional* control; in legislators' haste to offload responsibility, they deposited most bureaucracies into the executive branch. As a result, bureaus jump to the orders of presidents who often have different priorities than legislators.

Unlike most bureaucracies, the Sentencing Commission was unusual in that it was (fictionally) housed in the judiciary and enjoyed the assistance of an eminent scholar, Stephen Breyer.[20] Breyer seemed ideal: a former Senate staffer who was then a part-time law professor specializing in bureaucracies and Constitutional law, as well as a full-time appellate judge. Despite this rare combination of talent—if any bureaucracy had the resources to do good work, it was *this* one—the Sentencing Commission facilitated awful outcomes, and some of its machinery violated the laws in which Breyer was expert. In 2005, by which time Breyer was a Justice, his brethren concluded that the Guidelines as applied sometimes conflicted with the Constitution.[21]

In the meantime, equipped with take-all-prisoners criminal legislation, police rounded up the usual suspects. Because there are so many crimes, policing can descend into arbitrariness, which helps explain how the traffic code devolves into crimes of "driving while black," just as the baroque tax code allows the phenomenon of being "audited while rich." No law allows (and some forbid) discrimination on the bases of color or class, but many judges tread lightly around policing. Indeed, conservative judges immunized police from all but the most egregious abuse claims, and allowed cops to gather tainted evidence under doctrines of "reasonable mistake." Once again, the justification was complexity; police could not be expected to know or follow every rule. Conservative judges also argued that police deserve the benefit of the doubt, with Antonin Scalia noting (in 2006) that gross police misconduct was largely a thing of the past.[22] This was either disingenuous or catastrophically underinformed; either way, Scalia's forgiving attitude helped ensure that misconduct would be a thing of the *future*.

Once detained, brutally or otherwise, suspects are handed off to prosecutors, who select charges from a menu whose options and prices have been greatly inflated by tough-on-crime initiatives. In theory, prosecutors make their choices apolitically and case-by-case. Judges assume this is true, but that's not really tenable, given that DOJ has always been politicized and most local prosecutors are elected. Discretion would be less terrifying if prosecutors had to test their cases in court. But the arrival of the Guidelines and mandatory sentencing, rampant overcriminalization, the corruption of the bail system, and the underfunding of public defenders' offices amplified prosecutors' coercive powers, and the plea bargain reigns supreme.

The sliver of cases not summarily resolved by means outside judicial control are then sent to trial courts, which barely deserve the name. Most actions, whether civil or criminal, are resolved out of court, determined by the variables of money, law, and evidence, in descending order of importance. Quite simply, law is beyond the financial reach of most Americans. Even at $200 per hour, the least any decent city lawyer can afford to charge ($300–$1,000 per hour is the usual range), the poorest 20 percent of Americans could afford zero days of legal representation and the next 20 percent, about a week. Only the richest 20 percent—really, just the top 5 to 10 percent—can afford to litigate comfortably.[23] Pure financial necessity forces almost all cases to settle, and quickly, though this is not a subject of universal interest among judges.

At least criminal defendants have the option of court, however nominally. For civil matters, including important areas such as consumer protection and employment rights, access to courts may be denied entirely, with claims channeled straight into the privatized system of justice known as arbitration. In fact, the *criminal* laws of the 1980s played an important role in the diversion of *civil* litigation, a development no one quite anticipated back in 1984–1986. By the early 1990s, fearing a flood of new criminal cases, conservative Justices began diverting civil cases into arbitration. The flood never materialized, but conservative Justices kept expanding arbitration's reach, so that essentially every breathing American has now relinquished rights to sue in court. Arbitration clauses are everywhere: in mobile phone contracts, employment agreements, insurance documents, software licenses, and so on. Courts say that these contracts are entered into freely and knowingly (perhaps judges read software agreements every time their devices update) and claim that arbitration affords a speedy and fair forum for resolving disputes arising under such contracts. Of course, undisguised corporate enthusiasm for these agreements, made in unlikely paradises of willing consent such as hospital admissions, suggested that judicial assumptions might be unwarranted. Not only are law's departments disconnected from each other, they are estranged from life and logic, too.

Returning to criminal litigation, one of its great surprises is the secondary importance of evidence. What matters most is having the resources to gin up a hefty file of *stuff*, reliable or otherwise. We supposedly live in a golden age of criminal forensics, but contrary to *CSI* and its brethren, much forensic evidence is rubbish. Police labs have been mired in scandal for years, most forensic methods are quackery, witnesses are often worse than useless, and even reliable techniques like DNA analysis are prone to misinterpretation. Although there are rules that allow courts to independently filter out garbage forensics and other shoddy evidence, judges rarely do so on their own initiative. The burden of discrediting evidence rests almost entirely with defendants, most of whom cannot afford that undertaking. Perhaps that doesn't matter overmuch—the law often doesn't understand what evidence means, though this is a tragedy for an institution supposedly devoted to facts.

With economic and evidentiary factors stacked against them, defendants usually travel a direct line from arrest to arraignment to sentencing. Although one justification for the Sentencing Commission was to reduce racial disparities in punishment, the new tools and discretion granted to police and prosecutors allowed more minorities to be rounded up, and given (often racially motivated) prior convictions, these defendants found themselves shoved into the more hellish parts of the Guidelines matrix. Compounding the debacle, Congress never decided what to do with the human cargo being laded onto the ship of state. One major goal of prison was to rehabilitate criminals, but legal changes in the 1980s withdrew the necessary funds and incentives. Congress also failed to consult with prison authorities to see if the prisoner influx could even be contained. Prisons quickly became overcrowded, some so severely as to violate Constitutional rights, prompting involuntary releases. Indeed, conditions deteriorated so badly that some prisons became crimogenic, making their residents *more* likely to commit crime upon release.

The whole tough-on-crime experiment was a fiasco. To succeed, the experiment needed a grounding in social realities (by the early 1990s, crime rates were falling for reasons unrelated to the crackdown) and demanded coordination across the many departments required to fulfill a policy affecting tens of millions. The whole process became impossibly complex, with each rule engendering an exception and a new rule, hypocrisy and inefficiency multiplying at bacterial rates. But law, having other lives to ruin, and other ways to ruin them, moved on.

The legal system is often wrongly compared to a Rube Goldberg machine. A Goldberg machine, however complicated, eventually achieves its designed purpose. It may take three hamsters, twelve lightbulbs, and a steam engine to fold a napkin in Goldberg's universe, but the napkin gets folded. The legal system has a great many more hamsters, lightbulbs, and steam engines, all strung together in an enormous factory of Goldberg machines, yet it can't fold the napkin, and sometimes sets it on fire.

The heart of law's complicated assembly is the rule of law, a concept usually rendered as a "government of laws, not of men." There's more to rule *of* law than rule *by* law, but the essential points are that every part of society must play by the rules, and that law must not descend into the arbitrary whims of legal officials. However, because modern American law is overly complex, enforcement is necessarily selective; because law insulates officials from the consequences of their decisions, law becomes unaccountable; by necessity, modern law can only be rule by men. And because legislators and judges have tolerated—indeed, facilitated—the concentration of so much power in the presidency, it's not so much the rule of *men* as the rule of *one man*. From 2017, that man commenced an open war with the very people who granted his office such incredible power: a spectacular instance of law failing to comprehend itself or the consequences of its work. The incomprehension is mutual, of course, because Trump no more understands the Constitution than a cat fathoms quantum mechanics. Some critics deem Trump an outlier; vindictive, feckless, and incompetent, but this underscores the essential point. An incompetent president cannot summon quasi-despotic powers by himself—he must *inherit* them. And that inheritance will compound and be passed along, because until law reforms itself, the estate tax on stupidity and despotism stands at zero.

Some of the best legal arguments are not arguments at all, but questions that inspire doubts about the parties and the system. How many police departments need to look like those of Baltimore, Chicago, Oakland, and Detroit before trust in police breaks everywhere? How many courthouse doors can be closed by plea bargains and arbitration before citizens realize that courts are transforming themselves into mere civic adornments? How unaffordable must justice become before "justice for all" curdles into a sadistic joke—when only 20 percent of people can afford a trial, or 10 percent, or 1 percent? Will people continue to respect a system that promises jury trials, reasonable bail, and humane punishment but delivers none of the above? Just how many self-defeating blunders need accumulate before society realizes that law has only a tenuous grasp on its operations? And what happens when the law's servants declare themselves above the law?

As law students know, the answer is: "It depends."

CHAPTER ONE

THE VALUE OF LAW: MORE THAN JUST A NUISANCE

> [T]he supremacy of the law is essential to the existence of the Nation....
>
> Dwight D. Eisenhower[1]

Karl Marx thought the workers' paradise would have no lawyers.[2] The lawyerless utopia was nothing new, though most visionaries sidestepped the question of what would happen to attorneys during the revolutionary Rapture. Marx's novel contribution was to predict that the legal class would not disappear as the violent precondition of revolution, but as a peaceful result. In Marx's view, legal systems existed to impose the will of the bourgeoisie on the proletariat, i.e., to transfer limited resources from labor to capital. As socialism would abolish both scarcity and the bourgeoisie, it followed that lawyers and, by implication, most law, would be superfluous. There would be nothing to argue about in the dictatorship of the proletariat—in dictatorships, there never is.

The belief that law was merely an exploitative and dispensable stage in social evolution revealed a crucial limit to Marx's theory, just as it reveals the limits of other schemes that would eliminate or radically curtail law, whether espoused by Marxists, anarcho-libertarians, or small-state

1

ultraconservatives. Law is civilization's essential technology; there is no complex society without it. The hammer and sickle, fire and the wheel, get humanity only so far—perhaps to the level of large tribes. But New York c. 2020 AD, or even Mesopotamia c. 1800 BC, requires a legal system. Marx was absurdly well-positioned to know this, not just as a lawyer (for he was that) but also as a social historian whose home base was the British Museum. Had Marx poked his head out of the Museum's Reading Room, he would have been confronted by thousands of ancient slabs, papers, tokens, statues, fragments of papyrus, and other accumulations inscribed with legal directives testifying to the link between law and civilization. True, many of these antiquities refer to matters of slavery and private property, slotting with perfect cogency into Marxist theory: barbarous relics. But they contained other features that did not fit quite as neatly into Marxist historiography: early consumer protection laws, prohibitions on violence, and demands for the just treatment of the poor and helpless by the rich and powerful.[3] Life is more than a game of Monopoly, and law is more than a set of rules to shuffle around a fixed sum of money. There was a reason why the vitrines displaying the wares of peoples without law were so barren.

In viewing law as primarily parasitic rather than generative, Marx failed to appreciate law's real potential. To understand law in trivial terms, as a mere instrument to oppress and exploit, or a transient artifact of capitalist evolution, does society a disservice. The purpose of law is not to add a civilized veneer to the whims of the powerful; law helps save us from that. Law also maximizes our ability to create while protecting others from our creations. Law can be tiresome, of course, just like flossing and cardio days, but like those chores it has greater purposes.

This isn't to say law is perfect or always achieves its highest aims, but starting from a position of perfect cynicism makes it hard to see where law errs; the view that law always does wrong precludes any belief that the law can ever do right. The general public is not cynical about law's potential; by expressing deep frustrations with legal institutions, it reveals its *high* expectations of law. There's a reason the *New York Times* reviews Broadway's productions of *Oklahoma!* instead of Tulsa High's; only those capable of greatness, and granted the privileges to achieve it, provoke passion or reward thoughtful critique. So, before embarking on a sustained meditation on the failures of American law *as practiced*, it's worth pausing to consider the value of law in the abstract, and what resources law might require to achieve its potential.

Law's most obvious value is its ability to restrain violence (a function Marx grudgingly accepted might persist in his otherwise unregulated utopia). Curbing violence was law's original task, and one so valuable that early societies treated law as a divine gift. Ancient pantheons invariably feature a law-giver, like Athena, who ended otherwise unceasing cycles of retributive violence by requiring feuding clans to resolve their disputes before a jury.[4] Law grants legitimate institutions a monopoly on violence, which ends vigilantism and creates order, a point Hobbes famously made when he declared that in the lawless state of nature, there could only be a war of all against all, in which life was "nasty, brutish, and short." Hobbes, who lived through a fierce phase in one of England's civil wars, understandably made physical safety law's paramount duty. But law could do more than bring tranquility; just as "nasty, brutish, and short" is only a snippet of Hobbes's thoughts, so the reduction of violence is merely a subset of legal possibility. What Hobbes said, more fully, was that life without a legal Leviathan would be *"solitary, poor,* nasty, brutish, and short," with "no culture of the earth...no commodious building;...no knowledge on the face of the earth; no account of time; no arts; no letters; no society."[5] Law provides the safety to build, but how much more can it do, and to what ends?

The Mundane Miracle: Making Life Easier

The Constitution doesn't get overly specific about the objects of American law, aside from some throat-clearing in the Preamble about insuring "domestic tranquility" (shades of Hobbes), securing the "blessings of liberty," and promoting the "general welfare."[6] When the Constitution provides details about anything beyond tedious matters like electors or the Census, it's often to list things law *can't* do. But the thrust of the Preamble, and the latent assumption of the Constitution as a whole, is that law exists to coordinate society. This is the dead minimum to which all legal systems must aspire—and it's a useful starting point because (anarchists aside) coordination is the only major legal aim on which broad and immediate agreement is possible. From this lowly base camp, we can attain otherwise unreachable agreement on other legal goals.

Given that law's most publicized operations are intensely divisive, social coordination may appear a fantastical aspiration. Whatever else they are, laws on abortion, race relations, and gay marriage don't seem to promote coordination so much as provoke discord. But reading the daily news alone risks a distorted impression of law's general operations. Headlines always feature the most exciting (i.e., divisive) matters, and it can seem that law is nothing but a series of bombshells, often lobbed by courts. Of course, cases like *Roe* and *Obergefell* are morally and politically significant, but they have been, and always will be, volumetrically *in*significant. Workaday traffic management generates more legislation in a month, and brings more court cases in a week, than abortion and gay rights have in forty years. Most of law is like this, governing conduct whose moral dimensions are functionally nonexistent and whose emotional content is nil. Legal drama will come in later pages, but by first considering law's less controversial operations, law's value becomes easier to see.

By coordinating society, law makes life efficient. Most of the time, we simply want law to *choose*, and have no real feelings about what choice it makes. Who has passionate feelings about which side of the street we drive on, so long as we all drive on the same side? Though Americans drive trillions of miles every year, I'm aware of no Supreme Court briefs challenging the gross injustice of right-hand driving, just as I know of no mass protests demanding that billions of appliances be free to swing between America's parochial 120-volt standard and the impossible chic of the 220-volt Europlug. Laws were made, life went on. Admittedly, "efficient coordination" is a prosaic, awkward

4

slogan compared to the customary and uplifting pith of justice, fairness, equality, due process, and all the rest. But it's important nonetheless.

Law's methods for coordinating society are sometimes easy to see (consider the stop sign), but the huge efficiencies achieved can be hard to intuit, especially because a chief efficiency is being freed from thinking about the mundane. When a lotion bottle promises 15 SPF, no one has to reach for the chemistry set, because law assures us of that quantum of protection. Law's price is to make Coppertone and the FDA responsible for checking SPF, but those entities can do so more efficiently than consumers, reducing net costs; a few pennies per bottle is convenience had cheaply. Most (though not all) regulations on product safety, accuracy-in-advertising, professional competency, and so on, partake of this morally neutral, economically efficient dynamic.

Indeed, without a vast range of boring laws, complex societies would grind to a halt. Most transactions are now anonymous and would be impracticable if law did not provide a substitute for the personal trust that formerly lubricated commerce. The more we trust the legal system, the more easily we can transact. Even in situations that warrant specific investigation, law greatly shortens the chain of inquiry. Consider the dreaded home remodel, which often seems like a project that law makes *more* time consuming, not less (permits, building codes, etc.). What this view overlooks is that remodels are only practicable in the first place because other people obey the laws that apply to them. Without regulations on licensing and financial responsibility, you would have to vet your general contractor *and* his insurer *and* do the same for all the subcontractors *and* their insurers *and* test the fitness of every brick and wire used, etc., etc. *ad infinitum.* In a regulated world, law allows you to focus on one question: Is your contractor a bozo? If he is, law also provides your means of redress.

Thus, law permits efficient, large-scale coordination, i.e., the civilization Marx assumed would magically organize itself. By announcing standards ahead of time, even if somewhat imperfectly, law allows citizens to plan their behaviors and to have those behaviors predicted in turn. You do not have to think about whether your tailor prefers payment in the giant stone currency of Yap Island and they do not have to think about whether you feel like paying them. The law says they must take U.S. currency and you must to give it to them; the suit is bespoke, the transaction is not. This holds at any scale, anywhere in the United States. (The legal philosopher Scott Shapiro advances a more nuanced version of this dynamic in his characterization of laws as sets of "plans."[7])

There's another benefit to this coordinated/efficient view of the law: if efficiency is a meta-purpose, law that creates undue complexity or reduces total output risks self-defeat. Until the 1960s, efficiency considerations did not figure overmuch in scholarly accounts of law's work, but since then, the law and economics movement (L&E) has placed efficiency at the center of legal discourse. L&E scholars enjoyed wild success, not only because they found important applications for economics in law, but because they showed, somewhat to traditionalists' surprise, that law had long worried about efficiency—implicitly, perhaps, but deeply.[8] Even before Adam Smith rearranged his pin factories, law weighed costs and benefits, assigning duties to those fittest to carry them out. Once L&E became mainstream, judges and lawmakers were freed to put economic theories, previously latent and under-evolved, at the center of commercial law. Even criminal law could be framed in terms of efficiency. Although criminal law is normally viewed in moral terms that don't apply to civil law (no sane contract describes remedies for its breach as "punishment"), criminal law can easily be viewed as efficient. In deterring or removing untrustworthy players from the system, criminal law smooths everyone else's transactions. By the 1970s, legislators and presidents had also explicitly incorporated efficiency into their directives; the cost/benefit analyses now embedded in regulations were inspired by law's efficiency revolution.

However, viewing law as an exercise in efficient planning (and perhaps one better done by PhDs, not JDs) raised hackles. Many Ivy League academics considered L&E almost fatally uncouth; the image of Justice, looking very much like Jeremy Bentham's withered corpse clutching a ledger, galled a profession whose self-perception involved legions of sky-dwelling, sword-wielding nymphs defending the rights of man and human dignity. It's true that law isn't *purely* about efficiency. The right to a jury trial is not really "efficient," not at first glance and sometimes not at last glance. And even if some basic rights could be framed in efficiency terms, it would be skin-crawling to do so. For example, the right to abortion may produce social efficiencies. Though this is one of the few important claims about abortion that can be empirically tested, it is not an argument to raise in polite company, let alone one likely to sway a Supreme Court Justice.*

In addition to being unable to easily justify certain bedrock values, L&E faces internal limits. L&E requires humans to be mostly rational, which they often are not. Even in the dullest commercial transactions where no high principles are at stake, sloth, pettiness, and obstinacy feature as major variables, illogical expressions that appear in the most distant corners of L&E's spreadsheet, if they appear at all. This creates problems, which law rather irritatingly facilitates. In many lawsuits, at least one side has—almost by definition—behaved irrationally. The prospect of trial exacerbates maladaptive behaviors, because humans want (or think they want) their Day in Court. Sometimes people ask more of law than mere efficiency, and when they do, what they want is *justice*.

What About Justice?

Efficiency can only be law's starting—not highest—aspiration: justice occupies the uppermost slot. After all, attorneys general don't lead the "Department of Efficiency" or even the "Bureau of Law," they run the Department of Justice. Lawyers work in the "justice system," and students pledge allegiance to a nation with "liberty and justice for all."[9] Justice, alas, is trickier than efficiency. Law should produce justice, but for all the talk, it's hard to quantify

---

* *Freakonomics* famously linked lower crime rates with the rise in abortion access; the book's prime mover was Steven Levitt (a University of Chicago economist) and its abortion chapter used work done with John Donohue (a Stanford law professor of the—you guessed it—L&E school).

justice, or agree on its meaning. It's also basically impossible to show that justice is an *explicit* Constitutional requirement. Though many people quite reasonably assume the Constitution grants them a freestanding right to justice, the Constitution is elusive on the subject.*[10] The Preamble is the only place where "justice" appears in anything like its operant sense—and the Preamble, like a corporate mission statement, has no legal effect. Courts will no more accept a claim based on a "right to justice" than they would a claim based on the Preamble's promise of a "more perfect Union." Even the Amendments, which are more helpfully specific than the body of the Constitution, do not list "justice" among the rights conferred. The closest the Constitution comes to promising justice is in the Fifth Amendment, which requires "due process," and the Fourteenth, which requires the same plus "equal protection." The reason so many important and controversial claims invoke those Amendments is because they open some of the few Constitutional doors to redressing free-floating complaints of injustice.[11] People vigorously debate the precise dimensions of those doors. But it is to the lasting credit of Americans and their legal system that justice remains an animating virtue.

Even if the word "justice" doesn't feature much in the Constitution, once we accept the uncontroversial proposition that law's general goal is to produce efficiency and coordination, then justice must be a legal goal. A population that does not believe its laws produce justice (at least most of the time) will not follow the law when doing so is inconvenient—and police, being a finite resource, cannot coerce everyone into compliance. Without justice, there can be no coordination and no efficiency, and law becomes pointless. But achieving justice requires adding another floor to the legal tower: the rule of law.

---

*   *Law & Order* looms too large over American legal culture to ignore, so let's just get this over with. From 1990 to 2010, the DAs in *Law & Order* milled around in front of the New York Supreme Court, whose entablature reads (on TV and in real life): "The True Administration Of Justice Is The Firmest Pillar Of Good Government," quoting a letter from George Washington to Edmund Randolph, the first attorney general. However, the actual quote refers to the "*due* administration of justice," which is not quite the same thing. If law makes mistakes right at the front door, what sort of errors are committed inside?

The Rule of Law: Fairness, Accountability, and Impartiality

There's broad consensus that rule of law is an essential component in worthy legal systems. However, ever since A. V. Dicey popularized the term in the 1880s, people have bickered about its meaning. ("Rule of law" is like "American values"—everyone's for it, until someone else explains their personal vision of its details.) In 2006, Tom Bingham, then the grandest judge in England, graciously admitted that he "was not quite sure" what the rule of law meant.[12]

Bingham was unique only in admitting his uncertainty about the precise contours of the rule of law. (From here on, I'll generally call it the "RoL," for economy's sake.) Most lawyers don't know much about the RoL as a formal concept, and op-ed writers ventilating about Bush II/Obama/Trump's disdain for the RoL usually know even less. But the term is fancy and vague, and therefore much in vogue, its usage in books having doubled since 1980, and in recent years the RoL has featured in the daily emissions of press and politicians alike, not always with felicity. In 2017, the online magazine *Slate* asked readers to pay for that outlet's political reportage because "[t]he Trump administration poses a unique threat to the rule of law," while that same year, Deputy Attorney General Rod Rosenstein celebrated Constitution Day by remarking that "President Trump honors that principle...by appointing Department of Justice officials who support the rule of law."[13] It's possible, but deeply unlikely, that *Slate* and Rosenstein both employed RoL correctly.

There's no need to be confused about the RoL's basics. The term is newish, but its principles are ancient. Aristotle grabbed the nettle when he argued that fixed laws of general application do better than ad hoc (and ad hominem) decrees.[14] The barons who signed Magna Carta, and their inheritors like John Locke, also knew this. Tom Paine encapsulated the idea with his famous "in America the Law is King": people should obey the law, but law shouldn't obey one person.[15] The idea has become a little more elaborate over time, but the basic concept remains and it's an essential part of good legal systems. When the EU cohered, it expressly incorporated the RoL into its members' legal systems.

Whether rendered as "the law is king," *Rechtsstaatlichkeit, primauté de la droit, praworządność,* or plain old "rule of law," the minima are always these: (1) everyone is (2) bound by laws (3) of general application (4) as applied by ordinary courts. President or prole, governor or governed, no person is above law's sanctions or beneath its protections, and if a person is hauled into court, that court must be of the regular variety—no special tribunals, Star Chambers, secret courts, or other exotica; at least, not without extremely compelling reasons provided in advance. Those are the basic requirements for the RoL, and without the RoL there can be no real sense of justice and the entire legal system would be denuded of value. The RoL is how law provides the fairness, accountability, uniformity, and impartiality we expect of good legal systems. Arguably, the RoL also requires the guarantee of some basic set of human rights, promoting the freedom and equality we expect from law. In America, the Bill of Rights does most of the work without independent resort to the RoL.

Although RoL has a solid, ascertainable meaning, and is an ideal worth fighting for, the term has an awkward history, especially at the Supreme Court—starting with 1803's *Marbury v. Madison* and running through 2000's *Bush v. Gore.* In the latter case, attorneys for both candidates claimed the RoL served their side; undeniably, the case had RoL implications. Yet the majority opinion declined to invoke the RoL and even the dissents barely mentioned the concept. This was perhaps wise, as the swift intervention of the Court to decide a deeply political matter that had not fully percolated through normal legal channels suggested that a special exception was being made, and special exceptions don't sit well with the RoL. A more charitable, but less plausible, explanation was that the Court felt uncomfortable invoking "rule of law" as the Constitution doesn't contain that phrase. (Then again, we would not expect it to; the term was popularized after Ratification.)

However, it's fair to read the Constitution to embody at least some RoL principles, even if not all Court decisions do. Certainly, the Fourteenth Amendment's Equal Protection Clause says that no citizen is *beneath* the law. Whether a person can be Constitutionally *above* the law is, regrettably, both less clear and increasingly urgent. There are a few snippets in the Constitution that seem to provide loopholes. Notably, the Pardon Clause allows presidents to excuse violations of federal law retroactively; the right president and right criminal can manipulate matters to end-run the RoL. The Constitution is also vague about the breadth of its protections, which encourages autocratic officials to shove ever-more people into the category of Citizens Lite, or to strip citizenship entirely, as with expanding process of "denaturalization." The technical debate on these matters is arcane, but focusing on legal values simplifies the issues considerably. Ambiguities should be resolved to minimize the number of people above the law or outside its protections. Anything else undermines the goals of efficiency, coordination, and fairness that are essential legal virtues, and threatens the RoL.

It could be objected that the definition of RoL proposed here fails because not all its requirements appear cleanly in the Constitution. But constitutions are not chunks of isolated words; they have contexts and structures. Although the Court has made some specific and authoritarian blunders in this area, its general view (including that of its textualist/originalist wing) is that the Constitution incorporates *some* version of the RoL. And one of the most important reasons to believe the RoL exists in the Constitution is because that document establishes a strong system of checks and balances. From here, legal values become entwined with legal methods, starting with judicial review—not a freestanding value, but necessary to achieving all other legal values.

Having the Last Word: Judicial Review

The Constitution enumerates many checks and balances (vetoes, overrides, impeachments, confirmations, the power of the purse), but does not explicitly list one crucial check: the ability of courts to void laws inconsistent with the Constitution. But there are good reasons to believe that judicial review has always been present in the Constitution, because without judicial review,

11

the RoL would be toothless, and the Jenga tower we've been carefully assembling in rough accordance with the Framers' instructions would fall apart. Naturally, any time the Constitution implies an important power without actually listing it—the right to privacy, for example—certain people get their dander up. (These people would do well to remember that the Constitution doesn't explicitly guarantee the right to *vote*; that's just a norm.[16]) Judicial review is no different, and even some judges attack the idea, with Justice Gorsuch making some notably strange remarks on the subject, although he seems perfectly fine with judicial review when the reviewing judge is Gorsuch.

Beyond Constitutional silence, the usual critique is that judicial review is an antidemocratic usurpation of an elected branch by an unelected one—and, superficially, this is true. At a deeper level, though, judicial review is *radically* democratic, in the sense of government responding to a citizen's needs. If government violates your rights, your representative, with 740,000 other people to serve, can only do so much (in practice, nothing). But if the government stifles your Constitutional rights as an individual, a federal judge must listen. In courts, the government-to-citizen ratio is 1:1—and judicial review gives that single judge the power to help you. This is a legal service worth having.

Judicial review was inferred by the courts, most famously in *Marbury v. Madison*, a strange case that deserves more than the cursory attention it receives.[17] Careful study of *Marbury* might have even persuaded the Court to be more circumspect in *Bush v. Gore* and in other cases that have unnecessarily weakened the judiciary's apolitical mythos.* In the standard telling, *Marbury* established courts' ability to declare laws unconstitutional—a pivotal moment for the RoL, triumph for separation of powers, cue the choir. But *Marbury* is both less and more than that. It's "less," because *Marbury* was not a pathbreaker on judicial review; the idea had been present in court decisions and political dialogue well before Ratification.[18] This crucial detail shows that judicial review wasn't some freebooting innovation; the Framers

---

* The critique here is about the *process* of *Bush v. Gore*, not the election's outcome per se.

knew about it, and could reasonably be said to have assumed its existence in the same way that they assumed, when requiring presidents to be at least age 35, that everyone understood 35 referred to Earth years, not Venusian ones. *Marbury*'s true contribution was in establishing that courts could provide *remedies* for unconstitutional laws, a precedent that would be genuinely important over time.*[19] In the event, no remedy was granted in *Marbury* itself, partly for political reasons. And this brings us to the other twist, mostly overlooked even in law schools: *Marbury* was a tawdry, cynical, partisan, unethical mess. It's *Marbury*'s facts that make the case intriguingly perverse as a RoL monument, and so relevant for showing how judicial review should be improved, because if *Marbury* has been sanitized into a monument by deliberate forgetting, courts can only risk so many cases like *Marbury* and *Bush v. Gore*.

To decode *Marbury*'s real meaning, and to understand why the case retains broad relevance today, requires historical context. *Today,* Supreme Court cases almost always arrive as appeals (save for a few types of cases, such as those involving ambassadors or the states).[20] The facts have been established by lower courts, leaving the Court with only theoretical questions. This bolsters institutional trust in the Court, which seems removed from any specific fray. But with *Marbury,* the Court was very much in the mix; before the expansion of the legal system, the Supreme Court conducted trials itself, including the highly political trial of *Marbury v. Madison*. The basic dispute concerned one William Marbury's appointment as a justice of the peace. Near the end of his administration, President John Adams granted Marbury his commission, but the documents were not delivered before Thomas Jefferson, Adams's successor and enemy, was sworn in. Jefferson's secretary of state, James Madison (the Madison of *Marbury v. Madison*), refused to deliver the commission. Marbury sued under the Judiciary Act of 1789 to get what was his. The Court held that Madison's non-delivery was illegal.[21] The traditional narrative ends here, so many people (mostly hungover

---

* As lawyers like to say, there's no right unless there's a remedy. It's no consolation to a prisoner convicted using wrongfully obtained evidence that a court bemoans an illegal search; what matters to the prisoner is that the court can release him.

law students) assume that Madison's refusal was the unconstitutional deed that established judicial review.

It wasn't. The unconstitutional germ was a provision of the Judiciary Act, which improperly granted the Court direct jurisdiction over the matter in contravention of the Constitution; because the Act was the vehicle for suit, William Marbury *lost*.[22] Well, isn't this just a technicality? Who cares? *Marbury* established that courts could void unconstitutional laws, victory enough. But the facts show that courts are anything but immune to pressure from other branches, and highlight the judiciary's vulnerability when its members associate too nakedly with politics.

Marbury began with the election of 1800, a fiasco resulting in a tie in the Electoral College requiring no fewer than thirty-six votes in the House to resolve. In the tumult, the outgoing Federalist government tried to cement its legacy by stuffing the judiciary with cronies. Federalists created appellate courts to house new judges and filled lesser positions with sympathizers, including Marbury. As it happens, Marbury's commission was signed by then–Secretary of State John Marshall—the same Marshall who wrote *Marbury* and who had himself been installed on the Court as part of the larger scheme that got Marbury his commission. And because *Marbury* was a trial, the new Chief *Justice* was also a chief *witness*, because it was Marshall who had executed Marbury's commission. Compounding the oddity, the case required Marshall to interpret the Constitution, a document outlined by Madison, the nominal defendant. (Madison expected the judiciary to be the weakest branch and seemed determined to make his own example.) Exacerbating the political complexity, the Republicans (led by Jefferson, Marshall's *cousin*, in this ball of Founding incest) had recently repealed the Judiciary Act of 1801, essentially firing a whole category of federal judges for substantially political reasons, were ginning up impeachments of other Federalist judges, and had adjusted the Court's 1802 Term with the intent of keeping the Justices out of the game during a crucial political period.[23]

To recap, in service of a purely political agenda, the parties of the day were willing to: (1) create new courts; (2) delete and reconstitute parts of the judiciary; (3) refuse office to appointees; (4) impeach judges; and (5) watch the nation's highest judicial officer preside over a case in which he and his cousin/president had been involved (along with Marshall's brother—don't ask). This is a lesson with contemporary applications, not historical duff. Allegations of naked politicking by current Justices helped lead to the Garland/Gorsuch intrigue, and after the Kavanaugh appointment, some Democrats made noises about packing the Court. Meanwhile, Florida's governor suggested that his final act before he left office in 2019 would be to make midnight appointments, dramatically recomposing the Florida Supreme Court, while by mid-2018, every member of West Virginia's Supreme Court had either resigned or faced impeachment.[24] To understand the consequences of these antics, and how the judiciary might wriggle free of their consequences in the future, requires returning to 1803, and *Marbury*.

Although *Marbury* is the most famous RoL case on the books, it's worth repeating that Marbury did *not* get his appointment. And, in a companion case, the Justices allowed Republicans to rejigger the appellate courts, on legally unconvincing grounds.[25] Despite all the RoL blather in *Marbury* about America having a "government of laws, not of men," in reality *Marbury* sanctioned the triumph of politicians over laws, but it did sneak in the *principle* that courts could provide remedies for unconstitutional conduct even if it had to trade away a few litigants' rights along the way.

For some decades, *Marbury*'s inconvenient heritage rendered the case something of an unusable oddity. Eventually, *Marbury* became too useful to leave on the shelf. Though the real *Marbury* was not a flawless monument to the RoL, the mythical *Marbury* came to serve that purpose. That, it turns out, has been mostly good enough—but it required building up a professional judiciary as far removed from politics and the facts of any given case as possible. The real *Marbury* should be a warning to judges about getting anywhere near politics (as some judges do), lest they give credence to allegations of bias and "so-called" judging. That advice is especially timely today, in an era of disputes over executive power, where the Court's nominee pool draws heavily on officials who have been recently, and often controversially, associated with the executive branch.

The Marketplace of Values

Many scholars read *Marbury* as an elegant piece of *realpolitik* that preserved judicial independence at limited cost—a bargain, in other words. It seems distasteful to view *Marbury* so, but *Marbury* reminds us that bargaining is a key aspect of all legal systems. Legal systems provide marketplaces for trading in values including fairness, institutional coherence, democratic legitimacy, and legal integrity. This is a crucial legal service, and in a way, "justice" is just the measure of marketplace efficiency: the ability to assign appropriate weights to each legal value in a given context. (This is why so many important cases use "balancing" tests.) This is, in a sense, what happened in *Marbury*: Marshall bargained away one man's job in exchange for a lasting institutional principle. Unfortunately, the legal market is inefficient because its participants are frequently irrational, underinformed, and badly incentivized. Fortunately, even highly inefficient markets still operate; trading in legal values remains open, though commodities aren't perfectly priced.

A flat-out disruption is different, where trading in some legal goods can stop entirely. Such disruptions are called "states of emergency." *Brief* states of emergency are not necessarily incompatible with law's goals. Major disasters provide the classic examples: in the face of unexpected catastrophe, authorities may employ extraordinary mechanisms like curfews, price controls, and militarized policing that are otherwise forbidden—and these measures are pre-authorized, and constrained, by previously made law. Prolonged states of emergency, however, pretend to offer law's benefits without any of law's hassles. Permanent emergencies are un-law—the exceptions that swallow every rule—causing all legal values to decay. Their only utility is to show what happens when real law disappears.

Illustration by Negation

Authoritarians constantly find themselves tempted to invoke powers disproportionate to an emergency or to simply invent emergencies to justify suspension of normal law. In places like Putin's Russia and Maduro's Venezuela, tactics are unapologetically overt, with the military wheeled in to dispose of inconvenient assemblies, especially those that demand the RoL.[26] Western officials generally avoid this ham-fistedness, although David Clarke, Milwaukee's rabble-rousing sheriff from 2002 to 2017, suggested using National Guardsmen to suppress "goon anarchists."[27] Inevitably, Clarke's premise was a "state of emergency," and though the protests in question involved only minor disorder, Clarke described them as a "riot" requiring "ALL non lethal force."[28] Antics like Clarke's do nothing good for the legal system, but also pose no immediate threat, because they are patently absurd.

Nevertheless, emergencies can cause problems even in a robust republic, and never more so than when transient catastrophes are cast as perpetual crises. War and terrorism are favorites for this, on the grounds that law cannot fulfill its primary duty of maintaining order and restraining violence in the face of disaster. But the facts that America has been at war forever and that terrorism might now be part of life are precisely why they can*not* justify a state of emergency. When continued long enough, anything extraordinary becomes ordinary, and can be dealt with through normal legal channels. The initial disaster may abate or it may become chronic; either way, the state of emergency ends or the RoL suffers. Sometimes the losses are minor, but it can be hard to tell in advance. Maybe today's fire is just a fire. Or maybe not: perhaps the fire was set by terrorists and terrorists are everywhere. English doesn't have candid terms for what happens next. German does: *Ausnahmezustand,* the "state of exception" in which the executive branch can set aside any law, including a constitution.[29]

America has not yet suffered a full *Ausnahmezustand,* but isn't free of embarrassments. During the Civil War, Lincoln suspended habeas corpus. (Regrettably, this was an inspiration for Nazi jurist Carl Schmitt.) Habeas corpus—essentially, the right to petition an ordinary court for release after an unlawful detention—is so fundamental to the RoL that it had been part of English law for centuries before its incorporation into the U.S. Constitution.[30] Lincoln justified his circumvention of habeas as necessary to protect the rail lines funneling troops to the front. As a lawyer, Lincoln understood the Constitutional problems; only *Congress* has clear authority to suspend habeas corpus, and only when a rebellion or invasion threatens public safety.[31] The initial detentions were not Congressionally sanctioned and, when a detainee appeal reached the courts, Justice Taney (riding circuit) took his side.[32] But the Lincoln Administration ignored judicial admonitions for a time and then took the extraordinary step of suspending habeas nationwide, affecting counties where no rebellion, invasion, or threat to public safety was involved. Over the course of the war, perhaps 10,000–30,000 people found themselves deprived of normal access to the court system.[33]

War is the emergency least kind to the RoL.[34] In the (sometimes false) choice between safety and principle, politicians believe citizens will choose the former, even though cynical uses of "public safety" underwrote everything from Robespierre to Stalin. The Lincoln Administration never went quite so far, though it did frankly admit that the RoL would be jettisoned temporarily, with Lincoln's lawyers citing Cicero's maxim about law falling silent during times of war—a breathtaking claim, rightly rejected.[35] Since then, courts have varied in their deference to the executive.[36] It depends on the war and the court, so maximalist presidents always have an incentive to push the boundaries, including what counts as "war." Treating the Constitution as Gumby was a particular hobby of the Bush II Administration during the War on Terror.[37]

All branches of government should be parsimonious with emergency powers, because powers tend to outlive the emergency. FDR's emergency powers greatly outlasted the Depression and the war that were their initial justifications. Later presidents continued the trend, so that in the four decades after FDR's first inauguration, presidents wielded special authority over trade, travel, security, and even the Post Office. In 1973, a Senate committee concluded that "Congress and the public [were] unaware of the extent of the [state of] emergency... [n]or ha[d] the courts imposed significant limitations" on the executive's "vast range of powers... *[which] confer[red] enough authority to rule the country without reference to normal constitutional processes.*"[38] And this, even though the relevant emergencies had ended and there was "no present need for the United States Government to continue to function under emergency conditions."[39] The Committee concluded that a "majority of the people of the United States have lived all of their lives under emergency rule."[40] After the Senate report, Congress tried to restrain America's legal freewheeling, reserving the right to rescind declarations of emergency.[41] Going forward, presidents would have to formally declare states of emergency, identify what powers were being activated, and provide general information. That any of this required codification suggested how far out of hand emergency powers had gotten.

The return to normalcy lasted three years. By 1979, Jimmy Carter invoked a state of emergency over the Iranian hostage crisis.[42] The hostages came home in 1981—so long that we've been through seven Irani and six American presidents, nineteen Congresses, and five Batmans, two of whom (Affleck and Clooney) made a caper flick about those very hostages (*Argo*), way back when the forty-fifth president was still hosting reality television. And yet, the Iranian emergency continues. Indeed, *many* "emergencies" continue— roughly thirty at the time of this writing. Abuse of perpetual emergency power is a growing problem. Yet, while the 1976 reforms required Congress to reconsider each emergency within six months, it never has.[43]

America's permanent state of emergency conflicts with the RoL, the Constitution, and relevant law. Congress is the prime lawmaker, not the executive.[44] Presidential emergency decrees of great duration violate Constitutional doctrines including separation of powers/non-delegation. Beyond that, the declaration of martial law, use of military force, supply of incidental military support, indefinite detentions, and the diversion of litigation into abnormal courts—all of which have been justified by threat of riot or terrorism—sometimes breach enacted laws (e.g., the Posse Comitatus Act), usually violate their spirit, and almost always undermine the RoL.[45] An emergency regime leaves nations hostage to notorious vagaries of presidential temperaments. It's no coincidence that the emergency regime overlapped with undeclared wars, the massive expansion of executive dictates, bureaucratic overreach, and the spread of exceptions that reduces American law into cancerous Swiss cheese. Whatever the partisan inclination, the non-law of emergencies should give everyone something to hate.

The Legitimacy of Doing Things Well

The psychology of permanent emergency degrades institutions, and the judiciary, as the weakest branch, suffers most. This erosion can happen even if the initial emergency is genuine and the proposed response is legal, as in 1937, when FDR contemplated packing the Court to overcome judicial objections to the New Deal. As it happens, the Constitution doesn't forbid adjustments to Court membership: Article III requires a Supreme Court without saying anything about its composition.[46] There could be one justice or one hundred; nine is just a number chosen by Congress in 1869. Reformulating the Supreme Court was not (and is not) only superficially legal, it had been done six times before, sometimes for nakedly political reasons.*[47]

It was therefore a surprise, including to FDR himself, that the court-packing bill failed. Just four months before, FDR had won a landslide re-election, 523 electoral votes to 8. Because the Court had struck down some New Deal proposals in the preceding year, FDR read his victory as a mandate to cut through judicial obstruction.[48] Every variable seemed in FDR's favor save one: respect

---

* FDR had an example in David Lloyd George's Britain. Almost three decades earlier, Lloyd George's party threatened to stuff the House of Lords with Liberal peers. Lloyd George's plan was even more dubious than FDR's, since it entailed: (1) co-opting the sovereign, the legal head of state, who creates peers; (2) neutering half of the legislature; and (3) potentially intimidating the judicial branch, whose most senior members sat in the Lords. A century on, the Tories are considering the same tactic to overcome anti-Brexiteers in the Lords. Constitutional spirals are rarely virtuous.

for the RoL. Usually, the RoL is too abstract to arouse much public and legislative feeling. But court-packing was too obvious, too crude, too consequential: FDR planned to neuter the Court, and citizens knew it, because *FDR told them that was the plan.*[49] Court-packing died its deserved death.

Perhaps citizens sensed that tinkering with the Court was a large step toward arbitrary rule. Emergency measures can promote some legal values, notably maintaining order, often faster than normal legal process. Law knows this, and sometimes adopts its own emergency responses, but the price is to undermine the very goals law seeks to achieve. The coda to FDR's court-packing shows how. Appalled by FDR's plan, the Court reversed course, the famous "switch in time that saved nine." The price was a lack of candor about the constitutionality of the bureaucratic state and a certain supinity about executive branch transgressions, which persisted for decades. The tragedy, it turns out, was that there was probably no emergency for either side—most of the New Deal had already survived judicial scrutiny, and much of the rest almost certainly would have.[50]

The public outcry over court-packing shows that the public will support legal institutions, even when doing so risks the public's immediate agenda. The willingness to stand firm, even when doing so is inconvenient or carries institutional risk, is not merely part of the RoL, but a value in itself. In law, the easy way is often the wrong way, because it makes nonsense of the rules. Law must have *integrity.* This is both a functional requirement and a freestanding legal virtue—and not always identical to justice in its visceral sense. Letting the guilty man go, defying popular legislation, or acting against personal and partisan interests, when the rules demand as much, are part of law's daily work. The public largely accepts this, according law leeway and respect it would afford few others were they to do the same. One of law's special abilities is to help the public believe that at least one institution does things properly.

So now we know the basic goals of a legal system—coordination, efficiency, justice, the rule of law, accountability, and integrity—and from there we have extrapolated the institutions and norms necessary for success; we have a framework. The next step is to fill in that framework: by establishing who has legitimate authority to make laws, how laws should be made, and under what circumstances laws we deem unjust may be disobeyed.

CHAPTER TWO

JURISPRUDENCE: MAKING AND BREAKING LAW

[S]o far as we approve of monarchy, that in America the law is king. For as in absolute governments the king is law, so in free countries the law ought to be king.

Thomas Paine (1776)[1]

The prophecies of what the courts will do in fact, and nothing more pretentious, are what I mean by the law.

Oliver Wendell Holmes, Jr. (1897)[2]

In 1945, a plane crashed into the Empire State Building. Normally, this kind of accident would trigger an avalanche of lawsuits. None came, nor could they, not because the plane's operators hadn't erred (they had) or because people weren't hurt (they were), but because the government operated the plane. Under the doctrine of "sovereign immunity," federal and state governments cannot be sued without their explicit consent. That, anyway, is the theory espoused by the Court. Actually, it's less theory than assertion, because the Court views sovereign immunity as "axiomatic"—something so correct and necessary as to not require proof.[3] That cannot be right. When the government injures its citizens, it owes compensation, and when courts excuse government, they owe explanations, not axioms.[4]

All we get is tautology: government can't be liable for wrongs because it is our sovereign, and an essential characteristic of sovereigns is that they are immune from liability. *Rex non potest peccare*, intone the jurists, "the king can do no wrong." Now, no one but the most toadying courtiers or servile White House counsels believes that kings are literally incapable of wrongdoing; were that true, there would be no need for immunity doctrines. Rather, the argument goes, to require the sovereign to explain itself, much less in its own courts, would infringe upon the sovereign's prerogative to do as it pleases, without litigious second-guessing by the mob. To which twenty-first-century Americans might reply: When did we agree to any of *that*? This a question the Court wants to avoid, because there is no candid way to discuss sovereign immunity without probing the foundations of law itself, including the significant problems of what law *is* and why we should heed the authorities when they behave badly.

Defenders of sovereign immunity have three options: identify a Constitutional basis for the doctrine; provide an explanation based on jurisprudence (the philosophy of law); or locate historical precedent. The first two options are not viable: there is no Constitutional basis for immunity and, if the goal is to avoid awkward questions, philosophy rarely provides the quick way out. That leaves history—and "axiom" notwithstanding, this is really what the Court relies upon.[5] The history can't be American, because the notion of a monarch above the law is a nonstarter (given the Revolution) and musings about the inviolable, unitary nature of the sovereign go nowhere (given separation of powers). *English* history, however, seemed to provide the needful thing, because sometime between the reigns of Edward I (d. 1307) and Edward IV (d. 1483), the common law decided that the king could do no wrong—or anyway, could not be sued if he did.

In rummaging through the historical lawn sale of the Anglo-American tradition, the Court let its *Antiques Roadshow* mentality run amok, and paraded trash as treasure. The ostensible purpose of sovereign immunity is to protect the king so that he can promote order, but real English history showed that immunity doctrines did anything but. Even as English lawyers elaborated the doctrine (for technical reasons utterly inapplicable to American law), their nation was beset by usurpers, who invariably justified their revolts on the grounds that the previous king *had* done wrong—by making laws poorly, trampling on the rights of Parliament, and mistreating his subjects.[6] People have *rights*, and sovereign immunity mocks those rights. Points taken, but when the usurpers gained the throne, they faced serious questions. What did it really mean to make law legitimately and well, and what grounds did they (or their potential emulators) have to hold a sitting sovereign to account? England lacked (and still lacks) a written constitution, so no one could flip to an index to find the answers. To answer these questions, England needed help from jurisprudence.

So does America, notwithstanding its written Constitution. The Constitution doesn't answer every important legal question, starting with the question of its own legitimacy. Even if legitimacy is granted, the Constitution has all the gaps and ambiguities one would expect of a document four pages long and twenty-four decades old. (Hence the debate over sovereign immunity.) Even basic matters like the proper making of law are not treated satisfactorily; for example, the Constitution does not explicitly forbid the imposition of secret laws. The Constitution is also entirely silent on how it should be interpreted, when it might be suspended, and what redress citizens have if government makes laws badly or goes entirely off the rails. Only jurisprudence can fill these textual gaps sensibly and well. In places where constitutions are either unwritten (Britain, New Zealand) or where constitutions compete (as they do within the European Union), jurisprudence is a core feature of legal curricula, helping lawyers fill in lacunae and resolve conflicts between governing documents without resorting to the rubbish heap of medieval precedent.

Unfortunately, most American lawyers don't get a proper education in jurisprudence. The subject doesn't even feature as a stand-alone class in the standard American law school curriculum.[7] This is bizarre, because to understand the basic principles of law—including what law *is*—requires philosophical grounding. Lawyers ignorant of jurisprudence are as strange as engineers innocent of physics. Perhaps jurisprudence is beside the point for corporate lawyers and divorce attorneys, but it's hardly irrelevant to judges, or the lawyer-legislators who constitute half the Senate and a plurality of the House.[8]

If jurisprudence is so important, why isn't it taught? Partly because American law assumes that the Constitution will answer any question if tortured long enough, and fears what might happen if that proves untrue. And partly because jurisprudence is just difficult. Scholars don't agree on basic concepts, including what constitutes "jurisprudence," much less on a grand unified theory.[9]* But jurisprudence is too valuable to ignore, and there's enough agreement to allow us to answer the crucial questions. What we need is a summary that captures the essentials, in a way that's accessible without being intellectually vacant—an "everyday jurisprudence."

Formal, or "everyday," jurisprudence must answer three basic questions: (1) Who decides? (2) How should law be made? (3) When can we disobey? The struggles over judicial activism, states' rights, and imperial presidencies all involve the first question: Who makes the law? Arguments about Congressional procedures, vague or ill-crafted laws, and bureaucratic overreach implicate the second question and sometimes the first. Government-sanctioned injustices, such as Jim Crow laws, implicate the last question, and sovereign immunity is wrapped up in all of them. Even less grand matters involve these issues. When a police officer demands a cavity search during a garden-variety traffic stop, must we consent, simply because a man wearing

---

* We'll spare ourselves most of this, but to give you a sense for how disputatious things are, the twentieth-century titans of the field, H.L.A. Hart and Ronald Dworkin, are still bickering *posthumously*. Dworkin's latest attack was published in *Harvard Law Review*'s 2017 volume—four years after Dworkin died, twenty-five years after Hart expired, and fifty-six years after Hart published the book that spawned the debate.

a badge demands it? If we must, can we reconcile ourselves to this as a legitimate exercise of authority; if we need not, should we be compensated? An intuitive theory of jurisprudence helps us parse these questions, suggesting what the answers *should* be, and in many cases, telling us what the answers *are*, without too many trips to the law library.

The Deciders

*Some*body must make law, and since law proposes to tell us what to do, its creators usually offer some justification for why we should obey. For most of history, lawmakers staked their claim on divine sanction. Because God appointed kings as His earthly viceroys, to disobey the king was to disobey God, and nobody wanted to disobey God (what with the fire and brimstone). This arrangement was a little too convenient for kings, and not convenient at all for their subjects, but it made for a bracingly succinct jurisprudence, so long as the monarch was absolute and his people credulous. Who makes the law? The king. How should law be made? However the king wants. When might disobedience be possible? Never.

After God absented himself from the scene, it was only a matter of time before people noticed the vacuum. If God no longer sanctified monarchs with burning shrubbery, halos, and other indicia of heavenly sanction, no monarch had a provable claim to rule. Kings could not show that they were God's elect, and the Pope was always free to offer an opinion to the contrary. Worse, neither side could prove that God existed in the first place. The system only worked while people believed the magic. After the Protestant Reformation and the Scientific Revolution, belief ebbed, and absolute monarchy died away. Henceforth, we would know that our government was legitimate because we had agreed to that government, not because some sceptered oddball claimed access to the divine. We would not fear our government, because it would be bound by the law as we are, and as kings never were. Or so go the authorized biographies of modern republics.

As in all biographies, there's awkward embellishment. Fast forward past the age of revolutions, during which monarchs were deposed outright or ostensibly reduced to decorative furnishings, and what do we find? A kingly corpse in democratic drag, emitting the same stench of arbitrary authority and propped up by the usual magic. This is a disappointment in which legal theorists played a part, by failing to fully banish the relics of absolutism. For a start, many jurists simply could not conceive of a world in which *someone* didn't have unlimited authority over the people. John Austin, who looms over nineteenth-century jurisprudence, called that someone the "sovereign," a term that conveys a lot about Austin's thinking. In Austin's world, a law would be valid if a supreme power issued an order backed with threat of punishment—that was that, and civil rights lawyers and their ilk had nothing to add. For Austin, laws were prescriptive rules and nothing more. Austin claimed that his "positivism" (as in: "you must *positively* do X and Y") cleared away the subjective clutter of traditional law, putting issues like morality and efficiency where they properly belonged: in the hands of philosophers and politicians instead of those of lawyers.

To the confident, mechanical-universe minds of the nineteenth-century elite, positivism had much to commend it—and still does, at least in the low-stakes cases that constitute most legal interactions. In minor matters, we are all positivists. We do not want pedestrians quoting St. Augustine to cops ("an unjust law is no law at all!") and then jaywalking. But jaywalking cannot be the measure of a legal theory, any more than ponds can be proving grounds for submarines. When put to harder tests, classical positivism shows its flaws, many of which trace back to its regressive conception of the lawful sovereign. Positivism grants the sovereign too much power while asking too little of the law. If positivism's sovereign were Queen Victoria advised by William Gladstone, we might shrug: not perfect, but good enough. But if the sovereign were Chancellor Hitler advised by Carl Schmitt, problems would mount.

Referencing Nazis usually brings more confusion than clarity, but for law, the Third Reich is a main hinge between nineteenth-century positivism and modern jurisprudence. Whole schools of legal thought collapsed in the wake of Nazism, including first-wave positivism, because while everyone *knew* the Reich was criminal, existing jurisprudence had trouble saying exactly why. In its formal aspects, the Reich broadly resembled other Western legal systems: it had written law issued by a government that (initially) enjoyed electoral and constitutional sanction, plus the usual legal trimmings of paperwork, courts, and law schools. Worse, the Reich arguably came closest to the positivist archetype: there was a clear sovereign who issued orders backed by definite threats. When the reckoning came at Nuremberg, positivism couldn't readily distinguish between justice and "just following orders." It could not even show why the Nuremberg trials were different than Reich law. Could it be that justice was only a question of power, and that law, like war, was just the continuation of politics by other means? Returning to cops and cavity searches, do badges and guns by themselves sanction invasive behavior?

Early positivists tried to maneuver around those problems in unconvincing ways, and failing the Nazi test was fatal to Austinian positivism. But there was a second problem, which was that Austin's theories were not descriptively accurate in places like America—and descriptive accuracy was supposedly a positivist forte. For one, positivism generally concedes the existence of only one sovereign (albeit operating through many minions), but in America many sovereigns compete: the federal government reigns over some areas; the states over others; and courts, legislatures, and executives share power; while all of government derives its power from the ultimate sovereign, the people.[10]

Before turning to America, where sovereign power can be hard to see because it's often diffuse or hidden, a word on modern Britain, where Austin's positivist tyrant is consolidated in plain view. The British Parliament has the theoretical power to do virtually *anything*, even to neuter the courts that interpret Britain's unwritten constitution. The formal constraint on (and legal enabler of) Parliament is hardly less appalling: a monarch sitting "by the grace of God," precisely the sort of entity modern nations were supposed to be well shot of. (At least the question of divine sanction is settled in Britain—Elizabeth II is God's elect, and should she have any doubts on that score, she may consult herself, in her capacity as Supreme Governor of England's state church.) Some might say that the potency of the "Queen-in-Parliament" is just theory driven by British perversity, a picturesque nod to an imperial past.[*11] But no; legally, Queen-in-Parliament is entirely real. But surely, Americans will object, this nonsense must be absent in a republic founded in opposition to royal prerogative.

Alas, not quite: at the beginning of the chapter, we saw government escape liability for flying a plane into a building, so at least some shreds of royal prerogative remain alive and well. Americans can only sue government when a legislature graces them with a waiver, or in the limited circumstances where courts have created their own exceptions to the doctrine of immunity. But while legislatures have waived some tort immunity (as Congress did, in major reforms following the Empire State Building crash), statutory waivers and judicial exceptions don't cover all wrongs—and some astonishing abuses have and continue to unfold. The government has escaped liability for conducting medical experiments on soldiers without obtaining consent and for interning citizens in camps based on ethnicity alone. As I was writing this chapter, New York federal courts were tossing a cadet's suit against West Point officers for fostering an environment that led to her rape. Grounds? Immunity. And rather astoundingly, right after that, Allergan Pharmaceuticals leased the Mohawk Tribe's sovereign immunity (quasi-sovereignty having been granted to indigenous peoples to afford tribes a measure of autonomy from a government that took everything else away). For Allergan, the goal was to protect an ocular drug from unwanted patent challenges, an extension of the American-born company's decision to lease Ireland's

---

[*]   Of the 6 initial parties to the European Community's Treaty of Rome 1957, 3 were monarchs (3.5 if you include the French president who is also, by law, Co-Prince of Andorra); of the Maastricht Treaty's 12 original signatories, 6.5 were monarchs. Humanity's back always seems to ache for the royal lash.

sovereignty for tax purposes.[12] Now, you not only have to worry about the king, you have to worry about who's renting him.

The Court not only defends sovereign immunity, it has been expanding the doctrine. But the Court's immunity jurisprudence is almost certainly indefensible. As the dean of Berkeley Law, Erwin Chemerinsky, has ably explained, nothing about the text of the Constitution, and little in revolutionary history or philosophies of good governance, support the Court's position. If anything, parts of the Constitution suggest that the Framers intended for the government to be legally liable to its citizens, at least in certain contexts (eminent domain and the Takings Clause, for instance).[13] This raises some questions about judges that are best answered in their own chapter. For now, let's assume that the Court's interpretation of the Constitution is right, or anyway, not crazily wrong. The question then becomes: Did any of us actually agree to a social contract that authorizes such awful outcomes? Some jurists would say this is venturing too far afield, but it's not. The whole of American law hangs from a Constitutional peg, and if that peg is rotten, it's hard to see how law enjoys robust claims to legitimacy.

Magic and the Social Contract

The Constitution suffers from a conspicuous absence of consent. Obviously, no one has signed the document in a long time and only a fraction of Americans have actively consented to the Constitution, mostly naturalized immigrants who must pledge to "support and defend the Constitution" as a condition of citizenship.[14] A few others take a similar oath as a condition of their offices, including lawyers, public servants, and elected politicians. But everyone else—which is most of America—sits as a Constitutional bystander, creating a theoretical nightmare. If the Constitution establishes our sovereign, but 90+ percent of Americans didn't agree to the Constitution and the laws that flow from it, can we be plausibly said to owe the Constitutional Deciders our obedience?

31

Absent explicit consent, the Constitutional contract can only be implied, by conduct or receipt of benefits. By voting for the local dog catcher, using a public road, or just remaining in the country, the reasoning goes, you buy the whole legal system. It's an argument at least as old as Socrates. While Socrates awaited execution, a disciple offered to smuggle the philosopher out of Athens. Socrates refused, saying he had no right to disobey Athenian law at a moment of convenience, having previously and voluntarily enjoyed so many of its benefits. One of the boons Socrates listed was state-supported gymnastics training, so perhaps the whole dialogue was sarcastic; we can't know the philosopher's feelings, though we can say that this was not the strongest argument Socrates ever advanced.[15] Nevertheless, many people still take the receipt-of-benefits argument seriously, if for no other reason than that, when grasping at straws, a short straw is better than none at all.

Another of Socrates' arguments, concerning migration, is more relevant and (with one near-fatal caveat) more persuasive. Being free-born, Socrates could have emigrated from Athens to another city-state with more appealing laws; his decision to stay could be deemed as consent to Athenian law. In Federalist America, interstate migration is easy, and the choices genuinely varied. Those who value a right to privacy and all that it entails can move to California, where that right is guaranteed by the very first item in that state's constitution.[16] Those who want maximum latitude to shoot quail can migrate to Texas, whose bill of rights explicitly protects hunting.[17]

In a surprising way, questions about government legitimacy—often dismissed as empty leftist agitation—lead directly to a conventionally rightist and very practical position: we should take federalism (in its rightist incarnation, states' rights) seriously. Federalism also partly answers the question of "who decides?" When we move across state lines from one constitutional regime to another, *we* decide. From there on, our authorized representatives decide for us. But at least we really did pick them, helping dispose us to complying with the laws of our chosen state, and if we come to find those laws intolerable, we can leave.

Consent to federal law is harder to imply. Emigrating from the United States is more difficult than migrating among the states. You must find a country to take you, which is very difficult, especially for those without considerable assets. Those who do have such assets must pay an expatriation tax so forbidding as to render the choice nugatory.[18] (The Treasury demands an exit tax that includes *un*realized gains—even wealthy people find this difficult to cough up.) Moreover, the exit tax accumulates before citizens have a legal right to emigrate, as citizenship and the tax accrue at birth, and minors are functionally barred from renouncing citizenship.[19] If exercising a choice comes with an eighteen-year delay and an involuntary penalty, then consent can't really be described as freely given. With all these difficulties, the "here-by-choice" argument collapses. Americans are not freely Americans in the same way Texans are freely Texans. (A version of this holds for residents of the Golden State, who are only semi-voluntary citizens of their state, being at the mercy of the state tax board literally forever; "Hotel California's" you-can-check-out-but-you-can-never-leave is ripe for reinterpretation on this basis.)

The disparate levels of consent between state and national citizenship lurk behind local resentments of federal authority, especially when Washington issues commands in tension with regional preferences. The social contract with Washington is less legitimate, in important ways, than the compact with a given state.[20] As it happens, it may never be possible to establish federal legitimacy in a satisfying way. Hans Kelsen, one of the most influential jurists of the twentieth century, recognized the problem. While he thought it possible to establish the validity and coherence of an entire legal system from one starting point (the *Grundnorm*), the starting point itself could only be *assumed*, not proved. The *Grundnorm* in the United States is generally associated with the Constitution, a document that Kelsen famously thought could only be "presupposed."[21] If so, the presidency, Congress, judges, and the laws and rulings promulgated under their authority all spring from some monstrous sleight of hand. Short of revising and reauthorizing the Constitution frequently (as Jefferson hoped Americans would), we must heave a sigh and admit that the Deciders draw some authority from magic, not a reservoir of pure logic and popular consent.

There is an escape hatch, though. The Constitution is so filled with gaps and ambiguities that it's reasonable to say that there are many different "Constitutions" to choose from. We may have to accept that legal magic saddles us with a specific set of words, but we have the tools at our disposal to make those words work for us. Among these are our own expectations, because courts are sensitive to them. That only works if we're willing to sanction another tool: judicial discretion. To see why people of every political leaning ought to support at least some "judicial activism" (notwithstanding judicial mistakes like sovereign immunity), we need only compare our basic expectations of how law should be made against the Constitution's explicit requirements. It turns out that there's more to making law well than simply going through the basic Constitutional motions.

How Should Laws Be Made?

The American legal philosopher Lon Fuller described the essentials of making good rules as the "internal morality" of law. Per Fuller, proper laws must be: (1) actually made, rather than decreed ad hoc; (2) written comprehensibly, so people can actually comply; (3) issued in advance; (4) in a public way; (5) without demanding the impossible; or (6) contradicting other rules; or (7) changed so frequently that compliance becomes impossible; and (8) enforced as announced.[22] Fuller's criteria serve a value system (the proposals are "normative"), but one Fuller plausibly claims is limited to the value of making law competently.[23] As a technical framework for guiding and evaluating law, Fuller's inventory is as morals-free as we can get without choking on the dry toast of analytic philosophy or flirting with the positivist disasters we've already covered. However, Fuller's shopping list is more extensive than the *explicit* provisions of the Constitution and, anyway, buying every

34

item on Fuller's list doesn't guarantee an attractive legal system, any more than dumping flour and yeast into an oven guarantees a baguette. But omitting any item does end in something few of us would consider good law and therefore risks failing to achieve the goals discussed in the last chapter, of social coordination, efficiency, justice, and rule of law.*

Moralists might say that Fuller set too low a bar, and yet, real laws still manage to trip over it. Consider the bedrock expectation that laws be published. Whether out of a sense of fair play, or simply in the name of efficacy, every literate government from Hammurabi's on at least gestured in this direction. Even hardcore positivists would admit there's still a right way to make bad laws, and it starts with publication. The Roman Republic did not flinch from clubbing a man to death for slander, but it would have suffered acute embarrassment had the Twelve Tables not been posted in the marketplace beforehand. (Table Eight, for the curious.) All very barbaric, and we congratulate ourselves for having no such laws, except that we can't be sure: the Constitution does not compel publication of federal law. Article I demands only that each Congressional house keep a "journal of its proceedings." The journals can be as cursory as Congress likes, though for the most part, Congress does publish its proceedings, including the fragmentary language that constitutes American law. Congress.gov explains why: "[t]here would be no justice if the state were to hold its people responsible for their conduct before it made known to them the unlawfulness of such behavior. *In practice*, our laws are published immediately upon their enactment."[24] Note the "in practice," the legalese equivalent of we-usually-do-this-but-don't-hold-us-to-it; we'll get to this in a moment.

A significant caveat is that when Congress publishes laws, the manner is so unsatisfactory as to render questionable its compliance with Fuller's rules. Laws often emerge in unreadable and inaccessible formats. The jumble of 2017's tax rewrite—a giant mix of scribbles, typos, omissions, and

---

* "Good," "valid," "just," and "proper" can have special meanings in jurisprudence, but unless otherwise noted, I'm using them in their general senses. If jurists have problems with this, I'd advise them to pause for a moment on the propriety of "jurist" versus "jurisprude."

inscrutable fragments—was an infamous, but not isolated, example.[25] Many laws are cryptic, piecemeal modifications of older law in the manner of "section II.A.(2)(iii) shall be struck and replaced with 'shall not be amortized unless subject to section III.G.(4)(iv).'" The results are unreadable, which prompted the compiling of the United States Code, a handy condensate now commonly cited by courts and referred to by interested civilians, which is terrific, except that the U.S. Code is *not necessarily the law*. Only what Congress passes can become law, and Congress has not passed the entire, current U.S. Code. Fortunately, the U.S. Code almost always compiles the bits and pieces of enacted law into an accurate whole, but that even Justices must resort to U.S. Code citations instead of the real thing essentially concedes that America's operative law contravenes Fuller's comprehensibility requirement.

Even with the benefit of the U.S. Code, law often remains so hard to parse as to be functionally useless. For example, to know when disability benefits kick in requires a voyage to 42 U.S.C. § 423 (promisingly captioned "Disability Insurance Benefit Payments"), which provides for benefits for those with "disabilities" (defined in § 432(d)(1)), except for those who have attained retirement age per § 416(I) or sundry disqualifying exclusions, but assuming those exclusions don't apply, you'll get benefits calculated per § 415 (subject to § 402(q) or § 415(b)(2)(A)(ii), but to figure that out may require a visit to § 403(f)(5)), except perhaps if § 416(i)(3)(B)(ii) kicks in, and on and on. Even then, one must then flip through the relevant code of regulations to see how these statutes have been implemented (20 C.F.R. § 404, which has 21 major subparts), and also ensure that no bureaucracy has offered some important interpretive release on the foregoing and that no court has offered its own gloss, and so on. Whipping any of this into useable form feeds an entire cottage industry of digests and commentaries, all of which are prohibitively expensive. The complexity of the modern government is no excuse for incomprehensible laws—nor does the government itself accept complexity as a defense in civil cases. The SEC requires companies to disclose information in "plain English," and if GE can produce a readable summary of global operations involving everything from lightbulbs to nuclear reactors, the government can produce a readable law.[26]

The failings of printed law are bad enough, but sometimes, government has forgotten to publish entirely, breaking all sorts of jurisprudential commandments. During the New Deal, agencies chartered by Congress and the executive tried to hold people accountable for rules the agencies had never made public, and in one case, for a rule which did not exist.[27] Courts swatted these regulations away and Congress duly imposed a publication requirement on the federal bureaucracy.[28] Today, it's rare for legal decrees to go unpublished, but those that do tend to be very important, usually taking the form of presidential directives executed by bureaucracies. These can serve as law where they reasonably relate to authority granted by the legislature or the Constitution, but the weak Congressional publication requirement does not extend directly to the executive.[29] The Bush II Administration took advantage of this gap to issue a secret directive allowing warrantless wiretapping.[30] Subsequently, Congress and judges concluded that the wiretapping order violated other important legal principles, but those issues only came up because Bush II's order got leaked. A stronger publication requirement would not by itself have prevented any of this, but it would have provided other and faster means to hold government accountable.

As Fuller's list grows more demanding, lawmaking failures accumulate. Again, the tax code is a prime example. It famously and flagrantly violates Fuller's requirement of clarity; it violates Fuller's demand for continuity because Congress constantly tinkers with tax law; it violates the rule against contradictions because it's riddled with internal conflicts; it violates the demand for consistent application for a million reasons.[31] The tax code also demands the impossible, by requiring some payers—notably, the growing body of self-employed persons—to predict their income in advance or face penalties. Not only does tax law require clairvoyance, it can require past-life channeling, since taxes can be applied retroactively, which violates Fuller's prohibition on such laws, though allegedly, not the Constitution's. (The Court typically views the menial workings of tax law as beneath the protections of due process or the Ex Post Facto Clause, on the grounds that retroactive taxation is not arbitrary, or not a criminal penalty…or something to that effect—the Supreme Court's disinterest in tax law is palpable.[32]) Arguably, the only Fullerian criterion the tax code truly satisfies is mere existence.

It's true that economic activity is more complicated than it was in 1913, when the income tax was introduced, but the modern world isn't 1,000 times more complex than it was a century ago. Tax laws are definitely 1,000 times longer, and page count probably understates things, since taxes have become so arcane, so distributed across sources, so interdependent, and so tied up in supplementary pronouncements as to render tax law incomprehensible—even to specialists. It isn't greed alone that causes so many people to file erroneous tax returns; American tax law is just badly written. Swedish law is better made and compliance is accordingly higher, even though Sweden has famously hefty taxes. In fact, many Swedes can forgo tax preparation entirely, because Stockholm does the preliminaries for them.[33] (Other Scandinavian countries do the same, and tax filing in these places is so simple that it's often accomplished *via text message*.)

The failings of tax law are the failings of modern law generally, against which we have three cardinal protections. We can vote, for one. For another, we should be able to rely on courts to defease laws that violate Fuller's standards, though this requires us to ardently support judicial independence, giving judges the spine to strike down bad laws. Our ultimate weapon is to disobey outright—but should we?

Natural Law, Deep Rights, and the Rule of Law

Disobedience, unlike voting and judicial review, is not an advertised feature of any operating legal system, so *initial* justifications for disobedience must come from outside conventional law. The "initial" is important: law is flexible and inclined to self-preservation, and courts will gin up reasons to explain why any popular, successful disobedience was lawful all along. "Natural law" is the oldest and largest repository of uncodified justifications. As such, it is regarded with suspicion, especially by certain conservatives wary of courts creating new (or "new") rights—George III was not amused to read a Declaration invoking the "Laws of Nature," believing that the only laws that existed were those His government had passed with His assent.

The gist of natural law is that the "laws of nature" serve as a cosmic constitution that overrides the positive laws of man (statutes, constitutions, and the like). Big guns like Aristotle, Cicero, St. Augustine, St. Thomas Aquinas, Calvin, Grotius, Hobbes, Locke, Rousseau, the great eighteenth-century revolutionaries, as well as contemporary scholars like Fuller and John Finnis, all embraced natural law theories. Paradoxically, this lengthy and distinguished pedigree creates its own difficulties. Natural law has a source problem, because natural lawyers *are* the sources: too many of them and too often in disagreement. The natural law of Aristotle is not *quite* the natural law of Aquinas, as Aquinas pointed out (pre-Christian darkness). Finnis's modern suggestion that "play" for its own sake is a basic good would have incensed Calvin (cards and dancing being Satanically debauched).[34] And so on. During the civil rights campaign, *both* MLK and the KKK reverted to natural law arguments.[35] And that's the problem in a nutshell. One person's sham is another's natural law.

Natural law is protean and unavoidably subjective, not the first qualities we want in legal systems, which is why Bentham condemned natural rights/natural law as "nonsense upon stilts."[36] Many argue that there's no logical proof for natural law, and they are correct, because there *cannot* be proof. Natural law violates David Hume's "is-ought" rule, which in philosophy is a Very Big Deal (though one we will gingerly avoid). Positivists loathe natural law on Humean grounds and hardline positivists dismiss the idea that subjective notions ("it feels wrong to jail a teenager for carrying 0.5 grams of pot") could overrule law enacted by objective means ("possession of any amount of marijuana is subject to jail terms"). Nothing, after all, is going to irritate a positivist more than a tradition whose most memorable tag is that "an unjust law is no law at all," even though this was MLK's justification for resisting legal directives in the Birmingham campaign. ("Soft positivism" accepts that moral considerations can be valid if a given law allows them to be considered by judges; a version of this is practiced by many courts, as we'll see.)

Given these problems, even modern thinkers sympathetic to natural law have been eager to trim the weedier margins of the field. Lon Fuller was no card-carrying positivist, but his "internal morality of law" tried its best to avoid the philosophical dandelions of ecclesiastical judginess and vaporous political correctness that forever threaten to engulf natural law. Interestingly, John Finnis, a full-blown natural lawyer, arrives at something like Fuller's criteria for making law well from a natural law position, though Finnis's jurisprudence has more distant objects in mind than just making law competently, including seven "basic goods" that make life worthwhile, nestled within which are "nine basic requirements of practical reasonableness."[37] Finnis's seven goods range from the obvious (life) to the indefinable (aesthetic experience) to the outright controversial (religious meaning), a problem that infects a lot of natural law. Once you get beyond the basics, natural law promotes more contention than concord.*[38]

Although natural law is potent when wielded by principled people, it provides the unprincipled with too many justifications to avoid irksome duties, so judges rarely accept natural law as a freestanding argument—at least, not officially. These facts render natural law mostly useless for our purposes, with two exceptions. The first comes from the Declaration of Independence, which directly refers to natural law as a justification for rebellion and as a source of American values like "life, liberty, and the pursuit of happiness." The Declaration isn't an official legal source (as it predates the ur-law, the Constitution), though we can't exactly ignore it, and some think Constitutional

---

*   Lest Finnis seem a little too flower-power, it's worth noting that Finnis likened homosexuality to bestiality. Finnis also found time to mentor Justice Gorsuch while the latter was at Oxford.

interpretation should account for the Declaration's rhetoric. As a practical matter, the closer a law comes to infringing on the version of natural law referenced in the Declaration, the more the judges will find ways to sanction disobedience.* This is especially true when judges feel a right is important enough to smuggle in through the back door of Fourteenth Amendment, especially its Due Process and Equal Protection clauses. In such cases, disobedience doesn't need to be justified on the basis that bad laws are no laws at all; it can be justified on the basis that bad laws are unconstitutional.

The door of due process tends to swing open in response to social trends. The Warren Court (1953–1969) was particularly fond of this technique, responding to changing norms about race and defendants' rights, and later courts have protected abortion access and gay rights on similar grounds. The events leading up to landmark rights cases often came as a result of formal disobedience—indeed, given the Constitutional requirement that judges hear only a live "case and controversy," disobedience is often a precondition to legal evolution through the courts. Of course, judges render verdicts by reference to more than polls and head counts at protests; they consult their own jurisprudence of rights, which has more than a tinge of natural law.

Much of the jurisprudence of real-even-if-uncodified rights comes from the law professor Ronald Dworkin, whose work hovers in the background of really consequential, really close Supreme Court cases. Dworkin was *sui generis.* He didn't believe there's much need to consult with external morality (unlike the natural lawyers) because he believed that morality is entwined in the law (unlike the positivists). Nor did he see the law as some finite collection of rules that runs out in novel circumstances, as might happen, say, when an autonomous drone kills an astronaut for the first time.†

---

* The notable exception being the "pursuit of happiness," which is too subjective for judges, who are more comfortable supporting rights to property (physical and intellectual). They're not wrong to do so; Jefferson cribbed his line from Locke, who originally demanded that law protect "life, liberty, and *property.*"

† To be rudely reductive, positivists would shrug, noting that the law is silent about space-robot manslaughter, while the natural lawyers would wonder if the drones have souls and mete out punishment accordingly.

Rather, Dworkin viewed law as an inexhaustible network driven by principles, history, and rules, roughly in that order. Out of this mix, judges can (almost) always find *one right answer,* no matter how novel or controversial the case. In Dworkin's view, the most serious legal disputes are about finding that answer.[39]

Even if Dworkin is correct (and many think he is), so what? One implication is that we need to, as Dworkin put it, "take rights seriously"—even rights that aren't enumerated.[40] Confronted with a case on reproduction, a purely textualist judge can search the Constitution and terminate the inquiry when "abortion" and "privacy" come up empty, but in Dworkin's view, that doesn't conclude the investigation. The debate isn't only—or even primarily—about the text. It's about principles, including life and liberty, and the arc of law's treatment of those principles. If this is correct, then judges ought to look at case law, statutes, social realities, philosophy—everything—to arrive at the One Right Answer. Moreover, citizens should support that effort, and not get exercised about judicial activism. Looking at everything, including matters beyond the text, seems to be an essential part of judging.

Another implication of a legal system that considers every data point for best fit against our rights and expectations is that it has a strong, perhaps automatic, claim to our obedience. The One Right Answer is the Best Answer almost by definition; we cannot reasonably ask for more. The counterargument is that our legal system does not always provide the One Right Answer, and some parts of it don't even try. Yet, some slippery internal reasoning notwithstanding, Dworkin offers a fairly convincing way out of the various messes created by positivists (blindness to tyranny, indifference to unenumerated rights), natural lawyers (subjective chaos), and social contract theorists (reliance on magic). Dworkin's model has shortcomings, however. It revolves almost exclusively around judges; the real-world mix of legislatures, bureaucracies, and so on are peripheral to Dworkin's thinking and not really justified by it.

Even as to judges, Dworkin isn't fully convincing, because of the enormous complexity his model entails. Getting the One Right Answer is like deriving a math function from scattered points. If there were only two cases about robbery, the equation would be simple: $y = mx+b$. If Case 1 assigned six months in jail for a stolen iPad ($750) and Case 2 assigned five years for a stolen Rolex ($7,500), then Future Case 3, involving a stolen Lexus ($75,000), would bring fifty years. But there are millions of cases, plus any number of principles/rights, so finding the One Right Answer is functionally impossible. Dworkin wriggled his way out of this problem by positing an ideal judge ("Hercules") who had infinite time, wisdom, and research assistance. The perfect judge does not exist any more than Hercules did. But that's not fatal. Hercules describes a condition to which we hope judges aspire; some seasoned judges get close enough. When they do, we really ought to obey, because they've taken our rights seriously.

The mythical Hercules was constantly cleaning up messes, including his own. (The Labors punished Hercules for killing his family.) Judges must do the same, because however distant from the ideal the average judge might be, other members of the legal system lie farther still. Cops don't have infinite time to ponder an arrest, public defenders don't have limitless assistants to defend every case, and legislators don't draw on a bottomless well of wisdom. At most, Dworkin reconciles us to the authority of one branch of government, not all of them.

We have tentative answers to the three questions that began this chapter. Who makes the law? A sovereign, albeit one whose legitimacy is doubtful. How should the law be made? In accordance with some minimum internal morality: publication, intelligibility, consistency, etc. And when might we disobey? When our essential rights have been violated and we might convince the sovereign's judicial representatives of this. And should the sovereign be immune when it errs? Rarely, if ever.

American law schools should require at least one proper class in jurisprudence. Some deans may object that the subject is irrelevant to students' future areas of practice. Perhaps, though most classes are irrelevant to students' future areas of practice, just as most academic research is irrelevant to the judges and legislators it seeks to influence. American law schools are not well functioning, and this poisoned taproot feeds many of the errors in the rest of law.

CHAPTER THREE

LEGAL EDUCATION: THE SCHOOL AS SCANDAL

> Of course, you get a lot out of law school—you learn
> a lot—but the most you get out of law school is debt.
>
> Lloyd Blankfein[1]

In 1292, Edward I ordered his judges to locate "apt and eager" students to study law.[2] The king was an industrious legal reformer, a man who wanted to be known as the "English Justinian," after the emperor who achieved lasting fame by codifying Roman law.[3] The emperor, however, enjoyed a crucial advantage over the king: when Justinian issued his eponymous code in the sixth century AD, he could draw on the army of legal theorists and skilled advocates that imperial law schools had been churning out for five centuries. All Edward had were politicized clerics, semiliterate barons, and courtly amateurs; there hadn't been a law school in Western Europe in eight hundred years. Nor would there be under Edward. Instead of settling law students into a scholarly curriculum at the emerging universities in Oxford and Cambridge, Edward opted for the apprenticeship model, which paired aspiring lawyers with seasoned practitioners and set them to observing and discussing whatever cases were underway at the royal courts. The apprenticeship model persisted for centuries, profoundly shaping legal education and culture. By concentrating on litigation exercises, early English legal culture inclined toward the disputatious, idiosyncratic, tactical, and obsessive about the judicial point of view. It was, in a word, familiar.

Through royal intervention, Edward confirmed that English law was more than a mere trade, but just how *much* more was unclear, then and now. By contrast, Continental schools ushered law into the universities at Paris and Bologna, where it stood alongside the great traditional disciplines, theology and philosophy.[4] Continental schools accepted that law wasn't quite the "calling" theology was, or the intellectual fortress philosophy always has been, but saw the importance of synthesizing law's practical applications and theoretical aspects, its mercenary impulses and its social duties. Over time, many Continental faculties subdivided law into specialties, producing legal experts in various subjects and with different levels of training (though rarely losing sight of law's jurisprudential superstructure). But American instruction began and remained adamantly generalist, and skeptical of theory, including of any general philosophy of law. Even when law became a graduate-level pursuit in the late nineteenth century, American law schools refused to specialize or synthesize the curriculum, though their professors did become more conventionally academic in their research.

In failing to reconcile trade with theory, and advocacy with social purpose, American law schools have settled for the worst of all worlds—an abstracted research faculty presiding over an outmoded trade school. The results have not been good. As vocational enterprises, law schools are failing. Many students flub the bar exam and will never practice law, while the rest require years of experience before they can produce competent work on their own (after which they become hermetic specialists). As research institutions, the kindest summary is that legal scholarship is a mixed bag. Professors generate copious product, some of which is outstanding and highly useful, but most of which is turgid, intellectually slack, or fatally out of touch. Justice Breyer (himself a former law professor) has commented that many law review articles had "left terra firma to soar into outer space," while Chief Justice Roberts speculated that the average article explores superfluities like "the influence of Immanuel Kant on evidentiary approaches in eighteenth-century Bulgaria, or something, which I'm sure was of great interest to the academic that wrote it, but isn't of much help to the bar."[5] As it happens, with that particular joke, Roberts exposed himself more than the academy.* But Roberts and Breyer had a point: legal scholarship has become so disassociated from actual law that not even legal academics read much of it.

American law schools, then, are something of a bust. This matters, of course, because law schools have a monopoly on the production of lawyers and therefore condemn the rest of the legal system to undue expense and dysfunction. Before getting to the reasons for why law schools fail, it's helpful to quantify the magnitude of the academy's mistakes, starting with the inability of many legal graduates to become practicing attorneys.

The Diploma Mill of Last Resort

The first problem with law schools is that there are too many of them. At the time of writing, the American Bar Association listed 203 accredited schools and 30-odd unaccredited schools.[6] The unaccredited institutions are law's equivalent of Long Island wineries: dubious. But so are a lot of accredited schools. Over the past decade, students caught on, and previously robust legal enrollment has shrunk by a quarter.[7] Nevertheless, law schools still welcomed 37,400 students in 2017, about 9 to 14 percent of whom will drop out, producing a graduating class of roughly 33,000 students in 2020.[8] This is still too many. The BLS estimates America only needs a net 65,000 more practicing lawyers for the decade ending in 2026.[9] Law schools will produce several times that number, a surplus that the mass retirement of Baby Boomer

---

   *   In fact, (1) Kant was active in eighteenth-century Prussia and no one would expect his work to have filtered to the European periphery until the nineteenth century, as indeed it did not and (2) "Bulgaria" didn't exist in the eighteenth century, being part of the Ottoman Empire until 1878—a fact that shouldn't have been obscure to a Harvard history major (as Roberts was).

attorneys will not offset. If law schools are vocational schools, they must be reckoned a failure, because the lawyer glut ensures that many students will never work in the profession for which they trained.

But *are* law schools vocational institutions? Notwithstanding commencement speeches about "higher callings" (speeches that tacitly prepare graduates for the non-law callings which preference and circumstance will require), the answer is "yes," at least measuring by students' early careers. When students can get jobs practicing law, they understandably take them. Within ten months of graduation, 68.7 percent of the class of 2017 practiced law, mostly at conventional law firms, though some will be fired (both for performance reasons and because the legal industry is cyclical) and others will simply depart out of boredom or disgust.[10] This might suggest that a third of graduates go on to fulfill the grand social missions featured in the deanly addresses and alumni newspapers, but that's not quite the case. Many graduates don't work as lawyers at all, a fact not entirely explained by weak demand.

One reason why so many recent law graduates do not practice law is that they can't. Many students, even from relatively good schools, fail the bar exam—a test for which law school does not really prepare them. A whole exam-prep industry has sprung up in compensation, run by companies like BARBRI and Themis (the latter named after an allegorical goddess of justice, naturally). Almost all law students who can take cram classes do (as I did); indeed, big firms, having modest faith in legal education, encourage new hires to take the classes and foot the bill. And yet, pass rates remain shockingly poor. Gross passage rates range from a low of 44 percent (California) to a high of 81 percent (Oklahoma), with a national average of 59 percent.[11] A huge chunk of law school product is "defective" in a given year. What these pass rates would be absent cram classes is unclear, though available data suggest cram work improves passage rates by perhaps 10 to 15 percentage points.[12] In practice, mass bar failures do reduce the problem of lawyer oversupply, however pitilessly.

Let's pause for a moment on the bar exam, the hurdle imposed by local bar associations before they allow graduates to assume the actual responsibilities of caring for other people's legal fates. Licensing tests are good ideas in principle, but the bar is an exercise in mindless brutality. For a start, the bar is mostly a standardized test, suffering the usual infirmities of the genre: bias and a lack of realism. (Drafting contracts and arguing motions are not multiple-choice exercises and if the response is that there's no other way to process 33,000+ applicants, consider that even the DMV manages to conduct both a standardized and practical test.) Worse, the legal content of any given state's bar exam is *not actually the law in that state.* The "multistate" part of the bar exam is exactly what it sounds like, but there is no such thing as "multistate" law: different states have different laws. But even though the larger states, notably New York, California, and Texas, could create their own bar exams, almost all states use the synthetic law of a multistate exam, which is worse than useless: the right answer for the bar might not be the right answer in *any* state, which wastes students' time and risks confusing them about the actual law.*

To "flawed" and "irrelevant," we can add "suspiciously harsh," because many states set passing scores so high that it's reasonable to question whether their exams serve not so much as tests of competence as guild-imposed attempts at price control (which may explain bar examiners' indifference to the surreal and unhelpful nature of the tests—for a monopolist, a test succeeds when enough people fail).[†13] Naturally, people who should fail do fail. But some people who should pass *also* fail. D.C. and California, two of the most demanding jurisdictions, have bar exams that mowed down candidates who, whatever their other limitations, are clearly not incompetent. D.C.'s exam claimed a future senator/secretary of state (Hillary Clinton); California's body count includes two future governors (Pete Wilson, Jerry Brown), a

---

*   Wisconsin is the only state that waives the bar exam, but only for students who graduate from a Wisconsin law school.

†   Bar exams seem to skirt awfully close to cartelism, which is generally illegal. It would be here but for the nexus between state governments and the bar examiners, and once again sovereignty rides to the rescue of a questionable government practice.

state attorney general/senator (Kamala Harris), and a dean of Stanford Law School (Kathleen Sullivan, shortly after she left the deanship for private practice); even New York, with laxer standards, took out both a future mayor and future president (Ed Koch, FDR).*[14]

Clearly, something is off with the bar exam, but the exam has been a fact of life for longer than most American law schools have existed. If legal educators deem the bar exam silly (and many professors do, openly), law schools are the institutions best placed to demand reform. So far, those demands have been late in coming and largely ineffective, and bar examiners have countered, with some justification, that schools have not been carrying their weight.[15] Certainly, the examiners have a point: schools should better prepare students—not just for students' sake, but because many schools are public institutions and their social mandate is to convert taxpayer dollars into working attorneys. Until schools fix the bar or themselves, every year will see many thousands of their students felled by the exam.[16] Too hard on law schools? Not if medicine is a guide; 94+ percent of medical school graduates pass each of their boards on the first try, and whatever the boards' failings, being too easy is not among them.[17]

The Shallow End of the Talent Pool

Disasters this large always have original sins, and for law schools, many trace back to the admissions process. Admissions officers preach the usual sermons of well-roundedness, but the key inputs for admission to better schools remain LSAT scores and GPA. (At bad schools, the only filter is access to credit.) There's been controversy about how accurately LSAT scores predict *success*, but they can certainly predict *failure*. LSAT scores run from 120 to 180, with both the mean and median sitting near 151.[18] Students scoring

---

*   All passed a bar in later sittings. For the record, my critique is impersonal. I passed California's bar on the first go, though I doubt that I, or most other licensed attorneys, could pass if tested tomorrow: the bar's material just isn't relevant.

much below 155 are deeply unlikely to flourish, but lower-ranked schools, both regular and for-profit, admit low-scorers anyway—arguably breaching the ABA's prohibition on admitting students who do not "appear capable" of graduating and passing the bar.[19] (Indeed, something like one-third to one-half of *admittees* fall below standard.[20]) Loose admissions had long been a problem, which the Great Recession magnified. With public dollars and private donations declining, law schools could tighten their belts or relax their standards; they preferred the latter. The relatively new for-profit law schools were the worst offenders, but standards slid almost everywhere, and the pool of admittees with LSAT scores below 150 is almost certainly larger than the pool scoring above 170.[21] Even some elite schools tolerated slightly lower scores, though their standards were so high that the change was inconsequential.[22]

What *is* consequential is that the bottom half of law schools routinely admits battalions of students who will not thrive. Many, of course, will just fail—and society will foot the bill. When marginal students do scrape past the bar (by luck, by re-sitting the bar time after time, or by finding an easier state and "waiving in" to their home state), their admission reduces professional standards, slowing down courts and transactions, and upping error rates. A recent twist to the scandal is the growing number of students who decline to take the bar, perhaps at schools' own invitation. In 2015, one student at Arizona Summit Law School alleged that a dean offered students cash to "defer" the bar exam, presumably because it was not hard for the dean to predict which students might fail—by 2017, the school's bar pass rate hovered near 20 percent. After three years, the ABA indicated it would revoke Arizona Summit's accreditation approval (though as of this writing, the school still trumpeted its accreditation, because an administrative appeal stayed the ABA's revocation, a fact that gives some weight to the student's allegations about the school's deceptive practices).[23] These opt-outs, dismal in themselves, lead to the even more distressing conclusion that already low bar passage rates benefit from sample bias. Were all bad students to see legal education through to its horrifying conclusion, pass rates would be lower still.

Perhaps diploma-mills need not fear lawsuits from indebted, unlicensed, and academically deficient graduates, though if these unfortunates are powerless, the ABA and state attorneys general are not—and those institutions should make their power better felt.

Improving admissions standards would also alleviate another crucial problem: underemployment. Outsiders, a category that includes law school applicants, wrongly believe that law school provides a ticket to a secure career. As we saw, despite heavy attrition and widespread bar failures, schools produce too many lawyers, leading to high unemployment. The class of 2017 reported at least 7.9 percent unemployment ten months after graduation, which only seems tolerable without context.[24] Over the same period, total unemployment was 3.9 percent, and unemployment for Americans with a bachelor's degree or better hovered at 2.5 percent, and for professional degree holders, just 1.5 percent.[25] Whichever comparison one chooses, new lawyers face troubling levels of unemployment. The aggregate figures also conceal an important division between the best and the rest. At the five or so really elite schools, unemployment barely exists as a concept: within a year of graduation, out of the 224 students in Yale Law's 2017 class, exactly two were unemployed and seeking work.[26] The rest of the best also enjoy secure futures, but after the top 20 schools, employment outcomes begin descending to the national average—good, but not the handsomest return on a graduate degree.

From there, things get somewhat worse in the top 100, before falling off a cliff. Results for the bottom half of schools are generally awful, with average unemployment of around 13 percent and some spectacular disasters like the University of La Verne, where 34 percent of new graduates were still unemployed ten months after getting their diplomas.[27] Charlotte School of Law was so bad that it was abruptly shuttered in 2017, leaving many students with debt and no degree, an embarrassment so severe that even the secretary of education, the freedom-includes-freedom-to-fail Betsy DeVos, agreed to liquidate Charlotte students' debts if they couldn't transfer to another law school to complete their degrees. Adding to unemployment is underemployment, a severe problem even for lawyers from so-so schools. Not all lawyers can find work *as* lawyers—at least 11.8 percent end up in jobs where a JD is described as an "advantage," though that advantage is not quantified or netted against costs.[28]

As vocational schools, then, only the best law schools can be considered (qualified) successes. Students who gain admission to those schools are already good-to-outstanding scholars, so it's reasonable to question what role legal education plays in their future success, especially given the strange curriculum and indifferent teaching that characterize American law schools.

Curriculum Mortes

We can now mostly part company with lesser schools, since their lax admissions standards, low bar passage rates, and grim employment results render curricular analysis moot. As we've seen, graduates of better schools do not normally have difficulty finding good careers. At Harvard, 95 percent of students pass the bar and, if they choose to work in private practice, usually command starting salaries of $180,000 or more.[29] The relevant question for the top schools is not whether their graduates can succeed, but if their curricula contribute to that success and do so at a reasonable price.

A good legal curriculum should begin before law school, and in many countries, it does. America is not among those countries. While virtually all doctoral programs expand on an undergraduate's major, the American JD does not—indeed, lack of substantive prerequisites makes law school a famous refuge for aimless college seniors. Nor could undergraduates voluntarily prep for law school, as American colleges do not offer a germane package of classes, much less a stand-alone major. (What formal "pre-law" programs that exist are offered mainly by lower-ranked colleges feeding criminal justice professions and the lesser law schools; as relatively few alumni of these programs will ever practice law, neither the "pre-" nor the "law" is entirely accurate.) Not that law schools care: Yale's bracingly candid

53

"JD Eligibility" section reveals that the nation's top law school asks only that students "[r]eceive, or expect to receive...a bachelor's degree."[30] In what? Up to the student, though Yale expects a 3.91 GPA in whatever was studied (a 4.21 is preferred, though).[31] Yale is exceptional in its GPA expectations, but unexceptional in its ambivalence to field of study. The ABA, for its part, practices militant agnosticism, suggesting only that students find a major that "interests and challenges" while improving "research and writing skills"— i.e., every major at a proper university.[32] English, biology, dance, whatever; anything goes.

The undergraduate/graduate disjunction creates gaps that law schools cannot remediate. Agnosticism about major could increase intellectual diversity, producing a range of attorneys suited to serve clients in many fields: theater majors–turned–entertainment lawyers or economics students–turned–banking attorneys, and so on. In practice, however, agnosticism homogenizes the applicant pool, favoring humanities majors who have easier paths to high GPAs than peers in quantitative disciplines.[33] With STEM issues proliferating across legal practices, the implicit bias toward humanities disserves clients. Nor are all humanities majors created equal when it comes to preparing students for modern legal work, and without prerequisites, legal deans cannot assume incoming students will understand law's social, economic, and political contexts. As it happens, political science has been the most popular major for future law students, which mitigates the last concern, but not entirely, and not for everyone.[34] Would it kill law schools to require statistics, rhetoric, philosophy, and basic economics? It might, by trimming a key applicant pool: college seniors who apply to law school as a last resort. In sum, law schools cannot assume admittees have appropriate backgrounds (or any interest in law).

Law schools ignore curricular gaps, assuming that any reasonably fluent English speaker can be molded into an attorney. The first year of law school (1L) goes about this by training students to "think like lawyers," which entails synthesizing some legal rule out of a packet of cases and then nit-picking differences between them. The standard fodder for this exercise involves archaic subjects like Torts and Property, golden moldies that are irrelevant to most future practices and convey little about the average client's goals or law's broader social role. After 1L, students have opportunities to study pragmatic subjects, though not deeply and rarely via clinical (i.e., real-world) work. Unsurprisingly, law firm partners complain that new attorneys lack relevant skills, especially in the business and regulatory practices that dominate private corporate practice. Having myself been a client of many law firms, the partners' critique rings true as far as it goes, though it doesn't go far enough: even technically proficient attorneys (including the partners doing the complaining) often dissatisfy because, lacking context, they do not understand what clients seek to achieve. (As an example, when soliciting a legal opinion about a new venture, a client's preferred answers are, in order: "legal," "legal, but with some changes," "probably not legal," and "could cause problems in theory." Law school only gives students the confidence to provide that last and least helpful answer; law schools teach "issue-spotting," not problem-solving.)

In some cases, lawyers do not even try to understand client needs, because nothing in their education trains them to inhabit the client perspective. "What Clients Want" is a course badly in need of inclusion in the 1L catalog. But even if lawyers knew what clients wanted, they might not be able to deliver. Perhaps the cardinal sin here is innumeracy. Obviously, much legal work involves math—loans, workplace comp, sales contracts, securities filings, democratic fundamentals like redistricting, and so on. Yet, it's common to hear lawyers and professors singing (happily) the refrain "lawyers don't do math" to excuse various acts of ignorance. But lawyers need to be numerate, because math is everywhere and the proper vocabulary and grammar of math are obviously numbers and equations, not legalese or its estranged parent, English. Lawyers should be fluent in all these languages. Many are not, nor are they expected to be.[35] All major graduate-entrance exams have a math section *except* the LSAT, and relatively few law students have done decent college-level math coursework. Some law schools offer a few Learning Annex–level classes in accounting or statistics, but this is a recent development and not much compensation—lawyers and judges make momentous math errors all the time.[36]

Law school's bizarre pedagogy compounds these problems. Most 1L classes use the "case method," popularized in the late nineteenth century by Harvard Law dean C. C. Langdell.* Echoing the methods of Edward I (albeit nearer the reign of Edward VII), the case method requires students to study judicial opinions, teasing out their rules and principles, evaluating their reasoning, and locating particulars that "distinguish" one case from another. This sets the tone for future litigators, with success dependent on the ability to evade one result by finding some minute-yet-somehow-momentous difference between two otherwise identical fact patterns. Nevertheless, in the era before the regulatory state, when much law was judge-made common law, the case method had the virtue of at least resembling mainstream legal research. Since the early twentieth century, however, common law has been substantially replaced by statutory law, enacted by legislatures or embodied in agency rules. Unlike the judicial opinions studied in the case method, statutes and regulations do not have "facts" to discuss or distinguish, nor (for the most part) do they have a "logic" to critique, or contrary "authorities" or dissenting opinions to contrast. Higher-level classes devote some time to the special techniques of parsing statutes and regulations, but not nearly enough.

Thus, law school's cherished case method wastes time and distracts young lawyers—even the future litigators—from learning what's essential. For example, Contracts professors have students trudge through the quicksand of *Pinnel's Case* (1602) to learn that the "law does not question the adequacy of consideration," i.e., that law will uphold a contract so long as any payment is made. Worth the time? Hardly. (Especially because that's not *quite* the gist of *Pinnel's Case*.) Sure, it's amusing to discover that learned judges once pondered whether a robe, a peppercorn, or a tomtit (a small bird) sufficed as genuine payment. Nevertheless, might not a case from a world where people

---

* Langdell also helped gin up the fancy Juris Doctor degree to replace the old "bachelor of laws" credential in another attempt to deodorize the vocational stench of law; by the 1960s, most law schools had replaced the LLB with the JD.

settled bills in pepper and birds be a clue that the material might be a little...
outdated? Yet, professors happily spend hours on this sort of thing, even
though chestnuts like *Pinnel's Case* aren't the law anymore—variants of the
Uniform Commercial Code (UCC) are. Adopted by state legislatures mid-
century, the UCC plainly describes the consideration rule and its exceptions.
Even so, students don't always encounter the UCC, except in snippets quoted
in a case. Nor are students likely to read a contract in full or—God forbid—
actually draft one, as many will be called upon to do once school ends. (I'm
sure a few professors require their students to draft a contract in Contracts,
and I'm equally sure they're wrongly derided as cranks.) What holds in Contracts holds in most classes, so that with the exceptions of Civil Procedure
and Evidence, lawyers who will do nothing but deal with statutes/rules rarely
study them directly. Quite shockingly, it's possible to drift through law school
without reading the entire Constitution, which only takes an hour to peruse
and cannot be said to be wholly irrelevant to the legal enterprise.

Although higher-level classes now grudgingly accommodate themselves
to new legal realities, the oddities of the 1L curriculum grow increasingly
consequential, as it's on 1L performance that whole legal futures can hinge.
During 1L, law firms select summer associates; the private sector has begun
designating its chosen. Still more consequential, it's around this time that
many law reviews pick staff and judges begin recruiting clerks; the victors
in these contests join the true legal aristocracy. The enduring power of these
victories can be seen in the biographies of people at the top of the profession:
Justice Breyer's official C.V. proudly notes his clerkship for Arthur Goldberg
undertaken when Breyer's boss, John Roberts, was all of nine years old.[37] But
if law reviews and clerkships are evergreen credentials, their absences carry
a whiff of damaged goods. Thus, performance in 1L, the least representative
part of the curriculum, can have the greatest weight in determining legal
futures. It's an unusual way to anoint a professional elite.

Valid as the critique of legal education's substance is, perhaps it's beside
the point. So long as law schools continue to place a low priority on teaching ability, it really doesn't matter if the professor teaches tort law or taro

cultivation. Of course, excellent professors exist, but this is largely by accident, as the University of Michigan's manual for aspiring professors makes
clear. Under the heading "Teaching Less Central," Michigan says: "It is difficult to overemphasize how much law schools are looking for applicants who
will write scholarly legal articles. *Teaching is often not even mentioned in the
hiring process.*"[38] It's true that many future professors first obtain "teaching
fellowships," but this is a misnomer; the purpose of the "teaching" fellowship
is not to impart the secrets of *teaching*; rather, these fellowships exist to help
future professors *publish*.

Money Matters

As the curriculum provides law students with a weird *Weltanschauung*, high
tuition narrows the futures into which that worldview might be expressed—
distortions with real consequences for the legal system. In 2017, private
tuition averaged $46,000 annually and, adding incidentals, the rack rate for
a law degree can exceed $200,000.[39] Presently, Columbia Law holds the title
of most expensive, and suggests a minimum budget of $97,580 per academic
year.[40] The full number is surely higher, as Columbia's estimate of "personal"
expenses runs just $3,900, and a subway pass alone is $600 to $1,000 for the
academic term.[41] Columbia and other private schools in the top tier are,
however, something of a steal as they can be generous with financial aid and
their graduates find good work. Less expensive private schools cannot say the
same: of institutions charging substantially below the average, perhaps only
Brigham Young has a decent reputation for quality and job placement. To
the extent legal education contains bargains, they're at public schools, which
average $26,400 for in-state tuition, though the best public schools charge
closer to private-school averages: the University of California–Berkeley
charges $49,364, the University of Virginia charges $58,300, and the University of Michigan asks $57,262; only the University of Texas–Austin (base
tuition: $35,015) is both highly regarded and comparatively inexpensive.[42]

Adding in undergraduate costs, a law degree can represent a $250,000+ investment, more than a new Bentley Continental and roughly equal to the average price of a home in the Midwest.[43] Again, some private schools distribute plenty of aid, a point alumni flyers belabor when clamoring for money, but there's no getting around it: becoming a lawyer is expensive.

It was not always thus. Law school tuition has risen faster than inflation since at least the 1980s. Tuition increases at private law schools have averaged just over 6 percent growth per annum for the past three decades, in line with private college tuition generally, which is trouble enough.[44] The real problem, though, is at public schools. Forced to offset dwindling public support with tuition dollars, public undergraduate tuition rose quickly, but public legal tuition rose faster still, averaging 8 percent annual growth on a nominal basis. In 1985, in-state residents faced average public law school tuition of $2,006 (or $4,700 in today's currency), just 27 percent of private tuition then; today, the public/private ratio is 57 percent ($26,400).[45] If historical trends continue, average public and private tuition will converge in the 2030s at something like $100,000 annually.[46]

Lawyers are not famously sympathetic, but the high cost of legal education affects everyone. Society's share is reflected in higher legal costs, reduced legal access, and distortions in government hiring pools.* Individuals also suffer, because lawyers often play roles even in routine life events. Many states require lawyers to be involved in real estate transactions, and in every state it's wise to hire lawyers to manage divorce and custody battles, employment disputes, DUI defenses, and so on. Eventually, everyone pays for high tuition via higher legal fees. Even humble firms handling routine cases charge at least $150 to $300 per hour. As monetary stakes rise, so do hourly rates—as we'll see in a later chapter, $1,500-per-hour rates are hardly

---

* The legal market is oversupplied and, in theory, this should *reduce* legal costs. But costs have gone up anyway. Why? For one, many new lawyers, as we've seen, are not capable, and therefore can't depress prices. For another, the enormous costs of law school make it difficult (if economically non-rational) for some graduates to accept lower paying jobs, further reducing price competition.

unknown.[47] Major corporations can bear these fees, but even so, costs trickle down—however minutely—in the form of lower earnings, which depress share prices in the portfolios of the roughly 50 percent of Americans who own stock, and in marginally higher prices for consumers who buy these corporations' products.[48]

Escalating tuition also raises the costs for, and depresses the quality of, public-sector legal work. Although lawyers begin high on government pay scales, government offers a fraction of private salaries, paying junior lawyers around $52,300.[49] Career government lawyers generally top out at $135,000—25 percent less than a new lawyer earns at a top firm. To make the public/private gap more pungent, consider that the hiring bonus alone for ex–Supreme Court clerks exceeds the Chief Justice's annual salary.[50] John Roberts is doing fine; he has a great job and comfortable lifestyle, due in part to his prior career at the legal behemoth Hogan & Hartson (now Hogan Lovells). But other public lawyers don't enjoy a Justice's prestige, nor the ability to pad income with book deals (as several Justices have). Government therefore struggles to recruit and retain talent. This is so even with the most civically minded students; some law schools will partly defray loan costs for public interest lawyers, but lawyers must eat and sleep, and restaurants and landlords do not accept good works as payment. As tuition keeps rising, government will attract fewer exceptional lawyers and increasingly rely on recruits who are independently wealthy (and thus radically different from the public they serve). Worse, government will hire more candidates who expect to monetize public service later. After all, nothing quite polishes the résumé, or tarnishes the profession's reputation, like a pivot from public service to private practice, from prosecuting white-collar crime to defending it at a white-shoe firm.* With a few well-funded exceptions like the NRA and ACLU, legal activist groups fare even worse than government in this regard.

---

* The metonym of "white-shoe" for elite law firm comes from the old Ivy League habit of wearing white bucks. It was also a code for "anti-Semitic," though Jewish lawyers had the last laugh, with Wachtell Lipton now the most expensive and profitable (and arguably best) firm in America.

It was with some of these factors in mind that public law schools were established in the first place, and even for people who do not place a high value on diversity (however construed) or equality of opportunity, the steep rise in public tuition puts social missions in jeopardy. Over time, stronger lawyers will be tempted to migrate out of government, reducing quality and creating the appearance (or reality) of ethical conflict, and government work will be seen as distinctly second-class. Government's comparative asset is prestige, but few government positions are *that* prestigious and government's overall cachet has been waning since the 1960s and is now in free fall. With a few significant exceptions, such as federal prosecutors, government attorneys are already outgunned, intellectually and financially, by private lawyers. If, as many believe, private interests outmaneuver government, legal tuition provides a powerful explanation.

The Ivy Tower

Above the pedagogical humdrum drifts the *ukiyo* of law-school-as-research-institution. (I suppose this would make professors "mind-geishas," which is not as inaccurate as it seems.) As we've seen, the official posture of hiring committees toward teaching is somewhere between indifference and hostility, so if law schools can justify themselves as more than vendors of credentials, they need to produce a lot of research. And they do. But is that scholarship any good, or is it, as Justice Roberts suggested, obscure and irrelevant? Or, more pointedly, is the scholarship good enough to offset the failings of law-as–trade school? A little of both, as it turns out. Top law faculty produce extremely good work, even if some of it has no immediate practical value nor suits the Chief Justice's taste. (Certainly, this book cites its fair share.) But top faculty are just a tiny slice of the legal professoriate, perhaps 5 percent.

Valuing scholarship is fraught because most scholarship lacks immediate, tangible application and academic merit is subjective. Many attempts to evaluate academic output have been philistine embarrassments, as happened back in 1983, when one Professor Ellman measured "productivity" as a function of published pages. Volumetric analysis led to the felicitous implication that Ellman's own institution—ASU Law—rated seventh.[51] That ASU Law has never been anywhere near seventh on the leaderboards is perhaps most ably evinced by Ellman's ridiculous index, whose methodology would imply that McDonald's is America's "best" restaurant and Thomas Kinkade (mall-town's "Master of Light") its suburban Michelangelo.

However, it's not entirely impossible to describe and evaluate legal research. Law has more practical dimensions than, say, art, and the purpose of most legal research is to help law evolve. Such evolution is usually visible, given law's culture of precedent, publication, citation, and open reasoning. If a professor successfully pushes for modifications in federal sentencing laws, those changes appear in statutes; if professors convince judges to rethink "cruel and unusual punishment," court decisions will reflect that. Credit might not always be given explicitly, but specialists can tell when professors influence policy. Sometimes, influence is plain. After the Great Recession, Elizabeth Warren, whose work as a law professor had focused on bankruptcy and consumer protection, pushed for a consumer financial protection agency. It now exists, and when Obama nominated the Consumer Financial Protection Bureau's first head in July 2011, no one had to run to Lexis to discover CFPB's muse: Professor Warren stood next to the president. While liberal professors are more numerous and visible to the public, conservative and libertarian scholars have also achieved great sway, notably after the Reagan revolution. During Clarence Thomas's confirmation hearings, Joe Biden brandished a copy of Professor Richard Epstein's writings on property rights, asking Thomas if they had influenced the nominee's views.[52] Thomas demurred, but it's not hard to see Epstein's effect on Thomas or other conservative judges.

It would be a mistake, then, to write off legal academics as unfixable hermit kings. American law professors do not have the influence they once did, or as some foreign professors still do, but there's nothing about the job that consigns its holders to irrelevance. Liberal academics helped create the regulatory state in the 1930s and conservative professors led the pruning effort in the 1980s. Felix Frankfurter helped launch the ACLU while associated with Harvard; conservative professors shaped the Federalist Society and have influenced judicial nominations for decades. More recently, Professor Cass Sunstein helped the Illinois legislature "nudge" citizens to save more for retirement and undertook similar projects in the first Obama Administration; Professors Eugene Volokh, Guido Calabresi, Richard Posner, and Erwin Chemerinsky have also influenced their own fields.

Although an intellectually diverse group, these influential academics share a commonality—they often express their views *outside* conventional academic channels, even to the point of leaving the academy altogether. Law schools provide a secure base to generate ideas, but consequential academics generally branch out, intellectually and vocationally, into the judiciary (Frankfurter, Calabresi, Posner), public intellectualism (the above, plus Chemerinsky and Volokh), consumer advocacy/legislation (Warren), and most famously, the presidency (Clinton and Obama). The list continues, though not for as long as one might hope and not just because society produces a fixed percentage of geniuses. That law professors *can* influence law is true. That most *don't* is also true, and the production of unread (and unreadable) work is a function of who professors are and how they publish.

Preach, but Do Not Practice

In the beginning, law professors were practitioners: private lawyers, some judges, and the odd legislator. Their interests were practical, because they were practical men.[*53] Teaching played a large role, and publishing favored useful exercises like summarizing and clarifying the law. (These areas are now

---

[*]   All men, until 1897—and it would be another twenty-two years before a woman entered the tenure track of a major law faculty. Achieving balance has been slow: women now represent just over a third of law faculty overall.

somewhat disdained, though they remain urgent—a school is still a *school* and law has hardly grown more concise and lucid.) Even when law professors became more conventionally academic in the 1910s–1930s, many remained pragmatic, seeking to directly influence legislation by writing model laws in fields where legislatures were disposed to listen.[54] These efforts produced successes like the UCC and the original Federal Rules of Civil Procedure.[55]

Times have changed. Hiring committees grudgingly tolerate candidates with practical experience, but working at a firm for much longer than five years—which is to say, long enough to get good at practicing law—is considered a negative. This is unusual among professional schools; there are no professors of "theoretical dentistry." (Business school, a somewhat unflattering example, is the only other graduate program where many professors teach something they've never done, or done well.) Purely academic professors don't really know how to write or pass laws, or win cases, because inward focus leads them to see legislatures, courts, and law itself, as abstractions. The results flirt with absurdity, as during the legal tussle over on-campus recruitment in the "don't ask, don't tell" era. When law schools sued to be able to limit military recruiters on campus, the professors hired outside firms to file their briefs, which is not uncommon for procedural reasons. But did professors actually *write* their briefs? Harvard's press release was elliptical, noting that the professors' submission was "written...by a team of attorneys" from O'Melveny & Myers, with "input" from forty-odd professors.[56] The authorship of other schools' briefs was equally murky. Whoever the actual authors, they failed: the Court not only ruled in the government's favor, it did so 8–0 (Alito was recused), expressing acidic views on the logic and persuasiveness of the schools' submissions.[57] It's one thing to take on a noble cause and lose; it's quite another to be called out for making a bad effort in the process.

Law professors mechanically inform students that they toil in a practical profession, without taking that advice to heart. As a result, the influence of pure academics is declining, and not just because professors skew liberal and government is not always controlled by Democrats.

Between OCD and Irrelevance: Law Reviews

Legal scholarship is made worse by its overdependence on law reviews, which mediate most legal scholarship and cement legal elites. Every law school sponsors at least one legal journal and industry groups sponsor others, so that America has at least 940 legal journals, likely more than the rest of the world combined.[58] Factoring in multiple issues per year, and multiple articles per issue, the total volume of American legal publication is immense—likely exceeding the total number of published opinions produced by *all* federal appeals courts in a given year.[59] Knowledge is commendable, but pouring so much into the strange mold of law reviews distorts scholarship. By convention, many articles are roughly the same length regardless of topic or interest; their style is formulaic; their content, predictable. Like music's sonata-form, these constraints lead to technically proficient and mostly forgettable results, with a few spectacular exceptions.

It's hard to envision sudden improvement, because uniquely among academic journals, law reviews are dominated by student-editors.[60] As law students have no real depth in any legal subject, journal editors can't always tell if a submission is novel or potentially influential, so they focus on the variables they can comprehend, like the submitter's existing prominence or utility as a mentor. The main result is that reviews favor the already famous, which limits a key academic good: intellectual diversity. Once articles are accepted, unworldly editors can offer little useful feedback (not that many professors would take it); therefore, time is spent on copy editing tasks of sometimes ludicrous (b)anality, like checking to see if commas are improperly italicized after case names. (I indict my younger self here.) Professors, often journal alumni themselves, have been complaining about all of this since law reviews got up and running a century ago. And such is the grip of law reviews on legal scholarship that these complaints about law reviews appear...in law reviews, more of them than ever, and immune to professorial critique.

Does anyone benefit from this strange industry? Certainly, the professors and the students do—professors get the prestige of publication, students the cachet of journal membership. Law firms also gain a valuable screening tool. Journals are competitive, with membership indicating students' intellectual aptitude and, given all that proofreading, an ability to maintain focus in the face of mind-numbing tedium (a much-valued quality in young lawyers). Legal egos profit, too; the prestige of reviews is so central to lawyerly self-perception that Sonia Sotomayor *still* lists her law review work even though she has achieved at least one other distinction of note.[*61] Tenure committees also find journals helpful, as publication records weigh heavily in hiring decisions. Indeed, given the unusual structure of legal education, tenure panels must focus on journal publications. Aspiring law professors have comparatively little time to amass a publication record; it's rare to publish more than one student article during law school, much less the book-length dissertation required by other doctoral programs. Judicial clerkships, law's customary "post-doc," are also not conducive to scholarship—they're intense and offer little opportunity to write anything but opinions for supervising judges and, of course, clerks cannot claim credit for those since that would expose the seamy underbelly of the judicial system, as we'll see in Chapter 6. (Some judges also flatly prohibit publication during clerkships.) A résumé's attachment of "published works" must be filled somehow, and quickly; journals provide the easy way out. The growing proportion of PhDs in legal academia may help, but only somewhat—in the publications arms race, journals will always be willing dealers.

These critiques would be modest if it could be shown that law reviews produce benefits equal to their costs. A crude measure of influence is to evaluate law reviews like any other ad-free periodical, weighing regular subscription fees against costs. It would not be surprising if only a handful passed that commercial test, but it's almost certain that *no* major academic law review does. *Harvard Law Review*, which has the widest circulation, claimed just

---

[*] Of recent Court justices, three were not members of the main law review of their institutions: Kennedy, Thomas, and Gorsuch. Make of that what you will.

1,722 paid subscriptions for 2012, for $344,400 in gross revenues, assuming all subscriptions were full-price, which they were not.[62] University of Virginia's well-respected journal had 304 subscribers. And so on. Law reviews have other revenues; a favorite is to sell authors excerpt editions to use during job auditions.* But the mission of law review is not to compete with Kinkos, and reprint revenues are modest anyway. Against these measly total takings, law reviews have significant costs, offset by heavy subventions by their parent universities, like free rent and research services and, most importantly, the implicit subsidy represented by salaries of professors who write the articles. Over time, these subsidies—supported, at public institutions, by tax dollars—will grow, because whatever problems print newspapers have, law reviews are doing worse. Since 1972, *HLR*'s subscriber base has fallen almost 80 percent, matching steep declines at peer journals—and declines began almost two decades *before* the journals became available through online databases like Lexis or started posting free articles on the web.[63] The journals' perpetual deficits doesn't mean they should be abolished, any more than MoMA should be bulldozed because ticket sales don't cover operations. But it does raise a question: Why *aren't* law reviews doing better?

In a word, content. Reviews, like the legal curriculum, are out of step with the broader industry. At the beginning, reviews included many works with immediate practical application.[64] The term "law review" says it all: these journals originally aimed to *review* the current state of *law*. However, as law professors became more academic, emphasis shifted. Practical articles were consigned to trade publications, like the ABA's *Litigation*, while law reviews emphasized creative nonfiction loosely tethered to real law, plus reams of material on the narrow, if admittedly consequential, world of Constitutional law. (Notably, specialist publications with professorial editors, like New York

---

* Four law school journals—at Harvard, Penn, Columbia, and Yale—own a special cash cow, the *Bluebook,* the default manual of style for legal citation. Most lawyers buy a copy, providing those four journals with healthy incomes. Inevitably, the *Bluebook* itself has been the subject of legal controversy, when it was alleged that Harvard had not been properly sharing the *Bluebook*'s revenues. As *HLR* staff go on to so many prestigious positions, it's amusing to consider that a slice of the nation's legal elite might have participated in some giant fraud.

University's *Tax Law Review*, are well-read and thriving.) The result is that law reviews have become fora for academics to talk to other academics, and given the prevalence of self-citation, sometimes just to themselves.

It's not even clear if academics find journals particularly useful, as prestige journals are insistently generalist while modern law (and modern law professors) are specialists. But law reviews cannot be otherwise, because their editorial staff are mainly 2Ls who lack depth in any specialty. Now that databases can search all law reviews, generalism is less worrisome; useful articles will be found wherever they live. The problem is that most articles are so abstruse that judges, lawyers, and even other academics find them useless no matter where they appear. In one sample, the average number of judicial citations per article—a crude proxy for practical utility—was: zero.[65] (Fine: 0.4.) When citations occur, they usually appear in other law journals.[66] Professorial influence can accrete with enough time and enough articles, so focusing on short-term citations (or making too much of self-citation) can mislead, especially since review articles are often intentionally avant-garde. Louis Brandeis's article on rights to privacy came out in 1890, but judges first embraced the idea around 1905, and privacy's real heyday came later still. It may be that articles posted today will have Brandeisian influence in 2035, but the odds are long.

Reform Only Happens if You Try

Just as there's no mystery to how legal education can be bettered, there's also no chance improvement will happen soon. Nevertheless, reformers should consider a few basic steps. The fifty least selective law schools are not schools at all and should be closed. The middling tier should consider alternative curricula, including something like a JD-lite. Many legal matters are routine and low-stakes and, just as medicine has authorized the nurse practitioner to handle many tasks, law can do the same—as happens in countries like

France. This would require a restructuring of American law, but the benefits could be considerable. Traditional JD programs could be more selective, improving normal legal representation while sparing ill-equipped students the trauma of failing the bar. Consumers would also benefit from reduced costs and greater access to legal advice in straightforward matters. There's plenty of low-intensity work that "super-paralegals" could handle, such as misdemeanor bail hearings. If the objection is that defendants' rights might be imperiled by inadequate counsel, consider that the current arrangement often supplies no legal help at all. Creating different tiers of legal education would resolve some of the tensions between vocationalism, scholasticism, generalism, and social responsibility that have simmered in Anglophone law schools forever.

As for legal scholarship, academic inquiry doesn't thrive under limitations, and none are proposed. Rather, there should be a shift in emphasis. Tenure committees should seek a more diverse faculty. Only among legal faculty is it radical to propose that corporate lawyers teach corporate law. Deans should also recruit more former officials, and not as unproductive trophies in a low-expectations retirement home. There should also be more PhDs, including professors with quantitative backgrounds, and junior faculty should be granted the luxury and time to publish works outside of law reviews. Some of this is underway, but reforms need to go faster. Legacy faculty should be bought out; if the worst outcome is some faculty litigation the schools lose, well, at least they'll know the old professors had practical skills after all.

More than anything, law professors should interact with the system of which they are ostensibly a part, because the standard model for teaching does not fully incorporate reality. Why theorize about how judges think when you can take a litigation-oriented class from a sitting judge? Easterbrook, Posner, and Calabresi lectured while on the bench, and many other judges would welcome the chance to teach classes. Agency lawyers could teach regulatory law, prosecutors and public defenders could handle criminal law, and so on.

The gulf between theory and practice is far wider than it needs to be, nowhere more so than between academic models of how law is made and actual lawmaking. This is not just the fault of law schools; seasoned judges and even legislators themselves may not understand the process. Congress, it turns out, is stranger than even cynics are prepared to believe.

CHAPTER FOUR

LEGISLATURES: OUTSOURCED SAUSAGE-MAKING

All legislative Powers herein granted shall be vested in a Congress of the United States, which shall consist of a Senate and House of Representatives.

U.S. Constitution[1]

I have come to the conclusion that one useless man is called a disgrace, that two are called a law firm, and that three or more become a Congress.

Peter Stone[2]

The birthplace of federal law is a nondescript box—"the hopper." The hopper is a creature of the House and, as befits its home, mindlessly democratic. Any representative can introduce a bill by simply tossing a stack of papers within. A bill to rename a post office or one to unwind the Affordable Care Act, the Wastebasket of Democracy accepts all without judgment. The only limit is bulk, with oversize documents consigned to the more capacious embrace of the House Clerk.[3] The Senate lacks a hopper, because a functional furnishing would be déclassé, and thus unacceptable to the dignity of America's "upper house." Of course, the Senate is neither dignified nor, as it happens, "upper." (It's called the "upper house" because it once met *up*stairs, not because the Constitution makes it some Americanized House of Lords; "former attic people" would be just as accurate.) Never mind, Disneyfied pseudo-chivalry is the Senate's cultural preference, and the chamber duly grinds along with the efficiency of a Bourbon court. To merely introduce a bill requires a senator to attract the attention of the body's presiding officer at an appointed time, request leave to present, and pray that none of the other ninety-nine senators objects (which can trigger a delay; this is how Rand Paul briefly shut down the federal government in 2018).[4] Only after this preposterous ritual concludes may the Senate Clerk receive the bill.

By these two systems, which effectively capture the different paces and styles of House and Senate, Congress proposes America's laws. After proposition, a bill must be passed in identical form by both chambers, a failure-prone process of quarreling, reconciliation, and brute force. If the two chambers concur, the bill travels to the White House for signature or veto. In outline, the process described resembles textbook descriptions of federal lawmaking, a bit stranger in detail, true, though a certain weirdness should be expected from an institution that commissioned its first residence from a physician-turned-architect who believed he could reanimate George Washington's corpse using warm blankets and an invigorating transfusion of lamb's blood.[5] While it's tempting to pursue the Dracula on the Potomac motif (or to ponder the metaphor of the Capitol dome, a decorative shell that contains the smaller, load-bearing elements), we must press on to the actual workings of Congress. For it is in the details that Congressional reality departs radically from textbook models, judicial theories, and common perceptions, and where notions of a representative, deliberative legislature founder.

The general awfulness of Congress is a subject of near-universal agreement, though popular explanations vary in emphasis on partisanship, corruption, or plain incompetence. These explanations are not without merit, but they bypass the structural and historical reasons for Congressional dysfunction: Congress cannot produce satisfying, or even technically competent, laws, because it is trapped in an old framework whose anachronisms become more constricting and inapt each year. Unfortunately, that old framework is Article I of the Constitution, which is functionally unamendable; there can be no hard reset. All Congress can do is patch and improvise, and it has. Regrettably, the legislature's workarounds are inherently compromised, undermining Congress's ability to perform four crucial tasks: representing the public, crafting proficient legislation, checking the other branches of government, and making laws that are legitimate and command respect of the governed.*

The Dead Hand of History

When Congress first sat in 1789–1791, its structures and capacities stood in reasonable harmony with the duties of a small nation's legislature. The task of being responsive and representative was assigned to the House, a chore which the original body could plausibly achieve. In the 1790s, with a complement of roughly sixty-five representatives against some 800,000 free white adult males and 3.2 million non-enslaved persons total, ratios of represented-to-representatives ran from about 12,300:1 to 49,200:1 (and lower still, counting only those eligible to vote).[6] In numerical terms, a representative in the early Republic was not distant from today's town councilman, close to his constituents and their issues. That changed with time; population grew quickly, but the House did not, so that by 2016 the ratio of represented-to-representatives degraded by ~95 percent to 740,000:1.[7] By definition, representatives cannot enjoy anything approximating intimate knowledge of their constituents, undermining Constitutional assumptions.

The more dramatic violation of expectations belongs to the Senate. The

---

* Congress serves as the focus because it makes laws of national application. The dynamics of state legislatures are roughly parallel.

Framers envisioned that body as a modest protector of smaller states against the predation of their larger siblings, and also a patrician, contemplative counterweight to the volatility of the House. Again, time eroded the Framers' expectations. In 1790, the smallest states were overrepresented by a ratio not much worse than 10:1; today, the ratio is as high as 66:1, changing the Senate's character from mildly counter-majoritarian to flatly antidemocratic.[8] Meanwhile, Senate rules, originally drafted by Jefferson and still semi-operant, were designed to permit extended debate among *un*-elected patricians, not to be weapons at the disposal of directly elected senators, some hailing from states sufficiently tiny that private interests can sometimes dictate national policy.

These Congressional dynamics, already challenging, will only become worse. Though the number of representatives could be increased by legislative fiat, Congress has not done so in over a century; today's House of Representatives hardly deserves the name. The composition of the Senate, meanwhile, cannot be changed save by Constitutional rejiggering, which small states can block, and as population disparities grow more severe, the Senate will be increasingly vulnerable to extortion and obstruction. Two brief illustrations suffice for how unbalanced Congress is: setting the Constitution aside, and allocating based solely on population, at least three states would have *zero* representatives each and California alone would have as many senators as the smallest twenty-one states *combined*.[9] (To put it another way, the ten largest states, comprising roughly half the population, can be filibustered by coalitions of states representing as little as 11 percent of the population.)

While growth and the direct election of senators upended the Framers' original assumptions and designs, the vast expansion in Congressional remit created a severe mismatch between the legislature's responsibilities and its capacities. Congress's original duties were fairly limited, focused on external policy plus a limited set of nationally important matters, like the Post Office and national defense. But in 1790, even national defense was a light burden: the Continental Navy had been disbanded and the army had just one regiment defending the frontier. Nor did citizens particularly expect Congress to intervene in daily life; lawmaking was understood to be primarily the responsibility of state and local officials. So while early Congresses did pass some momentous legislation (not least because any federal legislation would have been momentous in an era where none had existed before), the national legislature didn't find itself overly taxed and legislative output was modest by contemporary standards.[10]

Almost everything has changed radically. The institution that once presided over a nation hugging a thinly populated rind of the Eastern Seaboard now governs over 325 million people spread across possessions stretching from Point Udall, Guam, to Point Udall, St. Croix, 9,497 miles apart. (The eponymous Udalls were brothers, both serving in government.) Supervising defense appropriations today is by itself more complicated than managing the entire nation of 1790: the number of Americans in uniform today greatly exceeds the enfranchised population when the 1st Congress convened. The public, previously content to be left largely alone by federal government, now expects Washington to provide retirement security, health insurance, and guarantee the smooth operation of a $20 trillion economy. To simply keep government open requires immense legislative maintenance. Yet in 1913, with federal responsibilities already large, Congress essentially froze into its present form, refusing to meaningfully expand even as legislators ordered up the New Deal and Great Society.[11] The result is a body whose work far exceeds the capacities of 535 people.

To cope with its hugely increased mandate, Congress improvised. First, it outsourced, to presidents, judges, bureaucrats, staffers, and so on, though doing so stretched Constitutional boundaries and upset the carefully ordered balance of powers. However, there remained things only Congress could do. So Congress undertook an internal reordering, rewriting procedural rules to overcome the imbalances that had accumulated over the decades. Unfortunately, many of these internal reforms made matters worse, and Congress, already overwhelmed, found it ever harder to make laws responsively, deliberatively, and competently.

There's Nothing More Prolific Than an Idiot

Many people deride Congress as a do-nothing body, which is partly true, though the bigger problem is that even what Congress does do, it doesn't do well. The 115th Congress (2017–2018) provides a good example: it proceeded through 11/12ths of its first year without producing anything of real consequence, suddenly disgorged a messy tax bill, and then keeled over twice, first in a two-day government shutdown in January 2018 and, three weeks later, in a brief "funding lapse." Yet, if the 115th achieved little in its first year, it was still active, mainly in failing to repeal/repair/replace Obamacare, an activity which consumed most of 2017 and left the budget in limbo for months.

The budget provides a convenient example of how even central tasks now outstrip Congressional capacities. Presented by the White House in March 2017 and due for passage before October 1, the budget was not enacted until March 2018. When Congress finally coughed up the outstanding bill (after various procedural crises), the document totaled 2,232 pages and was circulated to the House just a day before the vote (violating an internal House rule about due time for reading and deliberation). The bill was a black box directing money to places literally unknown, with one representative commenting that "[i]n all honesty, none of us knows what is actually in this bill" and Senator Rand Paul noting that his printer was still churning out pages less than eighteen hours before the Senate took up the legislation; nevertheless, the budget was approved by both chambers essentially sight-unseen.[12] Nor was the FY 2018 budget anomalous; all big bills have become shambolic, last-minute affairs. The tax package of 2017, which immediately preceded the budget, was another exercise in hasty incomprehension. Congress drafted it so badly that a bill designed to cut corporate taxes across the board ended up hiking taxes on some businesses. The reason: while revising the bill (as usual, at the last minute), GOP legislators made a series of major miscalculations, and only barely hustled in partial corrections before presidential signature.[13] Pelosi's railroading of Obamacare through the House in 2009–2010 was positively contemplative by comparison, and if no one quite comprehended what was in the mammoth health care bill when it was passed, at least large chunks of the act had been previewed for weeks or months beforehand.

Monster bills are mercifully infrequent, but Congress must constantly wade through an enormous amount of *stuff* of greater and lesser importance— much more than it can be plausibly said to "read" or "debate." (Not that legislators always get the chance: in March 2017, drafters hid their Obamacare revisions in a locked room, and when others, including some Congressmen, obtained access, the room was empty of everything but metaphor.[14]) Out of all this material, some 12,000 items per Congress on average, 85+ percent simply die, either on the merits or more usually out of sheer neglect. Of the remainder, ~7 percent pass as unpresented resolutions (essentially, matters of internal affairs or empty rhetoric of limited public consequence), leaving at most 5 percent to become actual law.[15] In numerical terms, the 107th Congress was typical, with more than 10,700 items introduced, of which 383 became law, or 0.72 enacted laws per member.[16] The pace may not seem torrid, but it's more than Congress can handle. Modern bills average twenty pages, more important legislation sprawls over hundreds of pages, and all but the most basic bills contain numerous sub-provisions and amendments, some sufficiently substantial as to constitute bills in their own right. And marching behind all meaningful bills are reams of supporting materials, themselves bodies of quasi-law used by agencies and the judiciary to divine the meaning of the often-cryptic legislation to which they relate.

The little math exercise just presented is interesting because of what it *disproves*, and momentous because of what it *does* prove. The statistics disprove notions of a do-nothing Congress; many of those thousands of proposals may be trivial or inane, but each represents work by someone. And this leads to what the tally proves: whatever else a modern Congress is, it *can't* be just 535 elected officials. A mere 535 people cannot write, ponder, debate, nor vote on that much material—not by themselves. Nor do they. Congress has an army of unelected helpers, roughly 20,000 people writing and researching bills, dickering over procedure, fetching coffee, or, in the case of House Chaplain Father Conroy, S.J., hearing some very interesting confessions.*[17]

Notwithstanding its supporting cast, Congress still couldn't manage as a freestanding institution. Simply *reading*, much less writing or revising, a small subset of the most crucial bills consumes substantially more person-hours than legislators and their staffs have. That leads to the further conclusion that Congress also relies on *external* "staff": lobbyists, executive agencies, think tanks, and so on. Thus, whatever the Constitution says, America's supreme legislature cannot, and does not, only "consist of a Senate and House of Representatives," nor are all Congressional members "chosen" and "elected by the people."[18] The math puts paid to that idea. Various parts of the legal system pretend otherwise—to everyone's peril—but there it is.

An army of staff isn't alarming in itself. An expansive nation demands an expansive Congress; the real concern is *how* Congress managed its growth and what that means for republican government. Outsourcing reduced democratic accountability, as did internal reforms that dramatically altered the composition and organization of membership. Not all of these mutations have been well explained by Congress to the people it professes to represent, to the judges who interpret its laws, or even to many of Congress's *own members*. This helps explain why Congress is the most hated branch of government; the modern institution diverges radically from popular conception. But Congress needs to be understood. We have already seen that Congress can no longer properly serve its representative functions or digest all the material passing through it. However, laws are passed somehow, so the next step is to examine the compromises Congress makes simply to enact legislation *at all*, and assess the price

---

*   Don't Congressional chaplains, who open legislative sessions with a *prayer* (and are paid six-figure salaries by taxpayers for doing so) violate the Establishment Clause? Isn't Congress acting unconstitutionally *every time it starts its business*? Does Congress even care about the nation's supreme law or its founding principles? Does the Court? Didn't Madison, as we saw in the Introduction, think this was nonsense? Good questions, but neither Congress nor Court have provided good answers. While I was editing this book, Congress compounded the oddities by firing and then rehiring the House Chaplain. Legislators should take the hint and abolish the offices: *God doesn't want to be bothered by Congress.*

paid for those expeditious mechanisms, whether settled in the currency of Constitutional balance, institutional legitimacy, or jurisprudential integrity.

Not Very Good, and Not Enough of It

The Constitution vests in Congress "all legislative Powers."[19] That burden is at once heavy and light. It's heavy, because the Constitution makes Congress responsible for all federal lawmaking. It's light, because the Constitution does not require Congress to make any laws in the first place (aside from an implied obligation to authorize a census). Congress barely has a job at all, in the sense of enumerated tasks amenable to objective assessment. All Congress *must* do is: appoint its own officers, keep a journal, preside over impeachments, provide advice and consent to executive appointments, and "assemble at least once in every Year."[20] With a few exceptions, like slow-walking executive nominations, Congress does what little the Constitution specifically demands: a B+ job, at worst.

Naturally, people expect more than the Constitutional dead minima from their legislature, and there was a time when Congress delivered to the general satisfaction of the public. In 1937, people held Congress in reasonably high regard; 44 percent even ventured that Congress was "about as good a representative body as it is possible for a large nation to have."[21] In the following decades, various measures of satisfaction wobbled in a band of 30–60 percent, with fluctuations heavily linked to the nation's martial and economic fortunes; not always stellar, but hardly terrible. But from the 1970s, faith began to waver, and after 2005, Congressional reputation entered steep and secular decline. No year since 2009 has seen an average approval rating higher than 20 percent, with November 2013 marking the lowest approval ever recorded: 9 percent.[22] Perhaps more tellingly, net "trust and confidence" in Congress fell from 46 percent in 1972, to 2 percent in 2007, and since then has gone negative, averaging –27 percent since 2007. Notably, the share of people who *entirely* distrust Congress has risen from an average 6.6 percent from 1972 to 2007 to an average 19 percent since; if legitimacy is a core legal goal (as was argued in Chapter 2), this lack of confidence is worrying.[23]

Certainly, Watergate, partisanship, and cultural shifts account for some dissatisfaction. Yet, there's also a technocratic, objective complaint: as an *institution*, Congress just can't manage. Funding government is complex, but as central a task as can be imagined. Nevertheless, since 1976, when a change in budgeting rules made broad government shutdowns possible, Congress has closed the national shop twenty times, in total, at least 128 days of "service interruptions," some partial and some complete.[24] Unsurprisingly, doing *more* than the minimum proves beyond the abilities of many Congresses, and major new legislation has become near-extinct outside of extraordinary circumstances.

The public expects better. Surveys, including those by pollsters like the *Wall Street Journal*, reveal that roughly half of Americans want "government" to "do more to solve problems"; it isn't simply the case that everyone prefers for government to stay out of the way.[25] And whatever the Framers would have made of the CDC or Social Security, they also expected more. The Constitution's refusal to task Congress with many specific chores reflects the Framers' *high* expectations of Congress; Congress was granted great latitude to rise to new challenges, including the power to override many state laws, and to pass whatever laws are "necessary and proper" to the exercise of Congress's powers.[26] Congress was designed to be *primus inter pares*, the first branch, a mirror of public will, etc. It was also tasked with checking the ambitions of other branches—the presidency, which might tend toward authoritarianism, and the judiciary, which might act without democratic sanction. Alas, those ships, laden with Constitutional hopes, have sailed and sunk.

Neither Check nor Balance

For several decades, Congress has not satisfied its role as a check-and-balance; instead of protecting its powers, Congress has been *ceding* them. This represents a break. For 150 years, Congressional ambition kept the system in decent alignment; legislators really did guard their prerogatives.[27] The legal system presupposes that Congress still does, but this has been untrue since the 1930s, when Congressional "ambition" unraveled as the legislature's work swamped its abilities—and when legislative ambitions faltered, the system of checks and balances that underwrite the republic trinity began to wobble.

Relinquished legislative powers can only go two places: the judiciary or the executive. Judges have always had a quasi-legislative function, mainly exercised by filling in gaps: e.g., making common law where legislatures hadn't acted, or giving specific meanings to enacted law's vaguer provisions. Beyond that, nineteenth-century judges tended toward passivity and the Court rarely contravened the direct will of Congress, finding unconstitutional fewer than one law annually between 1792 and 1919, on average.[28] As the Progressive Era bled into the New Deal, the judiciary felt the Constitutional balance was getting out of whack (mainly as a result of bureaucratic expansion), and began to wield its veto more often and more consequentially, a process that was revivified in the Civil Rights era.*

Judicial vetoes aren't always conclusive; while Congress cannot override vetoes to resurrect inherently unconstitutional policies, it can salvage technically defective laws whose general policy aims are not unconstitutional, or revise stale laws to bring them into line with court rulings and popular opinions. (In the latter case, the override isn't so much a showdown as legislative housekeeping.) Through the 1990s, Congress often did just that, with judicial action facing legislative reaction—a classical check and balance.[29] When 1980's *Mobile v. Bolden* construed the Voting Rights Act to focus on discriminatory "purpose" (instead of discriminatory effect), Congress amended the VRA two years later, achieving the policy result legislators wanted.[30] In 1988, Congress salvaged part of the Civil Rights Act along the same lines.[31] And

---

* To be fair, not all strikedowns are created equal, and before the Reconstruction Amendments and the growth of federal law, judges had fewer tools and fewer targets. Also, a declaration of unconstitutionality doesn't vaporize a law; it merely renders the law a dead letter (and potentially able to return to life should courts change their minds).

in 1991, Congress revived antidiscrimination legislation, overriding at least seven Court cases from the then-recent past.[32] Not all overrides were dramatic; some were merely updates and tidying, but they reflected attentiveness and a certain Congressional attitude.

Since 1998, however, Congress has been wary, or politically incapable, of undoing/revising many judicial decisions, even when there's a Constitutional path to do so and Congress is controlled by the party favoring the voided law.[33] In the shrinking circumstances in which Congress responds to the judiciary, efforts seem halfhearted and tend to fail. The notable recent exception is the Lilly Ledbetter Fair Pay Act of 2009, which overrode 2007's *Ledbetter v. Goodyear*.[34] But the Ledbetter Act marked no renaissance for Congressional ambition. *Ledbetter* was 5–4, a relatively weak holding that Justice Ginsburg worked to make weaker still. Ginsburg dissented from the bench (a rare event bound to attract media attention), eroding the Court's authority from within and all but forcing Congress to act.[35] Ruling Democrats introduced the corrective Ledbetter Act, which stalled until candidate Obama made the Ledbetter Act a *presidential*, not Congressional issue. The previously becalmed repair suddenly sailed onto the new president's desk. But those were extraordinary circumstances, and it was not really Congress checking the courts, but the president-elect—and no one could miss the symbolism: Ledbetter was the first act Obama signed.[36] To be fair, Congress may not always have the votes to override the Court (or a presidential veto), but it's not as if the stars *never* align. Rather, it just takes more time and will than Congress and its committees now have, making judicial vetoes more potent—vetoes that private litigants, from the ACLU to the Mercers, can ask courts to wield.

The Ledbetter story also highlights the more important transfer of power, not to the judiciary, but to the executive. When the same party controls the White House and Congress, the president generally leads and Congress follows. Formally, Congress retains its Constitutional powers, though increasingly it does not so much *write* blockbuster legislation as block or amend executive proposals; Congress has become less author than editor. This

arrangement may seem natural, especially in an era where presidents dominate media coverage, only 35 percent of Americans can identify their own
representative, and less than half the public can identify the party in control
of the House or Senate.[37] But presidential predominance is new, hardly older
than the New Deal, and for good reason: an imperial/prime ministerial executive is Constitutionally anathema. If presidents and legislators mostly agree,
as Pelosi and Obama often did, the consequences may be minor, though it is
in those cases that presidents truly exercise prime-ministerial prerogatives.
But even when parties split control of government, presidents can still drive
policy, the prime example being the federal budget. Constitutionally, "revenue bills" (i.e., taxes) can only "originate" in the House—and appropriations
(spending, essentially) must also be set by Congress. But today, the executive writes the first draft of the budget, and that draft defines the debate: the
executive provides the default option, and many political battles are won by
default.[38]

Tellingly, the White House didn't steal budget-writing authority from
Congress; Congress gave it away—a recurring theme, as we'll see. As the budget is central to governance, it's worth exploring how Congress transferred
the power of the purse. Originally, budgets were approved piecemeal and ad
hoc, in negotiations between Treasury and Congress; as government grew,
that process became unwieldy. In 1921, Congress required the president to
submit a consolidated budget and created a new entity (what's now the Office
of Management and Budget, or OMB) to assist him, but Congress did not
similarly equip itself.[39] Over time, it became clear that Congress had armed
a nimbler opponent. Legislators therefore passed the Budget Act of 1974.
That act forbade presidents from "impounding" funds (i.e., refusing to spend
allocated monies, Nixon's version of a line-item veto that prompted the Act)
and established the Congressional Budget Office (CBO) as a counterweight
to OMB.[40] Yet, the Budget Act did not herald a dramatic return of power
to legislators. Impoundments never represented a large fraction of spending, so that victory was of limited import. Establishing the CBO was more
consequential, because it gave Congress resources to meaningfully evaluate

a president's budget and push back using hard data. Better still, the CBO has been a strong, rigorous, intellectually independent institution—emphasis on "independent." CBO says what it wants, not what members want, and CBO's analyses can profoundly affect legislative fortunes, as Republicans learned during their unsuccessful attempts to repeal Obamacare in 2017.[41] So, while the Budget Act returned some control to the *institution* of Congress, it did so by creating a new locus of power, one not composed of actual Congressmen.

Leaving aside the budget—which a capable president controls, as OMB's director reports directly to him—the other great power transfer between Congress and the executive has been to agencies, those acronymical subunits of the executive such as the VA, IRS, and FDA. Today, when Congress legislates, it mostly sets general goals (indeed, this may be as much as Congress is capable of). From there, the agencies decide the rules and provide the detail. Thus, the *functional* law, the law that citizens obey, is mostly written not by legislatures, but agencies. (This is why businesses and their compliance teams look to regulations first, not the enabling legislation.) That devolution of power, sometimes Constitutionally dubious, has become so important that agencies receive a chapter of their own (the next one, actually). What matters for now is that, by immediate impact and volume of law, agency lawmaking is at least as important as Congressional lawmaking. Agencies' rules sometimes diverge meaningfully from those Congress might have written itself, and those rules are far more changeable in interpretation and application, as Scott Pruitt's tenure at the EPA confirmed. Congress has given up more power than many people realize or than voters might like—an environmentalist may be able to vote a coal-booster out of office in two years, but could do nothing about a Secretary Pruitt. Agencies have also outright thwarted Congress, as in 2018, when the acting director of the Consumer Financial Protection Bureau, a Congressionally chartered agency, asked for a budget of $0, in an attempt at self-liquidation. The Constitution did not predict these developments, and it provides no direct means for citizens to undo these profound restructurings.

In theory, Congress can retrieve its Constitutional powers from the other branches at any time. In practice, this is exceedingly unlikely. Executives and the judiciary are more ambitious and energetic than Congress, less prone to division, and generally unwilling to return powers prior Congresses gave away. As for agencies, which arguably won the greatest powers from Congress, legislative reassertion is presently impracticable. Congress is outstaffed by almost 100:1 and Congress can no more compete with agency-land than Bermuda can repel an American invasion.[42] Congress is so poorly equipped that, until recently, it was largely unaware that agencies often fail to comply with the Congressional Review Act, which requires agencies to report rulemaking for Congressional appraisal.[43] A Congress that doesn't carefully monitor the powers it delegates is not an institution likely to retrieve those powers.

Paradoxes: A Parliamentary Congress and a Lawless Legislature

Congress's failure to adjust to new realities not only forced some legislative powers to be relinquished, it also made it very difficult to properly exercise what powers remained. To compensate for splintering caucuses and growing disproportions in small-state power, Congress has been forced to suspend standard operating procedures and concentrate power in a dictatorial leadership. The official headcount belies this; the Capitol still numbers 535 elected and roughly co-equal tribunes. Unofficially, ever fewer people control, or even participate meaningfully in, legislative activity; 150, at most, and not all of them elected.* Congress, already too small, has gotten even smaller.

The concentration of power in leadership breaks significantly from Congressional tradition. Congressional leadership now believes that quasi-parliamentary practices are the only way to ram legislation through a

---

* The rest are like guests seated at a wedding reception's more distant tables: at best, they fill out the room; at worst, they cause trouble.

fractious Congress, in which many members are insulated from public opinion (by gerrymandering and otherwise) and belong to two increasingly heterogeneous parties. The price has been another state of emergency; long-standing rules and norms have been tossed aside, and committees, the traditional centers of power and competence, have been partly sidelined. Rule by a tiny cadre of leaders—Speakers, whips, majority and minority leaders—is the new normal, but it's a remarkable breach, achieved by remarkable means.

From the 1840s to the 1960s, committees were the centers of Congressional activity, ruled by chairmen selected on a seniority basis who exercised substantial control over legislation in their areas of specialty. The legacy system seasoned its chairmen, affording them years to study their subjects and to practice writing technically competent laws. Insulated by seniority, and operating mostly outside public scrutiny, committee leaders were able to wheel and deal, and while this fostered some crooked behavior, it also let committees engage in the pragmatic and bipartisan trading that public contests among high-profile leaders now makes difficult. This worked while committee chairs reflected the broader sentiments of their parties, but in the Civil Rights era, this could no longer be assumed. Unity broke among then-ruling Democrats. Northern Democrats were more numerous and progressive than their Southern counterparts, but the Southerners were more senior, and that made all the difference.* Democrats found civil rights legislation tied up in committees led by party members from the South. However, Democrats, with a 60 percent share in both chambers and skillful allies in the White House (especially LBJ), were able to achieve their goals without blowing up the system.

By the early 1970s, Democrats had fewer votes to spare, and impatient with committee rule, they retooled the system. (Democrats dominate this telling because they controlled the House from 1955 to 1995, and their reforms prefigured changes under Republicans like Newt Gingrich.) In 1975, Democratic

---

* Democrats found it easier to accumulate seniority in the South, where they faced little challenge from Republicans until the 1970s.

leadership ousted senior committee chairs. Going forward, seniority would only be one among several considerations for chairmanships. Leaders also opened up Congressional workings: committee work became publicly accessible and it became much harder to tally floor votes without attribution; now the public could know who voted for what and why. These (little-d) democratic reforms—embodying the whole PowerPoint lexicon of transparency, accountability, and empowerment—would make the House truer to its role as the republic's more open, dynamic, and efficient forum. Or so the thinking went.

Like many ambitious overhauls, the reconfiguration of the House amplified old problems and created new ones. Weakening the seniority system was supposed to distribute power, but ultimately centralized it. The seniority system, for all its flaws, operated with mechanical objectivity, immunizing chairmen from leadership's directives. In the elective system, seniority and substantive knowledge are now just two factors among many, the most important of which is ideological alignment with, and endorsement by, leadership. The usual price of a committee chairmanship is accepting leadership's agenda, and because new chairmen may have little experience, leadership crafts much of a "committee's" work. (This helps explain intensifying partisanship and its attendant gridlock; it's not just ideological, it's structural.) For example, Gingrich's Contract with America, which set GOP priorities in the 1990s, bypassed the committee system almost entirely; so did Pelosi's 100-hour plan in 2007. Stuck on the sidelines, committees have become less entrepreneurial and less powerful. Understandably, even *meetings* became less likely: American Enterprise Institute's Norman Ornstein calculated that committee/subcommittee meetings declined from an average of 5,372 per Congress in the 1960s and 1970s to 2,135 in 2003 to 2004, and remain much less frequent than they were fifty years ago.[44]

The decline of committees did not quash dissent; it merely changed its outlet, requiring further reforms. The House's customary "open" rules, designed to facilitate debate and amendment, became primarily mechanisms of delay. To slow down contentious legislation, dissidents attached amendments to everything, and the number of votes on amendments rose from 55 (1955–1956) to 107 (1969–1970) and then 439 (1977–1978).[45] The docket congested and, with sunshine rules, became a public relations scoreboard. Savvy operators forced public votes on matters specifically constructed for embarrassment. A genuine bill to fund low-income housing could be saddled with a fraudulent amendment to euthanize puppies, and cynical legislators knew exactly how cynical local-TV anchors would spin things: not "Congressman X votes to save public housing," but "Congressman X votes to kill puppies." The House descended into theater—in 1979, live theater on C-SPAN.

As a result, the House found it increasingly difficult to move legislation along. In theory, stalls in the House shouldn't be hard to overcome—indeed, stalls should be mathematically impossible in a body that operates by majority rule, has an odd-numbered membership, and draws from only two parties. It's the last assumption that's become problematic: there aren't quite two parties anymore because the parties are not homogenous. Today, there is more than one Republican party (GOP-Classic; GOP-Tea Party/Freedom Caucus; Trumpists; whatever Rand Paul is), just as there was more than one Democratic party in the Civil Rights era and is today (the Warren/Booker wing; the Pelosi/Schumer axis; whatever Bernie Sanders is). And because the parties' centers of gravity are further apart, there are fewer centrist votes to draw upon to counteract resistance from a ruling party's more radical wing(s). This is not a problem when a ruling party has a huge majority. But when membership is closely divided, sub-factions become important and House leaders must assemble a working majority out of the parts on hand, just as coalition governments do in foreign parliaments. The problem is that as Congress—especially the House—has drawn closer to the multipolar world of parliaments, it failed to develop the customary tools and institutional knowledge necessary to make coalition government practicable, as Paul Ryan intimated in 2017.[46] Coalition government in other countries involves dynamic power-sharing, semiautomatic dissolution in the event of major legislative failure, and the legal option to neuter obstructionists.[47]

One technique that *was* available to House leaders was to manipulate the rule book one step at a time. Each tactic used to thwart leadership was met with a rule modification, so that reforms designed to streamline legislation made procedures even more baroque, prone to manipulation and the appearance of illegitimacy. New complexities diverted politicians' already limited time to procedure, not policy; mastering the laws of the House is not the same as mastering the laws of the nation. But that's how it went, and leadership—which controls the rules, because the Speaker de facto controls the Rules Committee—kept tinkering.

The rules now exceed ready understanding, creating problems for the whole legal system. The rules were once reasonably comprehensible to legislators, judges, reporters, and voters—in part because the rules were mostly static (indeed, wholly unamended in the first twenty-odd Congresses). The House did not appoint a dedicated rules specialist until 1927, when it designated an official parliamentarian. Even with this help, representatives couldn't manage their own procedures, codified in a rule book that eventually spread across 1,000 pages, further adjusted by endless precedential material.[48] A parallel story unfolded in the Senate. Today, rules are so involved that even seasoned politicians live at the mercy of technocratic parliamentarians, another unelected power center inside Congress. Parliamentarians hold passive powers—they are judges, not legislators—though their (advisory) decisions can have immense consequences. In July 2017, the Senate Parliamentarian effectively derailed one of the Republicans' various attempts to repeal the ACA.[49] That parliamentary opinions occasionally surprise legislators, even when bills are high-stakes, suggests one way in which Congress mystifies even itself.

As the rules became unwieldy, leadership pursued the extreme. The Senate famously defanged certain filibusters, a step christened the "nuclear option," but the fallout was limited to executive nominations. The House, seriously congested, went thermonuclear, essentially vaporizing its rule book as necessary. If the standard rules, whatever their other benefits, risked derailing legislation, those rules would be suspended. Suspensions were not unprecedented, though they had been primarily used to speed along uncontroversial or minor legislation where debate and amendment were unnecessary. Today, leadership relies on special rules to ram through almost everything of note: deliberation reduced to take-it-or-leave-it. Between 1987 and 2014, most major measures—important, complicated, and contentious legislation—were midwifed using special rules, for the simple reason that passage under "regular" order would not have been possible.[50] Whether these laws could have been better made if gestated in committee, subject to customary debate and bargain, was no longer germane. Leadership believed that getting anything done, however badly, was better than getting nothing done at all.

Does it matter that Congress operates in a permanent state of emergency? Legislators say that they're troubled by the death of regular order, and every Speaker since Gingrich has promised its return. But reversions to regular order never worked out and were always abandoned. The explanation is straightforward: the point of regular order is to protect the legislative power of minorities (including minorities within a ruling party, like the Tea Party). With population disparities and polarization granting minorities more power than the Framers anticipated, this is precisely what Speakers with slim margins cannot afford. Therefore, leadership staged a quasi-coup, and only a few players control nearly every significant piece of legislation that comes through the chambers, as well as the all-important party purse strings, which open and close for election funding depending on a candidate's docility. It's hard to know if the public understands or approves of these developments, though the perpetual appeal of the newcomer candidate vowing to "clean up Washington" suggests that voters prefer (or believe in the existence of) a system of distributed Congressional power. But all pledges of one-man revolution do, aside from win votes, is reveal that a candidate is ignorant of Congressional mechanics or a fully credentialed cynic about the electorate.[51] In the House 2.0, only *leadership* can effect major policy change, and only with plenty of Senate friends, more than most Speakers have.

The Senate has long allowed minorities, even minorities of one, to achieve the sort of counter-majoritarian delay that the House's special rules prevent. The most famous tactic is the filibuster, a tool of delay masquerading as debate. (Appropriately, "filibuster" comes from *vrijbuiter*, the Dutch word for pirate.) Although some bills cannot be filibustered, most can.* It requires a 3/5ths vote to end a filibuster, a threshold sufficiently hard to overcome that the Senate is now synonymous with obstructionism. Obstructionist rules have long existed in the Senate; what's changed is the willingness to use them. Filibusters, comparatively rare before the 1970s, became routine by the 1990s, and are now a permanent variable in the political calculus.[52] Even the threat of filibuster can crash the Senate or result in eye-watering legislative bribery. The effects leak beyond the Senate, because both chambers must pass the same bill for it to become law. Indeed, House reforms inadvertently made filibusters more potent; with the Senate now the key chokepoint, counting votes in the *Senate* has become an important job for the Speaker of the *House*. The results can be Constitutionally confounding. Revenue bills must formally originate in the House, but the House may have no choice but to pass whatever the Senate can agree on.[53]

It's easy to deride the Senate as a sort of legislative gas chamber, responsible for Washington's gridlock. (The 45th president disdained all of Congress as hopeless, but reserved special ire for the Senate.) The Senate is irritatingly slow—though in the Senate's partial defense, the Framers all but *designed* the Senate to frustrate most voters, at least in the moment. The Senate originally served to balance a House made volatile by the latter's need to cater to the masses.[54] But as we've seen, the antidemocratic imbalance now verges on the intractable.

Congressional Competence

Even if Congress were suddenly reformed—by rebalancing representation, returning power to competent committee chairs, and adopting an efficient and comprehensible set of rules (a fantasy in itself)—there would still be a

---

* Budget reconciliation bills can't be filibustered, for example. However, low-grade "filibusters" can block expedited consideration of budget bills; again, this is how Rand Paul briefly shut down the government in 2018.

major problem: the membership. The *Federalist Papers* (by James Madison, Alexander Hamilton, and John Jay, but here, most likely Madison) fretted about this from the beginning.[55] Madison particularly worried that short election cycles could make the House prisoner to populism, prone to high turnover, unstable policies, and a culture of inexperience—a responsive institution, perhaps, but not the wisest.[56] This could be partially relieved by biennial (rather than annual) elections, but the weightiest counter would be the Senate, a body more insulated from electoral pressures and composed of intellectual patriots who would "study...the comprehensive interests of their country," cultivate expertise, and develop prudent, sagacious laws.[57] One supposes that Madison was an optimist.

Assumptions and reality parted company some time ago. In its first century, House membership was indeed volatile. While incumbents had advantages, around one-third chose not to run again, and of those who did, 10 to 25+ percent lost; approaching half of representatives could be freshmen in a given season.[58] After the 1880s, incumbents had an easier time, and since the 1970s, voters have returned 90 to 95 percent of incumbents seeking reelection.[59] Today, the average tenure of representatives is just short of a decade, and almost 20 percent of representatives have served more than sixteen years.[60] Partisan gerrymandering helps cement representatives in place, though the trend toward long tenure predates many redistricting excesses. Meanwhile, the composition of the Senate is as stable as Madison could have hoped, but senators' ideologies are more changeable: the advent of direct elections a century ago and the hotly contested intraparty primaries from the 1980s foster the sort of intellectual lability that Madison feared of, and was actually realized in, the House.

From Madison's perspective, this would be the worst of worlds, of intellectual volatility mixed with professional incumbency. The potentially saving grace is that incumbency might allow legislators to master policy and write laws with greater technical facility. Has incumbency delivered those benefits? Doubtful. A decade of service today means something different than it once did. Even if incumbents can be reasonably sure of reelection, politicking takes enormous effort, greatly reducing time for the real work of government. Campaigning is now so intense and expensive that ex-Representative Tim Roemer suggested it consumes between 30 and 50 percent of a member's calendar, and other Congressional insiders concur.[61]

The modest data we have on how representatives spend their time confirms Roemer's estimate. One of the more on-point surveys suggests that representatives break their time into thirds, with campaign work running through most of it. The first third is spent on "constituent service," a marriage of help-desk work and low-wattage campaigning that consists of answering letters and helping wrangle government benefits for voters.* Another third vanishes into humdrum administration and the grinder of media events, the latter a form of de facto campaigning. That leaves just one-third for core policy-making work, at best.[62] This fraction, already modest, can be reduced further by random events, anything from illness (a serious matter for the many elderly members of Congress), to tragedies like the 2017–2018 assaults on Congressional members, but not, you will be gratified to learn, by jury service (an inconvenience from which Congress exempts itself).[63]

The many demands on representatives' time make for a long apprenticeship. Buffeted by distractions, it can take representatives many terms to fully understand the legislative process, which is why senior legislators encourage newbies to stay quiet for a few years. Given leadership's power, many new legislators follow this advice, unless they arrive in a wave that changes leadership itself, as happened with the Gingrich revolution in 1994. And once representatives understand policy and process, they may only have a few years to use that knowledge, given the Republicans' introduction of term limits for their committee chairs. (Chairs who have termed out and face

---

* Many voters believe that their Congressmen can order federal agencies to fix some constituent-specific problem. That's not precisely true, for legal, ethical, and practical reasons, though for routine problems like an administrative error by Medicare, communications from a Congressional office may prompt agencies to review the problem and produce a solution that satisfies a voter.

return to back-bench obscurity often decline to seek reelection, reducing the institutional capacities of Congress.)

Legislating is a difficult and novel job, and nothing about elections or Congressional mechanics ensures competence. Most professions, from medicine to hairdressing, impose minimum educational and vocational requirements; some also screen for ethical and financial probity. The legislative career, however, has *no* substantive filters: the Constitution requires citizenship, periods of residency, and minimum ages (25 for representatives, 30 for senators), but that's about it.[64] Stupidity, bankruptcy, or criminality may (or may not: Google "James Traficant"; it's worth it) be political nonstarters, but they aren't legal barriers. Therefore, the only certain thing about a new legislator is that he or she was more appealing than the alternative (and not even that in the case of ties, which some states decide by coin flip).[65] A taxidermist today, a Congressman tomorrow—the Constitution shrugs. To compensate, one might expect Congress to provide new members with exhaustive courses on the legislative process. But Congress makes few gestures at training. New representatives take a seminar that lasts about a week and focuses on administrative topics like website maintenance, Congressional expense policies, and (cursory) ethics, with virtually nothing on the substance of legislating.[66]

The absence of training degrades the technical quality of law. There's no perfect vocational analogue to Congress; like all specialties, legislating requires training. The ability to draft a law rarely features in campaign ads, of course, with candidates preferring to tout the special advantages their experiences will grant them in Congress. Such claims should be greeted skeptically. Consider military service, a popular legislative credential. A former SEAL might be more ambitious, patriotic, and have better knowledge of Navy special operations than the longest-tenured civvie on the House Armed Services Committee, but that committee deals with everything from base leases to missile contracting, at levels of great abstraction. A given term's work may not touch on SEAL operations; it may not, for Constitutional reasons, even be able to resolve a problem the SEAL-turned-legislator knows to be urgent. In any event, leadership controls the agenda, so the SEAL's committee toil may be fruitless. Indeed, it may not even produce a substantive education. Representatives serve on an average of 5.3 committees/subcommittees, while senators serve on 13.8, but if a committee conducts a two-hour meeting weekly, a legislator's hourly policy budget can be exhausted simply by showing up.[67] Should a backbencher eventually join the leadership, he will do so without having gained much policy experience.

Even if legislators somehow master a subject in their long (and frankly pointless) apprenticeship, they must still translate that knowledge into written law. For decades, the natural qualification was legal practice. Lawyers share a culture and vernacular, making it easier for lawyer-legislators to communicate with the overwhelmingly legal community that interprets law: judges, bureaucrats, tax lawyers—the lot. Lawyers also know the frailties of the English language, because to practice law is to appreciate all the ways words can fail, through manipulation or misconstruction, or by unintended interaction with other chunks of legalese. Having a Congress without a lot of lawyers would be as odd as having an embassy in Thailand without any Thai-speakers. This is one reason why lawyers traditionally made up more than half of Congress, ranging from 48 percent in 1809–1811 to 79.5 percent in 1849–1850.[68] Despite lawyers' natural advantages, there's been a precipitous decline in lawyer-legislators since the 1910s, especially among Republicans (who substituted businesspeople for lawyers). Today, lawyers comprise just 36.5 percent of Congress, and while law is still the most represented profession, it's at levels well below the historical average.

The effect on *policy* is subtle. Adjusting for party, lawyers and non-lawyers do not vote in significantly different ways, save on matters that affect the legal system directly. For example, GOP lawyer-legislators favored public legal aid more vigorously than party peers, and lawyer-legislators generally seem more supportive of judicial independence and the rule of law.[69] The last two values are incontrovertibly important, though they are not the only loss. With just a third of Congress trained in law, the natural inference is that (however bad legal education may be) Congress has less institutional capacity to read or understand the bills it circulates. Non-lawyers may find concatenations of "provided, howevers" and "notwithstanding the foregoings" hard to parse, and fail to appreciate how sloppy commas and misplaced modifiers can lead to enhanced sentencing or costly litigation.[70] Vampire Weekend asked (or sang), "who gives a fuck about an Oxford comma?" Maine's dairy industry certainly does: in 2018, a $10 million dairy case hinged on the absence of an Oxford comma in a Maine statute.[71]

All of these structural incapacities make it hard for Congress to draft laws well, in accord with public expectations and jurisprudential criteria. Even legal specialists have a hard time understanding the results, and some judges (and academics) have either given up or retreated into fantasy. Justice Scalia sponsored a grand myth that the legislature, most of which is untutored in law and anyway overwhelmed, not only "authors" national laws, but does so diligently and in full agreement with Scalia's own Latinate treatises on drafts-manship.* The work of law professors Abbe Gluck and Lisa Bressman started to put paid to that notion.[72] But *every* thinking judge should have accounted for what Gluck and Bressman have started to prove, and to the extent Scalia & Co. did not, they were either silly or disingenuous. Equally, commentators at the other end of the political spectrum nourish the fiction that the nation's artless laws, produced in a haze of compromise and procedural manipula-tion, can be rendered legible by casting the oracle bones of legislative history to divine "Congressional intent." Well, what "intent" can 218 representatives and 51 (or 60) senators be said to have, when they barely glance at laws that are, anyway, written in a language legislators do not speak? As Gluck and others have shown, much of the "statutory interpretation" done by judges is, and can only be, aspirational fiction. Then again, judges feel they must do *something* to untoss the word salad served up by Congress.

Clearly, Congress would be better served if more of its members had

---

* David Foster Wallace inadvertently undermined Scalia's project in his glowing review of Bryan Garner's *A Dictionary of Modern American Usage*. That review that surveyed the huge, passionate disagreements affecting the dictionary-land that Scalia sometimes implied was as an Arcadia untroubled by schism, but which is absolutely not (in part due to the work of Sca-lia's future collaborator, Garner).

proper training in the business of legislation. (This doesn't have to be at the exclusion of other experience; people can have more than one job and postgraduate degree, and it's not much to expect our leaders to be—to put it indelicately—smart.) Reversing the lawyer-legislator decline, or at least providing compensatory training, would help. But given the other dysfunctions afflicting Congress, perhaps this is beside the point, as legislators probably don't read or write bills in the first place: staff do.

The Hidden Congress

Perhaps no group wields as much influence over public life, with as little recognition (or scrutiny) as Congressional staff. Elected officials keep staffers away from the public gaze, lest citizens realize how little legislators "legislate," though everyone in the broader Congressional universe appreciates the staff's importance. Lobbyists, for example, treasure staff directories and compile detailed profiles of senior staffers, reinforcing anecdotally what we know mathematically: in important ways, staffers *are* Congress.

The staff-driven Congress is a modern innovation. In its first century, Congress had almost no staff; legislators did most things for themselves. Legislators who wanted assistance had to pay out of pocket. Few cared to do so, and other than some personal aides (often spouses, a practice now banned), the Capitol's only helpers were some institution-wide professionals such as the Librarian of Congress, plus the odd committee helper. After 1885, Congress provided a modest staff allowance and assistants trickled in, though it was only after the New Deal and World War II that staff really expanded, in parallel with government itself.[73]

Most staffers are personal, serving individual members. A representative may hire up to eighteen full-time staffers, while senators can theoretically retain as many as they like within their budgets, though the average senatorial allowance of $3.5 million effectively limits staff to around fifty people.[74] From the perspective of substance, eighteen staffers for a representative is not much, since almost half of the staff toil on public relations, constituent service, and administration, leaving at most ten staffers to cover the thousands of bills a member is expected to read and vote on.[75] (Even fifty is not much for a senator.) The pressures are only partially alleviated by the modest institutional staff who serve specific committees, leadership, or the entire Congress.

Staffers are central to the legislative process, as it is they who review law, research the issues, and gather input from various interested parties, presenting findings to their bosses, who then gesture in general policy directions for draft bills.* Staff members write those, too—a combination of personal staff, committee staff (or staffs; sometimes more than one committee is involved), and the Offices of Legislative Counsel (OLC). Congressmen do debate concepts among themselves, though staffers often negotiate the all-important details with other staffers. Staff also prepare the whole Kabuki around a bill's presentation, and many of the words spoken by Congressmen—speeches, questions at hearings, public announcements, and so on—tend to be staff-written. Staffers can have as much power over legislation as a member wants, short of voting on the bill itself. Functionally, many elected officials are the equivalent of Hollywood's producers, the people who rarely write, edit, direct, or act in this year's Best Picture but who will nevertheless be granted the relevant Oscar (or Razzie).

There is nothing inherently wrong with this system so long as constituents understand it and legislators are candid about the dynamics. Unfortunately, much of the legal system depends on the fiction that Congressmen know what they're doing when they vote and speak. They may not: it's not uncommon to see a Congressman on C-SPAN reading his statement for what is obviously the first time, chuckling at staffers' canned jokes or stumbling over unfamiliar concepts. Nevertheless, the pantomime is deposited into the record, where bureaucrats and judges (the latter assisted by their own staff of clerks) digest the result as "legislative intent."

---

*   There are exceptions: e.g., Barney Frank, Elizabeth Warren, and Orrin Hatch could legislate solo in their areas.

Though dependency on staff is extreme, the prime worry is not that there are too many staffers; rather, the concerns are that staff are too few and too badly managed. Some 20,000 staffers may seem like a lot, but it isn't, not for an institution legislating for 325 million people and spending $4 trillion of their money. This is especially so given that perhaps 6,000 staffers really participate in lawmaking, and only about a tenth of those are experienced, dedicated legal drafters.[76] One would expect more staffers, yet Congress keeps cutting, so even as the national population increased by a third between 1987 and 2017 and the economy roughly doubled in size, staffer population *declined* by 30 percent.[77] Cuts to substantive staff were perversely heavy, with notable declines in committee staff (in keeping with the effort to neuter committees generally) and to the Congressional Research Service, which provides essential policy studies for both members and the public. Only the Capitol Police, charged with keeping members secure, expanded.[78] Cutting staff makes no sense, not least because staff represent the only part of Congress that can easily grow with the nation.

Quantity is not the only staff problem. The abysmal pay Congress awards its helpers makes retention exceptionally difficult. Staff assistants, the most common subspecies, earn as little as $30,000 to $33,000 per year, significantly below market wages.[79] (As one reporter tartly noted, Congressional aides can make less than the Senate's janitors.) Senior staffers make $100,000, and the most experienced staffers (mostly employed by leadership) collect $172,500, the maximum salary allowed.[80] Even at the high end, staff salaries don't go that far in Washington, D.C., and crucially, staff earn far less than they could as lobbyists, lawyers, or other private-industry actors. The consequence of low pay is that staffers tend to be younger and prone to turnover, so that while Congress's *elected* members have become perpetual incumbents, many of its core *workers* lack experience and continuity.[81] Congress could alleviate some of these problems by raising staff pay, not to market rates (various legal restrictions make that impracticable), but enough so that more important staff work becomes viable as a career instead of a pit stop.[82]

Lobbyists

The Congressional culture of self-diminishment does not apply to lobbyists. Unlike Congress, lobbyists have no desire to reduce their influence and no restrictions on paying for the best. Lobbying was a sleepy affair until the 1990s, a small industry focused on trade groups, unions, and a few companies deeply affected by government action (telecoms, defense contractors, and the like). Lobbying has since expanded dramatically, and there are now lobbyists for everything, even lobbyists for lobbyists (the Association of Government Relations Professionals f/k/a the American League of Lobbyists). Today, lobbying is an industrial counterweight to Congress, with 11,545 registered lobbyists reporting $3.37 billion in expenditures in 2017; the actual totals being slightly higher because sunshine laws exempt smaller lobbying efforts from disclosure.[83] Lobbying overwhelmingly promotes corporate priorities, with business outspending unions and public interest groups by more than 30:1.[84]

Corporate America defensively asserts that $3 billion is insignificant relative to the size of industry itself, which is narrowly true. Even bigger spenders like Alphabet (aka Google) devote a minuscule fraction of their resources to lobbying; the search company spent $15.4 million on lobbyists in 2016 (making it the eleventh biggest spender) against revenue of $90.3 billion.[85] The better metric, however, is lobbyist spending relative to *Congress*. Total lobbying spend is at least 79 percent of Congress's operations budget and there are also almost certainly more lobbyists than staffers working on substantive issues.[86] Compounding their advantages, lobbyists can focus on specific issues and draw on their clients' research resources, which collectively eclipse those of the Congressional Research Service. Lobbyists tend to know much more than the lobbied, and however knowledgeable the staffers at House committees may be, they will never know as much about cans as the Can Manufacturers Institute (CMI).[87] The energetic can lobby busily writes to Congress, even POTUS himself, about all manner of issues—and it turns out that cans are constantly at risk from unintended legislative spillovers. Who knew? The can lobby, which is the point.

Lobbyists provide expertise that an increasingly inexpert legislature needs, but in keeping with the adversarial nature of the American legal system, lobbyists only represent one point of view. Although staffers know this—obviously, the Vinyl Institute wants what's good for vinyl—it can be hard for overworked, generalist staffers to know the boundaries between fact and agenda. When the vinyl folks offer studies demonstrating the risks of switching from traditional, well-tested PVC ingredients to ostensibly greener, but less-studied inputs, does anyone expect staffers to offer intelligent opinions on the risks of hydrogen chloride and the wonders of chlorosulfonated polyethylene? Of course not, no more than anyone can expect staffers to know, without an alert provided by CMI, that a Section 232 "national security" inquiry posed grave risk to *beverage cans*.*[88] Lobbyists provide necessary education in arcane areas, but that education can be lopsided. Except in hotly contested matters, as when telecoms, Google, and consumer advocates first tussled over net neutrality, Congress may never hear all sides of an issue, much less from all interested parties. Congress will, however, hear from itself—or at least, its former self. Ex-legislators and staffers make up only a small fraction of lobbyists, but it's a highly influential fraction, usually at a firm's helm and able to get return calls from the Capitol. All this is perfectly legal, by the way, however much it gives off the appearance of impropriety.

Whether lobbying just looks corrupting or *is* corrupting is hotly disputed. The public seems to think the corruption is real, while legislators deny that lobbyists have much influence at all. The impartial academic research is mixed and will always be inconclusive, because the legislative process is too complex to parse statistically and legislators have no incentive to be overly transparent. Nevertheless, the general weight of the evidence suggests that the classic cases of lobbying corruption—in which lobbyists secure new legislation to their clients' benefit—are fairly rare, confined to those high-stakes

---

*   When drafting, I chose the Can Manufacturers Institute for amusement value; since then, cans have become a live issue with Trump's steel tariffs, which the commerce secretary defended on TV by waving around a steel can and assuring viewers that tariffs would only raise costs by a few cents. But lobbyists had been aware of this issue long before.

issues that command extraordinary spending. This can happen, as when chunks of lobbyists' text are copied wholesale into bills (as happened with a Monsanto-sponsored GMO bill). Where lobbying seems to enjoy greatest success, however, is less in ghostwriting new laws than in achieving beneficial technocratic tweaks and, perhaps most importantly, preventing changes to old laws—a sort of for-profit filibuster.[89]

On the whole, lawful lobbying may not be as utterly corrosive as some believe, though it does cause problems, of which three deserve particular consideration. First, while lobbyists generally cannot effect major changes in the text of a law or its enactment, lobbyists can usually get officials to read statements into the record, allowing private actors to influence the legislative history that courts use to interpret laws. Simply reading a lobbyist's gloss into the Congressional Record hardly seems like gross corruption, costs legislators virtually nothing, and if any political consequences arise, they'll emerge years or decades after the fact when the original parties are safely distant. Second, lobbyist influence on *formal* legislation—acts of Congress—may be limited, but the influence on quasi-law, like regulatory pronouncements, is much greater; indeed, Congress sometimes *requires* bureaucrats to consider lobbyist input when making regulations. We'll take that up in the chapter on bureaucracy. Finally, if citizens (and possibly legal actors such as judges) *believe* lobbyists corrupt the process, then lobbying degrades the legal system by limiting trust and reducing compliance. Lobbying may not be the fatal enemy that many sunshine groups decry and might even, in arcane matters, do some good—but there are always costs.

How a Bill Really Becomes Law

Congress has become a very different body than the one envisioned in Philadelphia in 1787 or described in classrooms today. It's formally true that there are 535 members of Congress, that they constitute the nation's supreme legislature, and that they write bills which, after debate, may be passed by both

House and Senate and, if signed by the president, become federal law. In reality, the executive branch sets many of the most important agendas, and a concentrated Congressional leadership drives bills forward, relying on staff (and sometimes lobbyists) to do analysis and drafting. Quality ranges from low to nonexistent, and mistakes are frequent, but nevertheless, products are rammed through the House in a parliamentary-style dictatorship in flagrant contravention of "regular order" to await their Senate fates. Bills that escape the Senate then return to their true birth parent, the White House, to be signed by the president and distributed to the agencies that implement the law by writing quasi-laws themselves.

All the while, many Congressmen, judges, and some parts of media play Let's Pretend, indulging the filmstrip ideal of *How a Bill Becomes Law*, a world in which Congress is still Congress. But the conventional understanding of Congress no more applies to the workings of Capitol Hill than Newton's mechanics explain a singularity. Congress is less than it was, and catering to old schemas distorts the rest of the legal system that's tasked with interpreting and enforcing Congressional will. It's a tricky problem, compounded by Congress's general incapacity, and one the ever-expanding administrative state has decided to resolve in the only rational way possible: by ignoring Congress.

CHAPTER FIVE

BUREAUCRACY: EMPIRE BY FORM

[H]owever many people complain about the "red tape," it would be sheer illusion to think…that continuous administrative work can be carried out in any field except by means of officials working in offices…. The choice is only that between bureaucracy and dilettantism….

Max Weber[1]

But recognition of the inevitability of comprehensive bureaucratization does not solve the problems that arise out of it.

Joseph Schumpeter[2]

The first platypus arrived in Europe in 1798.[3] It was dead, but its husk still created an uproar: What *was* this strange creature? It looked like a duck sewn to an otter. Some thought it was exactly that: a hoax, cobbled together from parts of real animals. As further carcasses arrived, the possibility of hoax withered and the probability of taxonomic crisis grew; the platypus defied classification. The platypus had mammary glands, and animals with *mammary* glands were quite obviously *mammals*. But it transpired that the platypus laid eggs, something mammals emphatically didn't do (much less through a combined anus/urethra/vagina, an almost deliberate provocation). All this was very upsetting, and what it upset was the taxonomic system European naturalists had neatly and lovingly elaborated. Nevertheless, explorers kept shipping back platypus carcasses, with seemingly malicious zeal. The system tottered, but in science, nature has the final say. Wigs were clutched, sighs heaved, and taxonomies redrawn.

The American legal system has its own platypus to contend with: the federal bureaucracy, a highly inconvenient hybrid. Classical constitutional taxonomy concedes only three kinds of federal animal—the executive, the judicial, and the legislative—assigning to each a special character forbidden to the others. That is not to say that the early republic was devoid of bureaucratic activity (a misapprehension some conservative pundits happily abet), only that what we would now describe as bureaucratic activity was more neatly distributed among the three branches. When poultry farms emitted noxious effluents, the public could ask the town council for an ordinance; if citizens suffered injury, they could ask judges to order compensation and an injunction. If chicken farmers refused to obey judges and legislators, the local mayor could arrest the poultrymen. All this slotted, with reasonable cogency, into the constitutional taxonomy. But the days of Hesiodic simplicity are long over. The chicken of 1800 has mutated into the McNugget, a globular amalgam of poultry parts and sundry chemicals sourced from multiple states and processed in plants belching invisible gases, whose toxicity can only be evaluated by careful study. And as chickens evolved, so did the legal means to regulate their quality.

The modern bureaucratic state that emerged to monitor our McNuggets can be seen as either meddlesome overreach or technocratic triumph, depending on what aspects are emphasized. Consider the many agencies that touch the humble McNugget before it reaches consumers: USDA (when the nugget is still in avian form); FDA (when the poultry transubstantiates into the nugget and is adorned with various additives); CBP (if chicken parts or

105

chemicals have been imported); DOL (the factory workers' safety); IRS (the workers' taxes); DOT (the trucking of nugget to and fro, unless the nugget arrives via Amazon/Postmates drone, in which case, FAA gets involved); FRS, FDIC, and CFPB (if nugget payment is made by bank card); SEC and FTC (if the nugget production involves a large publicly traded company, as it most certainly does), plus many state and local analogues.* Critics point to many acronyms traumatizing the humble nugget and pronounce an evil. But consider the other side: a sack of nuggets costs maybe $15, can be had on demand, and despite the billions of deep-fried chicken bits consumed each year, newspapers hardly burst with stories of nugget-related catastrophe. To which bureaucracy's opponents reply: the free market makes all this happen *despite* the bureaucrats, and the price to ponder is not a measly fifteen bucks, but $4 trillion, the cost of federal government, most of which is bureaucracy.[4] The debate can proceed in this inconclusive fashion for eternity, but at no point does either side dispute the extraordinary *magnitude* of bureaucratic impact. That matter is beyond debate.

As bureaucratic platypuses expand in range and number, critics realize that they cannot succeed by picking off the offending animals piecemeal (though, of course, they'll take potshots when they can). The solution can only be extermination, using some technique that makes *all* platypuses unviable, germ warfare conducted by paperwork. The justifications and weapons for this war reside in the Constitution, which *seems* to say that platypuses— which promiscuously mix powers of government meant to be separated—are illegal abominations. Of course, it's always been true that Constitutional animals have never been wholly pure. Sometimes, one branch will display the traits of another, as when judges quasi-legislate by elaborating the common law. But legal taxonomists mostly overlook these incidental incursions, on

---

* In English, those would be: the U.S. Department of Agriculture; Food and Drug Administration; Customs and Border Protection; Department of Labor; Internal Revenue Service; Department of Transportation; Federal Aviation Administration; Federal Reserve System; Federal Deposit Insurance Corporation; Consumer Financial Protection Bureau; Securities and Exchange Commission; and Federal Trade Commission.

the theory that a flying squirrel isn't a bird simply because the squirrel makes the occasional, brief glide. The problem is that bureaucracies exhibit the behaviors of all three branches of government continuously. Critics loathe this, and the most puritanical among them believe there is but one solution: thou shalt not suffer a platypus to live.

The case against bureaucracies—let's call it the "Constitutional Foul"—has a considerable intellectual pedigree, though it's essentially a fundamentalist argument, partaking of all the qualities of its genre. The Foul's logic is sound, *if* one grants certain problematical premises, chiefly that the Constitution is an infallible gospel that clearly forbids platypuses entry onto the American ark. (As we've seen, it may not be true that the Constitution is gospel at all.) The Foul is also vehement and narrow-minded to the point of obscuring other, more widely shared concerns about bureaucratic governance. Its implications are extraordinary, because shaving off every Constitutionally iffy bit of platypus would leave an unviable corpse—modern government would vanish. And like all fundamentalist arguments, the Foul seems too insane to be realized, because even those who despise the EPA would be reluctant to employ a weapon that would also unwind Social Security, Medicare, and the VA. The electorate is unlikely, in the name of ideological purity, to contentedly watch the Foul's WMD wipe out *all* dispensers of federal goodies. But for Constitutional jihadists, sidestepping a timid electorate is precisely the Foul's appeal. The Foul doesn't require 165 million votes, or 270 electors. The only precondition to victory is to persuade five Justices that the Foul is fair.

For many decades, swinging five Justices seemed impossible. Although the Supreme Court embraced a version of the Foul in the 1930s (in a case involving poultry inspections), the results were calamitous. FDR thundered about court-packing and the Justices rapidly changed course. They not only abandoned the Foul, but over succeeding decades abetted bureaucratic expansion using dubious legal fictions to gloss over bureaucracy's more egregious legal behaviors. Occasionally, the Court would summon enough energy to shave the margins of bureaucratic power, but the efforts were small and halfhearted. The Court never fully disavowed the theoretical foundations of the Foul, though as the decades passed in comparative tranquility, observers ceased to question the legal viability of bureaucratic governance.

Bureaucracies became a fact, like gravity or the platypus. But unlike the laws of nature, the laws of man are not immutable. Naturalists could not undo the real platypus, but judicial surgery can certainly lop off parts of the bureaucratic platypus until it looks like a more constitutionally conventional animal (even if the animal dies in the process). And not only can judges do this, but so can presidents, and Congress. Indeed, this movement is already underway. We can no longer take for granted that bureaucracies are a fixed part of the legal ecology, so it is time to reconsider how well bureaucracies serve goals of legality, democratic government, and public welfare.

Finding the Platypus a Home

The first challenge in tackling bureaucracy is to figure out where "bureaucracies" sit in the Constitutional taxonomy, to figure out what parts might be trimmed (if bureaucracies reside in the judiciary, they can't legislate; if they're legislative, they can't judge; and so on—*mutatis mutandis*, as lawyers say). Unfortunately, the Constitution doesn't refer to "bureaucracy," the U.S. Code doesn't define the term, and *Black's Law Dictionary* can't be bothered to conjure a meaningful entry. And "bureaucracy" itself is somewhat blinding, because if bureaucracy is just the parts of government that people hate, then there's no point in discussion; why defend something universally despised?

Partly for this reason, the term "bureaucracy" has been abandoned in academic literature, in favor of terms like the "administrative state" or "regulatory state." Unfortunately, these terms are legally meaningless. They also bring the important Constitutional debate to a halt because if bureaucracies *only* "administer" or "regulate," there's no Constitutional problem—if they administer, dump them in the executive and close the case; if they regulate, make them a legislative responsibility and hope for the best. These terms, while helpfully avoiding the pejorative connotations of "bureaucracy," are a little too neat; they are logical dead ends, because they presuppose one conclusion while foreclosing another.

Fortunately, we don't have to go far in the lexical search to find promising leads—no further than bureaucracies themselves, which now prefer to call themselves "agencies." This actually gets us somewhere, because "agency" has meaning. In law, agents are persons authorized by a principal to fulfill certain functions. All legal agents have principals; there is no "free agency" in law. Agencies, staffed by evocatively named civil servants, serve *someone*. But whom? Congress? Presidents? We the People? Some glowing abstraction? Does the EPA report to Gaia?

Because there are so many different federal agencies, operating under various authorizations, all generalizations are tricky, including a universal answer about who serves whom. Nevertheless, we can venture a response, because while the government lacks a universal definition of agency, it has a default definition. Federal law deems agencies to be divisions of the federal government that aren't Congress, courts, or the governments of federal possessions, plus a few oddball exceptions not relevant here.[5] Logicians can torture various outcomes from this, but the most straightforward read of the Administrative Procedure Act (APA) is that if agencies are anything, they are part of the executive. In a three-branch government, there's nowhere else for them to go.*

Dumping agencies into the executive solves one problem, but creates

---

*   The APA and bureaucracies warp normal English words into nonsense. For example, the APA defines an agency "rule" so broadly that the term includes virtually every regulatory issuance: statements of general policy, legal interpretations, procedural descriptions, etc. The APA's definitions are alien and confusing, so this chapter uses words in their common senses whenever it makes sense to do so. Here, a "rule" is something that tells citizens what to do ("don't pollute"); a "hearing" is a procedure with judicial features ("after arguments and taking evidence, the EPA finds that Acme Corp. polluted"); and an "enforcement action" is exactly that ("the EPA hereby fines Acme for dumping plutonium in the river").

others. First, not all agencies truly report to the executive. Many "independent agencies" exist, and what they are "independent" of is presidential interference. For example, the one thing the Federal Election Commission manifestly should *not* do is report to a president (or any other partisan), though this would seem to create some third-and-a-half branch of government.*[6] Second, not all agencies are authorities "of Government," save in some formalistic way. Many agencies depend on private firms to carry out their missions; functionally, they are *semi*-governmental, and have both public and private constituencies. Finally, for those agencies that really are part of the executive, the Constitution suggests they may only execute and enforce laws—anything more would perpetrate the Foul. Critics agree that most agencies are part of the executive, but argue that bureaucracies commit the Foul by going beyond mere enforcement of law.

To get a sense for the merits of the Foul, it's helpful to describe agencies' origins and work. In general, agencies are chartered by a Constitutionally established part of government, charged with certain goals, and then sent off to report to one of the classic three branches (typically, the executive). For example, Richard Nixon created the EPA by executive fiat, and Congress subsequently ratified the new bureaucracy, commanding it to protect the environment. Congressional instructions, however, are usually vague— and this is where problems really mount. In the EPA's case, the agency itself notes that "[a] number of laws serve as EPA's foundation for protecting the environment and public health," *but* that "most laws do not have enough detail to be put into practice right away."[7] Indeed, the laws may never have "enough detail"—some of the EPA's core enabling legislation is more than

---

[*] Some statutes expressly place agencies beyond direct presidential reach, but no statute can place an agency beyond the limits of the tripartite Constitutional scheme. Agencies are part of *some* single branch, in other words, but as they carry out functions of *all* branches, to whatever part of the trinity bureaucracies formally belong, the same Constitutional problems obtain. Most of the contemporary discussion about "independence" focuses on the president's (in)ability to remove heads of independent agencies. This is a confusing issue (even Obama got it wrong when he described the IRS as independent, which it is not). But for our purposes, independence is not a major issue going forward.

forty years old and still hasn't been amended to provide a clear scheme for protecting the environment. The EPA therefore supplies the operative details itself, via rules, interpretive releases, and so on, a gap-filling process called "rulemaking."[8] The results are often so substantive that they effectively *are* the relevant legislation, committing a Foul. Once the EPA has set its rules, it enforces them with fines, sanctions, and other correctives—an executive function that raises few Constitutional questions. Frequently, these enforcements create disputes, which the EPA litigates, either in regular courts (no problem) or, more importantly, in its *own* courts, using its own judges and procedures (definitely a problem).[9] Many agencies follow this basic model. What agencies are, then, are miniature governments, arranged by topic instead of by specific Constitutional provision and geography (as judges and legislators are).

The Wide State

Using the APA's anything-but definition as a rough guide, agencies constitute most of the federal government: 97 percent of its civilian employees presiding over ~99 percent of its budget.[10] Unfortunately, we cannot say precisely what all these agencies do, and this is a frequent critique by agencies' foes. Can we really be satisfied with a legal system when we have no idea what a large chunk of that system is up to?

Exasperatingly, the government itself lacks a firm grasp on what its various constituent parts do. For a start, government doesn't even know how many agencies *exist*. The General Services Agency (GSA), one of the several agencies for agencies, runs a website that refers to "the 60 agencies...Governmentwide" (note the definite article), but then links to at least 66 agencies.[11] Other government sources count anywhere between 137 and 445 agencies.[12] Unsurprisingly, the Government Accountability Office (GAO, another meta-agency) has struggled to describe what these agencies do (there being "no comprehensive list of federal programs"), how much they spend (given a lack of comprehensive funding data); and whether the forgoing is lawful (as some interagency programs "award out-of-scope work…and [do] not comply with laws and regulations").[13] The Administrative Conference (meta-agency number three, if you're counting), which is responsible for "efficiency, adequacy, and fairness" of federal agency processes, tried to quantify agency-land in its *Sourcebook of United States Executive Agencies*.[14] The effort was a little late. Agencies have been around in recognizable form since at least the nineteenth century, and the Conference since 1964. The *Sourcebook* arrived in 2012.*[15] Even then, the *Sourcebook* was incomplete, as the Conference freely admits. The prospect of all these agencies, running around in uncountable numbers doing unknowable things, excites Constitutional purists. Somewhere in this confusion, they are certain, agencies are committing legal and factual sins, some of which will be so loathsome in their particulars that even moderate Justices might be tempted to finally call Foul.

Is Foul Fair?

In isolation, the Foul manages to be both unmoving (to the vast majority of the population) and extremely serious (to specialist lawyers who understand the implications). The Foul is unmoving in the sense that most citizens, even die-hard conservatives, don't obsess over Constitutional abstractions so long as they receive sufficiently compensating benefits, like Social Security or health care. To clarify by extremes, if NIH credibly announced it was about to cure all cancers, how many people would be eager to probe NIH's Constitutional foundations? Five, tops. But five is all it takes at the Supreme Court, and this is what makes the Foul important in radical disproportion to its pragmatic appeal.

---

* The Conference does excellent work, but is badly understaffed—no staff, in fact, from 1995 to 2010, as a result of Gingrich's decision to axe the Conference, saving .0001% of the budget. If the thrift was near-undetectable, the intent was not.

Savvier critics like Columbia Law's Philip Hamburger appreciate the dynamics, and declare the Foul "central" to their anti-agency campaigns, because the Foul "confronts administrative power on its own [legal] terms."[16] Hamburger understands that a successful challenge *must* be legal, because the customary economic critique—that bureaucratic regulation is inefficient and unwieldy—has too many flaws. As a logical matter, the economic critique fails because it "usually accepts the legitimacy of administrative power."[17] As a practical matter, the economic challenge is hard to prove, and can only be done one agency action at a time—an undertaking that would require billions, if not trillions, of hours of work. And as a political matter, the economic critique has never really swayed any large chunk of Congress or the electorate. As Hamburger realizes, the legal challenge is much simpler and deadlier. To succeed, Hamburger and his allies only need one good case to lure five Justices into holding that bureaucracy violates the Constitution, a document the Justices can parse more easily than econometric data. It helps that most of the Justices have limited practical understanding of how bureaucracies work, freeing their minds of countervailing clutter.*

Hamburger's claim is sweeping: that "*all*" administrative power "is unconstitutional."[18] The argument is that the Constitution vests exclusive legislative power in Congress, meaning that whenever agencies promulgate rules that impose legal obligations—which they do, all the time—they violate Article I.[19] The unavoidable implication, given bureaucratic pervasiveness, is that America is basically lawless. (This is a hard line even for this book, but on his self-designated turf, Hamburger is not unpersuasive.) Bureaucracies obviously disagree with Hamburger, countering that they exercise powers delegated by Congress, merely giving precise form to legislative mandates. Under existing judicial doctrine, if a mandate has an "intelligible principle," courts turn a blind eye to the delegation. If Congress orders a steak and agencies

---

* The notable present exception is Clarence Thomas, who worked in agency-land for almost a decade. His experience seems to have been so bad that he, the only Justice with substantial relevant experience, is ready to kill off the entire bureaucratic enterprise.

serve up a porterhouse or ribeye, courts won't intervene. Hamburger thinks that's too indulgent. Perhaps, but if the Court abandons the intelligibility doctrine, the entire bureaucracy vanishes, and with it, the rules and laws that enable modern life to be *modern*. Until the Court is more thoroughly recomposed, this sort of total victory seems unlikely.

By contrast, a more modest, though still substantial, victory is eminently achievable even with the current Justices. All that's required is to persuade the Court to strike down agency actions whenever Congressional designs are either unstated or ambiguous. Agencies should not, the argument goes, be allowed to serve steak if Congress merely ventures that it's hungry, much less if agencies only intuit that Congress might be peckish. In such cases, unelected officials make law untethered to any Congressional design, contravening democratic principles. That's a reasonable academic argument, but again, it's not clear how much people care so long as *someone* is making laws (and steaks) and making them well.

Making laws is one thing, but punishing people is another, and this is where the Foul gains visceral appeal. A nation that has courts for simple traffic violations will not smile if it learns that legal judgments are being meted out without full judicial ceremony. But this is precisely how bureaucracies operate, imposing fines, mandating behavioral changes, and reducing or revoking social benefits, minus the customary process of normal courts: the independent judge, jury, and corpus of standard procedural and evidentiary protections.[20] The matters range from small (one person and a few thousand dollars) to giant (affecting entire industries and involving hundreds of billions of dollars), though from the perspective of those fighting in administrative courts, all actions are serious.

Some of the most routine administrative hearings involve small-dollar Social Security claims. When a person applies for Social Security disability benefits, the Social Security Administration makes an initial decision, after which matters can be contested and appealed; in 2015, roughly 2.3 million matters started up this quasi-judicial ladder.[21] Administrative hearings are presided over by administrative law judges (ALJs). Unlike normal judges, who must be free of (directly) conflicting interests, ALJs *always* have conflicts, because they are employed by the litigating agency—Social Security, in this example. This is bad enough, and worse, Social Security's ALJs are severely overworked and in some cases, they appear to be either incompetent or cynically indifferent.[22] Despite these flaws, this is how almost all appeals from initial disability determinations are decided; an ALJ's decision effectively ends the appeals process, unless a claimant makes the uneconomic decision to continue his crusade in federal court after exhausting administrative remedies.[23] Yet, even though agency adjudication sometimes verges on farce, as when Social Security denied benefits to a disabled adult partly on the basis of evidence proffered by physicians (one of whom was a *pediatrician*), some of whom had apparently not examined the claimant, there's been little public backlash.[24] Nor is there likely to be. Social Security cases are decided one by one. There are no small-town victims keeling over by the cartload to inspire another *Erin Brockovich*, nor are there gruesome moments captured on body cams to provoke media outrage. Bureaucratic hearings grind their victims up quietly, one at a time.

As quasi-judicial hearings take on increasingly criminal flavor, the contrast between normal and bureaucratic courts becomes disturbingly stark, and the alignment of incentives perverse. The SEC, for example, is also equipped with its own courts, wherein the agency can pursue securities charges. The SEC frames these cases as "civil" matters, and while that's technically true, it doesn't reflect the real texture. Everyone understands that an SEC insider trading charge is a fundamentally criminal allegation, a reality the SEC's penalties confirm. A $5 million penalty, censure, ban from the industry, and public opprobrium are no mere parking tickets. They are functionally criminal sanctions, and criminal sanctions demand real courts and real due process. But the SEC offers only Due Process Lite, an abbreviated ceremony whose pretrial procedures are shorter and less protective of defendants than those of normal criminal actions, and with the outcome decided by an SEC officer, rather than an independent judge. This works rather better for the SEC than it does for defendants, given that the SEC's success ratio for in-house proceedings is 90 percent versus 69 percent in normal courts.[25]

Some argue that because agency hearings like those run by the SEC and Social Security Administration involve mere money (doggedly ignoring what happens in immigration courts), there's less need for a full-dress court proceeding. That's really an "unsympathetic defendant" argument in disguise—the argument that some people deserve less due process because they're loathsome bankers, or mooching disability claimants, or whatever. The law should not countenance those kinds of arguments, not when any matter of consequence is involved. The Due Process Lite argument also ignores the policy failures to which agency adjudications are prey. A key goal of prosecution is to punish the wrongdoer alone, and for this, there's nothing more targeted than a prison sentence. But only real courts can order prison time, so while prison may be the socially preferable sentence, it may not be the one agencies seek.* Because agencies have a harder time securing wins in proper courts, they often prefer to litigate in-house, even if that means the culpable parties evade responsibility. In the SEC's case, this creates an incentive to pursue financial penalties, which can be awarded in-house. The problem here is that penalties are mostly borne by companies and their insurers, not wayward executives. Worse, company money belongs to shareholders—the very people the SEC is supposed to protect.† The virtues of agency adjudication, speed and ease of resolution, can easily become vices.

Agencies can also affect core rights, like free speech. In the case of broadcast licenses, which come with restrictions on what can be transmitted to the public, the implications for speech are obvious. In the cases

---

* Obviously, if agencies can't order prison time, they can't order the death penalty—not for human persons, anyway. But agencies can put *corporate* persons to death, by antitrust and other regulatory mechanisms, which may not seem like a big deal until you consider the thousands of employees and shareholders who might bear the price of a wrongful sentence.

† Given the length of legal proceedings, many shareholders will have bought their shares *after* the misconduct. Therefore, they not only paid a higher price for their stock, they also pay again in the form of a settlement to prior shareholders.

of agency guidance—advisory opinions and no-action letters—effects are subtler. For example, candidates and broadcasters often consult with the FEC and FCC on how they may interact with, and what they may say to, voters and viewers. The effects are generally minor, but in most circumstances, the law has no patience for anything remotely resembling a pre-clearance requirement on speech, whether for Citizens United or the *New York Times*.

The most extreme concerns over agencies' quasi-judicial powers involve residency and physical liberty. Immigration courts, for example, operate within the DOJ. These are political, not impartial, proceedings. The DOJ brings these cases and appoints the judges; the DOJ is in turn controlled by the attorney general, who reports to the president. This is about as blurred as powers can be, and these cases can be naked exercises in policy. The fate of Attorney General Jeff Sessions, for example, depended on pleasing his explicitly anti-immigration boss. It is no more an accident that Sessions reopened 350,000 immigration cases that the Obama Administration had closed or declined to pursue them in the first place; nor is it an accident that Sessions rerouted certain cases to himself, so that he could set internal precedent. Thus, for immigrants, the AG is prosecutor, judge, jury, policy-maker, and Supreme Court rolled into one.

Moreover, following 9/11, there have been murky hints that bureaucracies may substitute for conventional courts even when a citizen's freedom is at stake.[26] So far, this has happened only in special military contexts involving "enemy combatants." It seems highly unlikely that federal courts would tolerate such tribunals absent extraordinary circumstances (and perhaps only for preliminary status determinations—citizen, enemy combatant, etc.—though these can hardly be dismissed as unimportant). However, boundaries between war and peace in the age of terror have gotten a little blurry, and due process can evaporate depending on what the ever-flexible definition of "enemy combatant" is on a given day—a decision that is initially made by the White House, and to which courts afford considerable deference as a matter of "war-fighting" discretion.

The civil liberties problems posed by these agency tribunals are substantial (and suggest why partisans of all stripes should be leery of this set of agency powers), but the fixes are helpfully straightforward and would not seriously impair the broader bureaucratic mission. Congress or federal courts can order agencies to abandon quasi-judicial proceedings, requiring agencies to litigate in regular courts. That would require expanding the federal judiciary to assume the work now overseen by the roughly 2,000 ALJs.[27] This is not as impracticable as it seems. The financial barriers are modest; federal judges don't earn that much more than senior ALJs. The logistical barriers are higher, since the Senate would have to rouse itself to confirm new judges, but even that obstacle has a workaround: magistrate judges could handle much of the minor caseload, and magistrates do not require Senate confirmation.[28] Dealing with administrative incursions on free speech presents more serious challenges, but does not require structural changes, so long as litigants are willing to risk the ire of the regulating agency by resorting directly to courts instead of begging agency permission. Arguably, accepting a limited version of the Foul and reforming agency hearings would improve, not undermine, the bureaucratic agenda.

Forms Follow Functionaries

Quasi-judicial hearings are not red meat for bureaucracy's opponents— the core of the Foul revolves around the much bigger and more challenging question of whether agencies should make law. Making law, or more precisely, making rules that have the force of law, is central to the agency enterprise.[29] To strip agencies of the power to make and unmake rules would neuter bureaucracies. There is no way to predict whether this will serve or undermine any policy agenda in the moment. In the Obama era, agencies explored the limits of their powers to promulgate rules protecting the environment; greens celebrated while conservatives fumed. In the Trump era, agencies used those same powers to summarily roll back dozens of rules while promulgating new and laxer regulations on emissions and drilling; opposing camps suddenly found themselves reconsidering their bureaucratic sympathies.[30]

However many rollbacks an anti-regulatory agency might sponsor, bureaucracy's opponents would happily exchange all of them for the single victory of stripping rulemaking authority from agencies. Without agency rulemaking, Congress would have to pick up the regulatory slack, and as we've already seen, Congress can't even manage the work it has now. One senses that this is the point for Constitutional fundamentalists: if agencies don't make the rules, no one will. But this is precisely why we must now part with the most unyielding versions of the Constitutional argument. Modern economies could not exist without bureaucratic regulation; if the choice is between boring, regulated McNuggets and the glorious laissez-faire of poultry discharged from the business end of a food truck's woodchipper, the regulated McNugget wins every time. Nevertheless, accepting that regulation is necessary and expedient does not mean that agency rulemaking cannot be improved, or made to sit a bit more comfortably within Constitutional boundaries and social expectations.

The APA allows agencies to make rules in two ways: via "formal" processes and by "notice-and-comment." Formal rulemaking is labor- and fact-intensive, requiring public hearings, evidentiary records, and other steps promoting accountability and quality. Until the 1970s, many important rules were issued this way, allowing for more scrutiny and thoughtfulness than was usually possible in conventional legislation.[31] However, the process was never speedy, and critics argued that it led to bureaucratic paralysis. The favorite example remains the great peanut butter saga of 1959–1970, a struggle pitting an allied FDA and public, which wanted high peanut content in nut butters, against industry, which did not. Eventually, manufacturers agreed to nuttier butters, but refused to go higher than 87 percent peanuts; the FDA preferred 90 percent.[32] The hearings dragged on for months, the transcript ballooned to 8,000 pages, the two camps entrenched, and when the FDA mandated 90 percent, industry sued, triggering tedious litigation (which the FDA ultimately won).[33]

The cumbersome machinery of formal rulemaking led critics, including progressive academics and agency staff, to argue that formal rulemaking should be reserved only for special occasions—if it took over a decade to resolve a spat over actual peanuts, what did that say about more important regulations? What this argument elided was that the peanut butter rule dragged on for so long precisely because the stakes were peanuts. Jiffy was not the FDA's top priority; it had other things, like thalidomide, to deal with in those years. Nevertheless, the peanut butter story was too good not to use as a cudgel, so even though formal rulemaking had long been viewed as the gold standard for policy and an implicit legal requirement for most rulemaking, shortly after the peanut butter war ended, the Court decided that agencies could make rules less formally, absent an explicit statutory command to the contrary.[34] The Court's logic was notably feeble, a triumph of expedience over logic, midwifed by ignorance, fiction, and a simple desire to unclog the bureaucratic drain and get tiresome cases off the docket—foreshadowing the Court's work on its major bureaucracy cases in the coming decades. Indeed, the great expansion in regulation, and associated quality issues, may have been a by-product of the Court's *sua sponte* musings in one forgotten case from 1972 in which the Justices were "deeply uninterested," and where the only Justice with relevant experience was famous for being flighty and alleged by some scholars to be afflicted with "dementia."[35] So is hypertrophic bureaucracy the creation of judicial grandpas making crazy, unprovoked remarks? Possibly.

However achieved, with formal rulemaking made optional, agencies rapidly switched to notice-and-comment rulemaking, which remains their default mode. Compared to formal rulemaking, notice-and-comment is much less involved and faster (if not actually fast). The procedure is this: agencies propose rules, the public and lobbyists offer comments, agencies consider that feedback, and the draft rule is tweaked (or not) before issuance in final form. Even with notice-and-comment's abbreviations, agency rulemaking has the potential to be both more democratic and higher quality than conventional legislation. Agencies have large staffs of experts, and before issuing rules, they have obligations to consider public input, employ practices like cost/benefit analyses and, in certain contexts, to consult best available science. Congress, by contrast, has less domain expertise, no obligation to consider public input, and may pass laws as stupid and futile as it likes, though if jettisoning thought hastens some parts of the legislative process, the process of assembling coalitions more than offsets the time saved. Agencies, with fewer political cats to wrangle, can and do greatly outproduce Congress.

After notice-and-comment sped up rulemaking, the critique shifted from sclerotic underproduction of rules to chronic overproduction. The volume of rulemaking has become so large as to risk self-defeat. Between 2000 and 2015, federal agencies emitted 61,161 regulatory pronouncements, for average totals of 3,823 items and 23,543 pages per year.*[36] Adding new rules to historical accumulations plus the parallel volumes of local and state regulations produces a rulebook so large as to defy comprehension or compliance. As we saw in Chapter 2, a legal system that demands the impossible risks illegitimacy. And while it's true that any one citizen need only comply with some tiny fraction of all those rules, finding *which* tiny fraction is no small feat.

Even when it's clear what subset of rules applies, the adventure has only begun, because most rules are bewildering and counterintuitive. Consider sales taxes. Many state legislatures authorize sales taxes through complex laws, but even these laws cannot be applied without further rules and interpretation by tax agencies. The net results often defy comprehension. We move now from chicken nuggets to Italian food. Let's say I patronize a pizza place in California, but instead of summoning a simple slice, I want a calzone and soup (it's

---

*   Some rules are insignificant, others affect all parts of the economy, and some are anti-rules, in the sense that they repeal prior regulation, but overall, a fair total runs over three thousand annually.

California, after all). Will sales tax apply? It's a basic question, deserving of a straightforward reply. None is possible. California's Sales and Use Tax Law of 1933, Chapter 2, applies sales tax generally. Fine, tax will be charged. However, California generally exempts from sales tax food for "human consumption."[37] This is a minor complexity, but at least it generates a tax break, and if the inquiry ended here, most people would be satisfied. The inquiry, unfortunately, keeps going. As it happens, food *will* be taxed if prepared with heat. Fine, calzones are hot, and thus taxed. What about the soup? If the soup is minestrone, it's taxed; if gazpacho, not. Unless, that is, I've bought a calzone and gazpacho together—in that case, the gazpacho is taxed as part of a hot "bundle" (or mess, by this point). Fortunately, we can always count on tax schemes to have loopholes, and lo!, it turns out there's a tax exemption for "bakery goods."[38] As calzones are baked, they seem to qualify for tax-exempt status.

So far, so good, except that looking at enacted law—the law passed by a legislature—is not enough. (This is a critique in itself.) California's tax regulator, the Board of Equalization (BOE), issues all sorts of interpretations and regulations that gloss enacted law. Consulting BOE's missives, it appears that the "bakery goods" exemption doesn't apply to *savory* baked items, which BOE helpfully explains are the kind of items that contain meat and cheese but not fruits and/or cream.[*,39] Thus, a lamb samosa is taxable, a cream-filled donut is not. (Though who knows? The relevant section on baked goods is titled "Croissants.") Perhaps the pastry lobby got its claws in BOE, but leaving that potential bit of corruption to one side, the rules present another imponderable: What if the calzone is meatless? (Again, I'm in California; specifically, San Francisco.) Calzones have tomato sauce, and tomatoes are biologically fruits, so arguably the calzone should be tax-exempt. Then again, tomatoes are culturally considered savory, so honoring the spirit of the law would mean paying sales tax. Of course, rhubarb is the other way around, a vegetable treated as a fruit—tax regulations abound with these sorts of conundrums—and I'm sidestepping

---

*   I wrote this before California legislators gutted the BOE in frustration over allegations about the agency's corruption and mismanagement. But we don't even know how *many* new agencies will fill the gap or what they'll do with the calzone.

the BOE's (perhaps-definitive-perhaps-not) guidance about "pasties," taxation of hot vs. cold sandwiches provided by "river rafting companies," and other exhausting minutiae. The law offers "safe harbors," vendor-specific guidance, and circumstantial tests to help streamline compliance, but these end up being headaches themselves and are not worth getting into.

The taxable status of the calzone is too complicated, even for the BOE. The BOE cannot always explain why some items get taxed and others go tax-free, although this is basically the BOE's job.*[40] The result is totally unsatisfying, not just as a matter of jurisprudential clarity, but also as a policy matter. Faced with complex regulations, cautious vendors will find it expedient to simply charge sales tax on everything. The BOE will hardly complain about bonus revenue, but citizens should, and not just small-government conservatives. When vendors over-collect food taxes, the burden falls heaviest on families that spend a large fraction of their budgets on food, i.e., lower-income families.[41] By being too complicated, a regulatory regime designed by progressives achieves regressive results.

Agencies do not intend to make incomprehensible or self-defeating rules, but increasingly poor personnel policies all but guarantee that they will. Making, revising, judging, interpreting, and enforcing rules—and doing it well—takes more time than agency employees have. Despite substantial economic and population growth, direct federal agency employment is not much greater now than it was in the late 1970s.[42] The decline in the regulator-to-regulated ratio is one for which all the efficiencies of copy machines and computers cannot compensate. The obvious solutions are increased staffing or reduced regulatory scope, depending on ideological preference. But the electorate demands a lot of agency-administered programs, while

---

*   The vagaries of food taxes were brought to light by William Weissman, a tax lawyer who published an article pondering why he was taxed for a hot chocolate bought from a Starbucks inside a Target, but not for one bought at a Starbucks inside his office building. California's tax regulator provided a very long and convoluted defense, though it noted that it was "not clear why" the two purchases were treated differently. Then again, this is an agency that deems boiled lobster as not hot food, because the "primary purpose of placing [lobster] in hot water is to kill it," which supposes some sort of purely sadistic, non-nutritional tax purpose for shellfish boiling.

right-leaning Congresses have pledged to limit government hiring. That leaves agencies in a bind.

The solution has been a dissatisfying third way that emphasizes outsourcing, which keeps official head counts flat. Outsourcing some tasks is fine, of course, and agencies have always done this. Social Security issued millions of checks, but no one expected government to manufacture the paper on which those checks were printed. Today, however, agencies contract out even their core functions, with some agencies outsourcing almost all their work. The EPA is particularly aggressive, spending just 22 percent of its budget on internal payroll. Almost all the remainder goes to third parties: 29 percent to contractors and 45 percent as grants (mostly to state agencies, who themselves outsource).[43] The results are additional, often inefficient, layers: Congress gives EPA a mandate, EPA interprets the mandate and hands it off to local contractors, who then provide mandates to subcontractors. The subcontractors issue their own guidelines, and since they pay the people doing the actual work, the subcontractors frequently have more control over regulatory implementation than the nominal regulator; for Constitutional critics keeping score, that's not one delegation to gripe about, but at least three.

Constitutional questions aside, outsourcing reduces EPA to a think tank with a checkbook, which isn't automatically bad. However, the one thing that think tanks cannot outsource is *thinking*. To think, EPA needs data to understand whether its/your money is being used wisely, if outsourcing is a good idea in the first place, and whether EPA's regulations are well considered and properly implemented by its bevy of subcontractors. Nevertheless, EPA outsources some of its thought process, too. Regulations are supposed to be data-driven (indeed, an old executive order requires them to be so), yet up to 94 percent of EPA data comes from third parties, in some cases from groups whose own EPA funding may be determined by data they or their associates collect.[44] EPA has even used contractors to determine whether it should use contractors, and if this upsets you, feel free to call the EPA hotline. The operator might know something about outsourcing, as EPA has outsourced some hotline services, too.[45]

Outsourcing raises serious questions about the principal/agent dilemma mentioned earlier in this chapter. Agency contractors have dual responsibilities, but these responsibilities are not equal. A contractor's duty to an entity like EPA is largely defined by contract, and *contractual* obligations are generally limited to whatever's on the page: if an EPA contract requires five tons of waste to be shoveled out, and it costs a dollar more to shovel a sixth ton of sludge, the contractor need not shovel that extra ton. Indeed, contractors have good legal reasons not to shovel that extra ton, because they owe *fiduciary* duties to their shareholders and directors, and spending an extra dollar arguably breaches that fiduciary duty. This is an extreme example, but more realistically, contractors have few obligations to save EPA money, alert agencies that work ordered might be unnecessary, or undertake all the other things that true fiduciaries must. Contractors also can, and do, donate to agencies' political masters, who can push contracts in the direction of favored vendors (defense contractors in the 1980s being notorious examples). Outsourcing offers chances for efficiency, but risks breaking the principal/agent bond.

The Meta-Agency: OIRA

As outsourcing degraded the integrity of regulation from below, demands for accountability pinched regulators from above. All administrations since Carter's have heavily interposed themselves in the regulatory process. Every regulation with "significant" impact (save those generated by the few agencies whose independence is guaranteed by statute) must be submitted to the Office of Information and Regulatory Affairs (OIRA), which is part of the Executive Office of the President. OIRA does nothing about the Foul, but in theory, it could provide a mechanism for imposing democratic accountability. However, OIRA's obscurity grants presidents a measure of plausible deniability, as the White House's ability to veto regulations is not well known, a fact that undermines the democratic narrative. It also does not help that agencies sometimes game the process, failing to submit rules when required or manipulating rules to avoid scrutiny; for example, the IRS summarily issued crucial Obamacare guidance via *blog post*.[46]

OIRA review is triggered when it is "likely" than an agency will issue a rule having an annual "effect" (note the squishy language) on the economy of at least $100 million, cause significant confusion, adversely affect national interests, or fiddle with entitlements.[47] About 450 rules per year meet these standards, and once these rules are submitted, OIRA generally has ninety days to respond. Though agencies usually brief OIRA before formal submission, the official three-month review period is just not much time. "Significant" rules are just that, and most cannot be digested in ninety days. While revising this chapter, the shortest rule under OIRA review was two pages, which even the most disorganized White House could process in thirteen weeks. Many proposed rules, however, ran over 150 pages, and the longest, more than twice that.[48] One would imagine OIRA to be a large organization to handle this much material. It isn't: OIRA has about forty-five staffers.[49] Twice as many people primp the roses and vacuum the carpets at the White House, but forty-five is the number the White House deems sufficient to impose coherence and accountability on the massive federal bureaucracy.[50]

With so few staff, it may seem impossible for OIRA to carry out its mission, though it should be noted that OIRA's workings are something of a mystery. The Government Accountability Office (GAO) described OIRA's processes as "not well understood or documented."[51] The legal academy has often been caught short, and after serving as head of OIRA from 2009 to 2012, Cass Sunstein (a justly respected law professor) reflected that his own prior writings on OIRA were often "wrong or at best incomplete."[52] With the benefit of experience, Sunstein characterizes OIRA mostly as a regulatory clearinghouse and interagency ombudsman, with one eye on cost-benefit analysis, but not (as many do and have) as a body that reviews rules with an emphasis on political calculation. Sunstein's views may have been true for the Obama Administration in which Sunstein worked, but seem flatly implausible as to other administrations. After all, if OIRA were merely a bland referee and hand-holder, Reagan wouldn't have made OIRA a priority shortly after assuming office, and other presidents wouldn't have kept OIRA floating around the West Wing simply to keep the spreadsheet contingent happy.

OIRA's actual purpose seems not so much to sort, parse, and improve rules as to rubber-stamp uncontroversial rules and to discreetly suborn or kill politically sensitive items, at least when OIRA operates in a disinterested or cynical administration. The degree to which OIRA practices ignore-suborn-or-kill rather than study-and-improve is difficult to detect in the official statistics. Between 2000 and 2016, about 20 percent of rules moved along without much change, 70.2 percent were modified by review, and 7.2 percent were withdrawn or returned, in line with the narrative of OIRA as a technocratic clearinghouse.[53] When OIRA modified rules, interventions ran the gamut from minor tweaks to genuine and important improvements. But review often went beyond that, sometimes adjusting rules so drastically and strangely that the real purpose seemed to be to score political points.

The most misleading statistic, however, may be OIRA's kill rate, certainly higher than the 7.2 percent reported in government spreadsheets. When rules die, they often do so off the books, in opaque pre-review "consultations," in which OIRA informs an agency that a rule will be dead on arrival.[54] Given the disparities in staff and expertise between OIRA and the submitting agencies, these consultations can only be political, not technocratic, exercises. A chief argument for bureaucracies is (or, anyway, was) that they make rules well because they make rules apolitically. If agencies adjust their rules to satisfy OIRA/White House politics, technocratic values may suffer substantially. However, with OIRA in play, agencies cannot simply jam new rules into the Federal Register without at least thinking about the political consequences—in other words, agencies are not entirely immune to democratic forces.

Making It Worse by Helping

The degree to which agencies advance or thwart democratic good-governance is central to the debate about bureaucracies. Most of this debate now occurs via litigation, which focuses on two questions. First, can an elected Congress delegate its lawmaking power to unelected agencies? Second, if it can, have agencies faithfully executed the tasks delegated to them?

Constitutional fundamentalists have long argued that the answer to the first question is "no," on the grounds that Article I and principles of democratic accountability bar Congress from delegating its powers. The resulting destruction of the bureaucratic state, the (stupider) fundamentalists assure us, is entirely incidental. Of course, there's something palpably insincere about vindicating democracy by asking an unelected judiciary to defy the will of an elected legislature. But there's nothing literally unprecedented about the fundamentalist argument: the Court used non-delegation doctrine to thwart FDR in the early phases of the New Deal, and while the Court beat a hasty retreat in 1937, it never officially abandoned the doctrine. The Court kept its nukes, though perhaps only three Justices are bold enough to reach for the red button.

The more immediate threat to the administrative state is the erosion of something called "*Chevron* deference," after a leading 1984 case (involving Justice Gorsuch's mother).*[55] With anti-delegation sidelined, the Court now asks whether an agency has performed its duties competently and in accord with often-vague Congressional instructions. To decide those questions, *Chevron* and its progeny tell judges when and how much benefit of the doubt to afford agencies. In the typical case, *Chevron* encourages judges to "defer" to agency interpretations of Congressional legislation, which helps

---

*   Justice Gorsuch is a noted skeptic of bureaucracies and *Chevron*. His view is that bureaucracies are untrustworthy, a fact awkwardly confirmed by his mother's tenure at the EPA in the first Reagan Administration, which was so aggressively chaotic that Reagan sacked Mother Gorsuch and the House censured her in an unrelated matter. In a final twist, it was Ann Gorsuch's EPA that promulgated the rule leading to the *Chevron* case.

bureaucracies define the limits of their own power.[56] The animating presumptions are that agencies are experts whose close relationships with Congress make them better interpreters of legislative will than judges, and whose reasonable good faith may be presumed. Courts reserve the right to strike down actions that exceed the clear terms of an agency's mandate (or are simply too zany to be endured), but *Chevron* is generally understood to provide a safe space for agencies. That's the capsule summary, and it all seems quite reasonable and easy. The reality is more complicated, and about as useful as a thirty-page recipe whose each step reads "boil cake until tasty."

Critics claim that *Chevron* is not merely nonsensical, but a sham used to justify whatever the Court feels like doing. If the Court agrees with agency policy, it showily proceeds through the *Chevron* process to discover that everything is hunky-dory (and the agency wins). If the Court dislikes the policy, *Chevron* is conveniently forgotten, and the Court deploys its full, withering scrutiny (and the agency loses). If that seems too cynical, consider these facts. In their academic capacities, Scalia and Breyer wrote competing glosses on *Chevron* issues, but as Justices, each sometimes adopted *the other's* theory, seemingly because doing so produced more ideologically palatable results.[57] Scalia and Breyer are not alone. Scholars have noted that the Court has deployed *Chevron* erratically—in one large sample, using *Chevron* in only about a quarter of cases in which Court doctrine suggested that *Chevron* did apply.[58] Empirical studies have also shown that judges appointed by Democrats validate liberal agency actions more frequently than conservative policies, while Republican appointees do the reverse.[59] In many cases, "deference" is preference.

Chevron is now besieged. Skeptics conjure up ever-more excuses to ignore *Chevron*, working up to killing *Chevron* outright. Dispensing with *Chevron* would be intellectually tidy, though it's generally believed that agencies would be immediately exposed to a flood of unwinnable litigation. Many supporters of the bureaucratic status quo prefer to punt, though leaving *Chevron* in its current shambles carries a price of its own. Until the Court replaces *Chevron* with a clear, consistent, and realistic standard for judging agency rulemaking, rules of national importance can be settled only when private litigation arrives at the Court and five unelected Justices shake their Magic 8-Balls.

As for democratic values, *Chevron* doesn't do much for them now, its prolonged death throes will do even less, and its interment will almost certainly defy the popular will, so long as the public likes safe medicines and a functioning TSA. Whatever the inherent tensions between bureaucracy and democracy, the Court is making them worse.

At the risk of a fraught simile, bureaucracies are like guest workers who have overstayed their visas. They have become part of society and supply essential labor that the Constitution's natural citizens cannot, or will not, perform. But the legal status of bureaucracies has always been uncertain, and agencies persist only through acts of willful blindness, legal contortionism, inertia, and expedience. To protect these essential institutions, law degrades itself, covering for lapses better solved by direct action. Certainly, bureaucracies have powers—like administrative hearings—that should be handed over to other branches. The remaining powers, indispensable to modern government, would work better if their legal status were clearly confirmed. Some states have made modest efforts to provide Constitutional bases for some of their bureaucracies.[60] But achieving this at the federal level would require an inconceivably difficult rewrite of the Constitution.

There is no entirely satisfactory solution to the Constitutional problem posed by bureaucracies. The Constitution did not contemplate a society where government finds itself regulating drones piloted by AIs to deliver junk food. Yet, here we are, stuck with another version of the same problem that plagues all of American law: Is it more important to preserve the exact meaning of an antique document or to find ways to accommodate the institutions that, after decades of accretion, now govern society? Ultimately, this is a problem judges have handed to themselves, and the fate of the bureau-cratic enterprise mostly lies with them. Will they slice and dice the platypus or will they just leave it be? Certainly, judges could clean up the legal habitat, starting with *Chevron*. Or the judiciary could bow out of the game entirely, leaving it to Congress to rein in agencies that exceed their briefs—under the Congressional Review Act, Congress has the tools. Unfortunately, none of this will happen. Creating deliberate ambiguity over the administrative state amplifies judicial influence over the entire government. This is probably as some judges prefer, for judges have long seen themselves as not only the cen-ter of the legal universe, but the brightest stars within it.

CHAPTER SIX

JUDGES: ROBOTS, UMPIRES, OR GODS?

> Judges are like umpires. Umpires don't make the rules; they apply them.
>
> John Roberts[1]

O ne of litigation's grim joys is "impeachment," an attack on a witness's credibility.[2] Impeachment is not a free-for-all; the process is governed by rules of evidence which, like the rules of civil procedure, criminal procedure, and court practice, are mostly written by judges.[3] At the federal level, primary responsibility for drafting for procedural rules (whose name belies their power) resides in the Judicial Conference, a body headed by the Chief Justice—the very position for which John Roberts was auditioning when he testified to the Senate Judiciary Committee that judges "don't make rules."[4] Thus, judges *do* make rules—not only procedural rules, but a lot of substantive *law*: many of the doctrines governing torts, contracts, antitrust, insider trading, and criminal defense are judge-made or were transformed into statutes by legislatures working from judicial precedent. So, ladies and gentlemen of the jury, to visit impeachment upon John Roberts: Was Roberts merely ignorant when he claimed that judges don't make rules, or was he trying to mislead?

It couldn't have been ignorance. Roberts is a Harvard-educated litigator who was already sitting on a lower federal court; he knew what judging entailed. As for misdirection, why bother? Even the dimmest senators realize that judges do more than call "balls and strikes."[5] Some suggested that Roberts deployed his umpire metaphor as a coded message; liberal judges had been derided as "activists," so emphasizing passivity would signal reliable conservatism to the GOP, which controlled the Senate. But again, what was the point? Every senator knew Roberts was conservative: Roberts launched his career in the Reagan White House, had been nominated to a federal judgeship by Bush II, and in just two years had produced such pleasing results that the same president tapped Roberts to replace the recently deceased Chief Justice Rehnquist (himself a Nixon appointee and Roberts's own mentor). If "umpire" was code, Senate Democrats needed no Enigma machine to crack it.

Clearly, Roberts was doing something else, and it was this: trying to put an unthreatening face on judicial power. In the circumstances of a Court nomination, Roberts's effort was considerably misplaced, but it partook of a standard, almost reflexive enterprise: judicial myth-making. All judges wrap themselves in myths, whose collective aim is to suggest that when judges don their robes, they shed all human failings, becoming perfect machines for justice: wise, impartial, industrious, ethical, efficacious, apolitical, and restrained. The goal is to divert scrutiny and pressure, because potent as the judiciary is, it's also quite fragile. Unlike Congress, the judiciary's greatest powers are self-granted or the products of historical accident, and all federal (and many state) judges wield these powers without electoral validation. Unlike the executive, the judiciary can deploy no force on its own, and lacks budgetary autonomy. Judicial power ultimately draws on the faith people grant judges, and that faith requires a Solomonic myth. And it *is* a myth, in the sense of a story left unverified. There are surprisingly few mechanisms to screen for Solomonic virtues before judges take the bench, limited means to remove judges who fall short of the ideal, and no simple way to explain that a powerful judiciary is integral to a fair legal system. There are only tales, to help people believe what the system does not really try to prove or guarantee: that judges are excellent guardians of justice. That many judges are good, and some spectacular, does not mean the judiciary itself is perfect or that the judicial mythology doesn't overreach.

Many judicial myths are not so much lies as embellishments. For example, the picture of judges as functionaries with limited powers—not unlike Roberts's umpire—has an honest core. The Constitution limits courts to deciding a live "case or controversy," so judges cannot simply make whatever laws they want, whenever they want; they can only shape law by deciding whichever cases happen to land on their dockets.[6] As to individual judges, this is a powerful restraint, but as to the judiciary *overall*, the case-or-controversy requirement is hardly restrictive. American litigiousness ensures that all important issues will eventually find themselves before *some* court, and important cases will eventually wend their way to the appellate courts where judges, including the Justices, can solicit opportunities to make law by hinting at areas for future litigation. As for the notion that judges simply decide isolated cases, that's another partial truth. When the Court decided *Citizens United*, it formally decided a single matter, but the effects quickly spilled beyond one PAC. (And arguably, the Court decided *Citizens United* using reasoning unnecessary to resolving the immediate issue—in other words, it was deciding an issue, not a case.)

Judicial decisions are among the most enduring acts of American government: not only are federal judges life-tenured, the entire judiciary is devoted to precedent, making its decisions highly stable. By contrast, acts of Congress and presidents can be unwound by veto/override, by new officeholders often elected with a specific mandate to undo their predecessors' work, and, of course, by judges. Appellate judges wield more power than they care to admit. And even judges lower in the hierarchy exercise near-plenary powers over their own courts, with extraordinary latitude to shape the course of litigation, supplemented by the open-ended power of contempt, the discretionary authority to punish those who displease or defy the court.*[7] "Limited powers," then, is the truth, but not the whole truth and nothing but.

---

* Contempt penalties are usually fines or an overnight stay in jail, although one Pennsylvania litigant found himself in jail for fourteen years for contempt of court.

One reason judicial mythology is so lovingly tended by the bench is because judicial power is largely self-regulated, fettered only by judges' own intelligence and integrity, and pushback from colleagues. These are no small things, but they are purely internal controls, and the other branches cannot easily undo judicial work. When a court strikes down a law, an override requires joint action by the legislature and executive, which is tricky enough and, as to core Constitutional rulings, there's nothing anyone can do short of the flatly impracticable means of amending the Constitution. Nor are there convenient mechanisms by which the incompetent, abusive, or just plain dim judge can be called to account. For federal judges, the Constitution guarantees tenure during "good behavior," a standard sufficiently vague that federal judges can serve as long as they like. Removing a federal judge against his will requires impeachment, a process so difficult that it has been visited on just fifteen judges in American history.[8] And not only are there few external mechanisms to remove failing judges, there are few good internal mechanisms. At most, inferior federal judges can be reversed, or their dockets rejiggered to focus on minor cases where damage can be contained. State judges, often being elected, are more democratically accountable, but this is a weak control, as state judgeships often carry the longest terms in their governments and, being down-ballot positions, re-elections present modest challenges even for judicial specimens whose intelligence and ethics are less than sterling.[9]

No wonder that judges labor to reconcile the public to these substantial and discretionary powers by presenting themselves as wise arbiters faithful to laws whose meanings are, if not always clear, ascertainable by means of unquestionable rigor. Roberts's umpire routine merely took part in the larger tradition of judicial rhetoric. Roberts's schtick got called out only because of the intense scrutiny that attaches to the nation's highest judicial position. Mostly, judicial mythmaking escapes scrutiny, and judges work hard to keep reality from the public by enforcing a hieratic culture of deference and omertà. But the mythology is partly self-defeating. A profession that cherishes intellectual honesty degrades itself when it shapes its image falsely;

this is especially so when certain judicial myths strain reasonable credulity. Worse, many judges believe at least some of their superhuman mythology, fostering overconfidence and the errors that trait always brings, including unwarranted reluctance to examine their own behavior or that of their colleagues. ("Deference" to trial courts and "heeding precedent" from higher courts are, in part, aspects of the mythology: always give a fellow judge the benefit of the doubt and then some.) Assuming the public can stand it, judges should jettison their self-created myths. The judiciary should stand on its record, and if (as is possible) that record isn't sufficient justification, then the record, not the judicial mythology, should be reinforced.

There is one myth, however, for which judges cannot be held responsible, and it is perhaps the most toxic myth of all: that the American way of judging is normal. The public may assume so, but by global standards, the American judiciary is unusual in almost all its particulars, starting with judicial preparation and selection.

Becoming a Benchwarmer

Although judging is a specialty like neurosurgery and plasma physics, America assumes judging can be picked up on the fly. The most extreme examples are judges who aren't lawyers: twenty-two states allow the practice, and in eight of them (including Texas and New York) non-lawyers can hand out jail time. Shockingly, only 47 percent of state trial judgeships require a law degree, though these are mostly minor positions; for "general jurisdiction" trial court judgeships the figure is a somewhat more reassuring 79 percent.[10] The remaining states do require judges to be lawyers, though as we saw in Chapter 3, law school is not the most robust quality control, and is anyway significantly undermined in the many states that allow judicial elections. So long as a candidate wins the vote, *any* law degree will do, and judges may be elevated even if bar associations have deemed the candidate "unqualified."*[11] Voters may even elect lawless candidates, as happened with Roy Moore, when he was returned to Alabama's highest court despite being previously removed for unethical conduct and defying, of all things, court orders.[12] The federal system is not free of embarrassment but, being more prestigious and highly scrutinized, the pedigrees of federal judges are almost uniformly excellent. Excellence, though, is a norm, not a rule. The Constitution requires no educational (or really, any) qualifications of federal judicial candidates and, as recently as 1957, the Supreme Court included a Justice without a law degree.[13] Until recently, though, federal judicial candidates have been quite good, and since the Eisenhower years, presidents have employed the American Bar Association's prescreening before making nominations—save for Bush II and Trump.[14] But presidents may nominate whomever they like, and sufficiently partisan and craven Senates can and have confirmed judges whose pedigrees would render them unfit for legal office in other countries.†[15]

Even lawyers with outstanding legal educations and rated "qualified" may nevertheless find themselves woefully unprepared for their first years on the bench, because there's no job that quite prepares any private lawyer to be a judge and no rigorous training program to compensate for that reality. As former federal appeals judge Richard Posner observed, the transition to the bench is "abrupt," and while judicial education has improved since Posner joined the bench in 1981, it remains weak.[16] The Federal Judicial Center notes that "[t]here are *no* mandatory educational requirements or standards for federal judges," though it adds hopefully (if vaguely) that "the majority" of

---

*   Associations like the ABA sometimes err, and a few candidates initially ranked as "unqualified" turned out to be excellent judges. But the ABA errs on the side of the false negative, which is the safer practice, albeit one that can occasionally knock out the brilliant, but unorthodox, judge.

†   Trump may fill the largest number of judicial vacancies since the 1990s, and of his first nominee list, about 8 percent were rated "unqualified" by majorities of the ABA reviewing panels—not catastrophic, but 10x more "unqualified" candidates than the average nominee pool from 1989 to 2016.

judges "take advantage" of the Center's training programs, which include a "selection of educational publications and DVDs"; the Center also "invites" (but doesn't require) new judges "to attend two one-week orientation sessions" and perhaps some brief follow-ups.[17] So: optional *and* inadequate. States, by contrast, do generally require training, though programs tend toward the cursory, ranging from a few hours to three weeks. That's astoundingly brief, considering that *manicurists* in California must accumulate 400 hours of experience before taking their final licensing examination and striking out unsupervised.[18] (Cosmetologists need 1,600 hours, but they're Supreme Court Justices to the manicurists' trial judges.)

Unsurprisingly, rookie judges may be completely at sea, not least because even jurisdictions that do require judicial training allow new judges to postpone it. For example, Justices of the Nevada Supreme Court can defer the inconvenience of a four-day seminar for up to two years after taking office.[19] (That 2016's seminar took place in Reno provided no incentive to rush.[20]) The absence of pre-bench training is a problem for new judges, though for new trial judges most of all, as trial work is perhaps the most alien sort of legal practice, fast-paced and filled with rules many lawyers never encounter in depth, if at all.

The system's near-total inattention to judicial training has produced some stunning embarrassments. One federal appointee, lacking trial experience, was confounded by routine oral motions, scurrying back to chambers to research basic questions that a trained judge could handle automatically; another recently appointed judge in California has been known to solicit advice from colleagues via text message in open court. Even appellate judges, operating at a slower pace and prepared by a law school curriculum that focuses on appellate law, have significant training gaps. Many appellate judges are appointed directly to their posts and have little or no intuition for how trial courts operate—even though the essential work of appellate courts is to review trial court decisions. This culture of amateurism would be a source of greater social unease were it widely known. No one, for example, would be eager for the family physician to perform heart surgery. But

American law, committed to the view that every lawyer can acquire *any* legal skill, sails along untroubled.

Much of the world would view the American system of judicial (non-) education as bizarre to the point of negligence. Non-Anglophone countries groom future judges as they would candidates for any other profession. In France, the conventional route to judgeship is to obtain bachelor's and master's degrees (customarily in legally inclined fields), pass a rigorous screening test, and undertake a further thirty-one months at the *École Nationale de la Magistrature.*[21] French magistrates therefore begin their careers with considerable advantages over their American peers. France's technocratic system also helps transform the myth of an apolitical judiciary into something closer to a reality. Rank-and-file judges are processed technocratically, based on scores and openings. And while the Élysée nominally appoints high judges (as the White House does), the French executive seeks guidance on whom to appoint from a council dominated by legal professionals, and can only select from a pool of candidates vetted and trained by the judiciary itself.[22] Versions of this model, in which judges perform quality control prior to political appointment, prevail in many European peers and also in Japan.[23] Moreover, when foreign judges advance, they usually do so on objective bases including experience and test scores, rather than political connections and ideology. Only British-derived systems depart radically from this technocratic mentality, and even within the Anglophone community, America presents an increasingly odd example. In Britain, fortress of ancient and strange traditions, some judges now gain experience as part-timers before making judging a career, and merit-based examinations are becoming an important filter.[24] None of this is to suggest that *seasoned* American judges are incompetent (though a few are). It's merely to underscore that, in their early years, American judges operate at an unnecessary educational disadvantage and are promoted using more subjective metrics. Contrasted with foreign professional benches, the "apolitical" aspect of American judicial mythology becomes particularly stark.

Indeed, it is *because* American judges are political that they spend so much time insisting that they are not. The favorite tactic here is for judges to refer to the executive and legislature as the "political branches," implying that the judiciary is otherwise. This is flatly unbelievable at the state level, where many judges are elected, sometimes with party affiliations listed on ballots.[25] Appointments slightly disguise political considerations, though it defies credibility to assert anything less than that politics plays a major role in judicial selection. No president has appointed a cross-party Justice since 1971, when Nixon shoveled Lewis F. Powell, Jr. onto the Court. Party affiliation notwithstanding, Powell was not what anyone would call a flaming liberal; rather, he was a Southern Democrat ("far from a liberal on racial issues," though he evolved rapidly) and anything but an economic progressive, going so far as to espouse the theory that Ralph Nader's *Unsafe at Any Speed* was treasonous to capitalism.[26]

Judicial politics are no longer as overt and malodorous as they were during the Gilded Age, when hacks and cronies populated courts. Norms have changed and, anyway, the nation's better law schools churn out enough materiel that executives can always rummage up *some*one who, while ideologically aligned, has a pedigree sufficiently impressive that accusations of pure partisanship become harder to make. (With exceptions: in 2017, Trump nominated a candidate unable to answer questions about basic courtroom practice; the candidate withdrew under fire.[27]) Nevertheless, political considerations remain active, and influence detectible. The NRA, for example, offers occasional endorsements and, for top courts, considerable financial support, including a reported $1 million for a PR campaign during Neil Gorsuch's nomination to the Supreme Court.[28] Organizations on different sides of specific interests like abortion, drug legalization, and free speech do the same for their preferred candidates. And in the era of digitized opinions and big data, influence groups feel more confident about what their money will get, avoiding the ideological migration that left some nominators with buyer's remorse (as happened with Blackmun, Stevens, Souter, and even Rehnquist, to varying degrees).[29]

Of all the interest groups, none has been as influential as the Federalist

Society ("Fed Soc," in the community). Fed Soc's defining mission is to tilt the judiciary rightward, and it has been enormously influential; arguably, Fed Soc is the Right's greatest political success since Nixon's Southern strategy. The Society grooms a collection of ideologically sympathetic candidates, sometimes starting in law school, and presents its nominees to Republican administrations, making clear that any deviation from the approved roster of debutantes will carry heavy political consequences. Fed Soc has been so successful that, since the 1980s, right-leaning administrations have adopted the group's judicial lists wholesale; today, when the GOP is in full control, Fed Soc functionally operates as the Senate Judiciary Committee and White House combined.[30] Some judges associated with Fed Soc haven't been shy about returning the favor, as when Neil Gorsuch gave a speech to the Society shortly after becoming a Justice. Gorsuch also gave a talk to a different conservative group, and the dynamics of influence and loyalty may be partly inferred from the reputational risk in giving that speech, as the venue—Trump's Washington, D.C., hotel—was then at the center of a Constitutional suit against the president.[31] Gorsuch's speeches were not illegal or strictly unethical, though at least one of them was hardly apolitical or well-advised.

Once on the bench, politics continues to play a role (sometimes masquerading as "judicial philosophy"), and this is particularly noticeable among judges auditioning for promotion to higher courts. Auditioners to the Supreme Court, regardless of party, produce more "tough on crime" outcomes relative to other judges with comparable outlooks and profiles; the same seems to be true of district court judges aspiring to appellate positions.*[32] Auditioners' tough-on-crime performances aren't exactly exchanges of a few months of a prisoner's life for better shots at more prestigious judgeships, but neither are they savory. Even judges who can be promoted no further sometimes allow politics to influence their reasoning. Antonin Scalia's vaunted originalism/textualism famously warbled in and out of tune

---

* Aspiring judges know that what probably matters most is attending Yale or Harvard, working in D.C., toadying to executive power, and hoping to God that their 40s and 50s overlap with their party's control of government. These creatures can be spotted as early as 1L.

depending on the case.[33] Anthony Kennedy was also accused of practicing issue-specific politics (on matters such as gay marriage), most prominently by Scalia. That was doubly hypocritical of Scalia, given his own inconsistencies and his snark that Kennedy had no philosophy or logic to betray to politics.

By allowing politics to play a major role in judicial selection and by treating judgeships as political offices instead of civil service jobs, America has a judicial pool that is more overtly partisan and less meritocratic than that of most peer countries. Of course, no judge anywhere is entirely apolitical and, for the most part, state judges are no worse than acceptable and federal judges can rarely be described as less than pretty good. But judges are not, self-sponsored myths notwithstanding, umpires without affiliations. We'll see that they aren't perfect instantiations of wisdom and logic, either, but before we get to that, let's examine the routine of judges once they take the bench.

The Holy Trinities

In keeping with national preference for triplets, American courts generally sit in an ascending hierarchy of trial court, appeals court, and supreme court.* In trial courts (called "district courts" in the federal system and usually termed "superior courts" in the states), a single judge presides over randomly assigned cases. American trial courts usually hold "general jurisdiction," which means they can hear cases about anything, though some matters, either niche or low-stakes, are diverted to specialist courts (e.g., family, tax, small-claims, and traffic courts). Some courts divide themselves into civil and criminal divisions, but the *judges* themselves are usually generalists, as the common practice is for judges to rotate through the divisions, spending six months hearing criminal matters, then six months

---

* There's state-level variation, with older states having the weirdest nomenclature. In New York, the lowest court is the Supreme Court; the intermediate court is the Supreme Court—Appellate Division; the highest court is the Court of Appeals.

hearing civil matters, and so on. Federal courts are essentially general-ist, with a few exceptions, notably the bankruptcy courts. Thus, in many courts, a judge might start his day with murder proceedings and end it with an intellectual property dispute. This arrangement is uncommon outside Anglophone countries. Foreign law favors specialization and courts reflect this; Germany, for instance, has *five* high courts presiding over different areas of law.[34]

Americans are so accustomed to their system that its fundamental odd-ness can be hard to appreciate, especially the American system's faith in the single, omni-competent and all-powerful judge. In many countries, trials are not only separated by field, but overseen by more than one judge, to help correct mistakes as they occur; appeals also work their way up specialized channels. Specialization and contemporaneous review exist for a reason, and are central features of medicine, engineering, accounting, construction—really, everywhere save American judging. Business would consider Ameri-can court practices lunacy; no CEO would dare launch a new soda without soliciting input from six dozen specialists from the legal, marketing, R&D, finance, distribution, and sales departments. No wonder judicial mythology emphasizes superhuman abilities: the infinite variety of human dysfunction is a lot for one mortal to properly judge.

Should trial courts somehow err (or seem to), litigants may proceed to the courts of appeal, whose authority binds inferior courts within an appellate circuit. Federal appeals are heard by three-judge panels, randomly assigned, and their decisions can be appealed to the entire circuit (a rehearing en banc). Circuits have jurisdiction over the same types of cases, but each rules over its own geography, and the fiefs often disagree. Therefore, federal law, which is supposed to be nationally uniform, actually varies from place to place. A securities claim brought in Jersey City will be governed by the interpreta-tions of the Third Circuit, while six miles away, Manhattan proceeds under the precedent of the Second Circuit, which might be quite different. The same holds for some state appellate circuits, whose rulings bind only certain divisions (and then only some of the time; in states like California, things are even stranger and more complicated). This is a recipe for confusion, and circuit disagreements—along with matters of general importance—can be appealed to the relevant supreme court for harmonization, or finality, at any rate.

Aside from specialty matters such as state death penalty cases, a supreme court hearing is not guaranteed. After the 1890s, many supreme courts gained greater control over their dockets, able to decline appeals unless enough justices vote to grant leave.[35] At the U.S. Supreme Court, the process is called *certiorari* ("cert") and requires four votes. This step has become an intensely strategic game to vacuum up cases that will shape the law in high-stakes matters, while also allowing ideological blocs to dodge cases where they might not be able to achieve their desired result.[36] (Cert decisions are heavily influenced by clerks, who do the initial review—more on this in a bit.) Cert also greatly reduces total workload, which benefits the Justices, though not necessarily justice: at the Supreme Court, cert has lightened the load much too greatly, with the Court now doing full dress on just eighty cases a year, substantially fewer than it once did.[37] That pace is too slow to unify federal law or resolve other urgent matters, but it does leave time for more exciting work, like presiding over mock-divorce proceedings inspired by *Much Ado About Nothing,* a 2012 event requiring no fewer than three Supreme Court Justices and four appellate judges, one of the latter being Merrick Garland, who had his own brush with much ado about nothing four years later.*[38]

Though cert allows the Court to take a stately two to three full cases per week worked (justice takes a summer break), other courts must take cases as they come, which can overwhelm. State courts are by far the busiest, handling an influx of more than 86 million cases each year. Up to two-thirds of those

---

* This theatrical production was something of a hotbed for failed Court candidates. In addition to Garland's failure, Douglas Ginsburg's nomination to the Court also died, back in the Reagan years (pot smoking); David Tatel was also considered a strong candidate in 2000 (but his presumed nominator, Al Gore, lost the election partly thanks to the Court). The last member of the quartet was Brett Kavanaugh, the only actor to escape the curse (barely).

are minor matters—traffic violations, small-claims, and petty crimes—and though logistically taxing, such cases are dispatched easily enough. Nevertheless, 15 to 30 million larger cases remain, including at least 3.8 million serious criminal cases, against 11,000 general jurisdiction judges.[39] That's an immense volume, even deducting for the large number of cases that are straightforward or resolved out-of-court. Federal trial courts also face heavy loads: more than 440,000 pending cases against ~665 full judges.[*][40] Some 11 to 15 percent of district court cases are appealed to federal intermediate courts and their 167 judges, and ~13 percent of these are appealed to the Supreme Court—which has other things to do, and other people to do them.[41] But all judges have a lot to do—more, in their minds, than they can handle alone.

Santa's Little Helpers

Judges—especially on elite courts—cope with their dockets by outsourcing labor to clerks and other staff. This strategy receives little media attention, and judges strive to keep it that way, both for reasons of routine confidentiality and because their sometimes extreme reliance on clerks would undermine judicial mystique and public confidence. But clerks are an essential part of judicial work, especially (and perhaps perversely) at the highest courts, where matters are most consequential and workloads lightest. Clerks conduct research, prepare judges' questions for oral argument, draft many judicial opinions either in part or full, and at the highest courts, shape the docket by reviewing cert petitions. Thus, depending on the court and its master, much of what the public thinks is the substance of judging is done by people who are not judges—people who are, in fact, barely lawyers.

---

[*]   Federal lower court judges break into a few categories: Article III judges ("real" federal judges, in the dismissive parlance of elite lawyers), plus several hundred lesser judges who handle specialty/smaller matters or components of larger cases. The caseload figures exclude the bankruptcy courts, which handle over 750,000 cases annually and are the busiest part of the federal court system.

"Barely lawyers," that is, because most clerks are recent law school graduates with little experience, so fresh from school that they have either not taken the bar or not yet received their results, and thus cannot claim the title "attorney." Without a law license, a clerk could not represent a client in so much as a suit about a defective waffle iron. Yet, working in chambers and supervised (however nominally) by a judge, clerks can deny a prisoner's civil rights claim or draft a death penalty opinion. That notwithstanding, most clerks are bright and diligent, because competition for clerkships is intense. But today, so is competition for clerks. For more than thirty years, judges have stampeded, snapping up promising students sooner and faster. In the early 2000s, the clerk frenzy prompted judicial organizations to impose the "Plan," which laid out a calmer, more thoughtful hiring process. The Plan (which has gone through several iterations) has been about as successful as UN sanctions on North Korea. Aggressive judges routinely go rogue, grabbing choice students well ahead of the Plan's official timeline, with some judges and professors conspiring to place students before the first year of law school ends.[42] This harried process is necessarily a lightly informed chain of many links, each of them weak. Recruiting so early in law school means judges can only be guided by school reputation, a limited set of grades, and a smattering of professorial endorsements (themselves lightly informed), capped by a brief interview that often ends in an offer that many judges expect students to accept immediately. Thus, a profession that prides itself on deliberation shops for clerks like *Ab Fab*'s Patsy and Edina bought hats—fast, furiously, and with a hope that a prestige label guarantees quality and fit.

In this chaotic and otherwise unreflective process, one fact rarely goes unnoticed: a clerk's partisan inclination. Students send political signals by including extracurriculars (Fed Soc, a gay rights group, etc.) on their résumés, catering to whatever politics they believe their prospective employers hold. And everyone knows which professorial recommendations cut ice with conservative versus liberal judges, just as everyone knows which judges are conservative and liberal "feeders" to the higher animals in the legal food chain. Doubtless, some judges pay no attention to a clerk's politics, though the generally widespread congruence between judicial and clerkish ideologies reinforces what everyone believes but labors to prove by other means: whether labeled as judicial philosophy, worldview, or what have you, politics are part of judging.*

A major reason for the clerk hiring frenzy is that judges perceive clerks to be indispensable, though this is as much a product of cultural shift as higher workload. Until the early twentieth century, clerks were uncommon; the Supreme Court, for example, employed none until 1885 or so. Today, the Justices have four clerks each (and the Chief is permitted five). Federal appellate judges also usually take four clerks, and district judges hire two or three. Most judges supplement clerks with interns/externs (who spend a semester processing simpler work) plus the customary secretaries and helpmeets.

In addition to the clerks, courts employ staff attorneys, who serve a courthouse generally (rather than specific judges). These staffers process higher volume matters, mostly indigent lawsuits/pro se/prisoner rights cases/ benefits disputes and other items too small to detect from the legal Olympus. Having categorized these matters as "lesser," many judges briskly approve whatever outcome staff attorneys recommend (not always competently), freeing judicial time for more intellectually fascinating tasks.[43] The exceptions to staff-driven justice reside in lowlier state courts which, despite much heavier workloads, have neither the cachet nor resources to hire (m)any clerks. But those who can hire clerks do; no ambitious judge wants to go without.

Like all entourages, clerkly harems foster unhealthy dependence. Society grants courts considerable power because it expects that power to be exercised by officials of remarkable wisdom, experience, and probity—i.e., it's bought the judicial myth. But that myth, if it applies, applies to *judges*, not clerks. Clerks are overwhelmingly in their mid- or late 20s, with virtually no life or professional experience; they aren't sages on the mountaintop. Rather, clerks' outstanding virtue is excellence in the standard (though deficient)

---

* A few judges deliberately hire across partisan lines—though this act of "bipartisanship" simply confirms that judges *do* have partisan preferences. The famous example here is Scalia, though he dispensed with liberal sparring partners in his later years.

legal curriculum, and if all they were doing was preparatory research, society would have no objection. But clerks do a lot more than research, and the damage is most obvious when clerks write opinions. Lacking other tools, clerks tackle cases like glorified term papers: the grader's preconceptions must be flattered, the research must be exhaustive, the logic dense, every objection countered, and the actual outcome... well, that's often of decidedly lesser importance. The result is as formalistic and overengineered as you'd expect, and it's often difficult to tell (or care) what a clerk-written opinion means. The results can also be extremely unimaginative, since few points will be deducted for slavishly following precedent. A confident judge, by contrast, will produce an opinion that focuses on the core issues, dispatch those cleanly by employing only the essential arguments and, having a respect for her own time that clerks invariably lack, keep things short. That's a better result all around; the law is made more clearly, comprehensibly, and flexibly, with an emphasis on justice.

Just as clerks can degrade judicial opinions, they can deform judicial psyches. Many judges treat their staffs like serfs. Judges force clerks to work exceedingly long hours, swear them to secrecy about even nonconfidential matters, and some require clerks to toil on extracurriculars like speechwriting, drudgery for pet causes, and personal errands. Judges also insist on a culture of bow-and-scrape that vanished from other workplaces long ago; many judges insist on being called "Judge" in all circumstances and insist on pomp and servility. This is outright regressive: in the eighteenth century, American judges eschewed English wigs (too royalist); in the nineteenth, many forwent robes (same); but in the twentieth (when clerks arrived), every judge was in a robe.[44] Chief Justice Rehnquist went so far as to slap gold stripes on his togs, because he saw a production of *Iolanthe* in which the Lord Chancellor had gold-striped robes and presumably thought: *I'm the boss, so why not?*[45] To be sure, clerks have not deformed all judicial egos, and some judges are extraordinary mentors. But some judges are nightmarishly abusive, in ways that violate the law (Kozinski's sexual harassment, for example) and basic decency (screaming and other emotional terrorism are not uncommon).[46] It's difficult to see how this much imperium doesn't pollute other judicial work. Condescending and lawless chambers promote condescending and lawless judging.

Bartleby, the Judge

Now that the cast is assembled, the question becomes: How do judges decide? Measured as a fraction of cases filed, *trial* judges rarely "decide" much, in the sense of resolving cases by determining responsibility and levying penalties. Unless parties have agreed to a bench trial, it's *jurors* who decide guilt and innocence, and in civil trials, jurors also shape the damage award, while in criminal matters, legislatures require judges to follow an unappetizing and robotic recipe book. Anyway, trials themselves are exceedingly rare; by the 2000s, they were fewer in *absolute number* than in the 1960s (despite a rise in filings), and today, up to 97 percent of civil matters never reach trial, including an increasing fraction diverted to arbitration.[47] The umpires of John Roberts's fantasy league see most of their games rained out in early innings.

Unlike real umpires, though, trial judges have some control over the weather. They, and the rules they've written, can and do encourage, and sometimes outright coerce, settlement—judgments by other means. Especially in civil matters, it's not uncommon for judges to muse in pointed fashion about how parties really ought to work things out among themselves, sparing an overtaxed court system the bother of another case.

Were it true that out-of-court settlements represented deals struck by free and knowledgeable parties, we might celebrate the "nudge from the judge" as a triumph of economy. But, as we'll see in later chapters, plea bargains, arbitration awards, questionable mediations, and so on are the frequent and unjust results—precisely the sorts of arrangements that should provoke unease in a judge and prompt her to invoke the many and venerable equitable doctrines that would retrieve powerless parties from the grip of a parallel justice system biased against them, or to simply retain control of the case from the beginning. At least these sins are mostly of omission; it's hardly unknown for judges to shove litigants out of court by making perfectly clear when they believe a party is being "unreasonable" in demanding a day in court, a practice that is prejudicial in various senses of the term.

Even when judges don't actively shut the courthouse door, they unintentionally shape legal outcomes through lackadaisical case management. The meter is always running in litigation and judicial delays can compel parties to settle cases that both sides would otherwise wish to see through. This happens more frequently than it should, though it rarely makes headlines or attracts the attention of the Supreme Court. In business, every minute shaved off an Amazon Prime delivery represents a victory in the existential war against chaos and inefficiency. But judges operate at great remove from MBA culture; they manage their calendars as they like, and frequently what they like is delay that postpones work and induces parties to settle. Little about judicial culture penalizes pokiness, and modern management principles seem anathema.

Consider, for example, the rules for federal judicial administration. Within a federal district, administrative duties fall to the chief judge, who is selected not for managerial aptitude or interest, but on the basis of being the most senior active judge under 65 when a chiefship opens. To borrow from Tom Paine, this system is as likely to produce good judicial managers as heredity is to produce a good mathematician or CEO. Nevertheless, the system proceeds mostly unreformed, save for a few tentative experiments, like circulating statistics to shame judges into clearing their dockets. But shame is not a concept with much currency among gods, and to the extent it has an effect, it can make things worse: there's some evidence that judges will find ways to "tidy up" their statistics by resolving slews of cases before target dates, a practice with all the dangers that attend arbitrary deadlines.

Inattention to case management makes litigation slower and worse than it should be. Things move along faster than in *Bleak House*, but not nearly fast enough; in district courts, median time from filing to disposition is 7.6 months for felonies and 10.4 months for civil cases.[48] But this disguises some unsettling variability. In one study, 40 percent of civil cases were resolved within six months and two-thirds within a year.[49] These encouraging statistics are offset by the fact that many cases are patently frivolous, and gimmes don't count for much. The remaining one-third of cases took more than a year to resolve, many requiring several years, and some taking more than a decade. By far the longest delays attach to jury trials. In civil cases, median time from litigation's commencement to a trial runs to 26.4 months, and fully 15.7 percent of cases (representing 56,548 cases as of December 2016) were more than three years old and getting older.[50] While it's true that some matters just take longer to resolve—securities cases, for example, are extremely complex, with every step contested—mismanagement is responsible for much of the delay. In a subsample of employment cases, roughly half were resolved within three months, while the rest took two to three years; that's an enormous difference for cases in the same field, even if the facts vary.[51] Some blame rests with the litigants, who can be dilatory and chaotic, but that's no excuse. Judges have an obligation to ensure the swift administration of justice, and they have tools at their disposal to herd the various legal animals set before them. However, in one study, less than half of federal civil cases showed the entry of a scheduling order/conference, basic mechanisms for litigation management.[52]

When the ringmaster fails to wield the whip, the results can appall. An extreme example involved straightforward federal drug charges in New York, in which the defendant was held for almost *seven years* during "pretrial proceedings." The Second Circuit made clear that the delay was a product of astonishing mismanagement and poor judgment, including, but (as lawyers say) not limited to: several months wasted on three mental competency hearings (the lower court believing that the defendant's desire for a speedy trial indicated some form of insanity); a 117-day interlude for stenographers to transcribe a one-day hearing; further postponement due to the court's and prosecutor's "congested calendars"; an inexplicable period during which the U.S. Marshals "lost track [sic]" of the defendant; and so on—all delays which the lower court had the power and obligation to correct.[53] Somehow, this did not grind the defendant down into accepting a plea (itself delayed by a year).

But not all litigants have such fortitude; many give up entirely, while others settle on less-than-ideal terms.

Assuming the litigants survive the delays (some literally die during the wait), judges become more active, ruling on pretrial maneuvers that can dispose of cases ("dispositive motions," in law's pedestrian poetry). Again, though, measured as a fraction of cases, these events are rare because the system disfavors them. In federal civil suits, plaintiffs need only set out a complaint that offers a "short and plain" statement of their case, which competent lawyers can usually manage.[54] From there, defendants can ask the court to dismiss the suit based on some fatal flaw—a prime example being that the plaintiff failed to state a valid claim for relief.*[55] However, even if a case seems weak, there's frequently no point in attempting a motion to dismiss, as the law essentially forbids skepticism by assuming (at this stage) that facts alleged by the plaintiff are true. Defendants bow to the system's preferences and in one sample, only one-sixteenth of cases saw a motion to dismiss for failure to state a claim, though when brought—usually because a case was obviously dead on arrival—around three-fourths of these motions were granted in whole or part.[56] Nevertheless, plaintiffs normally get a chance to repair their claims, and many do, so few cases risk death at this stage. Arguably, more should; I once saw litigation based on the plaintiff's contention that he had invented the toothbrush sometime around 1996 (the first toothbrush was invented in the Tang dynasty, circa the eighth century AD), which took longer to resolve than common sense might suggest. To help trim the lunatic fringe, the Supreme Court tightened pleading standards in 2007–2009, forbidding conclusory and implausible allegations, but the effects were fairly modest in absolute terms.

As the case unfolds, the parties exchange information, a process called discovery. Litigants bicker every step of the way, because discovery is invasive, expensive, disruptive, and frequently inconclusive—colonoscopy by

---

* For example, if a plaintiff alleges wrongful conduct, but fails to allege that the conduct harmed him, there's no claim; this sort of omission is readily avoidable.

paperwork. The general posture of judges toward discovery disputes is that of the weary parent chaperoning siblings who should be old enough to figure out how to share. What judges often fail to appreciate at an intuitive level is that discovery rulings can adjust economic contours so radically as to force one or another side into settlement. The dramatic inflation in legal fees renders the costs of litigation viscerally incomprehensible to judges who left private practice even a decade ago; costs aside, most judges and litigators, having never been in-house counsels, also have no idea of the organizational disruption these fishing expeditions create. Discovery disputes deserve the same probity and effort given to dispositive motions (which get more attention, because they are "sexy"). Yet, many judges consider discovery matters tawdry and insignificant, offloading them to clerks, magistrates, special masters, fate—anywhere, really, besides their own persons. When courts do resolve discovery disputes, orders can be so cursory and formulaic (often relayed during a conference call) that it's reasonable to question if thought was involved at all.

If the parties soldier through discovery, they may ask the judge to resolve the case through a motion for summary judgment. The original purpose of summary judgment was to speed up litigation (judgment was supposed to be *summary*). The experiment didn't work; use was less frequent than it could have been, because the standards evolved to heavily favor allowing cases to proceed, except when the claims were palpably unsupported. Anyway, of the roughly one-fifth of cases in which the procedure is invoked, many summary judgment motions are brought with the purposes of *slowing down* litigation, so that disputatious parties can test their opponents' cases on paper before proceeding to trial.[57] Some claims do expire in summary judgment, but if enough economically viable claims survive (as they often do), the judge will set a trial date for some point in the hazy future. If litigants eventually try the case, things unfold as on TV, albeit with less drama and many more mistakes. The jury reaches its results, which the loser may ask the judge to set aside, though success here is rare. (It does happen in special circumstances: until 2017, Alabama judges were permitted to impose death sentences over jury objections, and did so surprisingly often.[58]) From there, parties either accept the result or file an appeal.

The classic image of the trial judge is of the great arbiter, carefully deciding cases after secluded contemplation. The reality is more prosaic and ad hoc. In the few instances in which judges can formally decide a case, the law strongly counsels against doing so and reserves the right to review any decisions that buck the trend. By contrast, trial judges pay far less attention in the areas where they have near-plenary powers to shape litigation. Discretion in managing dockets, deciding discovery motions, and resolving evidentiary questions at trial is almost unlimited, and appeals courts show little interest in questioning trial courts' decisions. From a systemic view, these matters are deemed second-class, and command no interest, produce no fame, and provoke no lapidary opinions—and in many cases, no opinion at all. It's perverse that the areas in which trial judges have the greatest discretion to do good command the least attention. Then again, trial judges don't command much attention. Just look at the credits on legal dramas: judges are always listed as "extras."

Trial judges are like Greek household gods, critical to the household but of little importance outside it. Appellate judges are something else: law's Olympians, able to influence populations far larger than two squabbling litigants in a local courthouse. These are the judges on whom senators, public interest groups, law professors, and reporters lavish their attention. The essential questions about appellate judges are not whether or what they decide—eventually, every flavor of issue will reach some appellate court—the questions are how they decide and why.

From a mechanical perspective, appellate judges customarily decide by signed, written opinion—one of the great norms of modern legal systems.

Written, published opinions promote accountability and force their authors to justify decisions by name, which tends to improve quality of thought.* What these opinions do not fully illuminate is *why* the judge reached that decision. Again, in a system that presumes lawyers can justify any position, opinions only assure us that reasons exist for a given conclusion, without necessarily proving that those reasons were the best available, or even genuinely held. But the opinions are reasonable evidence and, combined with what we know of judges and clerks, corroborate the two major models for judicial decision-making: the formalist and the realist, or in lay terms, the traditionalist and the freewheeler.[59]

The traditionalist, represented by Roberts's robot-umpire, emphasizes precedent and pattern matching. If a tennis ball lands smack on the line: Is it good or is it out? The traditionalist scours the archives to see if some higher and prior authority has decided the issue; if the Supreme Court has ruled that a ball falling on the line is out, case closed. Only when the case presents true novelties does the traditionalist begin to think for himself. This second, and more laborious, step is frequently unnecessary. First, most cases are not novel—humanity is repetitive in its errors and disputes. Second, traditionalists are Ecclesiastical by nature, and rarely see anything truly new under the sun, only variations on fundamental patterns. So even if the case law on foul balls deals exclusively with baseball games, traditionalists may disregard the distinction as insufficiently significant. They see two balls, two lines, and one analogy. Only in the most unusual circumstances does the traditionalist take out a fresh sheet of paper—or to put it more accurately, does he admit to doing so.

---

*   In recent years, many courts have increased their use of the *per curiam* opinion, which omits authorship information and was formerly reserved for trivial cases, but now extends to some important cases. This reduces accountability and transparency; the trend is not good. Notably, the Second Circuit—traditionally, one of the most intellectually prestigious Circuits—rarely issues per curiam decisions. The Fourth, Fifth, Sixth, and Eleventh Circuits are fairly heavy users of per curiam decisions. Many Circuits have also taken to the practice of not "publishing" their decisions; the opinions are available to read, but cannot be used as precedent. The unpublished per curiam decision, therefore, risks being a garbage disposal for less intellectually confident courts.

By contrast, the freewheeler starts with the facts, forming an impression of what a just result might be. The ball lands on the line, but perhaps tennis is too different from baseball, or perhaps the line has been drawn crookedly, or new regulations have made the line much narrower than it was, or the penalty for a bad ball has risen from a yellow flag to death by guillotine: Given these facts, what would be the just call? Context supplies the answer. Unless there's controlling opinion clearly foreclosing that answer, the fair result will be backward-justified, since all judges acknowledge that precedent has at least some value (even if only as window dressing). In external form, the result may appear to be purely traditionalist, adorned with citations and deference to precedent, even though the outcome was achieved before precedent was fully consulted. It's not hard to cobble together plausible opinions this way, because modern databases can obligingly produce cases standing for almost any proposition. Nor, if the judge is wise, should this judicial model be particularly alarming, since *the whole point* of judging is to achieve a just result. From here, I'll call this the "Posnerian" model, after the former Seventh Circuit judge Richard Posner, who described variants of this process as his modus operandi in some cases.[60]

Both models credibly describe how judges decide. Indeed, both models may be *simultaneously* credible. To take an absurd example (a favorite tactic in judicial opinions), let's say the Supreme Court has dealt with a dozen cases on tennis matches, issuing some blood-and-thunder opinions about how Americans have a Constitutional right to speedy tennis, and thus all questionable balls will be deemed immediately out of bounds without further investigation, penalty set at $5. The traditionalist, confronted with a ball that lands partly on the line, will duly assess the $5 penalty. The Posnerian will do the same, because even if the line has been crudely drawn or the relevant law treats a different sport, various jurisprudential values—legal clarity, consistency, and so on—vastly outweigh whatever injustice attaches to a $5 penalty. These sorts of easyish cases make up a lot of legal work, but if they were all that judges dealt with, there would be no books about judicial philosophy.

Closer cases are more interesting. They're also more important, precisely because precedent provides no obvious outcome (or in cases like *Brown*, because the mechanical outcome—segregation now, segregation forever— would be crazy to follow). But it's likely that the traditionalist and the Posnerian resolve many hard cases the same way, given the influence of clerks and politics. Consider the traditionalist judge, bound by precedent but reliant on clerks to rummage up the salient case law. The traditionalist's clerks, knowing their boss's predilections and being eager to please, may treat their judge as a special kind of client, sifting the archives (consciously or unconsciously) in ways designed to flatter their judge's perceived ideology. In such cases, clerks' bench memos and draft opinions may *seem* to be necessary results of precedent, without actually being so. Unless a judge knows the relevant area well (less likely in novel circumstances) or undertakes exhaustive personal research (less likely still), the judge might never detect his clerk's motivated reasoning; the traditionalist's result may be Posnerian by different procedure. The key difference between the ostensible traditionalists and Posnerians is that the latter *realize* what they're doing and it's their judicial wisdom—not some clerk's mental map of his boss's political philosophy— that decides the case.* The Posnerian model gives traditionalists the hives, but to repeat what should be obvious to the robot-umpires, isn't *judiciousness* why we have judges?

Whatever methods different judges use (and even a single judge may use different methods in different cases), appellate judges always have their logic tested. Unlike trial judges, appellate courts work as panels, affording colleagues a chance to push back. A clerk's desire to please is greatly outweighed by a desire not to embarrass. Clerks may work unduly hard to undermine

---

* Another category of judge is the rogue. Going rogue is rare, and is usually confined to specific issues; the Ninth Circuit's Judge Stephen Reinhardt had strongly liberal inclinations in certain criminal and immigration matters and simply ruled as he saw fit, whatever the precedent. Despite being overturned by the Supreme Court frequently and *unanimously*, Reinhardt remained defiant, allegedly chirping that "they can't catch them all."

disfavored precedents or overstate their bosses' preferred positions, but they will not omit important precedents and contrary arguments for fear of being caught out. Intra-panel competition improves judicial rigor, but the existence of panels hardly guarantees perfect and ideology-free results. In a simplified world of two homogenous political parties, one party always dominates every three-judge panel—and the greater the domination, the more one might expect partisanship. There are suggestions this occurs.

Whatever the method, are the results any good? The fact that decisions can be appealed and reversed provides a tempting means to evaluate. But great care should be taken, as most cases involve too many factors to succumb to simpler statistical analyses. A reversal here and an affirmation there may not be comparable. Even the most basic statistics can mislead: in treating the Supreme Court as the final word in correctness, a casual examination might suggest that federal appellate judges are nincompoops. When President Trump and his proxies condemned the Ninth Circuit for questioning his travel ban, they made this and other errors. Trump attacked the Ninth as being "overturned at a record number," while Sean Hannity called it the "most overturned" court in the country.[61] (The "record," not that it means much, is a 100 percent reversal/vacation rate for cases taken, achieved by various circuits at various times.[62]) These sorts of attacks conflate reversal rates with total "error" rate, and use a small, biased sample: the Court takes few cases (well fewer than 2 percent of those on offer) and overturns a lot of what it does take.[63] Thus, between 1999 and 2008, for example, even the "best" circuit (the Seventh Circuit) was countermanded 55.3 percent of the time, while the "worst" (the Federal Circuit, which focuses on specialist matters like patents and suits against the government) was set back 83 percent of the time.[64] High reversal rates are normal: the Court, which controls its docket, often takes cases it *wants* to reverse. Unlike lower courts, the Court doesn't have to waste time on "jobs well done." These numbers aren't terribly meaningful, whatever Trump says.

Looking at circuit courts, which must review all issues ready for appeal, reversals of district courts run under 10 percent.[65] That seems encouragingly low, reflecting few mistakes, though arguably the rate is *too* low. Again, context matters. Except for pure questions of law, which are reviewed from scratch, appeals courts strive not to second-guess trial courts (though second-guessing would seem, to the layperson, to be the function of appellate courts). This reluctance manifests in forgiving standards of review, e.g., reversing when a trial court "abused its discretion." Applying this standard in a meaningful way requires practical knowledge of what factors really matter in trial litigation, information that many appellate judges do not possess, having never been trial judges or litigants. For example, most litigants would see chaotic and dilatory case management as "abuses of discretion," but appellate courts generally do not. Instead, they hold that the trial judge's discretion to manage his courtroom being "broad," mismanagement should be overlooked save when it has been so gross as to void a core right (there being, by implication, no freestanding right to *efficient* litigation).[66] Appellate courts, focused on grander legal questions, apply the forgiving "abuse of discretion" standard to trial judges' conduct that can prejudice a case more deeply and permanently than many purely legal errors: not only case management, but many evidentiary rulings, the scope of cross-examination, admission of expert testimony, breadth of discovery, and even judicial recusal in some circumstances.[67]

Appellate courts can bend in other ways to accommodate lower courts. If a trial court disqualifies a party's lawyer—hardly a minor matter—that order will stand if it has "*any* sound" basis. Even if a court abused its discretion in the colloquial sense (say, by changing a verdict form after submitting the original to the jury), appellate courts will stand aside if the error is "harmless." Sometimes deference will be granted, even when the consequences can be significant, as when courts opine on the reliability of a witness before jurors—conduct that will not be questioned absent "*clear error.*"[68] Leaving aside some legal niceties, the net result is that, in many contexts, appellate courts only intervene when the judge has essentially gone bananas, and even then, some trespasses may be forgiven so long as they are "non-prejudicial" or have any "plausible" basis (even if not well articulated by the trial court itself). The official theory is that the trial judge, immersed in the proceedings, should be free of Monday morning quarterbacking. The central exceptions to these rules involve purely legal questions, though most appeals on these grounds must wait until the complete resolution of the trial case, or when a failure to intervene obviously risks destroying a litigant's legal ability to continue. The standard justification for this posture of delayed intervention is that constant appellate course-corrections would bog down trial courts and encourage wasteful appeals. Assuming this is true, and that a quick course-correction before lengthy proceedings would not expedite matters, the appellate justification still remains questionable. After all, it's more an argument about achieving *judicial* efficiency rather than justice or truth (inverting judicial rhetoric and practice) and may even undermine just results, since trudging through the full hoopla of trial may exhaust litigants' resources and preclude appeals, even appeals that might be winners.

Human Error

Mistakes happen; the existence of appellate courts concedes as much. Judges, though they labor to seem otherwise, are only people. They are prey to the same cognitive biases as other people—e.g., confirmation bias (seeing what they want to see), anchoring bias (overreliance on certain bits of information), the blind spot bias (a bias that keeps people from seeing bias), and, especially, overconfidence bias (having bought into their own Solomonic mythology).[69] Judges even get "hangry," or at least tired: a small study of Israeli judges showed that they granted 65 percent of parole requests at the start of a session, dropping to almost zero by the end of the sitting, but after a snack break, judges returned to almost the same levels of leniency that prevailed in the clement afterglow of breakfast.[70] Judging requires sustained attention to detail, often furnished by people who are boring (the lawyers), aggravating (both lawyers and litigants), or just plain crazy. With sittings dragging on for hours, the carnival can be more tedious than mortals can bear. Until the robots take over, courts should make the same concessions to biology that industrial organizations do. Bathroom and snack breaks would be quick and near-costless means to improve justice.

Other reforms may be impracticable, and of these, the greatest challenge is to recompose an unhelpfully homogeneous judiciary. On conventional metrics, the judiciary appears to have made progress, with race and gender becoming somewhat more balanced. Until the 1970s, the federal bench was near universally white, male, and Protestant; today, it's about a quarter non-white, a third female, and religiously mixed (including many non-religious judges, though seemingly none on the Supreme Court).[71] Overall, judges of different ethnic and gender backgrounds reach generally similar results (as one would hope), so a more diverse bench may not change many legal outcomes. However, black judges seem to be more amenable to certain voting rights and affirmative action claims, and black judges appear—make of this what you will—somewhat more likely to be reversed (though race alone may not be the variable doing the most work here; partisan affiliation seems important).[72] Even so, what exceptions exist are no more than modest. Regardless, greater diversity would improve perceptions of judicial legitimacy. As courts better resemble the communities they judge, people might become more likely to obey—reason enough to celebrate diversity.

"Conventional diversity" is not, however, the greatest compositional problem facing the judiciary—age and vocational uniformity are. Judges are increasingly old, and this is now a serious problem. While much was made of the shift since the Reagan Administration of appointing younger judges to ensure long legacies, the aggregate impact has been mixed. Federal judges remain late-middle-aged when appointed, on average fifty, though once emplaced, they prefer to stay forever: the mean age of sitting federal judges has been increasing faster than life expectancy and half of active circuit judges are over sixty-five (and sixty-one for district court judges) and for all judges, the average is approaching seventy.[73] Part of this is attributable to "senior status," which allows older judges to remain on the bench, but with reduced caseloads. But a reduced caseload is still a caseload, and senior trial judges collectively manage almost a fifth of all cases.[74] By definition, these judges are at an age where fatigue and cognitive decline become real considerations. At least senior status partly acknowledges this, though no judge is compelled to take it, and many "active status" judges linger on well past normal retirement age.

Judicial aging will almost certainly get much worse, as the preferred method of leaving the bench is in a casket. Depending on the year, 55 to 80 percent of judges who leave the bench do so by dying, and this reluctance to officially retire, combined with longer life expectancies, will move the federal bench from old to ancient.[75] By 2010, several judges were well into their 90s (thus, born while the Model T was still in production), and Judge Wesley Brown was still serving—at 104—before he died in 2012.[76] Some elderly judges remain quite good; indeed, the two sharpest judges in the courthouse I briefly worked in were quite old (though given to prolonged, silent immobility, which caused bemusement and unease in our craven, 20-something eyes, worried that these judges had expired mid-hearing). But there's no regime to ensure this.*

Intellectual and vocational diversity are also in sharp decline. A key advantage of an appointed (rather than career) judiciary should be diversity of background, especially in a system in which courts have general jurisdiction and hear all manner of cases. Until the late 1970s, judges had comparatively varied backgrounds. Today, most federal trial judges are appointed directly out of public sector legal jobs. About 15 percent were public lawyers (frequently prosecutors), but the greatest shift is that almost half of federal trial judges are appointed directly from another judgeship (a lesser federal judgeship, like a magistracy, or from state courts).[77] Likewise, half of federal appellate judges had been judges before.[78] The trend is toward a de facto

---

* While running the Seventh Circuit, Judge Easterbrook was vigilant about his colleagues' acuity and encouraged testing, pushing some judges to take senior status, retire, or have their dockets focused on less serious matters. All chief judges should follow his lead, but most have not.

career judiciary, albeit one that lacks the advantages of formal training and apolitical advancement that characterize foreign career judiciaries. It's not the worst of all worlds, but it's not the best.

Career trial judges have most notably displaced candidates from private law, who were mainstays of the mid-twentieth-century nominee pool.[79] While most of today's trial judges worked for a law firm at some point, their tenures tend to have been shorter and their experiences further distant, than those of private lawyers appointed sixty years ago. As a result, modern judges have less intuition for the dynamics of private practice. What private lawyers are appointed today are usually ex-litigators, not the corporate and regulatory attorneys who supervise the work underlying much of modern litigation—and we saw the consequences of judicial misapprehensions about bureaucracies in the last chapter. Judges with business or STEM backgrounds are also rare, though many civil cases are about nothing but business, and most IP and criminal cases turn on technical evidence.* The risks of misunderstanding can be great. So can the level of sheer disinterest: the broader financial sector accounts for about 10 percent of GDP, yet the Court takes relatively few banking, insurance, or securities cases, and the quality of its efforts in these arenas is, to put it politely, mixed.[80]

The decline in curricular diversity is most noticeable and consequential at the Court, which once attracted an astounding variety of talents. Save Kagan, today's Justices were all appointed directly from the judiciary, and while they are near uniformly intelligent and capable, their prior careers were overwhelmingly judicial/academic.[81] It would be helpful to add other talents to the mix. Much of the Court's work depends on parsing statutes and assessing legislative mechanics, but ex-legislators are rare on any courts, and the Supreme Court has not included a former legislator since O'Connor retired in 2006. The Court also routinely evaluates the workings of the executives and federal agencies (and tacitly considers merits of litigated policies),

---

* The exception here is the Federal Circuit, which deals with patent matters and has several judges with relevant experience.

so Justices with pertinent experience would help. But the Supreme Court has not included any truly major public executive in many years, though many significant politicians once made historic Justices: Earl Warren (thrice governor of California); Charles Evans Hughes (governor of New York, U.S. secretary of state); Robert H. Jackson (attorney general); Harlan Fiske Stone (same); Arthur Goldberg (secretary of labor); William Taft (president); John Marshall (secretary of state); etc.[82] Although no one sensible wants a politicized Supreme Court, we have one all the same, so it might as well include some seasoned politicians with firsthand knowledge about the other branches.

Vocational concentration across all courts produces gaps in institutional knowledge, against which the legal system provides no real safeguards. Clerks rarely have practical experience in fields other than law, and can't do much to correct judicial misapprehensions about, say, commodity derivatives or semiconductor lithography. Litigators also have almost exclusively legal backgrounds, and might not notice judicial mistakes about accounting standards, DNA evidence, or legislative intent. And all lawyers may experience a certain *déformation professionnelle*, as the French call it—a tendency to view things solely through the eyes of their own profession. Corporate lawyers, for instance, often neglect the economic substance of a contract; judges do the same. There are exceptions, of course, like Delaware's corporate-oriented Court of Chancery. Even if Delaware hiked taxes, corporations would still be happy to make their home in Wilmington if for no other reason than that— unlike almost every other state—Delaware has laws that reflect corporate realities and judges who are expert in business matters. There's a demand for diverse, substantive background; it just goes mostly unsatisfied.

The bench also further homogenizes judges by abstracting them from the world evolving outside chambers. England furnishes one of the more amusing collisions of age, privilege, and insularity. In *Sutton v. Hutchinson*, a case alleging underpayment for services, Ms. Hutchinson, lately of the Spearmint Rhino, appealed to the Royal Courts of Justice, where Lord Justice Ward ventured: "The appellant is a lap dancer. I would not, of course, begin to know exactly what that involves. One can guess at it, but could not faithfully describe it."[83] Fortunately, the trial judge had helpfully recorded that "the purpose" of a lap dancer "is to tease but not to satisfy."[84] One need not patronize the Rhino (or entirely buy Lord Ward's schtick) to realize that judges are perhaps a little distant from regular life, especially its baser aspects—though it is, of course, base impulses that land people in court. In any event, this is a trans-Atlantic phenomenon: during the Supreme Court's mid-century obscenity cases, Justice Harlan, partially blind and insulated from normal life, was forced to have Justice Stewart (or their clerks, depending on the teller) narrate the proceedings in porno flicks.[85] ("By George, extraordinary!" appears to have been Harlan's repeated refrain.)

All very droll, but these anecdotes reflect a serious discontinuity from real life and the community mores that judges police. A Court that still communicates by hand-delivered paper memo can have limited feel for how the unrobed masses use email, what expectations of privacy they have, and what search or discovery standards ought to be.[86] The blunders are especially evident in oral argument. Cell phones, for example, appear to perplex some Justices. Though cell phones have been in wide use for a quarter-century, they seem as mysterious to judges as jet planes would have been to John Marshall. During oral arguments, Justices have asked fairly basic questions about cell phones.[87] The social aspects of these devices apparently confounded Roberts and Scalia, both of whom wondered why anyone might have multiple cell phones, intimating that an outlandish profusion of (two) devices could suggest criminal behavior.*[88] Here, all the interpretations are odd: (1) Roberts had forgotten that normal working humans often have two phones;

---

* To get your blood pressure up, here's the exact colloquy:
Roberts: Why would he have two cell phones?
Attorney: Many people...have multiple cell phones.
Roberts: Really? What is—what is your authority for the statement that many people have multiple cell phones on their person?
Attorney: Just observation....
Well, Justice Roberts, what's *your* authority that one cell phone is "normal"? Is it "just observation"? In the interests of bipartisanship, Breyer joked that he didn't know what kind of phone he had, or how to unlock it. Or seemed to joke: that it's not clear says a lot.

(2)(a) Roberts has one government-issue cell, and uses it for work and personal calls; (2)(b) Roberts uses his personal, unsecured cell for work calls (risking government information); or (3) Roberts has no cell (and thus lives under a very lonely rock). To this we could add (4), that President Trump, who has multiple cell phones, is presumptively suspicious, though Trump is what older lawyers would call an "aggravated case."

Comic or sinister, the larger point of this abstraction from technology-in-reality is that laws on searches, seizures, privacy, etc., frequently turn on communities' "reasonable" expectations. Age and isolation leave judges less capable of making that assessment competently. As late as 2014, Scalia intimated he knew of no one with multiple cell phones and the transcript records "laughter," when the correct response should have been "awkward silence" or "muted gasps."[89] (Also, his friend Justice Ginsburg has two, and probably has for a while, given that one of them is a BlackBerry.[90]) Younger lawyers have their favorites: Sotomayor's "*the* iDrop" (a conflation of Dropbox and iCloud and adding the fogeyish definite article); Scalia's worries about people ripping HBO off the airwaves (not realizing that HBO is not broadcast); Kennedy's bucolic view of coding (musing that "any computer group of people" might churn out code); and Roberts's bafflement at technological complexity (describing intellectual property as complex, because it involved "a lot of arrows"); and on and on.[91]

The Justices are the most abstracted from real life, but many appellate judges hardly do better. Trial judges, confronted with daily life, are reasonably tethered—but unlike appellate judges, trial judges rarely make the law, and I've certainly litigated before some whose technological grasp was grandparental, at best. The laws of privacy, police searches, big data, artificial intelligence, and especially free speech, are all affected by new technologies and social expectations—and judges may not have the experience to decide wisely.

A judge does not have to be an electrical engineer to appreciate the role of technology in society, but judges should lead lives in which technology plays something like its normal role. Cloistered judges may not understand, at an emotionally profound level, how important new technologies are, with harmful consequences to emerging technologies and the economic growth and communities they foster.* Half of the average user's social media posts probably violate privacy, libel, emotional distress, and related laws as currently construed. What will judges do about that? Will they hold teenagers accountable for "publishing" deliberately unflattering comments about friends or make a codefendant of Facebook over noxious posts? How about Twitter: Is #fakenews libel per se?† What will judges make of Bitcoin—are crypto-users so alien that they must, like people with two cell phones, be potential accessories to money laundering and drug running? We'll find out. The Old Ones will let us know.

The judicial office also promotes an unhealthy level of arrogance and secrecy.[92] Justice requires humility, but the whole apparatus of servility fosters a sense of infallible righteousness. Justice also requires openness. It's one thing to be discreet, which the judiciary is—commendably, of all government institutions from the CIA to the White House, the judiciary leaks least. But discretion does not require a code of absolute silence. Judicial culture is far too paranoid about its workings, with some judges embargoing lunch menus in the belief that the future of free speech could be divined from some judge's choice of salad dressing. Worse, even lawful whistleblowing doesn't happen, so that misconduct and intellectual decline go largely unreported. The long-overdue revelations about Alex Kozinski provided an especially

---

* In 1984, the VCR almost died a legal death, potentially tanking the content revolution, from videotapes to peer-to-peer. Sony, a device manufacturer (of Betamax recorders, then VCRs), caught a break—barely. The studios' legal argument was complicated (because Sony was not a direct infringer and the case implicated the First Amendment) and Sony benefited greatly from the intervention of…Mr. Rogers; even so, Sony's victory was just 5–4. Arguably, the Court did a corresponding disservice in 2014's *ABC v. Aereo*, which held Aereo liable for time-shifting cable broadcasts; the company died. And it was at this time that Breyer was fretting about a service that might one day store and share vast amounts of music—a non-hypothetical called Spotify, founded in 2008.

† Libel per se is a public written statement that comments negatively about, among other things, a person's ability to competently carry out its professional duties—applied to the *New York Times* by an exiled White House minion, #fakenews is libelous per se, legally defensible only by recourse to the First Amendment as interpreted by activist and "so-called" judges. Who knew law, like health care, could be so hard?

depressing reminder.[93] Kozinski may or may not be an outlier, but the culture of secrecy means we can never really know. Indeed, for our most important courts, we cannot easily *see* their ostensibly public workings, while the Court forbids cameras, even though C-SPAN has been televising Congress's workings for forty years and the press corps has been stalking the West Wing for a century. The judiciary should be beyond political account, but it shouldn't be invisible. Extreme secrecy only fuels the already powerful conspiracy theories about activist and unaccountable judges. After all, in the TV age, only two types of people have their likenesses publicized by chalk sketch: the FBI's Most Wanted and the Justices.

State court judges have been a mixed bag from the start, and until judicial elections are reformed, or voters take a greater interest down-ballot, state benches will remain extremely uneven. Federal judges are different. For almost a century, they have been among the best members of the legal system. Nothing guarantees that they will remain so. The benefits of life tenure are being eroded by extreme longevity and associated decrepitude. Many countries avoid this problem by imposing fixed terms (judges of Germany's highest courts serve twelve-year terms) and/or mandatory retirement ages. Even other Anglophone countries, enchanted by backwardness, find ways to ease out judges with comparative facility. And English-speaking or otherwise, most nations screen judges more rigorously from appointment onward.

The Constitution makes it hard for judges to change life tenure systemwide (though they could interpret the Constitution's "good behavior" requirement to forbid drooling senility). Judges can, however, self-police and foster a culture in which retirement is the rule, not the exception. Judicial leaders should also address the growing divergence between judicial pay and private sector compensation, which in the next two decades will become unsustainably large, at least for lawyers in their prime. Presently, the gap is narrow enough for the considerable prestige of federal judgeship to bridge, but judicial prestige, as with the prestige of all government work, is in secular decline. Judges should ask for better pay and get it. They should also rely less on their clerks, impose a proper training regime, take court management seriously, and urge executives to make more intellectually diverse appointments.

The rule of law depends on a strong judiciary, which in turn depends on the respect of the governed. The magic works only so long as the flock is prepared to believe that the magicians are worthy of the gift. By failing to enact adequate institutional safeguards and conducting a torrid affair with an untenable mythology, the judiciary promotes weaknesses whose consequences travel beyond any single courtroom. The effects, however, have been rather grimly mitigated by the arrival of private adjudication—the Blackwater to the judiciary's geriatric Green Berets.

CHAPTER SEVEN

ARBITRATION: PRIVATIZED JUSTICE

> Do I believe in arbitration? I do. But not in arbitration
> between the lion and the lamb, in which the lamb is in
> the morning found inside of the lion.
>
> Samuel Gompers[1]

The most famous judge in America isn't a judge: she's an arbitrator. Judy Sheindlin—aka Judge Judy—presides over America's top syndicated TV program.[2] *Judge Judy* promises "real people" and "real cases" and delivers just that, because to appear on the show, contestant-litigants must agree to let Sheindlin conduct binding arbitration of their disputes. Sheindlin's syndicated parade of dysfunction has aired since 1996, meaning that Judge Judy has been in her seat longer than Justices Kavanaugh, Gorsuch, Kagan, Sotomayor, Alito, and Roberts have been in theirs (and nearly as long as Breyer and Ginsburg). Besides extraordinary tenure, Sheindlin has resolved far more cases (at least 6,000) than the Court has over the same period and attracts a considerably larger audience than even the most popular Justice (the Notorious RBG).[3] In shaping America's impression of civil litigation, Judge Judy's only real peer is the pioneering Judge Wapner of *The People's Court*, the John Marshall of the boob tube.

It would be fun to give *Judge Judy* the full Barthes/Derrida treatment, "interrogating" mythologies, analyzing signifiers and signified, and deconstructing all around. There's the psychodrama of Sheindlin's ex-husband succeeding Wapner on *The People's Court*. There's also Sheindlin's own legal history, including various lawsuits ranging from grimly prosaic allegations of bias to oddballs such as a $500,000 suit over Sheindlin's alleged theft of tableware. And then, of course, there's the meta-issue of the show *itself* requiring that any disputes about its workings to be resolved by arbitration (understandable given the cutlery suit). *Judge Judy* provides material enough for dissertation-level fireworks about the show-as-portent-of-legal/cultural-collapse, sure to guarantee tenure (at, let's be honest, Brown).[4] But if *Judge Judy* would entrance social studies departments, the legal elite prefers to overlook the gross spectacle entirely.

Nevertheless, *Judge Judy* demands something between overinterpretation and willful blindness, because the show offers a fundamentally truthful (if exaggerated) picture of the arbitration system, the giant parallel world of private justice. Arbitration is nothing more than a contractual arrangement to resolve cases by means faster, less formal, and less rigorous than court justice. *Judge Judy* does exactly that. The show's seemingly made-for-TV oddities very much feature in "real arbitration" (which, to repeat, *Judge Judy* legally is): low stakes, a glaring lack of procedural standards, disregard for written opinions, disconnection from precedent, and a narrow-minded focus on the case at hand without reference to notions of public policy or legal development. Of course, the show differs from mainstream arbitration in important ways, though surprisingly, usually for the *better*. *Judge Judy* resolves its cases swiftly, publicly, and mostly at its own expense; the contests are roughly equal; the parties knowingly consent to arbitration; and its mistress is a former judge of a real court. "Proper" arbitration cannot always say the same.

Judge Judy's greatest cultural significance is in embodying the migration of jurisdiction from public courts to private arenas. The shift has accelerated considerably since the 1980s, making actual mass arbitration synchronous with arbitration-television. Though the transition to privatized justice is well known to the professoriate, it commands little public notice. This is notwith-standing the fact that most Americans are party to an arbitration clause, often dozens of them, embedded in form contracts for everything from telephones to food delivery. What these clauses require, if invoked, is that the parties forgo normal civil court proceedings in favor of private resolu-tion before hired "judges." We are all potential contestants on the real-world equivalent of *Judge Judy*.

And rest assured, virtually everyone *has* signed arbitration agreements. If you shop on Amazon (as most households do), you are party to an arbitration agreement.[5] If you have a bank account, a credit card, maintain student loans, are employed by a large corporation, or use medical services, you are likely party to further arbitration agreements.[6] Essentially all cell-phone users are covered by arbitration clauses.[7] Not all financial firms use these clauses, but those that do tend to be large, so the clauses affect a disproportionate amount of economic activity. In a Consumer Financial Protection Bureau (CFPB) sample, arbitration clauses covered 44.4 percent of checking deposits and 53.0 percent of outstanding credit card loans, and 85.7 percent of the student loan contracts studied required arbitration.[8] Some 56.2 percent of nonunion private sector employees are subject to clauses, and larger employers were particularly likely (65.1 percent) to use these clauses.[9] Doctors, hospitals, and nursing homes have also discovered the pleasures of arbitration agreements. Not many consumers know that they are party to arbitration clauses, and fewer still truly understand what rights have been waived—perhaps less than 10 percent.[10]

These agreements, usually embedded deep in form contracts or online "conditions of use" essentially foreclose recourse to courts should you wish to sue a wayward counterparty. That corporations very much want you to relinquish court access can be inferred from the fact that General Mills seemingly tried to construe the mere act of opening a Cheerios box as "con-sent" to arbitration.[11] Though likely tenable as a matter of law (at least when coupled with a coupon), the Cheerios gambit collapsed due to freakishly bad publicity. But the Cheerios debacle notwithstanding, corporations continue pushing arbitration onto their customers and employees, upending the system of civil litigation.

This unseemly rush into arbitration, where every "I Accept" click or unscrewing of a toothpaste tube vaporizes access to public justice, raises some obvious questions. Why are corporations so eager to arbitrate—is arbitration *that* good, or are courts *that* bad? Why would courts acquiesce to diminishment of their social roles? What might be lost when justice migrates from public to private fora? Judges (driven by the conservative wing of the Supreme Court) and corporations have their answers ready, all premised on the speed, efficiency, and choice offered by arbitration, which they portray as an unalloyed good. The academic consensus runs the other way: the displacement of real courts represents a catastrophe, especially for employees and consumers.[12] The academics generally have the better of the argument. Mass arbitration degrades the law. It also tilts outcomes, because if consumers and employees aren't guaranteed to *lose* in arbitration (though some groups make that claim), they certainly find it very difficult to really *win*.

Arbitration arose to serve specific purposes and remains a fair and useful mechanism for the kinds of disputes that occasioned its invention. To fully appreciate where modern mass arbitration went wrong, it's helpful to know why anyone ever wanted arbitration in the first place.

Arbitration—Early Successes

Before there were judges, there were arbitrators, people who helped members of their communities resolve disputes.[13] In many parts of ancient Europe, arbitrators allowed disputants to be heard and have their injuries addressed, preserving community harmony. Their methods were necessarily crude, and sometimes coercive, but so long as the community was preserved, the outcome was deemed good enough. Even as modern procedural machinery developed—the whole complex of lawyers, judges, courthouses, forms, and rules—the communitarian impulse behind arbitration remained. In many traditions, Islamic legalism being a prime example, arbitration remains esteemed for its ability to facilitate the sort of conciliation and comity that litigation's war-by-paperwork makes difficult.[14]

In other traditions, including Anglo-American law, which emphasized individualism, personal vindication, and procedural objectivity, communitarian justifications for arbitration were always weaker. Western courts arose partly because informal arbitration could not always serve these values, especially as disputes extended beyond a single community. As courts institutionalized, they naturally viewed arbitration as a relic: ad hoc, semi-literate barbarity rendered moot by progress. Judges also disliked arbitration because it threatened their monopoly on justice, and the political and social establishments that sponsored judges tended to agree. It helped that the late seventeenth century, when European courts really took off, was technophilic and understood courts as the latest word in doing justice: Why walk when you can ride; why arbitrate when you can litigate?

However, courts could not solve *every* case, and arbitration flourished in special circumstances. Merchant shippers, for example, had limited time ashore to deal with courts; their disputes involved arcane matters (as anyone with the misfortune to know a weekend sailor is aware); and their community was sufficiently self-policing that it could resolve cases without resort to the state. These factors, coupled with the transnational aspects of many maritime disputes, rendered courts unusually ill-suited—and sometimes jurisdictionally incapable—of providing help. Even the crustiest English lawyers appreciated that arbitration was a "civilized" and "normal" process in maritime use, and not the second-class "abhorren[ce]" that arbitration was in other contexts.[15]

Maritime arbitration persists, as does labor arbitration, which thrived after the Civil War. Again, circumstances all but demanded arbitration. Postbellum courts recoiled at forcing people to work, and did not savor the proto-socialist prospect of forcing capitalists to employ anyone. Most importantly, capital and labor often both wanted arbitration, and had the means to establish a fair system. The essential point is that early arbitration succeeded because it was specialized, and provided not just a cheaper product, but a *better* one.

By the early twentieth century, a final set of special circumstances arrived: the disarray of federal courts in an era where federal (i.e., interstate) commerce had become crucial. The federal courts sank into chaos, crippled by archaic rules; indeed, district courts lacked a unified code of civil procedure until 1938. For a time, *courts* felt second-class. Larger merchants and their lawyers pushed Congress to relax the judicial monopoly so that companies could avoid court hassles and be assured that arbitration clauses would be respected in the many states in which business was conducted.[16] In 1925, Congress passed a law (now known as the Federal Arbitration Act, or FAA) to help.[17] Just four pages long, no one expected that the FAA would reconfigure the entire legal system. Rather, Congress intended to make arbitration provisions binding in the sorts of classic, multi-jurisdictional commercial disputes long subject to arbitration, with the FAA's express reference to "maritime" disputes highlighting continuity with established practice.[18]

The FAA was a significant development, but one firmly rooted in conventional arbitral principles. Nothing in it seemed to augur a major break. The Act had been solicited by commercial interests that wanted a guarantee that they could reliably arbitrate among themselves; they did not ask for a mechanism to force arbitration on those outside their communities. Nor did the Act seem to propose anything so radical as modify the laws of contract generally, which were set by state courts and legislatures.[19] Indeed, it's doubtful the law's original drafters foresaw that the FAA would—or even could—reach into purely *intra*state matters. The general view at the time was that if Peoria slaughterhouses sold beef to a Chicago supermarket, any resulting dispute lay beyond the FAA. It was years *after* the FAA was passed that the Court developed the idea that essentially all commerce was "interstate commerce," allowing federal policy to override state law when Congress desired.[20] Moreover, the FAA hardly seemed to express any desire to intrude on the substance of commercial litigation.*[21] The courthouse doors remained open, and for some time, it was doubtful that any arbitration clause not wanted by both parties would shut those doors.

Indeed, courts could never be fully excised from deciding civil suits, a fact the FAA confirmed. The Act explicitly granted courts supervisory roles over arbitration and confirmed courts' longstanding powers to overturn biased, unhinged, or otherwise defective arbitral awards. Crucially, the FAA explicitly declined to modify existing contract law, leaving courts free to void arbitration clauses on grounds like unconscionability.[22] Those who read the FAA's text, and not subsequent case law, would not expect that strong parties could use the Act to force weaker parties (consumers, employees, etc.) into unfair arbitrations. Yet, that is precisely what has happened over the past thirty-five years. The blame can be leveled squarely at the Court, which rewrote the FAA in a series of momentous and ill-considered decisions.[23] These cases had little basis in the FAA's text, betrayed basic principles of statutory interpretation, and made daring assumptions about arbitration that proved largely untrue.

The Court's Arbitration Revolution

For decades, the Court generally left the FAA alone, before reversing course in 1984's *Southland*. In that case, the Court—without evidence—concluded that Congress declared a "national policy favoring arbitration" (dubious) and that the FAA "withdrew the power of the states to require a judicial forum for the resolution of claims which the contracting parties agreed to resolve by arbitration" (wrong).[24] Intriguingly, the majority opinion was politically mixed, and the strongest dissents came from conservatives O'Connor and

---

* Today, substantive laws intended by Congress to preempt state law may do so, but "procedural" laws (which the FAA arguably is) that express no desire to preempt (which the FAA does not) generally aren't read to override state law. Decades after the FAA's enactment, the Supreme Court decided that the FAA was preemptive.

Rehnquist, who criticized the majority's legal logic and worried that *South-land* would concentrate federal power at the expense of state sovereignty.

After *Southland*, the Court continued souping up the FAA until the power to compel civil arbitration was essentially absolute. Over the next thirty years, the Court overrode state laws, forced essentially noncontractual claims (like antidiscrimination suits based on statutes) into arbitration, made class-action arbitrations impracticable, and undermined every traditional defense to arbitration contracts. These developments may seem recondite, but they had enormous practical consequences for consumers and employees, who now find themselves stuck in arbitrations they don't want and to which they did not knowingly agree. The consequences for intra-corporate contests were more limited, as modern arbitration was designed for corporate disputes. In high-stakes matters, corporations also frequently reserve the right to litigate in normal courts or provide for arbitration procedures that, save for being conducted privately, substantially replicate conventional court practice.[25] As a result, the Court's arbitration jurisprudence meant that corporations could force weak opponents onto *Judge Judy*, while bigger players could treat themselves to Cadillac justice.

Modern Arbitration—Weakness as Strength

Because the Court's arbitration cases make little *legal* sense, they can only be justified by the policies they claimed to serve: freedom of contract, fairness, and efficiency. Forcing parties into arbitration, the Court mused, simply reflected the prior bargain made by the parties, would not be an unfair substitute for court proceedings, and would speed resolutions. None of the Court's policy arguments have withstood contact with reality, with grievous consequences for consumers and the judicial system the Court nominally leads.

Starting in reverse order, arbitration is not efficient for many parties. A process is only efficient if it generates a lot of product relatively cheaply.

The correct "product" should be justice, which many arbitrations can't produce, but then again, in many contexts, arbitration clauses don't even produce many *arbitrations*. For example, between 2009 and 2014, AT&T's wireless base ran between 85 and 120 million users.[26] Yet, over that same period, AT&T's wireless customers, bound by arbitration clauses, filed a mere 134 arbitrations against the company.[27] The same sort of calculations hold for credit card companies, banks, and the like: very few arbitrations.[28] "Efficiency" seems to be a term defined by the stronger party, translating to "quashes almost all legal action at almost no cost." If that's the efficiency the Court had in mind, it could just as easily void a criminal defendant's right to jury trial. (Actually, the Court's done just that, as we'll see.)

The counterargument is that consumers bring near-zero arbitrations against telecoms, card companies, and banks because they have no disputes with these companies. This defies common experience and consumer satisfaction surveys.[29] It also can't be reconciled with prosecutions brought by government. In 2017, government settled two suits against telecoms for "bill cramming" and unauthorized charges, one for $90 million against T-Mobile and another for $88 million against AT&T (which, recall, had endured just 134 piddling arbitrations filed against it in a five-year period). Rather gallingly, government-as-consumer sued Sprint, recovering $15.5 million because Sprint had overcharged for court-ordered wiretaps; not only had telecoms fleeced private customers, they had overcharged taxpayers to (legally) spy on them.[30] Government has also regularly sued financial firms, extracting gigantic settlements from institutions like Wells Fargo and Countrywide. One reason government brings suits against abusive businesses while consumers do not is that the government isn't bound by arbitration clauses and has the resources to prosecute mass wrongdoing in a way lone consumers cannot.

The Court's response reduces to let-them-eat-arbitration, even when arbitration can offer no practical relief. This is especially a problem in matters in which each individual wrong is small, but the collective harm large—i.e., class actions. While it's true that there's no *legal* barrier to commencing a solo arbitration against a cell phone company for $378 of fake charges, there's also no way to make a $378 arbitration economically viable. First, consumers would have to frame a complaint based on their cell contracts, and reading those contracts requires a lawyer's assistance at $500 an hour, as cell contracts are functionally unreadable by most of the population.*[31] Cell contracts are, one might suspect, even designed to deter comprehension and there is only a single documented case of a consumer reading one all the way through and understanding it. That person was Judith Resnik, a Yale Law professor, who loathes consumer arbitration in a way that makes Nabokov's hatred of Freud seem tepid. In a lather, Resnik once attempted to prove her point by not only reading a cellular contract, but attempting to *negotiate* one afresh. (Vendors declined.) But even if consumers read a contract, and could point to a potential breach of some provision within, that's not enough: consumers must then prove instances of overcharging, rummaging up bills and data stored within corporate archives, and perhaps some evidence that the cell carrier had a practice of overcharging. Doing so would take a skyscraper of Resniks—in other words, a Manhattan law firm. Consumers therefore face a non-choice: pay $500 per hour to litigate a $378 claim or find a lawyer who assigns such a low value to his time that the customary one-third contingency fee of $125.99 seems worth it.

This is a problem the law has seen before and solved. When individual stakes are low, but many people have suffered the same injury, law allows for the class-action suit. These suits aggregate plaintiffs and damages, making it economically viable for lawyers to participate. The Federal Rules of Civil Procedure expressly permit class actions, which is partly how tobacco and asbestos companies were brought to heel.[32] In theory, arbitration can accommodate class actions, though industry had a well-publicized disaster when

---

*   As of early 2018, the AT&T wireless contract ran to 19,345 words and had a Flesch-Kincaid score of 34, close to the point where it's comprehensible only to the roughly one-third of Americans with proper college educations. For context, the higher the score, the easier a document is to read—Flesch himself scored the *Harvard Law Review* at 32, and mass periodicals score in the 40s and 50s.

it conducted a class arbitration: after the Pacific Gas & Electric Company contaminated Hinkley, California's groundwater, residents sued and the cases went to arbitration. After the first batch of plaintiffs won $120 million, PG&E settled the first-wave cases for $333 million, and Steven Soderbergh made the story into *Erin Brockovich*.[33] Tobacco, asbestos, and groundwater suits involved claims external to contracts, but industry learned its lessons, and reinforced its arbitral armor: contracts banned class-action arbitrations, effectively eliminating court cases from large swathes of economic life.[34] Some observers thought this was overreaching, but in 2011, the Court upheld class-action waivers in arbitration contracts in a case against AT&T.[35] This must have been an easy case, for at least Chief Justice Roberts. Roberts had, after all, already briefed the class-waiver issue in his prior career as a private attorney, asking the U.S. Supreme Court to reconsider an inconvenient anti-arbitration ruling by a California court.[36] The Court declined. After Roberts joined the Court, it heartily embraced a more expansive view of arbitration. All Chief Justice Roberts had to do was make a little law, precisely the sort of thing that he testified judges *don't* do.

By shutting down class-action arbitrations, the Court functionally voided rights embodied in state and federal law, and in the Federal Rules of Civil Procedure. The net effect is that when disputes involve small amounts, corporations may safely extract extra dollars from consumers, facing judgment only in the comparatively infrequent cases in which they are sued directly by government watchdogs or convicted in the court of public opinion by media exposés. It's perhaps worse than that, as the Court suggested in 2012 that not only contract claims, but potentially *tort* claims, can be shoved into arbitration, which might derail future Erin Brockoviches. The pertinent case, involving allegedly fatal neglect in nursing homes, produced a brief opinion limited to pooh-poohing a West Virginia statute that forbade compelled arbitration of personal injury and wrongful death claims.[37] A regime that guts class actions and consigns abused (or dead) seniors to lopsided arbitrations may not, it's reasonable to say, be producing social goods with optimum efficiency.* But those sorts of goods and that sort of efficiency were not what the Court focused on when it began its torrid affair with arbitration.

What did worry the Court in the 1990s, as it busily expanded the arbitral frontier, was *judicial* efficiency. Chief Justice Rehnquist fretted that federal courts would soon be overrun by litigation.[38] Rehnquist accordingly asked Congress to build new courthouses and appoint new judges. His core tactic, however, was not to expand capacity, but to reduce throughput: he wanted *some* new judges, but *many fewer* cases. In 1991, the Chief urged Congress to reconsider its rapid federalization of criminal law, radically curtail inmates' ability to file federal habeas petitions, and greatly limit "diversity jurisdiction" cases (interstate disputes not premised on substantive federal law).[39] Some of these ideas were worthy, others callous, and all ideological hobbyhorses for Rehnquist, who preferred legal issues to be devolved to the states and stay there. They also reflected a serious, if ultimately misplaced, concern about rising judicial workloads.

Congress granted Rehnquist his new courthouses and largely ignored his other pleas, so Rehnquist engaged in self-help. He could do fairly little to unilaterally reduce the judiciary's criminal docket; the Constitution made that difficult. The *civil* docket was another matter, were the Court willing to set aside some legal principles in the name of the greater (or anyway, its own) good. The Court therefore made it much easier for parties to force each other into arbitration, and thus away from courts. It did so without any legal basis, as Rehnquist (circa 1981 to 1984) had himself pointed out.

As a practical, rather than ideological, matter, the gambit proved unnecessary: what Rehnquist didn't appreciate in 1991 was that federal court filings were in a bubble. The S&L crisis and criminal drug epidemic, which had driven so much federal litigation, would shortly peak. Litigation would soon return to growing roughly in line with population and GDP. The tangible

---

* I say this as a former defense litigator who found class-action firms (at least for securities litigation) to be the very lowest form of legal life. But even slime molds play important roles in the ecosystem.

result of Rehnquist's reforms was a series of overbuilt and frequently desolate new courthouses, wastes of taxpayer money made uglier by the architecture, done in a style charitably described as exurban Hyatt. The intangible result was a doctrinal shift toward arbitration. That, it turns out, was uglier still.

Arbitrators and Their Procedures

What made the intangible result so ugly was arbitration itself, because there were never any guarantees that nonjudicial fora would be just or effective. At its best, arbitration complements courts. But arbitration never substitutes for courts—because it can't. Critically, arbitrators cannot enforce anything; only state actors have coercive power. Should a party withhold documents or refuse to obey arbitral decisions, parties must return to court.*

The lack of state power is the only truly universal feature of arbitration. Beyond that, arbitrations can be as close to, or far from, normal court procedure as an arbitration clause requires. Arbitration clauses can exclude attorneys, curtail discovery, limit motion practice, require or forbid written reasons for judgment, constrain appeal, shift fees and costs, require proceedings to occur at the South Pole; whatever the (stronger) parties prefer. Only when the procedures selected are embarrassingly cursory or abusive are courts likely to intervene, and then only reluctantly. In one case, arbitrators failed to hold a preliminary hearing, set a discovery schedule, nor required parties to produce documentary evidence prior to the main event. This triggered a complaint to a federal district court, which refused to intervene, stating that these procedural defects did not constitute a viable claim.[40]

All American law suffers from underdeveloped structural safeguards, but the problem is especially acute in arbitration. Though, as we've seen, there are

---

* The absence of state power partly explains why arbitrations have no juries. Even if the corporate lawyers who draft arbitration clauses wanted juries (and they don't, because they believe juries favor the smaller parties), private arbitrators cannot force twelve citizens to sit around for $12 a day as courts can.

no mandatory requirements for being a federal judge, the confirmation process and attending publicity make for a pretty talented bench. And once on the bench, judges operate within standardized rules of procedure, conduct open hearings, and face reversal on appeal. No such checks apply to arbitrators, so the need to screen for talent and temperament is arguably far greater than it is for judges. Yet, as the Bureau of Labor Statistics notes, "[t]here is no national license for arbitrators," "[f]ew candidates receive a degree specific to the field of arbitration," and "a bachelor's degree is often sufficient."[41] Many states do not require certification or training for mediation/arbitration work; those that do often content themselves with training programs running twenty to sixty hours. Even some of the better voluntary certification courses, like those offered by USC ("one of the top 10 ADR programs in the world" per an industry rag), do not require candidates to have a law degree and advertise the brevity of their coursework—completable in "as few as two semesters," as one of USC's programs enthuses.[42]

Arbitration is almost entirely self-regulating, a characteristic denied to utilities, emergency rooms, and most other providers of social necessities. Arbitration firms, which range from tiny to giant, have equally variable standards. Standards at smaller firms can be extremely loose. Larger, more prestigious firms do pride themselves on having talented arbitrators (including former state court trial judges), but even the largest, most reputable firms, like the American Arbitration Association (AAA), allow non-lawyers with "senior-level" experience and "appropriate" degrees to become arbitrators.[43] As in most markets, some very good firms exist, including JAMS (f/k/a *Judicial* Arbitration and Mediation Services), a corporation founded by a judge, whose standing rules and procedures tend to follow normal court practices and which declines to preside over the sleazier sorts of arbitration, such as those that require adjudication in inconvenient places, discourage counsel, or eschew written decisions.[44] Notably, when corporations arbitrate among themselves, they prefer JAMS and its peers.

The singular advantage arbitrators have over judges is that many have significant subject matter knowledge; indeed, this was an original justification for maritime arbitration. For example, construction arbitrators know more about building codes, cement drying times, and architectural practice than the average judge. The degree of specialization can be astonishing: nested in AAA's seven major specialty areas exist many subspecialties, including practices as hyper-specific as Olympic athletes and sports doping (in fact, the U.S. Anti-Doping Agency has designated AAA as the primary venue for Olympic doping disputes).[45] For intercompany litigation, this can produce more knowledgeable decisions, especially when an arbitration panel includes experts in both subject matter and legal procedure.

However, the recycling of industry insiders into arbitrators raises the possibility of bias. Arbitrators who come from industry may unconsciously favor their old employers; a doctor-arbitrator may be far more skeptical about malpractice claims than, say, a tax lawyer. The evidence for this proposition is mixed, but the consequences may be the same regardless, because the fundamental problem is perceptual: a justice system *perceived* to be rigged suffers many of the same legitimacy deficits as one that is *actually* rigged. Moreover, it's easy to show that arbitrators always have at least some structural conflict of interest that judges do not, because arbitrators only get paid if a dispute is arbitrable. Somewhat oddly, "arbitrability" is an evaluation courts often allow *arbitrators* to make.[46] Courts view this bias as minor, since it's a bias toward arbitration as an institution, not "classic bias" like overtly favoring a particular side. That judicial logic is not persuasive, however, if arbitration systematically disfavors one class of litigants (and we have and will see that it does). If so, structural bias becomes the kind of bias courts normally disallow.

Because arbitration is confidential, rates of classic bias—corruption, favoritism, prejudice, and so on—are not fully knowable. We do have glimpses, however, when arbitrations enter the public record via subsequent public litigation, as when courts hear petitions to vacate arbitral judgments when arbitrators exhibit "evident partiality." As the ABA notes, these cases are "difficult to prove and rarely succeed."[47] They are hard to prove because there's no freestanding rule that arbitrators keep a complete record of the proceedings—or indeed, *any* record. As for success, the procedural barriers to overturning arbitration are so high that few challenges are brought and, seemingly, even fewer succeed.[48] But arbitrators do have conflicting interests, even if we don't know to what extent, and can't do much about it.

In real courts, litigants may move to disqualify a judge at almost any time.[49] In arbitration, litigants have only two opportunities to challenge bias, and the mechanisms are nonoptimal. The first chance is at arbitration's beginning. This is a weak protection, as there are no hard rules on what must be disclosed, conflicts are self-diagnosed, and "trivial" conflicts of interest don't necessarily disqualify.[50] Worse, this regime sterilizes bias challenges, since merely disclosing bias (even *actual* conflicts of interest) can foreclose remedial action, even if parties didn't read or understand the disclosures. After disclosure, bias cannot be challenged until arbitration concludes— even if, during the course of arbitration, it seems likely that a court *will* find bias.[51]

Clearly, in cases that must be relitigated due to bias, arbitration is less efficient than court proceedings—but excepting these outliers, is arbitration faster and cheaper than court? Generally, yes, for the same reasons that Greyhound buses are faster and cheaper than the *QE II*: fewer amenities. In commercial arbitrations involving larger sums, the median time between filing a demand and the rendering of award runs about 11.6 months, versus 24.2 months just to get to trial in district court.[52] Arbitral pace is even speedier compared to the busier district courts (e.g., New York's SDNY) and always-congested state superior courts.[53] Boosters of arbitration ice their cake by noting that arbitrations slice a further two years off the appeals process, though appeals are rare because there are so few grounds to appeal arbitration, so the pro-arbitration argument here is akin to a dietician commending amputation as an efficient means of weight loss.[54] As for legal savings, the same logic holds: less law practiced means lower legal bills overall. The dollar savings, while hard to quantify, are likely nontrivial. Arbitration can indeed save time and money, at the cost of process and thoroughness. For knowledgeable parties, especially those facing the prospect of multiyear litigation, this exchange may be attractive. If legal savings are large enough, arbitration can be rational, even if a party believes it has a much better chance in court. These are not arbitrations that should provoke much worry.

Arbitrations that *do* raise concerns include those that involve the numerically largest group of potential litigants: consumers and employees. For the many small-dollar cases that arbitration clauses make uneconomic, there is simply no litigation. Gains in speed and cost are ∞ percent (or mathematically undefined, to be precise), though this doesn't represent a true improvement. Were bloody-minded holders of small claims to arbitrate anyway, the process is genuinely fast. But small claims courts are also fast. These courts, which handle low-dollar cases (usually $10,000 and under, depending on state), dispense with baroque procedures, and by statute must conclude preliminaries (if any) quickly, before conducting a brisk trial (often thirty minutes, about as long as a *Judge Judy* episode); most cases are resolved in three or fewer months.[55] Even corporations, generally averse to full-scale litigation, seem to prefer small-claims courts, and it's standard for lenders to exclude small claims from arbitration waivers, as courts can more expeditiously enforce debt collection than arbitrators.

Arbitration's friends extend their argument by citing the economic gains—invariably gigantic—that arbitration offers. That contention withers under scrutiny. For the smaller claims that comprise most potential arbitrations, small claims courts *already* provide expedient fora, and there's not much fat to trim. The customary fallback, especially in consumer cases, is that arbitration clauses permit standardized contracts and therefore reduce legal fees, with the savings shared by both parties. But that might not be true. When a court settlement forced some credit card companies to temporarily abandon arbitration clauses, life went on without consigning card issuers to oblivion or consumers to noticeable extra costs.

Where consumer arbitration clauses can achieve genuine efficiencies is in mooting *frivolous* class actions, proceedings that increase costs/lower profits for everyone but the class lawyers. However, corporate defendants should not be "repairing" class-action law by preprinted form, as they lack appropriate incentives or a Constitutional mandate. The proper locus for reform is Congress, which has reformed certain types of class actions without judicial–corporate freelancing.[56]

Whether or not arbitration is procedurally fair or economically efficient (not that some Justices really care), the Court argues that arbitration preserves freedom of contract, a cardinal virtue in market economies. This is something of a red herring, as the Court has allowed interference with contractual freedom when it believes that doing so serves public policy. Whatever else decisions upholding bans on prostitution, gambling, and drug dealing are, they are not laissez-faire. Intellectual inconsistency aside, consumers are not freely contracting with many of the companies that require arbitration. For a start, form contracts are often not contracts at all, in the traditional legal sense of being agreements to which both sides freely consent. Many contracts provide that their terms and conditions may be changed at any time, so that the cell contract signed in the store may not be the operative contract when the wrong occurs and it's time to litigate.

Clearly, no "freedom of contract" exists when one party can shift contractual terms on the fly; equally, no freedom exists when consumers have no practical choice but to sign a contract. For example, telecom is a necessity as much as water and food. The Justices, as we saw in Chapter 6, may not appreciate the centrality of cell phones and Internet to modern life, but these goods are essential all the same. Consumers have few choices when it comes to telecom providers (partially due to limp antitrust enforcement by other parts of the legal system). Because essentially all major telecoms require arbitration, consumers must give up court access to secure a basic necessity—and if telecom doesn't qualify as a necessity, consider that the increasingly oligopolistic health-care industry also uses arbitration when it can.[57] It's no surprise that concentrated industries like telecom and financial services simultaneously have terrible consumer reputations and great enthusiasm for arbitration.

A slightly weaker version of this holds for employment by major corporations, which have hopped on the arbitration bandwagon. If Americans can choose among employers, few can choose to be unemployed. Increasingly, workers have no choice but to sign contracts that include arbitration clauses designed to reduce employers' potential liability for wrongful conduct. This is not pure corporate villainy: by being so permissive about these liability-minimizing clauses, the Court may have put CEOs in a position where the profit-maximizing principles of corporate law encourage use of arbitration clauses. In 1992, just 2 percent of nonunion private sector employees were subject to mandatory arbitration, but as the Court expanded arbitration possibilities, more employees were saddled with arbitration clauses—56.2 percent by 2017.[58] The figure will certainly rise, especially after May 2018. That month, Justice Gorsuch dealt employees another blow, construing the FAA to trump the National Labor Relations Act (designed to protect workers, not that Gorsuch cares), allowing employers to squelch collective litigation.[59]

Bad Law and Bad Policy

Judicial enforcement of one-sided contracts that foreclose just outcomes—in this case, arbitration clauses—offends some of the oldest principles in Western law. In the fourth century BC, Plato suggested that magistrates might not want to enforce unjust contracts.[60] (Rather aptly, Plato assumed magistrates would be responsible for voiding such contracts after the failure of an arbitration.) Roman law similarly forbade certain grossly unfair contracts. English lawyers, immersed in the classics, adopted the same ideas no later than the sixteenth century, including the "doctrine of unconscionability," and exported those notions to colonial America. After the Revolution, American courts continued to void contracts on equitable grounds. The Court referenced the idea in nineteenth century, and it became part of statutes everywhere when the states adopted the Uniform Commercial Code.[61] In 1965, *Williams v. Walker-Thomas,* still a staple of first-year Contracts classes, made the doctrine famous and helps many students feel better about their sometimes-grubby profession.[62] (It's the "furniture usury" case, for former 1Ls.) As legal pedigrees go, this is about as venerable as it gets.

Unconscionability is a doctrine with limits, not some tool for hippie judges to void contracts with Big Business. Contracts are not unconscionable merely because they are form contracts or one party has superior bargaining power. A court can void contracts only when the contract has been procured via means either unethical, unknowing, or unfree, or when the result of enforcement would be grossly abusive.[63] Thus, arbitration clauses negotiated between large corporations are not unconscionable. Neither are clauses between consumers and companies where consumers receive some reasonable compensation for giving up their right to court.[64] But the worst arbitration clauses are one-way provisions extracted without a consumer's knowledge, free consent, or adequate compensation. They are, practically speaking, licenses to pilfer a few hundred dollars a year from consumers, raising serious questions of unconscionability; some state courts have held as much. The Court, however, says such contracts are fine, though a fair reading of the FAA and centuries of sensible precedent say the Court is wrong.[65]

The Court's enforcement of questionable arbitration clauses opens divides between what the law says and how the law works, undermining legal legitimacy. Recall that Fuller's jurisprudential principles require law to be intelligible and predictable; the Court's disregard for the FAA's plain text and venerable precedent disserves those goals. The Court further undermines legal legitimacy by trampling on states' Constitutional rights to determine their own contract law (traditionally a big deal for federalism-minded conservatives when they're not pushing their arbitration agenda) and by shunting important policy goals into arbitration's black hole. Previously, claims enforcing statutory rights, including the right to be free from discrimination and harassment, were thought non-arbitrable. Legislatures adopted those employment laws to advance the policy of fair employment. Parties generally cannot contract out of legislative mandates: an employee cannot be required to agree to sexual discrimination any more than a person can contract to sell himself into slavery. *If, and only if,* arbitration provides a truly adequate substitute for courts—and we know it often cannot—can arbitration of statutory claims be considered just. Otherwise, it's just a court-sanctioned back door to evade the law.

As arbitrations are confidential, many of these statutory violations occur without public scrutiny. The problem here is that public enforcers—agencies like the FTC, SEC, CFPB, etc.—have long relied on private claims to give them notice of when industries misbehave. Law enforcement becomes more time consuming and expensive, with agencies partly shut off from private discoveries; policy goals suffer; and law's legitimacy—here, that important statutes will be enforced—withers.

Closeted arbitrations also thwart legal development, because even when arbitrators provide written justifications for judgments, those ersatz opinions are rarely as structured and rigorous as those produced by judges/clerks. They are also not public, and never precedential; they just do their work and disappear. Once a case slips inside arbitration's event horizon, no information emerges. We cannot fully know how or on what bases the parallel justice system resolves cases until all arbitration firms mutually agree to release data (which they have not done, and will not do). The consequences of private justice for public policy have not attracted enough attention. Our common-law system is premised on the evolution that occurs one public precedent at a time, building and clarifying the law openly. Presently, there's so much litigation that arbitration poses no great threat to precedent, but as whole areas of the law vanish like species of butterfly in clear-cut rainforests, the effect will become large.

Promises Unfulfilled

In contrast to consumer disputes, arbitration in its classic contexts has more benefits than costs. Arguably, the benefits are growing as international trade expands. Resolution of arcane, trans-border disputes between large corporations needs arbitral outlets because national courts lack the structural capacity to handle these disputes quickly and without the appearance of bias. NAFTA's arbitration provisions have their flaws, but forcing Canada and Bombardier to litigate against Boeing and Washington in American courts (or vice versa) may lead to more friction than would international arbitration. Rapid inflation of legal costs also makes arbitration attractive for domestic tussles that involve more than small claims, but less than bet-the-company trials for which legal costs are a tiny fraction of the sums at risk.

For everything else, arbitration risks the integrity of the legal system, usually without sufficient compensation. The Court premised its arbitration cases on the idea that out-of-court procedures would be faster than normal litigation. But the judiciary should have used the tools already at its disposal before ginning up tenuous doctrine. Courts already have procedural rules that allow judges to expedite discovery, push cases along quickly (the "rocket docket"), and to herd litigants into pretrial mediations and settlement conferences before either side becomes too entrenched in its litigation position.[66] Speeding up litigation doesn't require napalming entire classes of legal claims; it just requires judges to use the tools they already have, though more energetically.

Nor is arbitration some sideshow in the greater legal discussion. As John Marshall noted in *Marbury*, "the very essence of civil liberty certainly consists in the rights of every individual to claim the protection of the laws, whenever he receives an injury."[67] One purpose of an open, rule-driven adjudication is to assure citizens that they will be heard fairly. Anything less compromises the rule of law, with savings far exceeded by the costs. Indeed, the rule of law is sufficiently important that the capitalism-minded World Bank compiles an annual index.[68] In a $20 trillion economy, the benefits of a stable and transparent legal system are worth hundreds of billions, at least. Yet, the entire federal judiciary costs just $7 billion, not even enough to buy 55 percent of the *Gerald R. Ford* aircraft carrier or to fund federal healthcare programs for fifty hours.[69] Adding judges to expedite litigation would be a rounding error in the budget. So whatever metaphor one chooses—the arsenal of democracy or health of the body politic—proper justice is hardly an unaffordable luxury, even adding in whatever extra billions court litigation demands in legal fees and delays. Perhaps Rehnquist believed he struck a good deal by pawning courts' monopoly on justice, but the savings haven't materialized. Courts, their many limitations notwithstanding, serve functions arbitration cannot. *Judge Judy* should be entertainment, not litigation's new normal. But it is, and undoing the slide into arbitration will require, among other things, addressing legal costs, which are such an important rhetorical device for arbitration fans.

CHAPTER EIGHT

LEGAL ECONOMICS: PUTTING A PRICE ON PRICELESS

Justice is open to all, like the Ritz hotel.

Sir James Matthew (Irish jurist)[1]

Every June, commencement speakers dutifully inform new lawyers that justice is priceless. When that bromide lands, cynics can see the future reflected in students' eyes. Those that moisten belong to the handful of lawyers about to embark on a lifetime of public service. Those that roll belong to the vastly larger group, those trudging toward careers whose worth will be measured in billable hours. And the eyes that narrow belong to the future partners of elite law firms, the few who realize that "priceless" is the adjective of the auction house. "Priceless" assures bidders that they are competing for a prize so valuable that its worth can only be determined by a contest whose weapons are tenacity and money, a struggle determined when the gavel falls, revealing the identity of the winner and cost of her victory. The potentially remorseful bidder can take solace, for however many dollars changed hands, a bargain was had, any sum being minute against the infinity of "priceless." And that's just for a Matisse; what number could encompass "due process" or "life, liberty, and the pursuit of happiness"?

The frenzied salons at Sotheby's and Christie's are not, of course, the images commencement speakers hope to conjure. But they are the right images all the same. Legal services are not priced for Walmart; legal help is beyond the reach of many Americans. The crisis of legal expenses has been growing for decades, and will get worse, with legal prices rising almost 50 percent faster than general inflation.[2] Speakers who know this can hardly admit it: as law school deans, prominent judges, and eminent politicians, many have been complicit in driving up legal costs. At most, these luminaries can make noises about pro bono work and donations to legal aid societies. Those are worthy things, but they *defray*, not deflate; charity no more arrests legal inflation than Oprah's Pontiac giveaway changed the price of cars.

That legal costs receive less attention than the latest mutation of *Roe* or the dramas of the Senate Judiciary Committee does not mean that legal economics are unimportant—quite the contrary. Money is an awkward subject, and idealists do not want to admit that costs shape Americans' rights more profoundly than most laws or theories. Indeed, legal costs will soon become the *most* important variable in the calculus of rights, save the Constitution. Nothing less than the legal system's legitimacy is at stake, though inflation is not a subject the legal establishment is keen to tackle. But how did law come to be so expensive and why do Americans spend so much on it? The specific reasons are numerous, but the basic dynamic is this: almost everything about American legal culture favors spending more, and almost nothing counsels spending less.

Law has always been a pricey undertaking wherever practiced, but nowhere more so than in contemporary America. The common law's archaisms are sometimes blamed, and while there's some truth to this, it's really an excuse masquerading as an explanation—America can hardly junk its entire legal system, so the subtext of the common-law defense is that high prices are unavoidable. Yet, legal services are cheaper in other common-law countries, which shows that law can be made more affordable in America without pawning liberty or resorting to kangaroo courts. Indeed, those degradations may be the natural product of *failing* to address legal inflation, as the rise of "inexpensive" arbitration shows. Curbing costs, however, requires a shared sense of urgency that has gone missing, and the first step in achieving that urgency is to realize that legal costs burden everyone.

Everybody Pays, Somehow

Because law is inescapable, its costs are inescapable. This is true even for people who will never hire a lawyer. The corporations who supply life's necessities engage in constant legal activity, with costs passed on to everyone. If Alcoa's lawyers jack up rates, the price of tinfoil rises. If Google and Apple embroil themselves in litigation, shareholder returns fall. And if government finds itself in need of more and more expensive lawyers, the mix of taxes and benefits will change. Like the billable hour, each increment may seem small, but the cumulative effect is large.

The total costs of American legal beavering cannot be precisely calculated, but all reasonable estimates produce substantial figures. By Bureau of Economic Analysis (BEA) estimates, the American legal industry's "value add" (its rough contribution to GDP) is ~$260 billion.[3] Because much legal work nestles within in-house law departments, a full measure of the legal economy is larger, perhaps as much as $440 billion (ten times the size of the waste management industry).[4] And then, of course, there's the government, which is essentially a legal creature with its own considerable expenses, but that lies beyond the present discussion.

Most of law's $260–$440 billion is billed to corporations, but individuals spend about $100 billion on legal services directly.[5] On a rough per-capita basis, that $100 billion accounts for almost 1.5 percent of gross median personal income (or ~1.7 percent of after-tax income).[6] By itself, that seems neither negligible nor dire, but it understates the true pain of legal costs. The per-capita cost of weddings is low, but that doesn't mean weddings are cheap; it just means that even Elizabeth Taylor gets married only so many times in one life (eight, for Ms. Taylor). Like weddings, when legal events occur, they can easily absorb much of an American's annual income, as the following table shows.[7]

Table 8.1: Typical Costs—Common Legal Events

Event	Legal Costs for Plaintiff or Initiator	Legal Costs for Defendant/ Respondent	Typical Duration
Simple Contract	$300–$1,500	N/A	1–15 days
Simple Business Formation (LLC)	$500–$3,000	N/A	1–30 days
Prenuptial Agreement	$2,500–$7,500	N/A	1–6 weeks
Contested Divorce	$15,000–$30,000+ plus judgment	$15,000–$30,000+ plus judgment	6–30 months
Contract Litigation	$91,000	$50,000–$150,000+ plus judgment	6–24 months
DUI Defense	N/A	$5,000–$10,000+	6–8 months
Simple Bankruptcy	$1,500–$5,000	N/A	3–6 months
Employment Dispute	$10,000– $50,000+	$80,000 + judgment ($10,000–$50,000+)	6–24 months
Medical Malpractice	$10,000–$100,000+	$50,000+ plus judgment ($100,000+)	24–44 months
Automobile Tort	$17,500–$50,000+	$50,000+ plus judgment	20 months

These prices lie out of reach for many. Here, it's appropriate to offer a brief and necessarily discouraging word about legal aid, subventions offered to lower-income persons who require help with civil legal matters.* Well over 60 million Americans qualify for legal aid, should they need it. However, in 2016, public legal aid budgets totaled just $1.6 billion (~0.5 percent of legal spending), of which federal government typically supplied 25–35 percent via the Legal Services Corporation (LSC). For fiscal 2018, the White House requested $0 for

---

*   Legal aid focuses on civil needs, and is discretionary. By contrast, "indigent defense" provides counsel to criminal defendants in certain cases and is a Constitutional right; the latter is discussed in Chapter 9. Some proceedings, such as traffic violations, do not receive either type of aid.

LSC, though Congress ultimately appropriated $385 million.[8] These figures are enhanced by pro bono work, though it's hard to estimate the total value of donated time (and perhaps only 36 percent of lawyers hit the ABA's aspirational target of fifty hours per year).[9] Whatever the precise dollar equivalents are, subsidized assistance is meager. Up to 70 percent of low-income households need aid in a given year; many do not know where to look, and those who do will often be turned away: depending on the state and the type of case, aid applications are denied anywhere from 50 to 99 percent of the time.[10] While legal aid changes the lives it does reach, it does not change the macroeconomics of law.

The reality is that Americans must expect to bear their own legal expenses, and many cannot, even those in the middle class. In 2014, the scholar Deborah Rhode reported that "a majority of the [legal] needs of middle-income Americans remain unmet."[11] But even those with ready cash to cover a retainer and expected fees for a "typical" case might still not be able to *afford* legal help, because there's no guarantee that an engagement will not grow more complex or will produce a satisfactory result. Will an employment discrimination case take fifteen, fifty, or five hundred hours of attorney time—and will the result be a win, a loss, or something in between? The most seasoned lawyer could not hazard anything more than an educated guess, because every legal event turns on factors beyond the exclusive knowledge and control of a client and her attorney. A legal bill is the product of hourly rates and time spent, and there's always considerable uncertainty around the latter variable, for reasons we'll take up later. Hourly rates are at least knowable in advance, and even if they are not the main drivers of the cost crisis, they provide a sensible place to begin.

Renting Minds by the Minute

Most lawyers bill by the hour; more precisely, by six-minute increments.* Many lawyers assume hourly billing is just another of their profession's

---

* To answer the inevitable question: yes, lawyers will round the last 3.51 minutes of work up to 6 minutes flat.

ageless traditions, while many clients suspect that the practice was created by lawyers to inflate bills. In fact, the billable hour was introduced just sixty years ago, partly at the behest of clients who wanted objective means to evaluate legal bills, and partly to help lawyers keep track of their time and charge appropriately. Today, everyone hates the billable hour (though no one has forwarded a practical alternative), but when it was introduced, all sides greeted the practice as a bold and necessary innovation. The experiment has not been a resounding success, but no comparable effort at reforming legal economics has been made since.

The billable hour replaced a long-standing practice of charging fixed fees, a convention that (now) seems attractive, but which always had severe shortcomings. The model was simple in theory: clients described the work they needed and legal professionals set a fee. From Independence to the mid-nineteenth century, fees were not only fixed, but often capped by state laws.[12] For example, in the 1790s, Pennsylvania set a maximum fee of $4.00 to handle a suit to judgment.[13] In Delaware, a contract or plead-ing might cost $1.50 or so, with many fees set at a maximum of a penny per twelve-word line.[14] Using Delaware rates, a lawyer who drafted 2,000 words per day could earn about twice the wage of a semi-skilled laborer.[15] This hardly condemned lawyers to penury, but at statutory rates, no lawyer could count himself a gentleman and no brilliant gentleman would deign to be a lawyer. The customary workaround was a gratuity based on a law-yer's reputation and success. John Adams received "gifts" and Alexander Hamilton almost certainly did, too, though the musical doesn't dwell on this tidbit.[16]

As the nineteenth century economy liberalized, rate caps disappeared and the profession destabilized. Lawyers, prone to inertia, kept charging fixed fees. But legal work had grown more complex and time-consuming, so lawyers found themselves losing money on unexpectedly long engagements. Worse, as law became a proper profession, clients cut off gratuities; one does not, after all, tip a doctor for a successful surgery. By 1958, middling lawyers earned less than middling doctors (possibly, God forbid, less than dentists).[17]

As we saw, both lawyers and clients agreed that the future lay in the billable hour. At first, hourly billing simply helped legal wages equilibrate with those of other professions. As the decades passed, rates kept rising, especially for elite attorneys. By the mid-2000s, media marveled at the $1,000-per-hour lawyer; just a decade later, senior lawyers in San Francisco and New York commanded almost double that. At historical pace, the $10,000-per-hour lawyer should arrive no later than 2047 (and well before on the coasts). As consolation, that figure is quoted in 2047 dollars; deflating to today's dollars, that's perhaps $4,600, or $77 per minute. If this prediction seems too bold, consider that the future might have arrived already: some experienced advocates demand $1 million for a Supreme Court brief, and in 2016–2018, New York law firms competed for the best attorneys in the range of $10–$11 million.[18] At 2,400 hours per year, that works out to $4,600 per hour, as it happens, though these eight-figure attorneys were paid for both their labor and the small businesses they had built. But we still can't be sure that no one charges $10,000 per hour today. Wachtell Lipton, America's highest-earning firm per capita, presents a simple and usually substantial bill for services rendered, recording a unitary number that reflects various factors including hours worked and a premium for the firm's "value-add" (hearkening to the days of lawyer gratuities, but this time with the servers setting the gratuity).* Is the hourly rate $1,500 or $15,000? Only Wachtell knows.

Wachtell is exceptional in every sense, but rank-and-file law is hardly cheap. Median hourly rates approach $350 per hour, and though half of lawyers charge less by definition, it's difficult to find competent counsel for less than $150–$250 per hour anywhere, and virtually impossible in big cities.[19] Legal time has been appreciating at roughly the same rate as luxury goods—a category to which law will soon belong, if doesn't already.

---

* Silicon Valley firms also generate revenue by collecting stock in start-up clients, either by conditioning representation on the right to invest or by discounting hourly rates in exchange for equity stakes, but this is a niche strategy—"not scalable," as Valley-types would put it.

Why Hourly Rates Are High

In the equilibrium charts of Econ 101, prices relate to supply and demand, with hourly rates at the intersection of the two curves. The microeconomic model is accurate as far as it goes, but only becomes revealing when the supply curve is decomposed into its constituent parts, starting with the cost of legal education. New attorneys with debt owe an average of $96,000 if they attended public school and $134,000 if they attended a private institution, to which economists would add another $150,000 of opportunity costs (representing the amount new college graduates could have earned by work- ing instead of going to law school).[20] In theory, prospective lawyers should demand an extra $35,000–$50,000 annually as compensation for going to law school.[21] Adding that to baseline wages for recent college graduates, aspiring lawyers shouldn't (to paraphrase Linda Evangelista) get out of bed for much less than $100,000 per year. And on average, they don't, not at big firms.[22] But tuition doesn't explain the rates billed to clients. A lawyer who earns $150,000 for a 2,200 hour work-year makes less than $70 per hour, a lot less than the $250–$450 per hour that bigger firms charge for that same sixty minutes. (This chapter focuses on the major firms because they account for a large fraction of total legal expenses and set compensation trends.) Some of the distance is closed by factoring in mundane costs of benefits, administration, overhead, and so on. These costs tend to be higher than average, as law firms cluster in expensive cities to be near clients and courts. But a generous allowance for routine overhead still leaves a gap.

A particularly disturbing explanation for the remainder is the private subsidy of public expense. A federal judicial clerk in New York earns from $70,000 to $95,000 (depending on experience), below the economically rational average salary, barely enough to cover student loan payments and an outer-borough apartment, and far less than the $160,000–$180,000 base salary at top firms.[23] For clerkships to be viable, someone must cover the difference, and private firms do the heavy lifting, paying clerkship bonuses of around $50,000, amortizing the additional opportunity costs of clerkship.[24] The longer a lawyer clerks, and the more prestigious the court, the bigger the bonus: $75,000 for a double clerkship and $300,000–$350,000 for the rarest prize, a turn at the Supreme Court.[25]

A similar dynamic holds for legislators, regulators, and federal prosecutors. Ex-officials bring prestige and (firms and clients hope) special knowledge and influence, as when a former U.S. Attorney switches from prosecuting white-collar criminals to defending them against his old colleagues. Salary enhancements range from modest to embarrassingly generous. To put it bluntly, government lowers its own costs by imposing an implicit tax on users of private legal services, with a whiff of corruption thrown in as a transaction fee.

Another factor, less frequently discussed, is the inefficiency of the legal market—the opacity and difficulty of simply *finding* legal representation. When individuals require an attorney, they often take whatever referrals their networks provide; there's no legal Amazon, with customer reviews and two-day shipping. Even if there were, many individuals need lawyers in moments of crisis, and have little time to shop around, no leverage to negotiate (not that many lawyers would haggle), and focus less on cost than on making bail or fending off a sudden custody suit. Corporations operate in a slightly more efficient market, having greater knowledge and bargaining power, but they still can't do that much about price. As law firms consolidated, companies found themselves turning to the same 100–200 firms, and outside the biggest cities, companies might now have fewer than a dozen plausible choices, all charging near-identical rates. Because switching costs are very high, corporate clients can do little to mitigate rising costs except to demand occasional discounts or pay bills tardily—passive-aggressive tactics that firms anticipate and offset by inflating rates accordingly. The inefficiency of finding a lawyer probably adds more frustration than inflation, though. The main drivers of hourly rates are educational debt, opportunity costs, overhead, and public subsidy.

There is, of course, legal profit, and law firms have a mostly undeserved reputation as exceptional money spinners. With margins of 30–50 percent gross (and perhaps 15–20 percent net), the better law firms' takings align with those realized by Apple and Goldman Sachs, while many law firms outside the richest 100 have margins closer to those of a public utility.[26] Perhaps some of that profit can be reasonably described as economic "rent" due to state bars' local monopolies on law, but the empirical evidence for this is weak, and even cutting firm margins to the S&P 500's average wouldn't reduce hourly rates by much. Summing up all the variables explains why hourly rates are high, and perhaps *justifiably* so. Therefore, true cost containment depends less on restraining rates than on containing growth in the second part of the cost equation: time. For legal costs to stabilize, labor intensity must fall—i.e., lawyers must become more *productive*.

Management and Incentives

Robert Solow joked that the computer age could be seen everywhere but in the productivity statistics, and this is certainly true for law. Dictaphones have given way to Dells, but on the whole, most legal work remains no more efficient than it was forty years ago in the sense of fewer inputs per output—and quite possibly, litigation is getting *less* efficient. The usual excuse for productivity stagnation anywhere is that efficiency gains have been channeled into quality improvements. Thus, movies are more time-consuming and expensive to produce than ever, but the effects are slicker and make for better cinema. This has always been difficult to prove (Ridley Scott's career might demonstrate the reverse), though it's at least plausible. But lawyers have difficulty substantiating the quality excuse and clients have an even harder time believing it.

Why hasn't law become more efficient? The moral hazards of the billable hour usually take the blame, for translating waste into money. That's possible at the margins, but after sixty years of hourly billing, it seems that some new legal mammal should have supplanted the hourly dinosaurs, innovating away all those unjustified billions. Silicon Valley has plenty of lawyers marinating in a culture of "disruption" who know that the first firm to achieve radical improvements would instantly become the most valuable practice on earth. Yet, Silicon Valley firms have birthed no Elon Musk of the law.

The surprising answer to the efficiency riddle is *ethics*. Productivity-enhancing technologies require wagering huge sums. Uber and Lyft have transformed the way people get from A to B, but through mid-2018, they had collectively raised $15–$20 billion.[27] They may yet become profit machines like Google and Facebook, and their investors (disclosure: I'm one) might do very well. But innovation's speculative riches are foreclosed to law firms. American legal ethics prohibit non-lawyers from owning, controlling, or drawing profits from law firms, so lawyers cannot tap outside equity funding, the traditional means of financing innovation.[28] Nor can firms self-fund. Latham & Watkins, the world's biggest law firm by revenue in 2015, had a top-line of just $2.65 billion, with income about half that.[29] Even if L&W paid its partners nothing, the firm would need at least a decade (and perhaps three, given the legal industry's notoriously self-flattering accounting) to amass what Uber alone has raised, and L&W's partners would bear the risk of total loss.* Innovation also takes time, so even if the experiment succeeded, the partners who funded the enterprise might well be retired or dead before any profits were achieved.

Truly radical innovation therefore cannot be expected from within law, but nor should we expect substantial innovation from without. Again, ethics create stumbling blocks. Non-lawyers cannot practice law, so anything other

---

* It's also basically inconceivable that the structure or culture of law firms would allow for large speculative investments in the first place. Law firms are structured as pass-through entities, which allows profits to be taxed only once (when received by a firm's partners), but habits and regulations encourage the distribution of substantially all profits, leaving less capital for investment. Firms could work around the tax code to build capital cushions, but legal culture strongly favors distribution of as much profit as possible.

than the most basic and collateral work must be done inside a traditional firm. At most, companies like LegalZoom can sell standardized forms at low cost, but anything more risks lawsuits from the local bar association (and indeed, LegalZoom has had to fend off several). Perversely, the ethical rules designed to promote clients' interests make it impossible for lawyers to provide what clients want most of all: lower costs. Other nations have begun to dabble with allowing non-lawyers to invest in firms. But America, ostensible home turf for innovation, refuses to experiment.

Lawyers do not seem keen to even try, viewing experiments as pointless distractions from the (equally pointless) work of shuffling documents by the hour. Manufacturers can swap capital and technology for labor, but service businesses are famously resistant to productivity enhancements, or so goes the usual thinking. The hoary textbook examples are barbers, who can only cut so much hair, no matter how many computers they buy. Lawyers believe the same holds for law and confine themselves to tinkering at the edges. Firms gamely tout initiatives like telecommuting, outsourcing, knowledge management, or whatever else precipitates out of the *Harvard Business Review*'s word cloud in a given year. But partners' hearts aren't really in the game. Lawyers believe that law is no mere service, but something of an art, and art (Andy Warhol notwithstanding) can't be mass-produced.

Yet, much of law, especially corporate law (legal argot for transactional work), is less art or service than product—indeed, a *commodity* product amenable to efficiency improvements. Capital constraints foreclose radical innovation, but some improvements require little more than cut-copy-paste. For example, all hedge funds use the same suite of documents; to be reliable counterparties, funds must use nearly identical documents. Taking basic documents and making slight, client-specific tweaks would greatly reduce costs. But once again, there are ethical barriers. Lawyers can only bill for new work and accordingly, they *do* new work, even if that only consists of reviewing, in great and unnecessary detail, documents that have been reviewed hundreds of times before. This is obviously unsatisfactory. No one bats an eyelash when Sony sells a million identical TVs and charges the same price for each, on the grounds that mass-production lowers unit costs, allowing everyone to share in gains. Clients wouldn't mind the Sony model applied to law. Moreover, clients often choose a firm precisely because its template documents represent the best of their type, hiring Firm X on the grounds that its U.S./Mozambique software licensing agreement is the finest ever drafted, needing only a few client-specific tweaks to achieve the desired result. Lawyers should be able to charge (repeatedly) for a best-in-class product, and clients would happily license firms' intellectual property at healthy rates, though less than what firms charge for fully "custom" work—and in the process, lawyers could achieve higher margins and be liberated to work on more useful tasks. But ethics forbid this model, and lawyers waste lifetimes pondering whether round is still the perfect shape for a wheel.

Some clients, exasperated by what feels like a charade, have pushed to return to fixed fees. This is the past recast as the future, and doomed to fail absent major changes. Legal culture would require a near-total overhaul, because lawyers are anal, completist, and risk-averse. Clients might accept the risk of minor imperfections, but lawyers won't and can't. For junior lawyers, a mere typo can be a source of profound embarrassment, while a substantive mistake is seen as a potentially career-ending disaster. Most errors are minor, and their economic consequences far lower than the costs incurred to avoid them—perfect is always much more expensive than very good. But perfectionism is not paranoia. Opponents will gleefully exploit any blunder, and law's adversarial culture is so deeply entrenched that even senior partners revel in exposing mistakes made by their own teams, however trivial. (No other profession gets as much emotional mileage out of the well-placed [sic].) Fear of malpractice claims exacerbates these tendencies. In tort law, negligence suits can fail when a defendant shows she took all reasonable steps to avoid an accident. The same holds for legal malpractice, and because negligence is determined by reference to "reasonable" and "industry-standard" practices, law's culture of anality and duplication becomes self-reinforcing.

Lawyers work to reduce not only their risk, but their clients', and this absorbs endless billable hours because it requires predicting and managing the future. Prenuptial agreements must accommodate marriages of uncertain duration; wills and trusts try to dictate the fates of up to three post-mortem generations; and incorporation documents govern entities whose lives are notionally perpetual. Lawyers must strive to account for all the calamities fate and human nature supply, so documents swell to cover every conceivable contingency, including the possibility that the law itself might change. Other industries cope with uncertainty by using probabilities derived from large data sets and by spreading risk around, as when insurers write thousands of life insurance policies based on actuarial tables. Lawyers have no comparable tools, in part because lawyers *are* the risk-management tools of last resort. Insurers, for example, cannot model everything, and when the imponderable arrives, they expect their attorneys to have drafted emergency exits into underwriting agreements.

Grim though the lawyers' positions may be, the private garden of corporate law is at least theoretically amenable to productivity improvements. If ethical rules and legal culture changed, clients could insist on more efficient practices by waiving certain malpractice claims and sanctioning legal work that involves something less than gross overkill. Those strategies are viable only when clients have unilateral control. In regulatory and litigation matters, clients are just one voice among many.

It Only Gets Worse

All the factors that make private law expensive are magnified in truly adversarial proceedings, supplemented by new and costly variables. In contested matters, the stakes are often higher, the facts unique, the incentives perverse, participation nonconsensual, the issues more complicated, and the other players at best indifferent and most of them outright hostile. Not surprisingly, the bills are larger.

Some of the growth in total legal spending is a product of the regulatory state that expanded in the wake of the Progressive Era. Before 1890, businesses could reasonably assume that most of their activities were unregulated; if Consolidated Biscuits wanted to dye its crackers magenta or acquire a competitor, it simply did so. By the mid-twentieth century, expectations flipped; the default assumption is that *every* activity falls into some regulatory scheme or requires fancy footwork to qualify for an exemption. The tricky questions are which regulations apply and how, matters on which clients seek constant guidance. Because many regulations are vague and heavily fact-dependent, lawyers must toil to provide even qualified answers to basic questions. (The process must be repeated with each change to the law; for many companies, it's an annual endeavor.) To obtain additional assurances, clients can instruct their lawyers to solicit "no action" letters, which describe a client's proposed conduct to a regulator and ask if it will provoke an enforcement action. Because an adverse reply can be worse than not asking at all, great care and expense are spent on these inquiries. Alternatively, clients can ask lawyers themselves to provide a semi-definitive answer, thereby establishing grounds for an advice-of-counsel defense should litigation arise.[30] Given lawyers' own potential liability (and that of their insurers), firms are reluctant to provide definitive advice, and the most formal expressions, "opinion letters," are pricey—$100,000 to tackle a single issue is not uncommon. Industries such as finance, which derive substantial revenue from operating at the regulatory frontier, pay willingly and well for these opinions; it's no coincidence that Manhattan law firms grew and prospered in tandem with Wall Street. And because Manhattan firms set salary expectations for the legal industry generally, the financial-regulatory complex helped push up prices for everything else.

Legal culture reaches its full neurotic bloom in litigation. Anality and risk aversion, always severe, become near-crippling, and proofreading becomes a $500-per-hour obsession. Thought experiments multiply, as lawyers try to predict not only the behaviors of the opposing party, but those of the judge, her clerks, the jury, and the courts of appeal. The field of inquiry also expands dramatically. What was once a mere contract, a piece of semiautonomous and mostly self-contained private law, is connected by litigation to the universe of precedent and interpretation. And with the advent of case law databases, the size of the visible universe expanded dramatically.

Before computers, research was comparatively brief. Most research began with, and often ended in, practice guides compiled by experts—the efficient commodification of intellectual property that ethical rules forbade in other contexts. The arrival of giant databases reduced these guides to starting points for journeys that could be endless. Clients hoped that computerization would speed research, but this was never going to happen. For cultural reasons, computerization might make legal research *better* (or anyway, more exhaustive), but it would never make anything *cheaper*. More cases online meant more cases to parse, more arguments to consider, more work to do. What if this case contained the magic key? Or the next? Lawyers burrowed into the world's least satisfying Wikipedia rabbit hole and remain there, with every new click producing hefty costs.

As exhaustive as legal research became, nothing added as much expense as discovery, the process of collecting and exchanging evidence. Corporate basements that once contained boxes of documents became server rooms whose capacity doubled every year, accumulating electronic junk that lawyers would be forced to sort. The great antitrust cases bookending the twentieth century show just how bloated evidentiary records have become. When the government broke up Standard Oil in 1911, the Supreme Court noted an "inordinately voluminous" record of 12,000 pages.[31] Nine decades later, the DOJ and various states sued Microsoft for antitrust violations. Though Microsoft's misconduct covered just five years and focused on perhaps four primary acts (versus forty years and thousands of misdeeds in the Standard Oil cases), the documentary record in the Microsoft litigation dwarfed its predecessor.[32] Microsoft disgorged millions of pages, employing "a team of 40 lawyers and paraprofessionals [each] working between 60 and 72 hours per week" for the exclusive purpose of rummaging up and reviewing documents—and that, just for *one* phase of the dispute.[33] The court exhibits and deposition snippets by themselves rivaled the entirety of the Standard

Oil files; *United States v. Microsoft* was to its predecessor case what Standard Oil was to a gas station.[34]

As technology had done for legal research, so it did for evidence, making enormous pools of data available without commensurate gains in usability. The functional practice in "discovery" (a process likened by one of my mentors to shoveling excrement from one side of a room to another, for eternity), is that the parties make insane demands of each other, asking for every scrap of evidence conceivably relevant to the case. The parties will squabble over "overbroad and unduly burdensome requests," often requesting court intervention at additional expense, and sometimes parties descend into spite, e.g., digitizing everything at unreadably low DPI or (in days past) setting up vast warehouses in Siberia with the heater switched off, leading to more fights.

Even when lawyers played fair, and with the benefit of reliable optical character recognition, keyword search, and other sorting protocols, masses of data proved hard to parse, as anyone who has sifted a Gmail account knows. Small cases were not greatly altered, but larger cases changed profoundly. A 2010 survey submitted to the Judicial Conference showed that major cases that went to trial averaged 4,980,441 pages of documents produced.[35] This understates volume, as parties only hand over what they must, meaning that lawyers had to winnow some unknowably large mass to get production down to 5 million pages. And even then, most of those 5 million pages were dross, not that either side could know without reviewing the lot. In the cases studied, the percentage of ultimately useful documents was abysmal: out of 5 million pages, an average of 4,772 pages (0.1 percent) were helpful enough to mark as exhibits for trial.[36] It's not correct that 99.9 percent of the discovery expenses were wasted, but nor is it true that discovery spending could be reduced by 99.9 percent.

As storage capacity grows, so will litigation expenses. In 2008, it cost large corporations a median of $17,507 to produce one gigabyte of data—$940 to round up the data, $2,931 for processing/formatting, and $13,636 for attorneys to review the results.[37] (The dead minimum cost per gigabyte in the study's sample was a still-forbidding $2,489.) The constant growth in email, attachments, databases, and so on, all housed in a limitless cloud whose capacity is measured by exabytes (each one equal to 1 billion gigabytes), suggests that discovery costs will keep rising.

Judges should do more to help contain costs, but as we saw in Chapter 6, courts do not treat discovery disputes as the central events they have become. American judges have the power to control discovery, but are reluctant to do so. Perhaps they fear that to judge discovery will prejudge a case. But judges also dislike discovery, and prefer to instruct parties to "work it out" (without fully appreciating how much the parties usually hate each other). When that fails, judges will farm out discovery disputes to magistrates, or to private "discovery masters" employed by the parties at additional expense.

Judges have the obligation to protect parties from abusive discovery requests based on nothing more than attenuated possibilities that seemingly irrelevant information *might* be important or open profitable avenues for exploration. In 2015, the Federal Rules of Civil Procedure tried to strike a balance by emphasizing that the burden of discovery be proportional to the nature of the case, but this will only be effective if judges take it seriously.[38] Little suggests that they will. Even before 2015, judges could tailor discovery, impose sanctions, and shift fees if they concluded that one party had been chasing a wild goose, though they rarely did so.

Growth in litigation expenses will eventually decelerate (but not reverse), whether or not judges intervene. Modern discovery can often cost almost as much as a case is worth. Parties will increasingly settle because the cost of litigating outweighs the value of justice which, as we've repeatedly seen, is hardly "priceless." The state of class-action lawsuits serves as a general warning about the impact of legal costs. These large cases are brought to vindicate the rights of millions of consumers (think of all the mail reading "Legal Notice: Purchasers of Defective Toaster Ovens Please Respond"). Legal expenses consume much of the value of these suits, so when plaintiffs win, they might receive fifty cents on the dollar, and in many cases, next to nothing.[39] Class actions have their special problems, but they reflect the future: a world where legal expense renders the value of victory at $0.

Cheaper Abroad

In legal costs, American exceptionalism (a term attributed to Stalin and not meant as flattery) remains alive and well, with legal spending per capita unusually high compared to peer nations. Qualitative differences between legal regimes make it harder to compare legal outlays than GDPs, but a rough sense can be had examining attorneys per capita and prevailing hourly rates.[40] America ranks first among its large peers. America has ~50 percent more practicing lawyers per capita than Canada, and American lawyers charge higher rates—around US$200–$300 per hour for freshly minted American lawyers versus an average US$160 per hour in Canada.[41] If anything, international comparisons may be too generous to the United States, because of the greater prevalence of fixed-fee contracts abroad.

Many of the factors that make American law costly feature less prominently overseas. Foreign legal education is generally cheaper, reducing hourly rates. Foreign law is often less complex, which may be surprising, given the common trope that Europe is an overregulated mess. But a Europe bound in red tape is an image drawn from the past and, for the purposes of our discussion, somewhat beside the point. Foreign regulations often cover more activities and regulatory levies can be higher, but the regulations themselves are often easier to apply, and that's what really matters for legal costs. For example, most peers have higher tax *rates*, but lower costs of tax *compliance*, because their tax codes are simpler, their bureaucracies speedier, and legal expense accordingly lower. For a hypothetical medium-sized company, the accounting firm PwC and the World Bank estimated that tax compliance would take significantly longer in America (175 hours) than in Canada (131 hours), Sweden (122 hours), the UK (110 hours), or Norway (83).[42] Some of the extra time is spent on accounting, but quite a bit represents legal work,

211

given the complexity and fragmentation of the American tax code. What holds for tax holds for American law generally; America ranks in the middle among OECD (Organisation for Economic Co-operation and Development) countries for regulatory burden and quality.[43] It's also likely that social dynamics such as income inequality and concentrated market share, both more prominent in America than in Europe, raise prices. While concentrated wealth slightly improves client leverage over fees, it greatly reduces appetites for hard bargaining. To protect their significant profits, American businesses find an extra $100 per hour or another million pages of discovery to be comparatively reasonable. Certainly, corporate general counsels, whose jobs depend on avoiding catastrophe, think as much. Whatever the reasons, it would appear that American companies spend almost 70 percent more on legal services, as a fraction of their revenues, than the global average.[44]

Fear is an unusually potent driver of American legal spending. American criminal sentences are harsh, so defendants who can afford lawyers have incentives to spend heavily. Prison is not the only worry; in America, background checks are routine and a minor conviction can foreclose a menial job. By contrast, European sentences are generally less punitive, and the economic consequences of conviction can be lower. In France and Germany, criminal background checks are generally limited to fields in which prior history is salient, like finance or policing.[45] Even Europe's high degree of urbanization and public transport might help; a garden-variety DUI can be devastating for workers living in American suburbs, while presenting lesser inconveniences to more urbanized Europeans. This is not to say Europe is a defendants' paradise, only that it harbors fewer incentives to litigate charges to the bitter end.

The higher stakes in American noncriminal law also encourage heavy legal spending. Although Europe has forceful regulators, when America assesses regulatory fines, the amounts tend to be large, as are awards at trial. Stories that make corporations shudder abound, from the McDonald's my-coffee-was-too-hot case (a $2.9 million verdict subsequently reduced to a still-impressive $640,000) to multibillion-dollar class-action settlements.[46] Punitive damages often comprise the bulk of newsworthy judgments (94 percent in the original McDonald's verdict, and 75 percent even after the award was trimmed), but this is mostly an American worry. Civil-law countries generally disallow punitive damages in private cases and many common-law nations restrict their use and amount. In America, fear of erratic and hostile juries further encourages corporations to spend heavily on defense. Again, this is a lesser concern overseas, where juries in civil cases are less common or simply not available.*[47] There's no way to directly measure the consequent increase in legal costs, but insurance premia, which quantify fear and liability, provide reasonable proxies. One study concluded that corporate liability insurance premia in America were 2.6 times that of a basket of Eurozone, mostly civil-law countries, with legal environment accounting for most of that difference.[48] Even among common-law nations, America remains an outlier, with liability insurance consuming significantly more resources than in Canada and Britain.[49]

In common-law countries like America, the price of a verdict is not always limited to the results of any one case. When litigation raises a novel issue, a loss can create precedent, and precedent paves the way for dozens of other suits and billions in additional damages. In civil-law countries, precedent is less of a concern; standard cases are judged on their individual merits with few larger implications. Continental jurists would find it unusual if half a dozen lawyers turned up in rural France to fight a €20,000 suit over an unsafe product, but in the heyday of tobacco litigation, Philip Morris was content to dispatch a Gulfstream filled with lawyers to fight smokers' lawsuits whenever and wherever they occurred.

---

* Confronted with similar cases, judges and juries generally do not return wildly different results, but overall, juries are more generous when they award damages and do account for most blockbuster awards. So corporations have reason to fear certain jury trials—though in analyzing legal spending, it doesn't matter whether fear of juries is rational or irrational, only that it exists.

Missing Restraints

One paradox of American legal economics is that litigation costs are high in part because the costs of commencing suits are low. At heart, America permits speculative litigation to a degree that most nations do not. Foreign courts generally expect a plaintiff to bring tailored charges supported by at least some evidence already in the plaintiff's possession, often with a degree of specificity (matching claims, witnesses, and documents) that is nearly impossible for American litigators to imagine.[50] When defendants reply, foreign courts expect equally solid responses, frowning on laundry lists of far-fetched or wildly contradictory defenses. These barriers serve to narrow the dispute rather than to prevent it entirely. (Once upon a time, American rules required more detailed pleading—but that time, rather pungently, was before 1938–1957; i.e., before the great inflation in American legal costs.) What can deter suits from ever beginning, or recommend their early termination, are cost-shifting provisions that require the loser to pay most (or all) of the winner's fees and costs. This practice is called the English Rule, and as the name suggests, it's not just a civil law phenomenon. Under the English Rule, wildcatting can be an expensive proposition.

Americans, by contrast, sometimes view the right to sue based on a hunch as something like a God-given right. The rules of civil procedure mostly ratify this sentiment: to commence suit, a plaintiff need only put the defendant on notice of the general nature of the suit and defendants may respond with similar vagueness.[51] A few types of cases, such as those involving fraud, must be alleged with "particularity," but this is no real barrier to the savvy lawyer. Regardless, each side is free to allege legal theories that are inconsistent or even mutually exclusive. Except where required by statute, there's no English-style verification requirement, no requirement for supporting evidence, and indeed, no functional requirement of preexisting factual or legal grounds for suit so long as it's "likely" that facts will ultimately be discovered to support the claim or a "nonfrivolous" basis for believing that the case will establish "new law" permitting relief.[52] The resulting canvas can be immense and one can reasonably question whether pleading does anything more than inform parties that someone is irked enough to sue. In 2007 and 2009, the Court tried to clamp down on the flimsy suits that the old rules allowed, requiring allegations to be at least "plausible." Much as the academy despised the Court's pleading reforms at the time, there's little evidence they had substantial effects. It's heresy in law schools to suggest that the Court might not have gone nearly far enough when it tightened pleading standards, but other countries have demanded more without sinking into barbarism.

Because American pleading is so permissive, the main deterrents to filing suit are the expenses a party might incur directly. But again, American law is unusually forgiving. Under the American Rule, each party expects to bear only its own costs, win or lose. In the case of speculative contingency fee cases (mostly used in personal injury cases and consumer class actions), the lawyer-investor bears the loss, further distorting incentives. Courts are reluctant to invoke special rules to shift fees (or sanction lawyers) when parties gin up pretty ridiculous claims and defenses.[53] As a result, there are few disincentives to commencing a suit and forcing the other side into an expensive discovery process. The upside is that it's much safer for small parties to sue bigger parties. In Europe, an individual smoker with a 60 percent chance of prevailing might never sue if faced with a 40 percent chance of a loss that would saddle her with British Tobacco's legal fees (certain to be substantial).

While American law makes it easy to bring wide-ranging lawsuits, it provides few incentives for judges to address the resulting bloat. The default posture for American trial judges is passivity. Any departure from that mold risks rebuke from higher courts, so the easiest thing to do is let marginal complaints and rambling discovery run their full course. Judges in civil-law countries cannot afford such indulgences. Civil-law judges preside over the discovery process, and in many countries are expected to personally review and summarize the evidence. They have no incentive to condone America's no-stone-unturned discovery practices. Moreover, because civil law litigation unfolds iteratively, rather than culminating in a grand trial, judges can whittle down a case's legal issues serially. The idea of collecting all the evidence based on an unsupported complaint, before disposing of preliminary legal issues, strikes many other nations as bizarre. And the American practice of allowing litigants to demand evidence without obtaining court approval, even from third parties (email services are a favorite target notwithstanding the Stored Communications Act), feels like another invasive lunacy. As a result, many peer nations have filed exceptions to the Hague Convention, which governs international evidence collection.[54] Countries including Germany, Switzerland, France, and even the UK, routinely refuse to help when Americans demand discovery within their borders.[55]

Sundry Oddities: Privatization, Perverse Incentives, and Firm Instability

A few final factors deserve brief consideration. Private legal spending is unusually high in part because many of the large cases prosecuted by private attorneys in America are delegated to public legal actors overseas. This is most evident in vindications of what are essentially public rights, which in America are frequently led by class-action suits seeking extraordinary damages. Private lawyers expect greater financial rewards than public actors, adding to costs. Occasionally, a class action will succeed beyond all expectations, and the prospect of lottery-like winnings seduces some plaintiffs' lawyers into frivolous lawsuits and unethical behavior; the nation's most prominent securities class-action lawyer, Bill Lerach, went to prison for hiring plaintiffs.[56] Other nations dispose of the morally hazardous waste of these suits by demanding greater energy from their regulators and prosecutors.

The second problem is that the conventional law firm model is a financially unstable, resource-destroying mess. Large firms pride themselves on reporting high profits-per-partner and many achieve this through imprudent leverage. Firms maximize partner payouts, leaving them thinly capitalized, often greatly indebted to banks, and highly fragile. Unexpected downturns have sent many firms into receivership, as happened to Brobeck.* Other firms, having temporarily maximized human gearing by hiring legions of associates (literally called "leverage" in the business), weather adversity by firing their troops en masse, destroying years of investment. Even in good times, firms waste their assets by treating junior associates like disposable widgets (FBU, or "fungible billing unit," was current slang when I was a litigator). Most firms expect associates to bill at least 2,000 hours per year which, factoring in administrative activities, requires 2,400 worked hours—anything less will be penalized, while anything more will receive a modest bonus. Associates are stressed, dissatisfied, and without any opportunity to cultivate the new client relationships on which they will be judged when it comes time to make partner. When that time comes—if they haven't already quit, disgusted by a profession that reduces the average corporate associate to a document butler—only one-third of associates can reasonably expect a partnership offer. The others, spent and broken, are tossed out. The results are high turnover, rapidly depreciating human capital, volatility, and higher legal costs as firms spend heavily to recruit fresh cannon fodder. It's no way to run a business, but law firms are not run by businessmen. They're run by lawyers, traditionally the less intelligent examples whose connections and expertise will not be missed when they are shuffled into firm management.

The rapid growth in legal costs is an inevitable product of American law itself. Real improvement requires reforming large swathes of the system's structure, culture, and incentives. The best targets for reform are obviously

---

* I was in court with Brobeck attorneys the day their firm went under. A few years later, after I'd left my old firm, it also collapsed after more than a century in practice. Legal deaths are not uncommon.

the rules and habits already discussed, those that have made law so expensive in the first place. The wrong targets—though these are the targets law has settled on—are to simply eradicate whole species of lawsuits, e.g., by shunting them into arbitration's memory hole or neutering them via doctrines of immunity.

All reform requires political consensus, which does not presently exist. Legal costs are not visible or urgent for most voters until the moment they arrive in the form of a personal event. Legal inflation is also not fully visible to American governments, because their wage bills are tacitly subsidized by private firms, while the public bears the greatest costs of judicial inefficiency. Other nations, which defray a larger fraction of legal costs for private citizens facing serious criminal *and* civil litigation, have stronger incentives to reform their legal systems, as governments bear costs of inefficiency more directly; Britain is one example: not as generous with civil aid as it used to be, but more generous than the U.S. is.[57] Since the 1990s, Britain has also required more active case management by judges and created specialized procedures more attentive to the nuances of differently sized cases.[58] In 2004, Australia allowed law firms to accept outside capital, affording law firms the flexibility to invest and streamline that has long been available to other industries. Australian firms took new capital and four even went public.[59] In 2007 and in 2011, the UK also liberalized outside investment.

These foreign experiments are too young, and overlapped too much with the Great Recession, to permit full judgment. British court reforms appear to have sped litigation; the outside investment rules in Britain and Australia are still fresh, and partly marred by one firm's disastrous acquisition of an insurance business (though the loss was borne by the firm's equity base, not its clients). The true outcomes will be known in time, but whatever the results, they reflected serious attempts to address inefficiencies in the legal market.

Achieving truly significant improvements in legal inflation will require a technological revolution, as all productivity enhancements do. Artificial intelligence presents the most obvious solution, and already shows real promise at performing routine legal work. By 2018, AIs were better at performing certain legal tasks than experienced lawyers, and their broader deployment could speed discovery, draft basic documents for human review, and so on. (AI is not very capital intensive, and many natural language technologies were developed for other markets.) AI may be the one area where efficiency improvements from without are possible. Whether legal AI will be *allowed* to realize its potential is a question of law firm incentives, professional ethics, and social values. So far, American bar organizations—state-by-state monopolies—have vigorously resisted change. The public might also resist AI's incursions, as law is among the most human of endeavors. Legal inflation may decide for us, though it would be better if we chose now—justice, after all, involves nothing if not a sense of free will. But on the present course, when Alexa and Siri replace Paul Clement and Clarence Darrow, we will have no option but to click "Accept" on the terms and conditions of our new legal world.

CHAPTER NINE

PROSECUTORS AND DEFENDERS: ANGELS OF VENGEANCE AND MERCY

> The prosecutor has more control over life, liberty, and
> reputation than any other person in America.
>
> Robert H. Jackson (1940)[1]

Jackson knew of what he spoke. A few months before his remarks on prosecutorial power, Jackson had become the U.S. attorney general, i.e., America's chief prosecutor. Pause, as Jackson did, to consider what it means to prosecute a federal crime. Merely bringing charges can result in a defendant's detention, financial ruin, and reputational collapse, all before a jury hears its first witness. The ensuing contest will hardly be equal, as the case caption attests: not *Jackson v. Smith*, one person pursuing another; but *United States v. Smith*, a nation against an individual. In the fight, the nation's resources will be directed by a single prosecutor's office, an entity whose charging discretion is virtually unlimited and whose accountability for misconduct is functionally nil. These unfettered powers are what prompted Jackson's comment.

The safeguard against prosecutorial despotism, Jackson believed, was a special temperament—a temperament, Jackson suggested, not unlike that of a "gentleman": dispassionate, reasonable, faithful to higher principles, and ruled by humility.[2] Jackson embodied those qualities as attorney general and (on leave from the Supreme Court) as the most famous prosecutor in the world, the chief U.S. prosecutor at the Nuremberg Trials. But that's the problem with enlightened despotism. Let the eyes unfocus, and the authoritarian field always reveals some encouraging example: a Frederick the Great, Lee Kuan Yew, or Robert Jackson. However, "enlightened" is the adjective and the exception. "Despotism" is the noun and the rule. The danger of power unaccountable, save to the consciences of the powerful, is precisely what law is supposed to avoid.

Jackson's vision of the gentleman prosecutor now seems quaint. Whatever else ex-prosecutors like Rudy Giuliani and Chris Christie might be, "gentlemen" is not the first descriptor that leaps to mind. As a prosecutor, Giuliani once indicted a firm for financial and tax frauds, dispatching fifty armed marshals to raid the firm and seize its assets, a well-publicized act that condemned the business to death before a verdict was ever obtained. Giuliani eventually got his conviction, but only temporarily: the firm's conviction was overturned; the IRS subsequently discovered that the firm's tax error was *over*payment; and various securities claims were vacated.[3] (In later life, Giuliani's blood-and-thunder instincts led him to opine that Darren Wilson should be "commended"; Wilson was the officer who shot Michael Brown in Ferguson, Missouri.[4]) Christie, meanwhile, had scandals simmering long before Bridgegate. In a prosecution for securities fraud, Christie's office wangled a settlement (fair enough), and then directed $5 million of the proceeds not toward the Treasury or the shareholder-victims, but to Christie's undistinguished alma mater—to endow a chair in, of all things, ethics.[5] Eighty years on, Jackson's musings about prosecutorial power ring true, as does his warning that lapses could make prosecutors "one of the worst" forces in society.[6]

Eighty years *before*, however, Jackson's speech might have seemed bizarre. Hard-charging, all-powerful Giulianis and Christies did not yet exist. What prosecutors the nation employed were weak and few until the early twentieth century: under-resourced, undistinguished men who occupied the lower rungs of the legal hierarchy, frequent subjects of professional and public scorn. That changed, especially during Prohibition, but the transition to the all-powerful prosecutor was (by legal standards) swift, almost unexpected. Certainly, the public supported vigorous criminal enforcement, but no one ever quite *agreed* to grant prosecutors untrammeled authority. Rather, the all-powerful prosecutor arose by means haphazard and circumstantial, the by-product of changes elsewhere in the legal system, some of which were originally intended to *curb* law enforcement's power. Because prosecutorial powers accumulated ad hoc, the norms, institutions, and expectations about prosecutors have never been settled, and because secrecy is among those powers, even the legal system itself does not fully appreciate the ways aggressive prosecutors can disserve their ostensible masters: justice and the public.

Not the Oldest Profession

For most of Anglo-American legal history, prosecution was a private affair. Most crimes, like murder and assault, were seen as wrongs against individuals, not against society. While the state provided judges, and enumerated crimes and penalties, it otherwise stood aside: law made victims or their survivors responsible for apprehending criminals and bringing prosecutions. Only when government supposed itself to be directly wronged, in matters like treason and sedition, did officials prosecute.

The emphasis on private, rather than public, prosecution derived from British policies, whose stated concern was protecting liberty. Prevailing wisdom held that state prosecution would constitute a dangerous infringement on freedom: inherently coercive, politicized, and potentially arbitrary. Government's incentives were all wrong, as a glance across the Channel revealed. Wouldn't the state be tempted, for political expedience, to prosecute the innocent? And in nonpolitical cases, was not the decision to bring or decline prosecution the *victim's* prerogative? Was it not possible that the state might co-opt a personal matter for its own ends, either displaying unjustified mercy or undue harshness (and perhaps bungling things either way)? The answers to these questions, Britain thought, were self-evident. With a few exceptions, such as minor crimes prosecuted by equally minor officials—the local constable charging a petty thief being archetypal—Britain did without dedicated prosecutors until 1880.[7] Even today, Britain retains private prosecutions on the theory that public prosecutors might not always be the best advocates for the wronged. Mostly, private prosecutions survive in bland trade disputes, as when taxi organizations prosecute unlicensed drivers and recording studios go after pirates, though in 1995, bereaved parents brought murder charges (rather than civil wrongful death claims) after the Crown dropped its own efforts.[8]

The American experience paralleled the British, though not quite as militantly or uniformly. Regions colonized by the Dutch and French employed public prosecutors early on (as did a few English-dominated colonies such as Connecticut and Virginia), acclimating citizens to the idea the state might vindicate private wrongs without catastrophic consequences for liberty. The Revolutionary elite had also read Cesare Beccaria's *On Crimes and Punishments* (1764), which argued that wrongs against a person could also be wrongs against society, logically requiring some form of public prosecution. By the 1820s, public prosecutors had spread across the states, though society had not fully committed to the concept. The public declined to provide prosecutors with resources out of cheapness, disinterest, a desire to protect liberty, or all three. For many years, public prosecution remained second-rate; when victims could, they hired private attorneys like Daniel Webster to pursue murder and other criminal charges.

As government expanded generally, public prosecution became routine and private prosecution became the anomaly, though it wasn't until 1973–1987 that the Supreme Court fully disallowed private prosecutions of crimes in federal court.[9] (In some states, private prosecutions of criminal law remain theoretically viable.) As government prosecutors became more competent, the public felt more comfortable leaving vindication in state hands. Prosecutors occasionally flailed, with the collapse of the OJ Simpson case providing a famous example. But since the Progressive Era, prosecutors have mostly gotten the job done. That, along with the expansion of civil litigation, muted worries about competence and the co-option of victims' rights. Even if the state flubs its charge, victims' survivors can bring parallel civil suits, though this backup system has been partially unwound by tort reform and immunity, renewing old concerns about undue dependence on state vindication of private wrongs.

The rise of institutional prosecutions made the need for publicly funded defenders obvious. The Constitutional right to publicly funded counsel in federal cases was established by the 1930s, but was not mandatory for state felony cases (vastly more numerous than federal cases) until 1963, when *Gideon v. Wainwright* overruled a contrary precedent from the 1940s.[10] Public defense is even younger than public prosecution, and its rules and norms are in greater flux. For example, many assume the right to public counsel is absolute—after all those *Miranda* warnings on TV about the "right to an attorney," how could they not? But the Court continues to define the contours of the right(s) to counsel. Among other limitations, courts have opined that the right to public counsel does not attach at all stages of criminal proceedings, nor does it guarantee particularly effective counsel.[11] (Only the most deficient lawyering, whether paid for by the state or defendant, is grounds for an "ineffective assistance of counsel" argument, or so the Court says.) Nor is government-funded counsel always required where incarceration is not imposed. The tattered right to public counsel also does not firmly attach in matters where penal consequences are derivative (such as prison time enhancements based on lesser convictions secured with or without benefit of counsel), in quasi-criminal matters such as deportation, and in civil matters where the penalties can be as painful as jail (child custody, notably).[12]

The questions of liberty that animated the private versus public prosecution debate have never been entirely answered, while the right to counsel seems increasingly limp. In the development of public prosecutions, prosecutors emerged the winners—perhaps too much so.

Spoilt by Choice

Prosecutors stand in unusual tension with America's adversarial legal system. Other lawyers represent, solely and zealously, their client's interests; doing so is an ethical duty and a core tenet of the adversarial system. If Samsung rips off an Apple innovation, Apple's lawyers can try to sue Samsung into oblivion without giving any thought to Samsung's customers, workers, shareholders, or the public interest. Prosecutors, in theory, cannot be so single-minded, because they serve many masters with different, sometimes competing, values: the state, the public, the victims, and above all, justice. The ABA's *Standards* for prosecutors provide that: (1) the "*primary* duty of the prosecutor is to seek *justice* within the bounds of the law, *not merely to convict*," (2) "[t]he prosecutor generally *serves the public* and *not* any particular government agency, law enforcement officer or unit, witness or victim," and (3) "the prosecutor *is not obliged* to file or maintain all criminal charges which the evidence might support."[13] State organizations and the U.S. Attorneys publish similar guidance.[14] If an otherwise upstanding teenager eggs a house on Halloween, a district attorney may decline to press charges notwithstanding the homeowner's cries for vengeance and mayoral bleats about zero-tolerance enforcement. Equally, a prosecutor may charge a shoplifter even if the local grocer, having just taken in *Les Misérables*, doesn't feel like spending a weekday testifying against the local Jean Valjean.

In a word, prosecutors have discretion. Discretion is the stated price of laboring toward multiple goals. With few real constraints, prosecutors can charge whom they want, how they want, with what they want. Discretion is what makes prosecutors so powerful, yet the *concept* of discretion has never been the subject of thorough public discussion or agreement. What little debate occurs focuses on narrow areas: whether prosecutors should forgo enforcement of federal drug laws against marijuana users, or hunt down or ignore nonviolent immigration offenders. These debates transcend the facts of any one case, and are primarily discussions about particular social policies, not prosecutorial discretion. Nevertheless, these debates hint at dissatisfactions with wide discretion.

Discretion in any field carries the potential for abuse. For prosecutors, the two categories of greatest risk are under-prosecution and over-prosecution. The former happens when prosecutors, for improper reasons, fail to charge suspected criminals; the latter, when prosecutors throw the book at defendants when doing so serves neither the facts nor society's interests. Save for a few hot-button issues (violence against minorities, political corruption, minor morals crimes, and some immigration matters), discretionary *under*-prosecution is not a major concern in America. Over-prosecution, however, is rampant. This is ironic: prosecutorial discretion derives from the state's ancient power to *dismiss* overzealous private prosecutions. Discretion was originally an instrument of mercy, not a license to go overboard.

Discretion becomes more potent as the option set grows and, on this front, American prosecutors lack for nothing. The past fifty years witnessed runaway expansion in criminal statutes, what scholars have described as a process of "overcriminalization."[15] In 1998, the ABA estimated that more than 40 percent of federal crimes created since the Civil War were enacted in the preceding quarter-century.[16] Since the ABA study, Congresses has been adding about 500 crimes every decade, with particular energy during election years.[17] Overcriminalization makes criminal codes tremendous, asymmetric resources for prosecutors. Citizens cannot possibly know all the criminal laws that affect them as they navigate the limitless world of daily life, but prosecutors presented with an arrest record work against a defined set of facts and, luxuriating in hindsight, can always locate relevant charges among the thousands available. A few scholars have suggested that we should be consoled that most criminal statutes involve a few types of classic misconduct (weapons, drugs, fraud), but that naïve view provides no comfort to citizens who suffer forfeiture proceedings in places like Ferguson, or are overcharged with various offenses to coerce a plea, or tangle with unscrupulous and vindictive Justice Department functionaries. There are just too many crimes.

In fact, virtually everyone will do something criminal, however unwittingly. Petted your dog during a car ride? That's good for a fine in D.C.[18] Played online poker for money? That's good for prison.[19] (Somehow that's embedded in a law nominally concerning *shipping port* security, not that Washington cares.) Heard that your state legalized pot and shared a couple of joints? The federal clink, if the U.S. attorney general is so inclined.[20] Didn't realize that states can't override federal law? Irrelevant. Violated *foreign* laws, say, Honduran fishery laws pertaining to the harvest and packaging of spiny lobsters? Too bad; Honduran law can provide a predicate crime for the Lacey Act: forty-seven-count indictment, verdict against defendants.[21] Does it matter that Honduras, between defendants' conviction and appeal, changed its interpretation of its own lobster laws to favor the defendants? No, the Eleventh Circuit says that's beside the point. Is it unsettling, and perhaps indicative of the legal fog in which citizens operate, that the lobster case required American judges to spend paragraphs figuring out what the word *"law"* means? What does it matter? Conviction affirmed; ninety-seven months in the pokey approved.

When presented with questionable conduct and unsympathetic defendants, prosecutors can always rummage up a charge, and usually many charges. Two people selling marijuana, for instance, seems to call for a simple drug-dealing charge: one wrong, one crime, one charge. But the Supreme Court has held that so long as each crime charged has a novel element to be proved, prosecutors may bring multiple charges for what is essentially the same conduct.[22] Our two defendants could face charges for trafficking, conspiracy, money laundering, tax evasion, and customs violations, because the same kind of conduct is often criminalized under many different statutes. And if a weapon was involved (or just happened to be nearby), the charging universe expands—and in a system where a sneaker can be a "dangerous weapon," finding additional charges presents no challenge.[23] Using the complex and punitive sentencing initiatives of the 1980s, prosecutors can also fine-tune charges to ensure a wide range of sentences, the better to extract a plea bargain—six months or six centuries, you can have your pick as long as you plead. Federalism also allows indictments to be carefully constructed so as to preserve options for other prosecutors, as state and federal laws frequently criminalize the same basic conduct in slightly different ways. Should a prosecution collapse in federal court, a district attorney can prosecute some variant in state court, or vice versa.* The advantages of a do-over, fully informed by the defendant's prior strategy, compound prosecutorial power.

Jury Rigged

In the federal system, the prosecutors are U.S. Attorneys and their assistants, who receive referrals from both federal agencies and from state police who suspect that a crime might have a federal component. In the states, prosecutors are generally termed "district attorneys" for a given county and receive referrals from local police and sometimes from federal agencies. Typically, law enforcement furnishes an arrestee and a case file, after which the prosecutor becomes master of the proceedings, deciding what charges to present, a bill that typically includes the arresting offense, plus any charges the prosecutor deems appropriate.[24] Occasionally, prosecutorial investigations produce suspects on their own, and in such cases, the prosecutor has total control from the start.

The mechanics of commencing prosecution depend on the type of case. For misdemeanors, prosecutors simply file charges. Procedures for more serious crimes tend to be more involved. In the federal system and many states, a prosecutor brings high-profile cases either by preliminary hearing

---

* A case on this issue of "separate sovereigns" was pending before the Court as of 2018.

(a procedure used by many states) or via grand jury (preferred by the federal government and some states).[25] Unlike a trial (or "petit") jury, a grand jury has sixteen to twenty-three members, instead of the trial jury's usual twelve, and decides by majority vote, rather than the unanimity required by most state and all federal petit juries.[26] Rather less grandly for those dragooned into service, grand jurors usually hear several matters in a term that can last anywhere from a few weeks to eighteen months, and for which they are paid a measly $50 per diem at the federal level, hardly a sum that focuses the mind (and which can be lower than the *legal* minimum wage, an indication of the generally lawless atmosphere of the grand jury). Should the prosecutor convince the grand jury, the body returns an indictment, the formal list of charges.

Grand juries might seem to provide at least some check on prosecutorial discretion, allowing society to weigh in on charging decisions, as was one of their original functions. The historical grand jury was not the prosecutor's pet it has become; it was an independent and entrepreneurial body that could conduct investigations itself, hear public and private complaints, and commence or quash proceedings. That institution is as dead as the Tidewater grandees who drafted the Constitution's Grand Jury Clause. The *United States Attorneys' Manual* still insists that one of the grand jury's purposes is to "protect[] ... citizenry from unfounded criminal charges."[27] But there's no way a modern grand jury can fulfill that role, because the prosecutor controls the entire process and there are no real safeguards against abuse. Law's usual protections against overreach are to make legal proceedings public, allow both parties and their lawyers to be present, and require judicial supervision. With grand juries, these protections do not really exist. Normal juror screening (voir dire) is a cursory feature, at best. If witnesses are called to bolster the prosecutor's case, they are not subject to cross-examination, which might reveal testimonial weaknesses or perjury. In many jurisdictions, if the witnesses are also potential defendants, they do not enjoy a right to counsel present in the room.[28] Judges play no real role and proceedings are secret.

The residence of grand juries in some parallel legal universe where normal protections don't obtain makes them an especially useful tool for inquisition. The investigatory powers of the grand jury (which the Supreme Court seems to believe can be disentangled from the police/prosecutorial apparatus) are incredibly broad, and grand juries may inquire on matters based on evidence that would be excluded in normal court.[29] A grand jury (read: prosecutor) "can investigate merely on the suspicion that the law is being violated, *or even just because it wants assurance that it is not*," which is extraordinary, and without many equivalents in non-totalitarian systems.[30] Prosecutors can use grand jury subpoena power to poke into whatever cranny they like. Worse, these special subpoenas are immune to challenges that might fell normal subpoenas, because the Court believes that applying the usual rules governing procedure and evidence would compromise the grand jury's secrecy and its ability to investigate.[31] This is perverse. Did the Framers really add a grand jury requirement so that the state could go hunting off-season and off-sides? No, a key goal was to allow community members to use independent judgment to check overreaching prosecutions.

Once the inquisition concludes, prosecutors present final charges and ask the grand jury to indict. The mechanics again operate at great remove from criminal trial practice. An indictment requires "probable cause," a much lower standard than "beyond a reasonable doubt."[32] What constitutes "probable cause" depends on the jurisdiction, but it's "not a high bar" and generally means that a reasonable person, considering the information presented, would conclude there's a "fair probability" that the defendant committed the crime.[33] The difficulty here is that the prosecutor, not an impartial judge, instructs the jury on the requirements of probable cause. Worse, the prosecutor has no obligation to elaborate on what the legal elements of a crime really mean or dive into pertinent defenses. For example, a CEO, having full access to financial statements, sells stock right before a plunge, and the prosecutor wants to indict. Was the CEO's sale insider trading? To the layman, it might seem exactly that, no further details required. But the law requires several factors to be present, including that the executive *improperly* traded on the basis of inside information—but if the executive merely followed pre-filed plans with the SEC, as is customary, the sale would not constitute misuse.[34] Prosecutors really should tell grand jurors these helpful tidbits, but there's no good way to know if they do, nor is a certain haziness about the law fatal to an indictment.[35] The jury votes, often blindly, and if twelve jurors (out of the usual twenty-three) agree, the indictment issues.[36] The statistics make clear just how lopsided this process is: in FY 2010, federal prosecutors declined to proceed in just *eleven* instances because grand juries failed to return a bill, an event called an *ignoramus*, and statistically much less likely than being struck by lightning.[37] As New York judge Sol Wachtler remarked, a grand jury would indict "a ham sandwich."[38] The whole grand jury process verges on farce, deodorizing prosecutions as "independent" while expanding prosecutorial power. For these and other reasons, all common-law countries but America and Liberia have essentially given up on grand juries.

The Ethics of Hard Charging

Prosecutors' tools are plentiful and the barriers to indictment low, but these factors do not by themselves explain why American prosecution is so vigorous. The level and intensity of prosecutions kept growing long after crime rates began their drop to generational lows, a mismatch for which population growth cannot account.[39] One straightforward reason for the frequency of prosecution is because that's what prosecutors' constituencies and careers demand. For many decades, the public has favored tough-on-crime approaches, a view that prosecutors seeking reelection or promotion to judicial positions keep front of mind.[40] For appointed positions, like U.S. Attorneys, elected officials understand voter preferences and nominate accordingly, if only to avoid catastrophic accusations of leniency, should a convict be undercharged or commit a vivid repeat. Once appointed, however, prosecutors proceed with almost no public accountability, at least when it comes to overcharging. Justice Scalia suggested that accountability might be achieved derivatively; if prosecutors turn into persecutors or otherwise misbehave, the public can punish the appointing executive at the ballot box.[41] But Scalia's claim is preposterous: the conduct of the U.S. Attorney for Wyoming is not a subject of intense study by Nate Silver at FiveThirty-Eight, and anyway, electoral sanction does not apply to politicians making appointments in their final terms. However, if appointed prosecutors are largely immune to public outcry, they must still satisfy intragovernmental constituencies; police and federal agents also expect, even demand, aggressive prosecutions. A prosecutor who declines to pursue a case based on factual weakness or legal technicality risks non-cooperation on future cases or even public condemnation by uniformed officers.* The net effect is that what accountability exists for prosecutors is a one-way ratchet, toward more vigorous prosecution.

Appointments, however, are better than elections. Almost all states vote in their senior prosecutors, allowing the public to express tough-on-crime preferences directly. Candidates cater accordingly, as democracy demands they should. However, prosecutors' special duties raise ethical questions about slavish fidelity to electoral whim, and campaign planks rarely feature rhetoric about well-rounded justice, though this is the prosecutor's prime duty. To the extent that any gestures to leniency are made, they tend to focus on matters over which state prosecutors have no decisive power, such as de-emphasizing immigration or petty drug cases (both of which are controlled by federal law). Doubtless, these vows of grace are not without virtue, but promising them creates ethical quandaries, as voters may be misled about local prosecutorial authority.

It is for all of these reasons that most countries do not elect prosecutors. They view prosecuting, like judging, as a profession to be insulated from politics, using appointment systems that rely on professional organizations to screen and regulate. Even common-law countries blanch at prosecutorial elections; England, for example, appoints Crown Prosecutors.[42] However, in

---

* By contrast, in some European nations, prosecutors are more independent from, or even control parts of, the police.

America, state prosecutorial elections have been standard since the Jacksonian Era. Supposedly, this holds prosecutors to public account, but prosecutorial misconduct is largely invisible, and again, electoral accountability usually points in one direction: toward aggressive prosecution.

These considerations are amplified by a political culture that emphasizes conviction "productivity" above all other goals, to the point where budgets are explicitly linked to convictions. For example, the U.S. Attorneys' Offices *say* that their goals are to prevent crime while "protect[ing] the rights of the American people" and "ensur[ing] and support[ing] the fair, impartial… administration of justice."[43] But their budgetary requests quantify those goals in terms of cases handled, emphasizing defendants found guilty.[44] The DOJ notes that 92.7 percent of its cases in 2014 were "resolved favorably," which in theory could include cases where, say, a prosecutor freed innocents, saved courts time and taxpayers expense, or upheld the law by dismissing charges where evidence was tainted. But no, looking at the math, "resolved favorably" really means convictions, and in 2014, U.S. Attorneys declined to prosecute in only 16.6 percent of matters received.[45] Perhaps metrics like justice are too hard to reduce to tabular form. Fortunately, the DOJ's budget request includes edifying "success stories." *All* of the substantive success stories involve convictions or penalties.

Against the enormous pressures to charge stands the prosecutor's conscience. Justice Jackson's "gentlemanly" virtues would be handy here, given the rubbery ethical rules that brace the prosecutorial backbone.[46] Prosecutors must obey the same basic rules as other attorneys, somewhat enhanced by, e.g., prohibitions against bringing cases without due cause. Nevertheless, the specific ethical guidelines applicable to prosecutors remain permissive and ambiguous—prosecutors can basically charge as they please, and where discretion is limited, it's mainly to *require* prosecutors to pursue the most serious viable charges.[47] The ABA's laudable standards quoted earlier are also optional; prosecutors do not even need to consider them. Chief prosecutors may voluntarily provide ethical guidance, and the DOJ publishes its *Manual* to that end, but these guidelines have no real force of law, and U.S. Attorneys have "plenary" authority over criminal prosecutions and may depart from DOJ defaults, rendering the *Manual* borderline advisory.[48] Equally disquieting is that most prosecutors' offices do not make explicit their decision to adopt, forgo, or modify ethical guidelines. And even if, say, DOJ's internal guidelines were breached, only DOJ has standing to sanction.[49]

Voters and defendants, in fact, have almost no direct recourse in the event of overzealous prosecution, thanks to our old enemy, sovereign immunity. Federal prosecutors enjoy functionally absolute immunity for their core duties.*[50] Even when prosecutors stray into collateral work, such as helping out with investigations, they still enjoy qualified immunity, a robust shield against misconduct.[51] The window for liability opens when prosecutions are "vexatious, frivolous, or in bad faith," and only when damage awards would not be "unjust" (for whom and in what way are not entirely clear). Misconduct cases are nearly impossible to win, and might not be economically viable in any event, with federal recoveries for costs and fees capped, and in some cases simply barred for individuals worth more than $2 million or corporations worth more than $7 million—i.e., the only litigants who can afford to sue prosecutors are financially deterred from doing so.[52] The only route to recovery for abuse of discretion requires clear proof of egregious circumstances—prosecutions that are vindictive or grossly violate constitutional rights—and the case law makes these so hard to prove that they are all but impossible to win, absent a media frenzy.[53] Worse, because prosecutorial immunity attaches to prosecutorial *acts*, those fulfilling prosecutorial functions (such as social workers who remove children from family custody) can also make claims of immunity.[54]

While the public cannot legally hold prosecutors to account, judges could. Prosecutors are frequently described as "quasi-judicial" (and by implication,

---

*   The Supreme Court had a chance to carve back immunity in a 2010 case involving prosecutors obtaining false testimony, but the parties settled before the Court decided, and the issue was avoided. But the sovereigns' positions were clear: the Obama Administration and attorneys general from twenty-seven states plus the District of Columbia encouraged the Court to protect full immunity.

are only "quasi-executive"), and surely this means the judiciary has a role to play in regulating prosecutorial behavior—not least because judges essentially manufactured prosecutorial immunity in the first place. Having laid the minefield, however, judges do not seem eager to wander through it, perhaps because doing so would call their own immunity into question. There is, however, one exercise of discretion judges *must* review—plea bargains—because judicial approval is required for the entry of most pleas.

All Plea, No Bargain

Plea bargaining excites scholars, arousing the sort of indignation normally associated with some novel injustice, though bargaining has existed for centuries. In the heyday of English private prosecution, plaintiffs routinely brought two charges for the same wrong—forgery being a common example—an aggravated charge that carried the death penalty and a lesser charge with a lower sentence, such as transportation to Australia. Were defendants to cooperate by making partial restitution, the plaintiffs would drop the more severe charge. This remains the essential dynamic: a combination of multiple charges and varying penalties, granting prosecutors the means to deal.

While plea bargains have always been common, their essential nature has changed. In the nineteenth century, perhaps three-quarters of prosecutions were bargained out, often representing a good deal for all involved, as sentences imposed were frequently light and the state had limited capacity to accommodate legions of long-term prisoners. As the list of crimes and punishments became more severe in the twentieth century, plea bargaining became more coercive and the outcomes more dire. The introduction of mandatory minimums in the 1980s encouraged ever more defendants to settle; today, plea bargaining resolves up to 96+ percent of criminal charges.

Doubtless, most plea bargains are, as they always were, a function of *some* guilt. If bargains truly matched guilt and sentence, with an appropriate discount for the expense saved and without undue coercion, there would be no great problem. There are reasons to doubt that those happy conditions prevail. Prosecutors have extraordinary incentives to bargain hard. The public expects convictions, which plea bargains assure. Public clamor in the 1980s and 1990s also pushed prosecutors toward punitive sentencing that sent the right signal, and when life terms and capital punishment became plausible outcomes for crimes that formerly bore ten to twenty years of prison time, the pressure on defendants to cave became irresistible.

Pleas also lighten the prosecutorial workload, which can be high. This might seem like a weakness that defendants could exploit, but most defendants lack the resources (including the resource of pure innocence) to go to trial. Even if more defendants insisted on trial, prosecutors always have the resources to try at least *some* cases, so defendants face a collective action problem—a prisoner's dilemma, of a sort. Defendants cannot be sure theirs will not be the case tried and they believe (with some reason) that prosecutors will pursue more punitive charges against anyone who refuses to plead, to send a message to other defendants who might not cooperate. The recent expansion of jail-without-bail also motivates defendants to settle. Many poor defendants unable to post bail or bond have already served time, lost their reputations and jobs, and therefore bargain for the only asset they have left: future freedom.

Plea bargaining's triumph cannot be laid solely at the feet of prosecutors. Judges could always winnow out unfair bargains, though they have their own reasons to prefer quick and easy pleas. Judges—especially state judges—face the same caseload and electoral pressures that make pleas attractive to prosecutors. Reputational risk creates its own incentives, as a bargain, unlike a trial, carries little risk of an embarrassing reversal by an appellate court. Perversely, the reputational incentive became more powerful with the Warren Court's expansion of defendants' rights and criminal procedure protections, which provided defendants endless and complicated grounds to challenge the conduct of criminal trials. While the cases of the

1950s and 1960s were rightly celebrated as defense victories, *as a whole,* they tend to work best for individual defendants with good lawyers and strong cases while creating perverse incentives for trial judges to sign off on all but the craziest pleas. The rise of sentencing guidelines with mandatory minimums also encouraged bargaining, and even after *Booker* made the Sentencing Guidelines merely the defaults, judges must work hard to modify sentences toward leniency—a deterrent to doing anything other than reaching for the rubber stamp. The shortest, best route to leniency still runs through the prosecutor.[55]

There is no doubt that a substantial majority of defendants should plead out, for reasons of simple guilt or rational cynicism. But 96 percent is not a "substantial majority," it's virtually everyone, suggesting that too many defendants take bad pleas because they lack alternatives. For some charges, the line between expeditious pleading and legal blackmail blurs. This is especially so given the development of appellate waivers, where prosecutors require defendants to give up many rights to appeal—as the DOJ notes, "[t]he advantage of a broad sentencing appeal waiver is that it will bar the appeal of virtually any Sentencing Guideline issue."[56] These waivers also subject defendants to the risk that the court itself may mete out a longer sentence, undoing the bargain without undoing the plea, while defeasing an appeal.[57] Unwilling pleas also subvert the old ideal that "every man has his day in court" and render nugatory the right to a jury trial—you cannot be said to have a "right to vote" if it requires a game of Russian roulette before you cast a ballot. But this is the dynamic prosecutorial power fosters. And curiously, the public defense system—the prosecutor's nominal opponent—has become an unhappy accomplice to the plea bargain regime.

Mercy's Underfunded Angels

Public defenders arrived about a century after public prosecutors and, from the start, one of their stated goals was to facilitate plea bargains. Naturally, some of this was just a PR ploy by defense advocates to overcome public unease with using taxpayer dollars to help criminals escape sanction. Public defenders have always been committed to shielding their clients from harsh sentences and wrongful convictions. That does not mean they have not accidentally made good on their original talking points.

What co-opted public defenders into the plea bargain regime is the substantial funding mismatch between prosecutors and defenders. In 2007, the last year for which comparable data were available, states spent $5.8 billion on prosecutors' offices versus $2.3 billion for public defenders.[58] Quite naturally, public defenders' offices are overwhelmed in ways that prosecutors' offices are not. Many states also rely on contractors to conduct public defense, invariably at below-market rates. New York's standard rates for felony defense are $75 per hour, which means the state can pay less per hour for murder defense than Manhattanites do to have a sink unclogged.[59] Other jurisdictions use fixed-fee contracts, paying a flat rate for a set number of cases regardless of their complexity, and these, like all such arrangements, encourage corner-cutting. Settlements of unseemly expedience are frequent—an egregious example being one California county that paid so little that only 0.5 percent of cases on that contract went to trial; no surprise, given that attorneys (including a newbie assigned to serious felonies) managed hundreds of cases each.[60] And unlike prosecutors, who frequently have in-house investigators to supplement the considerable police resources at their disposal, public defenders often have limited investigative help to build a defense.

Plea bargains, even bad bargains, tempt overworked defenders. The law assumes the defendant is the client of his attorney and master of his defense, but budgetary constraints render that mostly fiction. A defendant who pushes for trial can be an aggravation to his defender and to other defendants making claims on the same limited resource. Defenders' status as repeat players, constantly bargaining with the same prosecutors, compounds the pressure, as defenders do not want reputations for unreasonably resisting pleas (even when it's in the interest of any single defendant to negotiate hard).

Many defenders have won significant victories for their clients, including proving factual innocence. These are, however, extraordinary events and nothing about the public defense system, save the individual passion of an attorney, makes such outcomes as common as they might be.

Public Disservice

Given that a large fraction of defendants are factually guilty of *something*, it's fair to ask whether any of these critiques matter. For the legal system itself, the answer is a clear "yes." The whole system of public prosecution and defense violates the spirit of the law, and could eventually undermine the respect criminal law needs to survive. A system that promises judicious prosecution while focusing only on convictions, one that mandates no special set of ethics for prosecutors, insulates prosecutors from legal accountability, reduces the grand jury tradition to a charade, fails to provide adequate funding to Constitutionally mandated defense counsel, and conducts 96 percent of its business by backroom deal, is a system that sells its credibility far too cheaply. Arguably, the degradation of criminal law provides enough reason to demand reform.

Skeptics might ask to see more concrete harms. The whole culture of secrecy makes it impossible to present summary statistics; cases not brought to public trial, tested by adversaries, and resolved by judges and juries can't always be evaluated. Among the Rumsfeldian known unknowns, however, lurk enough known knowns to give anyone pause. We *know* that hundreds of convicts have been exonerated by DNA and, even without the magic of the lab, that prosecutors had good reason to doubt the guilt of many of these defendants.[61] We *know* that overzealous prosecutors have (per one federal judge) created an "epidemic" of Constitutional violations, including withholding crucial evidence, and charged defendants whom prosecutors had good reason to believe were legally or factually innocent.[62] We *know* that prosecutors have used their discretion to make an example out of defendants as a matter of policy, not the facts of a given case.[63] Aaron Swartz, a hacker who downloaded reams of academic articles in a misguided crusade to make intellectual property more available, committed a crime—though was that worthy of thirteen felony counts, a $4 million fine, and three decades in prison? We *know* that the academic groups who suffered the theft preferred to leave Swartz unprosecuted. But we also *know* that the U.S. Attorney disagreed, pushing forward until Swartz killed himself, a suicide his family blamed on relentless, overreaching prosecution.[64]

We also *know* that prosecutors emphasize crimes that produce quick pleas, just as we *know* prosecutions can have racially disparate effects depending on the type of crime.[65] We can also reasonably conclude that prosecutions for petty crimes considerably reduce resources available to pursue other wrongs with greater economic and personal consequences. We also *know* that prosecutorial discretion has long been tied to illicit purposes, tangled up in Jim Crow, and has been abused to protect other enforcers.

What we don't entirely know is why prosecutors occasionally go berserk, as when an Alabama prosecutor brought a case against a 76-year-old veteran for growing marijuana, fully aware that the defendant's decades-old robbery priors would result in an automatic life sentence without parole.[66] (Even Roy Moore thought it ridiculous.) But we do know that prosecutors failed to bring charges against Harvey Weinstein despite possessing evidence of his misconduct until public outrage prompted a new course, and that a New York DA proved unusually accommodating to Donald Trump, Jr. and his sister, having received a campaign donation from the family's corporate lawyer.[67] So we have our suspicions about "discretion." There are unknown unknowns, too, though until prosecutors become more transparent about their process, we can only guess—and that we have to guess is yet another reason for reform. So, the answer to whether the system requires reform is, at a theoretical and practical level: yes.

Necessary though reforms may be, nothing has been done to refashion the culture or incentives that make miscarriages of justice likely. Nor has anything been systematically done to meaningfully improve public defense, despite decades of begging by defenders and public interest groups. Out of desperation, entire defenders' offices have refused to take new cases or have sued to obtain adequate funding. (One defender took the grimly humorous step of invoking the bar's right to appoint one of its own to defend an indigent—said appointee being the governor of Missouri, who had refused adequate funding to public defense offices.)[68]

Reformatory inaction has high social costs. Overcriminalization, overcharging, and the culture of plea bargaining have led to extraordinary levels of incarceration, costing tens of billions, though as we'll see in Chapter 12, without much deterrent or reformatory effect. The present system also undermines law's integrity by reducing to rhetorical posturing all the promises of jury trials, indigent defense, judicious prosecution, the judge-as-final-arbiter, and so on. It's no real consolation that the lack of public outcry is as much a result of public attitudes toward crime as simple lack of knowledge. What would citizens make of prosecutors who carry no binding ethical responsibilities and cannot be held to legal account?

The system deserves judgment, but most of the public's criminal lawyers deserve sympathy. The world of criminal law is, by the standards of private law, unrestrained mayhem. Defendants rarely make for easy partners in the legal process: mental illness, a lack of fluency, poor education, and varying grasps of the legal system are routine challenges—and of course, some are violent, incorrigible criminals. For dealing with all of this, prosecutors and defenders collect modest pay and receive fewer social rewards than other legal servants like police. Prosecutors' jobs may not be as physically dangerous, but they are hardly safe. Serious physical attacks are quite rare, though intimidation is widespread, with almost half of prosecutors' offices receiving threats.[69] The DOJ doesn't collect comparable data for defense lawyers, but threats against them are routine, and perhaps even more frequent than against prosecutors.

It is precisely because the circumstances of criminal law are so awful that the legal system must be reformed. Legal systems exist to help us transcend the passions and frailties of the moment. A system that requires ethical behavior and holds prosecutors to account checks the very human tendency to assume, after prosecuting nine despicable criminals, that the tenth is no different. And a system that grants both sides sufficient monetary and temporal resources is one that can treat prison sentences as something other than trinkets to be auctioned on a legal eBay. These systems are not fictions: they exist in other countries. They should exist here, because they are, quite literally, the systems American law *requires*.

CHAPTER TEN

POLICE: THE THICK BLUE LINE

Freedom is about authority. Freedom is about the willingness of every single human being to cede to lawful authority a great deal of discretion about what you do.

Rudy Giuliani (1994)[1]

In January 2011, police in Framingham, Massachusetts, smashed Eurie Stamps's front door, tossed in a flash grenade, and stormed Stamps's home. Police had been tipped off that Stamps's stepson might be dealing drugs from "around" the house and obtained a search warrant, but Stamps himself was not a target, had no history of violence, and police had been specifically informed prior to the raid that Stamps posed no threat. Nevertheless, police ordered Stamps to the floor with his hands in plain view, and though Stamps complied, one officer thought it would be prudent to train his M4 assault rifle (safety flicked off) to keep the 68-year-old black grandfather under control. At some point during the chaos of the eleven-officer raid, Stamps's guard tripped or fell, unable to manage his cumbersome, military-grade body armor. The officer's M4 discharged, and Stamps, who had been contentedly watching television in his pajamas moments earlier, was dead. It was a tragedy made more senseless given that the prime target of the raid, Stamps's stepson, had been arrested outside the house *before* police broke down Stamps's door. While police did find drugs on the stepson, and arrested the raid's second target inside Stamps's house, Stamps had no drugs, offered no resistance, and had no real connection to the crime other than the misfortune of having the wrong stepchild.

Shocking as the details of Stamps's saga were, nothing about a SWAT team armed with military equipment to execute a routine search warrant was uncommon. Nor was it uncommon that the district attorney exonerated the officer, or that eight of ten claims in the Stamps family's subsequent lawsuit were initially dismissed. The only unusual feature of this "unfortunate matter" (to use the words of the town's lawyer) was that Framingham's insurance company agreed to settle the litigation, paying Stamps's family $3.75 million.[2] Most victims get nothing.

Militarized raids have become a regular part of American policing, with predictably tragic consequences. Special Weapons and Tactics teams were originally designed for extraordinary situations like hostage-taking, but they have become disturbingly ordinary. SWAT teams, unlike hostage takers, are everywhere: by the mid-2000s, 90 percent of large cities had SWAT teams, as did about 80 percent of small towns.[3] The police have become omnipresent, miniature armies kitted out with bomb suits, battering rams, night-vision goggles, armored personnel carriers, helicopters, drones, assault rifles, flashbang grenades, .50 caliber machine guns, and other military paraphernalia.[4] Police receive much of their stockpile from the Defense Department's 1033 Program, partially subsidized by the Department of Homeland Security. These gifts come with few meaningful restrictions or guidelines, save one: under standard agreements, any gear transferred to local police must be used within one year or returned.[5] Rather than give up their deadly baubles, police find reasons to deploy SWAT teams for even the most mundane work. Using statistical sampling, the ACLU concluded that at least 79 percent of SWAT deployments execute mere *searches* (mostly for drugs), which is about as practical as using a Black Hawk helicopter to pick up the kids from soccer practice.[6] Predictably, innocent people—a category that has included children, the pregnant, and the elderly—are injured or die, victims of literal overkill. Because of immunity doctrines, victims and their families have little redress. Nor do other police or public prosecutors care to investigate the particulars of most of these cases.

Didn't the Founding Fathers complain about English troops breaking down doors to enforce tax and customs laws, infringing on sacred liberty? Yes, they did—at exhausting length. And what, precisely, is the practical difference between the militarized policing of 2019 and Redcoat raids in 1776? In conceptual terms, both are objectionable; in practical terms, modern policing is a lot more deadly and invasive. And the whole of contemporary policing now drinks regularly at the well of militarized absurdity. The Los Angeles School District's in-house police acquired three grenade launchers and a "small tank" because, one supposes, recess gets rowdy.[7] In 2010, Phoenix sheriffs drove a tank into a man's house, though the crime in question was cockfighting. It was perverse enough that the outcome of this animal protection mission resulted in the extermination of all the chickens (plus a dog). But then there was the pilot of said tank—truly an epic day for self-government—actor Steven Seagal, who had been, like many others, deputized (many of them as part of a benefits-for-badges program).[8]

Militarization and pay-to-play are two aspects of a much larger problem with policing: America has a lot of cops with a lot of weapons, and no firm consensus about what the police mission is or what oversight is required. The police carry some—but only some—of the blame. Society calls upon cops to be social workers, assault teams, regulatory wardens, detectives, and civic ombudsmen—a clearly unviable combination. But rather than clarify police missions, or subject departments to accountability, government resorts to the tactics of the absentee parent, offering goodies like tanks and immunity. As for the consequences of this odd parenting strategy, it seems government would prefer not to know; government collects data through sporadic and incomplete censuses. Fragmented as the data are, a mosaic can be assembled, and the results do not encourage: police seem to find it difficult to fulfill basic missions like solving crime, while resorting to violence at rates other nations would deem scarcely credible. This raises all sorts of questions, starting with: How did a nation that rebelled against military enforcement of paper and tea taxes end up with a tank-driving Steven Seagal conducting a raid to break up chicken fights?

The Origins of Policing

By law's long standards, cops are new. For millennia, what public forces existed were special units specially tasked with suppressing insurrection, apprehending those who betrayed the state, and protecting the property of ruling elites. (Cynics would say *plus ça change*.) Even Imperial Rome, the most bureaucratic state in the West until the Enlightenment, hewed to this model, and the *cohortes urbanae* were essentially paramilitary forces designed to control riots and fight organized gangs, episodic events where one quasi-military force countered another.[9] "Policing" in its modern sense was largely unknown and seemingly unwanted well into the eighteenth century.

Therefore, unlike most issues about law and governance, which have been debated for millennia, there's been comparatively little time for societies to develop deeply held convictions about civilian policing. Even the ancient Greeks, normally inexhaustible in their opinions about governance, and whose *polis* serves as a root word of "police," had little to say, almost none of it good.[10] When Greeks needed to control unruly crowds or hold defendants awaiting trial, they delegated those tasks to slaves; no self-respecting Greek would want to exercise dominion over a fellow citizen. And the pillars of modern policing, routine patrol and intrusive investigations, were out of the question, at least where full citizens were concerned.[11]

The general absence of police did not mean criminals were left alone, only that citizens expected to handle policing themselves, just as they managed private prosecutions. Private parties could make citizen's arrests (a practice that remains legal in Britain and some American states such as California).[12] In England, a smattering of sheriffs handled the few crimes in which the state took a particular interest, e.g., insurrection, organized banditry, and poaching on aristocratic property. Sheriffs became somewhat more active in the thirteenth century, at the behest of reforming kings including, unavoidably, Edward I.[13] But even mild institutionalization filled Englishmen with apprehensions about remote and arbitrary authority, and it's no coincidence that the Robin Hood myth unfolds in the same century that Edward I granted more influence to sheriffs, including the very real Sheriffs of Nottingham.[14] The English, and their Colonial descendants, were perpetually chary about despots trampling on ancient liberties, fears confirmed when the tyrannical French inaugurated large-scale policing in the seventeenth century. Nevertheless, as populations grew and urbanized, the clutter of semiprofessional enforcers—sheriffs, constables, night watchmen (the latter recruited from the uninspiring category of "useful invalids")—seemed increasingly anachronistic and inadequate, even to passionate libertarians.

By the 1820s, British reformers decided to rationalize the system by founding a proper police force.[15] First, Britain's government needed to explain what the police would do, and how they would do it without becoming arbitrary tyrants. That was, and remains, tricky. Even the most basic duty, of enforcing law, raises difficulties. Citizens want laws enforced, but not always and not everywhere; people want to be able to roll a stop or jaywalk on occasion. Anyway, no police department could practice universal enforcement, so law enforcement necessarily becomes the exercise of coercive, discretionary power. That's precisely what worried Englishmen then, and worries some Americans now: with discretion comes the possibility for abuse.

So, when Sir Robert Peel unveiled London's Metropolitan Police in 1829, the first modern police department in the English-speaking world, his government tried to gain citizens' trust by carefully defining the goals and values of the new police. London furnished each officer with "General Instructions," stating that the principal police function was to "*prevent* crime and disorder." But success required the "willing co-operation of the public," and to reassure a skeptical public, Peel placed special emphasis on what police should *not* do. They should abstain from violence, deploying the "minimum degree of physical force which is necessary" to achieve a specific objective and "*only* when" other peaceful means had failed; refrain from "*even seeming to usurp the powers of the judiciary*"; not involve themselves in policy (the proper concern of legislators); and avoid "judging guilt."[16] And Peel's government, quite presciently, forbade police from engaging in a pantomime of arrests or violent showmanship as substitutes for actual prevention. The aim was to assure Londoners that police would not be alien or repressive. London reminded its officers that they served at public sufferance and should always exhibit "courtesy" and "friendly good humour" to the public of which they were a part, a point Peel drove home by dyeing police uniforms blue, in contrast to the army's red uniforms.[17] It was a shockingly progressive agenda, and London police eventually succeeded in part because they took Peel's admonitions seriously.

When American police departments cohered from the 1830s to the 1870s, many adopted Peel's principles. But policing was a harder sell to Americans, given Revolutionary discontents about standing armies conducting invasive searches under "general warrants" (blanket licenses to search and seize).[18] Accordingly, many American departments did not initially provide officers with uniforms or arms; Brooklyn's police, as just one example, did not carry guns until the 1880s. Nor did police sit entirely comfortably in constitutional schemas. Most state constitutions, and the federal Bill of Rights (subsequently "incorporated" against the states), place significant restrictions on the powers of search and seizure, and most police work is in direct tension with guarantees about the privacy of one's person and home, requiring a social consensus about balance which has not yet evolved.

Although many early police departments were incompetent and corrupt, they at least posed few major risks to life or liberty, a function of their smallness and political imperatives to leave the people alone. There was, however, one crucial exception: black Americans, specifically slaves. As legal property, slaves (and blacks generally) were excluded from the calculus of liberty. Capturing slaves and repressing their revolts were core functions for many early police departments. Indeed, Southern police vividly alleged the threats fugitive slaves posed to citizens' lives and property in order to drum up popular support for arming officers.[19] Northern police were also stained by slavery; they often cooperated with Southern colleagues to return slaves. Racial bias has been an original sin from which there has been no easy escape.

Over time, American police embraced the protection of all citizens (with varying degrees of sincerity), but this progress was offset by the development of a warrior mentality, where police stood separate not just from blacks but the public generally. It was the sort of internal army that Peel wanted to avoid, and it eventually employed the invasive practices against which the Founders rebelled: warrantless searches, arbitrary seizures, and paramilitary coercion.*[20] The public's expectations also changed, and the original mission of crime prevention expanded into something more amorphous, with police called upon to fulfill roles that lay well outside the scope of their original mission. But even that mission, in many places, developed in strange ways. Protecting citizens is just one goal to be weighed against other less licit imperatives like revenue collection, protecting the institution of policing, and selective repression. These developments erode legitimacy and divorce police from the public, problems the legal system amplifies by shielding police from accountability.

Structures and Staffing

American policing is highly decentralized, a product of historical assumptions that police bound to their communities would be more responsive and

---

* The best encapsulation of the dangers of military–police overlap comes from the *Battlestar Galactica* reboot, of all places. As *Galactica*'s chief informs his civilian president: "There's a reason you separate military and the police. One fights the enemies of the state, the other serves and protects the people. When the military becomes both, then the enemies of the state tend to become the people."

accountable than a central authority. This is an idea with merit, though localization must be balanced against the need for transparency and accountability. As a useful compromise, many nations conduct localized policing but centralize certain operations so that someone, even a distant someone, can collect data, implement policy, and ensure compliance. Although semi-centralization seems to produce higher satisfaction and better outcomes for both public and police, American policing remains resolutely fragmented. Some 15,388 state and local agencies employed about 724,690 sworn officials as of 2013, the latest year for which data is available (iffy data collection being a hallmark of highly decentralized institutions).[21] By contrast, just forty-three forces police England and Wales, and though localities have substantial influence over police, Parliament supplies two-thirds of policing budgets and exercises substantially greater oversight than Washington does over American departments.[22]

Supplementing local police forces are federal and private entities. Federal police comprise only a small part of all law enforcement, with just 120,000 full-time officers, ~80 percent of whom work at just two places, the Department of Homeland Security and the Department of Justice (which houses the FBI).[23] Private police forces, which are something of a throwback to the days of citizen self-help, are more numerous. Reasonable estimates suggest that 90,000 private organizations employ at least 1.1 million people, making private actors the largest component of American policing.[24] Most private policing involves the mundane protection of private property—mall cops, really. However, a small but growing fraction of private police wield powers similar to those of normal police, though without the same legal and political restrictions. In some states, private cops can obtain government permission to carry weapons, display badges, make arrests, and exercise other police-like powers.[25] And then, of course, there's Deputy Seagal with his tank, plus other weekend warriors including super-donor/sometime-cop Robert Mercer who, despite his base on the East Coast, served as a police volunteer in New Mexico. Under federal law, Mercer (and certain other "deputies") could carry concealed weapons, one of the privileges of leasing a badge.[26]

Save for federal police, most departments operate on geographic lines. The smallest geographic units are metropolitan forces, though urbanization means that cities have the numerically largest forces; New York City, for example, has by far the largest police department in America. The next level up are county forces, usually called sheriffs' offices. Sheriffs are elected (city police chiefs are appointed) and often have non-patrol duties, like managing jails and providing security for county government. In some cases, sheriffs also provide full police services to towns and unincorporated areas that lack their own departments. State governments also sponsor their own forces to patrol highways, perform investigative work, coordinate across county lines, and fulfill special functions as permitted by state laws—the Texas Rangers being a famous example of the last. Federal agents operate nationwide, but are limited to dealing with crimes that cross state lines or otherwise implicate federal interests. In theory, localization promotes accountability, though many cities are too large for this to be fully plausible. The value of localization is also complicated by federalization, now that Washington can invoke jurisdiction whenever it pleases, thanks to the rise in interstate commerce and the enormous expansion of federal criminal law during the wars on drugs, terror, and, most recently, immigration.

On TV, federal agents usually arrive to save a case from the incompetence or corruption of local police, and while this is a trope, it does reflect real quality variations between policing institutions, much of which begins with recruitment. The FBI, despite ups and downs, has generally been regarded as law enforcement's elite and, by selection criteria, that's accurate. FBI special agents must have at least a college degree and three years of work experience, be in excellent physical condition, and pass comprehensive background checks and skills tests. They must also train for twenty-one weeks at the FBI Academy, perform well during a long probationary period, and be willing to accept postings far from home. The whole process, selective and drawn out, deters lesser candidates, helping ensure that FBI agents are both qualified and committed.[27]

Requirements for local and private policing are vastly more forgiving.

While the FBI warns recruits of the rigors of application, the San Francisco Police Department's website chirpily notes that "Applying Is Easy!" and many forces advertise that jobs can be quickly had.[28] Although blue-ribbon commissions have been agitating for higher standards since the 1960s, including college-educated forces, minimum qualifications remain low. About 84 percent of local departments will accept recruits with a high school degree or equivalent. The Bureau of Justice Statistics (BJS) estimated that another 15 percent of departments had "some type of college requirement," though most departments are satisfied by coursework not leading to a degree, and others accept an associate's degree—only 1 percent of departments require a full four-year college degree.[29] Departments are always free to recruit above the minimum, and many do. Though data are incomplete and many surveys confuse attending college with obtaining a degree, it appears that 30 to 55 percent of newer recruits have some type of college degree (with considerable regional variation). Younger, better-educated recruits have raised departmental averages otherwise depressed by older cops hired when recruiters put less stock in college. Nevertheless, college is merely a preference, and departments can and do hire down to their minimums (educational and otherwise), especially when pressed. This has led to catastrophes, infamously in the case of the District of Columbia Police Department of the 1990s, whose recruitment binge led to bribe-taking, back-scratching, and sundry other corruption.[30]

While there's a strange level of controversy over the degree to which higher education benefits policing, it would be remarkable if schooling had *no* salutary effects. Indeed, several studies have found that better-educated officers provoke fewer citizen complaints and are less prone to use force.[31] Education may be the explanatory variable, though it's hard to disentangle associated factors like intelligence, motivation, social position, and higher average age at recruitment. Certainly, police should not be noticeably *less* educated than the general population, of which 32.5 percent have a four-year college degree (36 percent for those ages 25–44).[32] A chronically undereducated force would feed impressions that police are less capable than the citizens they serve, breeding mutual incomprehension and resentment.

After educational screening, departments test for aptitude and temperament. The aptitude tests don't seem particularly challenging; judging by sample questions in commercial study guides, someone with an eighth-to-tenth–grade education could pass with minimal preparation. The true hurdle is the background check, as many aspiring cops have criminal pasts. To satisfy hiring needs, 80 percent of larger police departments are willing to overlook minor misdemeanors; many departments will forgive DUIs, soft drug use, credit problems, and other indicators of potentially poor judgment.[33] The actual prevalence of waivers depends on department, but it's odd that a society busily drug-testing Taco Bell employees overlooks criminality in its police. At least, however, departments can screen criminal history. Determining if a potential hire has been terminated from another police job is much more difficult; there's (surprise, surprise) no truly universal database of officers fired from prior police jobs for misconduct, and even checking the patchwork databases that do exist may not be revealing, as some departments (governed by fear of suit and union rules) fire abusive cops but fail to disclose the misconduct in termination reports.[34] Various departments have found themselves saddled with bad cops fleeing other departments, only to fire them without disclosure, perpetuating the cycle.

After recruitment (assuming the hiree has not been an officer before) comes the police academy. The programs are surprisingly short, anywhere from a few weeks to six months, though this perhaps doesn't much matter, as curricula fall well short of the ideal. Instead of emphasizing seemingly critical subjects including methods of detection, criminal codes, civil rights, and the social functions of policing, the menu boils down to two subjects: guns and paperwork. For example, California's model curriculum requires a minimum of forty-eight hours on paperwork procedures, seventy-two hours on "firearms and chemical agents," but just two hours of training on the criminal justice system generally—i.e., barely enough time to screen one of the (six) *Police Academy* movies.[35] Standards for private police run even lower, in some cases verging on the nonexistent.

American police departments are, on the whole, less selective than those of peer nations. Europe's richer nations require more education for recruitment and promotion, have training programs that are more comprehensive and less obsessed with force, and impose more uniform standards.[36] For example, German recruits complete two or more years of specialized training in addition to holding either a college degree or a certificate from a policing-oriented high school, and senior police officials need a master's degree or better. British police have more stringent background checks, longer and more comprehensive training, and tougher screening tests than their American cousins.[37] Foreign departments have noticeably higher rates of solving crime, with fewer allegations of abuse, than American police. Education and training play roles, of course, but so do cultural expectations about what police should do.

Crime-fighting and Guardianship

In 2015, a presidential commission identified two competing models for policing: the "warrior" and the "guardian."[38] The warrior enforces law and fights crime, while the guardian has more general obligations of protection and service. The commission dredged up the term "guardian" from Plato's *Republic,* perhaps not realizing that Plato described proto-fascist liars who told people what to do at spear-point—or as Giuliani put it, "[f]reedom is about authority." (Giuliani had forgotten his Orwell; the correct quote is "freedom is slavery," but as Big Brother noted, "ignorance is strength.") Whatever the literary subtext, opinion polls suggest that the public views policing as tilting more toward the warrior/enforcer model, a view not always discouraged by police.[39]

In fact, warrior-style crime-fighting is not a major component of police work as a fraction of hours worked. Police spend less than 5 percent of their time dealing with violent crimes against persons (murder, kidnapping, battery), and another 15 to 20 percent on property crimes (burglary, trespass, vandalism); all the rest is a mix of traffic enforcement, social services, routine patrols, and paperwork.[40] The relative infrequency of violent crime as a direct component of police work is important, because fighting violent crime is a frequent justification for aggressive policing.

Perhaps police suppress serious crime by nipping minor crimes in the bud, and so a much larger chunk of police resources is devoted to vigorous crime-fighting in some attenuated way. This was the premise of "Broken Windows" policing (popularized by Giuliani), which cracked down on small-scale disorder, on the theory that a broken window would signal that the community would tolerate graver civic decay. Thus, the NYPD cracked down on petty crimes such as graffiti and turnstile-jumping (the criminal equivalent of the broken window) to prevent future and more violent crimes. But dealing with minor crimes is low-risk and requires little force, and it's hard to justify paramilitary policing because a fare-jumper *might* turn into the Zodiac killer.

Broken Windows was, in a way, a gussied-up version of the old thinking that more cops on the street would reduce crime. Politicians constantly promise more "feet on the beat," and while this may be effective as a political strategy, it's not clear that it's an effective policing strategy. Since the 1970s, empirical research has cast doubt on the utility of simply beefing up patrols. In 1972 and 1973, Kansas City tried to assess the impact of varying patrol intensity. The city established three study areas: the first as a control; the second, with preventive patrols eliminated entirely; the third, with policing radically increased.[41] Although patrol intensity varied from −100 percent to +300 percent, researchers found no significant difference in crime levels or citizens' fear of crime or satisfaction with police.[42] Subsequent studies in other cities came to similar conclusions.[43] More sophisticated research, which targeted small and especially violent areas (the police equivalent to the Army's "surge" strategy), did associate enhanced patrols with falling crime, but improvements eventually subsided.[44] Thus, politicians' chatter about beefing up patrols is mostly vacant, as should have surprised no one. In any event, most crimes are not detected by police on patrol. Rather, the *public* reports criminal activity—and when police solve crimes, they usually do so by building cases against suspects supplied by victims.

Even with public help, police are notably unsuccessful at bringing criminals to account. The conventional metric for "solving" crime is the "clearance rate," defined as taking a suspect into custody and remanding to judicial process.[45] Roughly 22 to 23 percent of known offenses are cleared by arrest, which is not impressive, especially as this overstates the true rate of crime resolution.[46] First, estimates suggest that fewer than 47 percent of violent victimizations and 35 percent of property victimizations are reported, so true clearance percentages might be much lower (there obviously being no way to fully know).[47] Second, police "unfound" (their term) many reported crimes, ostensibly because there is not enough evidence to support a charge, a decision about which police have unaudited and legally unaccountable discretion—discretion which has been abused at several departments.[48] The NYPD had a long practice of manipulating statistics to achieve more pleasing results, and gaming the numbers became particularly intense after New York launched its COMPSTAT program, which provided data reports that became potentially embarrassing media fodder. Other manipulations include reducing the severity of a reported crime (e.g., categorizing a rape as an assault, or a grand larceny as simple theft), or invoking the "exceptional instances" clause of the clearance definition to terminate a case—a procedure originally designed to close out cases where circumstances beyond police control made normal resolution impossible, as when a prime suspect or key witness died. Some departments seem to blatantly abuse these exceptions: between 2006 and 2008, more than three-quarters of crimes cleared by Sheriff Joe Arpaio's department in Maricopa County were cleared by exception, vastly higher than rates in nearby departments such as Phoenix (0.08 percent), Mesa (6.0 percent), and Glendale (11.0 percent).[49]

Accounting for all these factors, very few crimes result in arrest, likely less than 10 percent. Resolution of property crimes is especially low, perhaps under 5 percent, because police rely on victims to provide a suspect and most theft victims cannot do so. Police also view these matters as low-priority, as property owners who have suffered burglaries know—it's customary for police to warn theft victims that the case will never be solved (the implication frequently being that no attempt will be made), so filing a police report becomes a mere formality in the insurance claims process, not a step toward justice. Perhaps this is a reasonable posture for police when it comes to minor crimes, and justifies low resolution rates. But serious crimes also have fairly low resolution rates. Murders, among the most thoroughly reported and investigated crimes (dead bodies being harder to ignore than a stolen lawnmower), have a gross resolution rate of 61.5 percent nationally, which is fine but not outstanding. Some departments fall well below the already so-so average; Chicago has cleared fewer than 40 percent of its murders in recent years, and in 2017 the rate dipped under 20 percent, meaning that Chicago's murder clearance rate is lower than the nominal national average resolution rate for violent and property crimes.[50] By contrast, Canadian police solve 67 to 74 percent of murders, while German police "clear up" (their term) more than 90 percent of murders/manslaughters.[51]

Discretion's Uses and Abuses

Police have considerable leeway when confronted with criminal conduct. It is largely up to an officer whether to overlook a crime, make an arrest, or use force against a suspect. This is not how the system supposedly works, though when an officer exercises good judgment, discretion can be for the best. An unwitting trespasser might willingly move along if warned by police, or a motorist might be chastened into fastening a seat belt after a warning. When leniency satisfies goals of safety at low cost to enforcement, discretion does net good. However, police sometimes let infractions slide for dubious reasons; cops are especially loath to arrest other cops, for example, and some highway patrols were notoriously forgiving of speeders whose bumper stickers featured police charities. Discretion has occasionally slid into serious derelictions of duty, as happened in Chicago in the 1970s, where police refused to patrol the city's notorious housing projects, either out of genuine fear or perhaps motivated by the belief that the lower-class, largely minority residents in public housing did not deserve protection. As departments do not gather relevant data, it's impossible to quantitatively evaluate whether discretion brings net good or ill, though proxy data in some areas, like racial bias in arrest rates, suggest the widespread abuse of discretion.

Victims exercise their own discretion, which police never know about; we all do this when we fail to call in stolen Amazon packages and so on, and this can be socially efficient since the chances of apprehension are near zero, while the personal and public costs of filing a report usually exceed the value of merchandise. Victims also sometimes decline to assist with investigations, either out of fear or indifference, in which case officers usually drop a case. This can be immaterial, though in certain matters, especially those involving domestic violence, it can amount to making social policy on the fly. Some states have addressed this by requiring police to make an arrest whenever they have probable cause to believe domestic abuse has occurred, regardless of the victim's nominal preference. In general, though, police retain autonomy over arrest decisions.

Few legal officials have discretion quite as wide as the police. This is why Sir Robert Peel hoped laws would be enforced uniformly, and why some critics have called for mandatory arrest policies for all types of crimes, to ensure equal protection. (These proposals are unrealistic, given finite resources, and possibly a case where the medicine would be as bad as the ailment.) A thoughtful decision to arrest, or threaten arrest, balances a range of social interests: the likelihood of conviction, the seriousness of the crime, the opportunity costs of making a particular collar, victims' preferences, and suspects' rights. The calculation is subtle, requiring education many officers do not have and experience junior officers (the mostly likely to be assigned beat duties) necessarily lack. It also requires knowledge of law that is unhelpfully vague. Unscrupulous or merely ignorant police can invoke ambiguous laws regarding panhandling, public disturbance and assembly, and so on, discouraging conduct that they incorrectly deem illegal (or find subjectively wrong). The possibility for abuse is not trivial, amplified by "contempt of cop" arrests.[52] Nor is there much people can do, because most states functionally prohibit "interfering" with police work or resisting arrest (even when the arrest itself is improper). Given the time, expense, and vocational consequences of arrest, citizens may simply comply with an officer's order, proper or not, building resentment toward the law.

Officers have also used discretion to further criminal activity, sometimes in the name of the greater good, and sometimes not. In limited cases, police allow informants or even their own officers to participate in criminal activity as part of an undercover investigation.[53] Freedom of Information Act requests show that the FBI allowed "otherwise illegal activity" at least 5,658 times in 2011. Precise details were withheld, though they may not exist, as the FBI's internal controls are often lacking. The Bureau informed USA TODAY journalists that it couldn't so much as find files for prior years (though law requires meticulous record-keeping) and an Inspector General's report from 2005 suggested that some authorized criminality was not properly reported to supervisors.[54] These missing data are troubling, because FBI guidelines contemplate that agents might engage in practices such as money laundering and trading in controlled substances.[55] (For its part, the DEA doesn't seem to keep track of authorized criminality.) Given the seriousness of these activities, and the known lapses in internal control, the potential for disaster is not small. Local police departments also permit their own to participate in otherwise illegal activities. High-speed pursuits are an undeniable example, and whatever goes on in undercover vice operations is a fertile ground for speculation.

Another difficulty is that improper motives can be hidden behind the banner of discretion, and trading leniency for favors has been a traditional weakness in policing. The free cup of coffee presents no serious problems; indeed, it's often happily given to local cops, just as many donate to police-affiliated charities out of general gratitude.* However, anything beyond a small and isolated freebie usually comes with an expectation, and many departments lack clear rules about lower-level gratuities, so there's ambiguity about how many free pastries and coffees constitute too many. Departments also do not have strong guidelines about freelance work, which many officers perform. Potential conflicts of interest can be substantial. How will officers respond when dealing with a private enterprise, like a bar, which employs a fellow officer as a part-time bouncer? The murk can be considerable; worse, some police have been caught taking bribes, and directly participating in drug running, prostitution, perjury, and bank robbery. Major departments have suffered episodes of severe corruption; in the 1970s, the NYPD was one of the biggest drug dealers in the city, and in the 1990s, there were few types of crime that LAPD's Rampart Division did not practice, becoming notorious enough to inspire *The Shield*, FX's crooked-cops drama.

Fairness and Force

Two major categories of abused discretion deserve particular attention: discriminatory policing and widespread use of unnecessary force. Unlike bribery and extortion, these practices are semi-institutionalized, and they are protected both informally (by union power and the "wall of silence") and formally (by doctrines of legal immunity and "police officer bills of rights" codified in state law).[56] As a result, where the layperson sees bias or excessive force, the law frequently sees nothing, a divergence created by law's excessive deference to officer discretion and also by assumptions about police work that are not entirely supported.

Episodes of biased policing have been well publicized, especially after

---

* Police charities are often worthy institutions (I've donated minor amounts to a few), but they aren't entirely unproblematic, and some are mired in scandal. Moreover, if *any* citizen has a reasonable belief that a failure to donate will result in worse treatment, then no matter how good a charity's works, there's a problem.

2013, as the Black Lives Matter movement chronicled the stories of unarmed black suspect-victims like Trayvon Martin, Eric Garner, and Michael Brown. The existence of bias in individual officers and departments is beyond doubt, though *overall* prevalence is harder to quantify. As usual, direct nationwide data are missing, and what data are recorded sometimes contain errors that seem to be deliberate attempts to reduce racial skew, as when SFPD officers classified some Hispanic arrestees as "white."[57] While we can only infer from proxy indicators, it's undeniable that bias is a real problem. Minorities, especially black persons, are arrested at significantly higher rates than whites. Blacks account for 26.9 percent of total arrests (against 13.4 percent of the general population), the majority of arrests in murders/manslaughters (52.6 percent) and robberies (54.5 percent), and a hefty chunk of loitering violations (40.7 percent).[58] Blacks also comprise at least 33 percent of the incarcerated population generally, and in some states, much more; blacks constitute 68 percent of Maryland's incarcerated.[59] Social factors—such as the historical poverty and discrimination to which blacks are disproportionately subject—explain only some of the disproportion (disadvantaged people of all ethnicities being more likely to be arrested for many offenses). The rest of the difference requires explanation, which biased enforcement largely supplies.

The Constitution guarantees equal protection and forbids racial discrimination, so biased enforcement goes to the heart of law. Many departments, even in highly progressive cities, have fallen under the shadow of prejudice. For example, San Francisco police stop black motorists at approaching triple the frequency that population distribution would predict, and once stopped, the cars of black motorists are subject to nonconsensual searches at more than five times the rate for whites. Police do find contraband in blacks' cars, but only one-third of the time—notably, the lowest "hit" rate of any ethnic group.[60] In New York, the stop-and-frisk program, in full force from 2002 to 2013, captured a grossly disproportionate number of blacks and Latinos; the NYPD conducted more than 570,000 stop-and-frisks of minorities in 2011 alone.[61] Most were innocent (or innocent enough that the government declined to take further action; indeed, this was true for 88 percent of all ethnicities stopped).[62] A federal judge subsequently ruled that New York's existing stop-and-frisk program was unconstitutional, amounting to racial profiling.[63] (Nevertheless, versions of it continue.[64]) Following 9/11, local and federal police also targeted Muslim communities for enhanced surveillance, though these intrusions produced few (if any) significant arrests. Discriminatory policing both perpetuates prejudice *and* wastes police resources. But while yield rates in San Francisco, New York, and other cities were low, the sheer scale of searches ensured a steady flow of minorities into prisons. As Warren Buffett noted, "[i]f a cop follows you for 500 miles, you're going to get a ticket," and this is true, though a day of tailing a geriatric industrialist to write a $200 citation is not a terrific return on social assets, and the same holds for endless frisks to round up a couple of possession charges.[65]

Some activists explain discriminatory enforcement as an inevitable product of biased hiring policies, and if this is true, discriminatory enforcement is likely to be widespread and persistent. Racial/ethnic minorities comprise almost 40 percent of Americans, yet account for just 27.3 percent of police officers, and while the proportions have improved, progress has not been radical of late.[66] Departments that do not reflect their communities are often plagued by enforcement bias, as has been the case in Chicago, San Francisco, Los Angeles, and other big cities. Nor should citizens be beguiled by large numbers of minority officers if a department still fails to reflect its community. The Baltimore PD is almost evenly split between white and minority officers (though the city itself is less white than that), but that department's abuses were so bad that the DOJ intervened.[67]

As it happens, the academic literature is mixed on whether the race of an individual officer makes much difference in daily work, but this result is less important than the possibility that unbalanced hiring reflects institutional biases that will be recapitulated in the field and in legitimacy deficits suffered when departments do not reflect their communities. For these and other reasons, 44 percent of blacks report little or no confidence in their communities' police, versus just 18 percent of whites.[68] Minorities' distrust of police is crucial because minorities interact with police with disproportionate frequency, as both involuntary detainees and voluntary users of police services.[69] More balanced forces would help, though the standard response is that this cannot be achieved because minorities are unusually hard to recruit or fall below police hiring standards. As a statistical matter, some minority groups do have less education and more significant criminal records than the white majority (in which discrimination plays its own part). But even accepting this, the standard explanation is weak, given the low qualification thresholds for police, including forgiving attitudes toward prior convictions. In any event, it's possible to achieve near-complete parity with the community.[70] Atlanta police have done so, and that department is largely unburdened by the widespread bias scandals affecting many other big-city departments.[71]

Race is not the only way police can belong to a community. Formerly, officers lived inside the bounds of the cities they patrolled. In recent decades, residency requirements have been falling in police departments, and those that exist are often ignored. Today, 60 percent of officers in the seventy-five largest police forces live outside the limits of the cities that employ them, and in Boston, that included most of the police force's top brass, notwithstanding city hall's edict.[72] Many departments with alien forces experience high levels of discontent, while small towns with resident cops generally do not.

Entwined in the dynamics of alienation and discrimination are questions of excessive force, with minorities receiving disproportionately brutal treatment. Blacks are significantly more likely to be killed by police than whites, and minorities of all backgrounds account for over 60 percent of fatal police shootings when suspects are *unarmed* (here, in a dismal technicality, the minority becomes the majority).[73] Adjusting for the usual variables cited to explain away disparities—poverty, neighborhoods, etc.—still leaves a racial skew. What does narrow the gap considerably is frequency of police interaction, and as we've seen, minorities are substantially more likely to interact with police than are whites. Minorities still experience violence at a somewhat higher rate, but this reflects a larger problem, as suspects of any ethnicity face unusual dangers when meeting American police.

By global standards, American policing is violent. Data are again spotty and prone to faulty self-reporting, though journalists (especially at the *Guardian, Washington Post,* and *New York Times*) have done extraordinary work in assembling more comprehensive and disturbing accounts than those on official offer.[74] As researchers have noted, American police killed "more people in the first 24 days of 2015 than English and Welsh police have killed in the last 24 years."*[75] Black Americans are at high risk, but on a per-capita basis, even *white* Americans were fatally shot at twenty-six times the rate of German counterparts. American police also shot citizens at an estimated twelve times greater rate than Australian police and four times the rate of Canadian police.[76] Adjusting for factors like America's higher crime rate explains only part of the difference, and the unavoidable conclusion is that American policing is abnormally fatal. Besides guns, American police also have greater propensities to use clubs, fists, and chemical irritants. American police also use Tasers, a weapon barred or severely restricted in many other nations, given the dangers of unanticipated trauma and possible death from electric shock, though in America's unique case, Tasers represent distinct improvements over gunshots.[77] Even without Steven Seagal's action-hero antics, American police use force so intensely that the United Nations singled out America for violating the UN's general torture guidelines, which also cover police brutality.[78] As a party to some of the relevant international treaties, America had to issue a response, and the State Department furnished a subdued memo, which noted that while America was not in "full agreement" with the UN's high-minded musings (an understatement), some improvements had been made, including the settlement of a Chicago police torture suit sweetened by "a formal apology to torture victims."[79] Of course, this concedes that torture took place.

One reason for force disparities is America's unusual practice of physically detaining those suspected of minor crimes. In Western Europe, police

---

* Contrary to myth, British police can carry guns—hence the shootings. However, they receive considerable training in minimizing use of force and, as a general matter, do not carry guns on routine patrols.

generally issue tickets/court summonses for lesser infractions, which reduces stakes for both sides and makes violence less likely. For example, selling merchandise without a license is a trivial offense in most countries, and European cops confronted with a street peddler would simply write a ticket and move along. The same crime in America often provokes arrest—this is what happened with Eric Garner, whose sale of loose cigarettes resulted in a fatal chokehold. Both Garner and the arresting officer had records of misconduct, complicating matters, but the triviality of Garner's offense, combined with video showing that Garner had, at most, displayed some pert exasperation and minor resistance at being harassed for the umpteenth time by local police, suggest that the officer used force grossly disproportionate to any reasonable need. Indeed, force was almost necessarily excessive, as NYPD guidelines prohibited chokeholds as unacceptably dangerous. In other nations, Garner would have been simply ticketed, and in the unlikely event of death, the officer would have faced immediate sanction. But New York is not Frankfurt. Garner died, and the grand jury declined to indict the officer, a normal outcome for police (though not, as we've seen, for other citizens).[80]

As international comparisons suggest, "excessive force" is socially determined, and in America, the effective determiners are largely cops and judges. American law lacks a firm, universal definition, which is a problem in itself, though force is generally considered excessive when it exceeds what the *officer* "reasonably" believes necessary given the circumstances.[81] As a result, it's hard to calculate prevalence, though citizens, who have their own definitions, report excessive force at a rate of 6.6 complaints per 100 officers, of which only 8 percent were determined to justify disciplinary action.[82] The BJS has received complaints of data quality issues, and is looking into the matter, though in 2013, it spent all of $36,167 to commission a study.[83] We can safely say BJS overspent. Since 1994, the attorney general has been *required by Congress* to collect and publish various use-of-force data, but that exercise has not been properly undertaken, as the attorney general effectively conceded when DOJ announced, in October 2016, that it would finally implement a full data collection program.[84] So it takes $0 to conclude that DOJ fell down on the job, and one can venture at a further cost of $0 that it will continue to do so, because after October 2016, priorities changed. Jeff Sessions, the incoming attorney general, seemed deeply uneager to pursue the inquiry. During his confirmation testimony, Sessions fretted that federal nosing around in local law enforcement could undermine "respect" and "morale," an opinion delivered in the unfortunate context of discussing federal oversight of police in Baltimore (home of the Freddie Gray disaster), Ferguson (Michael Brown), Maricopa County (Sheriff Arpaio's tent-city internment camp for the un-American), and other problem departments.[85] In some technical way, Sessions wasn't wrong. After all, Sheriff Joe did seem distraught about his criminal contempt conviction for defying a court order to stop racial profiling, until the illimitable clemency of POTUS 45 lanced the boil.

It's clear that police deploy "excessive force," in the phrase's vernacular sense, with alarming frequency. But in the term's *legal* sense, police hardly ever use excessive force, or more germanely, they're rarely held accountable. As we've seen, law enforcement declines to prosecute itself, so civil suits must suffice. Although citizens have had a federal right to sue officials via a special waiver created during Reconstruction in the early 1870s, it wasn't until 1961 that the Supreme Court held that citizens could sue police officers personally for federal rights violations, ultimately including use of excessive force (somewhat counterintuitively, the right to sue departments is more limited—due to sovereign immunity). Defeat quickly followed victory, and in 1967 the Court ginned up what it called "qualified immunity," an offshoot of sovereign immunity.[86] With qualified immunity, government officers may escape liability for certain actions. The "qualified" bit is that immunity will attach only when an officer's action is "official," i.e., not in violation of the law. Should an official violate the law, he may be subjected to legal consequences.[87] This doesn't sound so bad, but it is.

First, though, the theory behind qualified immunity. Law wants officers to be able to exercise discretion without fear of lawsuits, which is important because much conduct will exist in a gray area between the clearly lawful and clearly unlawful. Fair enough, but the Court had initially imposed a difficult standard of proof, looking into an officer's "good faith," which was hard enough to gainsay (not least because the Court's language was somewhat inscrutable).[88] The Court then shifted to an even more stifling test, which granted officers immunity unless their conduct violated a *"clearly established* statutory or constitutional right of which a reasonable person would have known."[89] This is a different and more troublesome animal: the Court is not protecting shades of gray, so much as forbidding liability for any conduct that falls short of a very dark sort of black. This is because—as should be apparent by now—almost nothing in the law is "clearly established," much less in ways that "reasonable people" would have known. This is particularly so for Fourth Amendment jurisprudence (the usual grounds for suit), a highly confused and fluctuating area of law. What if 10 percent of judges, swimming against the tide, rule that shooting rattle-armed-and-highly-suspicious toddlers presents no Fourth Amendment problems, while 90 percent of judges go the other way? Is the toddler's right not to be shot while shaking a rattle "clearly established"? If the answer is "no," it's open season on toddlers.

Qualified immunity became even harder to overcome during the crime wave and drug hysteria of the 1980s and 1990s and the siege mentality post 9/11, with the Court ever more forgiving of abusive conduct. The current test is whether a victim had both a "clear" right and *"every* reasonable official would have understood that what he is doing violates that right."[90] (The Court, via Scalia, cited prior precedent for that formulation, implying that the "every" official qualifier had been part of the doctrine for twenty-four years; it wasn't—Scalia slipped it in.[91]) Not only must courts agree, perhaps so must cops (and unanimously, at that). Given that several million Americans suspect the Earth is flat, disagreement would seem to create almost insuperable barriers to recovery.[92] Justice Sotomayor described the present state of qualified immunity as an "absolute shield" that "tells officers that they can shoot first and think later, and it tells the public that palpably unreasonable conduct will go unpunished."[93] Fortunately, Sotomayor said this in dissent, otherwise it would be the one legal standard about which "every" cop would assuredly know.

Victims do sometimes receive compensation for police brutality, but regrettably, where victories are had, the law is usually not the prime mover. Only in special cases—a sympathetic victim, a media-savvy lawyer, and massive public outrage combined with body camera footage—do victims have a decent chance of prevailing. Most of these victories come by way of settlement, and are driven as much or more by fear of losing in the court of public opinion as in a court of law. Settlements do happen, and in 2014 alone, America's ten largest police departments spent $248.7 million paying for misconduct.[94] This is limited consolation. Much of that $248.7 million went to blockbuster settlements, often spread across many victims and years. But the *average* victim, assuming his suit survives pretrial motions, doesn't receive a giant windfall. Police understand that they are increasingly beyond account, and as the public begins to appreciate this, police legitimacy will fall and citizens will go out of their way to avoid police or simply submit, out of fear, to unreasonable requests that should be refused.

Latent in qualified immunity doctrine are assumptions about the special dangers of policing; in case after case, judges (often conservative) worry that cops should not have to consider liability when they face a potential threat. But this is a red herring. Certainly, cops shouldn't have to ponder lawsuits during a chase, but they should *always* consider Constitutional rights as one of the many variables they calculate, and not killing unarmed suspects in conditions of ambiguity is probably not too much to occupy the police mind, even during a pursuit. Anyway, policing is not unremittingly perilous. Conservative judges sometimes say so, and 93 percent of police believe that their jobs are getting more dangerous but, in fact, policing has become meaningfully *less* dangerous over the long haul, and being an officer carries lower risk of fatality than being a garbage collector or roofer (or, for God's sake, a *landscaper*), and is 90 percent less lethal than commercial logging.[95] We do not permit garbagemen to shoot guard dogs or loggers to put trespassers in chokeholds. Yet, we grant police something like this leeway, and it results in disproportionate danger to the public. For 2016, the FBI reported that 118 officers from any type of department were killed in the line of duty, of whom

66 died in violent circumstances and the rest by accident; meanwhile, officers fatally shot 963 people, a ratio of 8:1, in the most forgiving calculation.[96]

Death is not the only danger to police, and police reasonably fear violence, though statistically, they're not likely to be harmed even if directly threatened. In 2016, 57,000–68,000 officers were assaulted in the line of duty, but in only 4.2 percent of those assaults were guns used, while 78 percent of assaults involved no lethal weapon at all, and in 71.1 percent of cases, officers escaped without injury.[97] Even counting all assaults with weapons of any kind—guns, tire irons, the various cell phones and other shiny objects police have claimed as justification for shooting "armed and dangerous" suspects—produces some 16,500–20,000 officers actually injured. By comparison, between 2002 and 2011, the FBI estimated police threatened or used force on an average of 715,500 adults annually, with 535,300 citizens claiming excessive force.[98] Even subtracting a large number of serious criminals who required equally serious force to subdue, there's a large imbalance. The old saw used to be that it was better to let ten guilty men go free than imprison one innocent man; the contemporary version seems to be: better to shoot eight citizens or rough up thirty, than risk one officer.

Pandemic or Pandemonium?

Judging by public opinion, America has experienced an unrelenting increase in crime since 1989, when Gallup began polling the issue.[99] Curiously, August 2000 to October 2001 was a rare stretch when most Americans believed crime was *not* on the rise, though that period coincided with one of the few truly significant and well-publicized crime spikes in recent decades: the 2001 accounting scandals (relating to the dot-com crash, and the collapses of Enron and several other firms, some of the most costly financial crimes in history) and the 9/11 terrorist attacks, which murdered 2,977 people and will contribute to the early deaths of thousands of others (against an annual national homicide rate of roughly 15,000).[100] Leaving that aside, since 1993, on average, almost 65 percent of Americans in any given year believed that crime had risen over the past year; more recently, 57 percent believe crime has gotten worse compared to a baseline set in 2008.[101] Both Democratic and Republican politicians cater to this, spending heavily on police and pushing harsh sentencing laws and trimming civil liberties, policies pushed by, among others, Clinton, Bush II, and Trump. Courts, as we've seen, have also become more deferential to, and protective of, police.

But crime has not been rising, it's been falling, and by a lot. From a peak of 5,856 crimes per 100,000 people in 1991, crime fell 51.6 percent to 2,837 per 100,000 by 2016.[102] What's important is that crime began falling *before* many of the new cops, tougher sentences, or enhanced police discretion were deployed, and while crime continued to drop thereafter, much of the fall occurred before any crime initiatives could take hold. But policing expanded anyway. Since 1992, the nation added almost 200,000 new cops and the police/population ratio grew by over 7 percent, but if anything, crime declines *decelerated* as policing ratios peaked in 2008.[103] Since 2014, crime has been roughly flat, hovering near twenty-five-year lows. When Trump lamented American "carnage" in his campaign, crime rates were basically steady, with lower property crime rates offset by a modest increase in violent crime, and most of that increase was driven by just a few cities such as Los Angeles, Charlotte, San Antonio, and Chicago.[104] Chicago, whose civic structures have long been undermined by corruption and financial problems, by itself accounted for half the growth in the murder rate. A few cities are experiencing crime waves, but the nation is not.

The relationship between police and crime suppression is more complicated than just the number of officers. It may be that police have grown more effective, using methods like zero-tolerance policing and statistically driven management. But again, these policies were enacted *after* crime started dropping—sometimes long after. New York's crime rate started falling around 1991 or 1992, in line with national trends; at most, pilot experiments in cleaning up the subways had been underway for about a year and Rudy Giuliani, who championed the program, did not take office until 1994. Crime in New York was already waning, as it was in other cities that adopted New York–like models in the 1990s, and even in places like Los Angeles, whose police department barely functioned then, much less innovated. The research on these models is accordingly mixed; new initiatives might have contributed to the crime decline, but did not inaugurate the trend. What's also overlooked is that programs like stop-and-frisk themselves increased lawlessness, if for no other reason than that several hundred thousand unlawful detentions occurred during those programs and citizen complaints about police spiked (none of which, of course, were recorded as "crimes" in NYPD databases).

Many forces drove crime lower, of which police were merely one and perhaps not the most important. The economy improved in the early 1990s, but this explanation is incomplete: economic improvement in the 1980s did not suppress crime, nor did the Great Recession and its aftermath (2008–2014) spark a crime wave.[105] Adding up rising incomes, new policing tactics, higher incarceration rates, slightly reduced alcohol consumption, and marijuana decriminalization/nonenforcement still leaves a mystery. The proportion of younger men, who have a traditionally higher propensity for crime, did subside in the 1990s, though the giant Millennial generation has not triggered a criminal resurgence. The causes require investigation beyond our scope. (There may have been something unique about Boomers in their youths, an idea I've explored elsewhere.) What matters here is that crime fell notwithstanding police policies or procedures, which cautions against blind increases in police spending, as well as against tolerance for brutality, civil liberties violations, stop-and-frisk, and other extraordinary measures. The apparatus of emergency is in place, but the only state of emergency that exists is in law itself.

Asking Too Much

Police duties, and the law governing them, are amorphous—and police are essentially the victims here. Cops spend endless hours dealing with matters that are really the province of social services, handling tasks in which they are not specialists and which legislatures should assign to others, especially caring for the mentally ill. Police are also tasked with generating revenue for governments, a chore that's distracting, but not civically disastrous so long as fines and forfeitures are by-products of genuine law enforcement and not substitutes for normal taxation.

However, some governments rely on police to furnish large chunks of civic budgets, creating unhealthy incentives for extortion, especially when departments share in the proceeds. Ferguson provides an extreme example, where the DOJ concluded that "law enforcement practices are shaped by the City's focus on revenue rather than by public safety needs," leading to overheated policing of the city's municipal code and aggressive arrests (disproportionately of minorities), the essential purposes of which were drumming up cash.[106] Civil fines and fees have been imposed for seemingly minute violations of the local codes; one black woman in Ferguson who kept her family's old car as a sentimental possession had it towed on the grounds that it was a "derelict vehicle in the driveway"—she was ultimately assessed $1,200 in fines and never had the car returned.[107] Few cities are as bad as Ferguson, but about 6 percent of cities generate more than one-tenth of their revenue through police collections.[108] This is an abuse of both the public and the police. These levies are arbitrary, regressive, and, given the prevalence of bias, have outsized impact on minorities. These practices also divert officers from real work, and researchers have noted an inverse relationship between revenue generation and crime clearance rates in small towns—the more cops tax, the less they police.[109]

These practices also create an odor of corruption around other parts of government, including courts tasked with judging cases of police abuse. For example, the Nevada judiciary's budget substantially depends on traffic ticket revenue, and when ticketing fell off, Nevada courts had to cut back on judicial services, threatening the administration of justice.[110] While the funding crisis affected no rulings by the court on policing procedures, the appearance of bias and conflict is hard to avoid, and who knows what will happen when courts find themselves against the budgetary wall? Well, Ferguson does—its municipal court relied on police fines for its operational budget, and justice in Ferguson is not the force keeping Liberty's torch upright.

The most troubling version of cops-cum-taxmen involves civil forfeiture, whereby police seize properties based on the suspicion that the items have criminal associations—without needing to charge the owner with a crime. (Technically, the property itself is the "defendant" in these in rem proceedings, which produces strange case names like *United States v. Approximately 64,695 Pounds of Shark Fins.*) The usual criminal procedural protections don't apply to civil forfeitures, and the burden of proof rests on the property owner, who must show that seized items are untainted by criminal activity. In other words, you may be presumed innocent, but your bank account, house, and car are not. The particular moral hazard in this practice is that police share in some or all of the proceeds, creating unhealthy incentives while reducing accountability, as police can self-finance without voter consent. This is precisely the sort of arbitrary power that the freedom- and property-minded Founders loathed, and forfeiture traditionally existed only at the margins of American law, in customs enforcement and direct contraband seizures. The wars on drugs and terrorism were used to justify expanding the practice—another in the tiresome litany of extraordinary actions premised on dubious emergencies. Since 1985, when federal forfeiture kicked off, annual receipts increased from $25 million to ~$2 billion in recent years, and up to $4.5 billion in bumper years like 2013–2014; as of 2017, the forfeiture funds' gross assets stood at over $8 billion (because only ~40 percent of proceeds were disbursed to victims), though of course, it's hard to tell, as auditors identified significant deficiencies in the funds' internal controls.[111]

States have also gotten aggressive since 2001, and now reap several hundred million dollars through forfeitures. Many states' laws have historically disfavored forfeiture, but again, special circumstances provided a loophole—local police could seize assets and turn them over to Washington, whose forfeiture laws were more accommodating, and Washington returned the favor by granting police a cut that local laws would otherwise forbid. (The euphemism here is "equitable sharing," though the adjective applies only to law enforcement, and the only ones really "sharing" are citizens.) Thus, procedures that once applied to customs runners and drug lords have become part of standard practice, to relieve ordinary citizens, many of them innocent, of their property. Forfeiture represents a considerable source of funding and is extremely flexible, unburdened by legal hurdles (overseen, in any event, by courts who may themselves also benefit) and the tedious process of convincing voters to pay more in taxes. So this is the future, of police transitioning from de facto IRS agents into government-sanctioned shakedown artists.[112]

As police find themselves occupied by other tasks, the public has turned to private protection, especially for the property crimes police lack either the time, skill, or inclination to solve. Policing has not gone nearly as far down the road toward privatized justice as arbitration already has, nor is it as unaffordable as private lawyering increasingly is. But private police already outnumber regular police, and their menu of services is growing longer; it's not unreasonable to believe that many clients will soon pay for services formerly supplied by police, if only because the ultra-rich already do so, and their habits will trickle down to the merely affluent. In litigation, wealthy clients routinely rely on private investigators for both criminal and civil cases, and private police already handle many special crimes like wine counterfeiting and art theft and will, in due time, expand into more prosaic duties. Of course, private policing has a long tradition; the only difference is that before the mid-nineteenth century, private policing was the norm, just as private schooling was. Today, use of private services implicitly comments on the trajectory of public equivalents. Just as Stanford has eclipsed UC Berkeley, so Pinkerton's descendants may eclipse some public police. There's nothing wrong with this so long as it's a choice, not a necessity. However, if and when private police become much better than the public option, the implications for social and legal equality will become serious.

Whenever political discourse routinely invokes the unrelieved glory and nobility of a particular group, and even mild deviations prompt thunderous denunciations, we can be sure that unsavory compromises have been made. The police are a troubling case, because unlike the celebrated American farmer (the customary symbol of self-sufficient virtue, tariffs and subsidies notwithstanding), police have been granted the right to use force against fellow citizens and to deprive them of their liberty. This calls for the highest scrutiny, not unthinking deference.

Although police view themselves as under siege and without adequate support, the public and legal system actually grant officers extraordinary and undue leeway. The general public holds the police in higher regard than almost any institution save small business and the military, higher even than organized religion or medicine.[113] Citizens proffer generous funding; in many cases, police consume almost half of municipal budgets. Police require, and politicians supply, regular and degrading homage. When tribute is not forthcoming, police freely complain about their civilian bosses, sponsor political campaigns, and vent spleen in astounding ways, as when officers turned their backs on New York mayor Bill de Blasio during an officer's funeral. Certainly, police deserve respect for facing danger. But the troops face equal or greater dangers daily, without the overt politics or public disobedience.

The police describe themselves as the "thin blue line" separating society from disorder. It may perhaps be time to retire that phrase (not least because the case that made the phrase famous sentenced an innocent man to die).[114] The line is no longer thin, and it no longer wears blue, with many officers favoring paramilitary black, an apt if dismaying choice. This internal army was never contemplated by the Framers or the Constitution, which hardly expected (and arguably does not permit) armed agents to execute mass searches and seizures. The Framers would be shocked that courts have eroded the Fourth Amendment's warrant requirements to the point of meaninglessness, so that mere suspicion now allows millions of detentions, arrests, and property seizures to which citizens, who once had a common-law right to resist improper arrest, must now simply submit without complaint. Nor does the Constitution countenance the sort of routinely unequal and lethal enforcement regularly practiced by police, and while the Court may say otherwise, it does so by pawning intellectual credibility in service of paramilitary operators who require no further help from fellow civil servants also clad in black.

Nothing is less compatible with American traditions, or Peel's principles, than martial law, the suspension of regular order in favor of discretionary rule by militarized forces. Policing may be far from those shores now, but that's the direction in which it drifts, with sanction by courts and politicians citing crime waves that do not exist and intractable circumstances that somehow do not obtain in other advanced nations. The consequences for liberty are serious, and for evidence of their scope, one need look no further than the enormous prison state that warehouses the products of police zeal. We'll take up prison shortly. But one subject must be addressed first. Is any of the evidence that bridges the river of doubt, from arrest to conviction, even trustworthy?

CHAPTER ELEVEN

PROOF: THE EVIDENCE FOR EVIDENCE

> The basic purpose of a trial is the determination of truth....
>
> Justice Potter Stewart[1]

Is Minneapolis "on the edge of the Rockies?"[2] Google Maps says "no." A glance out of any Twin Cities window says "no." Jean Baudrillard said "yes." Then again, Baudrillard also contended that America was a "simulation" whose only reality existed in television and movies.[3] Baudrillard took a lot of flak for his pronouncements thirty years ago, though in hindsight, perhaps his real sin was radical understatement. Television, with its parade of infotainment and press briefings, has become more Walt Disney than Walt Cronkite. Cinema, after *The Matrix* debuted in 1999, also relinquished any remaining claims on reality. (Only an unembarrassed simulation would risk Keanu Reeves hauling around a copy of Baudrillard, though the movie winks at us by hollowing out the book so that Keanu/Neo can use it as a tote bag.) Virtual realities, alternative facts, creative accounting—anything goes in the era of post-truth simulation, with one exception. We still expect law to maintain some relationship with the truth—visitation rights, if not full custody.

Facts, truth, knowledge, and the relationships among them are complicated, and philosophers have developed a sophisticated discourse on these subjects. But lawyers are not philosophers, they're advocates, and epistemology isn't part of the curriculum—evidence is. Evidence is a wobbly blend of empiricism and armchair philosophy that converts factual claims into a legal truth: the verdict. Legal evidence is not about the facts, pure and entire; legal evidence is only what attorneys can convince courts to accept *as* fact. Baudrillard was partly right; we live in a legal *Matrix*.

Sometimes, law outright declines to take reality into consideration. For example, if police find a kilo of cocaine bearing a dozen clean prints from the defendant and damning DNA evidence, and obtain a willing confession, it's quite likely that the defendant is guilty of possession as a factual matter. But if the police seized the kilo in a warrantless raid prompted solely by racial animus, the kilo ceases to exist, and if the kilo is the prosecutor's only evidence, the legal truth switches from "guilty" to "not guilty." Many people applaud this, though if the exclusion of tainted evidence is morally good or socially useful, it does confirm that law openly manipulates reality.

Indeed, law must manipulate facts. By themselves, facts are inert, and require mechanisms to give them social weight and meaning—and in law, those mechanisms are called the rules of evidence. To achieve a satisfying social truth, law uses filters, but to filter sensibly, law must first understand the basic facts. Before applying a single rule of evidence, judges must understand that an atlas is a more reliable guide than Baudrillard, at least when it comes to the location of the Rocky Mountains.

Every case in an adversarial system must tease out reality from competing narratives, but law's history of locating truth is not reassuring. Although lawyers have had at least 4,000 years to develop good techniques to parse witness testimony (the oldest surviving legal text, the Code of Ur-Nammu, references perjury), good solutions eluded law. For many centuries, torture was the standard technique to locate truth. In ancient Rome, slaves often served as key witnesses in disputes between their owners. Roman law assumed slaves would lie to protect their masters, so the dungeon became an instrument of corroboration. *Ancien régime* France also allowed torture, with refinements—torment could last eighty-five minutes tops, with no leading questions allowed.[4] Continental jurists also attempted to mathematically grade the credibility of different types of witnesses. Testimony by nobles, clerics, and men of property counted for more than that of their inferiors, testimony by older men carried more weight than that of younger ones, and testimony by parties and their relatives was excluded as inescapably biased.[5] Today, science provides us with better means to sort evidence than the rack or the coat of arms, though various legal actors still make status-based assessments, believing or disbelieving cops because they're cops, and so on. Law's evidentiary process remains impressionistic, and has not kept pace with science or society, and a major problem is the law itself. Courts say they disdain tainted evidence, but the laws of evidence are themselves tainted.

Prove It

Each part of the U.S. legal system uses evidence differently, though only police, courts, and some agencies are bound by rules governing the collection, use, and analysis of data. Curiously, the institutions with the greatest powers to collect evidence also have the fewest rules governing its employment. Presidents head the largest evidence-gathering enterprise in human history, encompassing everything from the NSA to the CIA, though presidents are functionally unbounded by evidentiary limits when formulating policy, issuing executive orders, or giving commands for quasi-juridical detentions and assassinations. Presidents can and have given credence to evidence that would be inadmissible in court, that comes from unreliable sources, or that has been collected in violation of international and domestic law—as happened during the war on terror.

Congress also has considerable evidentiary resources, including research services, hearings, and reports furnished by private parties and other branches of government. It can also subpoena documents and testimony, conduct investigations, and impeach and try high officials. Though these are quasi-judicial powers, Congress is not subject to the procedural rules that obtain in normal courts; its operations lie largely beyond judicial review, and Senate impeachment trials eschew normal court procedure.[6] The relationship between evidence and the legislature and executive can be fairly described as "it's complicated." This creates special difficulties as questionable evidence seeps into the general legal system, including the laws of evidence that are codified by Congress. Law emerges from an epistemic morass, but there's nothing the rest of the legal system can do but play along.

Play along it does, with greater and lesser degrees of coherence and sincerity. For example, when agencies make rules, they have been required to consider the best available science; when agencies conduct in-house hearings, they employ a streamlined version of normal court rules. Police also have their own procedures governing evidence. Many of these procedures are driven by the potential for future litigation, because work premised on faulty or improperly collected evidence can be undone. Thus, while litigation represents only a small portion of legal activity, courts' evidentiary practices shape attitudes across much of the legal universe, making courts the natural focus for any discussion of evidence. But are court practices actually good at distinguishing fact from fiction?

Objection, Relevance?

In litigation, relevance is the master evidentiary rule. The rule is deceptively simple: irrelevant evidence is generally excluded, while relevant evidence is presumptively fair game.[7] And what's "relevant"? Per the Federal Rules of Evidence (FRE), information is relevant when "(a) it has any tendency to make a fact more or less probable than it would be without the evidence; and (b) the fact is of consequence in determining the action."[8] With that definition, the question might be better framed as: What *isn't* relevant? All the FRE require is "*any* tendency," and there are few situations in which another data point does not, in some tiny way, change the odds. The big data revolution makes this abundantly clear. If an Amazon shopper buys a Diet Coke today after a lifetime of drinking Pepsi, the shift might indicate incipient diabetes, psychotic meltdown, or a change in domestic partner. This data point has tiny weight, but it still carries *some* information, and number crunchers will update their models accordingly. Should courts follow the same algorithmic procedures when they consider evidence? Again, the relevance standard is "any tendency" to make a fact more or less probable, so in the right context, there's no logical reason why the switch to Diet Coke couldn't be germane. The rules before trial are even more expansive, allowing parties to request information "relevant" to the dispute, even if that information would not itself be admissible.[9] During police investigations and so on, "reasonable suspicion" alone can support a search for evidence (even if the suspicion is based on a factual or legal mistake).[10] The evidentiary dragnet trawls up a lot of information, whose yield courts must sift.

The relevance rule doesn't provide much help. Bodiless algorithms benefit from more information, but humans do not. Courts must therefore depart from a strict reading of the relevance rule to cut off what would otherwise be an infinite chain of inquiry. The question isn't whether evidence is relevant, but whether it changes probabilities *enough* to be worth the time.[11] Relevance decisions are informed by experience, wisdom, and other judicial virtues, but in a technical sense, decisions to admit evidence are guesses, because until evidence is introduced, there's no way to *know* how much new evidence changes probabilities. And the act of guessing itself changes the equation of a case, as the decision to admit or exclude evidence reflects judicial models of how a case will develop. This may not be "prejudicial" in the legal sense, but it's definitely a pre-judgment. The consequences are usually immaterial, but appellate courts rarely second-guess trial judges' evidentiary decisions, and biased judges can exclude relevant evidence to favor their own version of the case, with minority defendants the historical losers.*

---

* These decisions have high stakes, because even if an appellate court orders a retrial, circumstances will have changed. Scientific experiments can be repeated, and doing so under virtually identical conditions is a cornerstone of reliable scientific inquiry. Litigation is not repeatable in anything like the same way.

The relevance rule embodies many of the quandaries that afflict the laws of evidence. First, the most important evidentiary rules are unworkable at face value, and to function, law must allow judges the discretion to apply the rules. Law also provides a giant list of codified exceptions. For example, the rule against hearsay contains almost thirty escape-hatches, and the hearsay rule is itself an exception to the master relevance rule; indeed, it's reasonable to describe almost all the other evidentiary rules as exceptions to the relevance rule. Second, evidentiary rules, like the standards of proof, are fundamentally probabilistic, and humans lack a strong intuition about probability. Finally, as we've seen, evidentiary decisions are generally difficult to have reviewed and reversed, removing a safety net from one of law's most error-prone endeavors. Although evidentiary decisions are incredibly consequential, they are often made on the fly, argued by attorneys operating in real time before judges who must decide on the spot. The superstructure for processing evidence is a wobbly mess. Then again, so is most evidence.

Papers, People, and Problems

Documents and witnesses are staples of the litigator's diet. Documents are exactly what they seem: records of all types, paper, electronic, and otherwise. (But not red groupers, as far as the Sarbanes-Oxley Act goes, as we saw in the Preface.[12]) The essential problem with documentary evidence is incomprehensible volume: life leaves a vast sediment of receipts, contracts, emails, spreadsheets, and text messages. Computers are thickening that sediment at a tremendous pace: by 2020, there will be over 5,000 gigabytes of digital information per human, plus reams of paper documents.[13] Parsing documents has become exhausting, and it's easy to overlook crucial information. Many cases are therefore decided without all the facts.

The huge amount of documentary evidence creates not only epistemic issues, but equality problems. Parties with greater resources have greater evidentiary arsenals. This is especially worrisome in criminal matters, in which prosecutorial resources often greatly outstrip those of the defense. The Court relieved some of the pressure via the *Brady* doctrine, which requires prosecutors to share exculpatory evidence with the defense.[14] However, *Brady* has proved difficult to enforce and prosecutors sometimes fail to share. This is a problem with documents generally; one side often has exclusive control. The advent of metadata and backups has made it harder to tamper with, or deny the existence of, documents, but the problem remains.

Documents are, however, pretty reliable as evidence goes. Most documents are created long before litigation is even suspected, and are largely untainted by knowing cant. The cant comes later, when litigators quote documents selectively. While the rules allow rebuttal using the full document, doing so is cumbersome. Accidental misinterpretation is another problem, as documents rarely arrive with context. An email stating that "this corporation won't hire people because they're minorities" could be genuinely damning evidence of discrimination, or a mere typo ("won't fire…"), or something else (an exhortation to hire only on the merits, without reference to personal characteristics). Everyone has experienced the possibility for misinterpretation in text messages. Text lacks prosody, so important nuances get lost, and I'm not aware of any rigorous jurisprudence on the interpretation of clarifying emoticons like smiley faces, excrement piles, and eggplants. Understanding documents requires witnesses, and this is where trouble really starts.

Witnesses, unlike documents, are highly changeable. Witnesses know that legal proceedings are underway, and even if they face no immediate liability, they have agendas and interests that may affect testimony. Witnesses lie, because that's part of human nature. Indeed, researchers have noted that most people lie on a daily basis, and the most common reasons for lying are to conceal personal transgressions and to achieve personal gain, matters which are, of course, at the heart of litigation.[15] In more religious ages, the prophylactic against lying involved oaths, one hand up and the other on a Bible. To say this feudal ritual has lost some of its power is gross understatement. Many countries now abjure oath-taking as useless, consigned to the same rubbish bin as witness torture.

The secular supplement to oath-taking is the perjury prosecution. In 1968, a presidential commission concluded that perjury was widespread, and while not much follow-up work has been done, the general sentiment is that perjury remains common, though to an unknown degree.[16] ("It happens all the time," per one federal judge.[17]) We know that witnesses lie, a conclusion reachable by common sense, and because courts regularly overturn convictions because *police* give misleading testimony—indeed, police perjury happens frequently enough that it's been nicknamed "testilying." But overturning a conviction is different from holding witnesses accountable, and law seems reluctant to chase perjurers. In part, perjury is difficult to prove: perjury prosecutions come after the fact (when memories have degraded further, and parties have lost interest), and law requires that a misstatement be both material and intentional, and "confusion, mistake, [and] faulty memory" obviate the required intent.[18] All we can say definitively is that perjury is not a vigorous safeguard; no more than 185 people were arrested for federal perjury in 2008–2009 (0.1 percent of federal arrests) and many of them walked free.[19] Similar figures likely obtain in state courts. Lying is a low-risk enterprise.

Even witnesses who do not intend to lie are not bracingly reliable. The basic rule is that any idiot is "competent" to testify, so a witness's stupidity, drunkenness, or bias will not preclude him from proffering evidence.[20] Witnesses can also be manipulated, and this is a real problem in suspect identifications. Police lineups, for example, have long been plagued by manipulation. Law now forbids grossly biased lineups, so police cannot stock the tank with wildly implausible decoys (e.g., five white decoys and one black suspect) or overtly suggest which suspect a witness should pick out. But police can still manipulate in subtler ways ("take your time and be *really* sure"), and might do so unknowingly (by sending unconscious signals). Although researchers have suggested various improvements, such as requiring lineups to be conducted by officers unrelated to the case, police have been slow to reform.

Even with change, error rates will likely remain high, given that memory is fallible, especially in the stressful circumstances that often make people eyewitnesses in the first place. Another factor that's important, given racial disparities in arrests, is the cross-race effect: witnesses have greater difficulty in correctly identifying faces from outside their own racial group.[21] Adding these effects to other cognitive biases, varying incentives to lie, and the stress of testifying leaves eyewitness testimony much less reliable than jurors commonly believe. The Innocence Project conducted a review of convictions overturned on DNA evidence, and concluded that more than 70 percent were based on faulty eyewitness testimony.[22] That's only a sample, and one based on convictions known to be flawed. However, scholars have repeatedly observed memory's capacity to fail in research settings, and have even managed to create false memories in test subjects, many of whom insist that their implanted memories are true even after the trick was revealed.[23] As many witnesses are coached or otherwise prepared for trial, this creates unsettling questions of reliability.

Eyewitnesses remain central to litigation, and there are few protections against misleading testimony. In *Perry v. New Hampshire,* the Court considered the propriety of admitting an identification made shortly after the crime, where the witness identified a black man on site (who was, suggestively, standing next to an officer near the scene), but was unable to repeat the identification in a subsequent photo lineup.[24] Nevertheless, the Court held, 8–1, that due process rights were not violated because there was no indication of improper police conduct and because cross-examination and other "safeguards" granted the defendant adequate protection against dubious testimony. Perhaps, but only if cross-examination and other safeguards are rigorous and sensible.

In fact, many of the rules governing witnesses' testimony are concerned more with ritual than substance, and of these, the hearsay rule is perhaps the most important and troubling. "Hearsay" is testimony to establish a fact, given by a witness without direct knowledge of that fact.* For example, if a

---

* More properly, hearsay is "an out-of-court statement used to prove the truth of the matter asserted therein," which is an unilluminating mouthful to non-lawyers. I feel compelled to include the magic incantation, because every lawyer has this phrase burned into the brain during Evidence; my own professor, a former federal prosecutor, made us repeat the phrase in unison for weeks, moving his hands up and down like the little bouncing ball in karaoke subtitles.

witness saw the defendant's blue Ford run over a person, and says as much in court, that's "direct testimony." But if someone simply tells the witness those details, and the witness testifies accordingly, to prove that the defendant ran over a man with a blue Ford, that's hearsay. By default, hearsay is forbidden, being deemed too attenuated and unreliable to serve as evidence.[25] But hearsay is admitted all the time, pursuant to numerous exceptions. Some hearsay exceptions are sensible. For example, a county-recorded deed or NASDAQ's records may be admitted under the property and business records exceptions to prove ownership of a house or the closing price of Intel. NASDAQ is not in the business of recording false stock prices to exonerate small-town brokers, so there's no reason to believe such information is shoddy.

Unfortunately, most hearsay rules are not as sensible. There's a lot of historical detritus in hearsay law, much of it based on assumptions that have been shown to be dubious, or even false. For example, "excited utterances" are exempt from hearsay restrictions, so a person can testify to details relating to "startling events," presumably because the law believes that statements made "while the declarant was under the stress of excitement" are particularly credible.[26] Of course, recall of many types of information is compromised by stressful circumstances, but we're stuck with the exception, because some ancient judge thought it a good idea.[27] On the subject of ancient, "ancient documents" are also exempt. This exception is an unhelpful marriage of law's love of the past with the shady ethics of the small-town antiques dealer, as "ancient" is defined as at least twenty years old.[28] What's so special about twenty years—is it the case that people planning to plant misleading evidence only do so 239 months in advance, but not 241? The list of moldy treasures continues. A particular gem is the statement made "under the belief of imminent death."[29] This hearsay exception is limited to homicide prosecutions and civil cases to ascertain the cause or circumstances of death, and only when the original declarant is no longer available (presumably, because the "belief" of imminent death was accurate). Obviously, these special limitations implicitly admit that imminent-death hearsay might be particularly shaky, so it's not clear why law allows its use in the most consequential species of case, the murder trial. But the "imminent death" exception hardly brims with reason in any event.

Budding mystery writers could make a career out of the hearsay exceptions alone: the buried "ancient document," hearsay regarding "facts of personal or family history," reputations about "boundaries of land," statements made for "medical diagnosis or treatment" (who's ever lied to his shrink?), "excited utterances," and so on. And the aspiring Agatha Christie needn't worry if she accidentally includes "double hearsay" or bungles the details of a particular exception. The rules provide a catchall option, allowing hearsay's admission where the interests of justice require such and there are "equivalent circumstantial guarantees of trustworthiness."[30] As the original guarantee is near worthless, ginning up "equivalent" guarantees of trustworthiness isn't hard. Of course, one cannot spin a rich mystery out of hearsay doctrine alone. The mystery writer should therefore have her villain plant hair fibers, spent rounds, and fake tire treads. These might seem to be the kind of gratuitous flourishes that bring down a villain, because forensic science, unlike witnesses and hearsay, is supposed to be iron-clad. And so it can be in novels and movies. But in real life, forensics is anything but reliable. Perhaps Baudrillard is right: all is simulation, as fake as *CSI*, a show aptly situated in Las Vegas, the most unreal city in America.

Forensic Evidence

Forensics, loosely construed, has been around for a long time. The Bible refers to speech pattern analysis (in the Book of Judges, the Gileadites identify enemy Ephraimites based on their mispronunciation of "shibboleth"); Hippocrates commended physicians to study poisons to identify foul play; Romans autopsied Julius Caesar (conclusion: death by stab wound; stab #2 of 23 being deemed the fatal blow), and their lawyers analyzed bloody palm prints (to exonerate a murderer) and handwriting (to validate wills and contracts); and ancient Indian physicians assisted courts with matters concerning childbirth (finding: pregnancy lasts about ten lunar months or forty calendar weeks). Today, we look at ancient forensics and see a mess. At best, it confirmed the painfully obvious. More usually, it was false, tending to supply whatever conclusion was required by its sponsors: a mercenary and unscientific charade.

The rise of modern forensics in the nineteenth century supposedly changed all that, but the concurrent development of forensic science and modern police departments should be a clue that forensic science is, for the most part, not "science" at all. Proper science has no master and no supervening interest in a particular result; it is an independent witness. With the major exception of DNA evidence, however, almost all forensic science was created for, and remains sponsored and conducted by, law enforcement; *forensic* science is a witness with an agenda.[31] This important detail goes overlooked in many trials, as do the considerable inaccuracies of forensics generally. As a result, courts and juries can be misled, especially as technology has become an article of faith in the search for truth.

One particular challenge with scientific and forensic evidence is that each depends on probability and statistics, branches of math that are not intuitive, and in which lawyers have little training.* Two sadistic staples of college math departments suffice to show where intuition and math diverge. The first is the Birthday Problem, which asks how many people need to be in a room before there's a 50/50 chance that two share the same birthday. It's easy to intuit that this is a trick question, and that the number must be lower than, say, 183 (365 days, divided by two people, rounded up), but the number is much lower: just 23. The second example is the Monty Hall Problem, which involves a prize hidden behind one of three doors. You choose Door #3, but the host reveals that Door #1 hides nothing; is there any point to

---

* Probability and statistics are not interchangeable, though their differences are not germane for our purposes. Roughly speaking, probability is theoretical and can be used to describe *future* possibilities, while statistics takes *known* data and generates inferences. If we have a unbiased coin, probability tells us that the next flip has a 50% chance of heads even if we've gotten 999 heads in a row. Statisticians, after witnessing 999 sequential heads flips, would question the coin's fairness.

changing your choice given this new information? The answer is yes. Many people flatly refuse to believe this, and even after being forced to prove it in three different college classes, my ~~certainty is more-abstr~~act than intuitive. The endnotes link to a proof, but it's sufficient here to note two things.[32] First, our mathematical intuitions are often wrong. Second, our prior assumptions should be updated in light of new data. In fact, people perform versions of this constantly, including by adjusting first guesses as soon as it's clear there's a trick question involved.

Lack of mathematical fluency creates endless problems for law, often when attorneys use math to "quantify" certainty or doubt to meet a standard of proof (itself usually framed in probabilistic terms, such as "more likely than not"). In several cases, prosecutors have argued that the chances of innocence are infinitesimally small by multiplying a series of numbers, a strategy that only works if each event is "independent" (i.e., unrelated). If 50 percent of a town's residents own a car, 20 percent of cars are blue, and 10 percent of cars are Fords, then a prosecutor might argue that it's highly unlikely that the victim, run down by a blue Ford, was hit by anyone other than the defendant (who owns a blue Ford). The population of owners of such rarities *seems* to be a mere 1 percent (i.e., 50% x 20% x 10%), close to proof beyond a reasonable doubt. But if Ford *only* makes blue cars, then a blue Ford isn't quite so unusual—and neither is the suspect. (Roughly speaking.) A California case from the 1960s made precisely this sort of error.[33] Although that case became semi-infamous across Anglophone law, the error persists. In Britain, courts imprisoned several parents for the sudden deaths of their children, based on the same mistake, a series of injustices that prompted a rebuke to the Lord Chancellor by the Royal Statistical Society.[34]

Math errors routinely affect criminal cases, civil cases (employment discrimination), quasi-Constitutional cases (affirmative action and districting), and regulatory enforcement (antitrust and securities fraud). Lawyers can string together numbers all day long, but unless the variables are independent (and in both science and law, independence is a *fact* and therefore must be proved, not assumed), calculations will be wrong. This presents special problems outside courts, as when gut intuition dominates decisions to stop or arrest; the overrepresentation of minorities among convicts can make racial profiling seem valid, but as we saw in Chapter 10, even though more black drivers were stopped and arrested by the SFPD, they were *less* likely to have contraband.

Forensic conclusions always involve math, and this makes them prone to misinterpretation regardless of other factors. For example, experts often testify about whether evidence, like a fingerprint, is a "match." A "match" seems definitive, except that there's no such thing as a definitive forensic match, only a range of odds. (For this reason, prosecutors faced with proving matters beyond a reasonable doubt hate to get into the mathematical weeds because there's *always* mathematical "doubt.") Rigorous experts can only offer, based on various assumptions, a range of "confidence" subject to error rates. Even when those ranges are accurate, they're still prone to misinterpretation. An expert might be 99.999% confident that only 0.1% of the population exhibits a particular characteristic, so the prosecutor might summarily conclude that there's a 99.9% chance that the defendant committed the crime (or a 0.1% chance that he didn't). But this may not constitute proof beyond a reasonable doubt. Without any *additional* information, all that can be said is that in large cities, many people could share this characteristic; in Manhattan, at least 1,600 people might and when the island is swollen with workday commuters, up to 4,000, of which the defendant is only one.[35] Depending on other evidence, figures as low as ~0% or as high as 99+% could be derived.

All forensics operates on a spectrum of uncertainty, and of all forensics' many techniques, only well-conducted DNA analysis operates at the comfortable end of the continuum. Scientists developed DNA analysis independent of law enforcement, and the core principles have been well studied, peer-reviewed, and pose few conceptual problems. *Applying* DNA analysis is the tricky part. There are several testing regimes of varying quality, and none of them test the entire DNA molecule. In theory, comparing the full sequence of two DNA molecules could produce near-infallible identifications, but doing so is impracticable, so forensics labs test a set of snippets. The fewer the snippets, the greater the possibility of ambiguity or error. The most common test, used by the FBI, tests twenty fragments by default (increased from thirteen, after 2016), though DNA samples degrade over time and often, labs can test fewer than twenty fragments, raising the possibility of misidentification.[36] Compounding the difficulty, results must be interpreted by lab staff and by courts, and this is a problem because of conceptions about what DNA can prove. Genetic material can all but *dis*prove a match—to take an extreme case, if a genetic sample has XY chromosomes and no matching markers, then a female suspect can be freed as innocent.* This is one reason why DNA evidence has been so useful in exonerations. "Matches," however, merely describe ranges of possibility, and given testing's incompleteness, a certain number of false positives are expected. (Worse, with lower-quality DNA samples, labs must use amplification techniques, vaguely akin to blowing up a photo, with losses in fidelity.) DNA identification can be quite impressionistic, and different technicians sometimes draw wildly different conclusions from the same sample. In one study, only 6 percent of labs were able to correctly exclude a match in a mixed DNA sample, and when called upon to describe the odds of matches, labs varied wildly—in the words of one researcher, the results were as different as two fertility labs setting the odds of pregnancy at 50/50 or 1 billion-to-one.[37]

DNA analysis can provide useful and accurate information so long as the samples are good, the technicians reliable, and the results interpreted with integrity. Unfortunately, quality problems plague DNA analysis. Many samples are compromised, either through natural decay or by mistakes in collection. Most forensics labs are run by law enforcement, creating at least the appearance of bias. Training for technicians is often poor, the workload too great to allow for necessary care, and quality controls can be lax. Cross-contamination is not infrequent, where DNA from the suspect is introduced into samples from the victim (or vice versa), resulting in false matches that

---

* Women have XX chromosomes, and men XY, though in extremely rare cases, people who are genetically male can appear female (or to put it another way, apparent females can have XY chromosomes).

prove nothing more than that a suspect's DNA, unremarkably, matches his own. In the 2000s, audits of Houston's DNA lab revealed serious deficiencies in training and practice; audits also showed that Virginia's state lab had done questionable work, and other labs have been similarly afflicted.[38] Even the FBI has been affected. Following a lab technician scandal involving falsified procedures and inadequate testing (a disaster discovered only by accident), the Office of the Inspector General noted serious deficiencies in FBI lab work, including inadequate protocols that prevented reproducibility and lackluster internal controls. The Inspector General also found that the FBI, despite knowing of seriously compromised analyses, failed to properly inform almost half of the affected parties.[39] Although problems at crime labs have been well documented for many years, protocols have not been uniformly improved.

While poor methodology taints DNA analysis, genetic testing is at least sound in theory; most forensic science cannot claim that much. Fingerprint analysis has been widely used for over a century, developed by Sir William Herschel (son of the astronomer) to authenticate documents in British Bengal, and was considerably elaborated by Sir Francis Galton, providing police with new techniques.*[40] While fingerprint analysis performs adequately as a security feature in door locks and iPhones, it's probably inadequate on its own to prove anything "beyond a reasonable doubt." For one thing, it cannot be proved that fingerprints are unique; all experts can do is describe the chances that a print did not come from a suspect.

With clean samples and a large body of general print data as reference, it's at least possible to draw useful inferences. However, not many crime scenes offer clean prints, only a mix of incomplete, overlapping, smudged, or otherwise imperfect samples, which are subjected to equally imperfect analysis. The customary analysis involves three levels of detail: general shape (the loops, whorls, etc., formed by skin ridges), "Galton points" (the details of the

---

* Galton was a polymath who made several important contributions to math and science. He was also a eugenicist, and one of his aspirations was that his fingerprint refinements would support his notions about racial superiority/inferiority.

ridges themselves), and microscopic variation (siting of sweat pores, and so on). The loops and whorls aren't overly revealing and the microscopic details are often compromised in crime scene prints, so analysis tends to focus on Galton points, of which most humans have 75–175. Some countries require 24 or 30 points to correspond before declaring a match, but the U.S. does not, allowing investigators to make holistic judgments based on all three levels of analysis.[41] In other words, print analysis is pretty subjective, and technicians can and do disagree about the same set of prints. Technicians have even disagreed with *their own* prior analyses; in one study, technicians (unwittingly) reviewed matches they had made previously, and for ~10 percent of samples, came to different conclusions in the second round.[42]

The weakness of print analysis has brought a flurry of legal challenges, and the FBI felt compelled to defend law enforcement's cherished tool in the 2000s. To that end, the Bureau commissioned a large study, and in 2009 (and to no one's surprise), the study concluded that good prints could lead to highly certain identifications. Due to its flaws, the study was widely condemned. The controversy continued, and fingerprinting came under sustained attack. Science groups raised serious doubts about print methodologies and customary testimonial glosses ("the print is unique and we are confident that the fingerprint came from the defendant"), a practice that the AAAS described as "indefensible," noting that there is "no scientific basis for determining when the pool of possible sources is limited to a single person [i.e., the suspect]."[43] Naturally, defenders of the indefensible rose to the bait, and then-Senator Jeff Sessions, a member of the Judiciary Committee, waved away the brewing controversies, stating that "I don't think we should suggest that [print and other forensic analyses] that we have been using for decades are somehow uncertain."[44] Well, those methods *are* uncertain, and tradition doesn't change that, any more than Ptolemaic tradition made the sun revolve around the earth.

Sessions may think tradition suffices, but law requires expert scientific testimony to be credible. There are two basic tests, *Frye* and *Daubert*. The *Frye* test (from a case in 1923) asks if experts reached their conclusions using "generally accepted" techniques, though this is less an inquiry about accuracy than consensus.[45] (Galileo would not have survived *Frye*.) Some states still use a modified *Frye* test, but many state, and all federal, courts have moved on to the *Daubert* test, articulated in 1993. *Daubert*'s central inquiry is whether a method is "reliable," though this immediately causes conceptual problems, because in science "reliability" just means the ability to produce the same result over and over.[46] An otherwise perfect watch, set five minutes fast, is "reliable" and wrong. *Daubert*'s use of "reliable" irritates some scientists, but the rest of the opinion shows that what the Court was really interested in was validity/accuracy.[47] To that end, it suggested various indicia including testability, peer review, quality control, error rate, and the old *Frye* standard of general acceptance. Lower courts generally content themselves to apply these criteria mechanically, while missing *Daubert*'s spirit, which is: Could a given method be wrong? That requires independent thought every time, taking new research into account, but once a method has passed *Daubert* in one court, it tends to be grandfathered in without too much attention paid to subsequent developments. The cult of history and stare decisis strikes again, and *Daubert* turns into *Frye*, but with general acceptance determined by legal precedent, not science.

What kinds of forensic evidence, beyond fingerprinting, might fail a rigorous application of *Daubert*? Quite a lot. Bullet lead analysis, despite its known faults, was used for over a decade after *Daubert*, though it was finally abandoned in 2004. But other questionable methods persist: hair and fiber analysis, forensic dentistry, some blood tests, tread imprints, paint tests, etc. All these staples of TV and court have all fallen into serious doubt due to unacceptable error rates, poor quality control, lack of rigorous peer review, and the difficulty (or impossibility) of replicating results. Essentially all information, as we've seen, is relevant, so these methods can add something (especially at the detection stage), but because they carry the patina of rigorous science, they may unduly sway a jury—and judges should consider excluding them on grounds of prejudice.[48]

Safeguards: Cross-Examination, Confrontation, and Judicial Wisdom

The adversarial system is the core protection against dubious testimony, supplemented by judges' occasional and unprompted interventions. Adversaries can cross-examine witnesses, including the expert witnesses who present forensic evidence, to undermine credibility. Parties can also present their own witnesses to offer rebuttal, though many criminal and non-corporate litigants cannot afford to retain experts who command the same aura as lab techs from Quantico. The natural solution, advocated by ex–federal appellate judge Richard Posner, is for courts to exercise their existing powers to appoint neutral experts. Doing so would partly alleviate considerations of expense and also mute questions about bought testimony. (After all, parties hire experts to supply helpful conclusions, which are usually forthcoming.)

Parties can also employ the FRE to exclude evidence. The rules of hearsay, relevance, competence, and so on, all provide mechanisms to combat testimony, though as we've seen, these rules are so broad that they are often useless and, anyway, it's difficult to unring the bell if objections arrive after live testimony has been offered. Lawyers may also ask for evidence to be excluded when its "probative value *is substantially outweighed*" by dangers that evidence is too confusing, repetitive, dilatory, could "mislead[] the jury" (lacking practical options, the rule presumes the judge is immune to being misled), or if the evidence is "unfair[ly]" prejudicial.[49] There's a certain reticence to invoke the prejudice rule outside a few well-trod areas, though again, judges face little risk of being reversed.[50]

The prejudice rule is subjective and not a perfect protection. For a start, the rule allows some prejudice ("mere" prejudice is not enough), and perhaps even a lot of prejudice, given that the rule weighs importance against effect. That requires two determinations, of evidence's value and its potential to taint, determinations that occur in a partial vacuum, as there's no way to *know* before the evidence is introduced. Again, judges' mental models

295

shape cases, potentially taking the effective decision out of the jury's hands.* The law here is spotty, though the general thinking is that if judges believe evidence could overwhelm a jury's rational faculties, they should seriously consider exclusion. Especially vivid crime scene photos, evidence of gang membership, or one party's extraordinary wealth, have sometimes been excluded on grounds of prejudice.

Prejudice involves more than just vivid personal characteristics. Forensics and experts might seem to be steps toward the objective (and thus *anti*-prejudicial), but they seriously implicate the evidentiary rules' screen for confusing, prejudicial, and otherwise misleading evidence. Science has considerable mystique, which experts practicing quasi- or even junk science can borrow. The law here is a mess, with various evidentiary rules (and *Daubert*) blending together, but there's a strong argument that, aside from good DNA evidence, a lot of forensic testimony should be spiked by judges before a jury hears any of it.

Curiously, one type of expert testimony which probably *should* be permissible is often excluded: testimony by social scientists and psychologists about the unreliability of witnesses. Many federal courts are hostile to experts-on-witnesses, and the Eleventh Circuit bans them outright, on the belief that jurors understand the frailties of human testimony as matter of "common sense" and do not require expert help. That's ridiculous, because while jurors understand that witnesses make mistakes, the *frequency* of mistakes and the circumstances that contribute to them are hardly common knowledge.[51]

Functionally, the decision to admit or exclude almost all evidence rests with the trial judge, though the FRE override discretion for certain types of evidence in the interests of the public good. One important example is evidence of remediation. Law does not want to deter people from obtaining insurance, making repairs, or offering to settle cases; therefore, evidence of these events is presumptively excluded for some purposes. In a trip-and-fall,

---

*   Given the closed and overdetermined nature of verdicts, it's hard to know even after the fact.

it may be highly relevant that a shopkeeper repaired a sinkhole and offered a giant settlement, but the law draws a partial veil, potentially sacrificing the interests of specific litigants to promote the welfare of society at large.[52] This might be sound policy, but it's not motivated by fidelity to fact. And excluding evidence of remediation is not the only policy judgment law makes.

At Play in the Poisonous Orchard

Legal, social, and evidentiary principles become highly entangled when evidence in criminal cases has been obtained by unconstitutional means. In 1914, the Court held that evidence gathered in violation of the Fourth Amendment could not be introduced, establishing a strong "exclusionary rule," and subsequent cases applied that rule to violations of the Fifth and Sixth Amendments and required the states, originally unbound by the federal rule, to do the same.[53] The "fruit of the poisonous tree" doctrine extends the exclusionary rule by forbidding evidence that *derives* from unlawfully obtained evidence.[54] These rulings provoked fierce protests, because they freed criminals notwithstanding evidence of guilt, but were considered integral to policing the police and maintaining the integrity of the legal system.

The exclusionary rule has holes, which conservative majorities on the Court have been widening for several decades. The Court has granted police "good faith" exceptions in various circumstances, such as reasonable mistakes.[55] Mistakes are easy to fake, and officers have good reasons to fake them, as the "good faith" exception comes into play precisely because there's been a defective search (making *bad* faith a plausible assumption). The exclusionary rule also does not apply in civil trials, grand jury proceedings, and probation hearings. Furthermore, while tainted evidence can't be used in a criminal trial to prove guilt, it *can* be employed to impeach witnesses before a jury, opening a considerable back door.

The Court keeps tearing new holes in the exclusionary rule, claiming that it is a joy-killing prophylactic from a bygone era of widespread police abuses and limited civil remedies. The Court offered no support for its police-are-better-now sociology (which, in a different context, would fail the *Daubert* test). As for the expansion of civil remedies, the Court misreads its own work: we've repeatedly seen that the Court has been expanding immunity doctrines, weakening the very sanctions that the Court says provide deterrence and redress.

Today, the Court doesn't concern itself as much with the absolute rights and wrongs of a police search, but proffers a pseudo-pragmatic balancing test, asking whether "police conduct [is] sufficiently deliberate that exclusion can meaningfully deter it, and sufficiently culpable that such deterrence is worth the price paid by the justice system."[56] These exclusionary conditions might be satisfied, the Court suggested, if police acted deliberately, recklessly, or with gross negligence, something rather different than the old "good faith" test. It now appears that police can harvest poisonous fruits all day long, so long as their acts are merely negligent, and/or the products of unfixable incompetence or genuine disinterest. Worse, even if one enforcement agency collects evidence by means sufficient to trigger exclusion, it appears other law enforcement agencies can leverage that same information to build their own cases, creating yet another complexity.[57]

The exclusionary rule has never been solely about vindicating the Constitutional rights of defendants; it also protects the broader integrities of the Constitutional system, the judiciary, and the police. Perhaps the Court is willing to barter some of these values, but the Court should ask if it's selling legal integrity too cheaply. First, the Court cannot go lower than the floor set by the Constitution—nothing can be sold for less than the price of due process, a right implicated by defective searches. From there, it's an upward negotiation. When police ignore the Court's own jurisprudence on the Fourth, Fifth, and Sixth Amendments, they undermine the judiciary—and the Court should charge a premium for that. A strong exclusionary rule is important, not just for one defendant's sake, but for the judiciary's.

The Right to Confront

The Constitution provides another protection against questionable evidence: the Sixth Amendment's promise that a criminal defendant has the right to "be confronted with the witnesses against him."[58] The Confrontation Clause exists to allow cross-examination, which is supposed to be an essential advantage of the common law over the inquisitorial system. This should be one right that a proud common-law system defends to the hilt.

Unfortunately, the word "witness" is not simple—as we saw with hearsay, there are clearly cases in which the legal witness, the person on the stand, is merely a mouthpiece for the *true* witness, the person who saw what was going on. Direct witnesses are often unavailable, meaning that a strict interpretation of the Sixth Amendment might allow defendants to get away, or even create incentives to murder witnesses. So in 1980, the Court held that unconfronted/indirect testimony can be admitted if it comes with sufficient "indicia of reliability," such as falling within established hearsay exceptions (which, as we've seen, are frequently rubbish as indicators of reliability) or if there are other guarantees of "reliability."[59] Don't worry if that judicial logic seems murky; it was.

In 2004–2006, the Court tried to clean up its mess. To do this required understanding what a Sixth Amendment "witness" really is—or more precisely, *was*. So, the Court fired up the TARDIS for another of its *Dr. Who* adventures, and it's worth following the story, which illustrates how the Court arrives at many of its more ridiculous conclusions. In one witness-confrontation case, the majority, led by Scalia, tumbled out of the TARDIS to retrieve Webster's *Dictionary* of 1828, but of course the right date is 1791, when the Sixth Amendment came into legal being. But, you know, *close enough.* And what Scalia's majority concluded was that a "witness" is someone who offers "testimony," and "testimony" is information offered in solemn conditions that are, or seem, preparatory to legal proceedings, such as a formal interrogation initiated by police—but not, say, statements made while the police are responding to an emergency call. In other words, you have a right to confront whoever is on the stand (the officer), but not necessarily the person who actually possessed the information in the first place (the victim, say).[60] Now, this understanding of "witness" is generally consistent with the *Dictionary*'s fifth entry, though the third definition says that a "witness" is just someone who saw something, and Scalia's gloss is arguably in tension with the second entry, which just speaks to "that which furnishes evidence or proof."[61] In other words, the *Dictionary* doesn't really support Scalia's conclusion, it's a prop. And if you've seen *Dr. Who*, you know the props are cheap and unconvincing.

The Court sweated none of this, declaring that statements not produced with full legal ceremony—oaths, the looming clouds of litigation, police custody, whatever—aren't quite testimony.[62] Ergo, witnesses aren't always *really* "witnesses," and thus there's no Sixth Amendment problem. Hence, the Court condoned the admission of a recording of a 911 call that identified the suspect, noting that the recording was made during an ongoing emergency, not a police interrogation.[63] In fact, the call in question was not to 911, but *from* 911; it was a follow-up inquiry about the identity of the suspect, and thus at least a bit like an investigation.[64] This opened the gate to many potential abuses, though the Court breezily asserted that we needn't be bothered by unconfronted, "non-testimonial" hearsay because the Framers weren't either. But early Americans *did* worry about hearsay's frailties. Indeed one part of the hugely famous, hearsay-driven trial of Walter Raleigh (involving non-testimonial hearsay, a detail Scalia overlooked) was a major motivation for confrontation protections.[65]

Enough with *Dr. Who* jurisprudence. The essential point of the Confrontation Clause is that the accused must be able to test his accusers wherever possible; our rights here should be clear and robust. They are not, and this is a real problem in the age of forensic evidence, most of which is presented by testifying experts. But an expert is an intermediary, operating as a sort of Vanna White by turning letters to reveal information that other people have produced—and surely the accused should be able to test those other people, his true accusers. The Court has struggled with such cases, throwing trial judges into disarray. As Justice Kagan put it, the state of the law here "is—to be frank—who knows what."[66] We might or might not have a right to confront. It just depends on which Justice you ask, what dictionary he has, and what entry he flips to.

Hodgepodge Exceptions

The evidentiary rules are filled with many other gates and back doors, but only two need detain us. The first includes testimony about character, criminal history, and plea arrangements. The general rule is that these matters are too inflammatory and biased, and forbids them as direct evidence, but there are many ways to sneak in this kind of information, through witness impeachment and so on. The particular danger is that merely entering a plea discussion opens doors that cannot be easily closed, and given overcharging and prosecutorial browbeating, plea negotiations by uninformed defendants can create damning evidence for later use.[67] As prosecutors strongly prefer defendants to discuss and plead, this leaves defendants seriously compromised. For the most part, actual convictions can be excluded, save for sex crimes. Still, what law purports to exclude can often be smuggled into a criminal prosecution via other means. And in civil cases, the rules are even more porous.[68]

The second category of exclusion is based on privileges. The most important of these is attorney-client privilege, but it's not a blanket protection. The client owns the privilege, and only communications seeking legal advice are protected; simply cc'ing a lawyer does not provide a shield (though addressing "any thoughts?" to the cc'd lawyer might). However, soliciting advice about how to commit a crime or fraud falls outside the privilege, so a client cannot ask a lawyer how to carry out a murder or ask for help covering up a past crime. The bounds can be blurry, as substantively similar matters can fall into, or out of, the privilege depending on phrasing: if a landlord wants to evict a tenant, asking a lawyer how to do it lawfully or even asking if extreme harassment is lawful will be privileged, but asking for practical tips to evict a tenant "by any means" treads well into a gray area. Normally, careful phrasing can keep clients within the bounds of the privilege, though recent cases, involving certain famous lawyers and clients, show that privilege isn't foolproof. The privilege also opens up somewhat in fee disputes between attorneys and clients, so it's good to keep current on legal bills. Federal law also enshrines the marital privilege, and one spouse cannot be forced to testify against another, but this privilege can be waived by the witness-spouse; it's not absolute.[69]

Federal law generally does not recognize other privileges.[70] Other federal privileges exist mainly in popular imagination—journalists and their sources enjoy no absolute, evidentiary privilege, nor do priests and penitents. Some states offer additional privileges, for example shielding doctor-patient discussion, though often subject to considerable limitations. As for executive privilege, courts avoid that issue whenever they can, but executive privilege is not absolute, as every president since Nixon has been reminded.

Juries and Inquisitors

A major theoretical purpose of evidentiary rules is to ensure that that questions of liability and culpability are decided only on proper evidence. With almost all cases decided before trial, it may not seem like the rules of evidence have a real legal life, with a few exceptions like the exclusionary rule. But the rules *do* matter; litigation is always a possibility, and pretrial proceedings, which involve evidentiary disputes under the rules, influence many settlements. Losing a major pretrial evidentiary motion may by itself prompt a settlement. The rules adjust probabilities, and even if the rules embody no coherent theory, their effects are real enough.

By now, we can take it as given that the laws of evidence are largely detached from pure fact, so the final questions are whether we can or should dispense with most evidentiary rules. As a society, we'd clearly prefer to retain attorney-client privilege and Constitutional protections, but these protections were imported into the rules of evidence and would survive even if the FRE vanished. But what about hearsay and the rest? One temptation is to dump the rules entirely, with the standard rhetoric pointing to the civil law tradition, blissfully unencumbered by a complex, incoherent evidentiary apparatus.* The two systems have actually converged in recent years, in part because of European integration and legal reform, but civil and common law still retain different approaches to law, as their structures require. For example, in the civil tradition, when serious crimes occur, *judicial* police investigate, not regular police; the exclusionary rule has less practical importance. Depending on the civil law jurisdiction, a prosecutor might be assigned to advance the case, but generally, an investigating judge oversees the inquiry, interviews witnesses, visits crime scenes, and performs other tasks unthinkable to American judges. The investigating judge then compiles a dossier, turned over to the "sitting judges," who control the calling of witnesses and experts and generally run the show. The parties do have lawyers, but they're generally passive, and cannot choose, communicate with, coach, or directly question witnesses in the same freewheeling way that characterizes common-law practice.

Civil-law judges also try to resolve cases on the narrowest grounds, so rather than the common law's Tolstoyan survey of life stories, proceedings focus on whatever is most germane to a verdict. Contrary to general belief, some civil-law countries do have lay jurors as part of the judging panel, but there's always a professional judge to keep everyone on track. Judges will exclude certain evidence on constitutional and other grounds, especially now that EU treaties have been incorporated into members' legal regimes, and some countries have strict rules about witness testimony (parties are frequently deemed irretrievably biased and therefore excluded as witnesses). The overall expectation, though, is that the judges will flip through the

---

* Anglo-American skeptics derisively call this the "inquisitorial system"; their counterparts call the common law the "accusatorial system," which is hardly more flattering.

dossier, ask questions, and weigh evidence appropriately—without lawyers dickering over weird matters like excited utterances. The whole thing is so technocratic and placid that it defies even televisual fantasy. The French, lacking a system conducive to courtroom drama, had to import American TV shows, which distorted French imaginations rather badly (apparently, people started addressing judges as *"votre honneur"* instead of the correct *"madame la présidente/le juge"*) and the Ministry of Justice begged for home-grown dramas—the success of which you can test with a Netflix search.*
The civil system reposes substantial and coherent faith in judges to parse evidence wisely, which does not mean that judges grant all evidence equal (or sometimes any) weight, only that with judges in control, elaborate rules become less necessary.

Evidence in common-law countries reflects a less coherent view about judges and fact-finders. American law presumes a lone judge can rise above any prejudice—it perhaps has greater faith here than the civil systems, in which core investigation is carried out by one set of judges and decisions are rendered by a panel (usually a different one). By contrast, American judges see whatever the parties drag before them, and can only will themselves to unknow forbidden evidence. The American attitude toward juries is some-what contradictory, with lay juries viewed as a bulwark against tyranny, yet too childlike to handle raw evidence. This logical divide may be irrelevant, as the most critical matters, including the exclusionary rule, are handled away from the jury. For evidentiary rulings made in court, it seems that juries can't quite forget what they've heard. The trial proceeds anyway, unless the prejudice is "gross."

---

*   Fine, I'll save you the trouble. France's only major judicial drama is the infelicitously titled *Alice Nevers, le juge est une femme* (*Alice Nevers: The Judge Is a Woman*).

Almost all evidence is relevant, but not all of it is credible, and American law picks and chooses so strangely that the whole thing seems ad hoc, the product of historical accident. That's precisely what it is; for the most part, the FRE embody common-law doctrines developed centuries ago, often across the sea. The common law was supposed to be wise and case-specific; statutes are meant to be clear and broadly applicable. The FRE, and its state equivalents, are an unpersuasive hybrid. And so it is on an uncertain basis that we are judged, and in losing cases, punished.

CHAPTER TWELVE

REMEDIES: HOW MANY
WRONGS MAKE A RIGHT?

We can endure neither our vices, nor the remedies for
them.

Livy[1]

Most elevator "door close" buttons don't do much. Since the 1990s, the opening and closing of doors have been dictated by disabilities laws and floor management algorithms, not passengers' jabs at the control panel. "Door close" is a misleading relic, tossed into the same electronic midden as the crosswalk toggle and the office thermostat, other once-useful gizmos that have surrendered themselves to central programming.[2] As the alternative is a world of Larry Davids forever pushing our buttons, a few inconvenient seconds or uncomfortable degrees seems a reasonable exchange. Not everything can be given over to code, though. When we really need it, when we have suffered a grave wrong or been accused of inflicting one, we need a working button, one that connects us to someone who will listen to our pleas and has the power to help.

Law is that button, or should be. After all, law's ability to listen and to compensate (and sometimes to punish), is what makes law *law*, instead of philosophy, religion, or a utility-maximizing HVAC algorithm. And what transforms law into *justice* is proportionality: a convincing relationship between a wrong, its resolution, and community mores. Justice is the special province of courts, which can grant full, public hearings, and provide redress tailored to the facts. Of all parts of the legal system, only courts have both the mandate and the inclination to see us as individuals in distress, rather than a flock requiring passive optimization. Only courts can decisively intervene when the mechanical operation of law might work an injustice, or where other branches of government have participated in the wrong (as is often the case). Most importantly, courts can offer more than consolation: they can provide solutions—aptly called "remedies" and "relief"—indeed, they are often the *only* legal institutions that can do so. This is what we want of all institutional powers, from customer service reps to the legal system: the chance to make our case and receive our just deserts.

It is therefore one of the great legal tragedies of the past forty years that law has slowly transformed courts into elevator buttons, with our fates assigned to us by indifferent (or even malicious) programmers in other parts of law. Modern courts are frequently consigned to rubber-stamp whatever outcome other parts of the legal system fashion, be it in arbitration or plea bargaining. In the minute fraction of cases actually tried, legislation greatly circumscribes courts' discretion to fashion remedies. Penalties, especially criminal sentences, are set at whatever levels legislatures declare, implemented by whatever means executive branches prefer. This shift seriously undermines law, because remedies are the endgame in legal contests, and law only works if someone ensures that remedies are proportionate, tailored, and conscionable. We cannot accept some recitation from a Congressionally issued call script apologizing "for any inconvenience" followed by a decisive click. We need an interested human to listen, judge, and order a suitable fix. That process is now endangered.

No part of law has been as seriously compromised by buttonization as the criminal justice system, including prison and its related institutions.

Between Independence and the Gilded Age, American prisons had a true social mission: redemption. (In England, the primary mission was storage.) In this enlightened interlude, America was a leading carceral reformer, and the world came to investigate. Dickens made the journey (and left depressed, though he loathed America for years), but the most important visitor was Alexis de Tocqueville. It's been largely forgotten that de Tocqueville's original mission was to study America's penal institutions. Surely, the Frenchman hoped, the nation that paved the way for *liberté, égalité, fraternité* would have something useful to say about what might replace the Bastille. But de Tocqueville (himself a magistrate) and his companion Gustave de Beaumont were disappointed: "Whilst society in the United States gives the example of the most extended liberty, the prisons of the same country offer the spectacle of the most complete despotism."[3] And de Tocqueville's visit overlapped with the decades when America's jailers actually *tried*, with great earnestness, to be instruments of improvement. It says something that the word "penitentiary," with its New Testament aura of repentance and salvation, has become an anachronism; even the rhetoric of redemption has withered. All that remains is the despotism of the jailer, the cold calculation of the election-season pol, and the growing passivity of the judge. The business end of American law has abandoned its senses of mission and balance.

"Remedies" have been traditionally conceived as noncriminal, applicable only to matters like contract disputes. But all legal outputs, including criminal sanctions, are usefully viewed as remedies. Focusing on the *remedial* reminds us that the goal is vindication, not reprisal; repair, not revenge. For criminal law, that means rehabilitation, deterrence, and containment. For civil matters, that means compensation or prevention. Draconian sentences, the vindictive casino of punitive damages, and the empty injunction against future wrongs, seem unjust because they forget the remedial imperative, and because they do not tailor treatment to patient. But if cures are now prescribed mechanistically, administered arbitrarily and often punitively, are remedies becoming as bad as the diseases?

Fitting Punishment to Crime

For millennia, punishment was a matter of proportion, typically 1:1 and paid in kind, the doctrine of *lex talionis*, the law of "equivalent retribution." Hammurabi's Code records the first example, the famous formula of "an eye for an eye."[4] But even in ancient Babylon, proportion proved a subtle calculation; in a society of slaves, freed men, and full citizens, not all eyes were equal. Harming a social inferior triggered a fine in gold, while injuring superiors brought harsh punishment (chopping off hands, in the case of striking one's father).[5] Only when criminals and victims were exactly equal could equal punishment be just, though even these cases must have presented eventual difficulties; presumably, some official found himself judging a criminal who had blinded two people, with not enough body parts to satisfy.

With notions of equality fluid and with the supply of eyes fixed, law must constantly innovate, adjusting penalties to fit evolving contexts lest the public become disgruntled or disabled. This required the development of substitute compensation, and money provided the most flexible option imaginable. Hammurabi's Code already had suggested gold as recompense for injuries to slaves. As slaves were deemed currency in the flesh, the Code made no great conceptual leap. The real revolution was the idea that money could compensate for injuries beyond those to property. Formally saddled with the Torah's eye-for-an-eye literalness (perhaps picked up by Jews during their Babylonian Captivity), rabbis strove to make remedies more flexible, and declared money adequate compensation for many injuries, an idea that also prevailed in ancient Rome and in some Northern European cultures.[6] The subtext of money damages was that victims would have to settle for something less than literal justice, in the interests of the greater good. Thus, the id of *lex talionis* was supplemented by the ego of money damages, and then finally, the superego of mercy, famously embraced by Christ, who advised victims to "turn the other cheek." (His true meaning, as ever, was ambiguous, but tolerance is the popular interpretation.)[7] When Islamic law began to develop in the seventh century, it retained *lex talionis* but sweetened the clemency pot by suggesting that forgiveness or the acceptance of a lenient cash settlement might bring divine favor (though in cases of recidivism or sins against the state, harshness remained the rule).*[8]

Even as the scrim of money damages and clemency descended, much of *lex talionis* lingered on, a reflection of law's basic desire to make the punishment fit the crime. "Righting" some wrongs was obvious; medieval Europe put arsonists to the torch. Other crimes brought less ploddingly literal punishment. Poisoners, instead of being poisoned themselves, were boiled alive, though one supposes in metaphorical terms, boiling's biochemical torment came close enough. Parricide offered a real stumper, because it would be ridiculous to avenge an intra-family murder by offing *another* innocent relative. Roman law concluded that parricides should be sewn into a sack with a dog, rooster, snake, and ape, with the lot tossed into the nearest body of water, for reasons presumably obvious at the time. (It seems implausible—who has an ape handy?—though both the *Digests* and Livy refer to versions of the punishment.) Of course, the greatest crimes were against the greatest people, the entwined bodies of state and monarch, with England's preferred penalty to hang, draw, and quarter the convict, dismantling the condemned's body as the condemned had tried to dismantle the body politic. Contemporary accounts suggest that the execution in *Braveheart* was something of a parking ticket compared to the real thing. English judges kept playing at Hannibal Lecter until 1782, the same year that Joseph Haydn debuted his eminently civilized Symphony No. 73.

Yet, less than fifty years later, the most extreme versions of *lex talionis* disappeared in the West, save for the death penalty. And even capital punishment had been sanitized: in France, by the guillotine's efficiency; in England, by the withdrawal of executions from the realm of public spectacle. A core question in Foucault's *Discipline and Punish* is: What happened?[9] What, in the course of less than two centuries, diverted the course of juridical punishment

---

*   A few strict sharia regimes retain *lex talionis* in literal forms. Saudi judges ordered the surgical removal of a criminal's eye in 2000, and, in 2013, commanded that a man who paralyzed his victim have his own spinal cord severed unless he produced a substantial cash substitute.

from quartering, boiling, and other dungeon horrors into a regime of fines, prison, banishment, and rehabilitation? The short answer is: everything happened.* For civil cases, the expansion of the money economy rendered sheep-for-a-sheep/wagon-for-a-wagon an increasingly inferior archaism, and even in wrongful death suits, Anglo/Saxon/Teutonic law's *wergild* ("man payment") offered precedent for cash settlement. For violent crimes, decent English opinion found itself increasingly uncomfortable with traditional penalties, especially given their association with Catholic powers. If there was one thing that concentrated the mind of Georgian England, obsessed with "improvement" and eager to trumpet civilized liberty, it was the Continent, wallowing in popery and Inquisition.† But this created a problem. If criminals could no longer be hung or maimed with abandon, nor could satisfactory fines be levied against the impoverished lower orders, requiring a wholesale rethinking of punishment's logistics and philosophy. The result was the novel phenomenon of mass imprisonment.

Jails, Prisons, and Probation

America's corrections system has three major components: jails, prisons, and parole/probation. Jails trace back to ancient Egypt, and their basic functions have stayed constant: to hold suspects awaiting trial and to store convicts awaiting punishment elsewhere.[10] American jails are by far the busiest part of the carceral system; in 2016, 2,850 different local jurisdictions operated facilities that collectively processed 10.6 million "admissions" (including

---

*   Foucault's explanation paid special attention to the shift in state interests, from controlling bodies to controlling minds. Foucault's explanation retains its power in Europe, but the philosopher died in 1984, just missing America's new carceral experiment, which in its novel totality of slow-motion eradication squared Foucault's circle.

†   Inevitably, people less white than the Anglo-American average were left behind. In America, slavery remained a legal fact until the 1860s, and blacks are subject to unofficial legal disabilities to this day. And well into the twentieth century, Britain, with feckless candor, explained to UN busybodies why flogging, banished at home, remained a necessary expedient in its "backward" overseas dependencies; British Hong Kong mandated flogging into the 1980s.

311

repeat detainees).[11] For the most part, jails retain their character as waiting rooms; the mean stay runs to twenty-five days, so the average daily population is a just fraction of total admissions, about 731,300.[12] At any one time, about 65 percent of those 731,300 people await court action, while the rest have been convicted and either await transfer to long-term prisons or (if sentenced to less than a year) will remain in jail until release.[13] No jail is pleasant, and some, like New York's Rikers Island, are cesspools of misery and abuse. Others have, mostly by cruel accident, held defendants awaiting trial for scandalously long periods of time—one defendant in Alabama was jailed for ten years while awaiting trial.[14]

Jails receive little attention. Conditions can be bad, but on the whole jails are not overcrowded messes (only 17 percent run above rated capacity, compared to at least half of prison systems) and stays are fairly brief; the product of suffering multiplied by duration, in other words, is comparatively low.[15] However, jails are expensive. A year-long stay at Rikers costs New York up to $210,000, or almost seven times median personal income.[16] To put it more vividly, New York could lodge detainees at the grand Carlyle Hotel for the same daily rate, were prisoners willing to split a room. While the Carlyle isn't particularly secure, nor are many of the jailed particularly dangerous—indeed, many would be free pending trial were they able to afford bail. But jails do what little society asks of them, however expensively, and law shrugs.

Modern prisons are vastly more controversial, and part of the controversy derives from a lack of social agreement about what imprisonment should accomplish. The original purpose of prison was straightforward: to contain political enemies whose eminent status made execution impractical. Prison was substantially an *aristocratic* phenomenon, with troublemakers dispatched to places like the Tower of London and the Bastille, whose concurrent statuses as royal domains confirmed the nexus between prisoner and prince. But as elite imprisonment gave way to the impoundment of lesser peoples, society found itself saddled with a growing mass of incarcerated persons, and no consensus about what to do with them. Were prisoners merely to be stored, at great expense, or did they present opportunities for personal and public improvement?

The debate still meanders, but while society strokes its collective chin, the prison population has grown remarkably. In 2016, American prisons held 1.53 million people, plus another 257,000 in jail awaiting transfer to prison and sundry off-the-books detainees, bringing the total closer to 2 million.[17] America has more prisoners than any other nation, though in China's grim determination to eclipse American records, the People's Republic will claim the title around 2020, about a decade before it eclipses American GDP. Even then, America will have the cold consolation of first place in per-capita imprisonment rates among major nations.[18] No free country comes close to American imprisonment rates, which are five and six times higher than those of the UK and Canada, respectively.[19]

There's little comprehensive data on how much all this costs—as with police, Washington relies on a voluntary and incomplete census—but in 2013, total correctional spending was at least $80 billion, with prisons accounting for much of it.[20] Adjusting for inflation and other variables, correctional spending has probably breached $100 billion, which is more than twice the federal budget for housing and urban development (perhaps government's closest civil analogue to incarceration), though not cripplingly expensive against a $20 trillion economy.[21] However, even if the prison *population* continues its recent, modest subsidence, *costs* will keep rising, given the aging of the prison population and the concomitant rise in medical expenses. But direct outlays hardly capture the true costs of prisons, from the economic "deadweight loss" of 2 million unproductive people and their jailers to the profound degradations of all involved, including their families.

For Whose Good?

Against its costs, prison offers some compensating benefits, which are easy to describe, though hard to quantify and open to considerable moral disagreement and practical doubt. The usual justifications for punishments (including prison) are incapacitation, retribution, social condemnation, deterrence, and rehabilitation. Incapacitation, the removal of troublemakers, is straightforward and, assuming a criminal is rightly convicted and incorrigible, effective and largely self-justifying. Because detention is expensive and cumbersome, incapacitation before the mid-eighteenth century was more corporeal rather than carceral: criminals were executed, exiled, or condemned to penal servitude. Capital punishment was common, and Georgian Britain prescribed death for transgressions as minor as "grand larceny," the theft of goods worth as little as 12 pence (perhaps $150–$300 in modern terms).[22] Not surprisingly, thousands swung, and as Britain's "Bloody Codes" grew more drastic and comprehensive, encompassing almost 200 capital offenses by 1776, juries rebelled, exonerating the clearly guilty or strategically undervaluing the stolen property at just below the gibbet's threshold.

Jury protests threatened law's credibility and stability, so Parliament, while retaining the nominal threat of capital punishment, allowed death to be commuted to exile, a practice largely mooted by Britain's political integration of Ireland (c.1653) and Scotland (1707), but which had been refreshed by new colonial horizons.[23] Australia would become the largest and most famous recipient of Britain's criminal detritus, but North America served as Britain's first great overseas dumping ground, receiving roughly 50,000 criminals before 1776, supplemented by earlier shipments from Holland and France, to their then-possessions in the Mid-Atlantic and Louisiana. Penal servitude rounded out incapacitory regimes, with many governments using prisoners to build public works or making surplus convicts slaves to private owners (and thus not the state's problem).

America still employs versions of these non-carceral punishments. The federal government and thirty-one states retain the death penalty, though the range of capital crimes has narrowed and executions have become rare. Most of those on death row will die in their cells; in 2017, twenty-three convicts were executed.[24] (America has executed about 15,000 people in total since Independence, and while the pace of additions has decelerated over the past

decades, America is unusual among its peers in executing anyone at all.[25,26])
Exile continues, though exclusively as a punishment for noncitizens convicted of immigration violations such as illegal entry or the commission of
crimes that violate conditions of residency; in fiscal 2017, America removed
226,119 people.[27] Penal servitude also survives, now managed by the state,
in the practice of requiring prisoners to work for little or no pay (including
sporadic attempts to revive the chain gang).[28] But aside from deportation,
prison (including penal servitude) is and will remain the only numerically
significant form of modern incapacitation, at least until the Martian frontier
opens and the Red Planet becomes a celestial Australia.

Applied to heinous criminals and habitual recidivists, incapacitation
troubles few people, though storing incorrigible serial killers represents a
negligible fraction of prisons' work and cannot justify the sprawling penal
regime. Therefore, government holds its remaining prisoners under other
justifications, starting with retribution and moral condemnation. Retribution requires little elaboration; people accept the idea or don't, and data
have nothing to add. Proportionate moral condemnation is near-universally
accepted and self-explanatory, though for minor criminals, it's worth considering whether the inscription of a criminal record, an electronic scarlet
letter readily accessible to the public for a minor fee, might do most of the
work without the heavy costs of prison. If retribution and condemnation are
goals, convictions' social disabilities should be given due weight in the social
calculus, especially for lesser criminals.

The liveliest debates over punishment center on deterrence and rehabilitation, which monopolize conversations in progressive salons and op-ed pages
but which are, for some, secondary to the ancient purposes of punishment.
This disjunction may account for irreconcilable differences in Americans'
attitudes toward prison; parts of the public may be talking past each other.
But whether prison deters or rehabilitates, and the conditions under which it
might, are important questions, because they were the guiding assumptions
that helped produce, and still partly maintain, the vast prison state.[29]

Before the 1980s, the possibilities of deterrence and rehabilitation were, if not the most important features in a sentencing decision, at least considered. Judges and prosecutors had considerable discretion to adjust sentences to further these goals, with probation, psychological programs, parole, and extra years serving as carrots and sticks in the Skinner box of penal improvement. By both design and accident, discretion produced considerable variability in punishments for notionally equivalent crimes.

Progressives saw racial bias in sentencing disparities while conservatives decried inappropriate leniency, and both sides were correct, for different reasons. In a moment of bipartisanship with deeply unhappy results, lawmakers demanded more uniform sentences and got them. With political tailwinds provided by the (transient) crime wave of the 1960s–1980s and neo-Puritan hysteria over drugs, legislatures imposed mandatory minimums with abandon. Sentences would now be substantially determined by legislated tables. With a few important exceptions discussed later, these adjustments were technically valid. But as with many hasty and sweeping changes prompted by real or perceived crises, sentencing reforms disregarded important norms, this time about the proper competencies of the judicial and legislative branches.

The real impetuses for legislative sentencing could not be articulated in mixed political company without argument, so both sides decided to sell the policy as a matter of deterrence. Deterrence has two flavors: specific and general. Specific deterrence focuses on punishing one defendant with enough force so that he will not repeat his crime. The more colorful versions of specific deterrence are *lex talionis* filtered through the brain-death that is local TV news, e.g., slumlords who violate building codes have been sentenced to house arrest in their own tenements.[30] Most judges, however, content themselves that prison will be sufficiently unpleasant. By contrast, general deterrence does not focus on the specific criminal; rather, it translates "make an example out of him" into social policy. This, and only this, form of deterrence could justify the extraordinary sentences encoded by legislatures. A one-time carjacker with no priors will probably learn his lesson after three years in prison, but California statutes allow base sentences of up to nine years, which can be enhanced for gang ties, or the use of a gun, leading to decades in prison.[31]

General or specific, deterrence has practical limits. Deterrence obviously helps no existing victim, and even severe penalties may have no deterrent effect (a purse-snatcher with terminal cancer is beyond deterrence). As for general deterrence—from here on, "deterrence," as it's the motor of penal policy—the audience is society. Deterrence imposes more stringent penalties than proportionality recommends, 100 eyes for one eye, so that society receives the message clearly. As a matter of due process, deterrence ought to trigger presumptive suspicion, as penalties are driven not by the facts of a case, but by general social policies. And those policies, it turns out, have weak empirical bases. The harsh sentences of the 1980s and 1990s didn't seem to deter much, and there were reasons to suspect this would be true even before conducting the experiment. Deterrence presumes a rational proto-criminal who compares two expected values: (i) the crime's benefits (criminal gains multiplied by chance of success) and (ii) its costs (the effort involved plus the product of sentence length adjusted by probabilities of detection, arrest, and conviction).

White-collar criminals might perform these deterrence calculations, but street criminals probably don't, and perhaps can't. We can only extrapolate from those actually imprisoned (highly intelligent criminals might go uncaptured, biasing the sample), but many criminals lack the educational and intellectual resources to perform the mathematical gymnastics posited by deterrence theory. BJS surveys of jails and prisons from 2003 to 2017 showed that inmates were poorly educated (41.3 percent lacked a high school certificate vs. 18.4 percent for the population generally); suffered histories of mental illness (almost 50 percent of prisoners and 64 percent of those in jail, with 14 and 26 percent respectively being in "serious psychological distress," rates three to five times higher than for the general population); and had drug problems (around 60 percent versus ~5 percent in the general population).[32] This is not a population of Benthamite utility maximizers ripe for persuasion. Anyway, many criminals operate under other disabilities, including economic desperation, while others commit "crimes of passion," where emotion overrides deliberation, rendering deterrence irrelevant. The data allow a contrary argument, of course, that deterrence is *highly* successful among the affluent, educated, and sane, who are largely absent from prison statistics. But after the seventeenth century, such persons—perversely, the original staples of long-term punishment—added little to the prisoner tally, and are largely irrelevant to the deterrence debate.

Flawed as deterrence theory may be, even if one gamely plugs in the variables and pulls the lever, the results don't predict much success. The probability of capture, as we saw in Chapter 10, is extremely low. Deterrence will work only if penalties become unthinkably drastic or police dramatically improve capture/clearance rates. Direct experiments would be unethical, but certain natural experiments have unfolded, and their outcomes suggest that deterrence is a project of rapidly diminishing returns. In 1994, Californians instituted three-strikes laws whereby felons with two serious priors would, on conviction for *any* third felony, receive a sentence of twenty-five years to life, by default and almost without exception.[33] The law was widely publicized, long sentences were near-certain, and penalties dire; if there were an adjustment to the punishment variable that should have worked, this was it. Of course, crime was already declining nationwide by 1994, so three-strikes did not inaugurate the trend, nor is there much evidence that it provided much of an accelerant, in California or in the twenty-two other states that adopted similar laws from 1994 to 1995.[34]

Faster and more certain arrests, improved processing times, and prompt committals might work; there's evidence that criminals give these variables greater weight than harsh sentences. Speed cameras suggest the possibilities. With cameras, detection is instantaneous, conviction virtually certain, and fines are sent near-immediately. In England, speed cameras were generally effective, associated with a roughly 40 percent reduction in serious injuries.[35] Deterrence *can* work, but in the mixing board that is public policy, twirling the sentencing dial costs the most and does the least.

Mass Incarceration

Undeterred by theory or data, Congress authorized increasingly stringent penalties in the 1980s and 1990s, with a special focus on drug violations. Of course, Congress had already conducted similar experiments, first with Prohibition, then with the Boggs Act of 1951, which set mandatory minimums for narcotics crimes. Prohibition failed spectacularly, and Congress tossed the Boggs experiment two decades later, because the Act "had *not* shown the expected overall reduction in drug law violations."[36] But politicians as diverse as Ted Kennedy and Strom Thurmond had their reasons to try again, so mandatory minimums proliferated at the federal and state levels.[37] Police swept up lesser drug offenders and the mentally ill (frequently comorbid categories) with vigor. If the point was to amass human cargo to show that Steps Were Being Taken, the project succeeded. Drug sentences lengthened; in the federal system, from an average 54.6 months in 1980 to 74.2 months in 2011, even as other sentences declined by 3.3 percent, to an average 47.3 months.[38] Federal statutes passed in the 1980s also largely abolished conventional parole, so releases dropped across the board, while probation rates for federal drug offenders fell from 26 to 6 percent.[39] The population of incarcerated drug offenders increased, and now constitutes 46.1 percent of federal inmates.[40]

Although the Capitol's sahibs boasted that their drug safari would take down big game, modest possession charges of soft drugs like marijuana dominated enforcement and drove most of the growth in arrests (by 2007, more than 80 percent of drug arrests were for possession), and of the dealers who were sentenced, roughly half rose no higher in the criminal hierarchy than the peddling protagonist of *High Maintenance*.[41] On its own terms, the war on drugs failed, and one need look no further than Congress for evidence: legislators and aides were investigated for drug violations during the period when Congress debated harsher drug sentencing, and though a 1988 federal statute promised that America would be drug-free by 1995, in 2013, Washington, D.C., cops nailed Representative Henry ("Trey") Radel for trying to buy cocaine.[42] Radel received probation, unlike many other (less white, less prominent) residents of the District.[43] This is backward, of course: if there were any group one would want to deter by harsh sentencing, it would be *lawmakers*, not black youths far from the levers of power.

The most notable features of the tough-on-crime era were the U.S. Sentencing Guidelines, federal rules that greatly restricted judicial leeway to assign penalties outside the prescribed range. For many decades, judges had wide latitude to tailor sentences, with the Court noting in 1949 that "the punishment should fit the offender *and not merely the crime*."[44] After the 1980s, statutes transformed what had been a human and holistic undertaking into a mechanistic one. The Guidelines reduced convicts' lives to numerical points, derived from byzantine tables. While the Guidelines considered personal history, mitigating factors never seemed to matter as much as aggravating ones. Sentences were tabulated, and so long as they conformed to the mechanics of the statutory regime and were not grossly above Guidelines range, appeals became extremely difficult. This greatly altered the balance of powers, a change Congress tried to disguise by designating the U.S. Sentencing Commission as part of the judiciary and specifying that three of its seven voting members be judges. As a Constitutional maneuver, this was laughably cosmetic. The Commission isn't judicial discretion by other means; it's a hybrid agency operating by legislative delegation, a "junior varsity Congress," per Justice Scalia, and as such, an institution whose Constitutional viability should be highly suspect under the jurisprudence of Court conservatives.[45]

The Guidelines also made the rather confusingly named "probation officers" more central; these officers compile presentence reports to assist judges in assigning sentences. To populate the Guidelines matrix, presentence reports draw on arrays of facts about defendants, but those facts are not subject to normal rules of evidence and often do not relate to the crime of conviction.[46] These quasi-impressionistic reports amount to a referendum on the soul—Anubis replaced by a functionary, the Feather of Truth transformed into the Guidelines—operating at considerable remove from the actual crime and its facts. Nevertheless, the conclusions of these freewheeling assessments are presumptive, and judges must make a real effort to deviate. Accordingly, many judges adopt the presentencing report and move on, sometimes aping the language of the reports in a judicial cut-and-paste, after which the maw of prison gapes wide. Thus, the sentencing reforms of the 1980s and 1990s further detached punishment from any specific crime—not that juries would know. General practice forbids criminal juries from hearing of the potential consequence of their verdicts, save in state death penalty cases.[47] Of course, most punishments are set outside jury view anyway, during plea bargaining, save that after the 1980s, bartering was tethered to list prices provided by the unforgiving Guidelines.

As it happens, the Constitutional, jurisprudential, and practical problems of sentencing reforms were easily knowable in the resonant year of 1984, when Congress began its present journey, but it took two decades for the Court to act. It finally did, in 2005's *United States v. Booker*, which held the Sentencing Guidelines unconstitutional insofar as they imposed additional punishments based on facts not determined at trial.[48] The Court also returned some discretion to judges by making the Guidelines advisory, though without adjusting mandatory minimums or entirely freeing judges of the Guidelines. But *Booker* and its related cases were too little, too late; prison populations were peaking and millions had already served years under Guidelines sentences. As discontent grew over fruitless incarceration, Congress tried and failed to reform mandatory minimums in 2015. It tried again in 2017, under the ostensible direction of Jared Kushner, who has something of a familial stake in prison reform, given his own potential indictments and his father's prior imprisonment.[49] Meanwhile, other parts of the Trump Administration have renewed commitments to questionable policy, as when AG Sessions commanded federal prosecutors to seek the harshest sentences possible and directly repudiated the Obama DOJ's tentative experiments with drug leniency.[50] Given the importance of plea bargaining, the coerciveness of overcharging, and the lack of procedural and factual protections pretrial, Sessions partly circumvented the Court's *Booker* ruling in a manner which, while technically legal, hardly honored *Booker*'s spirit.

The sentences legislatures impose via judges are only one part of the equation, because many sentences are "indeterminate," i.e., can be partially remitted by parole—or used to be. The Guidelines functionally abolished parole for federal crimes committed after November 1987, and now allow release only after 85 percent of a sentence has run.* In the states, parole continues, doled out by boards whose members are generally appointed by governors. This means a prisoner's *effective* sentence becomes an executive, not judicial, determination. Yet, despite performing quasi-judicial tasks, parole boards are not bound by normal rules of evidence, possess discretion so immense as to negate any idea of due process, and are staffed by officers of limited professional qualification (which, if such qualifications exist, are sometimes withheld from the public). But these drawbacks are rendered almost irrelevant by case volume: on average, boards consider thirty-five parole applications per day, and sometimes up to 100, meaning that a decision made in as few as five minutes can translate into years of prison.[51] Disturbingly, most parole boards operate in closed sessions. Some, like Georgia, have public hearings, but classify the other workings of the boards as "state secrets."[52] Parole boards might be terrific, or they might be strip-mall Star Chambers; we can guess, but don't know.

What we *do* know is that parole boards are no longer in the parole business, not really. Parole rates dropped considerably from the 1980s to the 2000s; New York's parole board, for instance, granted 60 percent of eligible applications in the early 1990s, but fewer than 20 percent in 2010.[53] Several states have drastically restricted parole discretion and others have abolished parole, though parole boards remain in place, perhaps because they provide opportunities for Tammany-style patronage by local executives. Certainly, politics and parole can be deeply intertwined; after one Massachusetts parolee killed a cop, release rates dropped almost 40 percent.[54] Even if boards comply with the little law asks of them, they corrode the system from within:

---

* Federal sentences may be accompanied by "supervised release"; unlike parole, supervised release is tacked onto the base sentence. By contrast, probation is in lieu of prison, though violations can result in incarceration. Presently, 4.5 million persons are on probation or parole.

with parole board decisions fluctuating wildly, plea-dependent prosecutors become less reliable negotiating partners, judges and juries have their expectations frustrated, and time served is largely decided by dubious political operators. The whole exercise confounds, especially as the prison population is aging. Older convicts are more expensive to maintain and less likely to commit new crimes. From a fiscal view, parole boards should be kicking out as many old prisoners as they can.

All Stick, No Carrot

Bound up in all questions of sentencing and parole is rehabilitation, one of the original justifications for modern prisons. In the early 1800s, reformers believed that discipline and moral instruction would improve prisoners, with parole as inducement. By 1984, the Senate rejected the rehabilitation model as "outmoded," imposing mandatory minimums and jettisoning parole, thus eliminating important incentives.[55] Other reformatory options also evaporated, including in-prison education and substance abuse programs, though these programs have been shown effective in reducing violence and recidivism.[56] Although 84 percent of prisons do offer education, legislation in the 1990s reduced financing, and participation rates dropped as programs became harder to access and incentives disappeared.[57] But the viability of rehabilitation is decreasingly germane, as prison conditions deteriorate to levels where rehabilitation becomes flatly implausible. In 2016, federal prisons were 114 percent overcrowded, and state prisons ran to 99 to 102 percent of capacity in the aggregate and under forgiving assumptions, with some states (e.g., Illinois) running to 137+ percent.[58] Conditions vary from unpleasant to brutal, and prison staff have considerable leeway to alter the terms of detention by declaring lockdowns, imposing punitive solitary confinement, and revoking privileges, so yet again, the executive defines the practical contours of punishment.

Under the Eighth Amendment and UN conventions to which America is a party, prisoners have rights to proper medical treatment for physical and mental ailments, though most prisoners lack access to all but the most urgent and basic care. Nor will courts intervene unless a prisoner's medical needs are "serious" and staff displayed "deliberate indifference" to a prisoner's suffering; negligence, not even medical malpractice, qualifies.[59] In 2008, the bipartisan Second Chance Act adjusted course modestly, providing grants for education and rehabilitation, though annual budgeting never exceeded $100 million and the Act's funding appeared in jeopardy in 2018.[60] Even at the height of Second Chance, allotting $50 to each prisoner's education made clear that rehabilitation was not a serious priority, and conditions make some prisons crimogenic—i.e., inmates become slightly more likely to commit crime than before.[61] This statistic alone suggests how much America's carceral system fails even on its own terms. Prison is supposed to *reduce* crime, not foster it.

Prisons' self-defeating dynamics are policy questions beyond judicial reach; only when prison conditions hit rock bottom does the Eighth Amendment's prohibition on "cruel and unusual" punishment kick in.* Since the 1960s, prisoners and the DOJ have sued for, and received, judicial intervention to correct unconstitutionally abusive prison practices. As part of its tough-on-crime routine, Congress passed legislation in 1995 to make these suits more difficult.[62] However, as inmate populations grew, not even legislated barriers could protect the worst prisons. In the early 2000s, California's prisons had become so overcrowded that inmates lived in gymnasia and common areas, the inmate-to-toilet ratio hit 54:1, electrical and sewage systems failed, and guards feared riots.[63] Governor Schwarzenegger declared a state of emergency, allowing the state to "streamline" export of prisoners to facilities in other states or run by private contractors.[64] Litigation erupted from all corners, but California did little, leading to intolerable deterioration. Federal judges ultimately ordered California to reduce

---

* Although originalist judges are fond of dredging up historical sanction for harsh penalties, they have failed to note that large prisons did not really exist in 1791—in other words, prisons may not be "cruel" from the originalist perspective, but they are definitely "unusual."

324

its prison population—however it saw fit—to 137.5 percent of capacity, the maximum level deemed humane. California stonewalled, and after a decade, exasperated judges ordered California to release more than 30,000 prisoners (approaching the entire prison population of Virginia).[65]

California's persistent unwillingness to address its problems, some stretching back into the 1990s, cast doubt on executives' commitment to the rule of law; California only buckled when the matter became national news. The process was untidy and unsatisfactory to all involved, though, interestingly, California's crime rate continued to decline even after the mass release.[66] California claims the title for prison drama, but prisons in several states have been placed into DOJ or federal judicial receivership, a last-ditch remedy when state mismanagement becomes intolerable.[67]

The arrival of private prisons further complicated accountability problems— as, one might reasonably suspect, was the goal in using them. Private prisons emerged in the 1980s, and became a growth industry: between 1999 and 2015, their populations expanded by 83 percent, to 126,000 (at least).[68] Private institutions' overriding motive is profit maximization and the resulting less-than-no-frills model has led to lapses that render these institutions less safe for guards, inmates, and the public, than their government equivalents.[69] The federal government relies especially heavily on private vendors, but in 2016, Deputy AG Sally Yates, prompted by DOJ's dismal reviews of private institutions, ordered the Bureau of Prisons to wean itself from outsourcing.[70] Before that plan took hold, President Trump terminated Yates (for refusing to defend his travel ban) and AG Sessions reversed course on private prisons. By felicitous coincidence, the dominant firms in the private prison industry donated generously to Trump, and one firm had retained two of Sessions's assistants and relocated its annual retreat to a Trump resort.[71] And again, by coincidence, one donor's Cibola, New Mexico, facility, singled out as a particularly unfit by the Obama-era DOJ and slated for the chopping block, survived as a federal contractor, now housing ICE detainees.[72] Other inferences could be drawn, of course, though if AG Sessions had strong reasons to overturn the DOJ's exhaustively researched eighty-six-page report on the perils of private prisons, his one paragraph countermand declined to provide detail.[73]

When the Trump Administration arrived in 2017, prison populations had been mildly declining since 2009, due to dropping crime rates and a mix of reforms, leniency, budgetary cutbacks, court-mandated releases, and the outflow of prisoners arrested during the 1980s–1990s crackdown whose terms either ended or who qualified for parole. The trend might not survive, but even if it continues, it's not sufficiently powerful to meaningfully slim the swollen penal state, nor does it fix a system whose correctional institutions do not correct, whose deterrent policies do not deter, and which operates in a constitutional purgatory to which the angels of due process rarely visit.

Prison's Hinterlands

Less than one-third of the correctional system's population is in physical custody. The rest dwell in the system's dismal suburbs: 3.67 million probationers and 870,000 parolees.[74] Virtually any transgression can convert "community supervision" into incarceration, including acts that violate probationary terms—even those that are not inherently criminal, such as associating with forbidden people or failing to maintain employment. Most missteps will not be detected, but when they are, probation and parole officers have almost total discretion to decide whether public intoxication or tardiness for parole meetings warrants a swift return to prison. Probation and parole decisions, then, can be nearly as consequential as trials, though as we've seen, parole boards are nothing like courts. The tribulations of rapper Meek Mill, who was tossed back in prison for breaching probation terms—the violations included popping wheelies on a dirt bike and being accused of an airport scuffle (some charges were dropped)—brought probation's arbitrary quality into the limelight in 2017–2018.[75] Mill was ultimately freed after the intervention of everyone from Jay-Z to Patriots owner Robert Kraft, resources obviously not available to the average parole violator. Mill's case was also unusual in that a judge pushed for recommitment. (Its other aspects were common, including its prompt disappearance from national discussion.)

Mostly, though, probation decisions are made by executive officers, who usually get their way, especially when it comes to recommitments, which law formally views as bureaucratic applications of judicially imposed sentences, and unworthy of much scrutiny. That creates a large blind spot: each year, around 28 percent of carceral admissions result from probation/parole decisions, and the physical liberty of 1 in 55 adult Americans rests in the near-unlimited discretion of non-judges.[76] More troublingly, many probation officers are not public employees. Several states have outsourced these roles to private companies, whose employees often have less education and training than their public equivalents. This creates special problems, as parolees' poverty makes failure to pay probation fees a frequent reason for recommitment. Private firms have considerable incentives to relieve themselves of probationers who cannot pay, returning them to prison and thus government books, a standard procedure for dealing with nonperforming assets.[77]

Probation is just one part of the historical entanglement of economic status, debt, and punishment. Many of the earliest British prisons were debtor's prisons. The practice has been essentially recreated when probationers are recommitted for failure to pay private firms their probation fees. Technically, it's unconstitutional to reincarcerate for indigency alone, but some states allow private probation firms to make indigency determinations, a conflict of interest, given the incentive firms have to discharge themselves of insolvent supervisees.[78] By definition, indigents have trouble raising Constitutional objections, as mounting a court case whose root is lack of resources is quite obviously beyond most indigents.

The problem stretches beyond probation, affecting convicts unable to pay minor and collateral fines. Legal integrity and public safety suffer no real damage if an insolvent violator fails to remit a $200 levy, but some jurisdictions use minor lapses to reincarcerate offenders.[79] This is economically irrational, given the costs of prison beds, and also unlawful. It happens all the same. Presumably, the goal (assuming one exists) is to wring money from friends and family, just as it was in Georgian England. Americans once blanched at the Chinese practice of charging a family for bullets used in executions. But China's "bullet fee" is a myth. The American system of charging defendants for court costs, sometimes including the costs of public defenders and *juries,* is entirely real.[80]

The phenomenon of debt-punishment reaches its nadir in the bail system. Defendants are presumed innocent until proved otherwise, and the Constitution presumes that federal bail options will be provided (absent extenuating circumstances, like flight risk or public danger).[81] Custody without bail amounts to punishment without trial, which should be Constitutionally suspect. Of course, courts must tolerate transient intrusions on liberty prior to conviction, e.g., arrest, but after processing, the presumption is for some form of noncustodial supervision. In fact, defendants accused of petty crimes are often released on their own recognizance, no bail required. But many others must post bail, either by cash or bond. Bail typically ranges from $250 to $1,000 for misdemeanors and from $20,000 to $1 million for felonies.[82] Each jurisdiction sets bail according to its own reasoning (or whims), producing ludicrous disparities; California's Mariposa County sets bail for public intoxication at $10,000, while the same misdemeanor in nearby Fresno County bails at $75.[83] In New York City, median bail for misdemeanors was $1,000 in 2015 (in real dollars, essentially unchanged from 2000), while median felony bail was $7,500 (up 52 percent in real terms since 2000).[84] Almost all defendants who aren't released on their own recognizance receive bail options, but these can be meaningless in a country where roughly one-third of adults have no savings, one-third have less than $1,000 saved, and where young people and minorities (the groups disproportionately experiencing arrest) are in even worse financial shape.[85] The Eighth Amendment forbids "excessive bail" (as do some federal statutes), but "excessive" is a function of several factors, only one of which is the ability to pay.

Leaving aside serious suspected felons, unaffordable bail works an injustice by putting defendants in intolerable dilemmas. The longer defendants stay in jail, the fewer resources they have to fight their suits: they earn no income, have greater difficulty working with attorneys and witnesses, and lose the will to fight. With pretrial delays large and rising, even innocent parties increasingly find it rational to cop a plea when bail lies out of reach. In New York City, the rack rate for misdemeanors is between fifteen days and a year, and time served can be shaved down by cooperative pleas. Misdemeanants who are detained and cannot make bail can expect to serve an average eighteen days waiting for trial, with additional delays and more punitive sentencing always possible; pleas can be cheaper and more expedient, returning defendants (who are, post-plea, convicts) to their families.[86] The alternative is to rummage up bail money, which from a middle-class perspective (the perspective of judges, state legislators, and bureaucrats), seems eminently reasonable: Why spend an extra day in prison if $1,000 or $2,500 will spring you? But that might be a defendant's entire savings, and bail risks it all: should the defendant miss a court date, even for innocent reasons (like New York's sclerotic subway), bail may be forfeit.

Should defendants not have ready cash, they can rely on bondsmen, but this converts a possible loss into a certain one; the bond fee is a nonrefundable 10 to 20 percent. Bonds also carry hidden costs, as the industry has been plagued by abuses, including intimidation, coercion, over-collections, and the (occasionally improper) seizure of assets by legal process. There are good bondsmen, of course, but the industry generally marinates in a *Merchant of Venice* fog, with Shylock recast as Dog the Bounty Hunter. Dog, by the way, is as real as he is unreassuring, operating under the legal umbrella of permissive bounty hunting laws despite being himself an ex-con (sentenced for first-degree murder, shockingly) and disregarding trifles like international law, which resulted in his arrest in Hawaii and a request for extradition by Mexico, where he had hunted quarry.[87] To be clear, it wasn't A&E that made Dog's services to reality television possible, it was the bail system.

The arrival of Dog on the doorstep is alarming enough, but what's especially appalling about bail is that a federal study showed that 23 percent of felony defendants will have their charges dismissed, many will receive probation, and some unknowable (if small) fraction are innocent but plead guilty out of necessity—yet prohibitive bail means many of these people will spend meaningful time behind bars anyway.[88] Bail also creates problems for society generally, because incarceration is costly and bail is associated with future social dysfunction, against which bail offers only limited compensation, such as a minor increase in the likelihood that defendants make their court dates.[89]

Somewhere between bail and prison are pretrial diversions, whereby charges will be dismissed if defendants complete community service and pay fees and restitution. Diversion is largely discretionary, and prosecutors may not bother to offer it to defendants who seem unable to pay, though this creates a system of impressionistic, status-based justice. When diversion is offered, it comes with some of the same risks as bail, as failures to timely perform services or pay fees restart the prosecution cycle, effectively compounding punishment. Diversions were meant to be progressive and merciful, but they're increasingly just another source of revenue, and not one that aligns interests appropriately.

For very minor crimes and regulatory violations, fines serve as standard punishments. Fines are by far the most numerous legal penalties, and they raise few issues so long as they are affordable and proportionate. The problem, as with bail, probation, and diversion, is that fines occasionally mutate into harsher penalties. Defendants who cannot pay fees often suffer "stacking," by which late charges and processing fees compound base sums already beyond a defendant's reach, potentially triggering physical custody. Applied to indigents, stacking is about as socially useful as squeezing blood from a rock and charging taxpayers for the experiment, but it happens anyway.

Criminal punishment has evolved since *lex talionis*, and law now prefers to extract its due in money and time, and once these are remitted, the convict has paid his "debt to society." Unfortunately, it's hard to settle the bill in full, and many convictions trail penalty-enhancing strikes, employment disabilities, and prohibitions on voting. And then there are the fees and surcharges which, if not promptly paid, refresh the cycle of debt, requiring further settlement in the currency of years. Within the very broad limits of the Constitution, law has little to say about what sentences are appropriate;

that's a matter for sociologists and legislators (and, in a different tradition, scholars of jurisprudence). But when debts cannot be settled confidently, or their amounts and terms are determined by arbitrary means, society has not set a penalty, but a trap. And justice should not—indeed, given due process, cannot—tolerate a trap.

Civil Remedies

In civil matters, law offers three categories of remedy: compensatory damages, punitive damages, and injunctive and other equitable relief. Compensatory damages are just that, intended to restore parties to whatever position would have obtained had there been no wrong.[90] In cases involving money and other commodities, compensation presents little difficulty, except when defendants lack resources to pay or (as has become common) hide assets in shell corporations, rendering themselves "judgment-proof." But even in cases involving evasions, the problems are more practical than conceptual. However, not all cases involve fungible assets, requiring courts to make subjective or speculative calculations. What's a toe worth, or a life, or a Picasso? Moral and aesthetic values might be incalculable, but law must find a price, and that's usually whatever an item could earn in the market. Worker's compensation boards constantly value fractured digits and severed limbs, using calculations based on lost time and earning power. Courts employ similar methods, with upward adjustments for the plaintiff's pain, suffering, and peculiarities (David Beckham's foot is worth more than the average appendage, but less than it was fifteen years ago). These adjustments can lead to seemingly perverse outcomes: it has been cheaper to (accidentally) kill someone than to inflict nonfatal, exceedingly painful injuries requiring a lifetime of care, and while human life may be precious, the average wrongful death suit will not fetch the same legal price as, say, defacing *Le Rêve*. Although the professoriate loves these oddball examples, most civil cases are prosaic; money changes hands and life goes on.

When cases move into the brackish waters between civil and criminal law, punitive damages become available and problems mount. Law awards punitives when defendants' behavior is egregious, worthy of punishment and deterrence, and awards exceed any actual harm suffered. These are social verdicts—punishments, as the "punitive" indicates—and therein lies the risk of injustice. Normally, only governments can punish, and subject to the protections granted defendants in criminal cases. Punitive damages allow private parties to collect cash for public harms, at a much lower standard than the "beyond a reasonable doubt" applicable to criminal cases.[91]

Punitives have long been available in Anglo-American law, but the possibility for private misuse traditionally counseled limited application. In the thirteenth century (you knew Edward I wouldn't stay offstage for long), law allowed "lavish" damages for particularly loathsome acts, such as despoiling a church, abusing a government office, or "ravishing" a ward.[92] Over time, courts also tolerated punitive damages as a legal fiction, to allow plaintiffs to recover compensation for classes of injuries (like insults to honor) for which normal damages were not widely available. Historically, then, the purpose of punitive damages was to condemn *prior* acts of morally outrageous conduct, to inflict quasi-criminal penalties when the state was incapable of doing so (because the state itself was the wrongdoer), or to redress actual injuries when law did not provide a formal means of compensation (emotional distress being the usual example).[93] Deterrence, notably, was not a major feature.

Punitives have lost most of their original impetus, save for combatting wrongs committed by the state. Yet, perversely, punitive damages are now widely used in areas where legal evolution should render them moot, and rarely available in areas where they remain necessary. Modern law explicitly allows recovery for emotional distress and other "insults," eliminating one traditional justification for punitive damages. The rise of public prosecution eliminates another justification, as the state can vindicate itself more directly and efficiently than private plaintiffs can. Prosecutors may not pursue all crimes with sufficient vigor, but the cleanest solution to this problem is to give prosecutors proper tools and incentives, rather than rely on a thirteenth-century doctrine as a clumsy substitute. Of course, juries can still express outrage over *prior* acts, and award extra compensation that bears a reasonable relationship to proven harms. But to the extent punitive damages are awarded to *deter*, they become speculative, quasi-criminal penalties. As such, defendants should be afforded something closer to normal criminal protections, including proof beyond a reasonable doubt and the full safeguards of the Eighth Amendment. Dispensing with punitive damages, at least the component swollen by deterrence, could also advance the interests of plaintiffs generally. Giant punitive awards often trigger waves of tort reform that imperil basic civil claims under the pretense of combatting billion-dollar jackpots for the plaintiffs' bar. (The abuses of the securities bar led to restrictions on class-action financial litigation in 1995; by 2001, critics saw the legislation as an enabler of financial malfeasance.[94]) Fear of punitives also encouraged a rush to compulsory arbitration and settlement—so while punitives were originally a channel for community outrage, they now help push wrongs out of the community's legal view. None of this means that punitive damages should disappear, only that history and context counsel against promiscuous use.

The one area in which context has not changed, and where punitives can and should play important roles, are cases where conflicts of interest prevent the state from bringing appropriate charges. This suggests that punishing state officials would be an especially fit use of punitive damages—statutes do, in fact, allow for this—but only when immunity hasn't defeated the claim. Unfortunately, as courts expand the scope of sovereign and qualified immunity, the area in which punitives retain their greatest animating values is precisely where the door is closing fastest. The modern doctrine of punitive damages is not the worst of all worlds, but it's certainly backward, ahistorical, and illogical.

The final remedy is equitable relief, whereby courts order litigants to do (or not do) specific things. Equitable relief is available when normal damages don't work. For example, all real estate is, our brokers tell us, unique and irreplaceable. If a seller refuses to turn over the keys to the miracle condo with eastern light and fourteen-foot ceilings, the jilted buyer doesn't have to settle for cash; she can ask, and courts may give, the property itself. The equitable transfer of art, houses, the Hope Diamond, and other unique items is easily accomplished. What's harder is when plaintiffs ask courts to control *conduct*, often before a final verdict has been reached.

Injunctions and other equitable remedies are sometimes the only means to prevent injustice, though they carry risks of misfire. With temporary restraining orders (TROs), risks are small, because TROs only last a short time, preserving the status quo against imminent threats. For example, courts issue TROs against stalkers before adversarial proceedings commence, followed by a full hearing at the earliest possible date. The intermediate step is the preliminary injunction (PI), issued before any final determination on the merits, and often before evidence has been collected and contested. PIs usually involve more complicated facts, so there may be a substantial lag between an injunction and a decision on the merits. Therefore, courts dole PIs out with great care, requiring a plaintiff to show: (i) that he is likely to prevail on the merits; (ii) likely to suffer irreparable harm without court action; (iii) that the "balance of the equities tips in his favor" (i.e., the plaintiff will suffer greater expected harm if the PI doesn't issue); and (iv) that the PI is in the "public interest."[95] PIs involve enormous departures from normal practice, requiring courts to essentially prejudge cases before they have fully gelled (actual injury is a component of normal claims, and in the PI context, injury is necessarily incomplete, or even inchoate). PIs are "extraordinary" remedies in various senses, justified only by emergency—a classic example being the planned bulldozing of a historic building to make way for a mall.

Not all emergencies are equal, however, and here law reveals its preferences. First, law favors PIs that maintain the status quo, and while there are procedural, practical, and cynical reasons for this, as a logical matter, there's no reason to assume *ex ante* (the position from which courts approach PIs) that the status quo is particularly just, nor is it always clear what the status quo really is. Law also tacitly signals its preference for risking reparable injuries over avoiding injury in the first instance, which may seem unjust, but is wholly reasonable, given the dangers of courts meddling in the real world without first donning their procedural armor.

The law of PIs also tends to favor government interests. Private parties seeking PIs must post "security" to compensate their adversaries should their ultimate case fail, and when government is the adversary, security can be infeasibly large. This is especially troubling when public interest groups sue to vindicate public rights that government has trampled. The rules grant judges some flexibility to set the security at a level the "court considers proper" to satisfy the potential damage to a defendant, and courts can set security as low as $1, though no judge has an obligation to be creative, and a literal and unworldly application of the rule (by a clerk, say) might terminate a suit then and there.[96] Meanwhile, in their home courts, governments need *not* post security, on the assumptions that government is less likely to abuse PIs than private parties and that government is fundamentally creditworthy (true for the federal government, which can print dollars; much less reasonable for local governments, many of which are borderline broke). Finally, the requirement that PIs conform to the public interest also implicitly favors government, which speaks with more authority as to what the public good is. This factor can be decisive in matters of national security, where courts tend to be highly deferential, even when there are indications that the executive branch has end-run Congress and created dubious exigencies.[97] So there are really two streams of thought governing PIs. In contests against private parties, courts are stingy with PIs because of *where the case stands*. In contests against the government, judges are stingy with PIs because of *who the defendant is*.

After litigation runs its course, courts can issue final relief, either by permanent injunction or by enforcing consent decrees, where parties voluntarily contract (or rather, settle), agreeing to behave in certain ways. Regardless, ultimate enforcement resides in the court.[98] Smaller parties can only submit, but larger institutions sometimes refuse, often on matters of deep importance. The original *Brown v. Board* dispensed with "separate but equal" in public education, but many districts paid no attention, requiring further judicial action. Such interventions create multiple difficulties for courts. Courts must venture into a traditionally executive realm, managing matters beyond normal judicial competence; in doing so (functionally, if not quite technically), blending Constitutional powers. And when explicitly defied, courts must apply their will by force using the executive branch against itself. This represents a rather unnatural state of affairs unless two different executives are involved, as was the case in *Brown*.

After the Court decided *Brown* and *Brown II* (which required compliance with "all deliberate speed"), nine black students registered to attend a Little Rock high school.[99] Governor Faubus ordered the Arkansas National Guard to block those students from school. Eisenhower, having previously noted that "the Supreme Court has spoken and I am sworn to uphold the constitutional processes in this country," ordered in the 101st Airborne and federalized the Arkansas Guard.[100] Eisenhower's intervention resolved the immediate issue, but for many years, other schools nevertheless deliberately misinterpreted the Court's phrasing, even in comparatively progressive places like Boston—principle is never as potent as objections to actual remedies like busing. In the end, most districts grudgingly, if partially, integrated. A conspicuously defiant school district risked federal occupation, and one county against a nation is a losing proposition. But what if the federal executive resists court orders? Judges can hardly commandeer state militias to invade D.C. or borrow a tank division from the UN.

Beneath Contempt, or Above It?

The ultimate weapon courts have to enforce their will against the federal executive is the power of contempt, enforceable by fine or jail.* Fortunately,

---

* Congress also has contempt power, but it has a greater power, that of the purse, which courts lack.

the mere threat of contempt proceedings usually secures compliance. For agency officials, who spend careers litigating before a small pool of judges, self-interest and shame usually suffice. The political appointees who run agencies, and the elected officials who sit at the top of the executive, operate under different conditions and calculate self-interest on other metrics, as Governor Faubus did. As for shame, it's a norm, not prison. When officials lie beyond shame, courts must resort to the real deals: fines and jail.

When contempt sanctions issue against federal entities and officials, practical and Constitutional dilemmas can't be avoided. Fining an agency amounts to taking dollars away from a public institution, and this can be odd, or even counterproductive in cases where agencies require their full budgets to carry out court orders. Fines also raise the Constitutional stakes, because one or both of the other branches might be tempted to immunize errant departments by reimbursing contempt fines from the general pot. Deploying a contempt slush fund is an untested strategy, and it's not clear where it falls on the spectrum running from devious-but-technically-legal to clear Constitutional crisis. Most likely, slush fund reimbursements fall into a "shenanigans" category, with complexities taking so long to resolve that the relevant parties will have moved on before a final decision issues, allowing everyone to save face by withdrawing the issue as moot after a sanitizing interlude.[101]

Indeed, to the extent courts have a doctrine about these sorts of confrontations, it's that of face-saving. In virtually every serious case, either the court or the relevant agency has backed down before contempt fines kicked in, avoiding direct confrontation, so this area of law is not well developed. To play it out, the executive could argue that contempt fines are barred by sovereign immunity, though doing so requires a slippery reading of immunity law.[102] But even if government enjoys statutory immunity from fines, nothing protects those statutes against judges. The Court that manufactured foundational immunity doctrines could withdraw them. The special circumstances of contempt, where courts bear the insult, might focus judicial minds on the logical weaknesses of immunity in a way that, say, executive victimization of the general public has not.

When the executive really overreaches, courts may resort to jailing contemnors. Enforcement falls to federal marshals who, by habit and law, are obedient to the courts they serve and probably would not pause before cuffing agency officials. But structurally, marshals are part of the DOJ, itself headed by the attorney general, a presidential appointee who lives and dies by executive whim. In theory, the AG or (more circuitously) the president could rescue an errant Cabinet member, so a sufficiently abnormal and contumacious executive could trigger a Constitutional crisis. The possibility seems remote, but then again, contempt presupposes that the executive has *already* behaved abnormally; a particularly feckless and ill-advised executive might even, perhaps, stumble into a Constitutional morass without knowing it.

It takes two to have a Constitutional crisis, and courts generally prefer not to tango. They reserve the *right* to dance, of course, just as they reserve the right to undo the bureaucracy with the anti-delegation doctrine. But courts that can barely bring themselves to fine the executive have even less appetite to arrest it. So while courts regularly find government's rank-and-file lawyers in minor contempt (for the usual misbehaviors in court, e.g., missing deadlines), they rarely visit the same on government institutions and their senior officials. When courts do, they make every effort to assign nominal penalties, provide government second or third chances, and find reasons to discover that any government response, however tardy and lackluster, is satisfactory. On the rare occasions when trial judges become so exasperated as to reach for the big red button, appellate courts drop in to avoid a Constitutional showdown, sometimes on amazingly flimsy pretexts. Trial judges who stick firm may find themselves reversed, or even tossed off cases entirely, with their own brethren citing contempt rulings as evidence of "bias" against government, requiring recusal.

This is not the story told in law school, which focuses on one case in which the Court countermanded a presidential order in a time of war and the president meekly complied. That case exists, but it was immediately preceded by another matter, one that casts real doubt on judicial nerve. The cases were, essentially, nonidentical twins, decided at the end of the Truman

Administration. The first came in 1951, precipitating the first major contempt crisis since the Civil War. The vehicle was *Land v. Dollar*, and as a *casus
belli*, the nominal stakes could not have been more ridiculous; the case boiled
down to a squabble over stock in a shipping company. During the Depression, the company received a federal bailout and the government obtained
stock in the company, but no one could agree on whether the stock was sold
or merely pledged as collateral. In the event, the debt was repaid, the original
stockholders demanded their shares back and, after much wrangling about
the nature of the transaction, the D.C. Circuit concluded that the shares
should revert to their original owners. The government fought relentlessly,
taking a kitchen-sink approach: it contested the facts, then the legal conclusions, appealing to the Court (which denied cert three times), then tried to
reboot the case in a different court, claimed sovereign immunity to contempt
proceedings, and generally behaved like a brat. Ultimately, the D.C. Circuit
ordered the government to get on with it and give the stock back.

President Truman had previously commanded the secretary of commerce
to hold on to the stock however he could. Thus unlike most executive contempt cases, where layers of faceless bureaucracy stand between judges and
senior officials, *Dollar* presented the most direct standoff possible, a president and a Cabinet member versus the judiciary. (Why the Truman Administration felt compelled to take such a hard line isn't wholly clear, but there
were intimations that Truman's cronies were benefitting from positions at
the company, which they would lose should ownership revert.[103]) At last, the
D.C. court ordered the secretary to comply within five days or be jailed. Just
two days before intra-branch war erupted, the Court—which, recall, had
already dodged this case several times—parachuted in to de-escalate.

The Court's pretexts were flimsy, but it seems that the Justices did not
want to squarely confront claims of executive immunity to contempt, or
watch a lower court dispatch a Cabinet member to the clink, much less risk a
pardon that could further raise the stakes. Certainly, the Court didn't seem
keen to put the Constitution on the line over a chunk of stock, a hint shareholders took, settling with government at a steep discount. Justice Jackson,

339

who wrote separately about the case, was disgusted that the Court tolerated gross official disobedience, saying that the Court's reputation was itself "on trial," and that its decision would have an "evil influence," encouraging lawless defiance in the executive.[104] Who knew what tyranny Truman would work next?

Jackson didn't have to wait long: the following year, Truman seized American steel mills, claiming that labor disruptions threatened the war effort in Korea. Truman had possible legal grounds to seize the mills under the Selective Service Act, but invoking the Act would take time, and Truman— perhaps emboldened by *Dollar*—didn't feel like waiting. So the president acted by decree. A judge enjoined the seizure, and the matter reached the Court, where Truman famously lost. This time, he backed down and ordered the Commerce Department to comply. It's this second case, *Youngstown Sheet & Tube,* that law schools teach: the story of courts forcing a president to obey the law, even in wartime.[105] But 1952 was not 1951: by the time the Court decided *Youngstown,* Truman had (to his shock), lost the New Hampshire Democratic primary, his administration was mired in scandal, and Truman's favored successor—Chief Justice Fred Vinson, who had granted an emergency (and pro-administration) stay in *Dollar*—had declined to run in Truman's stead.[106] Certainly, *Youngstown* is an important case, but Truman was a dead man walking, the Chief Justice was slightly tainted, Truman's emergency wasn't real (the nation had a large steel inventory), and the case had been fully argued before the grandest court in the land. The judiciary had a much freer political hand in *Youngstown,* and it could make (via Jackson's concurrence) a profound statement about the limits of executive power. But *Youngstown* cannot be divorced from context. When paired with *Dollar,* the only firm conclusion that can be drawn is that judicial spine is stiff when presidents are weak; the obverse may be, but isn't necessarily, true.[107]

If, as we saw at the beginning of the chapter, the ability to provide redress is among law's most distinguishing features, then law's failure to properly infuse remedies with justice provides a serious count in the indictment against law itself. Each error drains law's reservoirs of authority, especially those of courts whose special responsibility is to ensure that outcomes are just. The particular danger here is that we must ultimately turn to the courts to curb the executive, in whom virtually all powers have been concentrated. Therefore, the crucial questions are whether a judiciary that routinely tolerates lesser inequities will still have the reflexes to resist the ultimate inequity, and whether it will still enjoy sufficient respect among the public to do so successfully. But there's really no question about whether courts will have to face this question; it's only a matter of time. Overreach has become the executive's way of life.

CHAPTER THIRTEEN

FAILING FROM THE TOP DOWN: IMPERIAL PRESIDENCIES AND CONSTITUTIONAL EROSION

> When the president does it, that means it's not illegal.
>
> Richard Nixon (1977)[1]

> The president can't have a conflict of interest.
>
> Donald Trump (2016)[2]

Here's the $64,000 question: What's *legally* wrong with the foregoing statements? It's actually hard to say, just as it's hard to say whether a sitting president can be indicted, forcibly deposed, required to turn over critical information to Congress, or be held in contempt.

Depending on the context, there may be nothing radically incorrect about the Nixonian/Trumpian statements, but this begs the question of what the context was. For Nixon, it (supposedly) involved national security, a legal nether-region over which presidents have *almost* unquestioned authority, although it took several court cases, a special prosecutor, and one of the biggest scoops in journalism to figure out where "almost" runs out. For Trump, the context involved demands that the president-elect divest from his ramshackle empire. Again, it takes legal digging to figure out that Trump's statement was at least *partially* true, and will take even more digging to figure out where the "partially" runs out. In the face of neo-absolutist assertions of executive power, it feels like the burden of proof is all wrong. The people shouldn't have to guess on what theory presidents exercise their powers; presidents should tell us. That presidents don't feel the need to do so, and instead force the public to flip through law books, demonstrates that the presidency deems itself a special case.

Other branches of government routinely state the legal bases for their activity. When Congress enacts laws, it provides a "Constitutional Authority Statement" specifying the Constitutional basis for writing a given law.[3] When courts decide cases, they state the precise reasons for their jurisdiction. When agencies issue regulations, they reference their statutory authority. But when *presidents* act, they formulaically intone that their authority derives from "the Constitution and the laws of the United States." This is zero-degree thought, the emptiness of "because I said so." *Which* part of the Constitution and *which* laws? Presidents decline to say.

Evasiveness grants presidents an enormous head start, allowing them to do as they please, while everyone else scrambles to assess legality. The burden of proof has landed on the people. Presidents seem free to act unless someone can provide incontrovertible proof to the contrary, and doing so takes time—long enough for presidents to get the nation into messy wars, establish special tribunals, spy on citizens, arrange slush funds, or cut deals with foreign powers. As a political fact, presidents can act unilaterally and forcefully, and when presidents entrench, they can only be moved by the full weight of the law, deployed by the other two branches of government, and usually with considerable public support. In Nixon's case, the combination probably still would not have sufficed without reinforcements furnished by the fourth estate, itself equipped with information provided by leakers from within the executive—and even then, Nixon was not removed by law, but by his own resignation. The modern presidency reduces America to a nation of legal Lilliputians, who can only bind the giant when acting in unison, and perhaps not even then.

The Founders would have unhesitatingly condemned the modern presidency as a tyranny. A quick comparison between the Declaration of Independence and contemporary presidential powers suffices as proof. The Declaration condemned the "absolute Tyranny" of George III, who had among other sins: refused to grant assent to laws, failed to support a robust judiciary, interfered with immigration, used kangaroo courts to try subversives, employed his military and "swarms" of officials to meddle with American life, and invoked sovereign prerogative to abrogate traditional liberties.[4] And now? Presidents issue signing statements that deny the force of properly enacted laws, resist judicial orders, issue decrees restricting immigration, convene "military commissions" to try "enemy combatants," commence war without Constitutionally required declarations, and preside over an enforcement regime that enjoys sovereign immunity when it transgresses against the people. How wide is the distance between George III and Bush II? Wide, but perhaps not wide enough, and getting narrower by the year. True, the people have pushed back against specific Constitutional overreaches. But resistance to an overbearing executive is mostly episodic; the *trend* among judges, Congress, and the public has been toleration of an increasingly powerful executive.

The False Flag of Necessity

Over the past century, almost all countries have concentrated power in their national executives, primarily at the expense of national legislatures and regional governments. In countries with fairly new constitutions, where civic norms have not fully entrenched, executive consolidation has been especially sharp. To a substantial degree, Hungary, Poland, the Czech Republic, and Russia have unwound the gains won in 1989–1992. But even countries with older constitutions or more deeply felt republican norms have drifted. In 2017, responding to Catalonia's burgeoning and largely democratic independence movement, Spain's (now ex-) prime minister Mariano Rajoy invoked emergency powers, deployed the Guardia Civil (once upon a time, Franco's pet goon squad), suppressed regional elections, and made political arrests.[5] To the northeast, Emmanuel Macron embraces a "Jupiterian" presidency— i.e., the president of France likens himself to the father of the gods (or to de Gaulle, which amounts to the same in certain quarters of France), and acts accordingly. In the many nations that use Britain's Westminster system, which has long granted prime ministers enormous powers, executive ascendancy is harder to spot, but the trend exists all the same. Britain, for example, stands just a slip of paper away from one-man rule: thanks to Tony Blair, the Civil Contingencies Act of 2004 allows a single minister in an emergency to suspend, in theory, virtually any act of Parliament save the emergency act itself and the Human Rights Act (an outgrowth of the *E.U.'s* constitutional guarantees).[6] The only, and completely unironic, constraint to this power is royal assent. Across the world—including America—the human sovereign has returned.

It should not (but apparently does) need to be said that concentrating so much power in individuals carries great risks. A terrible executive may provoke constitutional crisis or popular revolt—indeed, this is why Americans are American, and not British. Which raises the question: Why has this, or any other, nation tolerated the concentration of so many powers in one fallible person? An elective monarchy is a monarchy all the same, and prone to all its evils and weaknesses, as the Holy Roman Empire and Papal States demonstrated.

The response from executive apologists—many of whom have landed on the Supreme Court—is that a powerful presidency is a "necessity." As evidence, they point to the globalization of executive power, which they claim represents universal recognition that only executives have the agility to confront a world besieged by complexity and crisis. We'll deal with the historical obscenity of that in a moment, but for now, let's consider the arguments for executive power in the abstract. First, there's no *a priori* reason to think that modern executives are particularly nimble, much less so nimble as to warrant the upending of Constitutional balance. Executive power, after all, is wielded almost entirely through bureaucracies—hardly visions of lightning action, as we saw in Chapter 5. Equally, there's no reason to assume that a nimble executive (assuming such exists) will be competent, ethical, or judicious. Certainly, the division of powers embedded in many constitutions recognizes the possibility of the contrary. As James Madison noted, "[e]nlightened statesmen will not always be at the helm."[7] Anyway, the "nimble executive" proves too much: if contemporary life truly requires nearly unlimited executive discretion on matters of any real importance, the republican experiment is over.

Sensing this, champions of executive imperium assert that executives are not really destroying republican constitutionalism, so much as stretching its bounds in order to save it. *Wunderbar,* what could go wrong? Nothing, it seems; on the contrary, everything will go quite right. As proof, executive extremists curate a museum of blockbusters to foster the impression that presidents routinely transcend the Constitution to achieve the remarkable. Law professor John Yoo (best known for providing Bush II with rickety justifications for torture) provides a typical enumeration: Lincoln's Emancipation Proclamation, Teddy Roosevelt's trust-busting, and FDR's New Deal. Let's ignore the patent insincerity of a hard-right Republican justifying executive power based on anti-monopolism and the New Deal, and hear Yoo out. Here's what he wrote in 2008: "Our greatest presidents" expanded executive power, "for the most part...[in] a natural evolution which seemed then and now to be necessary....."[8] Now, that's not quite right. It's true that the executive actions on Yoo's list worked out pretty well, but with the exception of the Emancipation Proclamation, there were decent moral arguments for and against presidential action in the other cases. This is why the decisions Yoo lists were deeply controversial in the moment, hardly the "necessary" and "natural evolution" Yoo claims existed "then and now." Yoo also downplays or ignores that many of the executive actions he lists were confirmed by Congress and/or upheld by the judiciary—admittedly, sometimes after a tussle and after the fact, but confirmed all the same, and thus not unilateralism. Even accepting Yoo's premise—which basically boils down to the "Good King" hypothesis—one has to take monarchs as they come. After the regime change of January 2017, Yoo found himself possessed of new reservations.[9] But that's the problem with reading history backward, as Yoo does: there's no way to know *in the moment* whether a particular executive action is in fact necessary, nor whether it will better the republic and win history's sanction. All we can know in close-to-real-time is whether a particular action is a suspension of the ordinary legal order or not. As it turns out, many of the extraordinary measures employed by Yoo's boss, Bush II, were troubling and extralegal—as Yoo himself came close to admitting years later.[10] Perhaps future scholars will discover that Bush II's actions prevented catastrophe, but after almost twenty years, history is underway and unconvinced. Indeed, in 2014, the Senate described the "enhanced interrogation" Yoo facilitated as "brutal" and "*not* [] effective."[11]

The Decline and Fall and Rebirth of Executive Power

Because ardent supporters of executive power dip into history to make their selective case, it's worth understanding the origins and catastrophes of extreme executive power. The original model derives from the Roman Republic, whose Senate could grant extraordinary powers to a single person, the dictator. English borrowed the Latin word, but not its legal subtleties. Under Roman law, dictatorship could exist only when declared by the Senate (not the dictator), for a limited period (generally six months), to achieve a specific purpose stated in advance ("fend off Carthage"). Though dictators had considerable latitude, laws did not entirely dissolve; within Rome, citizens still retained legal rights to appeal—a nicety Yoo's former boss tried to jettison during the first phase of his War on Terror.[12] Though Rome appointed many dictators in its long history, most relinquished power in due course; they operated, to use an anachronism, *constitutionally*. The notable—indeed terminal—exception was Julius Caesar. Caesar had no legal claim to the dictatorships he sought, but the Senate, fearful and debased, went along, eventually appointing Caesar dictator for life. Had the Roman Senate resisted, things might have come out differently, at least for a time. Having fed power once, the Senate found it easier to do so again when Caesar's adopted heir, Octavian, won authority to rule as *princeps civitatis*, first citizen of Rome. Triumphalists like Yoo might respond that Rome, whose civic institutions were wobbling in the late Republic, received a great empire and peace when it cashed in republicanism for empire. Except that isn't quite true: Egypt, Rome's richest province, became the emperor's personal property, and Rome's subsequent history was punctuated by tyranny, rebellion, civil war, and decline. This might be of purely antiquarian interest, were not the idea of dictatorship revived repeatedly and with decreasing subtlety. After the French Revolution, the old requirements of a genuine threat to the homeland, continuation of normal judicial process, and fixed terms, lapsed. Dictatorship, born in legal chains, had shed them.

Worse, dictatorship became a constitutional feature. The notorious modern example is Article 48 of the Weimar Republic's constitution. Article 48 permitted the *Reichspräsident* to suspend certain civil liberties and govern by dictate "if the public safety and order...[were] considerably disturbed or endangered."[13] (These words will recur at home, I assure you.) From the start, Weimar Germany faced so many pressures, pulling its political parties in such radically different directions, that the Reichstag managed normal majority government only sporadically. Friedrich Ebert, Weimar's first president, repeatedly invoked Article 48 to steady the postwar economy, which worked for a time. Despite the Reichstag's ongoing instability, a better economy permitted a remarkable civic efflorescence from 1924 to 1929, but Weimar always teetered on the edge of dictatorship. As polarization grew and legislative deadlock persisted, many Germans believed that government-by-decree was the only practicable solution. When the Depression hit, Article 48 again became the prime instrument of governance, constantly employed by President Paul von Hindenburg to sidestep a Reichstag torn between left and right. In 1932, von Hindenburg and Chancellor Franz von Papen also used Article 48 to seize control of the Prussian state government, arguing that it was unable to maintain order. That maneuver was transparently fraudulent; Prussia had experienced some civil disturbances, but its real sin was resisting von Papen and von Hindenberg's policies.[14] German federalism therefore collapsed into mere fiction.

After further dysfunction in the national legislature, von Hindenburg and the conservative establishment decided to do unto Germany as they did unto Prussia. In their view, they had only three options: continued legislative disorder, bolshevism, or Nazism. The establishment theorized that Hitler would be most biddable, and tried to co-opt him into forming an extreme, but constitutional, government. Arguably, the establishment got a perverted version of its wish: Hitler gained power constitutionally, and his government was indeed extreme. From there, the legal status of the Nazi catastrophe became less clear; Hitler used intimidation and strategic arrests to cow the legislature into passing the Enabling Act, and what the Act enabled was dictatorship. As Weimar courts lacked robust powers of judicial review and the historical prestige of American courts, challenges to the Enabling Act went nowhere, and Germany descended into tyranny. Bizarrely, the Weimar Constitution continued on paper until 1945, after which Germany became an un-country under Allied rule. In 1949, Germany received a new Basic Law, which radically curtailed presidential power.[15]

Unlike Weimar or Rome, America does not have a constitution that allows rule by decree. Before the twentieth century, only one president consistently exceeded his lawful powers in a semi-Caesarean way: Abraham Lincoln. Indeed, Lincoln's presidency was something of a model to some rightist Weimar jurists, though they drew the wrong lesson—as do advocates of American executive power today. For some people, the salvation of the Union begins and ends the argument for the strong executive. But Lincoln's story is subtler and more reassuring than the ends justifying the means. While Lincoln did operate extra-Constitutionally, he faced a genuine emergency on home soil whose legal contours were not well defined, and did not seem keen on retaining emergency powers beyond the duration of the war. Even during the war, Lincoln usually tried to obtain legislative and judicial consent to his Constitutional freelancing. Most importantly, Lincoln did not pretend everything he did was either unquestionably legal and beyond account.

For example, during the first eighty days of the Civil War, Lincoln called up troops and spent without Congressional appropriation, actions beyond his Article II powers. However, Congress was then out of session and, once legislators returned, Congress "approved, and in all respects legalized and made valid" Lincoln's military actions "as if they had been issued and done under the previous express authority and direction of the Congress."[16] This was no Caesarean toadying. While Lincoln engaged in some dilatory gamesmanship to ensure that Congress would convene only once all of his supporters could be present in Washington, he never recomposed or physically threatened Congress to get his way, and often sounded Congressional leaders before taking executive action.

Lincoln wanted the other branches, properly emplaced and of their own will, to validate his actions. Even Lincoln's suspension of habeas corpus, a serious Constitutional breach, was eventually tidied up by Congress, this time in its own name.[17] For the most part, Lincoln's administration also litigated novel Constitutional issues in normal courts, and continued to hold free elections in the North, including Lincoln's own reelection in 1864, which he expected to lose.[18] Democracy continued, and the other branches remained active partners; the president did not feel he could act alone. So while Lincoln trod on the Constitution several times, he never denied that the Constitution should prevail, and the sooner the better. That, as much as the nobility of his cause, is what distinguishes Lincoln from true tyrants—Lincoln crossed the Potomac, not the Rubicon.

Even through the World Wars and Depression, the presidency was not entirely unbound. FDR accomplished most of his work through Congress.

Whatever its Constitutional infirmities, the New Deal was substantially passed (or confirmed) by Congress, not naked fiat. While FDR *believed* he had legal authority to proceed almost unilaterally in matters of urgency, he *acted* otherwise, returning time and again to Congress and voters for support. When World War II erupted and Britain begged for aid before America entered the war, FDR did not ship munitions on some unfounded theory of wartime powers, but asked his lawyers to ensure that the Destroyers-for-Bases swap, achieved by executive agreement, fit somewhere in the nooks and crannies of the law (a punctiliousness that greatly irritated Churchill).[19] Throughout his presidency, FDR's public statements carefully noted that his emergency economic directives were issued "under the Constitution and *under Congressional Acts*" (people could usually tell which ones), explicitly recognizing the Capitol's role. After Pearl Harbor, FDR traveled to Congress, and specifically obtained its authorization for war. During the conflict, FDR also largely accepted that he would have to litigate matters through normal courts, accepting losses as they came. So in two of the greatest wars America ever fought, one of them existential and the other potentially ruinous, presidents bent the Constitution but never declared themselves beyond it.

The White House Goes to War

All that changed in 1950, when Truman entered the Korean War without Congressional approval, based solely on a UN resolution.[20] There is nothing more dangerous than a nuclear state going to war, especially when that state is led by the only person in history to have actually used atomic weapons. War is a decision that requires contemplation and formality. Of course, in the event of an immediate and overwhelming attack on home soil, presidents may be forced to respond—though it proved no challenge to FDR to travel the 1.2 miles from White House to Capitol to receive Constitutional sanction to enter World War II. Apparently, this journey was beyond Truman, though the Korean War quite obviously involved no direct or imminent threats to American soil requiring swift, unilateral action.

If anything, American lives were lost *because* Truman acted. Some 36,574 American soldiers died in this undeclared war, but that's post hoc; in 1950, there was no way to be sure that the butcher's bill would not be vastly higher. North Korea was, after all, not just a client state of China (which fought directly), but also of the newly nuclearized Soviet Union, which covertly participated in the war. And though the Soviets did not then have the means to nuke the continental United States, they would shortly acquire them and could already strike America's European bases and allies. If there were a time for Congress to insist on its right to debate a war, rather than accede to presidential instinct, 1950 was it. But Congress did not declare war; indeed, it's *never* properly declared war since, despite constant military interventions, including the simultaneous occupations of two substantial nations.* Instead, Congress coughed up funds to support whatever interventions presidents had begun on their own initiatives garnished with the odd, Constitutionally ambiguous authorization.

Superficially, Congressional reticence over declaring war seems to mark no great break from prior practice; Congress has only formally declared five general wars, despite dozens of armed interventions since 1789. But *qualitatively*, 1950 was a watershed. The undeclared wars in Korea, Vietnam, Afghanistan, and Iraq bore no resemblance to the small, short, and near-riskless interventions of the nineteenth century. Does anyone remember American interventions in Sumatra, Samoa, Fiji, or Smyrna? Not really, and that is why these actions, legal or not, posed no great Constitutional risk.

Even as undeclared wars grew larger, their Constitutional moorings loosened almost completely. The War Powers Resolution of 1973, which authorizes military intervention without a proper war declaration, tried to offer a patina of legislative legitimacy.[21] But presidents have declined the invitation, stating only that their actions are "consistent" with, but not "pursuant" to, the Act.[22] The goal of this word game is to avoid conceding even an inch of presidential

---

* Major incidents in the past thirty years include: Libya (twice), Panama, Somalia, Yugoslavia/ Bosnia (thrice), Haiti (twice), Iraq (thrice), Afghanistan, plus whatever is going on in Syria, Yemen, etc.

authority; to invoke the Act might concede that presidents do not enjoy an unrestricted Article II power to fight whenever, wherever they please. As statements of executive power go, this is about as potent as it gets. Yet, Congress remains complaisant, because norms have changed, just as they did in Caesarean Rome. Even when American interests aren't in immediate peril and when hostilities risk open-ended and bloody quagmire, presidents believe they can act without much legislative pushback. And since 1950, they've been largely correct.*

Executive Legislation

In addition to usurping Congressional war powers, presidents have intruded substantially into other legislative domains. Article II requires that presidents "shall take Care that the Laws be faithfully executed"—i.e., the executive must enforce laws on an *as-is* basis.[23] However, presidents have taken to issuing "signing statements," offering commentary on whatever law they have just made official. Well into the twentieth century, signing statements contained little more than unobjectionable glosses or mild grousing.[24] On the few occasions where nineteenth-century presidents dared go further, suggesting that laws might be unwise or unconstitutional (and by implication, go unexecuted), Congress provided harsh rebukes. The memory of royal prerogative and its abuses remained comparatively fresh. Thus, when Andrew Jackson issued a statement about limiting the scope of a road bill, Congress denounced it as an improper line-item veto; when John Tyler issued a signing statement, legislators condemned it as a "defacement of the public records and archives."[25] As late as 1875, President Grant described signing statements as "unusual," an apt description of a Constitutionally suspect practice.[26]

In the twentieth century, presidents began to dabble with more, and more substantial, signing statements. Here again, Truman marked something of a

---

* A notable exception was Obama's request for Congressional approval for continuing operations in Syria. A Russian-brokered deal mooted the issue for a time.

turning point, issuing more than 100 statements, some offering vigorous objections to legislation. Since then, use has fluctuated, but the long-term trend is toward more intense use: Reagan issued 250 signing statements; Bush I issued 228; Clinton, 381; and Bush II, 161.[27] Given contemporary bill-bundling, a single signing statement can now affect many different issues; for example, Bush II's 161 statements offered more than 1,000 challenges to distinct provisions of law.[28] These statements have also risen from hollow press releases and modest nitpicking to attacks on the very constitutionality of laws. This is bizarre because "signing statements" obviously indicate that presidents have *signed* laws, thereby granting them legal life, yet statements challenge the very laws to which they are attached. Presidents try to justify the practice on the seemingly unobjectionable grounds that their statements merely clarify that the executive will not enforce laws that breach the Constitution, the document presidents swear to uphold. If that were the real purpose, presidents wouldn't bother with statements at all—grooms do not issue signing statements with their "I dos." But upholding, it transpires, is a selective business and therefore a false one; the only part of the Constitution signing statements deign to "uphold" is Article II. Any law that treads on the most expansive read of presidential powers in that Article risks a statement and potential nonenforcement.[29]

Bush II's statement binge prompted concerns about whether the executive was fulfilling its duty to faithfully execute the laws. As a candidate, Obama deplored Bush II's signing statements as unlawful legislation, saying that "[w]e're not going to use signing statements as a way of doing an end-run around Congress."[30] For the most part, Obama kept his word, issuing only 41 statements, though sometimes on important, multipart bills. As of mid-2018, Trump was issuing signing statements at roughly the same pace as Obama.[31] It's premature to conclude that signing statements have had their day. If Obama was comparatively circumspect about his powers, perhaps it was because he was cautious by disposition and by vocation, as a former Constitutional law professor. As for Trump, his slow pace almost certainly reflects the 115th Congress's near-total inability to produce significant legislation rather than some newfound executive restraint.

Even if the pace of signing statements continues to moderate, a problem remains, because the correct frequency for signing statements is functionally zero. As we've seen, executive enforcement is discretionary, but there's an important difference between making enforcement decisions on the *merits* of a specific issue and declining to enforce laws as a matter of presidential *policy*. To decline to enforce a law is, in effect, to nullify it. A special American Bar Association panel rightly condemned signing statements as undermining Constitutional principles and the rule of law.[32] It's easy to see why. Signing statements violate separation-of-powers by allowing presidents to selectively torpedo laws without resort to the official veto power. They also undermine the jurisprudential goals we saw long ago: How can laws be clear, predictable, and amenable to compliance if presidents enforce laws depending on mood, using documents whose legal status is uncertain and subject to revocation at any time? How can the rule of law be in place if presidents place themselves above law's rules?

In riposte, Congressional research agencies say they have been unable to detect widespread nonenforcement attributable to signing statements. Not only does this fail to remove the jurisprudential concerns, one would not expect much direct evidence of executive malfeasance. The fog of executive discretion always makes it difficult to identify the real reasons why executive employees do, or don't do, anything—though it seems unlikely (in most administrations, anyway) that executive branch staff simply ignore their boss's view. Moreover, some signing statements specifically intend to make impossible any probing of illicit nonenforcement. For example, in 2002, Congress passed a law requiring the executive to provide information to legislators, including instances when DOJ declined to enforce laws it deemed unconstitutional.[33] Here was a perfect opportunity to collect information about presidential discretion. While Bush II signed that law, he promptly affixed a statement to "construe" the law to preserve maximum presidential latitude and instructed agencies to "withhold information...which could impair foreign relations, the national security, the deliberative processes of the Executive, or the performance of the Executive's Constitutional duties."[34]

In other words, when Congress wanted to know what laws presidents declined to enforce as unconstitutional (the basis for virtually all important signing statements), the president refused on the grounds that this would impermissibly intrude on his Constitutional duties, reducing federal oversight law to Constitutional toilet paper. Bush II went even further by describing laws—which he had signed—as merely "purport[ing]" to direct executive agencies (most of which operate by delegation of *Congressional* power) to do this or that.[35] In legalese, "purporting" means "pretending," i.e., the executive denies that laws are laws except when and as the president chooses.

If a president actively disfavors a law, he can veto it *in toto*, and that's *all* the Constitution permits. When Congress tried to give Clinton pick-and-choose powers via a "line-item veto," the Court smacked the effort down as violating the Presentment Clause.[36] If the Court squarely confronts signing statements, it's hard to see principled Justices accepting that a president can universally decline to enforce a law (amounting, in substance, to a line-item veto) of his own volition and *against* Congressional wishes, given that the Court specifically ruled that Clinton could not wield such power when Congress tried to *give* it to him. The principles are the same, even if the precise legal grounds will differ. As for the objection that presidents need sometimes sign giant must-pass bills but somehow preserve the option to object to hidden and unconstitutional provisions within, the answer is that the executive can register his objections by participating in normal litigation.[37] But presidents don't want to do that, because the judiciary remains largely independent and the executive has more craven and clientelist resources to manufacture the required fig leaves. These helpers are the counsels' offices at the White House and DOJ, which exist largely to provide a legal basis for any action the president may want to take. These offices are supposed to advise presidents about where the edge of the Constitutional cliff lies, but often encourage presidents to take a running jump.

Indeed, it was the DOJ's Office of Legal Counsel (OLC) that birthed the modern, steroidal signing statement. In a 1986 memo penned by a young Samuel Alito (yes, *that* Alito), OLC argued that if signing statements proffered more substantive glosses, a "chief advantage[]" would be to *"increase the power of the Executive to shape the law."* With reason, Alito noted that this was a "novelty" that Congress would be "likely to resent."[38] Therefore, Alito laid out a cynical boil-the-frog strategy for rolling out increasingly powerful statements, reaching deeper into the validity of laws themselves. However, in articulating a grand vision of executive power, Alito laid various landmines for himself. Nine years later, a rather different president was in charge, issuing a torrent of signing statements to thwart Alito's ideological ally, Newt Gingrich—and therein lies the problem with signing statements: they are unstable. Alito was eventually compensated by his elevation to the Court, where he joined John Roberts. As it happens, Roberts trained at OLC and its sister institution, the office of the White House Counsel, where he disported himself by writing memos on how to dismantle the Voting Rights Act (about which his patron Bush II might say "mission accomplished"). The OLC and the White House Counsel are supposedly checks against hasty overreach, but in reality, they are more gas pedal than brake.

Do as I Say

The presidential arsenal includes executive orders, which command the bureaucratic apparatus to effect presidential policy. Obviously, presidents enjoy inherent authority to direct subordinates, and just as obviously, those powers are not unlimited, else America could have saved itself the trouble and kept Lord North and George III. Until the twentieth century, executive orders tended to confine themselves to bureaucratic management, with the Emancipation Proclamation as a momentous exception. From Teddy Roosevelt on, presidents issued more consequential orders, quasi-legislative in character and affecting private persons and rights.

As usual, champions of executive power cite the Emancipation Proclamation as the shining example of presidential fiats used for good, but presidents have been drawing against emancipation's moral credit without making many deposits. FDR's Japanese–American internment order of 1942 was a major withdrawal, and Trump's travel/immigration/border security orders from 2017 onward have made their deductions. Perhaps the largest class of debits are the Constitutional tensions created by an overreaching executive. Truman's actions precipitated the crises of *Dollar* and *Youngstown,* and some of FDR's orders were not Constitutionally pristine (though most enjoyed Congressional sanction). Eventually, the books will have to be balanced, and the ensuing receivership is sure to be unpleasant.

The Constitution on Hold

The typical euphemism for presidential centralization is the "unitary executive," which supposedly refers to the president's power to control the entire executive branch. In reality, it signals movement toward unitary *government* by the executive—legislative, executive, and, in the cases of military commissions and bureaucratic hearings, judicial. This degrades the law, whose overarching purpose is to foster social organization, a purpose made harder to achieve given the uncertain legal status of signing statements and the tendency of executive decrees to be made and changed on the fly (Trump undoing Obama's orders, which undid Bush II's, which undid Clinton's, and so on). Nor is unitary government compatible with separated powers, though so long as Congress exercises budgetary authority and the judiciary has the final say over Constitutional interpretation, and the people support them in doing so, there will be no plenipotentiary Dear Leaders. None of this means that it's impossible for America to experience a series of Constitutional failures that concatenate into political darkness. But these failures, while likely to be triggered by executive action, will always come from *outside* the Constitution: American presidents can't point to some Weimar-like Article 48 to claim the right to govern by decree. This has historically been important, because gross violations can't be tidied up as some part of the executive's "inherent" powers, however much OLC muses to the contrary.

This is one area in which the Founding Fetish provides helpful clarity. Almost everything about the American Constitution's history and text forbids executive tyranny, providing a bulwark that other, less successful constitutions have lacked. Nevertheless, the extraordinary powers now wielded by American presidents—to make war without declarations, control functional legislation via agencies and signing statements, establish military "commissions" to try suspected terrorists, and so on—push the nation toward the alarming condition of one-man rule. Unlike Lincoln, modern presidents do not acknowledge that they exceed their Constitutional powers, but implausibly assert that everything they do is flatly Constitutional (without pointing to any specific clause granting them such powers). The contemporary White House is much more powerful than the Nixonian morass that prompted Arthur M. Schlesinger, Jr. to write *The Imperial Presidency* in 1973. This is especially so as terrorism blurs the traditional boundaries between internal and external affairs. Foreign policy and military action have historically been the areas in which presidents enjoy the greatest deference by other branches, and terrorism refracts elements of both.[39] The other branches can push back, but Congress's habit of facilitating wars after they've begun, and the judicial tic of evading "political questions" and deferring to the executive whenever the Solicitor General incants "national security," open considerable space for executive action. Presidents have filled the vacuum accordingly, abetted by legal pyrite like John Yoo's torture memo, flowing out of the ever-accommodating OLC/OWHC.

In the moment, presidents often act with popular consent, but contemporaneous opinion polls are to republican government what the Billboard Top 40 is to the Pulitzer Prize for Music. Transient popularity is merely one (very historically troubled) indicator of legitimacy. More importantly, the public lacks all the facts in the moment and may rue swift actions of which they once approved. After all, since modern polling began, *no* president has been more popular than Bush II was immediately following 9/11, when he enjoyed a 90 percent approval rating.[40] As the true facts emerged, Bush II's approval slid, never breaching 50 percent after 2005 and hitting 34 percent when

Bush II left office. But by January 2009, the whole apparatus of domestic spying had been erected, American troops were in their eighth year in Afghanistan and their sixth in Iraq, and Gitmo, the Black Hole of Cuba, had received almost 800 long-term visitors (including at least one American citizen) with something less than Genevan courtesy.[41]

Notwithstanding subsequent exposés, the odd judicial smackdown, and voluntary discontinuation of failed and palpably illegal policies, the cloak of secrecy and executive privilege means that the full scope of legal errors remains unknown. Indeed, Senators Kyl and Graham argued that courts couldn't look into the issue. Those senators filed a freelance *amicus* brief with the Court, arguing that the Detainee Treatment Act of 2005 stripped the Court of its jurisdiction to review Guantanamo cases, an argument unsupported by the record (and fairly reeking of the scandals around *Marbury*), and duly rejected.*[42] The Act did, however, expand sovereign immunity for officials, including those performing "enhanced interrogations" where such were "authorized" and "determined to be lawful at the time," with determinations being made by executive branch lawyers.[43] In case this wasn't enough, Bush II issued a signing statement invoking the "unitary executive" and noting that the legislation would be construed to be "consistent with the constitutional limitations on the judicial power," a mysterious phrase not clarified until Kyl and Graham submitted their brief about jurisdiction-stripping.[44] And there, in one vignette, the endgame of signing statements, executive orders, emergency powers, OLC memos, and the rest, lies exposed: the evisceration of judicial review and the immunization of the executive branch. And for what? In Bush II's case, a rather dubious set of wars waged in the name of democratic norms.

Indeed, the aftermath of Bush II's "unitary executive" suggests why "nimbleness" may not be a virtue. After 9/11, the president surely needed to protect the nation with force, potentially pushing toward Constitutional frontiers as

---

*   The Detainee Treatment Act was shoved into the Hurricane Katrina relief bill, making it a truly banner day for the Bushites.

they were reasonably understood. No president need pore over First Amendment case law before shutting down a website offering a formula for anthrax and a map of the Pentagon's ducting; as has been said many times, the Constitution is not a suicide pact. But nor is the Constitution, not even Article II, a blank check. Nevertheless, during national security crises real and imagined (e.g., the dubious Gulf of Tonkin episode), presidents have repeatedly pushed past all sensible limits, launching undeclared wars. Few wars require immediate, almost unthinking, action. But as the most visible responder, presidents can whip up irresistible popular support in the moment, saddling Congress and the courts with faits accomplis and, eventually, the public with its regrets. That the greatest consequences have been borne by non-Americans is, in a legal sense, partial mitigation; presidents have few legal duties to noncitizens except those explicitly imposed by law or incorporated by treaty. But mitigation is not exculpation; a Constitutional sin is still a sin.

These considerations may seem somewhat abstract, literally far removed from the United States. Unfortunately, there's no reason to believe that legal wrongs will always occur at a comfortable distance. The essential premise of counterterrorism is that an attack will occur in America. Presidents may be tempted to deploy the federal military domestically, and indeed, a 2006 revision of the Insurrection Act provided that if "the President determines" that a natural disaster, terrorist attack, or "other condition" (as determined by the president) leads to "violence" such that local authorities "are incapable of maintaining public order," then he may "employ the armed forces."[45] These provisions, strikingly similar those in the Weimar Constitution, were walked back by the following Congress. But loopholes still exist; for example, the president may use the armed services to enforce federal law, on his own initiative in a self-determined emergency, if it is "impracticable" to proceed through the "ordinary course of judicial proceedings."[46] Well, what does that mean? A border crisis in California, where the governor is alleged to defy federal dictates and where legal resolution will be furnished by "so-called judges" ostensibly disabled by ethnic affinity? State regulation of recreational marijuana leading to a "crime spike"? Few judges would countenance such intrusions, but then again, the statute presupposes that judges will not be able to opine in the moment.

A particular challenge with emergencies, especially those involving terrorism, is that the executive must rely on secrecy, so illegal practices can be insulated from easy judicial and legislative review, or scrutiny from the public and the media. Secrecy has its purposes, but like attorney-client privilege, there are limits: systematic Constitutional abuses are not secrets; they're scandals. Congress could investigate, of course, but Congress is fairly supine when it shares a party with the president, and presidents are fairly obstreperous when Congress belongs to the other side. Courts, meanwhile, can take only live cases—which means that they can't act until someone leaks, or unconstitutional actions become painfully overt.

The complacent response is that America is not some banana republic. The executive doesn't "disappear" citizens or expropriate property willy-nilly, as Latin American dictatorships did. (Leaving aside denaturalizations, deportations, and civil forfeitures, to say nothing of the CIA's probable involvement, at White House direction, with the juntas and Operation Condor.) Nor does the executive maintain secret police or condone arbitrary detention and torture. (Leaving aside the NSA's warrantless wiretapping, the noncitizens dumped into Gitmo and various black sites, stop-and-frisk, and police brutality.) The executive doesn't detain people simply because it doesn't like the way they look or think. (At least, not anymore, or anyway, not as a matter of stated policy, except when it does.[47]) But that still leaves the executive with extraordinary powers. Surely, the executive has the burden of proof as to why it must bend the Constitution; just as surely, the unmagical words "national security" do not discharge that burden. Why hasn't law established more robust constraints on the executive, clarifying the status of war powers, executive orders, states of emergency, and signing statements? The practical answer is that the costs of executive power so far have been diffused into abstractions like civic erosion, the national debt, and indignities visited on other countries. No violation has been so palpably grave as to prompt a wholesale rethinking of the presidential powers that have accreted over the past century.

Showdowns and Secrecy

With so much authority, so many things to hide, and the great political tradition of scandal, presidents can trigger Constitutional crises even without troops on the streets. The most likely causes are presidential management of unpopular wars and foreign policy—specifically, the efforts to disguise their practical and Constitutional failings. Variations on these themes helped bring down Truman (Korea), Johnson (Vietnam), and Nixon (Vietnam/Laos/Cambodia), and badly damaged Reagan (Iran-Contra) and Bush II (Iraq/Afghanistan). Even Clinton suffered from the perception that his missile strikes in Sudan and Afghanistan were employed as a distraction from the Lewinsky case (well-timed and, given subsequent evidence the Clinton Administration labored to conceal, including by fiddling UN inspections, lacking strong factual basis). That most presidents since FDR have tripped over the same issue and been called on it stands simultaneously as a symbol of Constitutional (and journalistic) strength and the imperial presidency's specific weakness.

Whatever subject drives the crisis, when it comes, the key players will almost certainly be the president and the judiciary. The most direct route to conflict is presidential defiance of a major judicial order. Of course, presidents defy lesser courts on small matters constantly, but since the Civil War, no president has dared defy a firm ruling by the Court on any matter of great and independent significance. Presidents do push the limits, however, and in recent years, the unifying goal has been to protect the ever-growing body of secrets hoarded by the executive.

The cardinal case here is *United States v. Nixon*, wherein the president asserted sweeping executive privilege to resist a subpoena of the Watergate tapes. Tellingly, Nixon's personal attorney informed a lower court that the president had wanted him to argue that Nixon was "as powerful a monarch as Louis XIV," essentially inviting judges to reject the argument, which they duly did.[48] When the case reached the Court, it was clear at oral argument that Nixon would lose, but the Justices appreciated the stakes and wanted a unanimous decision. While the opinion itself was a bit muddled by the effort to achieve unanimity, the Court did hand down an 8–0 decision.*[49] That was good enough; Nixon resigned sixteen days later. However traumatic, the Constitution held.

The Lewinsky scandal provided the next major confrontation, where executive branch employees invoked various executive privileges to resist grand jury questions and other legal process. On March 20, 1998, President Clinton himself invoked executive privilege. Courts processed the lower-stakes claims first, and the privilege asserted by Secret Service agents seemed especially weak (the consensus being that they had been acting more as but-lers/procurers than agents on official business). On July 17, 1998, Rehnquist allowed lower courts to compel the agents' testimony. Ken Starr's grand jury issued a subpoena around July 25, setting up a confrontation, as presidents had long considered themselves immune to subpoena. But the political writ-ing was on the wall, and Starr underlined it by granting immunity to the Lewinsky family. On July 29, the president agreed to be voluntarily deposed, and Starr withdrew his subpoena, averting a Court case.[50] On August 17, Starr deposed Clinton; that same day, Clinton went on national TV and admitted his affair. The House subsequently impeached Clinton and the Senate conducted a trial, presided over by the Zelig-like Rehnquist. Clinton wasn't acquitted until February 12, 1999, but the Constitution had been out of danger long before, when Clinton decided not to challenge Starr's sub-poena. Ultimately, Clinton was cited for contempt of a lower court, fined, and had his law license suspended.

Crucially, in the Nixon and Clinton dramas, both presidents stood down instead of escalating into open defiance. It's not irrelevant that both

---

* The missing vote belonged to then-Justice Rehnquist, who recused himself because of his prior work in Nixon's Justice Department. It turned out that the Watergate tapes included references to Rehnquist, whom Nixon referred to as "Renchburg." Intriguingly, during Rehnquist's confirmation hearings to be Chief Justice, President Reagan ordered Rehnquist to assert executive privilege regarding the latter's Nixon-era DOJ work—one of only three times Reagan directly invoked the privilege; the other two involved an Interior Department oil lease and the EPA's practices under Gorsuch *mère*.

presidents were lawyers trained to view the Court with the same level of deference that older parish priests reserve for the Vatican, and may have found defying the Justices emotionally difficult—especially given that both presidents were, legally and factually, guilty of one or more sins that had been publicized to the point of undeniability.[51] As a result, the law of executive privilege is not well developed—the Court had not even articulated a real doctrine until *Nixon*—and only a few cases have been litigated seriously since.[52] Outside the White House, the general view is that executive privilege is not absolute, and applies with decreasing strength as matters get further from presidents and their core duties. Within the White House, the position varies by president, from maximalists (Nixon, Clinton, Bush II, e.g.) to moderates (Bush I, Obama, e.g.). The only plausible minimalist in the past forty years has been Reagan, whose administration declared that executive "privilege should not be invoked to conceal evidence of wrongdoing or criminality on the part of executive officers"; Reagan even turned over parts of his diaries during the Iran-Contra investigation.[53]

Presidents with fewer scruples or legal finesse may assert privileges that do not really exist. A particularly dangerous temptation may be to blend executive privileges with the pardon power; what information cannot be buried will be pardoned away. This combination could trigger a meltdown, and no sitting president has yet been foolish enough to try it on a matter of any consequence, though matters mixed rather uncomfortably in the ethical murk that was Clinton's Pardon Office. Judicial Watch, a right-leaning organization, was particularly curious about Clinton's pardons of donors like Marc Rich (a decision condemned by Jimmy Carter and rued by Clinton himself). Judicial Watch sued for records, but the case didn't arrive in court until after Clinton left office, and when DOJ lost one of its privilege arguments in 2004, the political moment had passed.[54]

With a sitting president, however, the stakes would be immeasurably higher. Depending on the gravity of the offense, the president's popularity, and remaining years in office, courts might reasonably choose to delay proceedings. That might not be particularly inspiring or just, but it could be pragmatic. The alternative, after all, would be to invoke the uncertain power of contempt, risking breakdown.

In 1958, President Eisenhower declared that the nation would have an annual celebration of the "principle of government under laws."[55] It took three years for Congress to actually *pass* the legislation formally establishing Law Day, but never mind.[56] Presidents can proclaim (nonbinding) days of observance as they please, and what pleased Eisenhower was to deposit Law Day on May 1, the same day that the Eastern Bloc celebrated international labor by rolling tanks down the streets. As a former five-star general, D-Day hero, Supreme Allied Commander, and since 1953 the civilian leader of the world's greatest military, Eisenhower could certainly have arranged his own parade, and rather better than Nikita Khrushchev, the jumpy ex–metal worker with a vocational school education then ruling Moscow. But gaudy displays of missiles and jets would be unbefitting a free people; anyway, if the point was to compare arsenals, better to brandish the greatest weapon in America's possession: the rule of law. It was a slap that glowed vividly, nowhere more so on Khrushchev's cheek. After all, the Soviet tanks in the 1958 May Day parades had crushed dissent in Budapest just eighteen months earlier, when Hungary dared defy its imperial master. And when not on parade duty in the spring of 1958, those same tanks were deployed around Moscow, to cow the Presidium into sanctioning the final consolidation of all state power into Khrushchev's person. So those were the options on May 1, 1958: dictatorship or democracy; the rule of man or the rule of law. Eisenhower made his choice, and was certain he would be vindicated.

Thirty-one May Days later, it seemed Eisenhower's vision would be realized. The Warsaw Pact was in disarray and even Moscow would soon enjoy its first direct election. There was a hitch, though; even as the Eastern

Bloc inched toward Western ideals, the West had migrated toward an Easternized executive—"oriental despotism," as a different generation would have tactlessly put it. And so Washington increasingly became what it beheld, a place where executives wield power over all areas of life, beyond normal account. The predictable consequences have been instability and power struggles within the executive branch—with the palace comes the intrigue. In the Trump Administration, plagued by leaks and in open conflict with the FBI and DOJ, the "unitary" executive is already at war with itself.

The greater executive power becomes, the larger the possibility for error. After decades of expansion, the presidency has become a near-impossible job, reposed in one beleaguered and often unstable person. The question is not whether executives will fail—many already have—but how serious and frequent future failures will be, and whether wrongdoers will have the grace to withdraw after making a serious mistake. A president unwilling to do so might unravel the system from above. But this assumes the system is not already unraveling from below, as the public slowly recoils from a legal system that falls short of its promises.

PROPOSALS MODEST AND OTHERWISE

> If we desire respect for the law, we must first make the
> law respectable.
>
> Louis Brandeis (1912)[1]

R ead quickly, there's nothing special about Louis Brandeis's words; a platitude with pleasing rhythmic balance, ready to be filed in *Bartlett's* and forgotten. Read slowly, Brandeis's words bloom into remarkable subversiveness. In the first clause, Brandeis suggests that the law should seek respect, implying that law is not respectable simply by virtue of being The Law. In the second clause, he suggests that to gain respect, law must "first make" itself respectable; the unavoidable implication, then, was Brandeis thought that law was *not* respectable—not yet. That's a remarkable sentiment from a man who was a natural contender for a seat on a prestigious court. Today, few in Brandeis's position would dare to be so bold, and in a sad twist, they have Brandeis to thank. Brandeis was a man of deep conviction, and an outspoken progressive (he pioneered the right to privacy on which so many of our present freedoms depend). When Woodrow Wilson nominated Brandeis to the Supreme Court, the Senate subjected him to the first public confirmation hearing for that position (over which hovered more than a whiff of anti-Semitism). Confirmation hearings should have been public all along, of course, but they became public for the wrong reasons—to drag Brandeis over the coals for daring to call a turd a turd. Law is not respectable, but it's not respectable to say as much.

The public has greater freedom of expression, and they see turds aplenty, if polls are any guide. Congress is a sour joke, widely loathed. Partisan preference plays a role, but citizens also sense that legislators cannot do their jobs. Simply passing a budget, much less on time, is often beyond Congress, and the tussles over the 2017 tax cut made abundantly clear that Congress operates by procedural shenanigans and the dismal expedient of not bothering to read the laws it passes. The federal bureaucracy, long an object of skepticism by the Right, now occasions unease among principled citizens of all political affiliations. Trump's ham-fisted lieutenants, marinating in corruption and incompetence, have made plain that fears about bureaucratic governance— its unaccountability, instability, and arbitrary process—were not fever dreams of Constitutional purists, but dangers waiting to be realized. While the judiciary retains public respect, its grandest court has seen net approval drift to zero. Worse, a growing plurality of Americans believes the justice system is not fair, and as the questions get more specific, distrust rises. Asked whether the justice system discriminates against the poor, an outright majority concur.[2] Were pollsters to regularly interrogate Americans about their feelings on legal costs, prosecutorial coercion, and other malfunctions, it's hard to imagine better results; indeed, one poll indicated that a majority of Americans wanted the civil portion of the justice system changed either "fundamentally" or "rebuilt" completely.[3] For all this, Americans still obey the law, more or less, though glum duty and fearful obedience cannot sustain law forever.

The exceedingly tiresome response from apologists for the status quo is that the legal system's dysfunctions compare favorably to the flagrant corruption of the Gilded Age, the politicized chaos of the early Republic, the legally sanctioned racism that prevailed into the 1960s, and other monsters dredged from history's depths. These apologias are descriptively true; they are also, in substance, morally off-putting demands that we accept "moderate" injustices while law sorts itself out. To state it plainly, "Better Than Jim Crow" is a grotesque reply to "Black Lives Matter." Certain scholars can explain all day long that the U.S. Code and the Constitution protect police from the consequences of brutality, condone an abusive bail system, permit shoddy evidence, require compulsory and iniquitous arbitration, tolerate unfettered executive discretion, and so on. Again, that's descriptively true of the state of the law at least as interpreted by courts. But the apologists *have* to be wrong about the true substance of the law, because if they're right, then the law enjoys no great moral claim to our allegiance.

At some point, the public will decide that legal dysfunction has risen to an intolerable level, and shift from polite requests for incremental reform to adamant demands for fundamental change. In the moment, the day of reckoning always seems distant. But entire legal systems mutate and collapse with surprising frequency. Professor Tom Ginsburg's team at the University of Chicago studied the mortality rate of constitutions written between 1789 and 2005, and came to the surprising conclusion that these supposedly eternal documents lasted nineteen years, on average. Even limiting the sample to the more stable polities of Western Europe, constitutional life expectancy typically ran to a mere thirty-two years; whole legal systems turned over twice in a lifetime.[4] The causes and outcomes varied, but stripping away confidence intervals, confounding variables, exceptions, and the rest, all that can be neatly said is this: constitutions will be replaced when important constituencies want something new, and this happens all the time.

As proprietors of the world's oldest written constitution, Americans might see profound Constitutional change as unlikely.[5] Yet the superficial endurance of the 1789 Constitution disguises significant and ongoing evolution. The four-page document on display at the National Archives has been radically altered several times, by the Bill of Rights (1791), the Reconstruction Amendments (1865–1870, abolishing slavery and guaranteeing equal protection), the Seventeenth and Nineteenth Amendments (1913 and 1920, providing for the direct election of senators and women's suffrage), and by the Supreme Court's incorporation doctrine (which applied much of the Bill of Rights to the states, starting in 1925). By the mid-twentieth century, America was, if not on its fifth constitution (the Articles of Confederation being the first), then at least on version 4.0 of the 1789 Constitution. It's hard to argue that these changes were anything but to the nation's benefit.

However, between 1917 and 1965, a new version emerged, centralizing power in the federal executive. It's this "Executive Constitution," uncodified and increasingly unwieldy, that governs us today. But this new constitution is radically different than its predecessors. The Executive Constitution pushes power *up*, to the president and his unelected camarilla, instead of pushing it down, to the people. And it unshackles the executive, because instead of the traditional parade of "thou shalt nots," the Executive Constitution's predominant character is of "thou may," a grant of discretionary authority to the executive branch.

Increasingly, the "executive branch" means the president alone. The "unitary executive" theory we encountered in prior chapters holds that the president has virtually unlimited power over the entire executive branch. Contemporary presidents claim authority to fire senior officials at any time, and have eroded the civil service job protections necessary to maintain a competent and mostly apolitical class of mandarins. On its present course, the Executive Constitution will shortly give way to a Presidential Constitution, barely distinguishable from royal prerogative. See what daylight you can find between the executive powers we've already covered and the British monarch's prerogatives circa 1790. The latter included the rights to declare war and dispatch troops, appoint and fire ministers, alter the civil service, be immune from wrongs, ignore statutes absent express language to the contrary, declare states of emergency, seize property, institute or quash legal proceedings, pardon at will, and claim ownership of all members of the genus *Cygnus*. Only the last prerogative sticks out. Does the wall separating American liberty from Georgian tyranny now consist of... swans?

The nation certainly does not need a Presidential Constitution slouching toward the Potomac and should forbid its further development. The nation would also do well to trim the Executive Constitution that already obtains.

Assuming for argument's sake that the present arrangement was made necessary by the World Wars and Depression, it has long outlived those exigencies and now generates parallel crises of its own. As we've seen, every war since 1950 has been undertaken at presidential initiative. In addition to their human costs, many of those interventions had unintended consequences; Vietnam and presidential policy in the Middle East, as examples, helped spur the destabilizing inflation of the 1970s. Trump's brewing trade war, commenced through the unilateral mechanism of "national security" orders, threatens to recapitulate the economic chaos of 1930s protectionism. The Executive Constitution was supposed to help us transcend military emergencies and economic crises, not contribute to them.

The Executive Constitution cannot be counted a resounding success, and one can reasonably question whether it counts as a constitution at all. Certainly, it does not seem compatible with jurisprudential goals or the rule of law, at least, not when the wrong president is in charge. (Of course, not having to worry overmuch about the wrong president is a chief virtue of a proper constitution.) And unlike prior Constitutional versions, no important part of the Executive Constitution has been ratified. Rather, it's been confected by means of intra-branch swaps and brazen power grabs, all without direct input by the states or public. Accordingly, the Executive Constitution's legitimacy and scope are unclear, as evidenced by the constant litigation challenging presidential authority and bureaucratic governance. It is essentially a revolution by paperwork, an arrangement not unlike de Gaulle's unilateralism, which François Mitterrand described in 1964 as *Le coup d'état permanent*. The difference is that de Gaulle's "coup" was entirely legal under the French constitution. America's Executive Constitution operates in a much more ambiguous space. Not only has it not been ratified, there's simply no way to reconcile it with the written Constitution. In substance, the Executive Constitution is a lawless reconfiguration of Constitutional power, a low-grade state of exception whose end product will be uncomfortably close to rule by decree.

Unwinding the Executive Constitution is hardly a cure-all, though it would fix a lot. Judges can impose limits, but only on a piecemeal basis—and only, as we saw with the Truman/Nixon/Clinton showdowns—when facing off against a president who is politically embattled and also capable of being shamed by contempt proceedings. A more durable, comprehensive solution must rest in the legislature. Congressional action is inconceivable while the same party controls the White House and Capitol. But when control is split, Congress has both the opportunity and incentive to reassert itself, taking greater command over two of the great levers of executive power: war-making and the bureaucracy. Rather than wait for presidents to embark on unilateral adventures, and be forced to choose between funding unwise and illegal wars or standing accused of "betraying the troops" (the twenty-first century's "stab in the back"), Congress can bind itself in advance, firmly refusing to fund undeclared wars. As for the bureaucracy, Congress can improve and stabilize governance by requiring formal rule-making in matters of importance and by imposing barriers to sudden policy reversals; better still, Congress could redistribute agency powers so that only enforcement remains under direct presidential control. These reforms may seem implausible, as likely as Vanilla Ice anchoring *Turandot*. But that's a comment on political will and imagination, not legal feasibility. Anyway, if the core of Europe could recompose itself into the EU, notwithstanding political differences and regional egos greater than those supposed to exist in the United States, surely America can manage more modest feats of Constitutional housekeeping. As we've seen, constitutions evolve more frequently and substantially than is commonly assumed, even in America. And just as Washington should recompose itself, so state and local governments should unwind their own experiments with executive authority. A decent separation of powers is not much to ask; indeed, it's a Constitutional requirement.

As for workaday improvements to matters less lofty than Constitutional rearrangement, I'll only briefly recapitulate some of the suggestions offered in the preceding chapters. Law schools should teach students practical skills and receive appropriate public funding to reduce legal costs; Congress should expand its membership and staff so that it can fulfill its duties with something like minimal competence; agencies should be relieved of quasi-judicial powers; the shoddy and untenable doctrines of compulsory arbitration should be undone; correctional institutions should correct; prosecutors should be bound by codes of ethics enforceable by the public and the courts; and doctrines of sovereign immunity re-interred in their fourteenth-century graves.

The governing ethos is simple: public law should make itself more accessible, and more accountable, to those it serves. Law is obligated to explain itself to the people, not vice versa. Statutes should be written clearly, court opinions at the appellate level digested by public services, and agency regulations written and posted in formats accessible to those affected. Some parts of law already do this. The DMV provides study guides, the IRS provides FAQs, and the judiciary has special procedures to make litigation easier for self-represented litigants. But *all* parts of the legal system should do as much or better. When law seeks to hold people to account, citizens should be given a reasonable sense of what the law is, what purpose it serves, and why it's being enforced. As we saw in Chapter 1, law has an internal morality, and it's time for judges to take that morality seriously and earn the title of "Your Honor." Judges should more readily accept arguments that challenge laws on due process grounds, and use their old common-law skills to question laws that are vague, overbroad, contradictory, or impossible to follow. It's a sad reality that law is more dazzled by technical sleights-of-hand than by arguments for fairness, and that mentioning "justice" (save as a rhetorical flourish at the higher courts) is disdained as an unsophisticated waste of time by attorneys eager to "get to the point." But justice *is* the point, a fact that bears constant repetition because it is so constantly ignored.

Informal citizens' review boards across all levels of the law could help, a sort of advisory jury of legal peers that reads proposed laws and opines on their comprehensibility. If laws regulating the hiring of nannies cannot be understood by nannies or parents, those laws should be revised until they're clear. The same holds for tax laws directed at small businesses, which entrepreneurs and CPAs should be able to understand, and for search and seizure laws, which both citizens and police should be able to fathom. These procedures would not only clarify law, but slow its mindless overproduction. It would also help if schools taught students how to interact with their legal environment, giving citizens an intuitive sense for what behaviors law seeks to control and how to find and understand relevant laws. And finally, the culture of expedience, of sidestepping good rules—a trait most powerfully embodied in the Executive Constitution—must go. In any other context, it would be dismissible tautology to insist that "rules are rules," but law's endless exceptions make it clear that rules *aren't* rules; they have become mere stage-effects.

It's difficult for the public to take laws seriously when law doesn't take the public seriously. And when law fails to afford citizens respect, or treats them as cattle to be herded one way or another without consultation, justice becomes a mirage.

Law cannot survive when people cease to believe in it. Unfortunately, few legal institutions seem moved to address the decay of civic faith. Rather, they assume that social inertia and the challenges of collective action will hold the system together in its current form. Over the short term, that's a reasonable wager, though a large one and made (as every public wager is) with other people's chips. However, the long-term odds may not be as favorable as commonly assumed. All legal systems require voluntary compliance, but the American system has become especially fragile because it depends on both willing obedience to formal law and near-universal participation in an uncodified system of shortcuts, participation that may be withdrawn at any time.

Appreciating the system's self-inflicted fragility requires only a brief thought experiment about plea bargaining, upon which the entire criminal justice system depends. What would happen if a philanthropist subsidized public interest firms, so that the share of defendants refusing pleas rose from 5 to 15 percent? The criminal justice system would grind to a halt. At the county level, a single billionaire could, on a whim, bring down the system by simply affording a modest fraction of defendants a real shot at the Constitutional right to due process. For example, Cook County (home to Chicago) has an annual public defense budget that barely approaches $80 million, a modest amount compared to the $500 million spent by that county's richest resident, Ken Griffin, just on art, and just in 2015.[6] Now, public defenders can't be created overnight, not even with $500 million, but competent corporate attorneys (of which Griffin has plenty) can at least bail out defendants and force district attorneys to take cases to trial, in numbers sufficient to weaken collective-action problems. This would be expensive; white-shoe firms cost more than public defenders, but the price gap is nothing a few extra yards of Jackson Pollock couldn't cover. A Ken Griffin public defense miracle probably won't happen, but that's not the point. The point is that large swathes of the law have allowed themselves to become brittle, and can be shattered by the intense activity of smaller groups or the low-intensity efforts of the broader public.

Of course, the most satisfying route to change is, and always will be, the franchise. Admittedly, the standard exhortation to vote has lost some of its power in the wake of *Citizens United*, election-meddling, and electoral disproportion, at least for national contests. For local legal offices, however, voting can be quite potent. Votes carry unusual weight in judicial and prosecutorial elections precisely because these offices are, in the circumspect parlance of social scientists, "low-salience"—i.e., not that important to most voters. But even national politics sometimes responds to public sentiment, at least when important donor coalitions have no strong preferences. Before tough-on-crime policies were instruments of political manipulation, they were a genuine response to citizens' fears over then-rising crime. Were the public to realize that crime has fallen dramatically for reasons substantially unrelated to *Rambo*-style policing and prosecution, politicians even modestly to the left of Jeff Sessions might be thrilled by the opportunity to steer a different course. The continuous growth in national debt and relentless progress of Social Security and Medicare toward insolvency mean that politicians *must* cut somewhere, soon. If public opinion allows, politicians will always choose senior benefits programs over a costly war on crime, whose premises and methods have proved flawed. At the state level, marijuana ballot initiatives have already signaled that the public has tired of one part of the war on drugs. As they have done with pot, so citizens can do for police brutality. Voters can demand that mayors hold chiefs to account, as indeed many mayors—exasperated by police unions and disobedient chiefs—would already like to do. In states that allow citizens to readily amend their constitutions, a wide range of legal issues can be implemented by ballot. California does this all the time. Admittedly, one of the worst pieces of legal tinkering in that state's history, the three-strikes law, was confirmed by plebiscite. But now that it has better data, the public is free to pursue more enlightened experiments.

Within the legal system, citizens already have more control than they appreciate or than most judges care to admit. Jury duty is a chore, but it grants citizens the chance to offer their own views about justice. And not only can jurors decide the facts, they can also opine on the justice of the law itself, by exercising the right of "jury nullification" to acquit defendants when jurors deem the criminal law unjust in itself. Nullification has been used for ill (notably to exonerate defendants accused of abusing minorities), but this is true of all powerful tools, and today, overcriminalization and overweening state power make nullification more likely to achieve justice. Judges prefer to hide the nullification right, tossing jurors who state that they will not apply laws with which they disagree, barring counsel from mentioning nullification, and allowing misleading jury instructions that suggest jurors must apply the law without exception. But the right remains and should be exercised when circumstances warrant. English jurors rebelled against the Bloody Codes and forced legal reform; American jurors can do something similar. Jurors can also consider the possible penalties in criminal cases, information that may be withheld at trial, but a sense for which can be readily obtained via a quick Google search while waiting to be called—after all, there's nothing else to do when trapped in government's holding pen. A general awareness of the frailties of forensic and other evidence can also inform decisions. None of this requires bending the law. To repeat, nullification is *part* of the law, a point our first Chief Justice made clear.[7]

The possibilities to do great justice in jury service are rare, because jury trials are rare, but law's desire to intrude on our every activity provides us with constant opportunities to push back. Merely being able to articulate basic rights with reasonable cogency can be enough to stop official harassment. Certainly, the police deserve our courtesy and respect as much as we deserve theirs, and when they behave as professionals, we should accommodate. But we never need to tolerate petty despotism. When police make unreasonable or unlawful demands, they can be politely reminded of what rights they propose to violate and of their liability under § 1983. This isn't particularly difficult. The Bill of Rights takes ten minutes to read, it costs nothing to put the local legal service agency's phone number in your wallet (you don't want to have to open your phone in front of police), and invoking § 1983 *very politely* may be sufficiently unsettling that officers discover they have other, better things to do. It doesn't matter if you have perfect recall of the latest Fourth Amendment cases; police don't either. And officers hardly want more paperwork if your supposed transgression is minor, much less the hassle of a § 1983 complaint and all the Internal Affairs attention it generates. Is this a strategy of privilege? Of course. But knowledge is a privilege, even if one not as powerful as wealth (or, to be frank, whiteness). Some privilege is better than none.

It's also within our control to view *good* laws as the outer limits on behavior. We need not take the most aggressive positions on our tax returns or subject every worker to an indefinite NDA. We can demand the same of corporate citizens. Companies that treat reasonable laws with disdain frequently find themselves sanctioned, broken up, or abandoned by consumers, and the transient profits had by poor corporate citizenship are usually outweighed by long-term costs. Many of the most aggressive banks in the 1990s evaporated after 2008, and others took years to recover stockholder losses (if they ever did). It's both socially reasonable, and financially prudent, to shun these companies. Many people, via their pension funds, university endowments, or other collective arrangements, have successfully amplified their voices: students persuaded universities to stop investing in countries that did business with apartheid South Africa, for instance.

All these efforts lie within our personal power, and are thus our responsibility. We can exercise our powers as opportunities arise and are also free to donate, agitate, and advocate for reform, and to defend those institutions that take our rights seriously. The alternative is that law will continue on its current course, toward a chaos of rules whose only unifying theme is discretionary power. Officials will stand above the law, insulated by law's complexity, doctrines of immunity, and expense, and the original promise of Revolution will stand revoked. Law will become for all what it has always been for some: an arbitrary and punitive sham.

It's best not to close fearfully. The law is bad, but not *that* bad, not yet. We can take steps, and when we do, it's useful not to obsess on the consequences of failure. Better to cultivate an informed, civilized outrage. Presidents, prosecutors, judges, members of Congress, senior bureaucrats, police, and all the other members of the legal caste may be described as the establishment, officialdom, the elite, or the powerful few. But their true relationship to us is as *employees*, as their paychecks confirm. And law itself, though it collects no paycheck, is just as much our servant as any salaried official. It's commendable for our employees to offer useful suggestions and to protect us from our ignoble impulses, but the legal system has confused the proper arrangement of a self-governing republic, and adopted airs well above its station. Exactly why must the assembled rise whenever some potentate, working at public sufferance and often not very well, enters a room? Because the natural order has been inverted, and the governed have allowed once-genuine respect to slide into habit, deference, and fear. Going forward, in every legal interaction, it's useful to remember who serves whom, and to remind our employees when they step out of line.

A BINDING ILLUSTRATION OF WHY PEOPLE HATE THE LAW

Mandatory Arbitration for Claims by Certain Users of This Literary Product

1. This Arbitration Agreement ("Agreement") is executed contemporaneously with, and as an inducement and consideration for, the sale and/or use of this product and its derivatives (collectively and separately, the "Product"). The Parties hereto (defined in Paragraph 2) acknowledge that this Agreement governs any and all uses of the Product and evidences a transaction in interstate commerce governed by the Federal Arbitration Act. Any use of this Product, including but not limited to reading any part of it and/or any material derived from it (each, a "Use"), shall be considered use sufficient to bind the Parties Compelled to Arbitrate (defined in Paragraph 2) to this Agreement.[1]

2. The Parties to this Agreement are:

    (A) the publisher(s) of this Product and the owners of its copyright (collectively or separately, as context requires, the "Proprietors") and

    (B) any user of this Product (broadly construed) who claims relief premised on Use, dissemination, and/or existence of the Product and who: (i) is identified by name in the Product or (ii) claims its identity is inferable from the Product or its derivatives (the persons identified in Paragraph 2.B, individually and/or collectively, the "Parties Compelled to Arbitrate" or "PCTAs").[2]

3. The use of the pronouns, including but not limited to "he," "she," "its," and "their" shall be construed expansively, as shall the use of conjunctions such as "and" and "or," the use of the singular or plural form (including plurals used as singular neuters), and the use or non-use of Oxford commas; such pronouns, conjunctions, singulars, plurals, and punctuations shall not be construed in any way that limits arbitrability under this Agreement. This Agreement to arbitrate shall be construed broadly, to favor arbitration. **The Parties acknowledge that this Agreement establishes the arbitrability of any claims brought by the PCTAs against the Proprietors.**[3]

4. To the fullest extent permitted by law, the PCTAs waive any claims arising from any Use, including the reading, dissemination, promotion, or existence of this Product. Such claims include but are not limited to claims, disputes, and controversies arising out of, or relating in any way to, the sale, purchase, advertisement, promotion, or use of the Product or of any goods or services (including websites) offered or provided in connection with the Product including but not limited to claims for equitable relief, claims based on contract, tort, statute, warranty, or any alleged breach, default, negligence, wantonness, fraud, recklessness, misrepresentation, suppression of fact, libel, defamation, slander, inducement, emotional distress, economic interference, and any other legal theory, including claims that arose before this Agreement or any prior agreement, or claims that might arise after the termination of this Agreement in whole or part (collectively, "Alleged Claims").[4]

5. Subject to Paragraph 4, any Alleged Claim brought shall, to the fullest extent permitted by law (including reasonable arguments for extension of existing law articulated by the Proprietors), be resolved by binding arbitration administered by the mother of Bruce Cannon Gibney (the

"Default Arbitrator"), according to rules established by her, at the place of Do Not Bend LLC's choosing, and the PCTAs explicitly waive any objections to venue in the Counties of San Francisco and New York. Should the Default Arbitrator be unavailable or decline, or should the preceding sentence be deemed by an authority of competent jurisdiction to be unenforceable (either event, an "Unavailability"), arbitration shall be conducted by JAMS, per its rules existing at the time a claim is brought. Any arbitration brought under this Agreement shall be, at the sole discretion of the Proprietors, confidential.[5]

6. Notwithstanding the rules of the Default Arbitrator, JAMS, or any other entity who might conduct an arbitration under this Agreement, the PCTAs explicitly agree to the following: (i) a PCTA must post cash or other security equal to One Million Dollars (US $1,000,000) concurrently with filing any claim and that such security is necessary to protect the rights, including rights and interests arising under the First Amendment, of the Proprietors; (ii) if any claim filed by a PCTA (including any claim that this Agreement is not enforceable or that the PCTAs are not bound to arbitrate their claims) is determined to be without merit (and the PCTAs agree that "without merit" shall include any order requiring arbitration of any kind whatsoever of *any* claim(s) brought by the PCTAs), the PCTAs shall pay, in addition to any other relief to which the Proprietors are entitled, an additional sum of One Million Dollars (US $1,000,000) to the Proprietors as liquidated damages for the inestimable value of the intrusion on Proprietor's free speech; and (iii) that during the course of any proceeding brought by a PCTA relating to the Product, the PCTAs (but not the Proprietors) waive any objection to the Proprietors seeking discovery, including discovery regarding the character and motivations of the PCTAs, and explicitly including information sufficient to establish: (a) bases for venue and jurisdiction; (b) counterclaims by Proprietors against the PCTAs; (c) grounds for recusal of any arbitrator or judge other than the Default Arbitrator deciding disputes related to or arising from the Product; and (d) discovery sufficient, in the

event recusal is deemed appropriate but is not invoked by the arbitrator/ judge, for the Proprietors to prepare a file for transmission to the appropriate institution for the termination, impeachment, or removal of such authority. *For the avoidance of doubt*, the provisions of Paragraph 6.iii.d shall not apply to the Default Arbitrator and any claims of bias as to the Default Arbitrator shall be brought *after* the conclusion of arbitration.[6]

7. Notwithstanding the foregoing, the Proprietors shall have the option to arbitrate or to bring any claims against the PCTAs in any court of competent jurisdiction. The Parties agree that any such decision will be made in the Proprietors' sole and complete discretion.[7]

8. Any challenges to the validity or enforceability of this Agreement shall be determined by the arbitrator in accordance with applicable law and the Default Arbitrator's rules (or the rules of JAMS, in the event of Unavailability).[8]

9. The Proprietors alone shall have the right to petition for consolidation of actions in their sole discretion.

10. The PCTAs explicitly waive any right to bring claims as a class, whether such claims are brought in arbitration or otherwise. The arbitrator may award declaratory or injunctive relief only in favor of the individual Party seeking relief and only to the extent necessary to provide relief warranted by that Party's individual claim. **The PCTAs agree that claims against the Proprietors can only be brought in a PCTA's individual capacity, and not as a plaintiff or class member in any purported class or representative proceeding.** Further, except at the request of the Proprietors, the arbitrator may not consolidate more than one person's claims, and may not otherwise preside over any form of a representative or class proceeding.[9]

11. Arbitration may be initiated by any Party by sending written notice of its intention to arbitrate ("Notice") by Federal Express 1-Day Overnight Mail to another Party's address of record. The Notice shall contain a description of a complete claim, dispute, or controversy and the remedy requested, describe the basis for the claim with particularity and furnish

all supporting evidence then in possession of the party demanding arbitration. In no event shall any demand for arbitration be brought if claims are barred by the applicable statute of limitations or laches. In the event of Unavailability, any claim requesting relief or an award greater than Twenty-Five Thousand Dollars ($25,000.00), shall be arbitrated before a panel of three independent and impartial arbitrators selected pursuant to rules of JAMS and this Agreement. Unless otherwise mutually agreed, each arbitrator *other than the Default Arbitrator* shall be a lawyer licensed by the State in which the venue lies per this Agreement, with twenty or more years of experience in the practice of commercial law and approved to be on a JAMS Panel, and any JAMS Panel shall include at least two arbitrators who are recognized specialists in issues involving the First Amendment.[10]

12. The arbitrator will deliver any decision or award in writing with a summary of the reasons for the decision or award, and the decision or award shall be final and binding on all parties, their successors, and assigns. The arbitrator may grant a motion to dismiss a claim or a motion for summary disposition of a claim. Judgment on the decision or award may be entered by any court having jurisdiction. Fees and costs of the arbitration will conform to the arbitrator's fee schedule in effect at the time of the arbitration and any and all fees and costs shall be borne solely by the party bringing a claim.[11]

13. This Agreement may be amended or modified by Proprietors at any time, with updates posted to www.nonsensefactorybook.com (the "Site"). Any amendments/modifications posted to the Site shall be deemed an integral part of this Agreement and the acts or conduct that make the PCTAs party to this Agreement shall bind them to any amendments/modifications posted on the Site.[12]

14. This Agreement is an election to resolve claims, disputes, and controversies by arbitration rather than the judicial process. **It is understood that the PCTAs waive any right to a jury trial or a trial in court**. The Parties understand that the rules applicable to arbitrations and the rights of parties in arbitrations differ from the rules and rights

applicable in court. The Parties acknowledge receipt of a copy of this Agreement.[13]

15. Should any part of this Agreement be deemed unenforceable, the Parties agree that any unenforceable part shall be severed in such a fashion to preserve the arbitrability of claims to the fullest extent the unsevered contents and applicable law allow.[14] The Parties also agree that any "footnotes" hereto are not part of this Agreement.

16. The Parties explicitly agree that this Agreement is an integral and necessary part of the Product, and that this Agreement is both a binding legal agreement and necessary to the exercise of the Proprietor's rights, including rights and interests protected under the First Amendment to the U.S. Constitution. The Parties further agree that the Product's functionality and purpose can only be achieved by the broadest possible construction of this Agreement to favor arbitration and the waiver of claims against Proprietors, and that is in the public interest and also equitable for all Parties, to do so.[15]

17. The Parties acknowledge that they have received good, valuable, and adequate consideration for entering into this Agreement, including but not limited to the sale and reading of this Product and its free previews.[16]

---

1   *Do these sorts of agreements really exist? Are they binding?* Yes. They appear everywhere—in shrink-wrapped software, inside user manuals, in credit card agreements, in system update pop-ups, and so on. As for whether these agreements are binding, each case depends on its particular facts, but courts have held that agreements buried inside products can be effective.

2   *This already seems exhausting. It's taken a paragraph to say this agreement is between you and some other people. Seems like there's a lot of time wasted.* It's worse than that. For important contracts, an associate drafts something, a partner reviews it, the process is repeated on the other end—and that's before anything hits litigation. One person's $500 hour of legal work might represent, to society, something like a $2,000 loss.

3   *Why is this paragraph trying to rewrite the dictionary, and why the sudden switch to bold?* The law is always struggling to control a future in which everyone fights about everything. Accordingly, contracts try to cover everyone and everything—including the (intentional) misinterpretation of their own words. That's partly why legal documents are so long. As for the bolded text, this is so litigators can argue that "it was right there in bold print!"

4   *Can people really waive away their rights?* Not all of them, but a lot—and contracts try to cover the waterfront.

5   *You can't be serious about your mother as the arbitrator.* As long as she's not cripplingly partial, she could serve. This operates toward the frontier of existing doctrine (but within it! or so I'll argue), which is why there's a fallback to a corporate arbitrator. Many contracts have fallbacks—lawyers tend to push it, but if they can't get away with Option A, they want Option B set by them, not some judge.

6   *Really?* Sure, why not? The pro-arbitration camp has always argued that one benefit of out-of-court proceedings is that parties can use whatever mechanisms they think best, and courts tend to agree.

7   *Wait, are you saying that you can have it both ways?* If we're being honest, that's what arbitration really is to begin with.

8   *Okay, so the arbitrator decides—why do we even have courts at all?* Good question. Presently, we have courts to tell us that these sorts of contracts are perfectly fine—arbitrability is usually left to the arbitrator. Courts say this helps everyone get the benefit of their bargain.

9   *So this contract applies to a whole bunch of people, but it can't be enforced by a bunch of people?* Yes. The law is pretty clear on this.

10 *This seems like you're stacking the deck.* Far from it—the glory of arbitration is that you can get subject-matter experts. It would be a missed opportunity if we had some arbitrator off-the-rack.

11 *This seems pretty normal.* It is normal—in the sense that having procedures and written opinions is normal in court. No one really knows if it's "normal" in arbitration—and there's no freestanding requirement that arbitrators do any of this.

12 *This is in here for show—no one does this, right?* Afraid so. You use a smartphone to surf the web, doubtless. Have a look at various "Terms & Conditions" and software license agreements.

13 *Haven't we gotten the point by now?* Until a theme has been through every variation, the legal symphony is not done.

14 *Again, is this really necessary?* Once upon a time, some lawyer forgot to put this in a contract, and the judge tossed the whole thing. So for eternity, lawyers will charge clients for shoving this into contracts. There's a lot of other historical detritus in legal documents generally, but lawyers feel compelled to keep it in—not only to protect themselves, but because if someone suddenly took an ancient clause out, it might signal a change—and for lawyers "change" means "unpredictable consequences" (which in turn means "potential liability").

15 *Really? An appendix is "integral" to the book?* Sure—it appears as an example in the text. In this sense, it's more "integral" than most. A phone still works without an arbitration agreement.

16 *Who said anyone received consideration?* The law and this appendix. The law generally requires "consideration" to be exchanged, but doesn't really care what that consideration is and doesn't enjoy poking around this subject—here, saying the magic words is enough. If there's litigation, and someone questions the consideration, lawyers will happily quote this language as a counter.

ACKNOWLEDGMENTS

First, I thank my readers. I hope the book has been worth your time.

I owe many other people my gratitude. It's strange that a ream of paper can generate so many debts, but it does, and I offer acknowledgments in roughly chronological order.

My parents are, as the law would put it, the "but for" cause of this book (but cannot be blamed for it). They're wonderful people. I'm lucky to have them as parents and for their support of my decision to leave law not long after their last tuition subsidy had been cashed. Then again, my parents probably saw the writing on the wall after a certain law professor tried to have me expelled for impertinence. (This may explain why few thanks are extended in *that* direction, although Professors Bainbridge and Volokh showed me how interesting law could be.)

My agent, Paul Lucas, has been a tremendous friend and guide, a zealous advocate and a close reader. He and the Janklow & Nesbit team have my thanks. They also have my trust, and for authors, who can say fairer than that?

The entire team at Hachette Book Group has been wonderfully supportive. My editor, Paul Whitlatch, is kind and gracious, equipped with a keen eye. He's faithful to the text, mindful of the reader, a pleasure to work with, and I rarely find myself in anything but accord with his suggestions. Few writers have the good fortune to say the same. The same can be said of his editorial colleagues, Lauren Hummel and Mollie Weisenfeld. Thanks also to publisher Mauro DiPreta for being a fierce advocate for serious books. As usual, Hachette's production team deserves credit for assembling a large book cleanly and confidently—thank you, Mike Olivo and Mandy Kain. Copy editors are not, I think, well-represented in acknowledgments, but they should be, especially when dealing with a book on law, a subject whose first language is not English. Marina Lowry has my gratitude. Thanks also to Hachette's marvelous in-house publicity and marketing team, including Michelle Aielli, Michael Barrs, Odette Fleming, Mark Harrington, Anna Hall, and Joanna Pinsker.

My special gratitude goes to my research assistants, April Reino and Wendy Lim, who have been everything an author could hope for: diligent, exhaustive, and committed to the facts. Their ability to find data based on my hazy recollections ("it's in the BLS database, as series 203483 or something or other") was astounding. This is my second book with them, and as they move on to new projects, I wish them the greatest success.

Angela Baggetta, my publicist, did a wonderful job with my previous book and I'm delighted to work with her again. Angela is factual, tireless, responsible, and effective. It's harder than ever to get books noticed, but she does, to her great credit.

My partner has been supportive beyond all reasonable expectation. While we disagree about some issues (and sometimes disagree significantly about how best to express a thesis), of the minds I've known well, my partner's is the most generous and agile.

Once again, I find myself thanking Luis Mendez and Dr. Clifford Sewell for providing me with the home and the health to do another book. Thanks also to Dan Halpern, a fine friend and great man, to whose many and deserved honors I add my own tribute, small in comparison, but deeply felt. My friends Betty and Alex Wilcox also deserve thanks, for reasons too strange to commit to the page. And to Michael, Troy, and the rest of Le Coucou, thank you. What can I say? My work is hardly perfect, but yours is, even if a certain one of its manifestations has disappeared from your menu.

As for the legal system, my experiences are obviously not unmixed, but there are some fine professors, judges, and advocates, and I've relied on their work in many places. What hope there is for the law rests in the fact that such people do so much and so well that they almost compensate for the rest of the legal universe.

And of course, there's my Fuzbo and my beloved Animal Family. *Vacaciones* are coming, little ones.

NOTES

Preface

1   Holmes, Sr., Oliver Wendell. "Valedictory Address." *New York Medical Journal*, vol. 13, p. 426 (1871). Doctor O.W. Holmes was father to the Justice of the same name.

2   *See infra*, Chapter 6 at note 47 and *passim*. Note for this section that the Sixth and Seventh Amendments provide the federal right and that while the right in civil cases has not been fully incorporated, most states provide such.

3   *Yates v. United States*, 135 S.Ct. 1074 (2015) (construing a provision of the Sarbanes-Oxley Act, 116 Stat. 745, codified in 18 U.S.C. §1519). Given Alito's concurrence, the margin was arguably closer than 5–4.

4   *See infra*, Chapter 7 and Appendix. Shrink-wrap software agreements, terms-in-the-box agreements, coupon-linked promotions (not unlike a book's free preview), gotcha provisions discovered without prompt returns, and so on, have all been used successfully to compel arbitration.

Introduction

1   Roberts, John. *2013 Year-End Report on the Federal Judiciary*. U.S. Supreme Court, 2013, p. 2, https://www.supremecourt.gov/publicinfo/year-end/2013year -endreport.pdf. Where it's reasonably clear that topical chapters provide the evidence, citations will be forgone in this Introduction—e.g., data on plea bargains are in the chapter on prosecutions; data unique to this chapter are cited.

2   Baker, John S., and Dale E. Bennett. *Measuring the Explosive Growth of Federal Crime Legislation*. Louisiana State University Law Center, The Federalist Society for Law and Public Policy Studies, 2004, p. 4, fedsoc.server326.com/Publica tions/practicegroupnewsletters/criminallaw/crimreportfinal.pdf; (citing Ronald Gainer, "Report to the Attorney General on Federal Criminal Code Reform," 1 Crim L. Forum, 99, 110 (1989)); Husak, Douglas. *Overcriminalization: The Limits of the Criminal Law*. Oxford University Press, 2008, pp. 9–10 (citing Gainer and reaching additional conclusions about overcriminalization across various jurisdictions). As Husak notes, the degree of prohibited conduct may not

be perfectly reflected by raw numbers (for example, 3,000 different jaywalking statutes are not as "overcriminalized" as one law banning "being human"), but as the jurisprudential discussion Chapter 2 makes clear, American overcriminalization raises troubling issues. Fields, Gary, and John R. Emshwiller. "Many Failed Efforts to Count Nation's Federal Criminal Laws." *Wall Street Journal*, 23 July 2011, www.wsj.com/articles/SB1000142405270230431980457638960107972 8920 (regarding "idiocy").

3   Fields, Gary, and John R. Emshwiller. "Many Failed Efforts to Count Nation's Federal Criminal Laws." *Wall Street Journal*, 23 July 2011, www.wsj.com/articles/ SB10001424052702304319804576389601079728920.

4   Baker, John S. *Revisiting the Explosive Growth of Federal Crimes*. Heritage Foundation. 16 June 2008, p. 1, https://www.heritage.org/report/revisiting-the -explosive-growth-federal-crimes; Baker, John S., and Dale E. Bennett. *Measuring the Explosive Growth of Federal Crime Legislation*. Louisiana State University Law Center, The Federalist Society for Law and Public Policy Studies, 2004, p. 3, fedsoc.server326.com/Publications/practicegroupnewsletters/criminallaw/crim reportfinal.pdf; *see infra* note 5, Dervan Testimony (4,450 statutory criminal offenses); *see also infra* Chapters 1 and 2.

5   U.S. Congress, House of Representatives, Committee on the Judiciary, Over-Criminalization Task Force of 2013. *Hearing on Regulatory Crime: Solutions*. 113th Congress. 1st sess. Washington: GPO, 2014 (statement of Lucian E. Dervan, Assistant Professor of Law, Southern Illinois University School of Law), p. 3, judiciary.house.gov/wp-content/uploads/2016/02/113-61-85566-1-1.pdf (citations omitted). John Coffee and others seem to have first made this point. Husak, Douglas. *Overcriminalization: The Limits of the Criminal Law*. Oxford University Press, 2008, pp. 9–10 and n. 24–25.

6   Cohen, Darryl T., et al. *Population Trends in Incorporated Places: 2000 to 2013*. P25-1142, U.S. Census Bureau, Mar. 2015, p. 1, www.census.gov/content/dam/Cen sus/library/publications/2015/demo/p25-1142.pdf. Local ordinances are minor and subordinate to state laws (in the case of conflict); the penalties tend to be fines. Regardless, ordinances must be obeyed.

7   Massachusetts General Laws, part IV, title 1, ch. 264, § 9; Alaska Statutes, title 4, ch. 16, § 30; Ng, Christina. "It Is Illegal to Be Drunk in Alaska Bars, Law Says." *ABC News*, 10 Jan. 2012, abcnews.go.com/US/illegal-drunk-alaska-bars-law/ story?id=15330748. Police say they only arrest the grossly inebriated; Alaska bargoers disagree.

8   Cali, Jeanine. "Frequent Reference Question: How Many Federal Laws Are There?" *In Custodia Legis*, 12 Mar. 2013, blogs.loc.gov/law/2013/03/frequent -reference-question-how-many-federal-laws-are-there/ (featuring guest post by LOC researcher Shameema Rahman).

9   Ingraham, Christopher. "Law enforcement took more stuff from people than burglars did last year." *Washington Post*, 23 Nov. 2015, www.washingtonpost .com/news/wonk/wp/2015/11/23/cops-took-more-stuff-from-people-than -burglars-did-last-year/ (comparing seizures and straight burglaries by dollar volume; "burglars" is not coextensive with thievery in the vernacular sense; thefts broadly construed were larger in dollar volume). Credit to economics

blogger Martin Armstrong for making the original comparison. *See also infra* Chapter 10.

10   E.g., Scott, Dylan. "The Senate Tax Bill's $250 Billion Problem." *Vox*, 7 Dec. 2017, www .vox.com/policy-and-politics/2017/12/7/16742046/senate-tax-bill-corporate -amt. The Senate was aware of some potential increases in tax, but grossly underestimated their impact. Professor Daniel Hemel at the University of Chicago has produced good research on this, but his Twitter feed (@DanielJHemel) is a particularly accessible and illuminating read.

11   *Plessy v. Ferguson,* 163 U.S. 537 (1896) (enshrining "separate but equal" until 1954's *Brown*); *Korematsu v. United States,* 323 U.S. 214 (1944); *Stanford v. Kentucky,* 492 U.S. 361 (1989) (execution of minors, overruled by 2005's *Roper*); *Buck v. Bell,* 274 U.S. 200 (1927) (sterilization); *Schenck v. United States,* 249 U.S. 47 (1919); *see also infra* Chapters 7 and 10 (arbitration and police brutality).

12   *Bush v. Gore,* 531 U.S. 98 (2000). The Supreme Court itself was sorely divided on the question, and only Kennedy and O'Connor did not file a concurrence or dissent.

13   *Pearson v. Chung,* No. CA-4302-05 (Sup. Ct. D.C., June 25, 2007) (aka "The Trousers Case"); *see also* Avila, Jim, et al. "The $67 Million Pants." *ABC News*, 2 May 2007, abcnews.go.com/TheLaw/LegalCenter/story?id=3119381&page=1.

14   Not all British possessions used common-law variants, but the largest and most important did—e.g., India, Ireland, Australia, and Canada (save Québec). A few used hybridized systems (e.g., Ceylon), adapted existing systems (e.g., Cyprus and some minor islands), or fudged it (e.g., Britain's Middle Eastern possessions).

15   U.S. Central Intelligence Agency. *The World Factbook*. Field Listing: Legal System. www.cia.gov/library/publications/resources/the-world-factbook/index.html. Wikipedia's page is somewhat more useful, and in my view, descriptively more accurate, though distinguishing between legal system types is not always easy. The four major systems are customarily: civil law, common law, "traditional law," and religious law (e.g., sharia, or canon law within the Holy See for certain purposes).

16   Madison, James. *Amendment I (Religion): James Madison, Detached Memoranda (Document 64, 1817)*. University of Chicago Press, 2000, press-pubs.uchicago .edu/founders/documents/amendI_religions64.html ("The establishment of the chaplainship to Cong[ress] is a palpable violation of equal rights, as well as of Constitutional principles....").

17   For details of the Supreme Court's architectural details, especially those of its north and south friezes, see Supreme Court of the United States. *Architectural Information*, www.supremecourt.gov/about/archdetails.aspx.

18   John, Arit. "A Timeline of the Rise and Fall of 'Tough on Crime' Drug Sentencing." *The Atlantic*, 22 Apr. 2014, www.theatlantic.com/politics/archive/2014/04/ a-timeline-of-the-rise-and-fall-of-tough-on-crime-drug-sentencing/360983/ (quoting former Senate Judiciary lawyer Eric Sterling; quotation source embedded within). Arit John's piece also provides a good overview of the 1980s–1990s tough-on-crime campaigns.

19   Saris, Patti B., et al. *Guidelines Manual 2016*. United States Sentencing Commission, 2016, pp. 419–421, www.ussc.gov/sites/default/files/pdf/guidelines -manual/2016/GLMFull.pdf. The original Guidelines ran to 329 pages.

20   Supreme Court of the United States. "Current Members." *About the Court, Justices*, www.supremecourt.gov/about/biographies.aspx.

21   *United States v. Booker*, 543 U.S. 220 (2005).

22   *Hudson v. Michigan*, 574 U.S. 586 (2006) at Part III.B. In the context of an exclusionary rule case, Scalia opined that police forces have grown more professional since the mid-twentieth century and that the need for the exclusionary rule (and other correctives, by implication) had declined. Scalia cited a scholar on this point; the scholar tartly noted, after the opinion, that Scalia had badly missed the point. Walker, Samuel. "Thanks for nothing, Nino." *Los Angeles Times*, 25 June 2006.

23   U.S. Census Bureau. "Wealth and Asset Ownership Tables." *Topics: Income & Poverty*, Tables 4–5, www.census.gov/topics/income-poverty/wealth.html (see data on household net worth). Author's calculations based on liquid assets. Summary data are also available via the St. Louis Federal Reserve Bank's FRED system, frequently cited as "FRED" in this book, usually followed by the alphanumeric code for the relevant data series.

Chapter 1

1   Eisenhower, Dwight. "Proclamation 3268—Law Day, 1959." 31 Dec. 1958, *The American Presidency Project*, www.presidency.ucsb.edu/ws/index.php?pid=87357.

2   Marx doesn't articulate a particularly coherent vision of law, other than its heavy, parasitic use by capitalists. E.g., Marx, Karl. *Communist Manifesto*, II; *see also* V.I. Lenin, *Collected Works*, Vol. 31. But the general interpretation is that Marx thought law would go, and hence lawyers; if the state "withered," (per Friedrich Engels, an idea that germinated with Karl Marx), the lawyers would do likewise. E.g., Jacob W.F. Sundberg, "On Marxism as a Legal Practice." *Washington University Law Review*, vol. 65, no. 4, 1987, pp. 822, 829 (citation omitted); Kelsen, Hans. *The Communist Theory of Law*. Frederick A. Praeger, Inc., 1955.

3   The most famous ancient codes, those of Hammurabi and other Mesopotamian rulers, were discovered after Marx left. But there were plenty of other ancient legal objects floating around; it's hard to know exactly what was on display when Marx was working on, e.g., *Das Kapital* or when he visited the Museum before his famous stint in the Reading Room, but the Museum had so many relevant objects (including the famous Rosetta Stone, essentially a tax document, dated circa 200 BC) that their import should have been hard to miss. Doubtless, the Reading Room also had a copy of the Old Testament, which has heavy legal overtones.

4   Aeschylus tells a version of this in the *Oresteia* (the *Eumenides*).

5   Hobbes, Thomas. *Leviathan*. Edited by J.C.A. Gaskin, New edition, p. 84, Oxford University Press, USA, 1998. Hobbes gave his Leviathan various duties, including the making and enforcement of law, subject to an understanding with his people. The discussion in *Leviathan* focuses on war and then proceeds

immediately to the nature of peace, itself enabled by law and the Leviathan. *Ibid.,* at 86 and succeeding chapters.

6   U.S. Constitution, Preamble.

7   E.g., Shapiro, Scott J. *Legality.* Harvard University Press, 2010.

8   E.g., *Indiana Harbor Belt Railroad Co. v. American Cyanamid Co.* (7th Cir. 1990) (discussing nineteenth century cases); Calabresi, Guido. *The Future of Law and Economics: Essays in Reform and Recollection.* Yale University Press, 2016.; Posner, Richard. "The Law and Economics Movement." *The American Economic Review,* vol. 77, no. 2, May 1987.

9   Pledge of Allegiance.

10 Werner, John F. "The New York County Courthouse." Supreme Court, New York County. 21 Mar. 2008, p. 3, https://www.nycourts.gov/courts/1jd/supctmanh/Courthouse%20History102012.pdf. Werner, the Chief Clerk of the Court, was a little elliptical about the mistake. The *New Post,* the first to catch and publicize the mistake, had a tonal error in the other direction. *See also* Washington, George. "Letter to Edmund Randolph." 28 Sep. 1789. https://www.loc.gov/resource/mgw2.022/?sp=177&st=text. (Randolph had been confirmed on the 26th.)

11 Limits exist on judicial discretion in this regard. E.g., *FCC v. Beach Communications Inc.,* 508 U.S. 307, 313 (1993) ("Whether embodied in the Fourteenth Amendment or inferred from the Fifth, equal protection is not a license for courts to judge the wisdom, fairness, or logic of legislative choices.").

12 Bingham, Tom. *The Rule of Law.* Reprint edition, p. vii, Penguin UK, 2011. Bingham had been Lord Chief Justice, Senior Law Lord, and Master of the Rolls (three of the highest, and not unrelatedly, some of the most ancient legal posts in Britain) and helped create the UK's Supreme Court.

13 Google ngram. Slate's slogan appeared in below-article ads in 2017, but has since been changed. Lovelace, Ryan. "Deputy AG Rod Rosenstein: President Trump 'Honors' the Rule of Law with Justice and Judicial Appointments." *Washington Examiner,* 18 Sept. 2017, www.washingtonexaminer.com/deputy-ag-rod-rosenstein-president-trump-honors-the-rule-of-law-with-justice-and-judicial-appointments/article/2634827.

14 Aristotle, *Politics,* Book III 1282b and *Rhetoric,* 1354b. Aristotle did note that particularly able rulers could be better than the average legal code; i.e., he wasn't a stranger to executive discretion.

15 Thomas Paine, *Common Sense,* available at www.learner.org/workshops/primarysources/revolution/docs/Common_Sense.pdf. The quote appears on p. 19 of the free digital version, and on other pages in other editions.

16 The Constitution forbids the *abridgement* of voting based on (certain) personal characteristics, but doesn't come straight out and say we *do* have a right to vote— not clearly. Of course, the right is reasonably inferred from the Amendments, and possibly from the Republican Guarantee Clause, though the Court hasn't said much about the latter.

17 *Marbury v. Madison,* 5 U.S. (1 Cranch) 137 (1803).

18 Judicial review had also appeared in England, in matters like *Dr. Bonham's Case* and in the writings of Lord Coke, CJ (sometimes only by implication) though the courts were deferring to Parliament by the mid-eighteenth century before

resuming judicial review in the twentieth. That scholars disagree about the case's true meaning is beside the point; the Revolutionary elite understood the case to involve judicial review. The Founders and Framers were also aware of judicial review closer to home, and cases involving the principle had been decided by American courts before Ratification in cases such as *Holmes v. Walton* (1780) (not formally reported) and *Commonwealth v. Caton*, 8 Va. (4 Call. 5) (1782). For a good contextual review of *Marbury, see* Treanor, William Michael. "The Story of *Marbury v. Madison*: Judicial Authority and Political Struggle." *Federal Courts Stories*, edited by Vicki C. Jackson and Judith Resnik, Foundation Press, 2010, pp. 29–56 (hereinafter "Treanor").

19 *Marbury v. Madison*, 5 U.S. (1 Cranch) 137, 162-63 (1803).

20 E.g., U.S. Constitution, art. III, § 2; 28 U.S.C. § 1251; *see also Chisholm v. Georgia*, 2 U.S. 491 (1795). *Chisholm's* functional outcome was undone by the Eleventh Amendment.

21 *Marbury v. Madison*, 5 U.S. (1 Cranch), 137, 162 (1803).

22 *Ibid.*, 174–190. The Judiciary Act of 1789 granted the Court original jurisdiction over Marbury's writ of *mandamus* and suits against an executive officer; the Court held that this contradicted the Court's constitutionally prescribed *appellate* role.

23 Treanor, pp. 34–36, 43; Surrency, Erwin C. "The Judiciary Act of 1801." *The American Journal of Legal History*, vol. 2, no. 1, 1958, pp. 53–65; Onuf, Peter. "Thomas Jefferson: Domestic Affairs." *Miller Center*, 4 Oct. 2016, millercenter.org/president/jefferson/domestic-affairs. Prominent judges actually impeached included Thomas Pickering (frequently drunk and perhaps worse; ultimately removed) and Samuel Chase (impeached but acquitted). The Judiciary Act of 1802, 2 Stat. 89–100, 156–57, adjusted the Court's term dates. For a brief overview, see "Landmark Legislation: Judiciary Act of 1802," Federal Judicial Center, https://www.fjc.gov/history/legislation/landmark-judicial-legislation-text-document-2.

24 Mahoney, Emily L. and Steve Bosquet. "Rick Scott starts process to pick Supreme Court justices. Political, legal fights loom." *Miami Herald*, 12 Sep. 2018, https://www.miamiherald.com/news/politics-government/state-politics/article218255400.html (noting that Gov. Scott's midnight appointments could shift the Florida court dramatically in favor of Scott's personal preferences); Criss, Doug, "The West Virginia House impeached the entire state Supreme Court." *CNN*. 14 Aug. 2018, https://www.cnn.com/2018/08/14/politics/west-virginia-supreme-court-impeach-trnd/index.html. Immediately before press, the Florida Supreme Court ruled that Scott could not pursue his stated plan, with various legal caveats; the matter remained in flux when this book was submitted. *League of Women Voters, et al v. Rick Scott, et al.*, Case No. SC18-1573 (2018).

25 *Stuart v. Laird*, 5 U.S. 299 (1803).

26 Associated Press. "Russia's New National Guard Will Be Tasked to Suppress Riots." *Daily Mail Online*, 6 Apr. 2016, http://www.dailymail.co.uk/wires/ap/article-3526740/Russias-National-Guard-tasked-riots.html; Associated Press. "Venezuelans Protest President Maduro's Plan to Rewrite Constitution." *USA TODAY*, 22 July 2017, www.usatoday.com/story/news/world/2017/07/22/venezuela-protests-opposition-slams-maduros-plan-rewrite-constitution/502263001/.

27   Israel, Josh. *Possible Homeland Security Pick Wants National Guard to Stomp Out Anti-Trump Protests.* ThinkProgress. 12 Nov. 2016, thinkprogress.org/sheriff -clarke-stop-peaceful-protests-10dc734b4409/.

28   Clarke, Jr., David A., "How to Stop Riots. 1) Declare State of Emergency. 2) Impose Early Curfew. 3) Mobilize Nat Guard. 4) Authorize ALL Non Lethal Force. 5) Tear Gas.Pic.Twitter.Com/LaBvrRbiz3." @SheriffClarke, 11 Nov. 2016, twitter .com/SheriffClarke/status/797275978691026944.

29   Schmitt, Carl. *Die Diktatur (On Dictatorship)*, 1921. Most famously, Schmitt began *Political Theology* with his definition of the sovereign as he who decides the exception. Giorgio Agamben's *State of Exception* provides a contemporary gloss. Schmitt is also playing a word game.

30   U.S. Constitution art. I, § 9. The original Magna Carta has also been construed as granting habeas rights, though this interpretation is controversial, and the use of habeas often had authoritarian overtones until the 1400s. Per William Blackstone, the term *habeas corpus* was in use by 1305; it was fully codified no later than the 1600s (by which time it had taken on its modern meaning, if not well before), by the Habeas Corpus Acts of 1640 and 1679.

31   U.S. Constitution art. I, § 9. The Habeas Clause doesn't expressly reference Congress, but it's understood from the context (Article I being concerned with Congress).

32   *Ex parte Merryman*, 17 F. Cas. 144 (C.C.D. Md. 1861). The administration argued that Congressional authorization was impracticable because Congress was in recess when Lincoln issued his order, but that argument was flimsy. *Merryman* itself was also messy—Taney blurred the weight of his decision (formally as a Justice in his circuit capacity) by emphasizing his position on the Court.

33   Ragsdale, Bruce A. "*Ex parte Merryman* and Debates on Civil Liberties During the Civil War." Federal Judicial Center. 2007, pp. 7–8; *see also* Neely, Mark E. *The Fate of Liberty: Abraham Lincoln and Civil Liberties*. Reprint edition, Oxford University Press, 1992.

34   I focus only on war's implications for the domestic ROL. The laws of war and international laws generally are complex and controversial: by nature, the difficulty of enforcement often shoehorns them into the binary outcomes of impotence or victors' justice. Plus, some scholars question whether they are really laws at all; a version of this doubt in other contexts animates things like Brexit.

35   Cicero's phrase is *inter arma enim silent leges,* or "among arms, the laws fall mute," which is generally rendered as "in times of war, the law falls silent."

36   Compare *Korematsu v. United States*, 323 U.S. 214 (1944) with *Youngstown Sheet and Tube v. Sawyer*, 343 U.S. 579 (1952).

37   The Bush II Administration achieved mixed successes at court (*Rasul, Hamdan,* and *Hamdi,* e.g.) but its general stance was to articulate doctrines of expansive executive power.

38   "Emergency Powers Statutes: Provisions of Federal Law Now in Effect Delegating to the Executive Extraordinary Authority in Time of National Emergency: Report of the Special Committee on the Termination of the National Emergency," 1973, S. Rep. 93-549, p. 6 and Foreword.

39   *Ibid.*, Foreword.

40   *Ibid.*, Introduction.

41 National Emergencies Act, 50 U.S.C. § 1601 *et seq.*; but for further complications, see also *Immigration and Naturalization Service v. Chadha*, 462 US 919 (1983) and subsequent statutory history (the legislation and case in combination, requiring a joint resolution rather than concurrent resolution to terminate emergency).

42 Executive Order 12170 (1979).

43 Korte, Gregory. "Special Report: America's Perpetual State of Emergency." *USA TODAY*, 22 Oct. 2014, www.usatoday.com/story/news/politics/2014/10/22/president-obama-states-of-emergency/16851775/. At most, there is a single reference to one Congressional reappraisal in May 1980 that may or may not have satisfied statutory imperatives.

44 The White House can make quasi-law via executive order in constrained circumstances and, of course, by controlling the bureaucracy. E.g., *J.W. Hampton, Jr. & Co. v. United States*, 276 U.S. 394 (1928) (finding that delegation is an "implied power" of Congress only so long as Congress provides an "intelligible principle" to guide the executive).

45 Scheips, Paul. *The Role of Federal Military Forces in Domestic Disorders, 1945– 1992.* U.S. Army, Center of Military History, 2005, history.army.mil/html/books/030/30-20/CMH_Pub_30-20.pdf at 55, 352, 432, 436, and generally (reciting a history of internal military deployments and relevant laws). Doyle, Charles, and Jennifer Elsea. *The Posse Comitatus Act and Related Matters: The Use of the Military to Execute Civilian Law.* R42659, Congressional Research Service, 16 Aug. 2012, fas.org/sgp/crs/natsec/R42659.pdf (noting scope of Posse Comitatus prohibitions and infrequency of legal action to address potential breaches).

46 U.S. Constitution, art. III, § 1.

47 Note that the Judiciary Acts of 1801, 1802, and 1866, e.g., had political aims, some of which were negated by circumstance or subsequent legislation. *See generally* Judiciary Act of 1789, 1 Stat. 73; Judiciary Act of 1801, 2 Stat. 89; Judiciary Act of 1802, 2. Stat. 156; Seventh Circuit Act, 2 Stat. 420; Eighth and Ninth Circuit Act, 5 Stat. 176; Tenth Circuit Act, 12 Stat. 794; Judicial Circuits Act, 14 Stat. 209; Judiciary Act of 1869, 16 Stat. 44 (the operative act).

48 "Franklin D. Roosevelt: Fireside Chat. March 9, 1937." The American Presidency Project, www.presidency.ucsb.edu/ws/index.php?pid=15381 (containing Roosevelt's statement that "I say that I and with me the vast majority of the American public favor.... chang[ing]" the number of Justices, and explicitly referring to the plan as "packing the court").

49 *Ibid.* (noting that FDR would "appoint Justices who will act as Justices and not as legislators" and challenging the Court's ability to "read[] into the Constitution words and implications which are not there, and which were never intended to be there"—which, of course, is judicial review and oddly the same basis under which liberal Justices are now being attacked by conservatives).

50 One swing Justice burned his papers, leaving an informational void, but FDR won many of his Court cases before the showdown and several of the holdout Justices (Butler, van Devanter, and then Sutherland) died over the next few years—which may seem unfairly post hoc, except that age and infirmity were some of FDR's stated reasons for packing the Court. FDR would have gotten what he wanted by 1939 or 1941.

Chapter 2

1   Paine, Thomas. *Common Sense: Addressed to the Inhabitants of America*. 1776.
     Annenberg Learner, www.learner.org/workshops/primarysources/revolution/
     docs/Common_Sense.pdf.

2   Holmes, Jr., Oliver Wendell. "The Path of the Law." *Harvard Law Review*, vol. 10,
     no. 8, 1897, p. 457.

3   E.g., *Price v. United States*, 174 U.S. 373, 375 (1899) (noting that immunity is an
     "axiom" of American jurisprudence and that cases on this point are so numer-
     ous as to not require citation).

4   The government's wrongs against its citizens are often appalling, as the following
     materials demonstrate. Chemerinsky, Erwin. "Against Sovereign Immunity." *Stan-
     ford Law Review*, vol. 53, Jan. 2001, pp. 1201–1224; *Korematsu v. United States*, 323
     U.S. 214 (1944); Cooper, Helene. "Reports of Sexual Assault Increase at Two Mili-
     tary Academies." *New York Times,* 15 Mar. 2017, www.nytimes.com/2017/03/15/us/
     politics/sexual-assault-military-west-point-annapolis.html; Thompson, Helen. "70
     Years Ago, a B-25 Bomber Crashed Into the Empire State Building." *Smithsonian*, July
     30, 2015, www.smithsonianmag.com/smart-news/july-1945-b-25-bomber-crashed
     -empire-state-building-180956103/; M. Reverby, Susan. "Ethical Failures and His-
     tory Lessons: The U.S. Public Health Service Research Studies in Tuskegee and
     Guatemala" *Public Health Reviews*, vol. 34, June 2012; *ResearchGate*, doi:10.1007/
     BF03391665. The American government also hired prostitutes to infect Guate-
     malan prisoners during disease prophylaxis studies; claims were dismissed on
     sovereign immunity grounds. The government finally paid compensation in the
     internment case in the 1990s.

5   *United States v. Lee*, 106 U.S. 196, 205–207 (tracing the history of the doctrine
     and noting that the "principle has never been discussed or the reasons for it
     given"). The *Lee* dissents strongly suggest that, while the majority points out
     differences between the workings of the doctrine in England and America, the
     inspiration for the doctrine in America is found in English history.

6   For a convenient history of Edward IV and ruptures in English succession gener-
     ally, see Dunham, William Huse, and Charles T. Wood. "The Right to Rule in
     England: Depositions and the Kingdom's Authority, 1327–1485." *The American
     Historical Review*, vol. 81, no. 4, 1976, pp. 738–761. *JSTOR*, doi:10.2307/1864778.
     and the narrative on Edward IV starting at p. 749.

7   Notre Dame appears to be the only major law school that requires a course in
     jurisprudence. Notre Dame School of Law. "Academics: Second and Third Years."
     The Law School, law.nd.edu/academics/degrees/j-d/second-and-third-years/. For
     most students, the course is brief, but students in certain sub-specialties must
     take a more intensive course. The link between jurisprudence and Notre Dame's
     Catholic mission is not coincidental.

8   Robinson, Nick. "The Decline of the Lawyer Politician." *Buffalo Law Review*,
     vol. 657, no. 4, Aug. 2017. *SSRN*, pp. 671, 692, papers.ssrn.com/abstract=2684731
     (noting that in the mid-nineteenth century, lawyers accounted for about 80%
     of federal legislators, declining to under 40% for the 114th Congress, but still

remaining the largest professional bloc; 51% of the Senate were lawyers and roughly 35% of representatives).

9   Dworkin, Ronald. "Hart's Posthumous Reply." *Harvard Law Review*, vol. 130, no. 8, 2017, pp. 2096–2130.

10 E.g., U.S. Constitution, arts. I–III and amdt. X.

11 Sovereignty is a major standard raised in nationalist rhetoric, from the 1930s–present. Indeed, Brexit was substantially motivated by resentment of Brussels busybodies infringing on the Queen-in-Parliament's prerogatives, with disgruntlement stretching back to *Ex Parte Factortame,* Numbers I–V (1989–2000), cases mostly upholding EU fishing regulations that supposedly trampled British sovereignty, which left invoking Parliamentary supremacy and backing out of the EU as the only escape hatches.

12 Thomas, Katie. "How to Protect a Drug Patent? Give It to a Native American Tribe." *New York Times*, 8 Sept. 2017, www.nytimes.com/2017/09/08/health/allergan-patent-tribe.html. Allergan's Mohawk maneuver was slapped down by courts, but versions of the strategy may yet be fruitful.

13 Arguably, provisions like the Takings Clause, which require the government to compensate citizens whose property is taken by eminent domain, seem to require the opposite conclusion—that government *can* be sued—if those provisions are to have meaning. The Supreme Court has mused that immunity was not thought to extend in full force to the states, per *Chisholm v. Georgia* (essentially overridden by the 11th Amendment).

14 "Naturalization Oath of Allegiance to the United States of America." U.S. Citizenship and Immigration Services, www.uscis.gov/us-citizenship/naturalization-test/naturalization-oath-allegiance-united-states-america.

15 *Crito* is the relevant Socratic dialogue.

16 Constitution of California. art. 1, § 1.

17 Constitution of Texas. art. 1, § 34.

18 Individuals who earn under a certain amount, or have less than $2 million in wealth, are generally exempt. An overview is available at the IRS website. Internal Revenue Service. "Expatriation Tax." *International Taxpayers*, 30 Mar. 2018, www.irs.gov/individuals/international-taxpayers/expatriation-tax#_Expatriation_after_June_17,%202008, *see also* 26 U.S.C. §877–877A.

19 Minors may renounce citizenship after age 16, but must do so in the presence of legal guardians, and the general view is that this is not a practicable option.

20 David Louk's *Whose Federalism?* (on file with the author) provides an empirical review of the sort which federalism scholars have long lacked.

21 Kelsen, Hans. *Pure Theory of Law.* The Lawbook Exchange, Ltd., 2005. Kelsen is a bit obscurantist on this and people dicker about whether the Constitution is the *Grundnorm* or *obedience* to the Constitution is, but for our purposes, it's close enough to call the Constitution America's *Grundnorm*.

22 Fuller, Lon L. *The Morality of Law.* Yale University Press, 1969 at Chapter II and p. 39.

23 *Ibid.* For a critique of Fuller, *see* Dworkin, Ronald M. "Philosophy, Morality and Law—Observations Promoted by Professor Fuller's Novel Claim." *University of Pennsylvania Law Review*, vol. 113, no. 668, 1965, p. 678.

24 "How Our Laws Are Made." Congress.gov, https://www.congress.gov/resources/display/content/How+Our+Laws+Are+Made+-+Learn+About+the+Legislative+Process; Sullivan, John V. *How Our Laws Are Made.* U.S. Government Printing Office, 2007, www.gpo.gov/fdsys/pkg/CDOC-110hdoc49/pdf/CDOC-110hdoc49.pdf.

25 Tankersley, Jim, and Alan Rappeport. "A Hasty, Hand-Scribbled Tax Bill Sets Off an Outcry." *New York Times,* 1 Dec. 2017, www.nytimes.com/2017/12/01/us/politics/hand-scribbled-tax-bill-outcry.html. The draft bill is largely incomprehensible—pp. 5–6 are particularly unintelligible. United Sates. Cong. House. Committee on House—Ways and Means, www.congress.gov/115/bills/hr1/BILLS-115hr1enr.pdf.

26 E.g., 17 CFR §§ 240.13a-20, 240.15d-20.

27 Griswold, Erwin N. "Government in Ignorance of the Law: A Plea for Better Publication of Executive Legislation." *Harvard Law Review,* vol. 48, no. 2, 1934, pp. 198–215. *JSTOR,* doi:10.2307/1332538.

28 "Administrative Procedure Act." 5 U.S.C. § 552.

29 *See infra,* Chapters 5 and 13.

30 Risen, James, and Eric Lichtblau. "Bush Lets U.S. Spy on Callers Without Courts." *New York Times,* 16 Dec. 2005, www.nytimes.com/2005/12/16/politics/bush-lets-us-spy-on-callers-without-courts.html.

31 Joint Committee on Taxation. *Complexity in the Federal Tax System.* JCX-49-15, Joint Committee on Taxation, 6 Mar. 2015 (discussing complexity and noting its role in failures in voluntary compliance).

32 Lunder, Erika K., et al. *Constitutionality of Retroactive Tax Legislation.* R42791, Congressional Research Service, 25 Oct. 2012, p. 16., fas.org/sgp/crs/misc/R42791.pdf, especially note 3 and accompanying text.

33 "Swedes and Taxes." *Sweden.se,* 2 May 2013, sweden.se/society/why-swedes-are-okay-with-paying-taxes/.

34 E.g., Finnis, John. *Natural Law and Natural Rights.* 2nd edition, Oxford University Press, 2011 at pp. 139–140.

35 Martin Luther King, Jr. *Letter from a Birmingham Jail.* Stanford Martin Luther King, Jr. Research and Education Institute, 16 Apr. 1963, kinginstitute.stanford.edu/king-papers/documents/letter-birmingham-jail; *Eldon Edwards: The Mike Wallace Interview.* Interview by Mike Wallace, 5 May 1957. University of Texas at Austin, Harry Ransom Center, hrc.utexas.edu/multimedia/video/2008/wallace/edwards_eldon_t.html.

36 Bentham, Jeremy. "Anarchical Fallacies; Being an Examination of the Declaration of Rights Issued During the French Revolution." *Works of Jeremy Bentham,* edited by Sir John Bowring, vol. VIII, W. Tait, 1839 at art. II.

37 Finnis, John. *Natural Law and Natural Rights.* 2nd edition, Oxford University Press, 2011, p. 281.

38 Laughland, Oliver, et al. "Oxford scholar who was mentor to Neil Gorsuch compared gay sex to bestiality." *Guardian.* 3 Feb. 2017, https://www.theguardian.com/law/2017/feb/03/neil-gorsuch-mentor-john-finnis-compared-gay-sex-to-bestiality.

39 Dworkin, Ronald. *Taking Rights Seriously.* 5th printing edition, Harvard University Press, 1978; Dworkin, Ronald. *Law's Empire.* 1st edition, Belknap

Press of Harvard University Press, 1986. This is an immensely reductive presentation of Dworkin's Right Answer, i.e., the outcome which best explains and justifies an outcome based on harmony with prior law and the moral principles behind it. Note that everyone except Hercules has their own "right answer," but unlike the mythical judge, it's not The Right Answer.

40   The phrase was most memorably conveyed in Dworkin's 1977 book, *Taking Rights Seriously.*

Chapter 3

1   Elkins, Kathleen. "Goldman Sachs CEO: The most you get out of law school is debt." *CNBC.com*, 18 Aug. 2016.

2   Stein, Ralph Michael. "The Path of Legal Education from Edward I to Langdell: A History of Insular Reaction." *Chicago-Kent Law Review*, vol. 57, no. 2, 1981, pp. 429–454, esp. 430.

3   *Corpus Juris Civilis.* Technically, only the *Codex Justinianus* is the "Code of Justinian," but the whole collection is generally referred to by Justinian's name.

4   Bologna is generally credited as the oldest university in the West and law, notably, has always been an important part of its curriculum; the university's motto is *Petrus ubique pater legum Bononia mater.*

5   Roberts, John. *C-SPAN: A Conversation Chief Justice Roberts.* 25 June 2011, www .c-span.org/video/?300203-1/conversation-chief-justice-roberts; Breyer, Stephen G. "Response of Justice Stephen G. Breyer." *New York University Annual Survey of American Law*, vol. 64, no. 33, 2008–2009, p. 33. Richard Posner eloquently made the point about the academic divide in *Divergent Paths.*

6   For a current list of schools, see American Bar Association. "ABA-Approved Law Schools, In Alphabetical Order." *Section of Legal Education and Admissions to the Bar*, https://www.americanbar.org/groups/legal_education/resources/aba _approved_law_schools/in_alphabetical_order.html. Figures for 2016 can be seen in the Standard 509 Information Reports on the ABA website. The number of schools varies slightly by year, but hovers at just over 200 (including programs that count toward the total but which are not necessarily freestanding schools).

7   American Bar Association. "2017 Standard 509 Information Report Data Overview." *Section of Legal Education and Admissions to the Bar*, 2 Apr. 2018, www .americanbar.org/content/dam/aba/administrative/legal_education_and _admissions_to_the_bar/statistics/2017_509_enrollment_summary_report .authcheckdam.pdf; *First-Year-Enrollment/Total Enrollment/Degrees Awarded 1963–2013*. Statistics, American Bar Association, www.americanbar.org/con tent/dam/aba/administrative/legal_education_and_admissions_to_the_bar/ statistics/enrollment_degrees_awarded.authcheckdam.pdf. Data are for JDs. First-year enrollment is down slightly more than total legal enrollment, for 2017 versus 2007–2010; total JD graduate production rate has slipped somewhat less. Admissions and applications follow the pattern.

8   American Bar Association. "2017 Standard 509 Information Report Data Overview." *Section of Legal Education and Admissions to the Bar*, 2 Apr. 2018, www
.americanbar.org/content/dam/aba/administrative/legal_education_and
_admissions_to_the_bar/statistics/2017_509_enrollment_summary_report
.authcheckdam.pdf; author's calculations (based on historical ABA data sources,
including Standard 509 data, graduate production versus initial enrollment and
also calculated separately based on ABA provided attrition rates).

9   U.S. Bureau of Labor Statistics, U.S. Department of Labor. *Occupational Outlook
Handbook: Lawyers*. 13 Apr. 2018, www.bls.gov/ooh/legal/lawyers.htm#tab-6. A
counterargument could be made that should per-capita lawyer rates revert to
levels prevailing three decades ago, demand could outstrip supply in the 2020s,
but the legal environment of the 2020s does not seem likely to resemble the go-go
1980s.

10   *Class of 2017 Law Graduate Data: Employment Outcomes as of April 2018*.
American Bar Association, Apr. 2018, www.americanbar.org/content/dam/aba/
administrative/legal_education_and_admissions_to_the_bar/statistics/2017
_law_graduate_employment_data.authcheckdam.pdf. Figures treat "bar passage required" jobs as "practicing law."

11   National Conference on Bar Examiners. "2017 Bar Examination and Admissions Statistics." *The Bar Examiner Magazine*, vol. 87, no. 1, Spring 2018, www
.ncbex.org/pdfviewer/?file=%2Fdmsdocument%2F218. Data cited are for all
2017 sittings. Pass rates for the February sitting are notably lower, because they
include many sitters who have already failed once/are otherwise "off-track" and
are less likely to pass. Aggregating all jurisdictions, the pass rates for July 2017
was 65% vs. 59% for all sittings.

12   Themis Bar Review. "Summer 2017 Themis Pass Rates." *Pass Rates*, www.themis
bar.com/pass-rates. Themis winnows its data sets (to its credit, disclosing how)
to produce flattering results, but this does not affect the conclusion. Improvement ranges from 0%–27%.

13   *Hoover v. Ronwin*, 466 U.S. 558 (1984). Conventionally, bar examiners apply
standards set out by a state's supreme court (or its committees); under the "state
action exemption," *Parker* immunity allows bar exams to escape the Sherman
Antitrust Act. *See also*, Harrop, Donald E. "Formulation of the Two Part Analysis for State Action Exemption—*Hoover v. Ronwin*." *Campbell Law Review*, vol. 7,
no. 2, 1984, p. 22.

14   Music, Adam. "Nobody Wants to Fail the Bar Exam, but It Happens—Even
to Kamala Harris." *ABA for Law Students*, 20 June 2017, abaforlawstudents
.com/2017/06/20/success-after-failing-the-bar-exam/.

15   Olson, Elizabeth. "Bar Exam, the Standard to Become a Lawyer, Comes Under
Fire." *New York Times*, 19 Mar. 2015, www.nytimes.com/2015/03/20/busi
ness/dealbook/bar-exam-the-standard-to-become-a-lawyer-comes-under-fire
.html.

16   National Conference on Bar Examiners. "2017 Bar Examination and Admissions Statistics." *The Bar Examiner Magazine*, vol. 87, no. 1, Spring 2018, www
.ncbex.org/pdfviewer/?file=%2Fdmsdocument%2F218.

17   United States Medical Licensing Examination. *Performance Data*. www.usmle .org/performance-data/default.aspx#2016_step-3.

18   Lisa Anthony. *LSAT Score Distributions for 2015–2018 Testing Years*. 25 June 2018, https://www.lsac.org/docs/default-source/data-(lsac-resources)-docs/lsat -score-distribution.pdf.

19   American Bar Association. "Chapter 5: Admissions and Student Services." *Standards and Rules of Procedure for Approval of Law Schools 2014–2015*, p. 31, www.americanbar.org/content/dam/aba/publications/misc/legal_education/ Standards/2014_2015_aba_standards_chapter5.authcheckdam.pdf. Of the 185 schools ranked by *U.S. News* in 2017, incoming full-time students had a median score of 156, it's reasonable to conclude (given the lesser schools omitted from rankings, the likely tendency for non-full-time students to have lower scores, and reported distributions) that roughly one-third to one-half of law incoming students are at or near risk. Ross, Kelly Mae. "12 Law Schools Where Students Had High LSAT Scores." *U.S. News & World Report*, 27 Mar. 2018, https:// www.usnews.com/education/best-graduate-schools/the-short-list-grad-school/ articles/2018-03-27/12-law-schools-where-students-had-the-highest-lsat -scores. *See also supra* note 8.

20   *Ibid.*

21   Author's calculations based on *First-Year Class—2017*. Standard 509 Information Reports—ABA Required Disclosures, American Bar Association, Aug. 2018, www.abarequireddisclosures.org/.

22   *Ibid.*

23   Zaretsky, Staci. "Law School Dean Allegedly Begged Graduates Not to Take the Bar Exam—On the Day Before the Test." *Above the Law*, 28 July 2015, abovethelaw .com/2015/07/law-school-dean-allegedly-begged-graduates-not-to-take-the -bar-exam-on-the-day-before-the-test/?rf=1; Ward, Stephanie Francis. "Arizona law school loses accreditation approval, which may be a first for an operating law school." *ABA Journal*, 11 June 2018, http://www.abajournal.com/news/ article/arizona_summit_loses_accreditation_approval_which_may_be_a _first_for_operat/; Arizona Summit Law School. "Accreditation." https://www .azsummitlaw.edu/about-aba-accreditation.html (last visited August 7, 2018); Currier, Barry. "Memorandum: Withdrawal of Approval, Arizona Summit Law School" American Bar Association, 8 June 2018, https://www.americanbar.org/ content/dam/aba/administrative/legal_education_and_admissions_to_the _bar/18_june_arizona_summit_public_notice.authcheckdam.pdf. The relevant litigation, which was concluded without public verdict, was *Lorona v. Arizona Summit Law School, LLC*, No. CV-15-00972-PHX-NVW (D. Ariz. 2015).

24   *Class of 2017 Law Graduate Data: Employment Outcomes as of April 2018*. American Bar Association, Apr. 2018, www.americanbar.org/content/dam/aba/ administrative/legal_education_and_admissions_to_the_bar/statistics/2017 _law_graduate_employment_data.authcheckdam.pdf. Law.com also provides periodic updates.

25   U.S. Bureau of Labor Statistics. "Civilian Unemployment Rate (UNRATE)." *FRED, Federal Reserve Bank of St. Louis*, July 2018, fred.stlouisfed.org/series/UNRATE

(national unemployment); U.S. Bureau of Labor Statistics. "Unemployment Rates and Earnings by Educational Attainment." *Employment Projections*, 2017, www.bls.gov/emp/tables/unemployment-earnings-education.htm (unemployment by education level); Gould, Elise, et al. *Class of 2018: College Edition*. Economic Policy Institute, 10 May 2018, p. 20, www.epi.org/publication/class-of-2018-college-edition/ (2018 college graduate unemployment, based on historical moving average for 21–24-year-old college graduates). Unemployment for recent college graduates was 5.3%. For comparable statistics based on age, *see* U.S. Bureau of Labor Statistics. "Table A-10. Selected Unemployment Indicators, Seasonally Adjusted." *Labor Force Statistics (CPS)*, 2018, www.bls.gov/webapps/legacy/cpsatab10.htm (25–34 year-old unemployment).

26   Yale Law School. *Class of 2017 Employment*. law.yale.edu/student-life/career-development/employment-data/class-2017-employment (visited July 2018).

27   Author's calculations based on *2015–2018 Granular Employment Data*. American Bar Association, https://www.americanbar.org/groups/legal_education/resources/statistics.html. Data are for the class of 2017.

28   *Class of 2017 Law Graduate Data: Employment Outcomes as of April 2018.* American Bar Association, Apr. 2018, www.americanbar.org/content/dam/aba/administrative/legal_education_and_admissions_to_the_bar/statistics/2017_law_graduate_employment_data.authcheckdam.pdf. For the class of 2016, the figure was 14.1%.

29   E.g., *2015 Standard 509 Information Report*. Harvard Law School, 2015, (bar passage), hls.harvard.edu/content/uploads/2015/12/2015-ABA-Standard-509-Report.pdf; Harvard Law School. "Employment Statistics." *Additional Employment Data*, 2018, (historical bar passage and median compensation), hls.harvard.edu/dept/ocs/recent-employment-data/additional-employment-data/.

30   Yale Law School. "Details About the Application Process." *Application*, law.yale.edu/admissions/jd-admissions/first-year-applicants/application (visited July 2018).

31   Yale Law School. "Statistical Profile of the Class of 2020." *Entering Class Profile*, law.yale.edu/admissions/profiles-statistics/entering-class-profile (visited July 2018).

32   American Bar Association. "Pre-Law." *Section of Legal Education and Admissions to the Bar*, www.americanbar.org/groups/legal_education/resources/pre_law.html.

33   Rojstaczer, Stuart, and Christopher Healy. "Grading in American Colleges and Universities." *Teachers College Record*, Mar. 2010, p. 4, www.gradeinflation.com/tcr2010grading.pdf. Law schools do consider context, like the quality of the applicant's college, but they have been cagey about their treatment of quantitative vs. qualitative majors—not that it matters, because applicants don't believe that law schools account for this, and behave accordingly.

34   Nieswiadomy, Michael. "LSAT Scores of Economics Majors: The 2008–2009 Class Update." *Journal of Economic Education*, vol. 41, no. 3, June 2010.

35   Some numerate judges have recently taken lawyers to task for their "math blocks." E.g., Weiss, Debra Cassens. "Posner: Lawyers Bad at Math Are an Increasing Concern; Inmate's Blood-Pressure Suit Shows Why." *ABA Journal*,

29 Oct. 2013, www.abajournal.com/news/article/posner_math_block_lawyers _an_increasing_concern_inmates_blood-pressure_suit/. Posner focused on scientific illiteracy, of which innumeracy is a part.

36   *Ibid.; see also,* e.g., *infra* Chapter 11.

37   Supreme Court of the United States. "Current Members." *About the Court,* www .supremecourt.gov/about/biographies.aspx (accessed 4 Feb. 2018).

38   University of Michigan Law School. "How to Get a Job in Legal Academia." www.law.umich.edu/careers/typesofemployers/Documents/HowtoGetaJo binLegalAcademia.pdf. For a corresponding view, see University of Chicago Law School. "Paths to Law Teaching." *Career Info,* www.law.uchicago.edu/ careerservices/pathstolawteaching.

39   Author's calculations based on rack-rates and treat as "private" any school not offering in-state tuition discounts. *Tuition and Fees/Living Expenses/Cond. Scholarships.* Standard 509 Information Reports—ABA Required Disclosures, American Bar Association, Aug. 2018, www.abarequireddisclosures.org/.

40   *Ibid.;* "Tuition and Fees for 2018–2019." *Columbia Law School,* www.law.colum bia.edu/admissions/graduate-legal-studies/tuition-fees-and-financial-aid.

41   MTA/New York City Transit. *Fares and MetroCard.* web.mta.info/metrocard/ mcgtreng.htm#30day.

42   Author's calculations; *Tuition and Fees/Living Expenses/Cond. Scholarships.* Standard 509 Information Reports—ABA Required Disclosures, American Bar Association, Aug. 2018, www.abarequireddisclosures.org/.

43   National Association of Realtors. "Mean Sales Price of Existing Homes in Mid-west Census Region [HOSAVGUSMWM052N]." *FRED, Federal Reserve Bank of St. Louis,* 1 May 2017, https://fred.stlouisfed.org/series/HOSAVGUSMWM052N.

44   *Trends in College Pricing 2017.* The College Board, 2017, p. 13, Figure 4A: Aver-age Rates of Growth of Published Charges by Decade, trends.collegeboard.org/ sites/default/files/2017-trends-in-college-pricing_1.pdf. Data from 2013 to 2017 use author's calculations based on *Law School Tuition (1985–2013; Public/Pri-vate).* Statistics, American Bar Association, 2017, www.americanbar.org/groups/ legal_education/resources/statistics.html.

45   *Tuition and Fees/Living Expenses/Cond. Scholarships.* Standard 509 Information Reports—ABA Required Disclosures, American Bar Association, Aug. 2018, www.abarequireddisclosures.org/. Data from 2013 to 2017 use author's calculations based on *Law School Tuition (1985–2013; Public/Private.* Statistics, American Bar Association, 2017, www.americanbar.org/groups/legal_education/resources /statistics.html.

46   In-state decelerations after 2011–2012 may or may not be permanent. If tuition moderates, public and private tuitions won't converge until much later; nothing about state budgets offers much hope, however.

47   Randazzo, Sara, and Jacqueline Palank. "Legal Fees Cross New Mark: $1,500 an Hour." *Wall Street Journal,* 9 Feb. 2016, www.wsj.com/articles/legal-fees-reach -new-pinnacle-1-500-an-hour-1454960708. *See infra* Chapter 8.

48   The likely impact on after-tax corporate earnings is probably less than 0.01% overall, though for companies with major legal events or in highly regulated

spaces, legal prices can have meaningful effects, especially when compliance overhauls, behavioral changes, lobbying efforts, regulatory fines, and settlements/judgments are included. *See infra* Chapter 8.

49 Government pay is determined by the "General Schedule" (GS), a complicated system doubtless designed by a lawyer. Basically, GS has 15 basic levels of pay, each of which has 10 steps; lawyers start high, at GS-11, subject to a cost of living adjustment that may be up 27–31% extra in places like D.C. and New York.

50 Polantz, Katelyn. "Wilkinson Walsh Lures SCOTUS Clerks with $350K Bonuses, Hires in 3 Cities." *Law.Com*, www.law.com/americanlawyer/almID/ 1202796052352/Wilkinson-Walsh-Lures-SCOTUS-Clerks-With-350K -Bonuses-Hires-in-3-Cities/. Wilkinson is presently the record-holder, but $200,000–$300,000 SCOTUS bonuses are common.

51 Ellman, Ira. "A Comparison of Law Faculty Production in Leading Law Reviews," Journal of Legal Education, Vol. 33, pp. 681–692, 688 (1983). Ellman offered various metrics, but Arizona tended to rise conspicuously in many of Ellman's measures; 7th in pages per faculty member, in the text's given example. Whatever Ellman's disclaimers about his process and conclusions, the impression given is that ASU somehow ranked among the traditional elites.

52 *Nomination of Judge Clarence Thomas to Be Associate Justice of the Supreme Court of the United States.* U.S. Government Publishing Office, Sept. 1991, pp. 111, 113, 115, 127, 396–97, 429, 485, www.govinfo.gov/content/pkg/GPO-CHRG -THOMAS/pdf/GPO-CHRG-THOMAS-1.pdf.

53 Professor Cunnae (a pseudonym of L.S., Esq.). *A Timeline of Women's Legal History in the United States. Stanford Law School,* p. 7, wlh.law.stanford.edu/wp-content/ uploads/2011/01/cunnea-timeline.pdf. Lindgren, James. "Measuring Diversity: Law Faculties in 1997 and 2013." *Northwestern Law & Econ Research Paper No. 15-07; Northwestern Public Law Research Paper No. 15-17,* June 2015, tables 2, 12. *SSRN,* papers.ssrn.com/sol3/papers.cfm?abstract_id=2581675; American Association of Law Schools Education. *Law School Demographics.* 2018. www.aals.org/wp-content/ uploads/2018/01/LawSchoolDemographics.pdf (figures for full-time faculty).

54 Intense partisanship's impact on professorial influence is mixed. Arguably, partisanship makes it easier for highly ideological professors to influence fellow travelers. Centrists might struggle, but this isn't a complete excuse, because persuasion is a central legal competence. Anyway, legislative gridlock has made judges more powerful, a shift that law professors, of all people, should be able to exploit.

55 E.g., Weinstein, Jack. "After Fifty Years of the Federal Rules of Civil Procedure: Are the Barriers to Justice Being Raised?" *University of Pennsylvania Law Review,* vol. 137, 1989, pp. 1901–23, at 1901.

56 "HLS Amicus Brief Wins Legal Writing Award." *Harvard Law Today,* 6 Jan. 2006, https://today.law.harvard.edu/hls-amicus-brief-wins-legal-writing-award/. In a profession obsessed with taking credit, the failure to stake a claim is essentially an admission of nonparticipation and Judge Posner suggested that the professors did not contribute. Posner, Richard A. "A Note on *Rumsfeld v. FAIR,* and the Legal Academy," *The Supreme Court Review,* vol. 2006, no. 1, 2006, pp. 47–57,

pp. 54, 56. It should be noted that Yale, as ever, was the exception here; its professors contributed heavily to their brief.

57   *Rumsfeld v FAIR.* 547 U.S. 47 at Part II (2006).

58   Law Journal Data Tool. *Law Journals,* Washington and Lee University, School of Law. https://managementtools4.wlu.edu/LawJournals/Default.aspx. About 70% of American journals are student edited—i.e., "law reviews" in the traditional sense. Washington and Lee's data tool does not capture all foreign journals, but lists about six hundred. H.W. Wilson's EBSCO catalog also compiles journal data and is roughly consistent with domestic counts.

59   The Courts of Appeals publish 4,600–5,000 opinions per twelve-month period. The Administrative Office of the U.S. Courts collects periodic information on published and unpublished decisions in its Table B-12-U.S. Courts of Appeals Judicial Business series, http://www.uscourts.gov/statistics-reports/caseload -statistics-data-tables. By contrast, leading law reviews publish much more; e.g., Harvard Law Review publishes ~24 full articles per year.

60   Indices like that compiled by Washington & Lee suggest that roughly 70% of journals are student-edited. *See supra* note 58.

61   Supreme Court of the United States. "Current Members." *About the Court,* www .supremecourt.gov/about/biographies.aspx.

62   Davies, Ross E. "The Increasingly Lengthy Long Run of the Law Reviews." *Journal of Law,* vol. 3, no. 2, 2013, pp. 246, 249, 258.; Harvard Law Review. "Subscriptions." *Ordering,* harvardlawreview.org/ordering.

63   *Ibid.;* Westlaw and LexisNexis were launched in the 1970s and originally focused on judicial opinions; other content was added in the 1980s. Desktop access wasn't available until 1979 on Lexis and the services' displacement of paper-based research truly took off only with the arrival of moderately quick Internet access, circa 1988–1992. It is unlikely the databases impacted review circulation before then and, at least in the case of Westlaw, journals didn't appear online until 1994. LexisNexis. "Historical Milestones." *About LexisNexis,* 2018, www.lexisnexis .com.sg/en-sg/about-us/about-us.page; personal conversation between author's research assistant and Westlaw corporate representative.

64   A scroll through the tables of contents of the first volumes of, e.g., *Harvard Law Review,* shows a distinctly practical bent.

65   E.g., Crespi, Gregory. "Judicial and Law Review Citation Frequencies for Articles Published in Different 'Tiers' of Law Journals: An Empirical Analysis." *Santa Clara Law Review,* vol. 44, no. 3, 2004, pp. 897–959, pp. 903, 907 (analyzing a subset of journals and articles and noting citation rates of less than 1.0 per article occur even at top journals). *See also* Callahan, Dennis J. and Devins, Neal. "Law Review Article Placement: Benefit or Beauty Prize," *Journal of Legal Education,* vol. 56, no. 3, Sept. 2006, pp. 374–387 (discussing predictors of citation); Ayeres, Ian, and Vars, Fredrick E. "Determinants of Citations To Elite Law Reviews." *The Journal of Legal Studies,* vol. 29, no. S1, Jan. 2000, pp. 427—450. Posner and Landes have also done notable work in the area of academic influence. While citations are important and a subject of professional obsession, they aren't perfect metrics, and can understate influence; there's also a right-tail dynamic.

66 E.g., Crespi, Gregory. *Ibid.* (analyzing a subset of journals and articles). Even highly cited articles aren't cited that frequently. Shapiro, Fred R. "The Most-Cited Law Review Articles." *California Law Review*, vol. 73, no. 5, Oct. 1985, p. 1540. *Crossref*, doi:10.2307/3480410.

Chapter 4

1 U.S. Constitution, art. 1, § 1.

2 Peter Stone, *1776!*. 1969. The line is usually attributed to John Adams, but appears to have only been spoken by his character in *1776!*.

3 Library of Congress. "The Legislative Process: Introduction and Referral of Bills." *The Legislative Process*, www.congress.gov/legislative-process/introduction-and -referral-of-bills.

4 The mechanics are variable and complicated, but the usual routine is to pro-long "debate" (a one-person filibuster), requiring a vote for cloture under Senate Rule XXII, which then limits subsequent debate to 30 hours. In Paul's case, the funding bill was presented late and required an intervening day before a vote, absent unanimous consent. Note that one senator cannot hold the chamber at bay indefinitely, if the needful majority is arranged.

5 Thompson, Mary. "Death Defied." *George Washington's Mount Vernon*, www .mountvernon.org/george-washington/the-man-the-myth/death-defied -dr-thorntons-radical-idea-of-bringing-george-washington-back-to-life/.

6 Parts of the 1790 Census have been lost. However, secondary sources attest to most of the information. E.g., National Historical Geographic Information System. "U.S. Geographic Summary Data and Boundary Files." *IPUMS NHGIS*, www.nhgis.org/. "Adult" here is a shorthand for the Census category "free white males of 16 years of age and upwards, including heads of families."

7 U.S. Census Bureau. "National Population Totals And Components of Change: 2010–2017." *Population Estimates*, www.census.gov/data/datasets/2017/demo/ popest/nation-total.html#par_textimage_1810472256. Data presented treat all residents as constituents to whom Congress has representative obligations, reflecting broader social expectations.

8 Author's calculations. U.S. Census Bureau, "National Population Totals and Components of Change: 2010–2017." *Populations Estimates*, www.census.gov/ data/datasets/2017/demo/popest/nation-total.html#par_textimage_1810472256.

9 The ratio of representation is particularly pronounced in America: over 325 mil-lion residents against 435 lower-house legislators. The ratios in the UK and Ger-many are better by a factor of roughly 10. Britain has 66 million people against 650 seats in the Commons; Germany has 83 million people against 709 seats in the Bundestag.

10 *The Public Statutes at Large of the United States of America.* Vol. 2, Charles C. Lit-tle and James Brown, 1845. Several Congresses passed just two bundled statutes each, though publishing conventions combined several legislative acts as a single "statute," not unlike today's practice of multipart bills. But the point remains:

Congressional output was low. Little and Brown's publishing firm, interestingly, would become Little, Brown & Co., which became part of this book's publisher, Hachette Book Group USA.

11 Pub. L. 62-5 (1911). That statute set the formula; the additions of a few states afterward adjusted totals.

12 Kaplan, Thomas. "Congress Approves $1.3 Trillion Spending Bill, Averting a Shutdown." *New York Times*, 22 Mar. 2018, www.nytimes.com/2018/03/22/us/politics/house-passes-spending-bill.html.

13 Most obviously, the adverse tax treatments of grain sellers, retailers, and certain pass-through entities, politically favored constituencies, survived into the enacted law and were almost surely unintentional. For a technical description of the errors/ambiguities, from the business-friendly Chamber of Commerce, see Harris, Caroline L. "General Regulatory Guidance Requests," U.S. Chamber of Commerce, 7 Mar. 2018, and associated chart, https://www.uschamber.com/sites/default/files/chamber_regulatory_feedback_comment_letter_03.07.18.pdf. *See also* e.g., Faler, Brian. " 'This Is Not Normal': Glitches Mar New Tax Law." *Politico*, 24 Feb. 2018, www.politico.com/story/2018/02/24/tax-law-glitches-gop-423434.; Bryan, Bob. "Experts Are Starting to Find Massive Errors in the GOP Tax Bill After It Went Through Congress at Lightning Speed." *Business Insider*, 7 Dec. 2017, www.businessinsider.com/trump-gop-tax-reform-bill-mistakes-corporate-amt-2017-12; Levitz, Eric. "Senate Republicans Made a $300 Billion Mistake in Their Tax Bill." *New York Magazine*, 7 Dec. 2017, nymag.com/daily/intelligencer/2017/12/the-senate-gop-made-a-usd300-billion-mistake-in-their-tax-bill.html; Bernstein, Jonathan. "Why the Tax Bill's Errors Won't Be Fixed." *Bloomberg*, 12 Dec. 2017, www.bloomberg.com/view/articles/2017-12-12/why-the-tax-bill-s-errors-won-t-be-fixed; Levitz, Eric. "Senate Republicans Accidentally Killed Some of Their Donors' Favorite Tax Breaks." *New York Magazine*, 4 Dec. 2017, nymag.com/daily/intelligencer/2017/12/senate-gop-accidentally-killed-all-corporate-tax-deductions.html.

14 Bryan, Bob. "The GOP Is Keeping Its Obamacare Replacement Plan in a 'Secure Location'—and There Is Now a Hunt to Find It." *Business Insider Deutschland*, 2 Mar. 2017, www.businessinsider.de/obamacare-replacement-bill-secret-room-2017-3?r=US&IR=T. *See also* links embedded in *ibid*.

15 Author's calculations, for the 105–115th Congresses. Data available at www.govtrack.us/congress/bills/statistics.

16 Data available at www.govtrack.us/congress/bills/statistics. "107th Congress (2001–2003)." *Browse (Congress.Gov)*, www.congress.gov/browse/107th-congress.

17 Brookings Institution. *Vital Statistics on Congress, Chapter 5: Congressional Staff and Operating Expenses.* 21 May 2018, www.brookings.edu/multi-chapter-report/vital-statistics-on-congress/. Other sources provide higher staff counts, up to ~32,000, but the point remains. *See also* chaplain.house.gov/chaplaincy/index.html (the House chaplain). The Supreme Court has been mostly silent on this issue, though it accepted a similar chaplain in the Nebraska statehouse. *Marsh v. Chambers*, 463 U.S. 783 (1983).

18 U.S. Constitution, art. I, § 1, amdt. 17.

19 U.S. Constitution, art. I, § 1.

20 U.S. Constitution, art. I, § 4; *see also ibid.* art. I *generally* and amdts.

21 Coursen, Kimberly, et al. "Restoring Faith in Congress." *Yale Law & Policy Review*, vol. 11, no. 2, 1993, pp. 251–52. (citing Roper Center polls).

22 *Ibid.*; Gallup. "Congressional Job Approval." *Congress and the Public*, 2018, news.gallup.com/poll/1600/Congress-Public.aspx.

23 *Ibid.*; author's calculations. Net trust and confidence are calculated by subtracting "not very much" and "none at all" percentages from "fair amount" and "[a] great deal" percentages. Data are through September 2018; data series are not continuous before 1997.

24 Struyk, Ryan, and Joyce Tseng. "The History of Government Shutdowns in 1 Chart." *CNN*, 13 Jan. 2018, www.cnn.com/2018/01/13/politics/us-government -shutdowns-budget-chart/index.html; Scott, Dylan, et al. "The Second Government Shutdown of 2018, Explained." *Vox*, 9 Feb. 2018, www.vox.com/policy-and -politics/2018/2/8/16993196/government-shutdown-2018-second. Figures include full shutdowns and funding gaps that suspended one or more major government operations or were popularly understood as shutdowns; "total days" rounds down the nine-hour shutdown of February 9, 2018. Before the 1974 Budget Act consolidated the budgetary process, government did not fully shut down as appropriations were ad hoc (though individual programs could experience funding lapses).

25 Newport, Frank. "Americans Want More Than Just Budget Cuts." *Gallup*, 9 June 2017, news.gallup.com/opinion/polling-matters/211892/americans-budget-cuts .aspx (citing Gallup's own research and the *Wall Street Journal*'s; Gallup's polling showed Americans almost equally split, the *Journal*'s wording produced a majority in favor of government doing more).

26 U.S. Constitution, art. I, §8, art VI, par. 2.

27 Setting aside the Civil War, for obvious reasons.

28 Spaeth, Harold J., et al. The Supreme Court Database, Version 2017 Release 01. supremecourtdatabase.org; *Acts of Congress Held Unconstitutional in Whole or in Part by the Supreme Court of the United States.* Government Publishing Office, 2002, www.gpo.gov/fdsys/pkg/GPO-CONAN-2002/pdf/GPO-CONAN -2002-10.pdf. The SCOTUS database was searched for "act of congress declared unconstitutional" in the "Historical" and "Legacy" databases. Bill Eskridge did the path-breaking work on this in 1991, subsequently updated. *See,* e.g., William N. Eskridge, Jr., *Overriding Supreme Court Statutory Interpretation Decisions, Yale Law Journal* vol. 101, p. 331 (1991) (hereinafter "Eskridge Override I"); Christiansen, Matthew, and William Eskridge. "Congressional Overrides of Supreme Court Statutory Interpretation Decisions, 1967–2011." *Texas Law Review*, vol. 92, no. 6, 2014, p. 1317 (hereinafter "Eskridge Override II"). Constitutional strikedowns ranged from 0 to 4, annually, rising in the twentieth century as the Court become more active and took a broader view (which created a self-reinforcing upward trend). There are also important differences obscured by the basic numbers—a single override may undo many judicial decisions in important areas, as happened even in the Congressionally passive 2000s, with copyrights, taxes, bankruptcy, etc.

29 *See Eskridge Override I* and *Eskridge Override II; see also* Hasen, Richard. "End of the Dialogue? Political Polarization, the Supreme Court, and Congress." *Southern California Law Review*, vol. 86, no. 2, Jan. 2013, pp. 205–62. Eskridge and Hansen differ on methodology and finer points, but generally agree on the trend.

30 *Mobile v. Bolden*, 446 U.S. 55 (1980), essentially overruled by Pub. L. 97-205, § 3, 96 Stat. 134 (June 29, 1982).

31 *Grove City College v. Bell*, 465 U.S. 555, partially overridden by the Civil Rights Restoration Act of 1987 [Pub. L 100-259, § 102 Stat. 28 (1988)].

32 Civil Rights Act of 1991, Pub. L. 102-166 (essentially an overhaul of prior civil rights acts), legislatively overruling in whole or part, *inter alia, Patterson v. McLean Credit Union, Wards Cove Packing Co. v. Atonio, Price Waterhouse v. Hopkins, Martin v. Wilks, Lorance v. AT&T Technologies Inc., EEOC v. Arabian American Oil Co.*

33 *Eskridge Override II*, Part II. Eskridge distinguishes between types of overrides, some falling into the category of contemporary and straightforward disagreement, others having the character of "policy updates," and so on.

34 *Ledbetter v. Goodyear Tire & Rubber Co.*, 550 U.S. 618 (2007), *overridden in pertinent part by* Pub L. 111-2 (2009).

35 Greenhouse, Linda. "Justices Limit Discrimination Suits Over Pay." *New York Times*, 29 May 2007, www.nytimes.com/2007/05/29/washington/30scotuscnd.html.

36 Democrats already controlled the House and Senate before Obama was elected. While a veto from Bush II was likely, things never got that far: the bill stalled due to a GOP filibuster. Obama's championship stiffened Democratic resolve and helped flip essential Republican Senate votes, getting Ledbetter out of Congress.

37 Mendes, Elizabeth. "Americans Down on Congress, OK with Own Representative." *Gallup*, 9 May 2013, news.gallup.com/poll/162362/americans-down -congress-own-representative.aspx (ability to name member of Congress; knowledge was self-reported, so actual figures are likely lower); Pew Research Center. "Section 10: Political Participation, Interest and Knowledge." *Beyond Red vs. Blue*, 26 June 2014, www.people-press.org/2014/06/26/section-10-political -participation-interest-and-knowledge/ (party control of the houses of Congress). Phrasing and disclosures are in the full survey methodology attached to Pew's reports.

38 U.S. Constitution, art. 1, § 7; *see also* Louk, David Scott, and David Gamage. "Preventing Government Shutdowns: Designing Default Rules for Budgets." *University of Colorado Law Review*, vol. 86, p. 181 (2015). The budget and "revenue bills" are interdependent and should naturally tilt as a historical and Constitutional matter toward arising in the House.

39 Pub. Law 67-13 § 201, § 207 (1921). Mandated benefits programs also reduce latitude over the budget, though for those programs, it's more the case that contemporary Congresses have ceded power to their predecessors of the 1930s and 1960s.

40 Pub. Law 93-344 § 201, § 1001 *et seq.* (1974).

41 Newkirk, Vann R. "The GOP Escalates Its Battle with the CBO." *The Atlantic*, 22 July 2017. www.theatlantic.com/politics/archive/2017/07/republicans-cbo-hhs -score-bcra/534480/.

42   *Compare Table 5—Trend of Federal Civilian Executive Branch Employment by Type of Position Occupied and Work Schedule to September 2013.* U.S. Office of Personnel Management, Sept. 2013, www.opm.gov/policy-data-oversight/data-analysis-documentation/federal-employment-reports/employment-trends-data/2013/september/table-5/ *with* Brookings Institution. *Vital Statistics on Congress, Chapter 5: Congressional Staff and Operating Expenses.* 21 May 2018, www.brookings.edu/multi-chapter-report/vital-statistics-on-congress/. Summary data (available in OPM's "Sizing Up the Executive Branch" reports) show executive employment roughly stable since 2013. Ratio excludes the Post Office.

43   Congress held hearings on the subject in September 2017, although it had been informed of agency failures many years before. U.S. House of Representatives, Subcommittee on Regulatory Reform, Commercial and Antitrust Law. *Rulemakers Must Follow the Rules, Too: Oversight of Agency Compliance with the Congressional Review Act.* 28 Sept. 2017, judiciary.house.gov/hearing/rulemakers-must-follow-rules-oversight-agency-compliance-congressional-review-act/; Copeland, Curtis W. *Congressional Review Act: Rules Not Submitted to GAO and Congress.* R40997, 29 Dec. 2009, p. 32, digital.library.unt.edu/ark:/67531/metadc627172/m1/1/high_res_d/R40997_2009Dec29.pdf.

44   Ornstein, Norman. "Part-Time Congress." *Washington Post,* 7 Mar. 2006, www.washingtonpost.com/wp-dyn/content/article/2006/03/06/AR2006030601611.html.

45   Sinclair, Barbara. *Unorthodox Lawmaking: New Legislative Processes in the U.S. Congress,* 5th ed. CQ Press, 2016, pp. 140–141 (counting floor amendments decided on a teller or recorded vote). After 1971, the teller itself became something of a forcing mechanism; counts prior to its advent might seem slightly depressed as a result.

46   Alberta, Tim. "John Boehner Unchained." *Politico,* Nov./Dec. 2017, www.politico.com/magazine/story/2017/10/29/john-boehner-trump-house-republican-party-retirement-profile-feature-215741 ("We basically run a coalition government without the efficiency of a parliamentary system.") (quoting Speaker Paul Ryan).

47   As a contrasting parliamentary example, Britain's legislators can deploy votes of no confidence to break a government (per party rules), its plurality party can hand out ministries to form coalitions, and the Commons can (and between 1911 and 2015, did) restructure the Lords to overcome obstruction.

48   U.S. House of Representatives. *Parliamentarian of the House | House.Gov.* www.house.gov/the-house-explained/officers-and-organizations/parliamentarian-of-the-house (Parliamentarian's history); Wickham, Thomas J. *Constitution, Jefferson's Manual, and Rules of the House of Representatives of the United States, One Hundred Fifteenth Congress.* U.S. Government Publishing Office, 2017, www.gpo.gov/fdsys/pkg/HMAN-115/pdf/HMAN-115.pdf. Quasi-parliamentarians (going by titles such as "messengers of the Speaker's table") served between the 1850s and 1920s, but the office was informal and its power was more personal than institutional. None of this is to deny the power of procedure in earlier Congresses; only to comment on its institutional distribution.

49   E.g., Pear, Robert, and Thomas Kaplan. "Senate Parliamentarian Challenges Key Provisions of Health Bill." *New York Times*, 21 July 2017. www.nytimes.com /2017/07/21/us/politics/senate-parliamentarian-health-bill.html; Weixel, Nathaniel. "Senate Parliamentarian: More Parts of ObamaCare Repeal Will Need 60 Votes." *The Hill*, 25 July 2017, thehill.com/policy/healthcare/343737-senate-parliamentarian -more-parts-of-obamacare-repeal-will-need-60-votes; Levitz, Eric. "Parliamentarian Deals Trumpcare a Final Death Blow." *New York Magazine*, Sept. 2017, nymag .com/daily/intelligencer/2017/09/parliamentarian-deals-trumpcare-a-final -death-blow.html.

50   Sinclair, Barbara. *Unorthodox Lawmaking: New Legislative Processes in the U.S. Congress, 5th ed.* CQ Press, 2016. pp. 135–136, 261–263 and accompanying tables (for selected Congresses for which Sinclair had data). Unlike the House, Senate amendment procedures appear to be geared more toward legislating than obstruction.

51   Historically, rank-and-file Congressmen could sometime manage to slap an earmark on a bill, directing pork back home. Earmarks never represented a large fraction of total spending and rarely impacted national policy; they just weren't important, practically. After 2007, earmarking became politically toxic and, in 2010, Republicans symbolically banned earmarks outright, further reducing backbench power. In 2016, the GOP did float the idea of allowing "congressionally directed spending"—i.e., earmarks.

52   E.g., Dodd, Lawrence C., and Bruce I. Oppenheimer, eds. *Congress Reconsidered.* CQ Press, 2016, pp. 312–320 (noting character of filibusters evolved from the 1970s from obstruction/moderation to affirmative gain-seeking).

53   Courts can review bills that violate the Origination Clause, per *United States v. Munoz-Flores,* but Congress can't exactly litigate its way to budget agreement.

54   Publius (Madison or Hamilton). *The Federalist Papers—Nos. 60, 62.* 1788. *Congress .gov,* https://www.congress.gov/resources/display/content/The+Federalist+Papers.

55   *Ibid.* (No. 62).

56   Publius (Madison). *The Federalist Papers—Nos. 52 and 53.* 1788. *Congress.gov,* https://www.congress.gov/resources/display/content/The+Federalist+Papers. Madison contended that biennial elections would be sufficient to offset many of these concerns.

57   Publius (Madison or Hamilton). *The Federalist Papers—Nos. 62 and 63.* 1788. *Congress.gov,* https://www.congress.gov/resources/display/content/The+Federalist +Papers.

58   Carson, Jamie, et al. *Assessing the Rise and Development of the Incumbency Advantage in Congress.* www.vanderbilt.edu/csdi/events/IncumbencyAdvantageCSW .pdf. Congress and History Conference, Vanderbilt University at fig. 1 and accompanying text; Glassman, Matthew Eric & Wilhelm, Amber Hope, "Congressional Careers: Service Tenure and Patterns of Member Service, 1789–2017," Congressional Research Service, 2017, figs. 2–3 and accompanying text, https://fas.org/sgp/ crs/misc/R41545.pdf.

59   *See supra note* 59 (Glassman et al at Summary); Cillizza, Chris. "People Hate Congress. But Most Incumbents Get Re-Elected. What Gives?" *Washington Post,* 9

May 2013, www.washingtonpost.com/news/the-fix/wp/2013/05/09/people-hate
-congress-but-most-incumbents-get-re-elected-what-gives/. For a slightly contrary view, *see* Dodd, Lawrence C., and Bruce I. Oppenheimer. *Congress Reconsidered*. CQ Press, 2016, pp. 69–74.

60 Glassman, Matthew Eric, and Amber Hope Wilhelm. *Congressional Careers:
Service Tenure and Patterns of Member Service, 1789–2017*. R41545, Congressional Research Service, 3 Jan. 2017, fig. 4 and p. 8, fas.org/sgp/crs/misc/R41545.pdf.

61 Roemer, Tim. "Why Do Congressmen Spend Only Half Their Time Serving Us?"
Newsweek, 29 July 2015, www.newsweek.com/why-do-congressmen-spend-only
-half-their-time-serving-us-357995; *see also* Scherb, Aaron. "Member of Congress
Need to Spend Less Time Raising Funds." *The Hill*, 7 July 2011, thehill.com/opinion/
letters/170295-member-of-congress-need-to-spend-less-time-raising-funds.

62 *Life in Congress: The Member Perspective*. Congressional Management Foundation and Society for Human Resource Management, 2013, www.shrm
.org/about-shrm/press-room/press-releases/Documents/life-in-congress-the
-member-perspective.pdf. Sample size was limited, since few Congressmen
responded to survey requests. In the survey, Congressmen suggested they spent
relatively little time on "politics," but even if that's true, they still admit to spending only ~35% of their time on core policy matters.

63 2 U.S.C. § 30(a).

64 U.S. Constitution, art. 1 §§ 2–3.

65 Levenson, Eric. "Coin Flips, Poker Hands and Other Crazy Ways America
Settles Tied Elections." *CNN*, 4 Jan. 2018, www.cnn.com/2018/01/04/us/tie
-elections-history-lots-coins-draws-trnd/index.html.

66 Author's conversations. For a sense of training priorities *see* Moody, Chris.
"New Lawmakers Start First Day of School." *CNN*, 19 Nov. 2014, www.cnn
.com/2014/11/13/politics/freshman-orientation-congress/index.html; *Members'
Congressional Handbook—115th Congress*. Committee on House Administration, U.S. House of Representatives, 27 Feb. 2018, cha.house.gov/sites/repub
licans.cha.house.gov/files/documents/member_services_docs/Members%
20Handbook%20115th.pdf; "Bipartisan Program for Newly Elected Members
of Congress." *Institute of Politics, Harvard Kennedy School*, iop.harvard.edu/
get-inspired/bipartisan-program-newly-elected-members-congress (noting in
agenda two-day training course for new members, dealing with policy and non
-policy issues); Lewis, Lindsay Mark, and Jim Arkedis. "So You've Won a Seat
in Congress—Now What?" *The Atlantic*, 6 Nov. 2014, www.theatlantic.com/
politics/archive/2014/11/so-youve-won-election-to-congressnow-what/382421/
(noting that during orientation members will learn "a little" about how Congress works and participate in administrative rituals like the office-assignment
lottery).

67 Brookings Institution. *Vital Statistics on Congress, Chapter 4: Congressional
Committee Data* (Tables 4-4 and 4-5). 21 May 2018, www.brookings.edu/multi
-chapter-report/vital-statistics-on-congress/ (includes assignments to special
and other committees). *See also*, e.g., Sinclair, Barbara, *Unorthodox Lawmaking*,
5th ed., CQ Press, 2017, p 50 (noting 3.9 committee assignments and 8.1 subcommittee assignments per senator for the 108th Congress).

68 Robinson, Nick. "The Decline of the Lawyer Politician." *Buffalo Law Review*, vol. 65, no. 4, 2017, Table 2 (data for selected Congresses, and may not include absolute extremes).

69 E.g. *ibid.*, pp. 661, 713–14.

70 One example is *Lockhart,* which enhanced sentences for child pornographers with prior convictions "relating to aggravated sexual abuse, sexual abuse, or abusive sexual conduct involving a minor or ward." The question was whether "minor or ward" modified all the crimes listed or just the last one. *Lockhart v. Smith*, 577 U.S. __ (2016) (construing 18 U.S.C. §2252(a)(4)). Kagan's dissent is worth a special read. Some states have special rules for drafting, including Maine's rule on the serial comma.

71 *Maine Legislative Drafting Manual.* Legislative Council, Maine State Legislature, 2009, www.maine.gov/legis/ros/manual/Draftman2009.pdf; Associated Press. "Lack of Oxford Comma Costs Maine Dairy Company $5 Million." *USA TODAY*, 8 Feb. 2018, www.usatoday.com/story/money/2018/02/08/oxford-comma-lawsuit/320944002/.

72 E.g., Gluck, Abbe R., and Lisa Schultz Bressman. "Statutory Interpretation from the Inside—An Empirical Study of Congressional Drafting, Delegation, and the Canons: Part I." *Stanford Law Review*, vol. 65, no. 5, May 2013, pp. 901–1025.

73 Smith, Steven S., et al. *The American Congress*. Cambridge University Press, 2015, pp. 214–216 (committee staff); Fox, Harrison and Susan Webb Hammond. "The Growth of Congressional Staffs." *Proceedings of the Academy of Political Science*, vol. 32, no. 1 (1975), pp. 115–116 (personal staffs other than for committee chairmen).

74 Brudnick, Ida A. *Congressional Salaries and Allowances: In Brief.* Congressional Research Service, 11 Apr. 2018, pp. 5–6, 10, www.senate.gov/CRSpubs/9c14ec69-c4e4-4bd8-8953-f73daa1640e4.pdf. Senate budgets are proportional to home state population, maxing out at around $5 million; a limited number of temps may also assist representatives.

75 *Ibid.; see also* Strand, Mark N., et al. *Surviving Inside Congress*. Congressional Institute, 2008, p. 14 and Ch. 3.

76 Author's calculations based on Brookings Institute and Norman Ornstein's Vital Statistics, Strand's Surviving Congress, GAO surveys. *See also* Gluck, Abbe R., and Lisa S. Bressman. "Statutory Interpretation from the Inside—An Empirical Study of Congressional Drafting, Delegations, and the Canons, Parts I & II." *Stanford Law Review*, vols. 65 & 66, at pp. 901, 725, 921 (citing 6099 Congressional staffers with drafting responsibility), and n. 63 (surmising that true population of legislative counsels is less than 650).

77 *See generally* U.S. Census Bureau. *Population and Housing Unit Estimates.* www.census.gov/programs-surveys/popest.html; U.S. Bureau of Economic Analysis. "Real Gross Domestic Product [GDPC1]" *FRED, Federal Reserve Bank of St. Louis*, Jun. 2018, fred.stlouisfed.org/series/GDPC1; Brookings Institution. *Vital Statistics on Congress, Chapter 5: Congressional Staff and Operating Expenses.* 21 May 2018, Table 5-1, www.brookings.edu/multi-chapter-report/vital-statistics-on-congress/.

78 Data for Capitol Police run through 2005, the latest available.

79   E.g., Glassdoor, "United States Congress Staff Assistant Salaries." 6 Nov. 2016, www.glassdoor.com/Salary/United-States-Congress-Staff-Assistant-Salaries -E226176_D_KO23,38.htm; Rosiak, Luke. "Congressional Staffers, Public Short-changed by High Turnover, Low Pay." *The Washington Times*, 6 June 2012, www .washingtontimes.com/news/2012/jun/6/congressional-staffers-public -shortchanged-by-high/; U.S. Bureau of Labor Statistics. "Average Hourly Earnings of All Employees: Total Private [CES0500000003]" *FRED, Federal Reserve Bank of St. Louis*, Jun. 2018, fred.stlouisfed.org/series/CES0500000003; U.S. Bureau of the Census, "Mean Personal Income in the United States [MAPAINUSA646N]." *FRED, Federal Reserve Bank of St. Louis*, Jan. 2016, fred.stlouisfed.org/series/ MAPAINUSA646N. Fed data include all income; BLS data focus on hourly earn-ings; author's calculations assume a 2,000-hour work year. High turnover, special elections, and so on, depress the figures somewhat. However, staffers are better educated than average; adjusting for quality and geography, they just don't make much. Average pay tends to be higher, due to seniority or unorthodox classifica-tion. CRS Report R44322.

80   *See supra* note 81; *Vital Statistics on Congress, Chapter 5: Congressional Staff and Operating Expenses.* 21 May 2018, www.brookings.edu/multi-chapter-report /vital-statistics-on-congress/.

81   E.g., *Life in Congress: Job Satisfaction and Engagement of House and Senate Staff.* Congressional Management Foundation and Society for Human Resource Management, 2013, http://www.congressfoundation.org/storage/documents/CMF _Pubs/life-in-congress-job-satisfaction-engagement.pdf at fig. 36 and accompa-nying text (noting that 63% of D.C. based staff were "likely/very likely" to seek new work, with higher pay as a prime motivation). *See also* Petersen, Eric R. and Sarah J. Eckman. "Staff Tenure in Selected Positions 2006-2016." Congressional Research Service R44683, 9 Nov. 2016. There's considerable tenure variation by member office and some staff simply move between positions, but the median tenure in any given position is remarkably low—even for some senior, substan-tive staff.

82   For an interesting member-by-member gloss, see Drutman, Lee. "Turnover in the House: Who Keeps—and Who Loses—the Most Staff." *Sunlight Foundation*, 6 Feb. 2012, sunlightfoundation.com/2012/02/06/turnover-in-the-house/.

83   OpenSecrets. "Lobbying Database." *Lobbying: Overview*, www.opensecrets .org/lobby/index.php; *see also* Drutman, Lee. *The Business of America Is Lobby-ing: How Corporations Became Politicized and Politics Became More Corporate.* 1st edition, Oxford University Press, 2015, p. 8 (noting $3.6 and $3.3 billion in lobbying expenditures for 2010 and 2012, respectively, up from $200 million in 1983; nominal dollars).

84   Drutman, Lee. *Ibid.,* at pg. 13 (noting 34:1 ratio for 2012 lobbying expenditure business versus "diffuse interest groups and unions," up from 22:1 in 1998).

85   OpenSecrets. "Lobbying Database: Alphabet Inc." *Lobbying: Overview*, 2017, www.opensecrets.org/lobby/index.php; Alphabet Form 10-K, Part II, Item 6 (FY 2016).

86   Author's calculations comparing 2016 figures, the latest full comparison pos-sible; OpenSecrets. "Lobbying Database." *Lobbying: Overview,* www.opensecrets

.org/lobby/index.php; Brookings Institution. *Vital Statistics on Congress, Congressional Staff and Operating Expenses.* 21 May 2018, www.brookings.edu/multi -chapter-report/vital-statistics-on-congress/.

87   Can Manufacturers Institute. *Can Central.* www.cancentral.com/.

88   The VI consulted with Congress over this issue. Flexible Vinyl Alliance. *FVA, Vinyl Institute Urge Congress to Protect $50 Billion U.S. Vinyl Economy During Fly-In.* 21 May 2012, www.flexvinylalliance.com/wp-content/uploads/2013/04/7-Plain -Talk-about-PVC-Stressed-in-Hill-Meetings.pdf. For the cans, *see,* e.g., Budway, Robert. *Re: Comment on Section 232 National Security Investigation of Imports of Steel.* 17 May 2017, www.bis.doc.gov/index.php/forms-documents/section -232-investigations/1710-23-can-manufacturers-institute-robert-budway/ file.

89   *See generally,* Drutman, Lee. *The Business of America Is Lobbying: How Corporations Became Politicized and Politics Became More Corporate.* 1st edition, Oxford University Press, 2015, Chapters 2, 4 and pp. 219–220.

Chapter 5

1   Max Weber, *Economy and Society, vol. 1,* Guenther Roth and Claus Wittich, eds. University of California Press (1978), p. 223.

2   Schumpeter, Joseph A. *Capitalism, Socialism and Democracy.* 5th ed., Taylor & Francis e-library (2003), p. 206.

3   Hall, Brian K. "The Paradoxical Platypus." *BioScience*, vol. 49, no. 3, 1 Mar. 1999, pp. 211–218. *academic.oup.com*, doi:10.2307/1313511.

4   Congressional Budget Office. *Budget.* (FY 2018). www.cbo.gov/topics/budget.

5   5 U.S.C. §551.

6   The FEC is a specially chartered commission under 52 U.S.C. § 30106 *et seq.*; however, parts of the APA apply to FEC and the FEC is routinely sued for violating the APA, for bias, being the alleged patsy of an administration, and so on.

7   U.S. Environmental Protection Agency. "Laws and Executive Orders." *Laws & Regulations*, last updated 14 Sept. 2017, www.epa.gov/laws-regulations/laws -and-executive-orders.

8   *Ibid.,* (noting EPA's rulemaking power); *see also* 5 U.S.C. §§ 551(4)-(5); 553 (agency rulemaking generally).

9   5 U.S.C. §§ 556-57.

10   Jennings, Julie, and Jared C. Nagel. *Federal Workforce Statistics Sources: OPM and OMB.* R43590, Congressional Research Service, 12 Jan. 2018, p. 16, fas.org/ sgp/crs/misc/R43590.pdf; author's calculations. Figures exclude Post Office and uniformed military; were those included, employment figures would be higher. Budgetary figures subtract the ~$11 billion allocated to Congress/the judiciary from federal spending totals; whether grants/mandatory spending are included are not, the point remains. The GAO's Interagency Contracting Report provides a figure of $500 billion for total agency spending ex-transfers.

11   Office of Information and Regulatory Affairs, Office of Management and Budget. "About the Unified Agenda." *Reginfo.Gov*, www.reginfo.gov/public/jsp/eAgenda/StaticContent/UA_About.jsp. The site also refers to—and it's not clear if this is a subsequent change—"approximately 60" agencies, but still maintains a definite article in its first paragraph. Clearly, there's confusion in agency land and the total has fluctuated during the writing of this book.

12   USA.gov. *A–Z Index of U.S. Government Departments and Agencies*. www .usa.gov/federal-agencies/a (137 agencies, 238 cabinet departments); National Archives. "Agencies." *Federal Register*, www.federalregister.gov/agencies (445 agencies as of Q3 2018).

13   *Opportunities to Reduce Fragmentation, Overlap, and Duplication and Achieve Other Financial Benefits: Statement of Gene L. Dodaro, Comptroller General of the United States*. GAO-14-478T, Government Accountability Office, 8 Apr. 2014, p. 16, www .gao.gov/assets/670/662380.txt ("no [] list of federal programs" noted in discussion re: need to improve executive agency performance and transparency). *Agency Actions Address Key Management Challenges, but Additional Steps Needed to Ensure Consistent Implementation of Policy Changes*. GAO-13-133R, Government Accountability Office, 29 Jan. 2013, p. 3, www.gao.gov/assets/660/651640 .pdf (noting out-of-scope/noncompliant work).

14   Administrative Conference of the United States. "What We Do." *News*, 28 Mar. 2013, www.acus.gov/.

15   Lewis, David E., and Jennifer L. Selin. *Sourcebook of United States Executive Agencies*. 1st ed., Administrative Conference of the United States, Office of the Chairman, 2012, www.acus.gov/sites/default/files/documents/Sourcebook-2012 -Final_12-Dec_Online.pdf. For FY 1995, the Administrative Conference's budget was $1.8 million compared to federal spending of $1.6 trillion; for FY 2018, the AC's budget request was $3.1 million, against a $4.1 trillion total budget request by the White House.

16   Hamburger, Philip. *The Administrative Threat*. Encounter Books, 2017, p 2. Hamburger's full critique, which I have used to inform the discussion, is available in his book *Is Administrative Law Unlawful?*, but *The Administrative Threat* is a faster read for the curious. Hamburger features precisely because he is one of the most articulate legal critics of bureaucracy.

17   *Ibid.*

18   *Ibid.*

19   Hamburger states that eighteenth-century Americans accepted judicial common-law "legislation."

20   E.g., *Goldberg v. Kelly*, 397 U.S. 254 n.10 (1970) (listing cases where full dress procedures not required before benefits termination, but noting that evidentiary hearing required to satisfy due process); *Matthews v. Eldridge*, 424 U.S. 319, Part II (1976).

21   Social Security Administration. "Information About SSA's Hearings and Appeals Operations." *Hearings and Appeals*, www.ssa.gov/appeals/about_us.html; Office of Retirement and Disability Policy, Social Security Administration. "Annual Statistical Report on the Social Security Disability Insurance Program, 2015 -

Outcomes of Applications for Disability Benefits." *Social Security Administration Research, Statistics, and Policy Analysis*, 2015, table 59.

22   E.g., *Goins v. Colvin*, 764 F. 3d 677 (2014).

23   Of the 2.8 million initial receipts, only ~18,500 matters will eventually be taken to district courts, less than 1% of the initial application pool and less than 5% of ALJ decisions. *See supra* note 21; Social Security Administration. *FY 2016 Congressional Justification.* 2016, www.ssa.gov/budget/FY16Files/2016FCJ.pdf at Table 3.27 and accompanying text (data for FY 2014).

24   *Goins v. Colvin*, 764 F. 3d 677 (7th Cir. 2014), pp. 678–679.

25   Eaglesham, Jean. "SEC Wins With In-House Judges." *Wall Street Journal*, 6 May 2015, www.wsj.com/articles/sec-wins-with-in-house-judges-1430965803 (analyzing outcomes from October 2010 to March 2015).

26   *Hamdi v. Rumsfeld*, 542 U.S. 507 (2004) (plurality opinion). *Hamdi*'s application is constrained by its peculiar facts, involving a U.S. citizen detained as an enemy combatant in allegedly wartime conditions, and the Court's "opinion" is a mess. *See also Rasul v. Bush*, 542 U.S. 446 (2004); *Hamdan v. Rumsfeld*, 548 U.S. 557 (2006) (questioning military commissions); *Boumediene v. Bush*, 553 U.S. 723 (2008). Synthesizing the cases and trends, it would *appear* that absent a full war and Congressional suspension of *habeas corpus* that most cases would be processed through something recognizable as a court. Note that military commissions fall outside of most administrative schemes, though this is a procedural, not Constitutional, issue. E.g., 5 USC §551(1)(F)-(G).

27   This would not be a complete solution; in addition to ALJs, agencies employ more numerous AJs, but one has to start somewhere.

28   Indeed, after *Lucia* and continued dysfunction at the highest levels of the bureaucracy, magistrates might become even more attractive on this basis.

29   Rulemaking authority is conferred by the Administrative Procedures Act, 5 U.S.C. §§ 551–569.

30   Harvard University maintains a list of environmental regulation rollbacks (and supporting documentation) in the turbulent Obama-to-Trump transition. *See* Harvard Environmental Law Program. n.d. "Regulatory Rollback Tracker." http://environment.law.harvard.edu/POLICY-INITIATIVE/REGULATORY -ROLLBACK-TRACKER/. (last accessed 1 Sep. 2017).

31   For a survey of the merits of formal rulemaking and an argument for its revival, see Nielson, Aaron L. "In Defense of Formal Rulemaking." *Ohio State Law Journal*, vol. 75, no. 2, 2014, pp. 238–292.

32   *Ibid.*, Part II.B.1.

33   For a good popular narrative, *see* Blitz, Matthew. "Why Midcentury Lawyers Spent 12 Years Arguing About Peanut Butter." *Atlas Obscura*, 14 Oct. 2015, www.atlasobscura.com/articles/why-midcentury-lawyers-spent-12-years -arguing-about-peanut-butter.

34   *United States v. Florida East Coast Railway*, 410 U.S. 224 (1973).

35   *Florida East Coast* essentially followed the Court's *sua sponte* sanctioning of notice and comment in *Allegheny-Ludlum*. For an historical review, *see* Barnett, Kent. "How the Supreme Court Derailed Formal Rulemaking." *The*

George Washington Law Review, vol. 85, no. 1, Jan. 2017, pp. 1, 2–4 (citation omitted).

36 Carey, Maeve P. *An Overview of Rulemaking, Types of Federal Regulations, and Pages in the Federal Register*. R43056, Congressional Research Service, 4 Oct. 2016, Tables 1, 6, fas.org/sgp/crs/misc/R43056.pdf (tabulating "final rule documents"); author's calculations.

37 California Sales and Use Tax Law of 1933, § 6359. I'm being slightly ambiguous about where I'm buying and eating this, which (sometimes) matters, subject to the 80/80 rule . . . about which—who cares?

38 *Ibid.*, (hot prepared foods and bundles).

39 California State Board of Equalization. "550.1712 Croissants." *Sales Tax and Use Annotations, Taxable Sales of Food Products—Regulation 1603*, www.boe .ca.gov/lawguides/business/current/btlg/vol2/suta/550-1712.html.

40 Weissman, William Hays. "Why Is Buying Hot Chocolate So Confusing?" *State Tax Notes*, 4 Dec. 2007, www.taxnotes.com/state-tax-today/harmonization-taxes/ why-buying-hot-chocolate-so-confusing/2007/12/04/3vn2?highlight=Why%20 is%20buying%20chocolate; California State Board of Equalization. "550.1715 Fresh Crab and Lobster." *Sales Tax and Use Annotations, Taxable Sales of Food Products—Regulation 1603*, http://www.boe.ca.gov/lawguides/business/current/ btlg/vol2/suta/550-1715.html.

41 Eskenazi, Joe. "Soup to Nuts: Crazy Food Taxes Penalize the Poor, Benefit the Rich." *SF Weekly*, 4 Apr. 2012, archives.sfweekly.com/sanfrancisco/soup-to -nuts-crazy-food-taxes-penalize-the-poor-benefit-the-rich/Content?oid=21 84608&showFullText=true; Weissman, William Hays. "Why Is Buying Hot Chocolate So Confusing?" *State Tax Notes*, 4 Dec. 2007, www.taxnotes.com /state-tax-today/harmonization-taxes/why-buying-hot-chocolate-so-confusing /2007/12/04/3vn2?highlight=Why%20is%20buying%20chocolate; Gore Grandrath, Anita. "California BOE Replies to Article About Taxation of Hot Chocolate." *State Tax Notes*, 12 Nov. 2008, www.taxnotes.com/state-tax-today/sales-and -use-taxation/california-boe-replies-article-about-taxation-hot-chocolate/2008 /11/12/3n4v?highlight=Why%20is%20buying%20chocolate; Weissman, William Hays. "Buying Hot Chocolate: The Answer Revealed." *State Tax Notes*, 12 Nov. 2008, www.taxnotes.com/state-tax-today/sales-and-use-taxation/buying-hot-chocolate -answer-revealed/2008/11/12/3pn9?highlight=Why%20is%20buying%20chocolate.

42 U.S. Office of Personnel Management. "Executive Branch Civilian Employment Since 1940." *Data, Analysis & Documentation: Federal Employement Reports, Historical Federal Workforce Tables*, www.opm.gov/policy-data-oversight/data -analysis-documentation/federal-employment-reports/historical-tables/ executive-branch-civilian-employment-since-1940. Excluding the Post Office and Defense Department, agency employment is up about 11% since 1978.

43 U.S. Environmental Protection Agency. *Fiscal Year 2016 Agency Financial Report*. 15 Nov. 2016, p. 27, www.epa.gov/sites/production/files/2016-11/docu ments/epa_fy_2016_afr_2.pdf.

44 *Environmental Performance Data and Metrics*. ECOS, 18 Sept. 2013, p. 1, www.ecos.org/wp-content/uploads/2016/02/ECOS-attachment-to-letter-on

-e-reporting.pdf. States and their subcontractors collect most of the data; the states are EPA's major grant recipients.

45   E.g., "Call Center: Contract management Needs Improvement to Reduce the Risk of Overbilling." Office of Inspector General, EPA, Report no. 15-P-0042, 23 Dec. 2014, p. 1; 8x8. *EPA Selects 8x8 Virtual Contact Centre for Call Centre Hotline.* www.8x8.com/au/resources/customers/outreach-process-partners.

46   Graham, John D., and James W. Broughel. "Stealth Regulation: Addressing Agency Evasion of OIRA and the Administrative Procedure Act." *Harvard Journal of Law and Public Policy: Federalist*, vol. 1, no. 1, 2014, pp. 25, 39–40. It's possible the IRS issued guidance with White House complicity. The blog post was eventually added to the *Federal Register*.

47   Executive Order 12866 § 3(f) (1993).

48   E.g., Office of the Secretary of Defense. *Part 199—Civilian Health and Medical Program of the Uniformed Services (Champus).* Government Publishing Office, 2017. www.gpo.gov/fdsys/pkg/CFR-2017-title32-vol2/pdf/CFR-2017-title32-vol2-part199.pdf. (civilian CHAMPUS program related to military; 313 pages); *Subchapter B—Medicare Program.* Government Publishing Office, 2017. www.gpo.gov/fdsys/pkg/CFR-2017-title42-vol2/pdf/CFR-2017-title42-vol2-part405.pdf. (Medicare, 190 pages).

49   *OMB's Role in Reviews of Agencies' Draft Rules and the Transparency of Those Reviews.* GAO-03-929, Government Accountability Office, Sept. 2003, p. 3, www.gao.gov/new.items/d03929.pdf (Bush II staffing levels of 55 FTEs); Office of Management and Budget. "About OIRA." *Regulation and Information*, obamawhitehouse.archives.gov/node/14989 (Obama staffing levels); *The White House*, https://www.whitehouse.gov/omb/information-regulatory-affairs/ (Trump staffing levels).

50   Brower, Kate Andersen. "How the Permanent White House Staff Welcomes a New First Family." *Time*, 12 Jan. 2017, time.com/4632665/kate-andersen-brower-white-house/.

51   *OMB's Role in Reviews of Agencies' Draft Rules and the Transparency of Those Reviews.* GAO-03-929, Government Accountability Office, Sept. 2003, p. 110, www.gao.gov/new.items/d03929.pdf.

52   Sunstein, Cass. "The Office of Information and Regulatory Affairs: Myths and Realities." *Harvard Law Review*, vol. 126, no. 7, May 2013, pp. 1838–40, 1862, 1872. Sunstein is highly reputable, but his piece is something a little more PR-inflected than mere scholarship and its internal contradictions, while minor, raise a few doubts. Moreover, his description covers the Obama era, and the various efforts toward transparency, cooperation, and workmanship seem to have disappeared in the Trump era—a shift that undermines some of Sunstein's assertions about OIRA's *institutional* character. OIRA itself makes few statements of its purposes or goals; a good example of OIRA's cryptic and unhelpful self-presentation is at: www.archives.gov/files/federal-register/write/conference/oira-overview.pdf.

53   Author's calculations based on "Regulatory Review Dashboard," Office of Information and Regulatory Affairs, https://www.reginfo.gov/public/jsp/EO/eoDashboard.jsp.

54   E.g., Tomkin, Shelley Lynne. *Inside OMB: Politics and Process in the President's Budget Office*, Routledge, (2015), pp. 206–16 (discussing OIRA in the Reagan Administration). The tenor of preconsultations varies by administration.

55   "Mrs. Gorsuch Pollutes The EPA." *New York Times*, 16 Feb. 1983, www .nytimes.com/1983/02/16/opinion/mrs-gorsuch-pollutes-the-epa.html (editorial); Shabecoff, Philip. "House Charges Head of E.P.A. with Contempt." *New York Times*, 17 Dec. 1982, www.nytimes.com/1982/12/17/us/house-charges -head-of-epa-with-contempt.html.

56   The key cases in agency deference follow. *Chevron U.S.A., Inc. v. Natural Resources Defense Council, Inc.*, 467 U.S. 837 (1984) (imposing the original *Chevron* test); *Auer v. Robbins*, 519 U.S. 452 (1997) (elaborating on deference, notably on agency's self-interpretation); *United States v. Mead Corp.*, 533 U.S. 218 (2001) (determining that *Chevron* should apply in various agency actions, not just rule-making, when agency uses delegated authority to impose policies with force of quasi-law); *Skidmore v. Swift & Co.*, 323 U.S. 134 (1944) (finding that agency interpretations receive deference related to "persuasiveness"). When *Chevron/ Mead* don't apply, agencies fall back on *Skidmore*, a less deferential standard. The remaining deference discussion forgoes citations, and presents my synthesis of the leading cases. If you've made it this far into the endnotes, you probably are also aware of *Petroleum Refiners, Seminole Rock*, etc., and are good to go.

57   *Compare* Breyer, Stephen. "Judicial Review of Questions of Law and Policy." *Administrative Law Review*, vol. 38, no. 4, 1986, pp. 363–98 *with* Scalia, Antonin. "Judicial Deference to Administrative Interpretations of Law." *Duke Law Journal*, vol. 1989, no. 3, June 1989, p. 511. Crossref, doi:10.2307/1372576.

58   Eskridge, William N., and Lauren Baer. "The Continuum of Deference: Supreme Court Treatment of Agency Statutory Interpretations from *Chevron* to *Hamdan*." *The Georgetown Law Journal*, vol. 96, no. 4, 2008, at §II.B and pp. 1125–1127; doi:10.2139/ssrn.1132368 (applying *Mead's* interpretation as benchmark). The upshot is that the Court can be pretty willy-nilly applying *Chevron*.

59   Miles, Thomas J., and Cass R. Sunstein. "Depoliticizing Administrative Law." *Duke Law Journal*, vol. 58, no. 8, 2009, pp. 2193–2230, Part I. Miles and Sunstein do not claim that partisanship is the sole driver—indeed, agencies tend to win about half the time even when fighting against presumed partisan inclination. Rather, they assert that partisan preference produces disparities in rates of validation.

60   States have considerably more constitutional leeway to do this, however, per *Prentis v. Atlantic Coast Line*. While a majority of states have explicit separation-of-powers clauses, many states contemplate or allow for administrative power. For example, Florida's constitution creates a fish and wildlife commission (an agency) with the power to "exercise the regulatory and executive powers" of the state. Fla. Const. art IV, § 9. Virginia's constitution says that powers are to be separate and then promptly goes on to say "provided, however, administrative agencies may be created by the General Assembly with such authorities and duties" as the state legislature designates. Va. Const. art. III, § 1; *see also* ibid., art. IX.

Chapter 6

1   "Roberts: 'My job is to call balls and strikes and not to pitch or bat.'" *CNN.com,* 12 Sept. 2005, www.cnn.com/2005/POLITICS/09/12/roberts.statement/.
2   E.g., Fed. R. Evid. 607–609.
3   *See* 28 U.S.C. §§ 2071–77; Duff, James C. "Overview for the Bench, Bar, and Public." U.S., www.uscourts.gov/rules-policies/about-rulemaking-process/how -rulemaking-process-works/overview-bench-bar-and-public. Each subcommittee contains a judge, and judges have final say before rules requiring legislative enactment are transmitted to Congress. Courts also set their own "Local Rules," etc., under § 2071, state analogues, and courts' inherent management powers.
4   28 U.S.C. § 20711 *et seq.* (delegating to the Supreme Court/Judicial Conference the power to draft rules governing the business of federal courts, subject to conformity with acts of Congress); 28 U.S.C. § 331.
5   "Roberts: 'My Job...'" *Ibid.*
6   *See* U.S. Constitution, art. III, § 2.
7   Avila, Jim, and Glenn Ruppel. "Lawyer Freed After Longest-Ever Term for Contempt." *ABC News,* 17 July 2009, abcnews.go.com/2020/story?id=8101209 &page=1.
8   *Impeachments of Federal Judges.* Federal Judicial Center, www.fjc.gov/history/ judges/impeachments-federal-judges. Not all those impeached were convicted by the Senate.
9   The justices of state supreme courts generally enjoy terms of at least 6 years, with 8–12 year terms being fairly common, compared to terms of 4 years for governors; states use a mix of elections, appointments followed by retention elections, and appointments depending on the state and court. Federal Reserve governors are the only officials whose offices are nearly as potent and long-lived as those of judges. National Center for State Courts. "Selection of Judges." *Methods of Judicial Selection,* judicialselection.us/judicial_selection/methods/selection _of_judges.cfm?state=; The Federal Reserve. "Board Members." Board of Governors of the Federal Reserve System, www.federalreserve.gov/aboutthefed/bios/ board/default.htm.
10 Smith, Brendan. "Legislative Efforts Requiring Judges to Hold JD Meet with Mixed Results." *ABA Journal,* July 2011, www.abajournal.com/%20magazine/ article/is_there_a_lawyer_in_the_court/; Malega, Ron, and Thomas H. Cohen. *State Court Organization, 2011.* NCJ 242850, U.S. Department of Justice, Officer of Justice Programs, Bureau of Justice Statistics, Nov. 2013, p. 5, www.bjs.gov/ content/pub/pdf/sco11.pdf. (trial courts).
11 E.g., Supplesa, Mark. "Who Is Judging the Judges? Issues of Qualification." *WGN,* 2 Dec. 2013, wgntv.com/2013/12/02/who-is-judging-the-judges-issues-of -qualification/ (Illinois judge rated "unqualified" by local bar group; others submitted no qualifications whatsoever); Greenwood, Max. "Bar Association dubs fourth Trump judicial nominee unqualified." *The Hill,* 7 Nov. 2017, the hill.com/blogs/blog-briefing-room/news/359234-american-bar-association -dubs-fourth-trump-judicial-nominee; Main, Frank. "2 Major Bar Associations

Find Longtime Judge Unqualified." *Chicago Sun-Times*, 4 Nov. 2016, chicago
.suntimes.com/chicago-politics/2-major-bar-associations-find-longtime-judge
-unqualified/.

12　Taylor, Jessica. "Roy Moore, Culture Warrior, Will Be Favored to Be the Next U.S.
Senator from Alabama." *NPR.org*, 27 Sep. 2017, www.npr.org/2017/09/27/553856901/
roy-moore-s-long-controversial-history-in-alabama-politics.

13　Until the very late nineteenth century, it was common for even prominent attorneys to apprentice without taking a law degree, and several prominent Supreme
Court Justices in the early Republic lacked law degrees. The last Justice without a law degree was Stanley Forman Reed, who retired in early 1957; the last
to be appointed without a degree was Robert Jackson. *See* Smith, J.Y. "Retired
Supreme Court Justice Stanley Reed Dies at 95." *Washington Post*, 4 Apr. 1980.
www.washingtonpost.com/archive/local/1980/04/04/retired-supreme-court
-justice-stanley-reed-dies-at-95/7781e22a-4142-4652-a49e-2df404a0faed/.

14　Smith, Allan. "Trump is bypassing judicial ratings agencies before making his nominations—and it has led to a substantial increase in 'not qualified'
nominees." *Business Insider*, 15 Nov. 2017, www.businessinsider.de/trump-judicial
-nominees-increase-in-aba-not-qualified-ratings-2017-11.

15　*Ibid.*

16　Posner, Richard A. *Reflections on Judging.* Harvard University Press, 2013,
pp. 32–33 and Chapter 1 generally. Posner self-educated in the months prior to
taking the bench, but not all incoming judges can or do.

17　The Federal Judicial Center. *Education and Research for the U.S. Federal Courts.*
2014, www.fjc.gov/sites/default/files/2015/About-FJC-English-2014-10-07.pdf.

18　Department of Consumer Affairs. "Frequently Asked Questions." *California
Board of Barbering and Cosmetology,* www.barbercosmo.ca.gov/forms_pubs/
publications/faqs.shtml#ae1.

19　State of Nevada. *State of Nevada Judicial Education Requirement.* nvcourts
.gov/AOC/Programs_and_Services/Judicial_Education/Overview/. *See* Judicial
Education Requirements at Appendix A.

20　The National Judicial College. *Ethics, Fairness, and Security in Your Court and Community.* 20 July 2015, www.judges.org/ethics-fairness-security-in-your-court
-and-community-1610/.

21　École Nationale de la Magistrature. *Étudiants.* 2018, www.enm.justice.fr/?q
=Devenir-magistrat-etudiants. Numerically, the largest number of French judicial trainees take the first *concours*, which requires a "BAC +4," though about
75% have a Master's II—i.e., most candidates have what amounts to (in rough
terms) an American Master's degree. Conseil d'Administration. *Rapport du pré-
sident du jury des concours d'accès 2016.* 27 Feb. 2017, p. 21, www.enm.justice
.fr/sites/default/files/rub-devenir-magistrat/Rapport-president-du-jury-acces
-2016.pdf. For a brief overview in English, *see* École Nationale de la Magistrature. *National School for the Judiciary.* 2017, www.enm.justice.fr/sites/default/
files/publications/plaquette2017_EN.pdf. *See also Décret no 72-355 du mai 4
1972 relatif á l'Ecole nationale de la magistrature.* Waivers, especially for highly
specialized courts or for "internal" recruits drawn from public service, are possible but represent a minority of candidates.

22 E.g., *The French Legal System*. Ministry of Justice (France), Nov. 2012, p. 5, www .justice.gouv.fr/art_pix/french_legal_system.pdf. *See also* Malleson, Kate, and Peter H. Russell, editors. *Appointing Judges in an Age of Judicial Power: Critical Perspectives from around the World*. 1st edition, University of Toronto Press, Scholarly Publishing Division, 2006, pp. 176–195. I've simplified the rather baroque process and there are exceptions (e.g., small claims). The most notable exception is France's Constitutional Council, a not-quite-Supreme Court, which includes members appointed by legislators plus ex-presidents. Not all presidents sit for long, or at all; then again, judging doesn't have the same prestige in France as in America.

23 *See generally* Malleson, Kate, and Peter H. Russell, editors. *Appointing Judges in an Age of Judicial Power: Critical Perspectives from around the World*. 1st edition, University of Toronto Press, Scholarly Publishing Division, 2006.

24 Judicial Appointments Commission. *Qualifying Tests*. Judicial Appointments Commission, jac.judiciary.gov.uk/qualifying-tests. Tests are used for short-listing.

25 *Appellate and General Jurisdiction Courts*. American Judicature Society, 2013, web.archive.org/web/20141208194400/www.judicialselection.us/uploads/documents/Judicial_Selection_Charts_1196376173077.pdf; Lim, Claire S. H., and James M. Snyder. "Is More Information Always Better? Party Cues and Candidate Quality in U.S. Judicial Elections." *Journal of Public Economics*, vol. 128, Aug. 2015, pp. 107–123. *ScienceDirect*, DOI:10.1016/j.jpubeco.2015.04.006 (noting in partisan identified elections that party drives votes over candidates' quality).

26 Powell, Jr., Lewis Franklin. "Attack on American Free Enterprise System." *Supreme Court History: Law, Power, and Personality, Primary Sources*, www .thirteen.org/wnet/supremecourt/personality/sources_document13 .html; Greenhouse, Linda. "Black Robes Don't Make the Justice, but the Rest of the Closet Just Might." *New York Times*, 4 Dec. 2002. www.nytimes .com/2002/12/04/us/black-robes-don-t-make-the-justice-but-the-rest-of-the -closet-just-might.html. To varying degrees, Powell's views mutated on the bench.

27 Savage, Charlie. "Poor Vetting Sinks Trump's Nominees for Federal Judge." *New York Times*, 18 Dec. 2017. *NYTimes.com*, www.nytimes.com/2017/12/18/us/ politics/matthew-petersen-judge-nominee-withdraws-trump.html.

28 E.g., *NRA-PVF Endorsement Policy*. NRA Institute for Legislative Action, 11 May 2010, www.nraila.org/articles/20100511/nra-pvf-endorsement-policy (NRA's general endorsement policies, noting occasional endorsement of judicial candidates); Corriher, Billy. *NRA Working to Elect Pro-Gun Judges and Prosecutors*. Center for American Progress, 14 Feb. 2013, www.americanprogress.org/issues/ courts/news/2013/02/14/53076/nra-working-to-elect-pro-gun-judges-and -prosecutors/ (a left-leaning site, though reliable, and providing links to NRA's tax filings as evidence); Kumar, Anita. "NRA Freedom Action Foundation Buys TV Ads to Tout Guns Ahead of Supreme Court Hearing." *McclatchyDC*, 14 Mar. 2017, www.mcclatchydc.com/news/politics-government/congress/arti cle138273388.html. The NRA's ads just happened to air the week of Gorsuch's

confirmation hearings, and emphasized that a new Justice could provide a decisive gun rights vote.

29   Epstein, Lee, et al. "Ideological Drift among Supreme Court Justices: Who, When, and How Important." *Northwestern University Law Review*, vol. 101, no. 4, 2007, pp. 1483–1582, figs. 5, 7. Berkeley Law Scholarship Repository, scholarship.law.berkeley.edu/cgi/viewcontent.cgi?article=2999&context=facpubs.

30   E.g., Barnes, Robert. "Federalist Society, White House Cooperation on Judges Paying Benefits." *Washington Post*, 18 Nov. 2017, https://www.washingtonpost.com/politics/courts_law/federalist-society-white-house-cooperation-on-judges-paying-benefits/2017/11/18/4b69b4da-cb20-11e7-8321-481fd63f174d_story.html; Wheeler, Lydia. "Meet the Powerful Group behind Trump's Judicial Nominations." *The Hill*, 16 Nov. 2017, thehill.com/regulation/court-battles/360598-meet-the-powerful-group-behind-trumps-judicial-nominations.

31   *Supreme Court Justice Neil Gorsuch's Speech at Trump's D.C. Hotel Draws Criticism.* NPR. Interview by Ailsa Chang, 28 Sept. 2017, www.npr.org/2017/09/28/554331346/supreme-court-justice-neil-gorsuchs-speech-at-trumps-d-c-hotel-met-with-criticis; Fahrenthold, David A., and Jonathan O'Connell. "D.C., Maryland Can Proceed with Lawsuit Alleging Trump Violated Emoluments Clauses." *Washington Post*, 28 Mar. 2018, www.washingtonpost.com/politics/dc-maryland-may-proceed-with-lawsuit-alleging-trump-violated-emoluments-clause/2018/03/28/0514d816-32ae-11e8-8bdd-cdb33a5eef83_story.html.

32   Epstein, Lee, William N. Landes, and Richard A. Posner. *The Behavior of Federal Judges: A Theoretical and Empirical Study of Rational Choice.* Harvard University Press, 2013, pp. 361, 376–379. Being tough on capital/street crimes is audition material; the same does not hold clearly for white-collar crimes. Data for district court judges are less clear (possibly because self-fulfilling filtering removes some judges from the auditioner pool), but Epstein et al. suggest the dynamic still holds.

33   Purdy, Jedediah. "Scalia's Contradictory Originalism." *New Yorker*, 16 Feb. 2016. www.newyorker.com/news/news-desk/scalias-contradictory-originalism; Posner, Richard A. "The Incoherence of Antonin Scalia." *The New Republic*, 23 Aug. 2012, newrepublic.com/article/106441/scalia-garner-reading-the-law-textual-originalism.

34   Basic Law Arts. 93, 95(1). The Basic Law is functionally Germany's constitution. Depending on how one counts, Germany could be described as having six high courts.

35   E.g., Judiciary Act of 1891 (partial control); Judiciary Act of 1925 (expanding control); Supreme Court Case Selections Act of 1988 (deleting appeals as of right from state supreme courts). State courts often call the process a writ of review or leave to appeal.

36   This is more important if there are persuadable/swing votes for any given case.

37   Spaeth, Harold J., et al. The Supreme Court Database, Version 2017 Release 01. supremecourtdatabase.org. *See also* Supreme Court of the United States. "The Justices' Caseload." *About the Court*, www.supremecourt.gov/about/justicecaseload.aspx; Lane, Elizabeth A., and Ryan C. Black. "Agenda Setting and Case Selection on the U.S. Supreme Court." *Oxford Research Encyclopedia of Politics*, Dec. 2017. *politics.oxfordre.com*, doi:10.1093/acrefore/9780190228637.013.91. The

Court sifts through several thousand cases annually, but only renders decisions in a fraction of them: about 80 receive plenary review, and about 100 more are disposed of without plenary review.

38   Kashino, Marisa M. "Ruth Bader Ginsburg Presides Over the Divorce Proceedings of Claudio and Hero." *Washingtonian*, 1 May 2012, www.washingtonian.com /2012/05/01/ruth-bader-ginsburg-presides-over-the-divorce-proceedings -of-claudio-and-hero/. Granted that Justice Ginsburg is a famed workaholic; the same reputation hasn't stuck to some of her colleagues.

39   Author's calculations; Schauffler, Richard Y., et al. *Examining the Work of State Courts: An Overview of 2015 State Courts Caseloads*. Court Statistics Project, National Center for State Courts, 2016, pp. 1,3, 11, 13, 17, www.courtstatistics .org/~/media/Microsites/Files/CSP/EWSC%202015.ashx. and data set available at www.courtstatistics.org. Traffic offenses count for just over half of cases filed in state court; "larger cases" refers to the subset of cases including felonies, domestic relations, and civil matters other than small claims and are calculated using the NCSC's data, assuming (for felonies) that the states reporting more detailed criminal data are representative of the nation. Malega, Ron, and Thomas H. Cohen. *State Court Organization, 2011*. NCJ 242850, U.S. Department of Justice, Officer of Justice Programs, Bureau of Justice Statistics, Nov. 2013, p. 4, www.bjs.gov/content/pub/pdf/sco11.pdf. There are about 28,000 trial court judges of general and limited jurisdiction plus various lesser quasi-judicial officials.

40   *Authorized Judgeships—From 1789 to Present*. U.S. Courts 2017, www.uscourts .gov/sites/default/files/allauth.pdf; see *also* "Judicial Caseload Indicators—Federal Judicial Caseload Statistics 2017." *United States Courts*, 31 Mar. 2017, www.uscourts .gov/judicial-caseload-indicators-federal-judicial-caseload-statistics-2017.;   "U.S. District Courts—Judicial Business 2016." *United States Courts*, 2016, Table 3, www .uscourts.gov/statistics-reports/us-district-courts-judicial-business-2016.

41   Appeals rates vary by case type, one case can result in more than one appeal, and many appeals are not pursued (or at the Supreme Court, are not filed with any realistic hope of being granted cert), but the range is reasonable. Without tracking case by case, but calculating based on the raw number of district court filings, lodged appeals, and times to disposition, yields gross appeal rates of ~14% for 2012–2015. *See* "Federal Court Management Statistics [various years]." *United States Courts*, www.uscourts.gov/statistics-reports/analysis-reports/federal-court -management-statistics. Scholars examining granular data find appeals rates of ~11% (for 1988–2000). Eisenberg, Theodore, "Appeal Rates and Outcomes in Tried and Nontried Cases: Further Exploration of Anti-Plaintiff Appellate Outcomes," *Journal of Empirical Legal Studies*, Vol. 1, Issue 3, 2004, pp. 569–688. *See also* Neubauer, David W., and Henry F. Fradella. *America's Courts and the Criminal Justice System*. 11th edition, Wadsworth Publishing, 2013, p. 68 and Chapter 3 generally. For Supreme Court caseloads, *see also* Supreme Court of the United States. "The Justices' Caseload." *About the Court*, www.supremecourt .gov/about/justicecaseload.aspx. For judgeships, see *Authorized Judgeships— From 1789 to Present*. U.S. Courts 2017, www.uscourts.gov/sites/default/files/ allauth.pdf.

42 Author's personal knowledge. *See also*, e.g., Lat, David. "Clerkship Hiring Is Getting Earlier and Earlier." *Above the Law*, 11 Apr. 2013, abovethelaw.com/2013/04/clerkship-hiring-is-getting-earlier-and-earlier/.

43 Posner, Richard A. *Reforming the Federal Judiciary: My Former Court Needs to Overhaul Its Staff Attorney Program and Begin Televising Its Oral Arguments*. CreateSpace Independent Publishing Platform, 2017, p. 6 and Chapters 1, 5, and 7 *generally*. Posner focuses on his old Circuit, the 7th, but there's no reason to believe the phenomenon isn't widespread; certainly, personal knowledge suggests that it's everywhere.

44 Resnik, Judith. "Managerial Judges." *Harvard Law Review*, vol. 96, no. 2, Dec. 1982, pp. 374, 478. *Crossref*, doi:10.2307/1340797. Some judges did wear wigs after Independence, but were publicly abused and soon dropped the headgear.

45 Greenhouse, Linda. "The Chief Justice Has New Clothes." *New York Times*, 22 Jan. 1995. *NYTimes.com*, www.nytimes.com/1995/01/22/weekinreview/ideas-trends-the-chief-justice-has-new-clothes.html.

46 Green, Miranda. "Renowned Appeals Court Judge Facing Claims of Inappropriate Sexual Conduct." *CNN*, 9 Dec. 2017, www.cnn.com/2017/12/09/politics/alex-kozinksi-accusations/index.html; Berman, Dan, and Laura Jarrett. "Judge Alex Kozinski, Accused of Sexual Misconduct, Resigns." *CNN*, 18 Dec. 2017, www.cnn.com/2017/12/18/politics/alex-kozinski-resigns/index.html.

47 *See infra*, Chapters 7 and 9. Galanter, Marc. "The Vanishing Trial: An Examination of Trials and Related Matters in Federal and State Courts." *Journal of Empirical Legal Studies*, vol. 1, no. 3, Nov. 2004, pp. 459–570. *Crossref*, doi:10.1111/j.1740-1461.2004.00014.x. *Combined Civil and Criminal Federal Court Management Statistics (December 31, 2016)*. U.S. Courts, 31 Dec. 2016, www.uscourts.gov/statistics/table/na/federal-court-management-statistics/2016/12/31-1. *See also* Refo, Patricia Lee. "Opening Statement: The Vanishing Trial." *Litigation*, vol. 30, no. 1, Winter 2004. A rise in junk suits, tenuous civil rights/prisoner/pro se claims, etc., have also been cited, but even to the extent those explanations are true, they are only *partial*.

48 *Combined Civil and Criminal Federal Court Management Statistics (December 31, 2017)*. United States Courts, 31 Dec. 2017, http://www.uscourts.gov/sites/default/files/fcms_na_distprofile1231.2017.pdf.

49 *Civil Case Processing in the Federal District Courts: A 21st Century Analysis*. Institute for the Advancement of the American Legal System, University of Denver, 2009, p. 4, www.uscourts.gov/sites/default/files/iaals_civil_case_processing_in_the_federal_district_courts_0.pdf.

50 *Combined Civil and Criminal Federal Court Management Statistics (December 31, 2016)*. United States Courts, 31 Dec. 2016, www.uscourts.gov/statistics/table/na/federal-court-management-statistics/2016/12/31-1.

51 *Civil Case Processing in the Federal District Courts: A 21st Century Analysis*. Institute for the Advancement of the American Legal System, University of Denver, 2009, p.4, www.uscourts.gov/sites/default/files/iaals_civil_case_processing_in_the_federal_district_courts_0.pdf.

52 *Ibid.*, pp. 4–5.

53 *United States v. Tigano*, Docket No. 15-3073 (2nd Cir. 2018).

54 Fed R. Civ. Pro. 8(a)(2). The Supreme Court refined pleading standards in the *Twiqbal* cases, discussed *infra*. *Bell Atlantic v. Twombly*, 550 U.S. 544 (2007); *Ashcroft v. Iqbal*, 556 U.S. 662 (2009).

55 E.g., Fed R. Civ. Pro. 12(b)(6).

56 Cecil, Joe S., et al. *Motions to Dismiss for Failure to State a Claim After Iqbal: Report to the Judicial Conference Advisory Committee on Civil Rules*. Federal Judicial Center, Mar. 2011, pp. 8, 13–14. *U.S. Courts*, www.uscourts.gov/sites/default/files/motioniqbal_1.pdf (measuring motions brought within 90 days of initial filing). Totals measuring full case lifecycles would be higher.

57 Cecil, Joe, et al. *Trends in Summary Judgment Practice: 1975–2000*. Federal Judicial Center, 2007, p. 8, www.uscourts.gov/sites/default/files/summary_judgment_1975-2000.pdf.

58 *The Death Penalty in Alabama: Judge Override*. Equal Justice Initiative, July 2011, eji.org/sites/default/files/death-penalty-in-alabama-judge-override.pdf; "Alabama Ends Death Penalty by Judicial Override." *US News & World Report*, 11 Apr. 2017, www.usnews.com/news/best-states/alabama/articles/2017-04-11/alabama-ends-death-penalty-by-judicial-override.

59 Posner, Richard A. *Reflections on Judging*. Harvard University Press, 2013. *See especially* Chapter 4 (distinguishing between "formalist" and "realist" appellate judicial models).

60 Posner, Richard A. *Reflections on Judging*. Harvard University Press, 2013, Chapter 4 and *generally*.

61 "Full transcript of Trump press conference." BBC. 16 Feb. 2017, https://www.bbc.com/news/world-us-canada-38987938; Trump, Donald J. "…. The Ninth Circuit, Which Has a Terrible Record of Being Overturned (Close to 80%). They Used to Call This 'Judge Shopping!' Messy System." *@realDonaldTrump*, 26 Apr. 2017, https://twitter.com/realDonaldTrump/status/857182179469774848; Hannity, Sean. "As predicted, 9th Circuit—the most radical left wing ct & the most overturned Ct in the country, upholds suspension of Exec order." *@seanhannity*, 9 Feb. 2017, https://twitter.com/seanhannity/status/829840155469107206.

62 Hofer, Roy. "Supreme Court Reversal Rates: Evaluating the Federal Court of Appeals." *Landslide*, vol. 2, no. 3, Feb. 2010, Table 2, www.americanbar.org/content/dam/aba/migrated/intelprop/magazine/LandslideJan2010_Hofer.authcheckdam.pdf. The Ninth Circuit has long had a high reversal rate—but not always the highest. At the time Trump spoke, the Sixth Circuit held that honor, and the Sixth is composed entirely of states Trump carried and where a majority of judges were appointed by Republicans. Kantor, Alice, et al. "What Are Real Facts about the 9th Circuit?" *CNN*, 27 Apr. 2017, www.cnn.com/2017/04/27/politics/trump-ninth-circuit/index.html.

63 Lee, Michelle Ye Hee. "Are 80 Percent or 0.1 Percent of the 9th Circuit Court's Decisions Overturned?" *Washington Post*, 21 Mar. 2017, www.washingtonpost.com/news/fact-checker/wp/2017/03/21/does-the-9th-circuit-court-overturn-80-percent-or-0-1-percent-of-its-cases/.

64 Hofer, Roy. "Supreme Court Reversal Rates: Evaluating the Federal Court of Appeals." *Landslide*, vol. 2, no. 3, Feb. 2010, Table 3, www.americanbar.org/content/dam/aba/migrated/intelprop/magazine/LandslideJan2010_Hofer

.authcheckdam.pdf. Figures are for reversed/vacated. These numbers can be sliced and diced various ways, but as noted, they're not that meaningful, not by themselves.

65 E.g., "Just the Facts: U.S. Courts of Appeal," Administrative Office of U.S. Courts, 20 Dec. 2016, Table 2, www.uscourts.gov/news/2016/12/20/just-facts-us-courts-appeals#table2. Figures would be lower still factoring in bankruptcy courts.

66 E.g., *Jorgensen v. Cassiday,* 320 F.ed 906, 913 (9th Cir. 2003) (discussing "broad discretion" regarding case management); *Southern California Edison v. Lynch,* 307 F.3d 794, 807 (9th Cir. 2002) (noting limitations imposed by due process on discretionary docket management).

67 "Abuse of discretion" applies, *inter alia,* in these contexts: *Sprint/United Mgmt. Co. v. Mendelsohn,* 128 S. Ct. 1140, 1145 (2008) (discussing, in case of ambiguous per se ruling, evidentiary rulings under FRE 401, 403) (citation omitted); *Facebook, Inc. v. Power Ventures, Inc.* 844 F.3d 1058, 1070 (9th Cir. 2016), *cert. denied* 138 S. Ct. 313 (2017) (applying standard to discovery sanctions and noting that discovery generally is reviewed at the same standard) (citation omitted); *Dorn v. Burlington N. Santa Fe R.R.,* 387 F.3d 1183, 1192 (9th Cir. 2005) (applying standard to decision regarding scope of cross-examination, though finding abuse in the instant case); *Kayes v. Pacific Lumber Co.* 51 F.3d 1449, 1464 (9th Cir. 1995) (applying standard to dismissal of counsel).

68 E.g., *Kirola v. City & County of San Francisco,* 860 F.3d 1164, 1178-82 (9th Cir. 2017) (credibility determination reviewed for clear error); *Allen v. Iranon,* 283 F.3d 1070, 1078 n.8 (such findings entitled to special deference).

69 The work of Amos Tversky and Daniel Kahneman are the classics in the literature of cognitive bias. A good summary is provided in Daniel Kahneman's *Thinking Fast and Slow* (2013), which provides further references to the academic literature.

70 Danziger, Shai, et al. "Extraneous Factors in Judicial Decisions." *Proceedings of the National Academy of Sciences of the United States of America*, vol. 108, no. 17, 2011, pp. 6889–6892. *PNAS,* www.pnas.org/content/pnas/108/17/6889.full.pdf.

71 Federal Judicial Center. "Demography of Article III Judges, 1789–2017." *Exhibits,* 2017, www.fjc.gov/history/exhibits/graphs-and-maps/demography-article-iii-judges-1789-2017-introduction. Data are for Article III active as of 2017.

72 Sen, Maya. "Is Justice Really Blind? Race and Reversal in US Courts." *Journal of Legal Studies,* vol. 44, Jan. 2015, p. 43, Parts 4, 5. Different studies, with different emphases, find other variables more important and race itself not statistically significant. E.g., Posner, Richard, et al. *The Behavior of Federal Judges: A Theoretical and Empirical Study of Rational Choice.* Harvard University Press, 2013, pp. 223–25. Sen controls for quality, partisanship, etc., and still finds differences; Posner et al. note insignificant variance. For the impact of judicial race on certain case dispositions, *see,* e.g., Cox, Adam B., and Thomas J. Miles. "Judging the Voting Rights Act." *Columbia Law Review,* vol. 108, no. 1, 2008, p. 55 (noting black judges twice as likely to favor liability under VRA); Kastellec, Jonathan P. "Racial Diversity and Judicial Influence on Appellate Courts." *American Journal of Political Science,* vol. 57, no. 1, Jan. 2013, pp. 167–183. *Crossref,*

doi:10.1111/j.1540-5907.2012.00618.x (noting, in context of appellate panel influence, effect of black judges favoring affirmative action programs). The literature on race and judging is mixed and incomplete due to the relatively limited number of minority judges with long records, and most work has associated race with particular issues. The number of confounding variables is large (especially as the first major wave of minority judges was associated with Democratic appointment).

73   Data are for Article III judges only and includes senior status judges. Federal Judicial Center. "Demography of Article III Judges, 1789–2017." *Exhibits*, 2017, www.fjc.gov/history/exhibits/graphs-and-maps/demography-article-iii-judges -1789-2017-introduction; *see also* Centers for Disease Control and Prevention, National Center for Health Statistics. "Death Rates and Life Expectancy at Birth." 9 June 2018. *Data.gov*, catalog.data.gov/dataset/age-adjusted-death -rates-and-life-expectancy-at-birth-all-races-both-sexes-united-sta-1900. Author's calculation. Adjusting for socioeconomic and other variables brings judicial life expectancy into closer alignment, but this simply reflects another judicial difference: they're richer and more educated than average, factors associated with longer life expectancy. The Congressional Research Service also provides occasional updates on this subject.

74   ProPublica. "Life Tenure for Federal Judges Raises Issues of Senility." *ProPublica*, 18 Jan. 2011, www.propublica.org/article/life-tenure-for-federal-judges -raises-issues-of-senility-dementia.

75   Data are for Article III judges only. Federal Judicial Center. "Biographical Directory of Article III Federal Judges: Export." 2018, www.fjc.gov/history/ judges/biographical-directory-article-iii-federal-judges-export. The filename is "Federal Judicial Service." Between January 1990 and July 2018, the FJC data show 67% of Article III commissions "terminated" by death. However, 90% of those who died had taken senior status, muting the impact. Final termination by death after the 1990s is slightly higher than before; with senior status likely pushing up contemporary death numbers just as unexpected deaths pushed up departures in the era before modern gerontology.

76   Sulzberger, A.G. "Wesley E. Brown, Oldest Judge in Nation's History, Dies at 104." *New York Times*, 25 Jan. 2012. *NYTimes.com*, www.nytimes.com/2012/ 01/26/us/wesley-e-brown-oldest-judge-in-nations-history-dies-at-104.html; Sylvester, Ron. "Federal Judge Wesley Brown Dies at Age 104 in Wichita." *The Wichita Eagle*, 24 Jan. 2012, www.kansas.com/news/local/crime/article1084960 .html.

77   Wheeler, Russell. "Changing Backgrounds of U.S. District Judges: Likely Causes and Possible Implications." *Judicature*, vol. 93, no. 4, Feb. 2010, www.brookings.edu/ wp-content/uploads/2016/06/02_district_judges_wheeler.pdf; Wheeler, Russell. *Judicial Nominations and Confirmations In Obama's First Term*, Brookings Institution, 13 Dec. 2012, www.brookings.edu/wp-content/uploads/2016/06/13_obama _judicial_wheeler.pdf. Standard vocational analyses focus on position immediately prior (or within one year) of appointment. Biographical Directory of Article III Federal Judges, 1789–Present, Federal Judicial Center, https://www.fjc.gov/history/ judges/search/advanced-search; author's calculations. *See infra*, note 78.

78 *Ibid.*; McMillion, Barry. *U.S. Circuit Court and District Court Judges: Profile of Select Characteristics*. R43426, Congressional Research Service, 1 Aug. 2017, figs. 8, 16, https://fas.org/sgp/crs/misc/R43426.pdf.

79 Wheeler, Russell. "Changing Backgrounds of U.S. District Judges: Likely Causes and Possible Implications." *Judicature*, vol. 93, no. 4, Feb. 2010, www .brookings.edu/wp-content/uploads/2016/06/02_district_judges_wheeler.pdf; Wheeler, Russell. *Judicial Nominations and Confirmations In Obama's First Term*, Brookings Institution, 13 Dec. 2012, www.brookings.edu/wp-content/ uploads/2016/06/13_obama_judicial_wheeler.pdf. Standard vocational analyses focus on position immediately prior (or within one year) of appointment.

80 "Broader finance" refers to "FIRE" industries—financial, insurance, lending, and real estate. A narrower definition of finance produces about 5–8% of GDP on a value-add basis.

81 Kagan was Solicitor General, a position often referred to as the "Tenth Justice." She had also been nominated to an appellate court, but the nomination lapsed, and she went on to Harvard Law.

82 Of sitting Justices, only Thomas had a long career in the executive, as head of the EEOC. Other recent Justices have executive branch experience, but tenures have tended to be much less prominent than those of Stone or Jackson, to say nothing of Taft, Warren, etc. Note that some prior Justices served only briefly in their highest positions in the executive, though many had substantial careers just below the top.

83 *Sutton v. Hutchinson*, 2005 EWCA Civ 1773. Justice Ward was, of course, being lightly humorous.

84 *Sutton v. Hutchinson, ibid.*

85 Totenberg, Nina. "Behind the Marble." *New York Times*, 16 Mar. 1975. *NYTimes.com*, www.nytimes.com/1975/03/16/archives/behind-the-marble-beneath-the-robes -supreme-court.html.

86 Associated Press. "Kagan: Court Hasn't 'Gotten to' Email." *Politico*, 20 Aug. 2013, www.politico.com/story/2013/08/kagan-supreme-court-email-095724.

87 *City of Ontario, California, et al. v. Jeff Quon, et al.* 08-1332, 19 Apr. 2010, www .supremecourt.gov/oral_arguments/argument_transcripts/2009/08-1332.pdf.

88 *United States v. Brima Wurie.* 13–212, 29 Apr. 2014 (oral argument), www .supremecourt.gov/oral_arguments/argument_transcripts/2013/13-212 _d1o2.pdf.

89 *United States v. Brima Wurie. Ibid.*

90 Cohen, Julie, and Besty West. *RBG*, Magnolia Pictures, 2018.

91 *American Broadcasting Corp. v. Aereo, Inc.* No. 13-461, 14 Apr. 2014 (Supreme Court oral argument transcript), p. 12 (the "iDrop"), p. 35 (HBO conflated with broadcast); *Alice v. CLS Bank*, No. 13-398 (Supreme Court oral argument transcript), p. 12 (coders). Frequently, it's hard to tell what's actually going on and the Justices sometimes strike a pose, but there are just too many "poses" to dismiss.

92 *See*, e.g., Cohen, Joel. *Blindfolds Off: Judges on How They Decide.* American Bar Association, 2014. Foreword (by Judge Richard Posner) (focusing on judicial secrecy and "self-deception," and noting also "autonomy," "pretense of

impartiality," "mystification" (jargon), and political sensitivities). Other opinions are my own, including the term "arrogance."

93   Zapotosky, Matt. "Nine More Women Say Judge Subjected Them to Inappropriate Behavior, Including Four Who Say He Touched or Kissed Them." *The Washington Post*,www.washingtonpost.com/world/national-security/nine-more -women-say-judge-subjected-them-to-inappropriate-behavior-including-four -who-say-he-touched-or-kissed-them/2017/12/15/8729b736-e105-11e7-8679 -a9728984779c_story.html?utm_term=.4b091947cbcc.

Chapter 7

1   Gompers, Samuel. "The Samuel Gompers Papers: The Early Years of the American Federation of Labor 1887–90" Vol 2, (Stuart B. Kaufman, ed.) University of Illinois Press, p. 87 (1987).

2   "Verdict's In: 'Judge Judy' Tops in 2016–17." *TVNewsCheck*, 6 Sept. 2017, www .tvnewscheck.com/article/107030/verdicts-in-judge-judy-tops-in-201617.

3   Minimum number of *Judge Judy* cases based on author's calculations based on 22 seasons through 2018 and 250+ episodes per season for recent years; other sources note >8,000 cases decided. "Analysis Specifications—Modern Data (1946–2015)." *Washington University Law's The Supreme Court Database* (number of cases decided), scdb.wustl.edu/analysisOverview.php; author's calculations (using a fairly generous definition of "decided" for SCOTUS). The Court doesn't report the number of downloads, but hearsay reports suggests that number is not large, and YouTube clips of Justices speaking at public events rarely exceed 70,000 downloads. That said, RBG (alone among the Justices) is a pop culture phenom, with a movie, T-shirts, etc.

4   "CBS Interactive Terms of Use: Section 17 Disputes; Arbitration." *CBS Interactive*, 15 Nov. 2017, www.cbsinteractive.com/legal/cbsi/terms-of-use (providing for arbitration for use of website which handles applications to have case heard by Judge Judy); Sheftell, Jason. "Ex-Friend of Judge Judy: I'll Drop My Lawsuit if You Give Back My China Set." *Daily News*, 15 Mar. 2013, (chinaware suit), www.nydailynews.com/entertainment/gossip/judge-judy-sued-ex-friend -china-cutlery-sets-article-1.1289099.

5   "Conditions of Use." *Amazon's Help & Customer Service*, 21 May 2018, www.amazon .com/gp/help/customer/display.html?nodeId=201909000 (arbitration required where allowed by law save for small claims); Hyken, Shep. "Sixty-Four Percent of U.S. Households Have Amazon Prime." *Forbes,* 17 June 2017, www.forbes.com/sites/ shephyken/2017/06/17/sixty-four-percent-of-u-s-households-have-amazon -prime/#c657ab045860 (prevalence of Amazon shopping).

6   *Arbitration Study: Report to Congress, pursuant to Dodd-Frank Wall Street Reform and Consumer Protection Act § 1028(a).* Consumer Financial Protection Bureau, Mar. 2015 (hereinafter "CFPB Study") § 1.4, § 2 *generally*, Appendices,

files.consumerfinance.gov/f/201503_cfpb_arbitration-study-report-to-congress
-2015.pdf. For the financial and telecom sectors, the CFPB Study provides good
empirical data. Scholars and public interest groups also maintain ongoing lists
of major corporations across industries that require arbitration. A good example
is Public Citizen—and though some of that group's *statistical* conclusions about
arbitration outcomes require context, their list of companies requiring arbitration is perfectly good. "Forced Arbitration Rogues Gallery: Expose Corporations
That Are Rigging the Justice System Against Consumers." *Public Citizen,* www
.citizen.org/our-work/access-justice/forced-arbitration-rogues-gallery.

7   CFPB Study, § 2.3 (use may be direct or semi-direct, as by authorizing arbitration
when third-party debt-collection is invoked; from the consumer's perspective,
there's no difference: it's arbitration).

8   *Ibid.* The study is not a complete survey, but arbitration is everywhere.

9   Colvin, Alexander J.S. "The Growing Use of Mandatory Arbitration: Access to the
Courts is Now Barred for More than 60 Million American Workers." *Economic
Policy Institute,* 27 Sept. 2017, pp. 1–2, www.epi.org/files/pdf/135056.pdf.

10   E.g., CFPB Study, § 3.4.3 (credit card arbitrations); author's calculations (requiring both awareness and comprehension of clauses; under more generous calculations, consumer error rates would be ~20%). To be fair, surveyed consumers
often did not know what legal rights they have generally—i.e., with or without an
arbitration clause. *Ibid.*

11   Strom, Stephanie. "When 'Liking' a Brand Online Voids the Right to Sue."
New York Times, 16 Apr. 2014 (noting General Mills's aggressive posture
of construing "purchase" or "use" of a product as consent to its terms of use,
which included arbitration), www.nytimes.com/2014/04/17/business/when-liking
-a-brand-online-voids-the-right-to-sue.htm; Foster, Kirstie. "Explaining Our
Website Privacy Policy and Legal Terms." *A Taste of General Mills,* 17 Apr.
2014 (walking back the arbitration assertions), blog.generalmills.com/2014/04/
explaining-our-website-privacy-policy-and-legal-terms/. The exact chain of events
required (in General Mills's mind) to trigger arbitration is not entirely clear: the
language is expansive, but the firm perhaps intended that the use of its website/
coupons would be the trigger, though use of the product might itself suffice
under the plain words of the clause as reported.

12   Judith Resnik at Yale Law is a particularly persuasive exponent of this view. E.g.,
Resnik, Judith. "Diffusing Disputes: The Public in the Private of Arbitration, the
Private in Courts, and the Erasure of Rights." *Yale Law Journal,* vol. 124, no.
8, June 2015, pp. 2804–2939, www.yalelawjournal.org/pdf/d.2804.Resnik.2939
_nz7yew68.pdf.

13   Emerson, Frank D. "History of Arbitration Practice and Law." *Cleveland State
Law Review,* vol. 19, issue 1, Jan. 1970, pp.155–164, engagedscholarship.csuohio
.edu/cgi/viewcontent.cgi?referer=www.google.com/&httpsredir=1&article=272
6&context=clevstlrev.

14   Islamic arbitration is an outgrowth of the concept of conciliation embodied in
sulh (amicable settlement) and elaborated in the Koran and subsequent texts,
often before an *hakam* (arbitrator). E.g., The Koran, al-Baqarah 2:178, 2:182, 2:224,

2:228; an-Nisa 4:35, 4:114, 4:128, 4:135; al-Anfal 8:1. Nevertheless, as Islamic businesses globalized, their embrace of Western-style litigation increased, though internal and especially family law remain heavily influenced by arbitration.

15   E.g., *Pando Compania Naviera S.A. v. Filmo S.A.S.* [1975] 1 Lloyd's Rep. 560 QB 742 (noting that "[t]he shipping and commodities trades of the world are unusual in that they do not regard litigation *or arbitration* with abhorrence. On the contrary, they regard it as a normal incident of commercial life—a civilized way of resolving the many differences of opinion that are bound to arise") (emphasis added).

16   For a good history, see Szalai, Imre Stephen, "Exploring the Federal Arbitration Act through the Lens of History Symposium." *Journal of Dispute Resolution*, vol. 2016, issue 1, article 9, 2016, p. 119 and citations listed at n.3 (hereinafter "Szalai"), scholarship.law.missouri.edu/jdr/vol2016/iss1/9.

17   United States Arbitration Act (generally known as the Federal Arbitration Act), Pub. L. 68-401 (1925) subsequently re-enacted, amended, and codified at 9 U.S.C. § 1 *et seq.* (as codified, hereinafter "FAA").

18   *See* Szalai *supra* note 16 *generally; see also* Pub. L. 68-401 (1925) (original version of the FAA) at Preamble (noting applicability to "contracts, maritime transactions, or commerce among the States) §§ 1 and 2 (referencing "maritime transactions") and § 3 (referring to "courts of the United States," i.e., federal courts); *see also Arbitration of interstate commercial disputes: joint hearings before the subcommittees of the Committees on the Judiciary, Congress of the United States, Sixty-eighth Congress, first session, on S. 1005 and H.R. 646, bills to make valid and enforceable written provisions or agreements for arbitration of disputes arising out of contracts, maritime transactions, or commerce among the states or territories or with foreign nations,* 9 Jan. 1924 (e.g., statement of Rep. Graham).

19   E.g., Pub. L. 68-401 (1925) Preamble and §§ 3, 6, 9–10 (noting that courts retain jurisdiction over the case and are required to enter judgment and to determine enforceability of arbitration agreements).

20   *Wickard v. Filburn,* 317 U.S. 111 (1942). Things were a bit muddled post-FAA/pre-*Erie*. The Court began its "interstate" expansions with *Prima Paint.*

21   The Court began articulating FAA preemption in *Southland Corp. v. Keating,* 465 U.S. 1 (1984), discussed *infra. See also Volt Information Sciences, Inc. v. Board of Trustees of Leland Stanford Jr. University,* 489 U.S. 468 at 477–478 (1989); *Doctor's Associates., Inc. v. Casarotto,* 517 U.S. 681 at 686–687 (1996).

22   FAA § 2 (providing that arbitration will be enforced "save upon such grounds as exist at law or in equity for the revocation of any contract").

23   *Allied-Bruce Terminix Cos. v. Dobson,* 513 U.S. 265, 283 (1995) (O'Connor, J., concurring) (arguing that the "Court has abandoned all pretense of ascertaining congressional intent with respect to the Federal Arbitration Act, building instead, case by case, an edifice of its own creation").

24   *Southland Corp. v. Keating,* 465 U.S. 1, 10 (1984).

25   E.g., Eisenberg, Theodore, et al. "Arbitration's Summer Soldiers: An Empirical Study of Arbitration Clauses in Consumer and Non-Consumer Contracts." *Cornell Law Faculty Publications,* 2008, -scholarship.law.cornell.edu/lsrp_papers/106/

(noting corporations prefer arbitration against consumers); Eiseman, Neal M., et al. "A Tale of Two Lawyers: How Arbitrators and Advocates Can Avoid the Dangerous Convergence of Arbitration and Litigation." *ABA Journal*, 8 Apr. 2013 (noting rising incidence of litigation-like behavior in arbitration), www .americanbar.org/content/dam/aba/administrative/litigation/materials/sac2013/ sac_2013/62-4_a_table_of_two.authcheckdam.pdf; Neil, Martha. "Litigation over Arbitration." *ABA Journal*, Jan. 2005 (similar), www.abajournal.com/magazine/ article/litigation_over_arbitration/.

26   Resnik, Judith. "Diffusing Disputes: The Public in the Private of Arbitration, the Private in Courts, and the Erasure of Rights." *Yale Law Journal*, vol. 124, no. 8, June 2015, pp. 2812–2814 (citations omitted), www.yalelawjournal.org/article/ diffusing-disputes; author's calculations.

27   *Ibid.*

28   CFPB Study at §§ 1.4.3-1.4.7, 5.5 and Appendices A–B. For example, in CFPB's sample covering five major markets, companies invoked arbitration in under 1% of individual cases. In a six-market sample, from 2010 to 2012, AAA received an average of 616 case filings annually; in 2012 alone, for just the credit card sub-market, the sample recorded some 41,000 small claims courts filings. By contrast, when allowed to bring class-action suits, at least 160 million people were putative class members, and 34 million were scheduled to receive relief, suggesting that there were vastly more claims than arbitrations.

29   Telecom providers have some of the worst customer satisfaction ratings in industry; financial institutions do better, but not always well. "Benchmarks by Industry." *American Customer Satisfaction Index*, www.theacsi.org/index.php?option=com _content&view=article&id=148&Itemid=213 (disaggregating telecoms and noting that services have varying levels of satisfaction, but low satisfaction for ISP, subscription TV, and fixed-line services). MSN and Zogby Analytics also poll for customer satisfaction, with banks and telecoms regularly featuring in the Top 10 "Hall of Shame." E.g., Elliott, Christopher. "The 10 Worst Companies for Customer Service." *CBS's Money Watch*, 7 June 2011, www.cbsnews.com/news/the-10-worst -companies-for-customer-service/ (2009–2011 lists); Stebbins, Sam. "Customer Service Hall of Shame." *MSN Money*, 8 Sept. 2017, www.msn.com/en-us/money/ companies/customer-service-hall-of-shame/ss-AAqEFz8#image=13 (2017 list). *See also* "Which Industries Get the Most Customer Service Complaints." *Salesforce Desk's Success Center, Find Tips and Best Practices for Making Awesome Service Your Secret Ingredient,* www.desk.com/success-center/customer-service -complaints-by-industry (noting credit card companies have lowest customer satisfaction in banking sector in an informal survey by a division of CRM supplier Salesforce.com).

30   Federal Trade Commission. "T-Mobile USA, Inc: Case Summary." 1 Feb. 2017, www.ftc.gov/enforcement/cases-proceedings/132-3231/t-mobile-usa-inc (T-Mobile); Federal Trade Commission. "FTC Providing Over $88 Million in Refunds to AT&T Customers Who Were Subjected to Mobile Cramming— Over 2.7 Million AT&T Customers to be Refunded, Mostly Through Bill Credits: Press Release." 8 Dec. 2016, www.ftc.gov/news-events/press-releases/2016/12 /ftc-providing-over-88-million-refunds-att-customers-who-were (AT&T); Parker,

Ryan. "Sprint to Pay \$15.5 Million to Settle Wiretap Overcharging Case." *Los Angeles Times,* 9 Apr. 2015, www.latimes.com/business/la-fi-government-sprint -wiretaps-20150409-story.html (Sprint).

31   "Wireless Customer Agreement." *AT&T,* www.att.com/legal/terms.wireless CustomerAgreement.html; author's calculations using Word readability tools; Flesch, Rudolf. "How to Write Plain English—Chapter 2: Let's Start with the Formula." pages.stern.nyu.edu/~wstarbuc/Writing/Flesch.htm.

32   Fed. R. of Civ. Pro. 23. The watershed in asbestos was James Cavett's suit against Johns-Manville. The Master Settlement Agreement, reached between state attorneys general and tobacco companies, is the centerpiece of tobacco litigation but had been preceded by decades of private individual and class-action litigation which, by the mid-1990s, had begun to dispose the tobacco companies to reform their never-settle postures. Asbestos claimants had tougher sledding; the issue in many health-related cases is whether the plaintiffs are similar enough to constitute a class. But they are usually similar enough to provoke defendants' fears.

33   The initial settlement of over \$300 million came fairly quickly; other settlements came over time.

34   E.g., "Wireless Customer Agreement." *AT&T,* www.att.com/legal/terms.wire lessCustomerAgreement.html ("Any arbitration under this Agreement will take place on an individual basis; class arbitrations and class actions are not permitted").

35   *AT&T Mobility LLC v. Concepcion,* 563 U.S. 333 (2011) (discussing arbitration in context of preemption of state law regarding arbitration).

36   Silver-Greenberg, Jessica and Robert Gebeloff. "Arbitration Everywhere, Stacking the Deck of Justice." *New York Times's Dealbook Business & Policy,* 31 Oct. 2015, www.nytimes.com/2015/11/01/business/dealbook/arbitration-everywhere -stacking-the-deck-of-justice.html?hp&action=click&pgtype=Homepage &module=first-column-region&region=top-news&WT.nav=top-news &_r=0.

37   *Marmet Health Care Center, Inc. v. Brown,* 565 U.S. 530 (2012).

38   *Ibid.*; Savage, David G. "Rehnquist Says New Cases Tax Federal Courts." *Los Angeles Times,* 1 Jan. 1992, articles.latimes.com/1992-01-01/news/mn-1051_1 _federal-court-system.

39   Greenhouse, Linda. "Ease Load On Courts, Rehnquist Urges." *New York Times,* 1 Jan. 1992, www.nytimes.com/1992/01/01/us/ease-load-on-courts-rehnquist-urges .html.

40   *Flight Systems v. Paul A. Laurence Co.,* 715 F. Supp. 1125 (D.D.C. 1989).

41   U.S. Department of Labor. "How to Become an Arbitrator, Mediator, or Conciliator." *Occupational Outlook Handbook,* Bureau of Labor Statistics, www .bls.gov/ooh/legal/arbitrators-mediators-and-conciliators.htm#tab-4. BLS notes that other arbitral positions do require a law degree; it depends—but it's not legally required as a general rule.

42   "Standalone Alternative Dispute Resolution (ADR) Certificate." *USC Gould School of Law, USC University of Southern California,* gould.usc.edu/academ ics/certificates/adr/standalone/; "Application Instructions—Alternative Dispute Resolution (ADR) Certificate." *USC Gould School of Law, USC University of*

Southern California, gould.usc.edu/academics/certificates/adr/standalone/applica
tion/ (noting "you must have earned your bachelor's degree by the time you
enroll at USC Gould School of Law. No law degree is required"). Even the MDR-
ADR *degree* does not require a law school diploma, though the LLM in ADR does.

43   "Qualification Criteria for Admittance to the AAA® National Roster of Arbi-
      trators." *American Arbitration Association,* www.adr.org/sites/default/files/doc
      ument_repository/Qualification%20Criteria%20for%20Admittance%20to
      %20the%20AAA%20National%20Roster%20of%20Arbitrators.pdf.

44   "Hon. H. Warren Knight (Ret.), Founder: Biography." *JAMS: Resolving Disputes
      Worldwide,* www.jamsadr.com/knight/ (noting JAMS founded by an ex-judge);
      "Consumer Arbitration Minimum Standards. JAMS Policy on Consumer Arbitra-
      tions Pursuant to Pre-Dispute Clauses Minimum Standards of Procedural Fair-
      ness." *JAMS,* 15 July 2009, www.jamsadr.com/consumer-minimum-standards/
      (setting out "minimum standards of fairness" before JAMS will take a case).

45   U.S. Anti-Doping Agency. "Protocol for Olympic and Paralympic Movement
      Testing." 1 Jan. 2015, R-2, www.usada.org/wp-content/uploads/USADA_proto
      col.pdf.

46   Nussbaum, Carolyn G. and Christopher M. Mason. "Who Decides: The Court
      or the Arbitrator?" *American Bar Association Business Law Section.* March 2014
      (listing circumstances where arbitrators decide arbitrability) www.americanbar
      .org/publications/blt/2014/03/03_mason.html. Courts say they try to enforce
      the parties' original agreement, including the arbitration of arbitrability, but this
      has proved unwieldy and the law is a mess, not cleared up by *Howsam v. Dean
      Witter Reynolds, Inc.,* 537 U.S. 79 (2002), *Rent-A-Center, West, Inc. v. Jackson,*
      561 U.S. 63 (2010), etc., and "gateway" doctrines.

47   Sussman, Edna and John Wilkinson. "Benefits of Arbitration for Commer-
      cial Disputes." *American Bar Association,* p. 4, www.americanbar.org/content/
      dam/aba/publications/dispute_resolution_magazine/March_2012_Sussman
      _Wilkinson_March_5.authcheckdam.pdf (public draft).

48   *See generally* Mills, Lawrence R., *et al.,* "Vacating Arbitration Awards Study
      Reveals Real-World Odds of Success by Grounds, Subject Matter, and Jurisdic-
      tion," *Dispute Resolution Magazine,* Summer 2005.

49   *Compare* 9 U.S.C. § 12 (providing for vacatur of arbitral awards within three
      months of judgment) *with,* e.g., 28 U.S.C. § 144 judge (providing for district
      court judicial disqualification "whenever" in the course of proceeding a "timely"
      and substantiated motion is made). *See also infra* note 50.

50   The FAA explicitly provides for vacating arbitral awards based on "evident
      partiality." 9 U.S.C. § 10(a)(2). *Positive Software Solutions, Inc. v. New Cen-
      tury Mortgage Corp.,* 476 F.3d 278 (5th Cir. 2007), cert. denied, 127 S.Ct. 2943
      (2007) (finding vacatur not required for non-disclosed "trivial" bias). Arbitra-
      tion firms set their own rules for disclosure. The leading (and unhelpful) case
      here is *Commonwealth Coatings Corp. v. Continental Casualty Co.,* 393 U.S. 145
      (1968). The Court's opinion suggested that arbitrators should be held to high
      standards, but White's concurrence, which had significant effects because some
      courts thought it rendered the Court's opinion a mere plurality, emphasized

that the Court did *not* hold arbitrators to judicial standards, because arbitrators were "men of affairs" who could not disentangle themselves completely from potentially conflicting business. *Ibid.*, at 150 (White, J., concurring). The circuits are heavily split on how much bias is too much. E.g., *Positive Software Solutions, Inc. v. New Century Mortgage Corp.*, 476 F.3d 278 (5th Cir. 2007); *Ometto v. ASA Bioenergy Holding A.G.*, 2013 WL 174259 at p. 8 (noting that under Second Circuit standard, "the arbitrator is quite unlike a judge, who can be disqualified in any proceeding in which his impartiality might be reasonably questioned"); *Schmitz v. Zilveti*, 20 F.3d 1043, 1046 (9th Cir. 1994) (reasonable impression).

51 E.g., *Aviall, Inc. v. Ryder Sys.*, 110 F.3d 892, 895 (2d. 1997); *Smith v. American Arbitration Association Inc*, 233 F.3d 502, 506 (7th Cir. 2000) ("The time to challenge an arbitration, on whatever grounds, including bias, is when the arbitration is completed and an award rendered.") (citation omitted); *Freeman v. Pittsburgh Glass Works, LLC*, 709 F.3d 240 (3rd Cir. 2015) (discussing obvious bias/reasonable-person-might-conclude standard).

52 Weinstein, Roy, et al. "Efficiency and Economic Benefits of Dispute Resolution through Arbitration Compared with U.S. District Court Proceedings." *Micronomics Economic Research and Consulting,* Mar. 2017, p. 2 and associated tables, www.micronomics.com/articles/Efficiency_Economic_Benefits_Dispute_Res olution_through_Arbitration_Compared_with_US_District_Court_Proceed ings.pdf. This report, prepared by the Micronomics consulting firm, used data furnished by AAA and some of its *normative* conclusions are suspect. Nevertheless, that arbitration is faster than court litigation is not much debated. There is no comprehensive set of arbitral data available, because arbitrations are non-public, so data filtered by groups like Micronomics—whatever the biases of the filter—are the best we have.

53 *Ibid.*

54 *Ibid.* The guiding assumption in the cited material seems to be that appeals will not be undertaken in the arbitral context.

55 "50-State Chart of Small Claims Court Dollar Limits." *www.nolo.com,* 4 June 2018, www.nolo.com/legal-encyclopedia/small-claims-suits-how-much-30031 .html; *Judge Judy IMDb,* www.imdb.com/title/tt0115227/?ref_=fn_al_tt_1. *See also* "Standards of Judicial Administration Vol. II: Standards Relating to Trial Courts." American Bar Association's Judicial Administration Division, 1992, § 2.52 (aspirational 30-day standard), www.americanbar.org/content/dam/aba/migrated/ divisions/Judicial/MO/MemberDocuments/trialcourtstandards.authcheckdam .pdf; Goerdt, John A. "Small Claims and Traffic Courts: Case Management Procedures, Case Characteristics, and Outcomes in 12 Urban Jurisdictions." National Center for State Courts, 1992 (noting almost all small claims matters resolved within 90 days in sample).

56 E.g., Private Securities Litigation Reform Act, Pub. L. No. 104-67, 109 Stat. 737 (1995). The U.S. Class Action Fairness Act of 2005 also updated the FRCP, for which judicial collaboration may be assumed (without assuming such was decisive). 28 U.S.C. §§ 1332(d), 1453, 1711–1715.

57   "Arbitration in the Life Sciences and Pharmaceutical Sector." *Corporate Disputes Magazine,* Oct.–Dec. 2017, www.wipo.int/export/sites/www/amc/en/docs/2017 _pharmacdm.pdf.

58   Colvin, Alexander J.S. "The Growing Use of Mandatory Arbitration: Access to the Courts is Now Barred for More than 60 million American Workers." *Economic Policy Institute,* 27 Sept. 2017, pp. 1–2, www.epi.org/files/pdf/135056.pdf (private, non-union employees).

59   *Epic Systems Corporation v. Lewis,* No. 16-285.

60   Plato. *Laws.* Book 11. Plato discussed what we would call equitable grounds for non-performance, including illegality, impossibility, and duress ("unjust compulsion"), though does not directly discuss what modern lawyers would understand as "unconscionability." But the equitable drift is clear enough. Note that contracts of adhesion are not usually unconscionable per se; courts typically demand procedural or substantive defects.

61   UCC § 2-302 (Unconscionable contract or clause); *Williams v. Walker-Thomas Furniture Co.,* 350 F.2d 445 (D.C. Cir. 1965).

62   *Williams v. Walker-Thomas Furniture Co.,* 350 F.2d 445 (D.C. Cir. 1965).

63   The doctrine has mutated over the years, but these are the general categories of unconscionability.

64   For a summary, see UCC § 2-302 and Official Comment.

65   FAA § 2 (allowing courts to void arbitration clauses on grounds on "such grounds as exist in law or at equity"). Some say that FAA § 4 limits § 2, but that's not convincing, nor are the Court's opinions in *Concepcion* or *DirectTV.*

66   E.g., Fed. R. Civ. Pro. 16.

67   *Marbury v. Madison,* 5 U.S. (1 Cranch) 137, 163 (1803).

68   "Worldwide Governance Indicators." *World Bank's DataBank, 20 Sept. 2017,* databank.worldbank.org/data/databases/rule-of-law.

69   *Compare The Judiciary FY 2017 Congressional Budget Summary.* The Administrative Office of the U.S. Courts, Feb. 2016, p. i., www.uscourts.gov/sites/default/files /fy_2017_federal_judiciary_congressional_budget_summary_0.pdf *with Defense Acquisitions: Assessments of Selected Weapon Programs.* United States Government Accountability Office's Report to Congressional Committees, Mar. 2015, p. 87 www.gao.gov/assets/670/668986.pdf (Gerald R. Ford Class Nuclear Aircraft Carrier (CVN 78) unit cost) *and* "NHE Fact Sheet." *CMS. gov's Centers for Medicare & Medicaid Services,* (Medicare and Medicaid spending only), www .cms.gov/research-statistics-data-and-systems/statistics-trends-and-reports/ nationalhealthexpenddata/nhe-fact-sheet.html.

Chapter 8

1   The saying is generally attributed to Sir James Matthew, though it has been used in Anglophone legal communities for over a century, and recycled by contemporary judges in Britain and America. "Speeches—Launch of the Report on Multi-Party Litigation," *Courts Service—Ireland,* 27 Aug. 2005 at n.14 and

accompanying text, www.courts.ie/courts.ie/library3.nsf/16c93c36d3635d5180 256e3f003a4580/97b4a7362c75858f8025708f002f964e?OpenDocument.

2   Author's calculations; U.S. Bureau of Economic Analysis. "Personal consumption expenditures: Legal services [DGALRC1A027NBEA]." *Compare Federal Reserve Bank of St. Louis (FRED)*, 27 July 2018, fred.stlouisfed.org/series/DGAL RC1A027NBEA *with* U.S. Bureau of Labor Statistics. "Consumer Price Index for All Urban Consumers: All Items [CPIAUSCL]" *and Federal Reserve Bank of St. Louis (FRED)*, 10 Aug. 2018, fred.stlouisfed.org/series/CPIAUCSL.FRED, *and* BLS category GD011; BLS Series CRUUR0000SEGD01; "GDP by Industry Data." IO Series 541100 (07NAICS_GO_C_Price Indexes).

3   U.S. Bureau of Economic Analysis. "GDP by Industry Data." IO Series 541100 (legal services) (value add data for 2017), www.bea.gov/industry/gdpbyind_data .htm. The Census reports Code 5411 data slightly differently, and shows legal services revenue (for 2012) of $262 billion.

4   *Compare ibid.* and *ibid.* Series 562000 (waste and remediation) *and* Thomson Reuters. *How Big Is the U.S. Legal Services Market?* Thomson Reuters Legal Executive Institute, 2015, www.legalexecutiveinstitute.com/wp-content/uploads/2016/01/How -Big-is-the-US-Legal-Services-Market.pdf. National accounts (especially gross output) can risk double counting, but these figures provide a reasonable sense of scale.

5   U.S. Bureau of Economic Analysis. "Personal Consumption Expenditures: Legal Services [DGALRC1A027NBEA]." *Federal Reserve Bank of St. Louis (FRED)*, 27 July 2018, fred.stlouisfed.org/series/DGALRC1A027NBEA. The BEA, on which FRED relies, calculates "personal consumption" of services (including legal services) as the sum of household plus nonprofit spending; across all categories, the latter is a fraction of the former.

6   Author's calculations. U.S. Census Bureau. "Real Median Personal Income in the United States [MEPAINUSA672N]." *Federal Reserve Bank of St. Louis (FRED)*, 13 Sept. 2017, fred.stlouisfed.org/series/MEPAINUSA672N (2016 data). Divisor assumes all legal costs borne by adults, but no other adjustment for the income age threshold (15+) and population count threshold (18+).

7   Legal costs include lawyers' fees plus customary legal costs like filing costs, state process fees/fines, copying charges, etc., but exclude judgment. Costs for all those services vary greatly by state and even minor variations in complexity can move costs substantially, and in smaller-dollar matters non-lawyer costs may be a substantial fraction of total legal cost. Expense also varies greatly depending on the particulars of a given dispute and the venue for litigation, by up to an order of magnitude (or more). Nevertheless, these ranges are reasonably illustrative. Where citations are not provided, figures are author's estimates based on personal experience. Hoffower, Hillary. "You don't need to be rich to get a prenup – here's how much you should expect to pay." *Business Insider.* 20 Oct. 2018, https://www.businessinsider.com/how-much-does-prenup-cost-2018-10 (basic prenups at $2,500 per party to $7,500-$10,000 in more expensive jurisdictions/ more complicated financial patterns); Michon, Kathleen, "How Much Will My Divorce Cost and How Long Will It take?" Nolo.com, https://www.nolo.com/ legal-encyclopedia/ctp/cost-of-divorce.html; "Divorce With Children: How Much Does It Cost and How Long Does It Take?" Martindale-Nolo Research,

https://www.lawyers.com/legal-info/family-law/divorce/divorce-with-children
.html; "Does a DUI Lawyer Give You a Better Outcome? Is It Worth the Cost?"
Martindale-Nolo Research, https://www.lawyers.com/legal-info/criminal/dui
-dwi/does-using-a-dui-lawyer-give-you-a-better-outcome.html (noting average $2,400 in legal fees, plus substantial additional costs, for private DUI legal
defense); Marquand, Barbara, "How Much Does a DUI Cost?" Nerdwallet, 3
Feb. 2016, https://www.nerdwallet.com/blog/insurance/cost-of-a-dui/; Pyles,
Sean "How Much Bankruptcy Costs and How to Pay for It." Nerdwallet. 12 Mar.
2018, https://www.nerdwallet.com/blog/finance/bankruptcy-costs-pay/; Local
Rules, various U.S. District Courts (establishing presumptively reasonable fees
for bankruptcy); Median. Hannaford-Agor, Paula, and Nicole L. Waters. "Estimating the Cost of Civil Litigation." *National Center for State Courts, Court
Statistics Project*, vol. 20, no. 1, 2013, p. 8 www.justresolve.com/wp-content/
uploads/2014/10/Courtstatistics.org-study-Estimating-the-Costs-of-Civil-Lit
igation.pdf; "The 2015 Hiscox Guide to Employee Lawsuits: Employee Charge
Trends Across the United States." *Hiscox, Inc.*, 2015, p. 12, www.hiscox.com/
documents/The-2015-Hiscox-Guide-to-Employee-Lawsuits-Employee-charge
-trends-across-the-United-States.pdf; Rubin, Jessica B., and Bishop, Tara F.
"Characteristics of Paid Malpractice Claims Settled in and out of Court in the
USA: A Retrospective Analysis." *BMJ Open*, vol. 3, no. 6, June 2013. *PubMed Central*, doi:10.1136/bmjopen-2013-002985; Sage, William M. "Medical Malpractice
Reform: When Is It about Money? Why Is It about Time?" *JAMA*, vol. 312, no.
20, 26 Nov. 2014, pp. 2103–05. *PubMed*, doi:10.1001/jama.2014.15416; Median.
Lee, Cynthia G., and LaFountain, Robert C. "Medical Malpractice Litigation in
State Courts." *National Center for State Courts, Court Statistics Project*, vol. 18,
no. 1, Apr. 2011, p. 8. U.S. Government Accountability Office. *Dollar Costs Associated with the Bankruptcy Abuse Prevention and Consumer Protection Act of
2005*. GAO-08-697, June 2008, www.gao.gov/assets/280/277572.pdf; Li, Wenli,
et al. *Consumer Bankruptcy, Mortgage Default and Labor Supply*. CEMFI, 2017,
p. 42, www.cemfi.es/ftp/pdf/papers/pew/model-current.pdf; Elias, Stephen, and
Attorney. "The Chapter 7 Bankruptcy Process: An Overview." *Nolo.com*, www
.nolo.com/legal-encyclopedia/free-books/foreclosure-book/chapter6-5.html.

8   Houseman, Alan W. "Civil Legal Aid in the United States: An Update For
     2017." Consortium for the National Equal Justice Library. March, 2018, p. 5,
     http://legalaidresearch.org/wp-content/uploads/CIVIL-LEGAL-AID-IN-THE
     -UNITED-STATES-2017-5.pdf (hereinafter "Houseman"); "Fiscal 2018 Bud-
     get Request." Legal Services Corporation. 2018, p.2, https://www.lsc.gov/sites/
     default/files/LSC-FY2018-BudgetRequest-Digital.pdf; "America First: A Budget
     Blueprint to Make America Great Again" (aka FY 2018 Budget Request), Office
     of Management and Budget, p. 15, https://www.whitehouse.gov/sites/white
     house.gov/files/omb/budget/fy2018/2018_blueprint.pdf.

9   Houseman, p. 18.

10   Houseman, pp. 12–13 (noting, *inter alia*, that "seven of every ten low-income
     households have experienced at least one civil legal problem in the past year,"
     with a majority characterizing the legal problem as significant or severe in
     impact).

11   Deborah L. Rhode, "What We Know and Need to Know About the Delivery of Legal Services by Nonlawyers," 67 S.C. L. Rev. 429, 429 (2016); *see also* Deborah Rhode, *Access to Justice* 3 (Oxford Univ. Press 2004).

12   Chroust, Anton-Hermann. *The Rise of The Legal Profession in America, vol. 2* pp. 240–248 (1965) (hereinafter "Chroust"). Statutory rates emerged in England to guide the recovery of attorneys' fees as part of the "English rule" of cost-shifting. But in the United States, statutory rates primarily existed to impose ceilings on what lawyers could charge their clients. *See* Vargo, John F. "The American Rule on Attorney Fee Allocation: The Injured Person's Access to Justice." *The American University Law Review*, vol. 42, 1993. *Washington College of Law Digital Commons*, digitalcommons .wcl.american.edu/cgi/viewcontent.cgi?article=1586&context=aulr.

13   Chroust, p. 257.

14   Chroust, p. 256; 2 Laws of the State of Delaware Ch. 27 §§ 18–19 (1793). Much of what we now consider "corporate" law (or solicitor's work in England) was handled by notaries. "Attorney" connoted an ability to litigate (as with barristers). Note that the national dollar was established in 1792. 1 Stat. 246 (1792).

15   Author's calculations (based on *ibid.*) It's virtually impossible to compare 1790s and modern dollars, but an illustrative index of eighteenth- and nineteenth-century wages appears at "American incomes ca. 1650–1870." *Global Price and Income History Group*, gpih.ucdavis.edu/tables.htm. Modern wages by trade can be found at United States Department of Labor, Bureau of Labor Statistics. "May 2017 National Occupational Employment and Wage Estimates United States." www.bls.gov/oes/current/oes_nat.htm.

16   Leubsdorf, John. "Toward a History of the American Rule on Attorney Fee Recovery." *Law and Contemporary Problems*, vol. 47, no. 1, 1984. pp. 11–12, doi: 10.2307/1191435. *JSTOR*, www.jstor.org/stable/1191435?origin=crossref. Hamilton married well, but the gulf between his income (much derived from his legal practice) and New York's statutory maximum retainer of $3.75 suggests tips played a role. Laws of the State of New York, 24th Sess. (ch. 190, pp. 555–556); Chroust, pp. 249–250.

17   Special Committee on Economics of Law Practice for the American Bar Association. *The 1958 Lawyer and His 1938 Dollar*, 1958; Bureau of Labor Statistics. *Occupational Outlook Handbook 1959 Edition*. U.S. Department of Labor, 1959. *Hathi Trust*, pp. 60–61, 66, 199–200, catalog.hathitrust.org/Record/000046071.

18   Stewart, James B. "$11 Million a Year for a Law Partner? Bidding War Grows at Top-Tier Firms." *New York Times*, 26 Apr. 2018. *NYTimes.com*, www .nytimes.com/2018/04/26/business/cravath-kirkland-ellis-partner-poaching .html. The exact amounts will vary depending on the profit share at the relevant firms.

19   Author's personal knowledge. *National Law Journal* and Lexis-Nexis compile hourly rates (averages and medians); *see also* "2018 Report on the State of the Legal Market." Thomson/Reuters and Georgetown Law, Chart 6, (showing range of ~$375–$500 for larger firms, depending on metric).

20   McEntee, Kyle. *A Way Forward: Transparency in 2018*. Iowa State Bar Association, Young Lawyers Division, 2018, pp. 4, *Law School Transparency*, data .lawschooltransparency.com/documents/2018_Report.pdf; "High Demand, Low

Reward: Salaries for 2018 College Graduates Flat, Korn Ferry Analysis Shows." *Korn Ferry*, 14 May 2018, www.kornferry.com/press/high-demand-low-reward -salaries-for-2018-college-graduates-flat-korn-ferry-analysis-shows/; Poppick, Susie. "Here's What the Average Grad Makes Right After College." *Money*, 22 Apr., 2015, time.com/money/collection-post/3829776/heres-what-the-average -grad-makes-right-out-of-college/. Debt is for students who borrow.

21 This assumes a 20- to 30-year career, historical interest rates, and existing tax rates (which tend to be higher in the major markets in which lawyers work). It also assumes that practicing law offers no "non-monetary" compensations, a reasonable assumption for many private lawyers.

22 "Findings from the 2017 Associate Salary Survey." *National Association of Legal Professionals*, June 2017 (reporting median salary of $135,000). Average salaries are somewhat higher.

23 See U.S. Courts. *Judiciary Salary Plan: New York-Newark, Table NY.* 2018, www .uscourts.gov/sites/default/files/jsp_new_york_2018.pdf (providing court pay scales); U.S. Courts. "Qualifications, Salary, Benefits." *OSCAR*, 1 Feb. 2018, oscar.uscourts .gov/qualifications_salary_benefits (judicial clerks are generally JS 11-13); Olson, Elizabeth. "Law Firm Salaries Jump for the First Time in Nearly a Decade." *New York Times*, 6 Jun. 2016. *NYTimes.com*, www.nytimes.com/2016/06/07/busi ness/dealbook/law-firm-salaries-jump-for-the-first-time-in-nearly-a-decade .html (noting $180,000 entry pay at Cravath). Note that because of timing quirks, even clerks with experience tend to earn less than the maximum salary over any given annual cycle.

24 Lat, David. "Clerkship Bonus Watch: Will $75K Become The New Standard?" *Above the Law*, 20 June 2016, abovethelaw.com/2016/01/clerkship-bonus-watch -will-75k-become-the-new-standard/. The size of the bonus depends on the firm and the clerk, of course.

25 *Ibid.* (multiple clerkships); author's personal knowledge; Lat, David. "It's Official: Supreme Court Clerkship Bonuses Hit a New High." *Above the Law*, 15 Aug. 2013, abovethelaw.com/2013/08/its-official-supreme-court-clerkship-bonuses-hit-a-new -high/; Zaretsky, Staci. "Supreme Court Clerk Bonuses Hit An Incredible New High." *Above the Law*, 22 Aug. 2017, abovethelaw.com/2017/08/supreme-court-clerk -bonuses-hit-an-incredible-new-high/.

26 Firms often report higher profits per partner through accounting machina- tions, e.g., ignoring the implicit salaries their partners earn and simply report- ing everything as profit. More realistic calculations show many firms have much lower profits than they tout in legal journals. See Johnson, Chris. "Why Your Law Firm Isn't Anywhere Near as Profitable as You Think." *American Lawyer*, 6 Oct. 2017, www.law.com/americanlawyer/almID/1202799861132/. Profits for Apple, Google, and the S&P 500 are annualized five-year margins based on a period ending in Q1 2018 using data from yCharts. Gross margins for law firms are 40–60%, best case, versus 39% (Apple) and 78% (Goldman Sachs), on a TTM basis. The legal services industry as a whole does not seem wildly profitable. E.g., BEA Series N3262C0A144NBEA; REVEF54111ALLEST. Again, iffy data col- lection and reporting prevent anything like the degree of certainty possible with public firms.

27   "Uber." *Crunchbase,* www.crunchbase.com/organization/uber; "Lyft." *Crunch-base,* www.crunchbase.com/organization/lyft. The mix of financing streams is complex, but $15–20 billion is a reasonable estimate of what's been "invested" in the companies' growth and development. Debt figures and share shuffling would push the figures higher.

28   E.g., *ABA Model Rule of Professional Conduct,* Rule 5.4: Professional Independence of a Lawyer, www.americanbar.org/groups/professional_responsibility/ publications/model_rules_of_professional_conduct/model_rules_of_profes sional_conduct_table_of_contents.html. All states have similar ethical bans on outside ownership. Courts have also upheld various challenges to novel law firm financing mechanisms. E.g. *Jacoby & Meyers v. The Presiding Justices,* 852 F.3d 178 (2017).

29   "Firms Ranked By Gross Revenue." *American Lawyer,* 26 Sept. 2016, www.law .com/americanlawyer/almID/1202768367950/?mcode=0&curindex=0&curpa ge=ALL.

30   Advice-of-counsel can be either an affirmative defense or defeat the state-of-mind element and is available in many, though not all, cases. For a description of the general requirements of advice-of-counsel, *see,* e.g., *CE Carlson, Inc. and Charles E. Carlson v. Securities Exchange Commission,* 859 F.2d 1429, 1436 (10th Cir. 1988) ("The elements of such a defense require a showing of 1) a request for advice of counsel on the legality of a proposed action, 2) full disclosure of the relevant facts to counsel, 3) receipt of advice from counsel that the action to be taken will be legal, and 4) reliance in good faith on counsel's advice.") (citations and quotations omitted). Other circuits have slightly looser interpretations focusing on full disclosure and good faith reliance.

31   *Standard Oil Co. of New Jersey v. United States,* 221 U.S. 1, 30 (1911); Subrin, Stephen N. "Discovery in Global Perspective: Are We Nuts?" *De Paul Law Review,* vol. 52, no. 2, article 4, 2002, n. 29, via.library.depaul.edu/cgi/viewcontent .cgi?article=1502&context=law-review. Subrin furnished this comparison in a 2002 law review article. The Court's language is slightly ambiguous, but the figure does appear to be for the government record alone; if it's for the total record, the comparison would be even more vivid.

32   *United States v. Microsoft Corporation,* 253 F.3d 34 (D.C. Cir. 2001). Arguably, the case hinged on a single core issue: Did Microsoft abuse its power to win the browser wars?

33   Labaton, Stephen. "Delay Sought by Microsoft in States' Case." *New York Times,* 22 Dec. 2001, www.nytimes.com/2001/12/22/business/delay-sought-by -microsoft-in-states-case.html.

34   The DOJ maintains an archive of litigation documents at: Antitrust Division. "U.S. v. Microsoft Corporation." *U.S. Department of Justice,* 16 Oct. 2015 (updated), www .justice.gov/atr/case/us-v-microsoft-corporation-browser-and-middleware.

35   Lawyers for Civil Justice, et al. *Litigation Cost Survey of Major Companies.* 2011, p. 3, Statement Submitted to the Judicial Conference of the United States, 2010 (citing 2008 data), www.uscourts.gov/sites/default/files/litigation_cost_survey _of_major_companies_0.pdf. These groups had an interest in reducing discovery burdens, but there's no indication that their data are wrong.

36   *Ibid.,* pp. 3–4.

37 Pace, Nicholas M., and Laura Zakaras. *Where the Money Goes: Understanding Litigant Expenditures for Producing Electronic Discovery*. Institute for Civil Justice, RAND Corporation, 2012, Table 2.2, p. 20, www.rand.org/content/dam/rand/pubs/monographs/2012/RAND_MG1208.pdf. The *average* costs were even higher, at $26,605 per gigabyte.

38 Fed. R. Civ. P. 26(b)(1) and "Committee Notes on Rules—2015 Amendment." *Cornell Law School's Legal Information Institute*, www.law.cornell.edu/rules/frcp/rule_26.

39 There's considerable variance in payout and fairly little data. However, a good survey is Fitzpatrick, Brian T. and Robert C. Gilbert. "An Empirical Look at Compensation in Consumer Class Actions." *Vanderbilt Law School, Public Law & Legal Theory Working Paper No. 15-3, Law & Economics Working Paper No.15-6*, 6 Mar. 2015 (marked as draft and not for citation, but available online and apparently near-complete—see also complete works cited for additional survey), www.epiqglobal.com/epiq/media/ResourceFiles/AnEmpiricalLookatCompensationinConsumerClassActions.pdf. Fifty percent or less is the conventional wisdom in industry—one-third in contingency fees, and another 10–25% in administration overhead. *See also* Hensler, Deborah R., et al. *Class Action Dilemmas*. RAND Corporation, Ch. 15, 2000, www.rand.org/content/dam/rand/pubs/monograph_reports/MR969/MR969.ch15.pdf. *See also supra* note 37, at n. 36. Part of the difficulty is that plaintiffs might not collect what is owed, depressing total recovery rates.

40 America is likely a net exporter of legal services, though it's not clear how many of those "exports" are essentially a cost of doing business *in America*. Estimates of legal services as a percent of GDP are 1.3–1.8 percent in America versus 1 percent in Europe. *See* Barton, Ben. "A Comparison Between the American Markets for Medical and Legal Services." *Hastings Law Journal*, vol. 67, pp. 1331–1365, n.48 (2016) (citing the work of Yarrow and Decker).

41 Author's personal knowledge; McKiernan, Michael. "June 2016—The Going Rate." *Canadian Lawyer Magazine*, 6 June 2016, www.canadianlawyermag.com/author/michael-mckiernan/june-2016-the-going-rate-3292/ (prices converted using average USD/CAD exchange rates for 2016 provided by yCharts); e.g. Ward, Stephanie Francis. "Billable Hour Rates Rise but Who's Paying Full Price?" *ABA Journal*, 5 Jan. 2015, www.abajournal.com/news/article/billable_hour_rates_rise_but_whos_paying_full_price/. Firms do discount, but there's no evidence that the discount rates vary meaningfully between America and Canada. Also, adjusting for living costs using tools like purchasing power parity has only a minor effect on the American-Canadian differential.

42 PwC, and World Bank Group. *Paying Taxes 2018*. 2018, Table 3, www.pwc.com/gx/en/paying-taxes/pdf/pwc_paying_taxes_2018_full_report.pdf?WT.mc_id=CT13-PL1300-DM2-TR2-LS1-ND30-TTA4-CN_payingtaxes-2018-intro-pdf-button. The study is multivariate, and includes some metrics that are only indirectly related to law, including an important metric that reflects VAT processing times. However, America does not have a VAT, tending to reduce the contribution of this variable. *See also* "Paying Taxes Methodology." World Bank. http://www.doingbusiness.org/en/methodology/paying-taxes.

43 Globerman, Steven, and George Georgopoulos. *Regulation and the International Competitiveness of the U.S. Economy*. George Mason University, Mercatus

Center, 18 Sept. 2012, §§5.1, 5.3–.5.5, www.mercatus.org/system/files/InterntlCom petitiveness_Globerman_v1-0.pdf.

44 "US Companies Vastly Outspend Rest of the World on Legal Services, Acritas Survey Shows." Legal Executive Institute/Thomson Reuters, 21 June 2017 (citing Acritas study). Unfortunately, aside from the BEA and other government data cited earlier, most survey data about legal costs comes in the form of semi-promotional studies by consultancies. Nevertheless, the general direction and rough magnitude accord with government data, and these studies help fill the vacuum in academic research.

45 E.g., *Code du travail*, arts. 1221-6—1221-9 (France). German law does not specifically address background checks, but its Equal Treatment Act (AGG) and Data Protection Act (BDSG) greatly limit employer scrutiny, as do applicable collective bargaining agreements. In certain professions of high trust, employers may ask applicants for a *Führungszeugnis* (a sort of good behavior certificate) and leave it there. Some nations, like Spain, allow background checks but employers use them less frequently than in America. Other European nations, like the UK and Denmark, allow greater background checks, but EU members are limited by conventions of privacy. Limits on background checks vary by state in America, but employers have much greater latitude.

46 Shapiro, Daniel J. "Punitive Damages in Louisiana: A Year of Controversy." *Louisiana Bar Journal*, vol. 43, no. 3, Oct. 1995; Associated Press. "Big Jury Award for Coffee Burn." 19 Aug. 1994; Pfeifer, Stuart. "L.A. Woman Sues McDonald's Over Hot Coffee, 20 Years After Huge Verdict." *L.A. Times*, 9 Jan. 2014.

47 For discussion of judge/jury differentials, see Eisenberg, Theodore, and Michael Heise. "Judge-Jury Difference in Punitive Damages Awards: Who Listens to the Supreme Court." *Cornell Law Faculty Publications*, vol. 8, no. 2, June 2011, scholarship.law.cornell.edu/cgi/viewcontent.cgi?article=1198&context=facpub.

48 McKnight, David, and Paul Hinton. *International Comparisons of Litigation Costs: Canada, Europe, Japan, and the United States.* U.S. Chamber of Commerce, Institute for Legal Reform, June 2013, pp. 1–2 and Appendix, www.instituteforlegalreform.com/uploads/sites/1/ILR_NERA_Study_International_Liability_Costs-update.pdf. Measured as a fraction of GDP and controls for non-litigation costs.

49 *Ibid.*

50 E.g., Dodson, Scott. "Comparative Convergences in Pleading Standards." Penn. L. Rev., vol 158, no. 441, Parts I, II.B, (2010). America once had restrictive "Code" pleading, but from 1938 to 1957, "notice" pleading took over. Even contemporary British courts tend to expect more detailed pleading than their American peers.

51 Fed. R. Civ. P. 7–8, 10 (pleading); Fed. R. Civ. P. 9(b) (requiring "particularity" when alleging fraud); *Conley v. Gibson*, 355 U.S. 41 (1957) (upholding notice pleading); *see also Bell Atlantic Corp. v. Twombly*, 550 U.S. 544 (2007); *Ashcroft v. Iqbal*, 556 U.S. 662 (2009).

52 Fed. R. Civ. P. 11(a)-(b). Rule 11 sanctions are, frankly, a non-deterrent.

53 There are certain cases, like civil rights and bankruptcy, where fee-shifting is more common/required. But in general, each side bears its own expenses.

54   Hague Conference on Private International Law. *Convention on the Taking of Evidence Abroad in Civil or Commercial Matters*, 1970, Article 23, assets.hcch .net/docs/dfed98c0-6749-42d2-a9be-3d41597734f1.pdf (aka "The Hague Convention," ratified by the United States as 23 U.S.T. 2555).

55   For an overview of Hague Convention tussles, *see* Born, Gary B. "The Hague Evidence Convention Revisited: Reflections on Its Role in U.S. Civil Procedure." *Law and Contemporary Problems*, vol. 57, no. 3, 1994, pp. 82–83. *JSTOR*, doi:10.2307/1191967. *See also* "Status Table—20: Convention of 18 March 1970 on the Taking of Evidence Abroad in Civil or Commercial Matters." Hague Conference on Private International Law, www.hcch.net/en/instruments/conventions /status-table/?cid=82; Restatement (Third) of Foreign Relations Law § 442, Reporter's Note 1 (noting the considerable "friction" generated among other jurisdictions by American discovery rules).

56   Parrish, Michael. "Leading Class-Action Lawyer Is Sentenced to Two Years in Kickback Scheme." *New York Times*, 12 Feb. 2008, www.nytimes.com/ 2008/02/12/business/12legal.html.

57   Ministry of Justice and Legal Aid Agency, Legal Aid Statistics in England and Wales: January to March 2017, 29 June 2017; *see also* Bach Commission on Access to Justice, Sept. 2017, p. 4, Appx. 6. The relative difference is more pronounced in government-funded civil legal aid.

58   The Civil Procedures Rules 1998 (UK). No. 3132, L. 17 (1998).

59   E.g., Legal Profession Act of 2004 (NSW); Legal Services Acts of 2007, 2011 (UK); Ho, Catherine. "A Law Firm IPO? Not so Fast." *Washington Post*, 16 Feb. 2015, www .washingtonpost.com/business/capitalbusiness/a-law-firm-ipo-not-so-fast/ 2015/02/16/d8085ff6-b09b-11e4-827f-93f454140e2b_story.html?utm_term =.24849a10d221.

Chapter 9

1   Jackson, Robert. "The Federal Prosecutor." *Journal of American Judicature Society*, vol. 24, June 1940, p. 18.

2   *Ibid.*, p. 20.

3   Marcetic, Branko. "The Long, Cruel Career of Rudy Giuliani." *Jacobin*, Dec. 2016, jacobinmag.com/2016/12/rudy-giuliani-trump-cabinet-secretary-state-mayor/. Several of the principals of the firm did have certain convictions sustained, though many of the tax and securities charges were vacated or otherwise mooted. *United States v. Regan*, 946 F.2d 188 (2d Cir. 1991).

4   "Giuliani on Ferguson: 'Atmosphere of Unbalance' to Blame." *Fox News*, 12 Mar. 2015, video.foxnews.com/v/4107351747001/.

5   Morello, Carol, and Carol D. Leonnig. "Chris Christie's Long Record of Pushing Boundaries, Sparking Controversy." *Washington Post*, 10 Feb. 2014, www .washingtonpost.com/local/chris-christies-long-record-of-pushing -boundaries-sparking-controversy/2014/02/10/50111ed4-8db1-11e3-98ab -fe5228217bd1_story.html.

6   Jackson, Robert. "The Federal Prosecutor." *Journal of American Judicature Society*, vol. 24, June 1940, p. 18.

7   United Kingdom Parliament, House of Commons. Prosecution of Offenses Act 1879. The Act was passed in 1879 and the first Crown Prosecutor appointed the following year. In its early years, CPS handled few major cases; not until the twentieth century did CPS prosecute cases *en masse. See also* The National Archives. "History." *The Crown Prosecution Service*, webarchive.nationalar chives.gov.uk/20080612094118/http://www.cps.gov.uk/about/history.html. The focus here is on institutional prosecution; constables could and did charge criminals (often those caught in the act) with a variety of crimes, though these were not institutional "prosecutions" in anything like the modern sense: they were variable, sporadic, not the primary task of those bringing the charge, and obviously not disinterested.

8   United Kingdom Parliament. Prosecution of Offences Act 1985 (c. 23) § 6(1) ("Subject to subsection (2) below, *nothing in this Part shall preclude any person from instituting any criminal proceedings or conducting any criminal proceedings* to which the Director's duty to take over the conduct of proceedings does not apply") (emphasis added); Victor, Peter. "First Private Prosecution for Murder: 3 Held." *The Independent*, 23 Apr. 1995, www.independent.co.uk/news/first -private-prosecution-for-murder-3-held-1616684.html.

9   *Leeke v. Timmerman*, 454 U.S. 83 (1981). The Court had been leaning this way for a while. E.g., *Linda R.S. v. Richard D.*, 410 U.S. 614 (1973). Piecemeal abolition of private prosecution in various states has been ongoing for a century, but some states retain mechanisms to allow victims to assist public prosecutors. *See also Young v. United States*, 481 U.S. 787 (1987).

10   *Powell v. Alabama*, 287 U.S. 45 (1932); *Johnson v. Zerbst*, 304 U.S. 458 (1938) (counsel required for federal defendant); *Gideon v. Wainwright*, 372 U.S. 335 (1963) (extending right to counsel to all criminal defendants) (overruling *Betts v. Brady*, 316 U.S. 455 (1942)).

11   E.g., *Kirby v. Illinois*, 406 U.S. 682, 688 (1972) (holding that right does not attach prior to initiation of adversary judicial proceedings); *see also Missouri v. Frye*, 536 U.S. 134, 140 (2012) (noting that right does attach in "critical" stages of prosecution). The circuits are split on the details.

12   E.g., *Scott v. Illinois*, 440 U.S. 367, 373–374 (1979) (no right to counsel in misdemeanor cases where imprisonment not imposed); *Nichols v. United States*, 511 U.S. 738, 748 (1994) (same, and finding that in even in such cases without counsel, the conviction may be used to enhance a sentence for another crime or to revoke probation); *Ross v. Moffitt*, 417 U.S. 600, 601-02 (1974) (limiting right to trial to first appeals as of right; no right for discretionary appeals); *Lassiter v. Dept. of Social Services*, 425 U.S. 18 (1981) (regarding termination of child custody); other limits include no right to public counsel at civil proceedings, including civil contempt proceedings that may result in jail, *Turner v. Rogers*, 564 U.S. 431 (2011). *See also Terry v. Ashcroft* 354 F.3d, 1192, 1196 (10th Cir. 2003). Exact state practices vary, subject to Constitutional minima.

13   American Bar Association. *Criminal Justice Standards for the Prosecution Function* (Standards 3-1.2(b); 3-1.3; 3-4.4(a)) 4th ed., www.americanbar.org/groups

/criminal_justice/standards/ProsecutionFunctionFourthEdition.html (emphases added).

14   E.g., The State Bar of California. *Rules of Professional Conduct: Rule 5-110 Special Responsibilities of a Prosecutor* (including "Discussions") www.calbar.ca.gov/ Attorneys/Conduct-Discipline/Rules/Rules-of-Professional-Conduct/Current -Rules/Rule-5-110 (noting that a "prosecutor has the responsibility of a minister of justice and not simply that of an advocate"); Texas Government Code Annex. *Texas Disciplinary Rules of Professional Conduct: Title 2, subtitle G.* § 3.09 1989 (including Comment) www.legalethicstexas.com/Ethics-Resources/ Rules/Texas-Disciplinary-Rules-of-Professional-Conduct.aspx (similar); Office of the United States Attorneys. "9-27.000—Principles of Federal Prosecution." *U.S. Attorneys' Manual.* U.S. Department of Justice, www.justice.gov/usam/ usam-9-27000-principles-federal-prosecution (noting various interests to be considered in federal prosecution).

15   For a good philosophical overview of criminal law proliferation, *see* Husak, Douglas. *Overcriminalization: The Limits of the Criminal Law.* Oxford University Press, USA, 2008, *generally* and Parts 1.I.–III.

16   Task Force on the Federalization of Criminal Law. *The Federalization of Criminal Law.* American Bar Association, 1998, Part I. National Association of Criminal Defense Lawyers, www.nacdl.org/WorkArea/DownloadAsset.aspx?id=17464.

17   Baker, Jr., John S. *Revisiting the Explosive Growth of Federal Crimes.* No. 26, Heritage Foundation, 16 June 2008, www.heritage.org/report/revisiting-the -explosive-growth-federal-crimes. The 500 figure is a conservative extrapolation from Baker's post-1996–2007 survey numbers.

18   D.C. Code §§ 50-1731.02.1-.03.

19   Pub. L. 109-347 (2006); 31 U.S.C. § 5361 *et seq.*

20   21 U.S.C. § 801 *et seq.*, § 844.

21   *United States v. McNab, et al.,* 331 F.3d 1228 (11th Cir. 2003), amended and superseded by deleting n.24 but otherwise unaffected.

22   *Blockburger v. United States,* 284 U.S. 299 (1932). As a rule and as applied, *Blockburger* and its progeny (e.g., *Brown v. Ohio*) are not always clear, with nuances for matters such as "lesser-included" offenses, the timing of prosecutions, co-sovereigns, and so on. The point is: prosecutors have plenty of bites at what is essentially the same apple.

23   E.g., *Commonwealth v. Fernandez,* 43 Mass. App. Ct. 313, 315 (1997).

24   E.g., *Oyler v. Boles,* 368 U.S. 448, 456 (1962); *Newman v. United States,* 382 F.2d 479, 481–482 (D.C. Cir. 1967); *Washington v. United States,* 401 F.2d 915, 925 (D.C. Cir. 1968); *United States v. Ruggiero,* 472 F.2d 599, 606 (2d Cir. 1973) (citation omitted). A huge number of cases confirm the width of prosecutorial charging decisions.

25   U.S. Constitution, amend. IV Forty-eight states have grand jury mechanisms, but only 23 actively use grand juries. *Hurtado v. California* declined to enforce the Fifth Amendment grand jury requirement against the states. 110 U.S. 516 (1884).

26   Fed. R. Crim. Pro. 6-7, 31. The precise rule is at least twelve jurors must agree to indict.

27 Office of the United States Attorneys. "9-11.000—Grand Jury." *U.S. Attorneys' Manual.* U.S. Department of Justice, www.justice.gov/usam/usam-9-27000 -principles-federal-prosecution.

28 E.g., Fed. R. Crim. Pro. 6; *United States v. Williams,* 504 U.S. 36, 49 (1992) (noting that the Court has suggested, though not held, that right to counsel does not obtain at this stage, even if witness is subject of investigation); Brown, Stephen, and Christine Levin. "Preparing a Grand Jury Witness: Sweaty Palms, Racing Heartbeat." *Litigation,* vol. 37, no. 4, 2011, pp. 28–31. Some states allow counsel, though often subject to restrictions.

29 *United States v. Calandra,* 414 U.S. 338, 343 (1974).

30 *United States v. Morton Salt Co.,* 338 U.S. 632, 642–643 (1950) (discussing administrative proceedings and describing investigatory powers of grand jury) (emphasis added).

31 *United States v. R Enterprises,* 498 U.S. 292, 297–301 (1991). Although the Court denied that it was permitting *"arbitrary* fishing expeditions" (or malicious ones), it *did* allow fishing generally, subject to the weak constraint of Federal Rule of Criminal Procedure 17(c)'s prohibition on unreasonable and oppressive subpoenas; however, targets can only overcome this by showing *"no reasonable possibility"* that the subpoena will help the grand jury execute its broad mandate. *Ibid.* 301 (in context of relevancy dispute) (emphasis added). Pages cited are from the sub-parts of *R Enterprises* that constitute the opinion of the (otherwise fractured) Court.

32 *Kaley v. United States,* 517 U.S. __ (2014) at Part II (citing cases for proposition that grand jury indictment viable if that body is properly assembled and indicts based on probable cause).

33 *Ibid.* (noting, in federal forfeiture case requiring probable cause that "[p]robable cause, we have often told litigants, is not a high bar: It requires only the kind of 'fair probability' on which 'reasonable and prudent [people,] not legal technicians, act.'") (citations omitted).

34 *Compare* 15 U.S.C. § 78(j); 17 C.F.R. § 240.10b5; *Ernst & Ernst v. Hochfelder,* 425 U.S. 185 (1976) (securities violation) *with* 17 C.F.R. § 240.10b5-1 (affirmative defense on misuse).

35 E.g., *United States v. Drew,* 722 F.2d 551 (9th Cir. 1983) (construing "knowing" and "willful" in challenged indictment sufficient stand-ins for fraudulent intent as element of crime); *see also* Office of the United States Attorneys. "221. Sufficiency." *Criminal Resource Manual (U.S. Attorneys' Manual),* U.S. Department of Justice, www.justice.gov/usam/criminal-resource-manual-221-sufficiency; *see also* "222. Elements of the Offense" and "223. Requirement of Specificity."

36 Fed. R. Crim. Pro. 6.

37 Motivans, Mark. *Federal Justice Statistics 2010—Statistical Tables.* Office of Justice Programs, Department of Justice, Dec. 2013, pp. 1–56, table 2.3, www .bjs.gov/content/pub/pdf/fjs10st.pdf (noting 11 bills not returned); "Flash Facts About Lightning." *National Geographic News,* June 2005, news.nationalgeo graphic.com/news/2004/06/0623_040623_lightningfacts.html. Lightning risk is lifetime risk.

38 Gould, David. "Sol Wachtler." *Historical Society of the New York Courts*, www
.nycourts.gov/history/legal-history-new-york/history-legal-bench-court
-appeals.html; www.nycourts.gov/history/legal-history-new-york/luminaries-court
-appeals/wachtler-sol.html ("ham sandwich," also quoted in Tom Wolfe's *Bon-
fire of the Vanities*). Wachtler himself was eventually fell into the "ham sandwich" category and was duly indicted—and ultimately convicted; Schemo,
Diana Jean. "A Prison Term of 15 Months for Wachtler." *New York Times*, 10 Sept.
1993, www.nytimes.com/1993/09/10/nyregion/a-prison-term-of-15-months-for
-wachtler.html.

39 Federal prosecutions have subsided somewhat since 2011.

40 E.g., Bandyopadhyay, Siddhartha, and Bryan C. McCannon, "The effect of elections of public prosecutors on trials." *Public Choice*, vol. 161, no. 1/2 (October
2014), pp. 141–156; Wright, Roland F. "How Prosecutor Elections Fail Us." Ohio
State Crim. L.J., vol 6, p. 581, Table 3 (2009); *see also* Berry, Kate. *How Judicial
Elections Impact Criminal Cases*. Brennan Center for Justice, New York University School of Law (noting that *judges* facing reelection/retention contests
become more punitive toward defendants), www.brennancenter.org/sites/default
/files/publications/How_Judicial_Elections_Impact_Criminal_Cases.pdf;
Weiss, Joanna Cohn. "Tough on Crime: How Campaigns for State Judiciary Violate Criminal Defendants Due Process Rights." *New York University Law Review*,
vol. 81, 2006, pp. 1101–1136. Prosecutors face similar electoral pressures (real or
imagined, as small-town prosecutors often run unopposed), and adjust strategies accordingly, usually by promoting tough on crime policies and perhaps also
by adjusting their mix of plea bargains and trials to achieve the most pleasing
statistics. It also appears that prosecutors focus more on policies than concrete
statistics, though the two cannot be entirely divorced.

41 *Morrison v. Olson*, 487 U.S. 654, 730–731 (1988) (Scalia, dissenting) (suggesting
in a case involving a special counsel, that executive was ultimately accountable
to the people).

42 E.g., Crown Prosecution Service. *Advocates: Selection Of*. Last updated 2010,
www.cps.gov.uk/legal-guidance/advocates-selection.

43 *FY 2017 Performance Budget Congressional Submission*. U.S. Department of Justice, p.1, www.justice.gov/jmd/file/821011/download.

44 *Ibid.*, pp. 21–22.

45 *Ibid.*; Motivans, Mark. *Federal Justice Statistics 2014—Statistical Tables*. Office
of Justice Programs, Department of Justice, Mar. 2017, pp. 1–56, table 2.2, www
.bjs.gov/content/pub/pdf/fjs14st.pdf. "Matters" treated as suspects disposed of.

46 E.g., 28 U.S.C. § 530B (requiring federal attorneys to comply with relevant state/
local rule, but imposing no independent new duties).

47 Most prosecutorial ethics standards are phrased as "shoulds," not "shalls" or
"musts." E.g., Office of the United States Attorneys. "9-27.000—Principles of
Federal Prosecution." *U.S. Attorneys' Manual*. U.S. Department of Justice,
https://www.justice.gov/usam/usam-9-27000-principles-federal-prosecution;
American Bar Association. *Criminal Justice Standards for the Prosecution
Function* (Standards 3-1.1(c)). 4th ed., www.americanbar.org/groups/criminal
_justice/standards/ProsecutionFunctionFourthEdition.html. Most states do

the same, with a few exceptions. E.g., W. Va. Code § 7-4-1 (generally mandating prosecution).

48 Office of the United States Attorneys. "9-2.001—Introduction." *U.S. Attorneys' Manual,* U.S. Department of Justice, 19 Feb. 2015 (updated Apr. 2018) (noting AUSA's have "plenary authority with regard to [] federal criminal matters"), www.justice.gov/usam/usam-9-2000-authority-us-attorney-criminal-division -mattersprior-approvals; *ibid.,* "9-27.120—Application" and "9-27.140—Modifications and Departures" ("United States Attorneys may modify or depart from the principles set forth herein as necessary in the interests of fair and effective law enforcement within the district.") and "9-27.001—Preface ("These principles of federal prosecution have been designed to assist in structuring the decision-making process of attorneys for the government. For the most part, they have been cast in general terms with a view to providing guidance rather than to mandating results.") Occasionally, DOJ will issue memoranda pushing prosecutors to use discretion in certain ways, but as usual, couched in conditional language. *E.g.,* United States Department of Justice, Office of Public Affairs. "Attorney General Holder Announces New Policy to Enhance Justice Department's Commitment to Support Defendant's Right to Counsel." *Justice News,* 14 Oct. 2014, www.justice.gov/opa/pr/attorney-general-holder-announces-new-policy-enhance-justice-departments-commitment-suppoet; Memorandum from Deputy Attorney General James M. Cole to All Federal Prosecutors (Oct. 14, 2014) (suggesting that prosecutors "should no longer" seek plea agreements that require defendants to waive ineffective assistance of counsel arguments).

49 Office of the United States Attorneys. "1-4.000—Standards of Conduct." *U.S. Attorneys' Manual,* U.S. Department of Justice, 19 Feb. 2015, www.justice.gov/ usam/usam-1-4000-standards-conduct; *ibid.* "9-27.150—Non-Litigability." State bars can sanction prosecutors independently for ethical violations, but the standards are somewhat different.

50 *Imbler v. Pachtman,* 424 U.S. 409, 423 (1976) (noting, in § 1983 case alleging use of false testimony and suppressed evidence, that "concern that harassment by unfounded litigation would cause a deflection of the prosecutor's energies from his public duties, and the possibility that he would shade his decisions instead of exercising the independence of judgment required by his public trust"); *see also Taylor v. Kavanagh,* 640 F.2d 450 (2nd Cir. 1981). The dropped Supreme Court case was *Pottawattamie v. Maghee,* whose history and amici curiae were referenced in the news. "Supreme Court Drops Key Case on Limits of Immunity for Prosecutors." *Christian Science Monitor,* Jan. 2010, www.csmonitor.com/USA/ Justice/2010/0104/Supreme-Court-drops-key-case-on-limits-of-immunity-for -prosecutors.

51 *Buckley v. Fitzsimmons,* 509 U.S. 259, 273–276 (1993).

52 18 U.S.C. 3006A *et seq.* (aka the "Hyde Amendment of 1997"). Recovery limits are embedded in the Hyde Amendment through reference to 28 U.S.C. § 2412. The Hyde Amendment is badly drafted, there are few cases, and no one is quite sure what the standards are.

53 *See North Carolina v. Pearce,* 395 U.S. 711 (1969) (regarding judicial immunity's viability when conduct alleged to be vindictive, analogous to prosecutorial

immunity case). The other important thread is *Yick Wo v. Hopkins,* 118 U.S. 356 (1886) and its progeny. While *Yick Wo* is a law school classic, the practical barriers to suing prosecutors are so high they are rarely overcome, and because of its focus on discriminatory bureaucratic administration, *Yick Wo* isn't exactly squarely on point, prosecutor-wise.

54 *Ernst v. Child & Youth Services,* 180 F.3d 486 (3rd Cir. 1997).

55 The law on the Sentencing Guidelines changed after *United States v. Booker,* 543 U.S. 220 (2005) (*inter alia,* striking down part of federal law that required judges to sentence within a legislated range). These issues are discussed *infra* Chapter 12.

56 Office of the United States Attorneys. "626. Plea Agreements and Sentencing Appeal Waivers—Discussion of the Law." *Criminal Resource Manual (U.S. Attorneys' Manual).* U.S. Department of Justice, www.justice.gov/usam/criminal-resource-manual-626-plea-agreements-and-sentencing-appeal-waivers-discussion-law. The *Manual* also contains a helpful list of cases.

57 *Ibid.* (noting that such "could encourage a lawless district court to impose sentences in violation of the guidelines").

58 *Compare* Perry, Steven W., and Duren Banks. *Prosecutors in State Courts, 2007—Statistical Tables.* U.S. Department of Justice, Office of Justice Programs, Bureau of Justice Statistics, Dec. 2011, pp. 1–11, table 2, www.bjs.gov/content/pub/pdf/psc07st.pdf *with* Langton, Lynn, and Donald Farole. *State Public Defender Programs, 2007.* U.S. Department of Justice, Office of Justice Programs, Bureau of Justice Statistics, Sept. 2010, p. 22, table 1, www.bjs.gov/content/pub/pdf/spdp07 .pdf. Maine had no public defender and is excluded from defender statistics. The BJS data are neither complete nor perfect, but seem reliable as to general direction and rough magnitude.

59 E.g., NY Cty. L. art. 18-B § 722 (2014) (providing for appointments). *Compare* "Assigned Counsel Plan (18B): FAQ (Frequently Asked Questions)." *Appellate Division—First Judicial Department, Supreme Court of the State of New York, at Overview* (noting $60-75 hour range for appointed counsel), www.nycourts .gov/courts/AD1/Committees&Programs/18B/index.shtml#faq *with* "New York Plumbing Service Costs & Prices—ProMatcher Cost Report." *ProMatcher,* plum bers.promatcher.com/cost/new-york-ny-plumbers-costs-prices.aspx.

60 U.S. Department of Justice, Office of Justice Programs, Bureau of Justice Assistance. "Contracting for Indigent Defense Services: A Special Report." Prepared by Spangenberg Group, et al., p. 1, Apr. 2000, www.ncjrs.gov/pdffiles1/bja/181160.pdf.

61 Gross, Samuel R., and Michael Shaffer. *Exonerations in the United States, 1989–2012.* National Registry of Exonerations, 22 June 2012, pp. 1, 58, 66, www.law .umich.edu/special/exoneration/Documents/exonerations_us_1989_2012 _full_report.pdf; *see also* e.g., Wines, Michael. "Prosecutors Had the Wrong Man. They Prosecuted Him Anyway." *New York Times,* 17 Jan. 2018, www .nytimes.com/2018/01/17/us/prosecutors-new-orleans-evidence.html.

62 *United States v. Kenneth R. Olsen.* 737 F.3d 625 (2013) (Kozinski, dissenting) cdn.ca9 .uscourts.gov/datastore/opinions/2013/12/10/10-36063%20web.pdf Wines, Michael, *ibid.*

63 Kohler-Hausmann, Issa. "Managerial Justice and Mass Misdemeanors." *Stanford Law Review,* vol. 66, no. 3, Mar. 2014, pp. 611–693, 655 (noting role of policy,

which can cut either way); Yoffe, Emily. "Innocence Is Irrelevant: This Is the Age of the Plea Bargain—and Millions of Americans are Suffering the Consequences." *Atlantic*, Sept. 2017, www.theatlantic.com/magazine/archive/2017/09/innocence-is-irrelevant/534171/.

64   Estes, Adam Clark. "Aaron Swartz Isn't the First Hacker to Commit Suicide in the Face of a Federal Investigation." *Atlantic*, 14 Jan. 2013, www.theatlantic.com/technology/archive/2013/01/aaron-swartz-isnt-first-hacker-commit-suicide-face-federal-investigation/319484/; *United States v. Aaron Swartz*. Crim. No. 11-CR-10260-NMG, www.wired.com/images_blogs/threatlevel/2012/09/swartz superseding.pdf; Schofield, Jack, "Aaron Swartz Obituary." *Guardian*, 13 Jan. 2013, www.theguardian.com/technology/2013/jan/13/aaron-swartz. Swartz also suffered from depression, which might have contributed to his suicide.

65   Kutateladze, Besiki Luka, and Nancy R. Andiloro. *Prosecution and Racial Justice in New York County—Technical Report*. Document no. 247227, Prosecution and Racial Justice Program, Vera Institute of Justice, 31 Jan. 2014, www.ncjrs.gov/pdffiles1/nij/grants/247227.pdf. Race is only one, and not always the strongest, factor (though many factors are strongly interrelated).

66   Walters, Joanna. "Supreme Court Considers Taking Case of Man Given Life in Prison for Growing Pot." *Guardian*, 15 Apr. 2016, www.theguardian.com/society/2016/apr/15/lee-carroll-brooker-alabama-marijuana-sentence.

67   McKinley, Jr., James C. "Cy Vance Defends Decision Not to Pursue Case Against Harvey Weinstein." *New York Times*, 11 Oct. 2017, www.nytimes.com/2017/10/11/nyregion/cy-vance-defends-weinstein-decision.html; Bernstein, Andrea, et al. "How Ivanka Trump and Donald Trump, Jr., Avoided a Criminal Indictment." *New Yorker*, 4 Oct. 2017, www.newyorker.com/news/news-desk/how-ivanka-trump-and-donald-trump-jr-avoided-a-criminal-indictment.

68   Taketa, Kristen. "Missouri's Head Public Defender Assigns Case to Gov. Nixon, Cites Overburdened Staff." *St. Louis Post-Dispatch*, 3 Aug. 2016, www.stltoday.com/news/local/state-and-regional/missouri-s-head-public-defender-assigns-case-to-gov-nixon/article_37809be0-b7ee-56b4-b478-bf8dfe01720f.html (noting the defender's claim that the governor withheld funds).

69   Perry, Steven W. and Duren Banks. *Prosecutors in State Courts, 2007—Statistical Tables*. U.S. Department of Justice, Office of Justice Programs, Bureau of Justice Statistics. Dec. 2011, table 7, www.bjs.gov/content/pub/pdf/psc07st.pdf.

Chapter 10

1   "Freedom Is About Authority: Excerpts from Giuliani Speech on Crime," *New York Times*, 20 Mar. 1994, https://www.nytimes.com/1994/03/20/nyregion/freedom-is-about-authority-excerpts-from-giuliani-speech-on-crime.html.

2   Lodge, Richard K. "Police Investigation Details the Night Eurie Stamps, Sr. Died." *Metro West Daily News*, 1 May 2011, www.metrowestdailynews.com/x730839074/Police-investigation-details-the-night-Eurie-Stamps-Sr-died (describing the events); Haddadin, Jim. "Family of Framingham Man Killed by

Police Receives $3.75 Million Settlement." *Patriot Ledger,* 29 Sept. 2016, www
.patriotledger.com/news/20160929/family-of-framingham-man-killed-by-police
-receives-375-million-settlement; Haddadin, Jim. "Framingham Settles Lawsuit in Stamps Case." *Metro West Daily News,* 4 Sept. 2016, www.metrowestdaily
news.com/news/20160904/framingham-settles-lawsuit-in-stamps-case (describing
the settlement and referencing the "unfortunate matter"); Balko, Radley. "Still
Waiting for Justice after SWAT Team Member Kills Innocent Grandfather." *Washington Post,* 6 Jan. 2015, www.washingtonpost.com/news/the-watch/wp/2015/01/
06/still-waiting-for-justice-after-swat-team-member-kills-innocent-grand
father/?noredirect=on&utm_term=.d6ebbd5cdfd7 (opining on history of the case
prior to its appeal and settlement and discussing the legal issues); *Stamps v. Framingham,* No. 15-1141 (1st Cir. 2016).

3 "War Comes Home: The Excessive Militarization of American Policing."
ACLU, June 2014, p. 19, www.aclu.org/sites/default/files/field_document/jus14
-warcomeshome-text-rel1.pdf. *See also* Balko, Radley. *The Rise of the Warrior
Cop: The Militarization of America's Police Forces,* Reprint ed., *PublicAffairs,* 26
Aug. 2014.

4 *Ibid.,* pp. 3, 11, 19, 22, www.aclu.org/sites/default/files/field_document/jus14
-warcomeshome-text-rel1.pdf (citations omitted).

5 *Ibid.* p.16, Appendix B ("Agreement between the Defense Logistics Agency and
the [Applying] State of ___" www.aclu.org/sites/default/files/field_document/
jus14-warcomeshome-text-rel1.pdf.

6 *Ibid.,* pp. 2–4, www.aclu.org/sites/default/files/field_document/jus14-warcome
shome-text-rel1.pdf.

7 Szymanski, Mike. "Apology for Involvement in Police Weapons Programs Not
Enough for Protestors." *LA School Report,* 25 Apr. 2016, laschoolreport.com/
apology-for-involvement-in-police-weapons-program-not-enough-for-protesters/.

8 Fund, John. "The United States of SWAT?" *National Review,* 18 Apr. 2014,
www.nationalreview.com/2014/04/united-states-swat-john-fund/ (Seagal); Mider,
Zachary, and Zeke Faux. "Robert Mercer Got a New Badge. The Sheriff Got a
New Dodge Ram." 16 Apr. 2018, *Bloomberg,* www.bloomberg.com/news/articles/
2018-04-16/robert-mercer-got-a-new-badge-the-sheriff-got-a-new-dodge-ram.

9 Fuhrmann, Christopher J. *Policing the Roman Empire: Soldiers, Administration,
and Public Order.* Reprint ed., Oxford University Press, 11 Apr. 2014. Furhmann
is something of a corrective to the prevailing view that Rome lacked police, but at
most, Rome employed a motley array of provincial governors, detached legion-
aries, and mercenaries for ad hoc protection of Roman citizens (a minority of the
population in most places). Ancient Egypt has been cited as sponsoring police,
but these guardians fell into the ancient archetype of paramilitaries mainly concerned with protecting property and enforcing laws of personal importance to
ruling families, e.g., tracking down tomb robbers. China, having a longer history of bureaucratic centralization, had the only pre-modern forces that could
be plausibly be described as police. As early as the Eastern Zhou Dynasty
(c. 770–255 BC), Chinese "prefects" had the power to make arrests, refer cases for
judicial disposition, and even conduct basic detection.

10 "Police" proximately derives from the post-classical Latin *politia*, in the sense of civil administration, which was the word's common use before the very late eighteenth century; Latin's *politia* draws on Greek's *polis* (or a corruption/borrowing thereof). "Police." *Oxford English Dictionary On-Line*; *see also* "Police." *Online Etymology Dictionary*.

11 Athens had a few magistrates with specific "beats," but nothing we would recognize as a police force. Sparta stood as partial exception and employed the *Krypteia*, a sort of secret police, but their main duties were to keep helots—serfs who were not full citizens—in line.

12 E.g., Police and Criminal Evidence Act 1984, 1984 c 6098, Part III.24.4A (as updated in 2018) (providing that "a person other than a constable may arrest without a warrant" subject to certain limitations) (emphasis added), www.legislation .gov.uk/ukpga/1984/60/pdfs/ukpga_19840060_en.pdf; Cal. Penal Code § 837 (providing for arrests by "private person[s]" subject to certain conditions). Today, most private detentions occur either in the context of bounty hunting (under auxiliary authority, discussed elsewhere in this chapter) or via the "shopkeeper's privilege," which in some jurisdictions allows merchants to detain those suspected of shoplifting until police arrive. The perils of exercising these privileges is substantial, both in terms of physical danger and civil liabilities for injuries resulting from private detention.

13 Assize of Arms 1252 (Henry III); Statute of Winchester, 13 Edw. I, St. 1 (1285) (Edward, more germanely).

14 The myth gained currency (and was perhaps even invented) in the century after Edward I died, but it's generally understood to have taken place near Edward's reign. Of the thirteenth-century sheriffs, two sheriffs are still remembered: Reynold de Grey and John de Balliol, whose names will be familiar to British lawyers from Gray's [sic] Inn and Balliol College, the former sited on de Grey's land and the latter endowed by Balliol.

15 Glasgow claims it created the first police force, though that's not quite true.

16 The London Police's General Instructions embody what are known as "Peel's Principles of Policing," though Peel probably did not write the principles himself. The Principles are available at: Gov.UK. "Definition of Policing by Consent." 10 Dec. 2012, www.gov.uk/government/publications/policing-by-consent/definition -of-policing-by-consent.

17 Gaunt, Richard A. *Sir Robert Peel: The Life and Legacy*. I.B. Tauris, 2010, pp. 67–69.

18 The Fourth Amendment is read to prohibit general warrants, requiring specific warrants tailored to the circumstances, supported by oath or affirmation, and issued only when "probable cause" exists. The Constitution, which predates modern police, does not address policing specifically, though the Third Amendment's prohibition on quartering troops reflects the Framers' distaste regarding internal occupations by militarized forces.

19 Wagner, Bryan. "Disarmed and Dangerous: The Strange Career of Bras-Coupé." *Representations*, vol. 92, no.1, pp. 119–120, 2005.

20 The Declaration of Independence provides a useful list of grievances.

21 Reaves, Brian A. "Local Police Departments, 2013: Personnel, Policies, and Practices." *U.S. Department of Justice, Office of Justice Programs, Bureau of Justice Statistics' Bulletin*, 14 May 2015, table 1, www.bjs.gov/content/pub/pdf/lpd13ppp.pdf.

22 Gov.UK. "National Statistics: Police Workforce, England and Wales: 31 March 2015." 16 July 2015, p. 9: Police Workforce, by Type of Police Worker, as of 31 March 2015, England and Wales (citing current and historical data), www.gov.uk/government/publications/police-workforce-england-and-wales-31-march-2015/police-workforce-england-and-wales-31-march-2015; National Audit Office, "Financial Sustainability of Police Forces in England and Wales." 4 June 2015, p. 5 and fig 2: Central Versus Local Government Funding by Force Area in 2015–16, www.nao.org.uk/wp-content/uploads/2015/06/Financial-sustainability-of-police-forces.pdf#page=18.

23 Reaves, Brian A. "Federal Law Enforcement Officers, 2008." *U.S. Department of Justice, Office of Justice Programs, Bureau of Justice Statistics' Bulletin*, June 2012, pp. 1, 14–15, www.bjs.gov/content/pub/pdf/fleo08.pdf.

24 "National Policy Summit: Building Private Security/Public Policing Partnerships to Prevent and Respond to Terrorism and Public Disorder—Private Security/Public Policing—Vital Issues and Policy Recommendations." International Association of Chiefs of Police, 2004, p. 2 (estimating 90,000 organizations employing up to 2 million "security officers and other practitioners"), www.theiacp.org/Portals/0/pdfs/Publications/ACFAB5D.pdf *see also* United States Department of Labor, Bureau of Labor Statistics. "Occupational Employment Statistics—May 2017 Occupation Profiles." E.g., employment code 33-9032—Security Guards (noting 1.1 million private guards in this category).

25 E.g., Virginia Code § 19.2-13 (allowing for "SCOPS" private police with guns, powers of arrest, and in specialized cases, badges), CA Penal Code §§ 830.2, 830.32, 830.75 (UC campus police and private campus police); *see also* Jouvenal, Justin. "Private police carry guns and make arrests, and their ranks are swelling." *Washington Post,* 28 Feb. 2015, www.washingtonpost.com/local/crime/private-police-carry-guns-and-make-arrests-and-their-ranks-are-swelling/2015/02/28/29f6e02e-8f79-11e4-a900-9960214d4cd7_story.html?utm_term=.e76d64ced8a6. Practices vary among the states: Virginia, North Carolina, and South Carolina, for example, allow various combinations of arrest powers, sirens, special badges, and so on, while states like California allow for private security but disallow other police-like behavior (save on some campuses), though many still allow certain private individuals to carry weapons openly and/or allow for citizen's arrests.

26 Mider, Zachary, and Zeke Faux. "Robert Mercer Got a New Badge. The Sheriff Got a New Dodge Ram." 16 Apr. 2018, *Bloomberg,* www.bloomberg.com/news/articles/2018-04-16/robert-mercer-got-a-new-badge-the-sheriff-got-a-new-dodge-ram.

27 Federal Bureau of Investigation. "Career Paths: Special Agents." FBI Jobs, www.fbijobs.gov/career-paths/special-agents.

28 E.g., U. S. Department of Labor, Bureau of Labor Statistics. "How to Become a Police Officer or Detective." *Occupational Outlook Handbook,* www.bls.gov/

ooh/protective-service/police-and-detectives.htm#tab-4. The SFPD is fairly typical. City and County of San Francisco, Police Department. "Career Opportunities." sanfranciscopolice.org/career-opportunities.

29 Reaves, Brian A. "Local Police Departments, 2013: Personnel, Policies, and Practices." *U.S. Department of Justice, Office of Justice Programs, Bureau of Justice Statistics' Bulletin,* 14 May 2015, table 7 and accompanying text, www.bjs.gov/content/pub/pdf/lpd13ppp.pdf.

30 From the late 1980s, the DCPD lowered standards across several variables. For an accurate, though partisan, summary of the consequences of DCPD's hiring failures and general mismanagement, including its failure to raise education requirements from GED-level while other large departments were raising academic requirements, *see* Rowan, Jr., Carl T. "Who's Policing D.C. Cops?" *Washington Post,* 8 Oct. 1995, www.washingtonpost.com/archive/opinions/1995/10/08/whos-policing-dc-cops/73b5deea-03e8-4928-a342-652e4ef1b247/?utm_term=.aa19996b5ca2; *see also* Labaton, Stephen. "U.S. Accuses 12 Capital Officers of Protecting a Cocaine Racket." *New York Times,* 16 Dec. 1993, www.nytimes.com/1993/12/16/us/us-accuses-12-capital-officers-of-protecting-a-cocaine-racket.html.

31 Rydberg, Jason and William Terrill. "The Effect of Higher Education on Police Behavior." *Police Quarterly,* vol. 13, no. 1, 3 Jan. 2010; *Sage Journals,* journals.sagepub.com/doi/10.1177/1098611109357325; Stickle, Ben. "A National Examination of the Effect of Education, Training and Pre-Employment Screening on Law Enforcement Use of Force." *Justice Policy Journal,* vol. 13, no. 1, 2016, pp. 3, 12, www.cjcj.org/uploads/cjcj/documents/jpj_education_use_of_force.pdf (noting that education is an important variable, though pre-employment screening might be even more effective); Paoline III, Eugene A., and William Terrill. "Police Education, Experience, and the Use of Force." *Criminal Justice and Behavior,* vol. 34, no. 2, pp. 179–196, 1 Feb. 2007; *Sage Journals,* journals.sagepub.com/doi/abs/10.1177/0093854806290239 (finding that college education reduces verbal force and 4-year college notably reduces physical force).

32 U.S. Census Bureau. "Educational Attainment in the United States: 2015: Population Characteristics: Current Population Reports." Ryan, Camille L. and Kurt Bauman, Mar. 2016, p. 1 and Table 1, www.census.gov/content/dam/Census/library/publications/2016/demo/p20-578.pdf. Almost 60% have "some" college (ages 25+).

33 Reaves, Brian A. "Hiring and Retention of State and Local Law Enforcement Officers, 2008—Statistical Tables." *U.S. Department of Justice, Office of Justice Programs, Bureau of Justice Statistics,* Oct. 2012, p. 14, www.bjs.gov/content/pub/pdf/hrslleo08st.pdf.

34 *Final Report of the President's Task Force on 21st Century Policing,* May 2015. "Pillar 2. Policy & Oversight: Recommendation 2.15," pp. 29–30, www.theiacp.org/Portals/0/taskforce_finalreport.pdf (noting lack of comprehensive national database).

35 CA.Gov's Commission on Peace Officer Standards and Training. "Regular Basic Course Training Specifications: Regular Basic Course Minimum Hourly Requirements—Minimum Content and Hourly Requirements Regular Basic

Course (RBC)—Standard Format." 1 July 2018, post.ca.gov/regular-basic-course-training-specifications.

36 Some European departments recruit high school graduates and compensate for lack of a BA by recruiting from police-oriented vocational schools or by requiring longer training programs.

37 E.g., Metropolitan Police. "How to Become a Police Constable." www.metpolicecareers.co.uk/newconstable/becoming-a-pc.php; Dodd, Vikram. "New Police Officers Face Degree Requirement." *Guardian*, 14 Dec. 2016, www.theguardian.com/uk-news/2016/dec/15/new-police-officers-face-degree-requirement; Greater Manchester Police. "Sample of Training Programme." 19 Apr. 2017, www.gmp.police.uk/content/section.html?readform&s=6b8b2141790c8cb8802579fe0046f1ea.

38 COPS Office. *The President's Task Force on 21st Century Policing Implementation Guide: Moving from Recommendations to Action*, 2015, pp. 1, 11, noblenational.org/wp-content/uploads/2017/02/President-Barack-Obama-Task-Force-on-21st-Century-Policing-Implementation-Guide.pdf.

39 Morin, Rich, et al. "Behind the Badge: Amid Protests and Calls for Reform, How Police View Their Jobs, Key Issues and Recent Fatal Encounters between Blacks and Police." *Pew Research Center,* 11 Jan. 2017, p. 76, assets.pewresearch.org/wp-content/uploads/sites/3/2017/01/06171402/Police-Report_FINAL_web.pdf. Surveys of police revealed a slightly different view. *Ibid.* (noting that 8% of police view themselves as enforcers, 31% as protectors, and 62% as "both equally"; for the public, the figures were respectively 29% enforcers, 16% protectors, and 53% "both equally").

40 Data on police time varies by organization and internal department. The fragmentation of American policing makes it especially hard to obtain data on police use of time, but the figures presented seem reasonably constant across time and geography. Webster, John A. "Police Task and Time Study." *Journal of Criminal Law and Criminology*, vol. 61, issue 1, article 9, 1970, table 1 and accompanying text, scholarlycommons.law.northwestern.edu/cgi/viewcontent.cgi?article=5642&context=jclc (studying a mid-sized city and noting that violent crime accounted for 2.96% of time spent, property crimes 14.82% of time spent, with the rest devoted to other activities); *see also* Kappeler, Victor E. "So You Want to be a Crime Fighter? Not So Fast." *EKU Police Studies Online,* 12 Feb. 2013, plsonline.eku.edu/insidelook/so-you-want-be-crime-fighter-not-so-fast (summarizing selected literature, with general range of classic crime-fighting activities usually under 25% of total time/incidents).

41 Kelling, George L., et al. "The Kansas City Preventive Patrol Experiment: A Summary Report." *Police Foundation*, 1974, www.policefoundation.org/publication/the-kansas-city-preventive-patrol-experiment/. "Satisfaction" here refers to various metrics of same in the cited report.

42 Carr, Christine Marie. "The Kansas City Foot Patrol Project: An Evaluation of the Effectiveness of Foot Patrol in Violent Crime Micro-Places." 2014, at Chapter 2, mospace.umsystem.edu/xmlui/bitstream/handle/10355/43482/CarrKanCitFoo.pdf?sequence=1&isAllowed=y. Carr summarizes the literature and notes benefits were limited, and though some subsets felt safer, crime remained stable.

43 "The Newark Foot Patrol Experiment." *Police Foundation*, 1981, www.ncjrs.gov/App/Publications/abstract.aspx?ID=81779. For a contrary account, see Ratcliffe, Jerry H., et al. "The Philadelphia Foot Patrol Experiment: A Randomized Controlled Trial of Police Patrol Effectiveness in Violent Crime Hotspots." *Criminology*, vol. 49, no. 3, 8 Aug. 2011. Wiley Online Library, onlinelibrary.wiley.com/doi/abs/10.1111/j.1745-9125.2011.00240.x.

44 Carr, Christine Marie. *Ibid.*

45 U.S. Department of Justice, Federal Bureau of Investigation, Criminal Justice Information Services Division. "Offenses Cleared." *Uniform Crime Report, Crime in The United States, 2016*, ucr.fbi.gov/crime-in-the-u.s/2016/crime-in-the-u.s.-2016/topic-pages/clearances.

46 U.S. Department of Justice, Federal Bureau of Investigation, Criminal Justice Information Services Division. "Crime in the United States 2015." *Uniform Crime Report, Table 26—Percent of Offenses Cleared by Arrest or Exceptional Means by Geographic Region and Division*, 2015, ucr.fbi.gov/crime-in-the-u.s/2015/crime-in-the-u.s.-2015/tables/table-26; author's calculations. Figures for 2016 and other recent years, also from the UCR, are generally comparable.

47 Truman, Jennifer L., and Morgan, Rachel E. "Criminal Victimization, 2015." *U.S. Department of Justice, Office of Justice Programs, Bureau of Justice Statistics' Bulletin*, 22 Mar. 2018 (revised), at tables 1, 4, www.bjs.gov/content/pub/pdf/cv15.pdf. Census/BJS calculate unreported victimization by inference and survey; BJS figures are for "violent victimizations" and "property victimizations" and exclude homicide for methodological reasons. Sources conflict on the precise level of non-reporting and there are definitional differences between the NVCS and UCR, but the BJS figures are within the range of reasonable estimates and the best available.

48 Walker, Samuel and Charles M. Katz. *The Police in America: An Introduction*, 9th ed., 2018, p. 288.

49 *Ibid.*, pp. 293–294.

50 Main, Frank. "Murder 'Clearance' Rate in Chicago Hit New Low in 2017." *Chicago Sun Times*, 9 Feb. 2018, chicago.suntimes.com/chicago-news/murder-clearance-rate-in-chicago-hit-new-low-in-2017/. *Compare to,* e.g., U.S. Department of Justice, Federal Bureau of Investigation, Criminal Justice Information Services Division. "Offenses Cleared." *Uniform Crime Report: Crime in the United States, 2010*, 2010, ucr.fbi.gov/crime-in-the-u.s/2010/crime-in-the-u.s.-2010/clearances. The compared years are different, but Chicago's murder resolution rate is shockingly low.

51 David, Jean-Denis. "Homicide in Canada, 2016." *Canadian Centre of Justice Statistics*, 22 Nov. 2017, p. 5 (reported homicides) *Juristat*, www.statcan.gc.ca/pub/85-002-x/2017001/article/54879-eng.pdf; "Police Crime Statistics—Federal Republic of Germany, Report 2014." *Bundeskriminalamt*, 2014 at pp. 5, 71, www.bka.de/SharedDocs/Downloads/EN/Publications/PoliceCrimeStatistics/2014/pks2014_englisch.pdf?__blob=publicationFile&v=1. Each country defines "clearance" and "solve" somewhat differently. For example, Germany considers a case "cleared up" when a suspect has been identified (generally as a prelude to arrest), though few doubt that German police, e.g., solve a higher percentages of murders

than American police. *See also* Liem, Marieke, et al., "Homicide Clearance in Western Europe." Eur. J. Crim., pp. 1–21, 2018 (noting 70–95+%).

52 Lopez, Christy E. "Disorderly (Mis)conduct: The Problem with 'Contempt of Cop' Arrests." *American Constitution Society for Law and Policy's Issue Brief*, 7 June 2010, web.archive.org/web/20110305022631/http://www.acslaw.org/pdf/C21/Issue%20Briefs/ACS%20Issue%20Brief%20-%20Lopez%20Contempt%20of%20Cop.pdf.

53 The United States Department of Justice Archives. "Undercover and Sensitive Operations Unit, Attorney General's Guidelines on FBI Undercover Operations." 8 Mar. 2017 (updated), part IV, H, www.justice.gov/archives/ag/undercover-and-sensitive-operations-unit-attorney-generals-guidelines-fbi-undercover-operations#participation.

54 U.S. Department of Justice, Federal Bureau of Investigation. "Federal Bureau Investigation Annual Otherwise Illegal Activity Report." 31 Jan. 2012, www.documentcloud.org/documents/742049-fbi-oia-report.html (FBI's FOIA response); Heath, Brad. "Exclusive: FBI Allowed Informants to commit 5,600 crimes." *USA TODAY*, 4 Aug. 2013, www.usatoday.com/story/news/nation/2013/08/04/fbi-informant-crimes-report/2613305/; U.S. Department of Justice, Office of the Inspector General. "The Federal Bureau of Investigation's Compliance with the Attorney General's Investigative Guidelines." Sept. 2005, pp. 90, 108, www.documentcloud.org/documents/1513075-fbi-compliance-with-use-of-informant-guidelines.html#p121.

55 Office of the Attorney General. "The Attorney General's Guidelines on Federal Bureau of Investigation Undercover Operations." fas.org/irp/agency/doj/fbi/fbi undercover.pdf.

56 E.g., Ca. Gov. Code §§ 3300 *et seq. See also* Hager, Eli. "Blue Shield: Did you know police have their own Bill of Rights?" *Marshall Project*, 27 Apr. 27, 2015, www.themarshallproject.org/2015/04/27/blue-shield#.Etqk3UTYF.

57 "Report of the Blue Ribbon Panel on Transparency, Accountability, and Fairness in Law Enforcement." July 2016, p. 23, sfdistrictattorney.org/sites/default/files/Document/BRP_report.pdf.

58 U.S. Department of Justice, Federal Bureau of Investigation, Criminal Justice Information Services Division. "Crime in the United States 2016." *Uniform Crime Report, Table 21: Arrests by Race and Ethnicity*, 2016, ucr.fbi.gov/crime-in-the-u.s/2016/crime-in-the-u.s.-2016/topic-pages/tables/table-21. The FBI's data do not reflect all departments, but departments surveyed covered 257 million people, over three-quarters of the population; U.S. Census Bureau. "Quick Facts, United States." 1 July 2017, www.census.gov/quickfacts/fact/table/US/PST045216 (black population in US generally).

59 Carlson, E. Ann. "Prisoners in 2016." *U.S. Department of Justice, Office of Justice Programs, Bureau of Justice Statistics Bulletin*, Jan. 2018 (Revised 7 Aug. 2018), table 9 (sentences of over one year), www.bjs.gov/content/pub/pdf/p16.pdf, author's calculations; Prison Policy Initiative. "Blacks are Overrepresented in Maryland Prisons and Jails." www.prisonpolicy.org/graphs/2010percent/MD_Blacks_2010.html (includes jails).

60 "Report of the Blue Ribbon Panel on Transparency, Accountability, and Fairness in Law Enforcement." July 2016, pp. 28–30, sfdistrictattorney.org/sites/default/files/Document/BRP_report.pdf.

61 "Annual Stop-and-Frisk Numbers." New York Civil Liberties Union, www.nyclu.org/en/stop-and-frisk-data; *see also* Bratton, William J. "Crime and Enforcement Activity in New York City (Jan 1–Dec 31, 2013)." *New York City Police Department*, p.15, www1.nyc.gov/assets/nypd/downloads/pdf/analysis_and_planning/2013_year_end_enforcement_report.pdf. Minimum figures presented; possibly as many as 624,000.

62 *Ibid.*

63 *Floyd v. City of N.Y.*, 959 F. Supp. 2d 540, 605, 660–663 (S.D.N.Y. 2013) and 8 Civ. 1034 SAS (2013). For a general review, *see* Conti, Allie. "New York City Cops Still Don't Know Why They're Stopping People on the Street." *Vice,* 16 Feb. 2016, www.vice.com/en_us/article/jma9z3/new-york-city-cops-still-dont-know-why-theyre-stopping-people-on-the-street.

64 Programs like stop-and-frisk persist as "*Terry* stops," though these are at least more tethered to Constitutional doctrine.

65 "Warren Buffett on Driving Violations, Baseball and Jamie Dimon." *New York Times Dealbook,* 16 Oct. 2013, dealbook.nytimes.com/2013/10/16/warren-buffett-on-driving-violations-baseball-and-jamie-dimon/. Buffet, rather infelicitously, made the comment in the context of commenting on Jamie Dimon and J. P. Morgan's regulatory fines.

66 Reaves, Brian A. "Local Police Departments, 2013: Personnel, Policies, and Practices." *U.S. Department of Justice, Office of Justice Programs, Bureau of Justice Statistics' Bulletin*, 14 May 2015, table 5 and accompanying text, www.bjs.gov/content/pub/pdf/lpd13ppp.pdf; U.S. Census Bureau. "Current Population Survey." Note that Hispanics are treated both separately and as "white" by the Census; the two must be added together for general population data; BJS separates out the white/Hispanic sub-population. However, it appears that Hispanic officers have experienced stronger employment gains within departments.

67 U.S. Department of Justice, Civil Rights Division. "Investigation of the Baltimore City Police Department." 10 Aug. 2016, www.justice.gov/opa/file/883366/download; "Police Department Race and Ethnicity Demographic Data." *Governing,* Baltimore County Police Department, www.governing.com/gov-data/safety-justice/police-department-officer-demographics-minority-representation.html.

68 Morin, Rich and Renee Stepler. "The Racial Confidence Gap in Police Performance." *Pew Research Center,* 29 Sept. 2016, www.pewsocialtrends.org/2016/09/29/the-racial-confidence-gap-in-police-performance/#blacks-are-less-confident-than-whites-in-their-local-police.

69 Durose, Matthew and Lynn Langton. "Requests for Police Assistance, 2011." *U.S. Department of Justice, Office of Justice Programs, Bureau of Justice Statistics' Special Report,* Sept. 2013, Appendix Table 2, www.bjs.gov/content/pub/pdf/rpa11.pdf.

70   Doing so may take time, as especially aggressive hiring to achieve desired racial composition can violate civil rights laws. E.g., *Ricci v. DeStefano,* 557 U.S. 557 (2009).

71   Black/white. *Governing*'s "Diversity on the Force" provides additional context.

72   Silver, Nate. "Most Police Don't Live in the Cities They Serve." *FiveThirtyEight,* 20 Aug. 2014 (average data), fivethirtyeight.com/features/most-police-dont-live-in-the-cities-they-serve/; Ryan, Andrew. "Boston's Residency Rule Routinely Flouted." *Boston Globe,* 6 July 2014, www.bostonglobe.com/metro/2014/07/05/boston-residency-rule-for-city-workers-frequently-ignored-and-weakly-enforced/jBqf3ST8Pqkpsr5IDjSCZL/story.html.

73   Lopez, German. "Police Shootings and Brutality in the US: 9 Things You Should Know: There are huge racial disparities in how US Police use force." (Card 2 of 11). *Vox,* 6 May 2017, www.vox.com/cards/police-brutality-shootings-us/us-police-racism.

74   E.g., Swaine, Jon and McCarthy, Ciara. "Killings by US police logged at twice the previous rate under new federal program." *Guardian,* 15 Dec. 2016, www.theguardian.com/us-news/2016/dec/15/us-police-killings-department-of-justice-program.

75   *Sociological Forum,* vol. 30, no. 4, Dec. 2015 p. 1112; onlinelibrary.wiley.com/doi/epdf/10.1111/socf.12200 (using a combination of reasonable estimates, some prepared by media investigations, and assuming that killings in 2013 equaled those in 2011).

76   *Ibid.*

77   Markowitz, Eric. "Taser Takes Aim at Europe." *International Business Times,* 14 Dec. 2015, www.ibtimes.com/taser-takes-aim-europe-2217825. About 33 in 50 American officers are equipped with Tasers, while the figure for Europe is 1 in 50. Some European nations have recently expanded Taser programs, while others maintain bans or restrict use to specialist squads.

78   United Nations, Human Rights, Office of the High Commissioner. "Convention Against Torture and Other Cruel, Inhuman or Degrading Treatment or Punishment" www.ohchr.org/EN/ProfessionalInterest/Pages/CAT.aspx; (applying to government officials but excluding pain and suffering "arising" from or "incident" to a lawful arrest) United Nations Committee Against Torture Convention Against Torture, Periodic Report of the United States of America, 5 Aug. 2013, Question 25, Paragraphs 42, 49, 141 (referencing UN concerns) e.g., www.state.gov/documents/organization/213267.pdf.

79   U.S. Department of State, Diplomacy in Action. "One-Year Follow-up Response of the United States of America to Recommendations of the Committee Against Torture on Its Combined Third to Fifth Periodic Reports." 27 Nov. 2015, Pars. 3, 27, 47, 52, www.state.gov/j/drl/rls/250342.htm.

80   The ACLU was not able to obtain the grand jury records, so we cannot know the full reasons for the *ignoramus.*

81   McEwen, Tom, U.S. Department of Justice, Office of Justice Programs, Bureau of Justice Statistics. *National Data Collection on Police Use of Force,* Apr. 1996, pp. 5, 8, www.bjs.gov/content/pub/pdf/ndcopuof.pdf (noting no universal definition);

U.S. Department of Justice, Office of Justice Programs, National Institute of Justice, Bureau of Justice Statistics. *Use of Force by Police—Overview of National and Local Data*, 1999 p. 4, www.ncjrs.gov/pdffiles1/nij/176330-1.pdf; "NYPD Fails to Define 'Excessive Force,' New Report Says." *CBS News*, 1 Oct. 2015, www.cbsnews.com/news/nypd-fails-to-give-officers-definition-of-excessive -force-report-says/ (noting absence of unifying definition of "excessive force"); see Chapter 2 and *infra* this chapter for discussions of qualified immunity.

82 Matthew J. Hickman, "Citizen Complaints about Police Use of Force." *U.S. Department of Justice, Office of Justice Programs, Bureau of Justice Statistics*, June 2006, p. 1, www.bjs.gov/content/pub/pdf/ccpuf.pdf. *See also* Garner, Joel. "Progress toward national estimates of police use of force." National Institutes of Health, PLoS 13(2):e1092932, 2018. Note that "excessive" force might not always trigger a citizen-reported complaint.

83 Office of Justice Programs, National Institute of Justice. "NIJ Award Detail: Assessing the Validity and Reliability of National Data on Citizen Complaints about Police Use of Force." www.nij.gov/funding/awards/pages/award-detail .aspx?award=2013-R2-CX-0035.

84 E.g., Pub. L. 103–322, title XXI, § 210402 (1994) (Data on Use of Excessive Force); 42 U.S.C. § 13701 et seq., § 14131 (Quality assurance and proficiency testing standards) *et seq.*, § 14141 (Cause of Action) *et seq.*; Apuzzo, Matt, and Sarah Cohen. "Data on Use of Force by Police Across U.S. Proves Almost Useless." *New York Times*, 11 Aug. 2015, www.nytimes.com/2015/08/12/us/data-on-use-of-force-by -police-across-us-proves-almost-useless.html; United States Department of Justice, Office of Public Affairs. "Justice Department Outlines Plan to Enable Nationwide Collection of Use of Force Data." *Justice News*, 13 Oct. 2016, www.justice .gov/opa/pr/justice-department-outlines-plan-enable-nationwide-collection-use -force-data. DOJ characterized its project as filling a gap in statutory language and to collect data on various metrics include use of force, use of excessive force, etc.; whatever it was, DOJ gave up.

85 "Senate Confirmation Hearings: Day One." *Atlantic*, 10 Jan. 2017, www.theatlantic .com/liveblogs/2017/01/senate-confirmation-hearings-day-one/512642/13445/.

86 *Monroe v. Pape*, 365 U.S. 167 (1961) (§ 1983 liability); *Pierson v. Ray*, 386 U.S. 547 (1967) (laying groundwork for qualified immunity, though that term entered use later).

87 *See generally ibid.; Scheuer v. Rhodes*, 416 U.S. 232, 237 (1974), abrogated by *Harlow v. Fitzgerald*, 457 U.S. 800 (1982).

88 *Pierson v. Ray*, 386 U.S. 547 (1967).

89 *Harlow v. Fitzgerald*, 457 U.S. 800, 818–19 (1982) (emphasis added).

90 *Ashcroft v. al-Kidd*, 563 U.S. 731 (2011) at II.B (emphasis added) (citation omitted). Here's what it said: "A Government official's conduct violates clearly established law when, at the time of the challenged conduct, '[t]he contours of [a] right [are] sufficiently clear' that every reasonable official would have understood that what he is doing violates that right."; *see also Anderson v. Creighton*, 483 U.S. 635, 640 (1987) and *infra* note 91, regarding misuse of prior precedent by *al-Kidd*.

91 *Compare ibid.* to *Anderson v. Creighton,* 483 U.S. 635, 640 (1987) ("...the contours of the right must be sufficiently clear that *a* reasonable official...") (emphasis added). Because the Court now only looks to "objective reasonableness," the "a" versus "every" is, to some extent, window-dressing by Scalia.

92 Signe, Dean. "No, One-Third of Millennials Don't Actually Think Earth Is Flat." *Science Alert,* 4 Apr. 2017, www.sciencealert.com/one-third-millennials-believe -flat-earth-conspiracy-statistics-yougov-debunk. Title of the article notwithstanding, the survey showed that ~15% of Americans harbored some suspicions of flatness/were unsure.

93 *Kilsea v. Hughes,* 584 US __ (2018) (Sotomayor, J., dissenting).

94 Elinson, Zusha, and Dan Frosch. "Cost of Police-Misconduct Cases Soars in Big U.S. Cities." *Wall Street Journal,* 15 July 2015, www.wsj.com/articles/ cost-of-police-misconduct-cases-soars-in-big-u-s-cities-1437013834.

95 Morin, Rich, et al. "Behind the Badge: Amid protests and calls for reform, how police view their jobs, key issues and recent fatal encounters between blacks and police." Pew Research Center, 11 Jan. 2017 p. 65, (more dangerous) assets.pewresearch.org/wp-content/uploads/sites/3/2017/01/06171402/Police -Report_FINAL_web.pdf; "National Census of Fatal Occupational Injuries in 2016." *Bureau of Labor Statistics' News Release,* 19 Dec. 2017, www.bls.gov/news .release/pdf/cfoi.pdf; *see also* "Fact Sheet Police Officers August 2016." *Bureau of Labor Statistics' Injuries, Illnesses, and Fatalities,* 27 Apr. 2018 (Last Modified), www.bls.gov/iif/oshwc/cfoi/police-officers-2014.htm. The Pew report has some ambiguous phrasing, but an NPR interview by one of its authors confirmed the 93%-more-dangerous understanding.

96 "FBI Releases 2016 Statistics for Law Enforcement Officers Killed and Assaulted in the Line of Duty." *Federal Bureau of Investigation's News,* 16 Oct. 2017, www.fbi.gov/news/pressrel/press-releases/fbi-releases-2016-statistics-for -law-enforcement-officers-killed-and-assaulted-in-the-line-of-duty; "Fatal Force." *Washington Post,* www.washingtonpost.com/graphics/national/police-shootings -2016/.

97 "FBI Releases 2016 Statistics for Law Enforcement Officers Killed and Assaulted in the Line of Duty." *Federal Bureau of Investigation's News,* 16 Oct. 2017, www.fbi .gov/news/pressrel/press-releases/fbi-releases-2016-statistics-for-law-enforcement -officers-killed-and-assaulted-in-the-line-of-duty. "No weapon" excludes hands, fists, and other "personal weapons" that do not appear to be lethal weapons in the colloquial sense.

98 U.S. Department of Justice, Bureau of Justice Statistics, Office of Justice Programs. "Police Use of Nonfatal Force, 2002–11." Nov. 2015, www.bjs.gov/con tent/pub/pdf/punf0211_sum.pdf.

99 "Crime." *Gallup,* news.gallup.com/poll/1603/crime.aspx. Enron's difficulties and the rumors surrounding them became fully public two days before the poll, though financial crime was a subject of considerable media attention throughout that year.

100 "September 11 Terror Attacks Fast Facts." *CNN,* 5 Aug. 2018, www.cnn.com/ 2013/07/27/us/september-11-anniversary-fast-facts/index.html; Smith, Erica L. and Alexia Cooper. "Homicide in the U.S. Known to Law Enforcement, 2011." U.S.

Department of Justice, Office of Justice Programs, Bureau of Justice Statistics, Dec. 2013, www.bjs.gov/content/pub/pdf/hus11.pdf.

101   "Crime." *Gallup*, news.gallup.com/poll/1603/crime.aspx; author's calculations (65% figure); "A Divided and Pessimistic Electorate." *Pew Research Center*, 10 Nov. 2016, www.people-press.org/2016/11/10/a-divided-and-pessimistic-electorate/3-11/ (2008-2016 period).

102   A convenient summary through 2015 is available from the Brennan Center for Justice. Friedman, Matthew, et al. "Crime Trends: 1990–2016." Brennan Center for Justice at New York University School of Law, 2016, p. 1, www.brennancen ter.org/sites/default/files/publications/Crime%20Trends%201990-2016.pdf. Full data, including 2016 figures, are available from the FBI, collected at: "About Crime in the U.S. (CIUS)." *Federal Bureau of Investigation: Uniform Crime Report,* ucr.fbi.gov/crime-in-the-u.s/2016/crime-in-the-u.s.-2016/cius-2016.

103   Banks, Duren, et al. *National Sources of Law Enforcement Employment Data.* NCJ 249681, revised 4 Oct. 2016, www.bjs.gov/content/pub/pdf/nsleed.pdf; author's calculations (sworn officers, 1992–2012).

104   Friedman, Matthew, et al. "Crime in 2016: A Preliminary Analysis." Brennan Center for Justice at New York University School of Law, 2016, p. 1 and Table 1, www.brennancenter.org/sites/default/files/publications/Crime_2016_Prelimi nary_Analysis.pdf. Estimates suggested overall crime rates declined slightly in 2017; Grawert, Ames C. and James Cullen. "Crime in 2017: A Preliminary Anal-ysis." Brennan Center for Justice at New York University School of Law, 2017, p. 1, https://www.brennancenter.org/sites/default/files/publications/Crime%20 in%202017%20A%20Preliminary%20Analysis.pdf. The FBI's Uniform Crime Reports provide the most recent official data, which (as of press time) generally confirm the Brennan Center's headline totals; if anything, Brennan may have slightly overstated the crime rise.

105   It's difficult to pinpoint when the economy truly recovered from the Great Reces-sion. GDP achieved positive YoY growth by 2010 (ending the recession as a tech-nocratic matter), but middle-class incomes did not fully recover until almost a decade later.

106   Civil Rights Division. *Investigation of the Ferguson Police Department.* U.S. Department of Justice, 4 Mar. 2015, p. 2, www.justice.gov/sites/default/files/ opa/press-releases/attachments/2015/03/04/ferguson_police_department _report.pdf.

107   Martinez, Michael, et al., "Policing for Profit: How Ferguson's Fines Violated Rights of African-Americans." *CNN*, 6 Mar. 2015, www.cnn.com/2015/03/06/us/ ferguson-missouri-racism-tickets-fines/index.html.

108   Goldstein, Rebecca, et al. "Exploitative Revenues, Law Enforcement, and the Quality of Government Service." *Urban Affairs Review,* Aug. 2018, p. 1, www .law.nyu.edu/sites/default/files/upload_documents/YOU_policing.pdf.

109   *Ibid.;* McCoy, Terrance. "Ferguson Shows How a Police Force Can Turn into a Plundering 'Collection Agency.'" *Washington Post,* 5 Mar. 2015, www .washingtonpost.com/news/morning-mix/wp/2015/03/05/ferguson-shows -how-a-police-force-can-turn-into-a-plundering-collection-agency/?utm _term=.171c82f62327.

110 Whaley, Sean. "Drop in Traffic Tickets Has Supreme Court Near Broke, Chief Justice Says." *Las Vegas Review Journal,* 22 Mar. 2015, www.reviewjournal.com/local/local-nevada/drop-in-traffic-tickets-has-supreme-court-near-broke-chief-justice-says/.

111 Office of the Inspector General. *Audit of the Assets Forfeiture Fund and Seized Asset Deposit Fund Annual Financial Statements Fiscal Year 2017.* U.S. Department of Justice, Dec. 2017, oig.justice.gov/reports/2017/a1805.pdf#page=1; Asset Forfeiture Program. *10-Yr Summary of Financial Report Data.* U.S. Department of Justice, 2017, www.justice.gov/afp/file/10-yr_summary_of_reporting.pdf/download (fund inflows for fiscal 2012 and 2014) ("Treasury Summary"); Carpenter II, Dick M., et al. *Policing for Profit: The Abuse of Civil Asset Forfeiture.* Institute for Justice, Nov. 2015, 2nd Ed., pp. 5, 10, ij.org/wp-content/uploads/2015/11/policing-for-profit-2nd-edition.pdf. Total asset data for AFF/SADF of $8.3 billion are from the Fund's 2017 Annual Report, presented in gross terms. The Funds have paid out, of course, but even the net account balances at DOJ and Treasury increased by 485% from FY 2001–2014. From FY 2007–2016, victims received just under 40% of the fund's deposits; in 2016, the figure was 10%. Treasury Summary, p. 4.

112 For a good survey, *see* Stillman, Sarah. "Taken." *New Yorker,* 12 and 19 Aug. 2013, www.newyorker.com/magazine/2013/08/12/taken?reload=true. Toward the end of the Obama Administration, Washington made noises about reforming forfeiture practices, efforts promptly abandoned in 2017.

113 "Confidence in Institutions." *Gallup,* news.gallup.com/poll/1597/confidence-institutions.aspx.

114 The conviction was secured mainly by prosecutorial misconduct, however.

Chapter 11

1 *Tehan v. Shott,* 382 U.S. 406, 416 (1966).

2 Baudrillard, Jean. *Amérique.* Hachette, 2014, Apple e-book, p. 25. Baudrillard's mistake was pointed out when the first edition of *Amérique* came out in 1986, notably by Robert Hughes. The geographical error has not been corrected in nearly thirty years.

3 *Ibid.,* pp. 28–42.

4 Durmay, Benedetta Faedi. "Women and Poisons in 17th Century France." *Chicago-Kent Law Review,* vol. 87, issue 2, Apr. 2012, p. 359 (citations omitted), scholarship.kentlaw.iit.edu/cgi/viewcontent.cgi?referer=www.google.com/&httpsredir=1&article=3837&context=cklawreview.

5 Merryman, John H. and Rogelio Pérez-Perdomo. *The Civil Law Tradition: An Introduction to the Legal Systems of Europe and Latin America,* 3rd ed., Stanford University Press, 2007, p. 119.

6 Halstead, T.J. "An Overview of the Impeachment Process." Congressional Research Service, updated ed., 20 Apr. 2005, at CRS-4–6, www.senate.gov/reference/resources/pdf/98-806.pdf. Impeachments are governed by Senate rules.

In some aspects, they mirror practices in normal courts: the accused may be represented by counsel in and the presiding officer (the Chief Justice, in the case of a presidential impeachment) may rule on procedural motions and the admission of evidence, though these rules are not well developed and not, as a practical matter, binding or subject to meaningful judicial review.

7   Fed. R. Evid. 402 (relevant evidence presumptively admissible absent statutes, case law, etc. to the contrary).

8   Fed. R. Evid. 401 (emphasis added). State rules of evidence are broadly similar.

9   E.g., Fed R. Civ P. 26(b).

10   E.g., *Heien v. North Carolina,* 574 U.S. __ (2014) (allowing search even where suspicion based on mistake of law); *Hill v. California,* 401 U.S. 797 (1971) (allowing searches based on reasonable mistake of fact).

11   E.g., Fed. R. Evid. 102 (stating that the rules of evidence should be "construed so as to administer every proceeding fairly, eliminate unjustifiable expense and delay... to the end of ascertaining the truth and securing a just determination").

12   *Yates v. United States,* 135 S. Ct. 1074 (2015).

13   E.g., Mearian, Lucas. "By 2020 There Will Be 5,200 GB of Data for Every Person on Earth." *Computer World,* 11 Dec. 2012, www.computerworld.com/article/2493701/data-center/by-2020—there-will-be-5-200-gb-of-data-for-every-person-on-earth.html.

14   *Brady v. Maryland,* 373 U.S. 83 (1963).

15   Bhattacharjee, Yudhijit. "Why We Lie: The Science Behind Our Deceptive Ways." *National Geographic,* June 2016, www.nationalgeographic.com/magazine/2017/06/lying-hoax-false-fibs-science/. There's huge scientific literature on this, for the simple reason that most people lie.

16   For an older (though still accurate) summary, *see* "Perjury: The Forgotten Offence." *Journal of Criminal Law and Criminology,* vol. 65, no. 3, Sept. 1974, www.jstor.org/stable/pdf/1142605.pdf?refreqid=excelsior%3A73da5e276d8c249 11a2cadba6df5db08.

17   Schmitt, Richard M. "Lying in the Courtroom: 'It Happens All the Time.'" *Wall Street Journal,* 9 Oct. 1998, www.wsj.com/articles/SB907891358251126000.

18   18 U.S.C. § 1621 (federal perjury statute requiring willfulness); *see also United States v. Dunnigan,* 507 U.S. 87, 94 (1993) (listing exculpatory circumstances and listing Court precedent on same).

19   Motivans, Mark. "Federal Justice Statistics Tables." *Bureau of Justice Statistics,* 26 Jan. 2012 (revised), table 1.1, 2.2, www.bjs.gov/content/pub/pdf/fjs09st.pdf. Prosecutors declined to charge in over half the perjury/intimidation/contempt cases underway in the sampled period. Percentages are for Marshals arrrests.

20   Fed. R. Evid. 601. State laws differ.

21   E.g., Hourihan, Kathleen L., et al. "A Cross-Race Effect in Metamemory: Predictions of Face Recognition are More Accurate for Members of Our Own Race." *Journal of Applied Research Memory Cognition.* 2012, pp.158–162, DOI: | 10.1016/j.jarmac.2012.06.004, scinapse.io/papers/2013569428.

22   "Eyewitness Misidentification." *Innocence Project,* www.innocenceproject.org/causes/eyewitness-misidentification/. For a survey of known issues with eyewitness identification, see National Research Council, et.al. *"Identifying the Culprit:*

Assessing Eyewitness Identification." National Academies P, 2014, www.innocen ceproject.org/wp-content/uploads/2016/02/NAS-Report-ID.pdf.

23   Arkowitz, Hal, and Scott O. Lilienfeld. "Why Science Tells Us Not to Rely on Eyewitness Accounts." *Scientific American,* 1 Jan. 2010, www.scientificamerican .com/article/do-the-eyes-have-it/#. Loftus and Pickrell did the pioneering work; subsequent studies by Hyman et al. (1996) confirmed the finding, and Wade et al. (2002) and other researchers noted that between 20% and 50% would stand by false memories.

24   *Perry v. New Hampshire,* 565 U.S. 228 (2012) at Part I.A.

25   Fed. R. Evid. 801–807 (governing hearsay and its exceptions).

26   Fed. R. Evid. 803(2).

27   Payne, Stacey, et al. "The effects of experimentally induced stress on false recognition." *Memory.* Vol. 10, no. 1 (2001) pp. 1–6; *see also* Payne, Stacey, et al., "The impact of stress on neutral and emotional aspects of episodic memory." *Memory.* Vol. 14, no. 1 (2006), pp. 1–16 (surveying existing literature and noting differences in impact of stress on recall for different aspects of the same event). The pioneering book in the area is by Elizabeth Loftus, originally printed in 1979: Loftus, Elizabeth. *Eyewitness Testimony.* 2nd ed. Harvard University Press, (1996). If I recall my Evidence class correctly—and it was not a stressful class— the old judicial theory was that excited people didn't have time to think of a lie. As an evidentiary theory, that's questionable and also misses the point.

28   Fed. R. Evid. 803(16). The document must also be authenticated, but this isn't really a robust protection.

29   Fed. R. Evid. 804(b)(2).

30   Fed. R. Evid. 807(a).

31   Committee on Identifying the Needs of the Forensic Sciences Community. *Strengthening Forensic Science in The United States: A Path Forward.* National Research Council, Aug. 2009, pp. 14–28, 38–39, 42–44, 183–84, 197, 224, www .ncjrs.gov/pdffiles1/nij/grants/228091.pdf (hereinafter "NC Study"); Ellis, Emma Grey. "The War Over Forensic Science Started Long Before Jeff Sessions." *Wired,* 14 Apr. 2017, www.wired.com/2017/04/war-forensic-science-started-well-jeff-sessions/.

32   The usual way to solve the Monty Hall Problem—which is an imprecise variant of the game show—is to use Bayes's theorem. The *Angry Statistician* blog provides two ways of solving the problem. angrystatistician.blogspot.com/2012/06/ infamous-monty-hall.html.

33   *People v. Collins,* 68 Cal.2d 319 (1968). The California Supreme Court overturned the case.

34   Green, Peter. "Letter from the President to the Lord Chancellor regarding the use of statistical evidence in court cases." *Royal Statistical Society,* 23 Jan. 2002, www.rss.org.uk/Images/PDF/influencing-change/rss-use-statistical-evidence -court-cases-2002.pdf.

35   Author's calculations; Moss, Mitchell L., and Carlton Qing. "The Dynamic Population of Manhattan." New York University Press, Mar. 2012, p. 1, wagner.nyu .edu/files/rudincenter/dynamic_pop_manhattan.pdf.

36   "Frequently Asked Questions on CODIS and NDIS." *Federal Bureau of Investigation,* (accessed May 2018), www.fbi.gov/services/laboratory/biometric-analysis/

codis/codis-and-ndis-fact-sheet. The snippets are short tandem repeats, which do not code for protein generation, referred to by FBI as the "loci."

37 Coble, Michael D. and John M. Butler. "DNA Mixture Interpretation: State of the Art." *National Institute of Standards And Technology*, 8 Jan. 2015, pp. 30, 38, strbase .nist.gov//pub_pres/ASCLD-LAB-Jan2015-CobleButler.pdf#page=30&zoom =auto,-211,522; Worth, Katie. "The Surprisingly Imperfect Science of DNA Testing." *Frontline*, 24 June 2015, www.pbs.org/wgbh/frontline/article/the -surprisingly-imperfect-science-of-dna-testing-2/. Other studies have come to similar conclusions; *see* NC Study.

38 "Quality Assurance Audit for Forensic DNA and Convicted Offender DNA Databasing Laboratories." *FBI*, 12–13 Dec. 2002 (audit dates) (Houston), www.scientific.org/archive/Audit%20Document—Houston.pdf; *ASCLD / Lab Limited Scope Interim Inspection Report*. Commonwealth Virginia Division of Forensic Science, Central Criminal Laboratory, 9 Apr. 2005 (Virginia), www.scientific.org/archive/VirginiaProblems/ASCLDLAB-AuditReport.pdf; Dao, James. "Lab's Errors Force Review of 150 DNA Cases." *New York Times*, 7 May 2005, www.nytimes.com/2005/05/07/us/labs-errors-force-review-of-150-dna -cases.html.

39 Office of the Inspector General. *The FBI DNA Laboratory: A Review of Protocols and Practice Vulnerabilities*. U.S. Department of Justice, May 2004, Executive Summary and p. 55, oig.justice.gov/special/0405/final.pdf.

40 The first admission of fingerprints as evidence in American courts appears to have been in the events leading up to *People v. Jennings* (1911), case-law.vlex .com/vid/96-n-1077-ill-613164642.

41 For a good description of fingerprints in court, see *United States v. Mitchell*, No. 02-2859 (3rd Cir. 2004), Part II.B. Non-federal standards vary.

42 Ulery, Bradford T., et al. "Repeatability and reproducibility of decisions by latent fingerprint examiners." *PLoS ONE* 7(3): e32800, 2012, https://www.ncbi.nlm .nih.gov/pmc/articles/PMC3299696/. In the second round, technicians eliminated their false positives but repeated false negatives.

43 Thompson, William, et al. "Latent Fingerprint Examination." *American Association for the Advancement of Science*, Sept. 2017, p. 9, doi: 10.1126/srhrl.aag2874, mcmprodaaas.s3.amazonaws.com/s3fs-public/reports/Latent%20Finger print%20Report%20FINAL%209_14.pdf?i9xGS_EyMHnIPLG6INIUyZb66L5 cLdlb. The fingerprint debate has been proceeding inconclusively for over twenty years.

44 "Strengthening Forensic Science in the United States." Senate Hearing 111– 554, 9 Sept. 2009 (statement of Jeff Sessions), www.gpo.gov/fdsys/pkg/CHRG -111shrg54720/html/CHRG-111shrg54720.htm.

45 *Frye v. United States*, 293 F. 1013 (D.C. Cir. 1923) (describing standard as "sufficiently established to have gained general acceptance in the particular field in which it belongs").

46 *Daubert v. Merrell Dow Pharmaceuticals, Inc.*, 509 U.S. 579, 589 and n.9 (1993).

47 *Ibid.*

48 Fed. R. Evid. 403, 702–703.

49 Fed. R. Evid. 403 (emphasis added).

50 C. Park, et al. "Evidence Law: A Student's Guide to the Law of Evidence as Applied in American Trial." West Group, § 12.01, 540–541 & n.6 1998; *see also* e.g., *United States v. Dodds*, 347 F.3d 893, 897 (11th Cir. 2003) ("This Court reviews a district court's evidentiary rulings for a *clear* abuse of discretion.") (citation omitted) (emphasis added).

51 *United States v. Holloway*, 971 F.2d 675, 679 (11th Cir. 1992) (stating that the 11th Circuit has an "established rule" about the inadmissibility of experts-on-witnesses).

52 E.g., Fed. R. Civ. Pro. 407–408. The inadmissibility of settlement offers and remedial measures is not unlimited, however.

53 *Weeks v. United States*, 232 U.S. 383 (1914); *Mapp v. Ohio*, 367 U.S. 643 (1961).

54 *Silverthorne Lumber v. United States*, 251 U.S. 385 (1920); *Wong Sun v. United States*, 371 U.S. 471 (1963). "Fruit of the poisonous tree" was coined after *Silverthorne*, but the principle applied in the original case.

55 E.g., *Herring v. United States*, 555 U.S. 135 at p. 9 (2009) (finding mistakenly issued warrant does not trigger exclusion).

56 *Ibid.* The Court has used the term "good faith" rather oddly in this context; it's not exactly "good faith" in the normal legal or vernacular sense, as the Court admits.

57 Shiffman, John and Kristina Cook. "Exclusive: U.S. Directs Agents to Cover up Program Used to Investigate Americans." *Thomson Reuters*, 5 Aug. 2013, www.reuters .com/article/us-dea-sod/exclusive-u-s-directs-agents-to-cover-up-program -used-to-investigate-americans-idUSBRE97409R20130805.

58 U.S. Constitution, amdt. VI.

59 *Ohio v. Roberts*, 448 U.S. 56, 66 (1980).

60 The Court's first attempt to resolve the *Roberts* problem was in *Crawford v. Washington*, 541 U.S. 36 (2004), Part III.A. In *Crawford*, testimony was disallowed. In *Davis v. Washington*, the Court formulated the solemnity/legal ceremony exception, which is the main focus of the main text's discussion. *Davis v. Washington*, 547 U.S. 813 (2006).

61 "Witness" Webster's Dictionary—1828: Online edition. http://webstersdiction ary1828.com/Dictionary/witness.

62 This strain of thought reached its acme in *Michigan v. Bryant*, 131 S. Ct. 1143 (2012).

63 *Davis v. Washington*, 547 U.S. 813, 821 (2006) (holding that testimonial hearsay requires confrontation, but "nontestimonial" hearsay does not).

64 *Ibid.*, Parts I–II.

65 Fisher, George. "The *Crawford* Debacle." Michigan Law Review First Impressions, vol. 113, no. 17, pp. 22–24 (2014).

66 *Williams v. Illinois*, 567 U.S. 50, Part IV (2012) (Kagan, J., dissenting).

67 Prosecutors often demand a waiver of FRE 410 as a condition for beginning negotiations. And FRE 410 itself is not absolute.

68 Fed. R. Evid. 412 (sex crimes); Fed. R. Evid. 607–609, Article VI *generally* (witnesses and impeachment). Under the *Old Chief* doctrine, defendants can try to stipulate their way around this. *Old Chief v. United States*, 519 U.S. 172 (1997).

69 E.g., *Trammel v. United States*, 445 U.S. 40 (1980).

70 E.g., Fed. R. Evid. 501–502 (recognizing attorney-client, but providing no other privilege unless specified by statute, Constitution, or state law when applicable).

Chapter 12

1 Titus Livius. *The History of Rome.* Preface. This is the usual translation.
2 Mele, Christopher. "Pushing That Crosswalk Button May Make You Feel Better, but..." *New York Times,* 27 Oct. 2016, https://www.nytimes.com/2016/10/28/us/placebo-buttons-elevators-crosswalks.html.
3 De Beaumont, Gustave, and Alexis De Tocqueville. *On the Penitentiary System in the United States: And its Application in France.* Francis Lieber, transl. Carey, Lea & Blanchard (1833), p. 47.
4 King, L.W, translator. "The Code of Hammurabi." *Yale Law School's Avalon Project,* § 196 (establishing the basic penalty), avalon.law.yale.edu/ancient/ham frame.asp. Most of the Code attaches crimes directly to penalties.
5 *Ibid.* E.g. §§ 195, 200–205. The Code's penalties are all over the map, but this is the general dynamic.
6 E.g., "Twelve Tables." *Yale Law School's Avalon Project,* Table VIII, § 3, avalon .law.yale.edu/ancient/twelve_tables.asp. Romans often specified prices in terms of certain kinds of property, like livestock, which we might consider inflation-adjusted animal currency. Germanic and British tribes also used monetary penalties for some non-property wrongs.
7 This interpretation, while disputed, is in keeping with Jesus's passive posture toward secular law ("render unto Caesar," and so on). St. Augustine viewed it as a theological sally against heresy (either Jewish or Manichean). E.g., Augustine of Hippo. "Contra Faustum, Book XIX." *New Advent,* pars. 3, 19, 25, www.newadvent .org/fathers/140619.htm.
8 *Qisas* is the Koranic concept of retributive justice. Qur'an 2:178, *The Noble Qur'an,* quran.com/2/178-188 (suggesting forgiveness but noting that recidivism will receive a "painful" penalty); Qur'an 5:45, *The Noble Qur'an,* quran.com/5/45 (forsaking eye for an eye can serve as expiation for sins); Nair, Drishya. "Saudi Arabia: Man who Paralysed Friend to Have Spinal Cord Severed." *International Business Times,* 1 July 2014, www.ibtimes.co.uk/saudi-arabia-punishments-stab-paralise -spinal-cord-452683 (discussing physical penalties applied in twenty-first century).
9 There are a number of historical inaccuracies in Foucault's work, especially his conflation of accounts written by officials and reformers with the actual facts, but Foucault's general premise is valid.
10 Translations sometimes call ancient jails "prison," though they were not. Rome's infamous Mamertine Prison, built into a sewer, was merely a waystation—famously, for St. Paul, before his crucifixion. The Latin word for such institutions is *career* which, I regret to report, does not supply the root for "career" in its vocational sense.

11 Zeng, Zhen. "Jail Inmates in 2016." NCJ 251210, *U.S. Department of Justice, Office of Justice Programs, Bureau of Justice Statistics' Bulletin*, Feb. 2018, pp. 1–2 and Table 4, www.bjs.gov/content/pub/pdf/ji16.pdf.

12 *Ibid.*, Table 6.

13 *Ibid.*, Table 3.

14 Kovaleski, Serge F. "Justice Delayed: 10 Years in Jail, but Still Awaiting Trial." *New York Times,* 19 Sept. 2017, www.nytimes.com/2017/09/19/us/alabama-kharon-davis-speedy.html.

15 Zeng, Zhen. *Ibid.*, table 5. A minimum of 14 and up to 27 states (plus the federal system) run over capacity, and crowding is worse in larger prisons systems and middle-sized jails, so adjusted by population, prisons are the more overcrowded system. Carson, E. Ann. "Prisoners in 2016." *U.S. Department of Justice, Office of Justice Programs, Bureau of Justice Statistics' Bulletin*, Jan. 2018, Table 16, www.bjs.gov/content/pub/pdf/p16.pdf.

16 U.S. Census Bureau. "Real Median Personal Income in the United States [MEPAINUSA672N]." *FRED, Federal Reserve Bank of St. Louis*, 13 Aug. 2018, fred.stlouisfed.org/series/MEPAINUSA672N; Henrichson, Christian, et al. *The Price of Jails: Measuring the Taxpayer Cost of Local Incarceration.* Vera Institute of Justice, May 2015, p. 28, storage.googleapis.com/vera-web-assets/downloads/Publications/the-price-of-jails-measuring-the-taxpayer-cost-of-local-incarceration/legacy_downloads/price-of-jails.pdf, and Vera data available at www.vera.org/publications/the-price-of-jails-measuring-the-taxpayer-cost-of-local-incarceration; author's calculations based on total costs divided by average daily population. The minimum official price is $96,690; $210,000 reflects the all-in. Figures for median income are national; against the New York MSA income, the figure is 3.2x. New York's own calculations (for 2012) ran to $168,000. Salas, Nasha. "NYC's Jail Population: Who's There and Why?" New York City Independent Budget Office. 2013. http://www.ibo.nyc.ny.us/iboreports/printnycbtn20.pdf (average cost per inmate, fiscal 2012, based on data from New York City's Department of Corrections).

17 Carson, E. Ann. "Prisoners in 2016." NCJ 25119, *U.S. Department of Justice, Office of Justice Programs, Bureau of Justice Statistics' Bulletin*, Jan. 2018, table 1, www.bjs.gov/content/pub/pdf/p16.pdf; transferees are based on author's calculation based on BJS jail statistics *supra*.

18 Wagner, Peter and Alison Walsh. "States of Incarceration: The Global Context 2016." *Prison Policy Initiative*, 16 June 2016, www.prisonpolicy.org/global/2016.html; Walmsley, Roy. "World Prison Population List." *Institute for Criminal Policy Research*, 2016, 11th ed. www.prisonstudies.org/sites/default/files/resources/downloads/world_prison_population_list_11th_edition_0.pdf.

19 *Ibid.*

20 E.g., Bronson, Jennifer. "Justice Expenditure and Employment Extracts, 2013—Final," Bureau of Justice Statistics, 29 June 2018, data tables 1, 10, and associated files, www.bjs.gov/index.cfm?ty=pbdetail&iid=6308; Kearney, Melissa S., et al. *Ten Economic Facts about Crime and Incarceration in the United States.* Hamilton Project—Brookings Institution, May 2014, www.hamiltonproject

.org/assets/legacy/files/downloads_and_links/v8_THP_10CrimeFacts.pdf (2010 figures).

21   U.S. Bureau of Economic Analysis. "Gross Domestic Product (GDP)." *FRED, Federal Reserve Bank of St. Louis*, 27 July 2018, fred.stlouisfed.org/series/GDP; "HUD's Proposed 2019 Budget." *U.S. Department of Housing and Urban Development: Secretary Ben Carson*, www.hud.gov/budget.

22   Knowles, Julian B. *The Abolition of the Death Penalty in the United Kingdom: How It Happened and Why It Still Matters.* Death Penalty Project, 9 Nov. 2015, pp. 9–10, www.deathpenaltyproject.org/2015/11/09/the-abolition-of-the-death -penalty-in-the-united-kingdom-how-it-happened-and-why-it-still-matters/. Monetary comparisons this old are fraught, but in the mid-eighteenth century, a decent housekeeper earned about 15 pounds per year, and at 240 pence per pound (British coinage was non-decimal), 12 pence would be slightly more than a day's wages. "Five Ways to Compute the Relative Value of a UK Pound Amount 1270 to Present." MeasuringWorth.Com,www.measuringworth.com/calculators/ ukcompare/relativevalue.php (offering various methods of conversion).

23   Transportation Acts of 1717, 1784, 1785. The loss of America prompted the technical refreshment of Scottish transportation, but it was little used—by 1785, Britain was gaining more distant options.

24   Death Penalty Information Center. *Executions by Year—Number of Executions Since 1976: 1481.* Last updated 14 Aug. 2018, deathpenaltyinfo.org/executions-year.

25   Espy, M. Watt, et al. *Executions in the United States, 1608-2002: The ESPY File (ICPSR 8451),* version 5, Ann Arbor, MI: Inter-university Consortium for Political and Social Research, 2016, doi.org/10.3886/ICPSR08451.v5.

26   *Ibid.* For a useful visual, see Wilson, Chris. "Every Execution in U.S. History in a Single Chart." *Time,* updated 25 Apr. 2017, time.com/82375/every-execution -in-u-s-history-in-a-single-chart/.

27   *Fiscal Year 2017 ICE Enforcement and Removal Operations Report.* U.S. Immigration and Customs Enforcement, p.13, www.ice.gov/sites/default/files/documents/ Report/2017/iceEndOfYearFY2017.pdf (includes apprehensions at border). Internal exile is still practiced, mainly as vindictive intrastate policy affecting mental patients (only some of whom are criminal); California sued Nevada over the latter's habit of busing its problems into the Golden State. Nevada has also paid contractors in other states to take its convicts. Sabatini, Joshua. "SF Reaches $400K Settlement Proposal in Nevada Patient-Dumping Case." *San Francisco Examiner,* 5 Oct. 2015, www.sfexaminer.com/sf-reaches-400k-settlement-proposal -in-nevada-patient-dumping-case/ and Hubert, Cynthia, et al. "Nevada Buses Hundreds of Mentally Ill Patients to Cities Around Country." *Sacramento Bee,* 14 Apr. 2013, www.sacbee.com/news/investigations/nevada-patient-busing/article2577189 .html; Botkin, Ben. "Nevada Officials OK $9.2M Deal to Ship Inmates to Arizona." *Las Vegas' Review-Journal,* 10 Oct. 2017, www.reviewjournal.com/crime/nevada -officials-ok-9-2m-deal-to-ship-inmates-to-arizona/.

28   Bragg, Rick. "Chain Gangs to Return to Roads of Alabama." *New York Times,* 1995, www.nytimes.com/1995/03/26/us/chain-gangs-to-return-to-roads-of-alabama .html; "Arizona's 'concentration camp': why was Tent City kept open for 24 years?"

Guardian, 21 Aug. 2017, www.theguardian.com/cities/2017/aug/21/arizona-phoenix
-concentration-camp-tent-city-jail-joe-arpaio-immigration.

29   In practice, the sentencing reforms of the 1980s functionally eliminated
rehabilitation as an official goal, though it remains a nominal justification for
prison. Compare S. R. No. 98–225, pp. 75–77 (listing the purposes of sentencing,
including correctional rehabilitation) and 18 U.S.C. § 3533(a)(2)(D) (noting sentencing should reflect need for "correctional treatment") *with* 18 U.S.C. § 2582(a)
(noting that prison is "not an appropriate means of promotion correction and
rehabilitation").

30   Kroll, John. "Judge Pianka's sentence for landlord's code violations: You must
live in your own lousy building." *Cleveland Plain Dealer News*, 19 Dec. 2008,
blog.cleveland.com/metro/2008/12/judge_piankas_sentence_for_lan.html.

31   CA Penal Code § 215 (basic carjacking); § 186.22 (gang membership enhance-
ment, if crime at direction of gang); § 12022.53 (gun enhancements, ranging
from 10 to life).

32   Harlow, Caroline Wolf. *Education and Correctional Populations.* NCJ 195670,
U.S. Department of Justice, Office of Justice Programs, Jan. 2003, p. 1 and table
1 (education), bjs.gov/content/pub/pdf/ecp.pdf; Bronson, Jennifer, and Mar-
cus Berzofsky. *Indicators of Mental Health Problems Reported by Prisoners and
Jail Inmates, 2011–12.* NCJ250612, U.S. Department of Justice, Office of Justice
Programs, Bureau of Justice Statistics, 2017, pp. 1–7, www.bjs.gov/content/pub/
pdf/imhprpji1112.pdf; Bronson, Jennifer and Marcus Berzofsky. *Drug Use,
Dependence, and Abuse Among State Prisoners and Jail Inmates, 2007–2009.*
NCJ 250546, U.S. Department of Justice, Office of Justice Programs, Bureau of
Justice Statistics, June 2017, pp.1–14 (drug use), www.bjs.gov/content/pub/pdf/
dudaspji0709.pdf. Data are from different years because the BJS does not conduct continuous censuses on all issues. Many trends appear to be stable, though
educational poverty rose sharply in the 1990s. The Census American Community Survey, while arriving at slightly different figures, basically accords with the
BJS numbers.

33   Three Strikes was brought into both legislative and propositional being by CA
Penal Code § 667 (b)-(i) (1994 legislative version); § 1170.12 (effecting Proposition 184) *revised by* Proposition 36 (2012) (to require third strike to be a serious/
violent felony) and *abrogated* in limited circumstances by various constitutional
challenges. Judges did have discretion to overlook a third felony where it fell outside the "spirit" of the law, but no defendant could rely on this and judges weren't
overly keen in the event. Since prior felonies could elevate minor crimes into third
felonies, the law was harsh, punitive, and nearly certain: i.e., a good experiment.

34   E.g., Parker, Robert Nash. "Why California's 'Three Strikes' Fails as Crime and
Economic Policy, and What to Do." *California Journal of Politics and Policy*, vol.
5, no. 2, July 2012, cloudfront.escholarship.org/dist/prd/content/qt1n48f1rj/
qt1n48f1rj.pdf?t=nhxihu; Males, Mike. *Striking Out: California's 'Three Strikes
and You're Out' Law Has Not Reduced Violent Crime. A 2011 Update.* Center on
Juvenile and Criminal Justice, Apr. 2011, www.cjcj.org/uploads/cjcj/documents/
Striking_Out_Californias_Three_Strikes_And_Youre_Out_Law_Has_Not
_Reduced_Violent_Crime.pdf; Zimring, Franklin E., et al., *Punishment and*

Democracy: Three Strikes and You're Out in California. Part II, Oxford University Press, 2003. Most studies focus on the impact (if any) three strikes initiatives had on felonies/violent crimes.

35 There are many variables at work, including the greater safety of cars and growing traffic, but researchers have disentangled most of the variables and the conclusion holds: speed-cameras work. Allsop, Richard. *The Effectiveness of Speed Cameras: A Review of Evidence.* RAC Foundation, Nov. 2010, § 2.2., www.racfoundation .org/wp-content/uploads/2017/11/efficacy_of_speed_cameras_allsop_181110 .pdf; Tang, Cheng Keat. "Do Speed Cameras Save Lives." Special Economics Research Centre, London School of Economics, SERC Discussion Paper 221, Sept. 2017, www .spatialeconomics.ac.uk/textonly/SERC/publications/download/sercdp0221 .pdf.

36 S. Rep. 91-613, p. 2 (1969) (discussing, inter alia, the Boggs Act).

37 Among the bipartisan fiascoes were the 1984 Sentencing Reform Act (which required "truth in sentencing," requiring offenders to serve at least 85% of their mandated term and created the Sentencing Commission to guide judges); the 1986 Anti-Drug Abuse Act (mandatory drug minimums and the 100:1 crack/ cocaine disparity); the 1988 Anti-Drug Abuse Act (same song, but louder); and the 1994 Violent Crime Control and Law Enforcement Act (expanding criminal penalties but allowing judges discretion to lighten sentences for some minor drug crimes); and the Anti-Terrorism and Death Penalty Act of 1996 (more of the same, and helped link crime to immigration violations). The states followed suit. In 2010, government lightened up drug sentences, some retroactively, but from 2017 to mid-2018 Congress and Attorney General Sessions have shown no appetite for continuing the Obama-era experiment.

38 *Federal Drug Sentencing Laws Bring High Cost, Low Return: Penalty Increases Enacted in 1980s and 1990s Have Not Reduced Drug Use or Recidivism.* Pew Charitable Trust, 27 Aug. 2015, fig. 1 and pp. 4–5, www.pewtrusts.org/en/ research-and-analysis/issue-briefs/2015/08/federal-drug-sentencing-laws -bring-high-cost-low-return.

39 *Ibid.,* fig. 2.

40 Federal Bureau of Prisons. "Offenses." 28 July 2018 (updated), www.bop.gov/ about/statistics/statistics_inmate_offenses.jsp.

41 U.S. Department of Justice, Office of Justice Programs, Bureau of Justice Statistics. "Drugs and Crime Facts: Drug Law Violations." 14 Aug. 2018 (rev.), www .bjs.gov/content/dcf/enforce.cfm.

42 E.g., U.S. House of Representatives. "Historical Summary of Conduct Cases in the House of Representatives: Committee on Standards of Official Conduct, 1798–2004." ethics.house.gov/sites/ethics.house.gov/files/Historical_Chart_Final _Version%20in%20Word_0.pdf; *see infra* note 43.

43 "Rep. Trey Radel's (R-Fla.) Charging Documents and Plea Agreement." *Washington Post,* 20 Nov. 2013, apps.washingtonpost.com/g/page/politics/rep-trey -radels-r-fla-charging-documents-and-plea-agreement/605/;Debenedetti,Gabriel. "Florida Congressman Radel Gets Probation on Cocaine Charge." *Reuters,* 20 Nov. 2013, www.reuters.com/article/us-usa-congress-radel/florida-congressman -radel-gets-probation-on-cocaine-charge-idUSBRE9AJ0T720131120. Probation is

not unusual for a straight, first-time charge, but many of D.C.'s black defendants do not seem to receive such leniency.

44 *Williams v. New York,* 337 U.S. 241, 247 (1949) (considering New York's discretionary regime). Discretion can work to increase or decrease the sentence.

45 *Mistretta v. United States,* 488 U.S. 361, 427 (1989) (Scalia, J., dissenting).

46 U.S.S.G. § 6A1.3(a); Fed. R. Evid. 1101(d)(3); Fed. R. Crim. Pro. 32.

47 E.g., Florida R. Crim. Pro. 3.390(a); *see also* Bellin, Jeremy. "Is Punishment Relevant After All? A Prescription for Informing Juries of the Consequences of Conviction." *Boston University Law Review,* vol. 90, no. 2, n.41 and accompanying text, 2010. A few states like Virginia do allow juries to determine some sentences, but these are in the minority.

48 *United States v. Booker,* 543 U.S. 220 (2005). *Booker* was a messy, multi-front war of ideology and personal history. The formal stakes were the Sixth Amendment right to a jury trial, but lurking within which were important questions about law and order and the administrative state. Justices whose personal political convictions might militate for a particular outcome in *Booker* had to be careful not to give ammunition to their opponents when the war resumed on other Constitutional fronts—but that's what you get when Congress blurs powers for dubious reasons. Another compounding factor: Justice Breyer was a member of the Sentencing Commission during the critical years of 1985–1989, and was not uninvolved in the debacles that unfolded. Breyer's brother, as it happens, is a federal judge tasked with applying *Booker* in his own court and also served as a Sentencing Commission member from 2013 to 2016 and as Vice Chair until 2021; one can only imagine their Thanksgiving table talk. "Stephen Breyer." Cornell University Law School's Legal Information Institute, Supreme Court, www .law.cornell.edu/supct/justices/breyer.bio.html (noting Justice Breyer's position on the USSC); U.S. Sentencing Commission. "About the Commissioners: Acting Chair: Judge Charles R. Breyer" www.ussc.gov/commissioners (noting Charles Breyer's position on the USSC).

49 Krieg, Gregory. "Kushner vs. Christie: The Nasty Trump Transition Fight that Goes Back a Decade." *CNN,* 17 Nov. 2016, www.cnn.com/2016/11/16/politics/ trump-transition-jared-kushner-chris-christie/index.html; Mangan, Dan. "Rudy Giuliani Says Trump Son-In-Law Jared Kushner is 'Disposable,' Warns against Investigating Ivanka." *CNBC,* 3 May 2018, www.cnbc.com/2018/05/03/rudy-giuliani-said-trumps-son-in-law-jared-kushner-is-disposable.html. The two bills that failed were the Sentencing Reform and Corrections Act proposals of 2015 and 2017; in February 2018, a reboot emerged out of committee, over Sessions's objections.

50 U.S. Attorney General. *Memorandum for All Federal Prosecutors: Department Charging and Sentencing Policy.* U.S. Department of Justice, 10 May 2017, www .justice.gov/opa/press-release/file/965896/download. Other than the drug reversal, Sessions's memo ostensibly parrots the traditional guidance for U.S. Attorneys, but his drift was unmistakable.

51 Schwartzapfel, Beth. "Life Without Parole: Inside the Secretive World of Parole Boards, Where Your Freedom May Depend on Politics and Whim." The Marshall Project, 10 July 2015, https://www.themarshallproject.org/2015/07/10/life -without-parole.

52 O.C.G.A. § 42-9-53.

53 Schwartzapfel, Beth. *Ibid.*

54 Release rates dropped from 42% to 26%, an almost 40% relative decline. Schwartzapfel, Beth. *Ibid.*

55 S. Rep. 98–225, p. 38 (1983); 18 U.S.C. § 3582(a).

56 Davis, Lois M., et al. *Evaluating the Effectiveness of Correctional Education: A Meta-Analysis of Programs that Provide Education to Incarcerated Adults.* U.S. Department of Justice, Bureau of Justice Assistance and Rand Corporation, 2013, www.bja.gov/Publications/RAND_Correctional-Education-Meta-Analysis.pdf.

57 E.g., *ibid.*, p. 4.

58 For definitions of capacity, see U.S. Department of Justice, Office of Justice Programs, Bureau of Justice Statistics. "Terms & Definitions: Corrections." www.bjs.gov/index.cfm?ty=tdtp&tid=1. Calculations are based on BJS data and author's calculations; where states did not report, estimates assumed prisons operated at 100% capacity. Carson, E. Ann. "Prisoners in 2016." NCJ 251149, *U.S. Department of Justice, Office of Justice Programs, Bureau of Justice Statistics' Bulletin.* Jan. 2018, table 16 and associated CSV file, www.bjs.gov/content/pub/pdf/p16.pdf. Some states do not report prison capacity statistics to BJS and those that do have considerable interpretive leeway to expand "design capacity" (set out in the original prison plan) to a higher "operational capacity" (due to extra guards, conversion of non-housing spaces into bed spaces, etc.), and population statistics often exclude prisoners with shorter sentences or in transit.

59 *Estelle v. Gamble*, 429 U.S. 97, 104–105 (1976).

60 Justice Center, Council of State Governments. *The Second Chance Act.* U.S. Department of Justice, Bureau of Justice Assistance, Jan. 2016, csgjusticecenter.org/wp-content/uploads/2014/08/SCA_Fact_Sheet.pdf; Office of Management and Budget. *Budget of the U.S. Government: A New Foundation for American Greatness: Fiscal Year 2018.* U.S. Government Printing Office, 2018, www.whitehouse.gov/sites/whitehouse.gov/files/omb/budget/fy2018/budget.pdf; "ACLU Comment on Trump Budget." American Civil Liberties Union, 23 May 2017, www.aclu.org/news/aclu-comment-trump-budget.

61 As to prisons overall, the evidence is somewhat mixed, though on balance, crimogenic effect seems indicated. While firm empirical evidence is not yet available, the anecdotal evidence suggests the existence of at least some crimogenic effect, depending on circumstance. E.g., Pritikin, Martin H. "Is Prison Increasing Crime?" *Wisconsin L. Rev.*, volume 2008, no. 6, at Part III (speculating a rough 7% crime increase due to prisons versus hypothesized carceral-alternative forms of punishment); Touré. "A Former Inmate Talks About How Prisons Manufacture Criminals." *Vice.* 8 Sep. 2015 (interviewing former criminal who has become a New School professor and whose answer to "is prison crimogenic" was a flat "yes").

62 Prison Litigation Reform Act of 1995, 18 U.S.C. § 3626.

63 *Brown v. Plata*, 563 U.S. 493 (2011) at Part 1; *see also* Executive Department State of California. *A Proclamation by the Governor of the State of California.* www.cdcr.ca.gov/News/docs/3JP-docs-01-07-13/Terminating-Prison-Overcrowding-Emergency-Proclamation-10-4-06.pdf (describing conditions in 2000s, but

revoking state of emergency); Warren, Jenifer. "State Prison Crowding Emergency Declared: Schwarzenegger's Move Could Allow Forcible Transfers of Inmates to Out-of-State Lockups." *Los Angeles Times*, 5 Oct. 2006, articles.lat imes.com/2006/oct/05/local/me-prison5.

64 "Governor Uses Executive Authority to Relieve Prison Overcrowding, Proclaims Emergency to Allow Inmate Transfer." *CDCR News*, 4 Oct. 2006, /news.cdcr.ca.gov/ news-releases/2006/10/04/governor-uses-executive-authority-to-relieve-prison -overcrowding-proclaims-emergency-to-allow-inmate-transfer/; "Judge Blocks Prisoner Transfers Out of California." *Reuters*, 20 Feb. 2007, www.reuters.com /article/us-california-prisons-idUSN2021238220070220.

65 *Brown v. Plata*, 563 U.S. 493 (2011); Barnes, Robert. "High court upholds orders that may releases thousands of Calif. Inmates." *Washington Post*, 23 May 2011, www.washingtonpost.com/politics/supreme-court-upholds-order-that-may -release-thousands-of-california-inmates/2011/05/23/AFY2ou9G_story.html ?utm_term=.43f8ad728b75.

66 Worland, Justin. "What Happened When California Released 30,000 Prisoners." *Time*, Oct. 8, 2015, time.com/4065359/california-prison-release-department-of -justice/.

67 U.S. Department of Justice, Civil Rights Division. "Special Litigation Section Case Summaries." www.justice.gov/crt/special-litigation-section-case-summaries#gdoc -summ.

68 E.g., Geiger, Abigail. "U.S. Private Prison Population Has Declined in Recent Years." *Fact Tank,* Pew Research Center, 11 Apr. 2017, www.pewresearch.org/ fact-tank/2017/04/11/u-s-private-prison-population-has-declined-in-recent -years/. Private prisons peaked in Obama's final term and then began a modest decline. They're poised to resurge under Trump. Surveys, and thus data for private prisons, are usually incomplete; figures represent minimums.

69 Office of the Inspector General. *Review of the Federal Bureau of Prisons' Monitoring of Contract Prisons*. U.S. Department of Justice, Aug. 2016, p. ii, oig.jus tice.gov/reports/2016/e1606.pdf.

70 Zapotosky, Matt. "Justice Department Will Again Use Private Prison." *Washington Post*, 23 Feb. 2017, www.washingtonpost.com/world/national-security/justice -department-will-again-use-private-prisons/2017/02/23/da395d02-fa0e-11e6 -be05-1a3817ac21a5_story.html?utm_term=.58b455e1ffd5.

71 Brittain, Amy and Drew Harwell. "Private-Prison Giant, Resurgent in Trump Era, Gathers at President's Resort." *Washington Post*, 25 Oct. 2017, www.washingtonpost .com/politics/with-business-booming-under-trump-private-prison-giant -gathers-at-presidents-resort/2017/10/25/b281d32c-adee-11e7-a908-a3470754bbb9 _story.html?utm_term=.a5a554bcffc8; Gill, Lauren. "Trump Administration Giving Boost to Private Prison Campaign Donors, Leaked Memo Shows." *Newsweek*, 30 Jan. 2018, www.newsweek.com/trump-private-prison-campaign-donors-leaked-memo -795681; Watkins, Eli and Sophie Tatum, "Private Prison Industry Sees Boon Under Trump Administration," *CNN*, 18 Aug. 2017, www.cnn.com/2017/08/18/politics/ private-prison-department-of-justice/index.html.

72 Zapotosky, Matt. "The Justice Department Closed This Troubled Private Prison. Immigration Authorities Are Reopening it." *Washington Post*, 27 Oct. 2016,

www.washingtonpost.com/world/national-security/the-justice-department
-closed-this-troubled-private-prison-immigration-authorities-are-reopening
-it/2016/10/27/6e52855e-9b87-11e6-a0ed-ab0774c1eaa5_story.html?utm_term
=.ce7d2090ea00.

73 Sessions, Jeffrey. *Memorandum for the Acting Director Bureau of Prisons.* U.S. Department of Justice. 21 Feb. 2017, www.bop.gov/resources/news/pdfs/20170224 _doj_memo.pdf.

74 Kaeble, Danielle, and Mary Cowhig. *Correctional Populations in the United States, 2016.* NCJ 251211, U.S. Department of Justice, Office of Justice Programs, Bureau of Justice Statistics, Apr. 2018, table 1, www.bjs.gov/content/pub/pdf/ cpus16.pdf (estimates as of Dec. 31, 2016).

75 "Meek Mill Says He 'Would Be in Prison' Without High-Profile Support." *CBS*, 8 May 2018, www.cbsnews.com/news/meek-mill-interview-criminal-justice-reform/. Mills had a series of minor prior delinquencies, many of which were dismissed.

76 Author's calculations; Kaeble, Danielle, and Thomas Bonczar. *Probation and Parole in the United States, 2015.* NCJ 250230, U.S. Department of Justice, Office of Justice Programs, Bureau of Justice Statistics, revised 2 Feb. 2017, p. 1, www .bjs.gov/content/pub/pdf/ppus15.pdf. Figures are for adults.

77 Human Rights Watch has done a series of reports on the subject, e.g., "Set Up to Fail: The Impact of Offender-Funded Private Probation on the Poor." *Human Rights Watch*, 20 Feb. 2018, www.hrw.org/report/2018/02/20/set-fail/impact -offender-funded-private-probation-poor; "Profiting from Probation: America's 'Offender-Funded' Probation Industry." *Human Rights Watch*, 5 Feb. 2014, www.hrw.org/report/2014/02/05/profiting-probation/americas-offender -funded-probation-industry.

78 *Bearden v. Georgia,* 461 U.S. 660 (1983) (holding that indigent violators may not be incarcerated without a hearing demonstrating that the violator "willfully" failed to pay); *see also* American Bar Association. *Resolution 111-B: Proposed Resolution and Report.* Aug. 2018, p. 3, www.americanbar.org/news/reporter _resources/annual-meeting-2016/house-of-delegates-resolutions/111b.html.

79 Shapiro, Joseph. "As Court Fees Rise, the Poor Are Paying the Price." *NPR*, 19 May 2014, www.npr.org/2014/05/19/312158516/increasing-court-fees-punish-the-poor.

80 RCW § 12.12.030 *modified by* Washington Laws of 2018, § 269; Shapiro, Joseph. *Ibid.*

81 The Constitution doesn't directly speak to the presumption of innocence, but it was a long-standing feature of common law and is strongly implied by the Bill of Rights, facts the Supreme Court confirmed in 1895. *Coffin v. United States*, 156 U.S. 432 (1895). Meanwhile, the Eighth Amendment's prohibition on "excessive bail" confirms the expectation that bail will be available.

82 E.g., Supreme Court of California, County of Los Angeles. "Bail Schedule for Interactions and Misdemeanors." 2018, www.lacourt.org/division/criminal/ pdf/misd.pdf (L.A. misdemeanor bail schedules); Supreme Court of California, County of Los Angeles. "Felony Bail Schedule." 2018, www.lacourt.org/division/ criminal/pdf/felony.pdf (L.A. felony bail schedules). Other jurisdictions set bail higher and lower, but these ranges are not wildly atypical.

83 Krupnick, Matt. "Bail Roulette: How the Same Minor Crime Can Cost $250 or $10,000." *Guardian*, 20 Sept. 2017, www.theguardian.com/us-news/2017/sep/20

/bail-disparities-across-the-us-reflect-inequality-it-is-the-poor-people-who
-suffer.

84 Hood, Chauhan, P. et al. *Trends in Custody: New York City: Department of Correction, 2000-2015.* John Jay College. 5 Apr. 2017, fig. 27 and accompanying text, misdemeanorjustice.org/wp-content/uploads/2017/04/TrendsInCustody _FullReport.pdf; Federal Reserve Bank of St. Louis, Economic Research. "Consumer Price Indexes (CPI and PCE)" https://fred.stlouisfed.org/categories/9; author's calculations.

85 E.g., Elkins, Kathleen. "Here's How Much Americans at Every Age Have in Their Savings Account." *CNBC,* 3 Oct. 2016 (savings accounts), www.cnbc .com/2016/10/03/how-much-americans-at-every-age-have-in-their-savings -accounts.html. *See also* "The Precarious State of Family Balance Sheets," Pew Charitable Trusts, 29 Jan. 2015, pp. 1, 10–11, www.pewtrusts.org/-/media/ assets/2015/01/fsm_balance_sheet_report.pdf (noting that about half of families lack liquid resources sufficient to manage about a month of normal expenses).

86 Phillips, Mary T. *A Decade of Bail Research in New York City.* New York City Criminal Justice Agency, Inc., Aug. 2012, Part VIII, www.prisonpolicy.org/ scans/DecadeBailResearch12.pdf. The median time was 5 days, due to some long pre-disposition detentions; most defendants are not detained. The bail situations for felonies is much more stringent and arraignment times longer.

87 Siddique, Haroon. "Duane 'Dog the Bounty Hunter' Chapman Barred from UK: US TV Presenter's Celebrity Big Brother Appearance in Doubt after He Is Denied Visa Over 1976 Murder Conviction." *Guardian,* 12 Aug. 2012, www.theguardian .com/world/2012/aug/12/duane-dog-bounty-hunter-uk; "Bounty Hunter Duane 'Dog' Chapman Arrested." *Associated Press,* 21 Sept. 2006, *TODAY,* www.today .com/popculture/bounty-hunter-duane-dog-chapman-arrested-2D80555484. Due to state law quirks, Dog's *legal* conviction for first-degree murder arose from his *factual* status as an accessory.

88 Cohen, Thomas H. and Kyckelhahn, Tracey. *Felony Defendants in Large Urban Counties, 2006.* U.S. Department of Justice, Office of Justice Programs, Bureau of Justice Statistics, 26 May 2010, p.1 and Table 11. www.bjs.gov/index .cfm?ty=pbdetail&iid=2193.

89 Dobbie, Will, et al. "The Effects of Pre-Trial Detention on Conviction, Future Crime, and Employment: Evidence from Randomly Assigned Judges." NBER Working Paper No. 22511, August 2016, www.nber.org/papers/w22511.pdf.

90 Different cases feature variations on these basic types—e.g., in contract law, there's restitution (forfeiting gains/making whole) and quantum meruit (a quasi-contractual remedy to give a plaintiff fair compensation for services rendered). But the basic taxonomy is the same.

91 For punitives, the exact standard of proof varies by jurisdiction. Only Colorado requires proof beyond a reasonable doubt; thirty states require "clear and convincing evidence" (a looser standard) while the remainder use the "preponderance of the evidence standard" (the lowest standard, requiring only that it be more likely than not that a defendant is liable). Note that while some empirical research suggests that jurors do not seem to make heavy distinctions between the standards of proof for punitives, judges, litigants, and the law most certainly

do. Woody, William Douglas, and Greene, Edie. "Jurors' Use of Standards of Proof in Decisions about Punitive Damages." *Wiley Online Library*, DOI: 10.1002/bsl.2027, www.uccs.edu/Documents/egreene/WoodyGreene%20Standards %20of%20proof%20punitive%20damages.pdf.

92 Statutes of Westminster (II), Gloucester, and Merton; for subsequent developments, *see Wilkes v. Wood* (1763) 98 Eng. Rep. 489, 489; (1763) Lofft 1 (Lord Pratt CJ).

93 Scholars have questioned the degree to which "insults" were really noncompensable save through punitive damages, but this is a question of degree: punitives were awarded for insults where compensation would be impossible or inadequate.

94 The critics were misguided about securities, but not necessarily things like tobacco and asbestos litigation.

95 *Winter v. NRDC*, 555 U.S. 7, Part III.A (2008) (citations omitted). Depending on the commentator, *Winter* either clarified or raised the bar on the "irreparable harm" requirement, from the "possibility" of harm to the "likely" harm. Pretty clearly, harm is always possible, and courts had always required more than mere possibility, and something closer to a "pretty likely" standard.

96 *Environmental Defense Fund, Inc. v. Corps of Engineers*, 324 F. Supp. 879, 833 (D.D.C. 1971) (requiring $1 security). *See also*, e.g., Fed. R. Civ. Pro. 65 (security). *See also*, e.g., N.C. R. Civ. Pro. 65; 231 Pa. Code Rule 1531.

97 *Winter v. NRDC*, 555 U.S. 7 (2008) (Ginsburg, J., dissenting).

98 The quasi-judicial bodies in agencies also have versions of these powers.

99 *Brown v. Board of Education II*, 349 U.S. 294, 301 (1955). "All deliberate speed" was almost certainly ambiguous by intention.

100 Eisenhower, Dwight. "The President's News Conference." 19 May 1954. *The American Presidency Project*, www.presidency.ucsb.edu/ws/index.php?pid=9892.

101 Fines could be satisfied out of the Judgment Fund, which exists to pay routine judgments and settlements against the executive. Until 1996, the Fund was administered by GAO, a highly independent and integrity-minded department, which opined that the Fund could *not* be used to pay penalties (including most contempt fines). Since then, Treasury has run the Fund. Treasury has not issued similar guidance, and is a much more politicized entity than GAO; the possibility of shenanigans is thus much greater.

102 Much would depend on how courts interpret 5 U.S.C. § 702, which waives immunity for relief other than "money damages." Fines are "money," but they aren't exactly "money damages," because they aren't compensatory, but coercive/penal.

103 Krock, Arthur. "In the Nation: The Tangled Dollar Steamship Case." *New York Times*, 22 May 1951, timesmachine.nytimes.com/timesmachine/1951/05/22/ 89441278.html?action=click&contentCollection=Archives&module=ArticleEnd CTA&region=ArchiveBody&pgtype=article&pageNumber=30.

104 *Land v. Dollar*, 341 U.S. 737, 749-750 (1951) (Jackson, J., withholding assent).

105 *Youngstown Sheet & Tube Co. v. Sawyer*, 343 U.S. 579 (1952).

106 Rothman, Lily. "The Primary Election that Put New Hampshire on the Political Map." *Time*, 9 Feb. 2016, time.com/4204347/new-hampshire-primary-history/;

"Obituary: Vinson Excelled in Federal Posts," *New York Times*, 9 Sept.1953, archive
.nytimes.com/www.nytimes.com/learning/general/onthisday/bday/0122.html.

107 For a good treatment of judicial contempt showdowns, *see* Parrillo, Nicholas
R. "The Endgame of Administrative Law: Governmental Disobedience and
the Judicial Contempt Power" *Harvard Law Review*, vol. 131, no. 3, pp. 685–794,
Jan2018,harvardlawreview.org/wp-content/uploads/2018/01/685-794_Online-1
.pdf.

Chapter 13

1 Richard Nixon, Interview by David Frost 1977. Clip available at www.youtube
.com/watch?v=HiHN3IJ_j8A. For a transcript, see Street Law, Inc., and The
Supreme Court Historical Society. "Nixon's Views on Presidential Power:
Excerpts from a 1977 Interview with David Frost." *Landmark Cases*, land
markcases.org/en/Page/722/Nixons_Views_on_Presidential_Power_Excerpts
_from_a_1977_Interview_with_David_Frost. Nixon was speaking about more
than just the Watergate break-in during Frost's interview.

2 Shear, Michael D., et al. "Trump, in Interview, Moderates Views but Defies Conventions." *New York Times*, 20 Jan. 2018, www.nytimes.com/2016/11/22/us/
politics/donald-trump-visit.html.

3 House Rule XII, clause 7(c). For an example form, see rules.house.gov/sites/
republicans.rules.house.gov/files/115/PDF/Constitutional%20Authority%20
Statement%20Form.pdf. The Authority Statement may refer to any part of the
Constitution granting Congress its powers, but that's usually Article I. There's
no required level of specificity, but members often do point out the relevant
clause. Versions of this have been used by several Congresses.

4 Declaration of Independence.

5 Like all breakaway movements, the legal status of Catalan independence is subjective. But the apparatus of election interference, paramilitary deployment,
political arrests, sedition charges, and so on does not encourage.

6 Civil Contingencies Act 2004, Chapter 36, part 2, §§20, 23(5). The CCA's predecessors, the Emergency Powers Acts (of various years, mostly germinated as
a result of the World Wars and Irish troubles), were hardly more reassuring,
but their timing indicates a need that greater than that which occasioned the
CCA.

7 Publius (James Madison). *The Federalist Papers—No. 10*. 1787. *Congress.gov*,
www.congress.gov/resources/display/content/The+Federalist+Papers#TheFeder
alistPapers-10.

8 Yoo, John. "On Presidential Power." *WritersReps.Com*, 2008, www.writersreps
.com/feature.aspx?FeatureID=152. *See also* Yoo, John. "Presidential Greatness
and Constitutional Power." Frank G. Raichle Lecture Series on Law in American
Society 305 (2007) (providing a more nuanced articulation). Yoo's longer pieces
contradict his short-form pieces on some points.

9   Yoo, John. "Executive Power Run Amok." *New York Times*, 20 Jan. 2018, www
     .nytimes.com/2017/02/06/opinion/executive-power-run-amok.html.

10   Sullivan, Andy. "Even Torture Memo Author John Yoo Thinks Rectal Feeding
     Was Illegal." *Huffington Post*, 14 Dec. 2014, www.huffingtonpost.com/2014/12/
     14/john-yoo-torture-report_n_6323360.html.

11   *Report of the Senate Select Committee on Intelligence: Committee Study of the
     Central Intelligence Agency's Detention and Interrogation Program.* U.S. Senate,
     S.R. 113–228, pp. 12–13, 9 Dec. 2014, www.intelligence.senate.gov/sites/default/
     files/documents/CRPT-113srpt288.pdf; *see also* "Statement by the President:
     Report of the Senate Select Committee on Intelligence." *Whitehouse.gov*, 9 Dec.
     2014, obamawhitehouse.archives.gov/the-press-office/2014/12/09/statement-pre
     sident-report-senate-select-committee-intelligence (President Obama's gloss in
     the same vein at pp. 12–13 of the unified PDF).

12   At least after 300 BC, when it was made clear that the right of *provocatio* under
     lex Valeria continued during dictatorship. This is where Schmitt's distinction
     between commissarial and sovereign dictatorship becomes important.

13   *Verfassung des Deutschen Reiches,* art. 48 (usually called the *Weimarer Verfas-
     sung,* and hereinafter, "Weimar Constitution"). Coupled with Article 25, the
     president could also engineer a legislative dissolution.

14   The event is referred to as the *Preußenschlag.*

15   *Compare* Basic Law, arts. 68, 80–81, 91 (requiring presidents to work with legisla-
     tors to invoke emergency powers and limiting their exercise) *with* Weimar Con-
     stitution art. 48 (providing near-unilateral presidential power). The new Basic
     Law had to be ratified by the Allies and has never been ratified in a normal sense
     (details social contract theorists strive to overlook) and was, in turn, imposed
     on East Germany during unification (another matter politely swept under the
     rug, with Habermas supplying the vocal exception), and its civil liberties do not
     extend unequivocally (Nazis are functionally banned, a democratic limitation
     more than compensated for in pragmatic terms). But this was a reasonable price
     for undoing the legacy of Article 48. Occupation Statute (*Besatzungsstatut*) arts.
     4–5, repealed by the Treaties of Paris 1954 (Allied approval); Basic Law, art. 21(2)
     (parties). Any party that threatens Germany's democratic order may be banned
     by Germany's senior jurists, but in 2016, German courts held that the threat had
     to be concrete and refused to disband the NDP. Scholars quibble if the Basic Law
     is technically a "constitution," but this is an academic detail. It may be plausibly
     argued that consent to the Basic Law occurred during reunification, because the
     Basic Law was a condition of the deal, though as Habermas notes, it's not like the
     GDR had much choice.

16   U.S. Statutes At Large, vol. 12, ch. LXIII, § 3 (1861).

17   Habeas Corpus Suspension Act of 1863 (providing an indemnity against Lin-
     coln's prior actions and authorizing suspension under Congress's authority).

18   Lincoln, Abraham. *Memorandum on Possibility of Not Being Reelected.* 23 Aug.
     1864. Library of Congress, The Abraham Lincoln Papers, memory.loc.gov/
     cgi-bin/ampage?collId=mal&fileName=mal1/354/3549600/malpage
     .db&recNum=0 (noting that the chances of reelection were "exceedingly bad").
     Lincoln, rather oddly, sealed up the memo and had the Cabinet sign it.

19   Acquisition of Naval and Air Bases in Exchange for Over-Age Destroyers, 39 Opp. Att'y Gen. 484 (1940). The memo was by, of all people, Robert Jackson.

20   UN Security Council Resolution 84 (1950); *see also* Authority to Use Military Force in Libya, 35 Op. O.L.C. 12 (2011), www.justice.gov/olc/opiniondocs/authority-military-use-in-libya.pdf.

21   Some have questioned whether the Act is itself valid or useful. The Act cannot supersede the Constitution's declare-or-don't provisions about war, so some scholars have tried to rescue the act as merely providing a definition of "war." If so, the Act is Constitutional, but mostly useless. I leave out questions involving UN treaties, self-defense, and war (though I emphatically do not agree that international treaties can "amend" the Constitution).

22   E.g., Obama, Barack, and Speaker of the House of U.S. Representatives. *Letter from the President—War Powers Resolution Regarding Iraq.* 8 Sept. 2014, obamawhitehouse.archives.gov/the-press-office/2014/09/08/letter-president-war-powers-resolution-regarding-iraq.

23   U.S. Constitution, art. II, § 3.

24   Garvey, Todd. *Presidential Signing Statements: Constitutional and Institutional Implications.* RL33667, Congressional Research Service, 4 Jan. 2012, p. 1, fas.org/sgp/crs/natsec/RL33667.pdf (hereinafter "Garvey Study").

25   Garvey Study, p. 2 (citations omitted).

26   *Ibid.*

27   *Ibid.* at Summary. The Truman figure derives from UCSB's American Presidency Project.

28   *Ibid.*

29   *Ibid. passim*; *see also Da Costa v. Nixon,* 55 F.R.D. 145 (E.D.N.Y 1972) (stating that no executive statement denying efficacy of legislation could be valid).

30   "Obama 2008: Bush Used Signing Statements to 'Accumulate More Power,'" *Real Clear Politics,*18 Apr. 2011, www.realclearpolitics.com/video/2011/04/18/obama_2008_bush_used_signing_statements_to_accumulate_more_power.html; Meckler, Laura. "Obama Shifts View of Executive Power." *Wall Street Journal,* 30 Mar. 2012, www.wsj.com/articles/SB10001424052702303812904577292273665694712. While Obama used signing statements with comparatively less frequency, a few statements did have substantial implications.

31   Woolley, John T. "Presidential Signing Statements: Frequently Asked Questions." *The American Presidency Project,* www.presidency.ucsb.edu/signingstatements.php?year=2017&Submit=DISPLAY; author's calculations.

32   *The ABA Task Force on Presidential Signing Statements and the Separation of Powers Doctrine.* American Bar Association, Aug. 2006, p. 5, www.americanbar.org/content/dam/aba/publishing/abanews/1273179616signstatereport.authcheckdam.pdf. The ABA's opinion is mostly confined to statements that suggest that legislation is unconstitutional, might not be enforced, etc. *See also supra* note 29.

33   28 U.S.C. § 530D (2002).

34   Bush, George W. "Statement on Signing the 21st Century Department of Justice Appropriations Authorization Act." 2 Nov. 2002. *The American Presidency Project,* www.presidency.ucsb.edu/ws/index.php?pid=73177.

35 *Ibid.*

36 *Clinton v. City of New York,* 524 U.S. 417 (1998). The legal grounds for attacking signing statements would be different, but the structural constitutional objections would overlap. *See also supra* note 29.

37 The executive can always piggyback onto the inevitable third-party lawsuits that spring up after any major piece of legislation. And there have been cases—one even entitled *United States v. United States*—where the executive sues itself, though most of these cases involved a normal agency litigating against an "independent" agency.

38 Alito, Jr., Samuel. *Using Presidential Signing Statement to Make Fuller Use of the President's Constitutionally Assigned Role in the Process of Enacting Law.* Department of Justice, Office of the Deputy Assistant General, Office of Legal Counsel, 5 Feb. 1986 (emphasis added), www.archives.gov/files/news/samuel -alito/accession-060-89-269/Acc060-89-269-box6-SG-LSWG-AlitotoLSWG -Feb1986.pdf.

39 Presidents usually cite Article II on this point.

40 Gallup, Inc. "Presidential Job Approval Center." news.gallup.com/interactives/ 185273/presidential-job-approval-center.aspx.

41 University of California—Davis Center for the Study of Human Rights in the Americas. "List of Individuals Detained by the Department of Defense at Guantanamo Bay, Cuba, January 2002–May 2006." *Prisoners Transferred into Guantanamo (DoD Documents),* 2018, humanrights.ucdavis.edu/projects/the -guantanamo-testimonials-project/testimonies/prisoner-testimonies/prisoners -transferred-into-guantanamo-dod-documents (noting 759 prisoners detained from 2001 to 2006; more arrived after the study period). The American was Yasser Hamdi.

42 *Brief of Senators Graham and Kyl as Amicus Curiae in Support of Respondents (Hamdan v. Rumsfeld).* June 2006, www.scotusblog.com/archives/Graham%20 Brief.pdf; *Hamdan v. Rumsfeld,* 548 U.S. 557, n.10 and *generally* (2006).

43 Pub. L. 109-148 § 1004(a).

44 Bush, George W. "Statement on Signing the Department of Defense, Emergency Supplemental Appropriations to Address Hurricanes in the Gulf of Mexico, and Pandemic Influenza Act, 2006." 30 Dec. 2005. *The American Presidency Project,* www.presidency.ucsb.edu/ws/index.php?pid=65259. The title notwithstanding, the appropriations act contained the Detainee Treatment Act.

45 Pub. L. 109-364, *repealed in relevant part by* Pub. L. 110-181.

46 10 U.S.C. § 252. The president must determine that a rebellion or "obstruction" exists before invoking this provision.

47 Silva, Daniella. "Border Patrol Agent Detains Woman for Speaking Spanish at Montana Gas Station." *NBC News,* 21 May 2018, www.nbcnews.com/news/ latino/border-patrol-agent-detains-women-speaking-spanish-montana-gas -station-n876096. *See also supra* Chapter 10 on racial disparities in policing.

48 Library of Congress. *Executive Power—Magna Carta: Muse and Mentor.* www .loc.gov/exhibits/magna-carta-muse-and-mentor/executive-power.html.

49 Garvey, Todd. "Presidential Claims of Executive Privilege: History, Law, Practice, and Recent Developments." Congressional Research Service. 15 Dec. 2014, p. 25, https://fas.org/sgp/crs/secrecy/R42670.pdf (citation omitted).

50 "Starr Subpoenas Clinton to Appear Before Grand Jury." *CNN*, 25 July, 1998, www.cnn.com/ALLPOLITICS/1998/07/25/clinton.subpoena/; for an extremely useful chronology of the Clinton-Lewinsky saga, *see* "A Chronology: Key Moments in the Clinton-Lewinsky Saga." *CNN*, 1998, www.cnn.com/ALLPOLI TICS/1998/resources/lewinsky/timeline/. The agents claimed a derivative "protective privilege."

51 The Bush II and Obama Administrations also invoked executive privilege, but mainly to frustrate Congress and in cases where the stakes were lower or procedural quirks dissolved the crisis by themselves.

52 *See generally* Garvey, Todd. *Presidential Claims of Executive Privilege: History, Law, Practice, and Recent Developments*. R42670, Congressional Research Service, p. 1, fas.org/sgp/crs/secrecy/R42670.pdf.

53 Garvey, Todd. *Presidential Claims of Executive Privilege: History, Law, Practice, and Recent Developments*. R42670, Congressional Research Service, p. 21, fas .org/sgp/crs/secrecy/R42670.pdf.

54 *Judicial Watch Inc. v. Dep't of Justice*, 365 F.3d 1108 (D.C. Cir. 2004).

55 Eisenhower, Dwight. "Proclamation 3221—Law Day, 1958." 3 Feb. 1958. *The American Presidency Project*, www.presidency.ucsb.edu/ws/index.php?pid=10 7097.

56 36 U.S.C. § 113. For a chronology *see* "What Is Law Day? A Primer." *Before the Bar*, American Bar Association, 1 May 2017, abaforlawstudents.com/2017/05/01 /law-day-primer/.

Conclusion

1 "Justice Louis D. Brandeis." *Louis D. Brandeis Fund for Social Justice*, Brandeis University, https://www.brandeis.edu/legacyfund/bio.html.

2 *Compare The Evolving Landscape of Crime and Incarceration*. Greenberg Quinlan Rosner Research, 19 Apr. 2018, p. 3, storage.googleapis.com/vera-web -assets/inline-downloads/iob-poll-results-summary.pdf (focusing on criminal justice system) *and 43% Say U.S. Justice System Unfair to Most Americans*. Rasmussen Reports, 26 Mar. 2014, www.rasmussenreports.com/public_content/ archive/mood_of_america_archive/supreme_court_ratings/43_say_u_s_jus tice_system_unfair_to_most_americans (justice system generally, with bare plurality disagreeing that it is "fair" to most Americans and a majority disagreeing that it is fair to the poor) *with* M/A/R/C Research. *Perceptions of the U.S. Justice System*. American Bar Association, 1999, www.americanbar.org/content/ dam/aba/publishing/abanews/1269460858_20_1_1_7_upload_file.authcheck dam.pdf.

3 "New Nationwide Poll: Most Voters Distrust U.S. Legal System." Common Good. 26 June 2012, https://www.prnewswire.com/news-releases/new-nationwide-poll -most-voters-distrust-us-legal-system-160429725.html. The Common Good is nonpartisan (enough that the *Atlantic* did a brief entry on this poll), but CG's founder

has long agitated against the legal system and some of the survey's questions were a touch leading. Nevertheless, the poll largely accords with findings in other survey work (albeit slightly differently worded). E.g., *supra* note 2 and "The State of State Courts: 2017." https://www.ncsc.org/~/media/Files/PDF/Topics/Public%20Trust%20and%20Confidence/State-of-the-State-Courts-2017-slides.ashx.

4 *See* Ginsburg, Tom, et al. "The Lifespan of Written Constitutions." University of Chicago Law School. 15 Oct. 2009, https://www.law.uchicago.edu/news/lifespan-written-constitutions (mean and Western Europe). *See also* Elkins, Zachary, Tom Ginsburg, and James Melton *The Endurance of National Constitutions*. Cambridge University Press, 2009, pp. 126–29 (noting median survival period of nineteen years). We can, and the cited authors do, debate the meaning of "constitution," but if anything, their calculations err toward generosity. EU treaties radically changed constitutional norms in member states. Even Britain (whose unwritten constitution falls outside the survey's stated parameters), despite having an ancient constitution, experienced profound change after 1900—not only in its relationship to the EU, but as whole chunks of empire were added, subtracted, or had their relationship with the British sovereign radically modified (as happened with Australia, Canada, New Zealand, and Ireland—the last a previously integral part of the UK, and, to a lesser extent, Scotland).

5 For scholars with a *Guinness Book* mentality, San Marino's Statutes of 1600 might qualify as the oldest written constitution in the world, but at 24 square miles, with no currency of its own, and more cars than people, San Marino falls into the category of irrelevant oddities. The Vatican's present constitution arguably dates no further back than the Lateran Treaties and is anyway under revision by Pope Francis.

6 "Cook Co. Public Defender Says the Dept. Cannot Afford More Cuts." *CBS Chicago*, 26 Oct. 2017, chicago.cbslocal.com/2017/10/26/cook-co-budget-cuts/; *see also* Campanelli, Amy P. "Letter to Mayor Daley." Cook County Public Defender, 20 Oct. 2017, https://www.cookcountyil.gov/sites/default/files/public_defender_-_finance_response.pdf. Kapos, Shia. "Ken Griffin Showcases $500 Million Art Purchases at Art Institute." *Crain's Chicago Business*, 18 Feb. 2016, www.chicagobusiness.com/article/20160218/BLOGS03/160219824/ken-griffin-showcases-500-million-art-purchases-at-art-institute.

7 Jay's comments were made during *Georgia v. Brailsford*, 3 Dall. 1 (1794), excerpts from proceedings of which are available at The University of Chicago Press. "Amendment VII, Document 14: *Georgia v. Brailsford* (3 Dall. 1 1794)." *The Founders' Constitution*, 2000, press-pubs.uchicago.edu/founders/documents/amendVIIs14.html.

INDEX